PROCLUS'
COMMENTARY ON
PLATO'S
PARMENIDES

PROCLUS' COMMENTARY ON PLATO'S *PARMENIDES*

◫ ◫ ◫

Translated by
GLENN R. MORROW
and
JOHN M. DILLON
with
Introduction and Notes by
JOHN M. DILLON

PRINCETON UNIVERSITY PRESS

1987

UXORI DILECTISSIMAE

CONTENTS

PREFACE

IN 1973, Glenn Morrow, Adam Seybert Professor Emeritus of Moral and Intellectual Philosophy at the University of Pennsylvania, died, while still rather less than half way through a translation of Proclus' *Commentary on the Parmenides*. He had published the *Commentary on the First Book of Euclid* in 1970 and had plainly developed in his retirement a taste for the tortuous ramifications of Proclus' style and thought. Charles Kahn of the University of Pennsylvania, Morrow's literary executor, asked me if I would be willing to complete the work. I accepted the task without much thought, although I had various other commitments, since I felt that it would be a good excuse to give a close reading to a work that I might otherwise be tempted to avoid. The consequence was ten years of hard labour (though with many interruptions), the results of which I present to the world with relief not unmixed with trepidation.

Nicholas of Cusa is said to have valued Proclus' *Commentary on the Parmenides* above all other books (the Sacred Scriptures, we trust, apart), and it has been a major influence on many other thinkers, both in the Greek East, and later, through William of Moerbeke's translation (probably done in the 1280s), in the Latin West. The roll call begins with Damascius and "Dionysius the Areopagite," includes such figures as Aquinas, Ficino and Pico, and may best be seen, perhaps, as ending with Hegel[1] and Schelling.

As a useful interpretation of Plato's *Parmenides*, the Commentary began to be dismissed in the last century, as the new critical approach to Plato began to take effect. I present it here, not primarily as an exegesis of Plato's text (though from time to time Proclus' insights are useful, or at least challenging), but rather as a monument of Neoplatonic metaphysics, disguised, as so much Neoplatonic philosophy is, in the form of a commentary.

I have been enormously helped in the preparation of this translation by the unstinting aid provided by Prof. L. G. Westerink of SUNY Buffalo, who patiently checked every page of it and provided a host of corrections, often involving brilliant emendations of the text. For access to William of Moerbeke's Latin translation, and for many fruitful suggestions over and above it, as well as much enjoyable discussion of the problems, I am greatly indebted to Dr. Carlos Steel of the University

---

[1] As witness Hegel's praise of the *Parmenides Commentary* in his *Vorlesungen über die Geschichte der Philosophie I i* (*Werke*, 2d ed., vol. XIV, p. 206), and *Phaenomenologie des Geistes*, preface, vol. II, p. 55.

of Louvain, who is currently completing an edition of the Latin text, the first volume of which has already appeared,[2] with the second to appear shortly. Steel will then embark on a Budé edition of the Greek text, which will put the text at last on as sound a footing as can be hoped for. Ideally, this translation should have waited for that happy event, but in fact most of the necessary emendations in the text are already embodied in it, owing to the fortunate circumstances outlined above.

I am most grateful, also, to Professor Elizabeth Anscombe and Dr. Lotte Labowsky for allowing me to make use of their translation of the final portion of the commentary on the First Hypothesis, which is only preserved in Latin.

For the immense patience and energy in typing and retyping a vast and tedious manuscript I extend my heartfelt thanks and appreciation to my wife, Jean, to whom my share of the work is dedicated, and the secretary of the School of Classics of Trinity College, Dublin, Mrs. Rosemary Doran. I would like to express my gratitude also to Elizabeth Powers of Princeton University Press for her heroic work on my rather troublesome manuscript.

[2] Proclus: *Commentaire sur le Parménide de Platon: Traduction de Guillaume de Moerbeke,* Tome I: Livres I à IV, Leuven, 1982.

GENERAL INTRODUCTION

A. LIFE AND WORKS, WITH A BRIEF
INTRODUCTION TO
PROCLUS' PHILOSOPHICAL SYSTEM

I do not propose to devote much space to a survey of Proclus' career and philosophical position, since this has been done adequately elsewhere, not least by Glenn Morrow in his introduction to Proclus' *Euclid Commentary*, which may be regarded as a companion volume to this,[1] but for the convenience of the reader something should be said.

LIFE

Proclus was born in Constantinople, of a prosperous Lycian family from Xanthos, on February 8, A.D. 412.[2] His father, Patricius, a lawyer, was there on business at the time, but returned shortly afterwards to Xanthos, where Proclus received his basic education. It is plain that Proclus' parents were staunch pagans (Marinus describes them as "outstanding in virtue," *VP* 6) and it is interesting to observe how relatively comfortably Patricius operated in the empire of Theodosius II (408–450).

As soon as was reasonable (perhaps in his mid-teens), his father sent Proclus to study in Alexandria, with a view to his following him into the legal profession. There he lived with a prominent sophist, Leonas, who introduced him into the ruling circles of Egypt, including Theodorus, the governor at the time. At some point around year 430, Leonas was sent by the governor on a mission to Constantinople and took the young Proclus with him to continue his studies. Proclus was at this stage, it seems, already inclining to philosophy rather than law, and at Constantinople he seems to have come to some sort of decision about his future, which Marinus piously attributes to the influence of Athena (*VP* 9), but which may be more plausibly ascribed to the ex-

---

[1] See also the accounts of R. T. Wallis, in *Neoplatonism*, ch. 5, A. C. Lloyd in ch. 19 of the *Cambridge History of Later Greek and Early Medieval Philosophy*, and Saffrey and Westerink in the introduction to vol. 1 of their Budé edition of the *Platonic Theology*. The older work of L. J. Rosán, *The Philosophy of Proclus*, is still useful. Excellent also is R. Beutler's *RE* article, "Proklos," Band XXIII, 1(1957): cols. 186-247.

[2] Our almost exclusive source for Proclus' life is the hagiographical biography of his pupil (and successor as head of the School) Marinus. Marinus actually gives us Proclus' horoscope (*VP* 35) and thus an exact date for his birth. Marinus tells us also that he died on April 17, 485 (124 years from accession of Julian in 361). Proclus, in a way characteristic of Neoplatonic philosophers, tells us virtually nothing about himself.

perience of meeting students and professors of philosophy who had been through the schools of Athens. On his return to Alexandria, he enrolled in the lectures of the Aristotelian Olympiodorus and not long afterwards, becoming dissatisfied with the approach to philosophy he experienced in Alexandria, set sail in 430 or 431 for Athens in search of deeper truths.

What his father had to say about this is not recorded by Marinus, but it does not seem that his allowance was cut, so we may assume paternal good will. Once arrived in Athens, he attached himself to the Platonic School of Syrianus and the aged Plutarch, and made an excellent impression. Plutarch had officially retired, but agreed to read Aristotle's *De Anima* and Plato's *Phaedo* with the young man, and even took him in to live with him. No commentary by Proclus on either of these works survives, but Plutarch apparently urged him to write up his notes on their sessions, so this early experience probably had considerable influence on his doctrine of the soul.

After Plutarch's death two years later, Proclus moved in with Syrianus and in the next two years worked through the whole of Aristotle with him (*VP* 13), and following on that, the works of Plato. Since Marinus emphasises that he went through Plato "in proper order," we may infer, I think, that Syrianus observed something like the Iamblichean sequence of ten dialogues,[3] beginning with the *Alcibiades I* and ending with the *Philebus*, followed by the two "summits" of Platonic philosophy, the *Timaeus* and the *Parmenides*. This admittedly would not provide for either the *Republic* or the *Laws*, which Marinus in chapter 14 assures us that he studied as well, so space was found for them in the course at some stage. Marinus also tells us that by the age of twenty-seven, after about eight years of residence in Athens, Proclus had composed a commentary on the *Timaeus*, "and many other treatises." The problems of dating which this statement involves are discussed below (in sect. C). By the time of the *Timaeus Commentary*, Syrianus would appear to have died, to judge from the past tenses in which Proclus consistently refers to his views. The generally agreed date of Syrianus' death is "c. A.D. 437," though the evidence is not very definite. All we know (from Marinus, *VP* 26) is that, after the completion of their Platonic studies, Syrianus proposed to Proclus, and to his fellow-student Domninus, that he expound to them either the Orphic poems or the Chaldaean Oracles, as being the ultimate repositories of theological wisdom, but Proclus and Domninus could not agree as to which they wanted to read, and Syrianus died shortly afterwards.

Proclus then seems to have succeeded to the headship of the Platonic

---

[3] Cf. Procl. *In Alc.* 11.11, and *Anon. Proleg. to Platonic Philosophy*, ch. 26.

School at about the age of 25.[4] He held this position for almost fifty years, until his death in 485. During this period he seems to have achieved something of a position of prominence in Athenian society, despite the inevitably hostile Christian environment. As Marinus reports (VP 15) "he sometimes took part in political deliberations, attending public meetings and proposing resolutions with practical wisdom (ἐμφρόνως). He also consulted with magistrates on matters of justice, not only exhorting these men, but in a manner compelling them, with his philosophic plain speaking, to do their proper duty." He also took some part in public education. He even appears to have intervened on an international level. Marinus (VP 15) speaks of him "writing letters to those in authority, and thus benefitting whole cities," of which he mentions Andros as an example.

He enjoyed the protection of at least one prominent member of society, by the name of Rufinus (VP 23), who attended his lectures, but such protection could not shield him from one period of persecution (VP 15), when he found it prudent to withdraw from Athens for a year, and went to Lydia, where he occupied himself with studying and assisting in the preservation and revival of the local cults. Whatever caused the political storm, it blew over, and he returned to resume his accustomed activities.

All this public business did not seem to hinder him from getting through a prodigious amount of teaching and writing. Marinus tells us (VP 22) that he gave customarily five lectures or seminars a day, sometimes more, and wrote about seven hundred lines. In addition, he consorted with other philosophers and conducted informal evening conversazioni. He also was liable to be up half the night at his devotions—the religious side of Proclus must not be forgotten. His hymns were often composed at night, or early in the morning, sometimes as the result of a dream (VP 28).

This pace of life seems to have continued for upwards of forty years, until a few years before his death in his sixty-ninth year, when his health failed and he was able to do little more than compose a few hymns and converse with his friends until his death three years later (VP 26). He was succeeded in the headship of the school, first by his faithful disciple and biographer, Marinus, and then by a rather more substantial philosopher, Isidore.

---

[4] Possibly only after a short period of headship by Domninus, but this conjecture is based only on Marinus' reference to Domninus in ch. 26 as φιλόσοφος καὶ διάδοχος. However, in ch. 12, Marinus speaks of Syrianus finding in Proclus "the successor he had long been seeking," and the probability is that his reference to Domninus as διάδοχος in ch. 26 is non-technical, though Domninus may have shared in the headship in some way for a while. Proclus refers to him twice in the In Tim. (I, 110.1 and 122.18) as "our companion."

WORKS

As for Proclus' many works, their order, with special reference to the place among them of the *Parmenides Commentary*, will be discussed below, in section B. What we have, in brief, are first, three systematic works—two, the *Elements of Physics* and the *Elements of Theology*, relatively early works, the third, the *Platonic Theology*, certainly a late one. Then there is an impressive succession of massive commentaries, of which those that survive are the ones on the *Alcibiades I*, the *Timaeus*, and the *Parmenides* (in all cases abruptly truncated, possibly by an exhausted scribe). The commentary on the *Cratylus* survives only in summarized form, and even that gives up at *Cratylus* 407C. The "commentary" on the *Republic* is actually a series of seventeen essays on aspects of the dialogue, collected together. He also wrote a commentary on Book I of Euclid's *Elements*. We know, as well, of lost commentaries on the *Phaedo, Gorgias, Phaedrus, Theaetetus,* and *Philebus*. There were also commentaries on the Chaldaean Oracles, the basic "sacred text" of later Neoplatonism, and on the *Enneads* of Plotinus.

Then we have a series of monographs on particular topics, originally thought only to survive in the Latin version of William of Moerbeke (who also translated the *Timaeus* and *Parmenides Commentaries*), but recently rediscovered by L. G. Westerink in the guise of works by the Byzantine Isaac Sebastocrator, whom Westerink discerned to be simply plagiarising Proclus: (1) *Ten Problems Concerning Providence*, (2) *On Providence and Fate*, and (3) *On the Existence of Evil*. All have now received modern editions (see Bibliography).

In addition, Proclus composed a number of religious or theurgic works, of which all that survives is a fragment, *On the Hieratic Art according to the Greeks*, and a collection of seven hymns.

PHILOSOPHICAL SYSTEM

The question of what may properly be regarded as the philosophy of Proclus is a vexed one. He has traditionally been regarded as the major figure in the development of later, "Athenian," Neoplatonism. In so far as he is the great systematiser of this philosophy, this is a valid view, but it has become increasingly clear, as his writings have been studied critically, that very little of what he presents to us is original to himself—nor, to be fair to him, does he try to disguise his indebtedness to his predecessors, particularly to Syrianus. Indeed, when the faithful Marinus comes, in chapter 23 of his biography, to catalogue his master's innovations in philosophy, he makes the following remarkable statement:

He became the author of many doctrines not previously discovered, both concerning nature and the realm of Intellect and things still more divine. For it was he who was the first to assert the existence of a class of souls which can contemplate many Forms simultaneously, a class which he very properly postulated as intermediate between the intellect, which cognises in advance all things together in a simple intuition, and souls, which pass consecutively in thought from one Form to another. Anyone who wishes can come upon his original doctrines, if they go through his works, a thing which I have declined to do in the present context, for fear of excessively lengthening my account, if I were to go through everything.

Now Marinus, it may be argued, is a biographer of little brain, but one would think that, as the key contribution of his master to the development of Platonism, he could have come up with something more impressive than this (he hints vaguely at scores of other innovations, but one must assume that they were of the same order of importance).

This is, therefore, I think, a most significant passage. What we have here is the filling of a small gap by Proclus in the very comprehensive system of links and intermediate entities with which, first, Iamblichus, and then Syrianus, adorned the Neoplatonic universe. This intermediate class of soul, if it has a use, may have been postulated as the sort of soul possessed by such bodhisattvas as Orpheus, Pythagoras, Plato, Plotinus, Iamblichus or Syrianus, but it may be just a logical construction, Proclus having perceived the possibility of an intermediate term between Intellect, which is static and intuitive, and Soul proper, which is in motion and discursive (cf. perhaps, *ET*, prop. 184). In that case, he would seem to be postulating a rather self-contradictory entity, part intuitive, part discursive.

I dwell on this detail because it accords with the impression one forms from the commentaries. On the rare occasions when Proclus ventures explicitly to interpose his own opinion, it is always on a matter of detail, often of a theurgic nature, and not suggestive of the workings of a great original mind. Nevertheless, Proclus is what we have got, and to understand him we must possess at least an overview of the doctrines of the Athenian School.

The relatively simple metaphysical scheme of Plotinus, providing for just the three Hypostases—One, Intellect, and Soul—seems to have suffered elaboration already at the hands of his senior pupil Amelius (who had a special weakness for triads), but from the perspective of the Athenian School it is Iamblichus (c. 245–325) who began the major system of scholastic elaboration which is the mark of later Neoplatonism.

Already Plotinus had felt the tension between a totally transcendent One, negatively described, and a One which is in some way the origin of all things.[5] We also find in some of his works a tendency to elevate the Logos into something like a further hypostasis and a tendency to separate a higher and a lower Soul (the lower being Nature), but in general Plotinus resists the multiplication of entities, something he associates with Gnostic woolly-mindedness (*Enn.* II, 9.1).

However, he left many questions open for his successors, and especially when, with Iamblichus, Neoplatonism becomes something of a religion as well, the desire to accommodate the multitude of traditional (and not-so-traditional) deities, as well as entities deriving from the Chaldaean Oracles and the Orphic writings, together with a philosophic concern to fill in the gaps in Plotinus' universe, led to a multiplicity of elaborations.

Some Basic Principles

Despite its appearance of Byzantine stratification and complexity, Proclus' philosophy is a dynamic system, a system postulating continuous intellectual motion, and we should therefore begin by examining some of the basic laws governing the being of the intelligible, and indeed of the sensible, world.

The Derivation of Multiplicity from Unity

"All that exists," states proposition 11 of the *Elements of Theology*, "proceeds from a single first cause." This principle is then elaborated on below:

> There is a first cause of all existing things, whence they severally proceed as branches from a root, some near to it and others more remote.

The basic problem with which all Neoplatonic speculation is concerned, from Plotinus on, is how a multiplicity, and worse, a multiplicity of levels of being, can derive from a totally transcendent and Simple One. Plotinus had propounded the theory of undiminished giving by the One, the image of the inexhaustible spring, which creates without being affected by its creation (e.g. *Enn.* V, 3.12; III, 8.10). The universe thus produced from the One is a plenum, in which no gap can be tolerated (e.g. *Enn.* II, 9.3). From Iamblichus on, as I have said, this principle leads to a progressive multiplication of entities—not of hy-

---

[5] A tension well described by A. H. Armstrong in his book, *The Architecture of the Intelligible Universe in the Philosophy of Plotinus*, Cambridge, 1940 (repr. Hakkert, 1967), esp. chs. 1-3.

postases, since the basic distinction of henadic, noetic, and psychic realms remains, but of moments within each hypostasis. The principle which Dodds calls the "law of continuity"[6] is well stated by Proclus at *De Prov.* IV, 20 (= VII, 28, of Isaac Sebastocrator's version): "the processions of real beings, far more even than the positions of physical bodies in space, leave no vacuum, but everywhere there are mean terms between extremities, which provide for them a mutual linkage" (cf. also *PT* III, 2, p. 6.21ff. S-W).

Relations of Causes and Effects

This involves a system of production in which "every producing cause brings into existence things like to itself before the unlike" (*ET*, prop. 28), raising the question of the relations between causes and effects, another subject of basic importance for Proclus' system. This is dealt with in propositions 75–86 of the *Elements of Theology*, which should be read in this connection.[7] The first principle (prop. 75) is that "every cause properly so-called transcends its effect." The alternative would be that it is immanent in its effect, and so to some extent inferior to it. This principle that causes are not *in* their effects (though effects are in their causes, as we shall see) must cause us to qualify any talk of Neoplatonism having a doctrine of emanation; what we have is more a sort of *illumination* of the lower by the higher; causes, as we learn in *ET*, props. 26-27, are not diminished by their production.

Another principle of wide application is that laid down in *ET*, props. 56-57: "All that is produced by secondary beings is in a greater measure produced from those prior and more determinative principles from which the secondary were themselves derived" (56); and "Every cause both operates prior to its consequent and gives rise to a greater number of posterior terms" (57). The idea is that the efficacy of the higher causes is not limited to their immediate products (as, for instance, Intellect's production of Soul), but extends on down through the products of these products, and actually beyond, to entities not caused by its own immediate products. This interesting doctrine produces the remarkable result, for example, that Matter is dependent for its "existence" (such as it is—sub-existence, more accurately) on the One alone, while Nous is the cause of being for inanimate objects, to which Soul does not extend. In *PT* III, 6, we find an elaborate working-out of the theory in respect of the relations of the One to the three chief moments of the hypostasis of Nous—Being, Life, and Intellect (well set out by Dodds on p. 232 of his *Elements of Theology*). The doctrine is also given

[6] *Elements of Theology*, p. 216, commenting on *ET*, prop. 28.
[7] Cf. also *In Parm.*, pp. 745-746, a good summation of Proclus' theory of spiritual productivity.

an ingenious application at *In Parm.* 691.5ff., to the relations among Parmenides, Zeno, and Socrates.

Cyclic Creativity

While causes are not affected by their effects, every effect both proceeds from its cause and is implicit in it. As we learn in *ET*, prop. 30: "All that is immediately produced by any principle both remains in the producing cause and proceeds from it." Further, prop. 31 tells us, "All that proceeds from any principle reverts in respect of its being upon that from which it proceeds." These propositions, and those that follow (32-39), express the doctrine of cyclic creativity, enunciated by Plotinus in such passages as V, 2.1 or VI, 5.7, and thereafter basic to Neoplatonism. Werner Beierwaltes makes this the chief theme of his great work, *Proklos: Grundzüge seiner Metaphysik,*[8] and he is right to do so. The cyclic process of *rest* in the causal principle, *procession* from it and *reversion* towards it (μονή, πρόοδος, ἐπιστροφή) governs all activity both in the intelligible and in the physical worlds. The original rest in one's cause is a state of potentiality (δύναμις) which can also be viewed as the cause's potency (these two senses of δύναμις are combined in Neoplatonic thought) while both procession and reversion are required before actuality (ἐνέργεια) is achieved. Procession alone would result only in indefiniteness; an entity fixes its essence only through reflecting back on its cause. The cause has thus a double function, both producer of the effect and goal of perfection for it. The process of ἐπιστροφή is exceedingly complex, as every lesser cause is simultaneously acting as the goal of its own product's reversion and is engaged in reversion upon its own cause, and all are ultimately reverting upon the One.

A particular feature of this cyclical process of causation is the doctrine of causal series or 'chains' (σειραί) of entities on different levels of being dependent on a single cause. *ET*, prop. 21, declares: "Every order (τάξις) has its beginning in a monad and proceeds to a multiplicity (πλῆθος) co-ordinate therewith; and the multiplicity in any order may be carried back to a single monad"; and prop. 97: "The originative cause of each series (σειρά) communicates its distinctive property (ἰδιότης) to the entire series; and what the cause is primarily the series is in subordinate degrees (καθ᾽ ὕφεσιν)." Every entity, in fact, is in the 'chain' of some henad. To anticipate slightly, in later Neoplatonism, beginning with Iamblichus, the realm of the One was enriched with a multiplicity of rather contradictory-sounding entities called henads, which served as the supra-intelligible, but participated, first principles of all classes of being. The traditional Platonic Forms are upstaged by

[8] Klostermann, Frankfurt am Main, 1965.

these new entities, since the Forms are intellects, and thus not sufficiently unitary, it seems, to serve as first principles. The realm of the
One, where the first principle should preside in solitary state, thus becomes strangely cluttered, in the interests of logic and the principle of
plenitude.

The corollary of prop. 21 is worth quoting *in extenso*, I think, since
it gives a conspectus of how Proclus sees individual entities at each level
of being relating, first, to the monad of their own realm, and then to
what is above them:

> From this it is apparent that in the nature of body unity and plu-
> rality coexist in such a manner that the one Nature has the many
> natures dependent from it, and, conversely, these are derived from
> one Nature, that of the whole; that the Soul-order, originating
> from one primal Soul, descends to a manifold of souls and again
> carries back the manifold to the one; that to intellective essence be-
> longs an intellective monad and a manifold of intelligences pro-
> ceeding from a single Intelligence and reverting thither; that for
> the One which is prior to all things there is the manifold of the
> henads, and for the henads the upward tension linking them with
> the One. Thus there are henads consequent upon the primal One,
> intelligences consequent on the primal Intelligence, souls conse-
> quent on the final Soul, and a plurality of natures consequent on
> the universal Nature.

Proclus makes use of this doctrine of pluralities ruled over by monads
near the beginning of the *Parmenides Commentary*, at 620.5ff., in discussing Parmenides' doctrine of the One. The monad of each level has
a relation to its own *taxis* of reality analogous to that of the One to the
whole of reality (cf. *PT* II, 5, pp. 38.3ff. S-W).

Participation

Related to this process of cyclic creativity is the distinction between
'participated' (μεθεκτός) and 'unparticipated' (ἀμέθεκτος) aspects of
each hypostasis. The primal monad of each level of reality, beginning
with the One itself, is 'unparticipated'. It is a 'whole-before-the-parts'
(ὁλότης πρὸ τῶν μερῶν), as opposed to a 'whole-of-parts' (ἐκ τῶν μερῶν)
(cf. *ET*, prop. 67), which is its 'participated' moment, as being participated in by the individual entities on the same hypostatic level (e.g.
intellects or souls). All higher entities (e.g. intellects) are also participated in by the entities next lower to them (in this case, souls), though
Intellect itself, the intelligible monad, is not so participated. On the
other hand, it participates in the hypostasis above it (in this case, the

henadic realm) and indeed can be seen as the lowest element of that realm. *ET*, prop. 23, is a basic statement of this relationship. It lays down that "all that is unparticipated produces out of itself the participated, and all participated levels of an hypostasis are linked by upward tension to unparticipated entities."

The complexities of this relationship have recently been well discussed by A. C. Lloyd in a paper, "Procession and Division in Proclus." The motive for making this distinction between unparticipated and participated is to preserve the transcendence of higher entities, while allowing for the processes of creation. The extreme realism of Proclus' philosophical position leads to his postulation of distinct entities answering to each aspect of an hypostasis, but things become clearer if we think of them as just aspects after all. All of Proclus' triadic constructions are also unities.

The three moments of the hypostasis of Nous are illustrated vividly near the beginning of the *Parmenides Commentary* (Book I, 628.1ff.) where Parmenides, Zeno and Socrates are likened, respectively, to the 'unparticipated and divine Intellect', 'participated Intellect', and 'particular intellect' (ì.e. the individual intellect as participant in the generic Intellect). Other important passages are 745.40-746.20; 1041.20-30; and 1069.23-1070.15.

Potentiality-Actuality (Dynamis-Energeia)

This pair of concepts, as mentioned above, is involved with those of cause and effect, and procession and return. Δύναμις I have rendered 'potentiality', but (again, as mentioned above), the idea of power or potency is present in it, as well as the more strictly Aristotelian concept. The One, for a start, in Plotinus' doctrine, is the δύναμις πάντων (*Enn.* V, 1.7.9, cf. III, 8.10.1) in the sense both of potentiality and potency, though Plotinus elsewhere makes a clear distinction between the active potency of the One and the passive potency of Matter (*Enn.* V, 3.15.32ff.). In this latter passage, Intellect is presented as ἐνέργεια, the actualisation of the One's potentiality.

All this is naturally taken over by Proclus, though in an important passage, *PT* III, 9, p. 31.14ff., he exempts the One itself even from the possession of potency, assigning primal potency to the Limit of the *Philebus*, which he sees as a second One. *Dynamis* and *energeia* remain, however, as basic principles of the Procline universe. At *ET*, prop. 77, we find the axiom: "All that exists potentially is advanced to actuality by the agency of something which is actually what the other is potentially"—the basic Aristotelian "chicken-before-egg" principle viewed Neoplatonically. The being (*ousia*) of a causal principle implies its potency, and its potency must come to actualisation. *Dynamis* occupies the same role as does the life-principle, ζωή, between the moments of ὄν and νοῦς.

This will suffice, I think, as a conspectus of the basic concepts with which Proclus operates—which make his universe go round, so to speak. Let us turn now to a brief survey of the components of that universe.

The Hypostases

The One and the Henadic Realm

In their doctrine of the One, the Athenian School and Proclus actually retreat from an innovation brought in by Iamblichus to solve the problem of the tension already present in Plotinus' system between the One as totally simple and transcendent and the One as the source of all being. Iamblichus cut the Gordian Knot by postulating two Ones, the first completely unnameable (and thus unrelated to anything following it), the second still "unconnected to the triad" (of the noetic realm), but serving as the first principle of all existence (Damascius, *De Principiis* 43, I, p. 86.3ff.).

Proclus actually attacks such a concept in *ET*, prop. 20: "Beyond the One there is no further principle; for Oneness is identical with the Good; that is therefore the first principle of all things, as has been shown" (prop. 12). The One is both formal and final cause of the cosmos; it is in this capacity that it is the Good (cf. *ET*, prop. 8). Any further qualification would diminish it (as Plotinus says in *Enn.* III, 8.11). All Being springs from the One as first cause (*ET*, prop. 11). Oneness in general is that which holds together every level of existence—and every individual—and gives it form. Good expositions of this basic truth may be found at *In Parm.* I, 703.12ff. and in the first three chapters of Book II of the *Platonic Theology*.

As has been said above, however, the One is not alone in its realm. Proclus also, following Iamblichus, finds a place at this level for the principles of Limit and Limitlessness (*peras* and *apeiria*), derived from the *Philebus* (23cff.), and for a multiplicity of "henads."

An Iamblichean development that the Athenian School did adopt was the postulation of a dyad of antithetical principles, Limit and Limitlessness, immediately following on the One (cf. Damascius *De Princ.* 50-51; Iambl. *In Tim.* fr. 7 Dillon). At *ET*, prop. 90, Proclus declares: "Prior to all that is composed of limit and limitlessness there exist substantially and independently the primal Limit and the primal Limitlessness." He develops this principle over the following five propositions.

There is also a full discussion at *PT* III, 9. This dyad must be prior to the henads, since they partake of Limitlessness to the extent that they are multiple (cf. *ET*, prop. 159).

The henads themselves arise from an application of the law that a cause must produce what is most like itself before anything else, the law of plenitude. Being multiple, they form a bridge between the One and all multiplicity. They are *participated* entities, which the One is not, and form appropriate summits for all 'chains' (*seirai*) of beings (cf. *In Parm.* VI, 1043.9ff.). They are not themselves, of course, intellects, but the *noes* of the noetic realm are present in them 'causally' (κατ' αἰτίαν). The henads are necessarily more unified than intellects (cf. *In Tim.* III, 12.22ff.), and yet each is an individual in some mysterious way. There is a sort of hierarchy among them of more and less universal ones (*ET*, prop. 136), though presumably without their being divided into genera and species. They are limited in number (prop. 149), and equal to the number of real existents which participate in them (prop. 135). They exercise *pronoia* in the etymologising sense of 'pre-intelligence' (*ET*, prop. 120), but also, it seems, in the normal sense (prop. 122). They provide a place, above the level of Intellect, to situate the gods of traditional religion, and they can all be referred to as *theoi*.

The doctrine of henads is made more complex by the fact that Proclus provides for henads at every level of being, noetic, noetic-noeric, noeric, psychic, and so on (*ET*, props. 151ff.) but these must be seen as just principles of unity within each hypostasis (monads), not henads in the strict sense.

The fullest presentations of the doctrine occur in the *Elements of Theology*, props. 113-165, and *Platonic Theology* III, chs. 1-6. Both Dodds, in his commentary on the former (esp. pp. 257-260), and Saffrey and Westerink, in their Introduction to the latter, give very helpful expositions of both the history of the doctrine and its complexities.

Nous

Already Iamblichus had divided the Plotinian hypostasis of Nous into an 'intelligible' and an 'intellectual' level (κόσμος νοητός, νοερός), each triadically subdivided (see Proclus' account of this at *In Tim.* I, 308.18ff.; also Appendix C of my *Iamblichi Fragmenta*; in that appendix I also suggested that a noetic-noeric level should be assumed from the text, but I now find that an unnecessary speculation). Syrianus and Proclus filled out this scheme further by producing a three-fold division, inserting the 'intelligible-intellectual' (νοητὸς καὶ νοερός) realm between the previous two—again, an application of the principle of plenitude. Each of these levels is divided into 'moments', themselves triadic in structure, variously named to answer to different entities discerned by Syrianus in the Second Hypothesis of the *Parmenides*, which he conceived to contain a description of the hypostasis of Nous in all its complexity (see below, p. xxxiif.), but broadly answering to the pattern ὄν – ζωή – νοῦς, or πατήρ – δύναμις – ἐνέργεια. Books III-V of the *Platonic Theology* are largely taken up with the discussion of these triads.

All this proliferation takes its start from the distinction in aspects of Nous first established by Plotinus (cf. e.g. *Enn.* I, 6, 7; V, 4, 2; V, 6, 6), but never formalised by him, though it was later by Porphyry and Iamblichus. For the Athenian School, the moments of Being, Life, and Mind predominate variously throughout the hypostasis, each generating corresponding triads until the situation begins to resemble a hall of mirrors. There are three triads of intelligible-intellectual gods and a hebdomad of intellectual ones, all seen by Syrianus as mentioned in the First and Second Hypotheses of the *Parmenides* (cf. below, xxxiii). Superimposed on this is the distinction between the Unparticipated Monad of Nous, its participated levels, and finally its manifestation in "participation" at the next level of Soul.

The Platonic figure of the Demiurge similarly suffers triadic proliferation. There is a demiurgic level of being (the intellectual realm proper), and a "father of the demiurges" or demiurgic monad, who presides over it and over the "demiurgic gods" (though the Demiurge proper is identified with the seventh, or lowest, triad). We find a major discussion of the nature of the Demiurge in the *Timaeus Commentary*, in the lemma on *Tim.* 28C (I, 99-319) which includes a full survey of previous Middle Platonic and Neoplatonic opinions. All that we need note for the present purpose is that the role of the demiurgic level of being is to transmit the Forms of the noetic realm to Soul, and so to Nature and the physical cosmos. A most interesting application of Proclus' doctrine of demiurgic action is to be found at *In Parm.* IV, 844.11ff. (cf. my comments in the introduction to that book).

Soul

Once again, the psychic realm must have its proper monad (or henad), Unparticipated Divine Soul, which itself participates in Nous and presides transcendently over its own realm. In the *Elements of Theology*, when Proclus comes to discuss Soul (props. 184-211), we find no mention of such an entity, only of souls in the plural, but it is plainly presupposed, and is in fact mentioned earlier, in prop. 164. There we learn that the Unparticipated Soul "presides primarily over the cosmos" (πρώτως ὑπὲρ τὸν κόσμον ἐστί), but does so transcendently and so is distinct from the immanent World Soul, as well as from individual souls.

These latter are arranged in an elaborate hierarchy of angelic, dae-monic and heroic, human and finally irrational levels, all dependent on their proper divine henad, in the sense of being in its *seira*, or chain. The distinction of these levels of being, and of those in the realm of Nous, is relevant to the protracted discussions of Books III and IV of the *Parmenides Commentary* of the various levels at which the Forms manifest themselves. For the details see the introductions to those books. Proclus, of course, adopts the Platonic Theory of Ideas in the form in which it was bequeathed to him, of which he gives us a useful account at the beginning of Book IV (837-853).

Other than this, Proclus' views on the lower levels of Being, Soul, Nature, and Matter, and the multifarious beings contained in them, are not relevant to a study of the *Parmenides Commentary*, which is concerned only with the henadic and noetic realms. Soul and Nature are more the concern of the *Timaeus Commentary*. A description of them would, I think, unnecessarily lengthen this survey. Readers anxious for more detail should turn to Beutler's excellent *RE* article, "Proklos," to which I am much indebted in this brief account.

Discussions of particular aspects of Proclus' philosophy relevant to the *Parmenides Commentary* may be found in the introductions to individual books. I would draw attention here to the following: in Book I, his allegorical method (pp. 5-7); in Book II, the structure of the realm of Forms (pp. 94-98); in Book III, arguments for the existence and na-ture of Forms—"Of what things are there Forms?" (pp. 145-156); in Book IV, participation of particulars in Forms, together with discussion of various levels of Form (pp. 195-209); in Book V, dialectic, and in particular "Parmenidean" dialectic (pp. 326-331); in Book VI, the number and subject matter of the hypotheses of the *Parmenides*, involving a conspectus of the structure of Proclus' universe and those of his predecessors (pp. 385-390); and in Book VII, the detailed structure of the hypostasis of Nous—a subject more proper to a commentary on the Second Hypothesis, but appropriate (negatively) here (pp. 474-491). It can be seen from this survey how the *Parmenides* and the *Timaeus* (which is concerned with the Soul and all below it) could be taken by Neoplatonists to cover, complementarily, the whole gamut of existence.

B. PREVIOUS COMMENTARY ON THE *PARMENIDES*

Proclus himself, in the Preface to the Commentary (630.15-645.8) gives a schematic account of the history of the interpretation of the *Par-*

menides which there is no reason to contradict. He does not present it as a chronological succession, but it is easily understood as such. [9]

The earliest interpretation of the dialogue[10] was that it was a logical exercise with a polemical purpose, in effect a satire on the Zenonian method of argument, to be compared in this to the parody on Protagoras' doctrine in the *Theaetetus*. This interpretation is distinguished from one, which we find represented in Albinus (*Isagoge*, ch. 3; *Didaskalikos*, ch. 6); and Thrasyllus (*ap.* Diog. Laert. III, 58), which regards it as a logical exercise with a positive, educational purpose. It is possible, therefore, that the first interpretation was that of the New Academy, who would have found the *Parmenides*, on their interpretation, a most useful document for teaching the art of destructive argument, even as they found the *Theaetetus* a useful source document for a skeptical theory of knowledge.[11] But there is no question of any New Academic writing a commentary on the dialogue.

When the Platonic School returned to dogmatism with Antiochus, interpretation of the *Parmenides* must have altered. The first part would now be seen, not as a demolition of the Theory of Ideas, but simply as a purification of it from naive misinterpretations, while the second part was certainly seen as an exercise in logical method, very much as Parmenides himself advertises it in the dialogue. Thus Albinus in *Didaskalikos*, chapter 6, finds examples of various Aristotelian categorical syllogistic figures in Parmenides' arguments (e.g. the second at 145b, while the third he appears to extract from the second hypothesis as a whole,[12] as well as various hypothetical and "mixed" syllogisms (e.g. at 137dff., 145bff., 145a). Taurus uses 156d as the basis for a discussion of the notion of 'instant' (Aulus Gellius, *NA* VII, 13).

Among mainline Middle Platonists, then, there is no indication that anyone saw the second part of the dialogue as containing any positive metaphysical doctrine. But on the fringes of the Platonic movement it is possible that some people did. E. R. Dodds, in an important article,[13] argues that the elaborate structure of reality of the Neopythagorean

---

[9] He actually says 'εἰσί δέ τινες καὶ γεγόνασι τῶν ἔμπροσθεν', which seems to imply that he is envisaging contemporary differences of opinion also, though I find it unlikely that there were still partisans of the "logical" interpretation in Proclus' Academy.

[10] I have summarised these views in the introduction to Book I. Here I will merely discuss their possible identity.

[11] This we can gather from a remark in the *Anon. Theaet. Comm.* 54.38ff., that passages such as 150cff. proved, for some people, that Plato was an Academic, since he never dogmatises! See on this John Glucker, *Antiochus and the Late Academy*, pp. 38–41.

[12] "That which partakes in shape is, qualified; that which partakes in shape is limited: therefore, what is qualified is limited" does not correspond to any particular argument in the dialogue.

[13] "The *Parmenides* of Plato and the Origin of the Neoplatonic 'One'," *CQ* 22(1928): 129–142.

Moderatus (1st cent. A.D.)[14]—or rather, that attributed by Moderatus to Plato—is based upon a metaphysical interpretation of the second part of the *Parmenides*. The relevant passage is as follows:[15]

> It seems that this opinion concerning Matter was held first among Greeks by the Pythagoreans, and after them by Plato, as indeed Moderatus tells us. For he (sc. Plato), following the Pythagoreans, declares that the first One is above Being and all essence, while the second One—which is the truly existent (*ontōs on*) and the object of intellection (*noēton*)—he says is the Forms; the third, which is the soul-realm (*psychikon*), participates (*metechei*) in The One and the Forms, while the lowest nature which comes after it, that of the sense-realm, does not even participate, but receives order by reflection from those others, . . .

Dodds' proposal that this rests on an exegesis of the *Parmenides* is most persuasive. The "three kings" of the *Second Letter* (312e) might be seen as playing their part as well, but that curious document may itself be dependent on a metaphysical interpretation of the *Parmenides*. In this scheme, the First Hypothesis concerns a supra-essential One; the Second, a "One-that-is," or Nous; and the Third, Soul. It may even be that the Fourth is being asserted to concern Nature, or the physical world, but that is not so clear.

If Moderatus is being influenced by any previous authority here, that is not apparent to us. Nor does there seem to be any sign of such an interpretation of the *Parmenides* among "orthodox" Platonists before Plotinus (though Numenius and/or Ammonius Saccas may well have been influenced by it).[16] However, unless one wishes to deny this passage to Moderatus altogether, it seems to me that Dodds' elucidation of it is valid, and that we have here an indication of a metaphysical exegesis of the dialogue flourishing at least in the Neopythagorean tradition.

This Neopythagorean interpretation of the dialogue, on the other hand, does not seem to concord with the first of the "metaphysical" interpretations listed by Proclus (Book I, 635.31-638.2). This interpretation, he says, takes the subject of the dialogue as Being, as in Parmenides' poem. As I suggest in the introduction to Book I, this can

---

[14] Relayed to us, via Porphyry, by Simplicius, *In Phys.* 230.34ff. Diels.

[15] The passage is from a treatise of Porphyry's *On Matter*, so that is his primary concern here.

[16] Porphyry, in his *Life of Plotinus* (20) quotes Longinus as saying that Numenius, Cronius, Moderatus, and Thrasyllus wrote on the first principles of Plato and Pythagoras, though "falling far short of Plotinus in precision and fullness." Dr. Harold Tarrant suggests to me that this may betoken a metaphysical exegesis of the *Parmenides* by these authors, but it is really not much to go on.

hardly apply to anyone after Plotinus, and since it does not apply to Moderatus, one is left with the rather desperate suggestion that Plotinus' contemporary, Origen the Platonist, is intended, a man of whose views Proclus takes some cognisance, presumably because Porphyry did so.

The first Platonist to adopt unequivocally the "metaphysical" interpretation of the *Parmenides* is Plotinus. Plotinus does not, of course, write commentaries as such, but his programmatic treatise *Enn.* V, 1, "On the Three Principal Hypostases," becomes, in effect, from chapter 8 on, an exegesis of the latter part of the *Parmenides*, particularly of the First Hypothesis. Interestingly enough, Plotinus leads into this exegesis with a reference to the Three Kings of the *Second Letter*. In presenting this exegesis, which takes the One of the First Hypothesis to be the One above Being, that of the Second to be Intellect, and that of the Third to be Soul, Plotinus shows consciousness of presenting a new departure (while defiantly maintaining his accord with the most ancient and best authorities) when he says (8.9–14): "These teachings, then, are no novelties, no inventions of today, but long since stated, though not straightforwardly; our doctrine here is an exegesis of those earlier ones, and can show the antiquity of those opinions on the testimony of Plato himself" (MacKenna's trans., slightly emended). This will at least imply that he feels himself to be going against the consensus of mainline Platonism, though not necessarily against Ammonius, or even Numenius.

Plotinus' senior pupil, Amelius, at least had views on the subject matter of the hypotheses, as we learn from Proclus' doxography[17] in Book VI (1052.31–1053.35). I will not go through the scheme in detail, except to note that Amelius, as one might expect, follows Plotinus in his identification of the subjects of the first three hypotheses, though he goes on to find subjects for all the rest as well (eight, on his calculation).

There is no need to suppose, however, that Amelius wrote a commentary on the *Parmenides* as such (we know nothing of his views on any other aspect of it, unless one counts his doctrine that there were Forms of Evils). With Porphyry, on the other hand, the situation is rather complex. It is fairly plain, from his probable position in a series of anonymous doxographies (see below, p. xxxi) that he wrote a commentary on the dialogue, but doubt still surrounds the attribution to him of the *Anonymous Turin Commentary*, boldly claimed for him by the French scholar Pierre Hadot.[18] Hadot brings much learning to bear

---

[17] The doxography is anonymous, like everything else in the commentary, but all the figures concerned are identified by an industrious scholiast.

[18] "Fragments d'un Commentaire de Porphyre sur la Parménide," *Revue des Études Grecques* LXXIV (1961): 410–438, and *Porphyre et Victorinus*, vol. II.

on the question, but the parallels that he adduces still, I think, create no more than a probability. The Anonymous Commentary covers the text, in patches, from 137c to 143a, so that much of it coincides with the surviving part of Proclus' Commentary. It is therefore interesting to compare them where they can be compared.

The first point of contact comes at *Anon.* I, 25ff. Hadot, where the author is discussing the proper sense in which the One may be described as ἄπειρον (137d7). After rejecting the view of Speusippus and another authority whose name is corrupt that it is infinite in smallness (διὰ σμικρότητα), the author advances his own view that it is so because of its infinite power, and its being the cause of all existing things, and first principle of all things that follow upon it . . . and because it transcends even the notion of 'one' (διὰ τὸ αὐτὴν καταλείπειν καὶ τὴν τοῦ ἑνὸς ἐπίνοιαν)."

Now this view does indeed appear in Proclus, as Hadot points out, at 1118.19ff., in the course of a doxography on just this question. But there are complications. This view appears second in a list of four, culminating in that of Syrianus and Proclus. Working backwards, we find a view, probably that of Iamblichus, that the One is infinite because Nous is Limit, and it transcends Nous. Then comes the view that it is infinite "ὡς ἀπειροδύναμον καὶ ὡς πάντων γεννητικόν, and because it is the cause of unlimitness in all existent things, and extends the gift of itself throughout all existent things." The first view given is that the One is infinite because it is intraversable (ἀδιεξίτητον) and because it serves as a limit to all other things, while requiring no limit itself. Now this first view is also criticised by Plotinus in *Enn.* VI, 9.6, who then proceeds to adopt the second view listed here: "We must therefore hold that the One is infinite not by reason of its intraversability either in size or in number, but rather from the infinity of its power (τῷ ἀπεριλήπτῳ τῆς δυνάμεως)."

It is entirely probable that Porphyry would be in agreement with Plotinus on this. Plotinus also declares (5.3ff.) that smallness should not be regarded as being in question here, as it might be if one were discussing the mathematical point. The first view listed by Proclus is therefore pre-Plotinian, and the second view that of Porphyry. What we now observe, though, is a number of small inconsistencies between Proclus and the *Anon.* Proclus attributes to Porphyry (?) the view that it is infinite because it is not just the cause of existent things, but the cause of *unlimitedness* in all existent things (which, indeed, makes more sense). There is also no mention in Proclus of the idea that the One transcends even the notion of "One," a point made much of by the *Anon.* On the evidence so far, one might say that the commentary seems to be influenced by Porphyry, but could be that of a pupil.

The next point of contact, after a long gap in the text, occurs at 139c (sects. III–VI) on the question whether the One is other than the Others (its unlikeness to the Others is brought in too, although this is raised only at 139e7ff.). The text of the *Anon.* resumes at the point where the *aporia* is being raised as to whether God can in this case be said to be "other than" and "unlike to" Intellect. The answer to this is that the One (or God) does not differentiate itself from other things by unlikeness or otherness, but by possessing an "incomparable superiority" ἀσύμβλητος ὑπεροχή) to everything else, in virtue of which everything else is, as it were, nothing. The author then goes on to illustrate the unsuitability of applying the terms 'other' and 'same' to the One by using the comparisons of our talk of the sun's 'rising' and 'setting', where nothing at all is in fact happening to the sun, and of our thinking the land is moving as we sail past it, while in fact it is we who are moving.

These images find no echo, unfortunately, in what should be the parallel passage of Proclus (Book VII, 1184.9–1185.10). Here, an *aporia* is raised, not about Intellect in particular, but "how the One can be said to be transcendent over all other things, if it is not other than them?" The answer is that the One transcends and is separate from all other things, not by virtue of Otherness, but through an "unspeakable superiority" (ἄφραστος ὑπεροχή—a notable verbal echo of *Anon.* III, 7, one might argue, though Hadot does not note it). Proclus, instead of either of the *Anon.*'s images, points to the two usages of *aei*—"always," to signify sempiternity, in the case of the cosmos, and eternity, in the case of Intellect. He also does not follow the *Anon.* in laying any emphasis on the non-existence of everything else, a topic on which the *Anon.* expatiates at length. Indeed, apart from the partial coincidence of phraseology in ἄφραστος ὑπεροχή, there is no indication that Proclus is acquainted with the text of *Anon.*

The next point of contact occurs at 141a5–d6, the proof that the One cannot be "in time," and so neither older nor younger nor the same age as itself. This is all one lemma for the *Anon.*, though Proclus divides it into six, covering ten pages of Cousin's text (1233.33 to 1233.19). Once again, the position is less than satisfactory. First of all, Proclus begins with a discussion of how the One should transcend eternity as well as time, which is not reflected in *Anon.*, who turns directly to the question of the logical form of Plato's argument here.

This corresponds to Proclus' discussion from 1225.37 on (his second lemma), and both Proclus and *Anon.* then address the view held by some that Plato is simply being sophistical here. In answer to this, Proclus provides a three-stage doxography leading up to Syrianus (1226.2ff.), so that this would have been an excellent place to test Porphyrian authorship, but unfortunately *Anon.*'s text breaks off just as he has stated the problem (VIII, 35). We do at least have a minimal verbal coincidence (σοφιστικὸς ὁ λόγος, VIII, 33, and 1225.38), but that is not much to go on.

When the text resumes again (sects. IX-X) we are at the end of the First Hypothesis, discussing the unknowability of God, à propos, presumably, 142a3-8, but there is no point of contact between Proclus and *Anon.* here, and Proclus does not give a doxographical survey which would enable us to identify any Porphyrian doctrine.

After that, we are in the Second Hypothesis, and all hope of comparison ends. The confrontation between the two texts has been tantalisingly inconclusive. There are points of contact, but nothing, I think, that could not be explained by a common source in Porphyry, while nothing that is really distinctive about *Anon.* comes through in Proclus. But one might well make two points here. First, if this is not Porphyry, who on earth is it? It is not Iamblichus, and the pattern of Proclus' doxographical notices seems to show that the commentaries of Porphyry and Iamblichus were the only ones, apart from that of Syrianus, with which he was familiar. Occasionally there is a fourth opinion given, but this can usually be explained as someone Porphyry is refuting, and need not denote another full-scale commentator. Secondly, one might argue that Proclus might not in fact be using Porphyry's commentary at first hand, but only through Iamblichus or Syrianus. Incredible as this might seem, we should not underestimate the capacity of late antique commentators to bypass primary sources when secondary ones were available. Thus Proclus may only have been acquainted with the main points of Porphyry's exegesis and not with his literary elaborations. On the whole, I am prepared to leave the *Anon. Taur.* with Porphyry on the basis of the analogies which Hadot has brought to light, while being unable to share Hadot's certainty that he has solved the puzzle.

After Porphyry, we also have sufficient evidence that Iamblichus composed a commentary on the *Parmenides*. Apart from evidence of his views on the subject of the hypotheses (1054.35-1055.25, with the scholiast) we have about ten references to him in Damascius' *De Principiis* (the latter part of which we may now, following Westerink,[19] learn to term his *Commentary on the Parmenides*), which clearly come from a *Parmenides Commentary* (frs. 3-14 in my collection). The extent to which he contributed to the Syrianic-Procline view of the dialogue is not clear, but he certainly will have allegorised the characters and

---

[19] Proclus, *PT* III, pp. lxxxiii-lxxix. It is plain, in fact, that everything from ch. 127 of the *De Principiis* onwards (vol. II, p. 5 Ruelle) is a commentary on the *Parmenides*, beginning with the Second Hypothesis (142b1).

adopted a positive interpretation of the arguments of the first part. As regards the interpretation of the First Hypothesis, we have eleven doxographic passages in Books VI and VII, where a series of three authorities is presented, culminating in Syrianus, which leads to the probability that the previous two are Porphyry and Iamblichus. In a number of cases, it is possible to discern something, either in the content or in Proclus' way of referring to them, that is characteristic of one or the other, and I have adverted to these in the notes. Certainty can never be claimed here, but I think it likely that we have the opinions of Porphyry and Iamblichus on a series of passages, which show that they gave detailed attention to the text. However, there is no indication that Iamblichus anticipated the elaborate series of identifications of levels of being worked out by Syrianus for the First and Second Hypotheses.

I append here a list of these passages, to serve as a basis for further discussion:

PASSAGES ATTRIBUTABLE TO PORPHYRY AND IAMBLICHUS FROM BOOKS VI AND VII

	Porphyry	*Iamblichus*
VI	1053.38–1054.37	1054.37–1055.25
	1089.30–1090.13	1090.13–23
	1106.31–1107.9	1107.9–1108.19
	1114.1–19	1114.20–35
	1118.19–25	1118.25–33
VII	1140.26–1141.13	1141.13–1142.10
	1150.2–21	1150.22–1151.7
	1173.7–1174.3	1174.3–12
	1216.15–37	1216.37–1217.13
	1226.6–15	1226.15–26
	64K.25–66K.24	66K.25–68K.14

The existence of commentaries by Porphyry and Iamblichus, then, is assured. As to Plutarch of Athens and Syrianus, Proclus' immediate predecessors and teachers, the position is less certain. In the case of Plutarch, we know that he had views on the *Parmenides*, since we have his interpretation of the subject matter of the hypotheses (of which he identified *nine*) in Book VI, 1058.21–1061.20, but there is no evidence that he composed a commentary on the dialogue. He does not seem to figure in the doxographical passages (where he should be accorded comparable honour to Syrianus, if he had any views), and Damascius only mentions him in connection with the identification of the subject matters, though he frequently records the views of Syrianus. However, Plutarch's view of the subjects of the hypotheses formed the basis for that of Syrianus, so it is important. He sees only the first five as having positive subjects (God, Intellect, Soul, Forms-in-Matter, Matter), while the last four have only a negative role, as reductions *ad absurdum*, showing that the existence of all other things is abolished if the One does not exist. He also sees the subjects of Hypotheses II–V represented in the four divisions of the Line in *Republic* VI (1060.26ff.). But this does not amount to evidence for a commentary. Plutarch's interests, indeed, seem to have run more in the direction of psychology. The two works that he is recorded as reading with Proclus are Aristotle's *De Anima* and Plato's *Phaedo*.

Whereas Plutarch pretty certainly communicated his interpretation of the dialogue only orally, the situation with Syrianus is less clear. The fact that Damascius refers to him does not constitute independent evidence of a commentary, since Damascius is only using Proclus. Proclus refers to him repeatedly, but these references may simply be to his own notes of Syrianus' lectures. This is not to say, however, that Syrianus' influence is not paramount in the commentary. Proclus in fact makes no bones about the fact that he owes everything to his master (cf. his remarks in the Preface, 618.3ff. and in Book VI, 1061.20ff.), and the explicit references to him are probably just the tip of the iceberg. The question of Proclus' debt to Syrianus, though generally recognised now by scholars, still needs further exploration through a proper study of Syrianus' own philosophy. Dr. Anne Sheppard has made a useful contribution recently in the matter of the essays on the *Republic*,[20] but Syrianus' role in both the *Timaeus* and *Parmenides Commentaries* has yet to be fully stated. The more Syrianus emerges from obscurity, the more I think it will become clear that, in Dodds' words, "Proclus is not an innovator, but a systematiser of other men's ideas."[21]

Even the extent to which further systematising was required here may be called in question. The basis for Proclus' exegesis of the First and Second Hypotheses is the remarkable notion of Syrianus that each characteristic denied, or asserted, of the One represents a distinct class of gods. A useful table of them is provided by Saffrey and Westerink in the introduction to volume I of the Budé *Platonic Theology* (pp. lxviii-lxix), but it may be worth while reproducing it here, with due acknowledgement:

[20] *Studies on the 5th and 6th Essays of Proclus' Commentary on the Republic* (*Hypomnemata,* Heft 61), Göttingen, 1980, ch. 2.
[21] Introduction, p. xxv.

Parmenides	Attribute denied	Class of gods	In Parmenidem
141e7–142a1	One-that-is	intelligible gods	VII, 26K.1–46K.18
137c4–5	multiple	1st triad of intelligible-intellectual gods	VI, 1089.17–1097.20
137c4–d4	whole and parts	2d triad of intelligible-intellectual gods	VI, 1097.21–1110.15
137d5–138a1	shape	3d triad of intelligible-intellectual gods	VI, 1110.16–1134.12
138a2–b7	in itself, in another	1st triad of intellectual gods	VII, 1133.13–1152.14
138b8–139b4	at rest, in motion	2d triad of intellectual gods	VII, 1152.15–1172.26
139b5–139e6	the same, different	7th divinity (Demiurge)	VII, 1172.27–1191.9
139e7–140b5	like, unlike	hypercosmic gods	VII, 1191.10–1201.21
140b6–d8	equal,	encosmic gods	VII, 1201.22–1212.4
140e1–141d7	time	universal souls	VII, 1212.5–1233.19
141d8–e7	parts of time	'higher beings' (angels, daemons, heroes)	VII, 1233.20–1239.21

I have noted these divisions at the appropriate places in the special introductions to Books VI and VII, but it is useful, I think, to have them set out here. This whole scheme is the brainchild of Syrianus, to which Proclus contributes nothing further that is discernible.

The case is pretty certainly the same with the elaborate scheme of ascent through the levels of Form that is discerned in the first part of the dialogue, as expounded throughout Book IV (see the introduction to that book). Proclus presents Parmenides as posing his problems about the Forms simply in order to lead Socrates to a more sophisticated understanding of the multiplicity of levels at which the Forms manifest themselves. Each apparently insoluble puzzle, then, is only insoluble at a certain level. Advance a stage higher, and it solves itself. The Third Man argument, for instance, is an insoluble puzzle at the level of immanent forms, but Parmenides is here leading Socrates to an understanding of transcendent Forms (889.6ff.), where it no longer presents a problem. There are for Proclus no insoluble puzzles in the first part of the *Parmenides*. But such a scheme, though not attributed at any stage to Syrianus, must surely have formed part of the exegesis of a man who could derive such subtleties as he does from the text of the First Hypothesis.

Like Proclus, Syrianus commented on the whole dialogue, but, as I have said, we cannot be sure that he composed a written commentary. If he did not, then it would indeed be Proclus' chief distinction to have preserved and formalised his master's teachings, here as elsewhere.

C. THE PLACE OF THE
PARMENIDES COMMENTARY IN
PROCLUS' WORK

We know, or think we know, from Marinus, Proclus' biographer, (*VP* 13), that by the age of 28 (that is to say, by A.D. 440), Proclus had composed ("among many other treatises") his *Commentary on the Timaeus*. Whether or not Syrianus was still alive at this time is not certain. The date of his death is normally given as about 437, but on no very conclusive evidence. Proclus' references to him in the *Timaeus Commentary* are normally in the imperfect ("my own teacher used to say," "the view of my own teacher was"), which is ambiguous since it could simply refer back to Syrianus' views expressed in his seminar, but on the whole it seems more likely that Proclus only began to publish his commentaries after his master's death.

In the *Timaeus Commentary*, Proclus appears to make reference to a few previous works of his own. At I, 45.8 (ταῦτα μὲν οὖν καὶ ἐν ἄλλοις) we seem to have a reference back to his *Commentary on the Cratylus* (which is preserved in a summary form), where a similar but fuller discussion of the role of the Demiurgic Intellect in the universe is to be found in chapter 99 (48.13–51.13 Pasquali), but this is less than certain. A clearer reference is made to his *Commentary on the Philebus* (now lost) at I, 385.9 (δέδεικται δ' ἐν ἄλλοις). We also hear of συνουσίαι on the *Phaedrus* (III, 295.4), which might mean no more than oral lectures, but there seems little point in mentioning them unless they were recorded, and we know from other references (e.g. *In Parm.* 1128.37, ὡς ἐνδείκνυμεν ἐξηγούμενοι τὸν Φαῖδρον) that he wrote such a commentary.

There is evidence, then, that the *Timaeus Commentary*, while a relatively youthful work, is by no means Proclus' earliest (unless, of course, we assume these references to be later editorial insertions). On the other hand, it is certainly earlier than the *Parmenides Commentary*. There is an interesting reference forward to the latter at *In Tim.* III,

12.27-30: πόσαι δὲ αὐταὶ καὶ οἶαι (sc. certain intermediate natures), θείως μὲν οἱ θεοὶ γιγνώσκουσιν, ἀνθρωπίνως δὲ καὶ φιλοσόφως ἡ τοῦ Παρμενίδου διδάσκει μυστικὴ παράδοσις, εἰς ἥν καὶ ἡμεῖς τὴν ἀκριβῆ περὶ τούτων ἐξεργασίαν ἀναβαλλόμεθα. This passage definitely looks forward to a commentary on the *Parmenides*, but gives us no indication how soon the project was to be realised.

An indication that some time elapsed between the two commentaries is, as I have noted at various points in the text of the *Parmenides Commentary*, that there is a paternalistic and middle-aged tone about many of Proclus' obiter dicta in this work which would suggest that the author is a good deal more than twenty-eight. There are also a number of probable references back to the *Timaeus Commentary* (812.25, to *In Tim.* II, 43.27ff.; 925.20, to *In Tim.* II, 21.62ff.; 1174.25, to II, 135.21ff. or 160.6ff.; 1225.29-30, to III, 14.16ff.) as well as to commentaries on the *Sophist* (774.24-25) and on the *Phaedrus* (950.1; 1128.37). As for Proclus' two other works of commentary, the collection of essays on the *Republic* and the *Commentary on the Alcibiades I*, the position is not clear. The *Republic Commentary* contains clear references to the *Timaeus Commentary* at II, 20.10 and 335.20 (the latter to a lost portion of it), and a reference at I, 37.23 (εἴρηται μὲν οὖν διὰ πλειόνων ἐν ἄλλοις περὶ τούτων) is discerned by the scholiast *ad loc* to be a reference to the essay *De Malorum Substantia*, a commentary on Diotima's speech in the *Symposium* (lost), the *Commentary on the Theaetetus* (lost), and a Commentary on Plotinus' *Enneads* (lost), but the scholiast is probably only producing parallel passages, without a clear knowledge of their chronological order.

The *Alcibiades Commentary* seems to contain no clear references to any other work, but in one important respect it stands nearer to the *Parmenides Commentary* than to the *Timaeus Commentary*. For some reason, in the *In Parm.* Proclus eschews reference to any previous commentator except Syrianus, and even he is only referred to periphrastically as "our master" or "our leader." All others are simply οἱ μέν and οἱ δέ. By contrast the *Timaeus Commentary* is explicit in its references to the commentaries of Porphyry and Iamblichus, and refers frequently to opinions of Plotinus and Amelius, as well as occasionally to Middle Platonists such as Albinus, Plutarch, Atticus, Numenius or Severus. The *Alcibiades Commentary* makes explicit reference only to Iamblichus (6 times) and Syrianus (once) of previous commentators, and once to a passage of Plotinus. This may only be because there was little previous commentary on the *Alcibiades*, but it does appear more like the practice of the *In Parm.* By the time of the composing of that commentary, Proclus seems to have come to the conclusion that referring by name to previous commentators was somehow inartistic, and he reduces them to anonymity. If we had his lost commentaries on the *Philebus, Theaetetus*, and *Sophist*, we might well be able to trace various stages of development in this tendency, but as it is we can only note the striking contrast between his practice in the *In Tim.* and that in the *In Parm.*

I have indicated in the commentaries to the individual books the various passages mentioned above which point to the *In Parm.* being composed relatively late in Proclus' career, but we may review them together here. First of all, it is dedicated to a pupil of his, Asclepiodotus (618.18) who was admittedly one of his older pupils, since he acted as pedagogue to a younger pupil, Isidore, (Dam. *Vit. Isid.* 156.4 Zintzen), but a pupil none the less. Then there are a series of remarks on the proper attitude of pupils to masters and of the young to the old, which, while not impossible for a very priggish youth, would come much more naturally from a well-established middle-aged professor. Examples are Book I, 695.26ff., 697.23ff., 701.15ff., 722.15ff., and the homily on the nature of the ideal student in Book IV, 926-927.

In fact, however, the exact chronological position of the *In Parm.* in Proclus' work is not of great importance, since there is very little indication of any development in his philosophy over the whole extent of his published works. For instance, one may accept E. R. Dodds' judgement[22] that the *Elements of Theology* is early (*In Tim.* II, 195.27ff., seems to be a reference to *ET*, props. 67ff., among others—ὡς πολλάκις ἡμῖν ἐν ἄλλοις δέδεικται), and that the *Platonic Theology* is late (it refers back to the *In Parm.*, e.g. *PT* II, p. 61, 17 S-W; III, p. 83, 9 S-W), but between those two productions there is very little observable change. One may note a certain development in the elaboration of subdivisions of the intelligible world: for instance, the intelligible and intellectual realm, which is firmly established in the Commentaries, as well as in the *Platonic Theology* , finds no place in the *Elements*, nor does the subdivision into subordinate triads of the triad Being-Life-Mind. But since both these elaborations seem to be attributed to Iamblichus by Proclus in the *Timaeus Commentary* (I, 308.18ff.),[23] it can hardly be maintained that they were not part of Proclus' philosophical system at the time of the composition of the *ET*. More probably he did not feel it necessary to introduce these elaborations into a treatise on *elements*—though, as Dodds remarks (*op. cit.*, p. xvi), the omission of the whole intelligible-and-intellectual realm is hard to explain. It is firmly there, however, in the *In Tim.*, which is, as we know, an early work.

---

[22] Proclus, *ET*, Introduction, pp. xv-xvi. The first scholar to attempt a chronology of Proclus' works was actually J. Freudenthal, in *Hermes* 16 (1881): 214ff., who based his conclusions mainly on the cross-references that Proclus makes to his own works. In the case of *ET*, however, the format of the work really precludes any such references.

[23] See Appendix C of my *Iamblichi Fragmenta*, pp. 417-419.

For Proclus, the *Timaeus* and the *Parmenides* were the two summits of Platonic philosophy (*In Tim.* I, 54.14), to be reached after the progressive study of a series of ten dialogues, beginning with the *Alcibiades I* (cf. *In Alc.* 11.11) and continuing with the *Gorgias, Phaedo, Cratylus, Theaetetus, Sophist, Statesman, Phaedrus, Symposium, Philebus,* arranged according to their *skopoi*, or subject matter, to form a complete course in all branches of philosophy, from a knowledge of oneself (*Alcibiades*) to a knowledge of the Good (*Philebus*).[24] This scheme is actually that of Iamblichus, as Proclus freely acknowledges. It presumably constituted the normal course in the Platonic School from Iamblichus' time onwards. The fact of this being the established order of instruction does not necessitate that Proclus wrote his commentaries in this order, of course, though it might have influenced him to some extent.

All the indications, then, are that the *Parmenides Commentary* is a work of Proclus' middle age, and that it represents the summit of his achievement in the commentary form, as well as the most developed stage of his philosophy. He plainly did not rush into the task of commenting on the work which he regarded as containing Plato's inspired teaching on the highest realities in the universe. How far he was satisfied with the result we cannot be sure. According to Marinus (*VP* 38), he professed himself most satisfied with his commentaries on the *Timaeus* and the *Theaetetus*. No mention of the *Parmenides*. Certainly the *Timaeus Commentary* is easier to read, but there is something awesome about the intellectual achievement of deriving a constructive philosophical system, and indeed a blueprint of the intelligible universe, out of the text of the *Parmenides* that makes the latter more impressive.

One reason that Proclus may be unwilling to claim too much credit for the *Parmenides Commentary* might of course be that in fact very little of it is truly his. As I have argued in the previous section, the basic scheme of interpretation of the Hypotheses, and of the First and Second in particular, is that of Syrianus, as certainly is the interpretation of the arguments in the first part of the dialogue. But the *Timaeus Commentary* seems to be just as thoroughly based on the exegesis of Syrianus, so this is hardly a very plausible answer to the problem.

A final question requiring discussion is how far the commentary of Proclus originally extended. What survives extends only as far as the end of the First Hypothesis, less than half the extent of the whole dialogue, and it is already a mighty work. Raymond Klibansky, in announcing his discovery of Moerbeke's translation[25] wished to maintain

---

[24] This list is found in the *Anonymous Prolegomena to Platonic Philosophy*, a work of the 6th century A.D. The *Sophist* and *Statesman* are omitted in the MSS, but added very plausibly by Westerink after the *Theaetetus* to bring the number of dialogues up to ten.

[25] *Ein Proklos-Fund und Seine Bedeutung*, Heidelberg, 1929.

that the end of the First Hypothesis is as far as Proclus went. But this is to dismiss not only the references forward to proposed discussion of the Second Hypothesis (e.g. 725.1-2; 733.31; 1137.6-7; 1175.30-31; 1191.14-15)—which might, of course, remain unfulfilled—but the fact that Damascius' *Problems and Solutions*, from chapter 127 on, is explicitly a commentary on Proclus' *Commentary*, and that this extends to the end of the dialogue, making constant reference to Proclus' views (normally referring to him simply as αὐτός). Indeed, the conclusion to Damascius' work (not, admittedly, written by Damascius himself), reads "The Problems and Solutions of Damascius the Successor to the *Parmenides* of Plato, following step by step (ἀντιπαρατεινόμεναι) the commentaries on the dialogue of the Philosopher" (i.e. Proclus), and this is a true description of the contents. Klibansky is compelled to argue that Damascius is actually commenting on the *Platonic Theology*. Now certainly Proclus covers the same ground in the *Platonic Theology*, but Damascius actually contrasts his treatment of one question in the *Commentary* with that in the *PT* (II, p. 96.13-19) to the detriment of the latter—so there is no question, I think, of the *PT* being his source for the bulk of his references.[26]

The total commentary must indeed, then, have been a monstrous work, and it is not, perhaps, surprising that it suffered the fate of Proclus' other surviving commentaries (the *In Tim.* and the *In Alc.*), as well as of the *Platonic Theology*, in being truncated, perhaps by an overburdened scribe. The essence of his views on the rest of the dialogue can in fact be recovered, both from the *Platonic Theology* and from Damascius, by anyone who is interested.

D. THE PROBLEM OF THE
FORTY LOGOI OF ZENO

At a number of places in the Commentary, to be discussed below, Proclus seems to show knowledge of a treatise of Zeno's which is not derivable from the text of the *Parmenides*, and the inference seems possible that he has access to a document, whether genuine or otherwise, purporting to be the original book of Zeno, from which he is quoting here.

It may be useful, I think, to detail all the references which Proclus

---

[26] It must be admitted, as a problem for my view, that all the Greek manuscripts of the Commentary (though not, it seems, Moerbeke's original) begin with the heading Πρόκλου Πλατωνικοῦ Διαδόχου εἰς τὸν Πλάτωνος Παρμενίδην ἑπτὰ βιβλίων τὸ πρῶτον, which makes clear that their archetype contained only the seven books we have, but I would suggest that this only proves that the Commentary was truncated at a fairly early stage in the tradition. It may be noted that neither the MSS of the *Timaeus Commentary* nor those of the *Platonic Theology* make any mention of a definite number of books.

makes to Zeno's treatise, to see how many of them are susceptible of such an interpretation:

1. At 619.30-620.3, Proclus introduces us to Zeno's treatise: "Now Zeno, Parmenides' disciple, did not care to plead directly for his master's doctrine, since he thought it needed no additional confirmation, but attempted to give it secret aid by writing a book in which he ingeniously showed that those who suppose that beings are many encountered no fewer difficulties than were alleged against those who say Being is one. For he showed that the same thing will be both like and unlike, both equal and unequal, and in general that there will result the abolition of all order in the world, and that everything will be thrown into confusion."

Everything that Proclus states here is derivable from Plato's *Parmenides*, 127d–128e, except the statement at the end that Zeno showed that the same thing will be, not only "like and unlike," but "equal and unequal" ($\emph{ἴσον καὶ ἄνισον}$). One might say that this is an easy extrapolation from "like and unlike" (and that the final remark about "the abolition of all order in the world" is likewise a natural deduction from the text); but it need not be, and I think it may be regarded as a straw in the wind.

2. At 684.21-26 Proclus refers to Zeno's treatise as follows: "Such was Zeno, perhaps, in bodily appearance, 'tall and graceful in appearance,' but far more so in respect of his discourse ($λόγοι$). For what Parmenides had uttered in compressed form, Zeno unfolds and transmits in extended discourse ($εἰς παμμήκεις λόγους ἐκτείνων$)."

There is nothing here, certainly, that could not be derived from the text, though the adjective $παμμήκης$ is quite emphatic.

3. The next substantive reference occurs at 694.23ff. (= 29A15 D-K), in connection with "Socrates' questioning of Zeno: Zeno had put forth many arguments, *forty in all*." He then reports the first one, in terms entirely derivable from the text of the dialogue. Further down, however, he makes some remarks which would seem more natural if he had a text of Zeno in front of him. At 696.8-9, he says "Socrates has set forth the whole argument quite clearly and succinctly, having accurately identified the first hypothesis, and seen the purpose of the argument as a whole"; and then, at 696.16-18: "Zeno has developed each of these parts *at length* ($διὰ πολλῶν$)." Both of the latter remarks could, certainly, be deductions from the text of the dialogue (e.g. 128b1), but they are more naturally, I think, taken as the statements of someone who is comparing one text with another. As for the detail that the *logoi* amounted to forty, Proclus here is our earliest authority for this. Our

only other source, the sixth-century commentator Elias (also 29A15 D-K) gives no indication of deriving his information from Proclus, and may thus be regarded as an independent source.

4. At 696.28-29, we have a reference to "this and Zeno's other arguments," which seems to indicate Proclus' acquaintance with a series of them.

5. More substantially, in Book II, 725.22-39, we find a passage where an argument of Zeno's against plurality is given which could not be derived from the text. In Plato's text we simply have the statement that, if things are many, they must be both like and unlike. We have no indication how Zeno argued for this conclusion, or what he meant by it. Proclus explains this as follows: "If things are many, they will be *unlike* one another, since they will have no share in unity or sameness; but they will also be *like*, in that they will possess the common characteristic of not participating in any 'one' (characteristic)."

The terminology which Proclus employs here is certainly not primitive (talk of "participation" is hardly Zenonian), but the basic argument surely is. Indeed, using 'like and unlike' as if they described attributes of a subject would be absurdly primitive at any time after logic had been developed in the Academy and Peripatos (unless we are dealing with a very sophisticated forger). The argument can only be effective at a time before the logic of predication was understood. I would suggest, therefore, that Proclus had before him a document which, however reworked, is of Zenonian origin.

6. At 760.27-761.3, à propos 129b6-8, we find the following: "After the words about likeness and unlikeness, he shifts back to unity and plurality, drawing upon Zeno's own discourse (καὶ ταῦτα ἀπὸ τῶν Ζήνωνος λόγων λαβών). For just as Zeno had refuted those who separate the many from the One by showing that Likeness and Unlikeness become the same, so likewise he argues against them by starting from the One and from plurality, and shows that apart from the One the same thing will be many and the many one. For a plurality apart from the One is a many by the very fact that it does not partake of unity, for what is not controlled by unity is many; and since they have in common their not being one, they will be one by this very fact, for things that share a character in common are one by virtue of this common character. So that if not being one is common to them, the many will be one by virtue of not being one; and inversely their not being one will be one because it is present the same in them all."

Once again, Proclus professes to be checking the course of the argument in Plato's dialogue off against the sequence of arguments in

Zeno's original work. The argument presented is similar to the one presented above about like and unlike, and presupposes a similar level of logical primitiveness when one has abstracted the later (Procline?) terminology of participation.[27]

7. At 769.23-770.1, à propos Socrates' mention of Rest and Motion at 129e1, we find the following:[28] "These last two (sc. Rest and Motion) he has added to the pairs previously mentioned, since Zeno also had used them as well as the former ones to prove the absurdity of separating the many from the one. Zeno's refutation has been based not only on Likeness and Unlikeness, Unity and Plurality, but also on Rest and Motion. He showed that if the many are without unity, it follows that the same thing in the same respect is both at rest and in motion. Everything at rest is in a one something (ἔν τινί ἐστιν ἑνί), and everything that is in motion is departing from some one (position); so that if the many do not share in a unity, they will be unresting; and again, if they have in common the character of not sharing in some unity, they will be in some one (state); hence will be in this respect unmoving. The same things, therefore, will be moving and stationary; so that the many are not altogether devoid of unity. Such was Zeno's argument."

This argument uses the ambiguity of the expression ἐν ἑνί, which can be taken to mean "in a place," "in a state," or "in a position," to construct an argument of similar form to the previous ones.

8. At 862.26-34, while commenting on Socrates' attempted analogy of the daylight (131b) Proclus says: "It is clear that he has taken his example from the discourse of Zeno; for Zeno, in his endeavour to show that the many participate in some one, and are not devoid of one, even though greatly separated from each other, has said in his discourse that whiteness is present both to us and to the antipodes, just as night and day are."

This passage has a number of interesting aspects, which I have discussed in an earlier article,[29] but which may be repeated now. The point of the argument was presumably that 'white' is taken to be 'one thing', and yet the many say that there are many white things, so that, "if there

---

[27] The manuscript tradition, by the way, both Greek and Latin, becomes confused at 761.2-3 Cousin, as is perceived by Chaignet in his translation (p. 218). For καὶ πάλιν τὸ οὐχ ἕν ὡσαύτως ἐν τῷ ἕν πᾶσιν εἶναι ταὐτὸν / et omne quod non unum eodem modo in eo quod unum omnibus inest idem (rendering καὶ πᾶν τὸ οὐχ ἐν τῷ ἐν πᾶσιν ἔνεστι ταὐτὸν?), we should read καὶ πάλιν τὸ οὐχ ἕν ὡσαύτως ἕν, τῷ ἐν πᾶσιν εἶναι ταὐτὸν, since what we need is "and inversely their not being one will be one, because it is present in them all."

[28] This passage I have discussed already in the *Archiv für Gesch.d.Phil.* 58 (1976): 221-222.

[29] "New Evidence on Zeno of Elea," *AGPh.* 56 (1974): 127-131.

are many," 'white', which is *one*, would have to be in various different places at once. The Antipodes are brought in, I assume, as being the most remote people from us, but they are a strange and notable feature, since, if Zeno really mentioned them, this would be their earliest attested mention. Certainly, the form of the argument, with its ignorance of predication, is primitive enough to be Presocratic.

9. In Book V, 1024.12ff. Proclus tells us that Zeno used to call some of his arguments "true" and others "tactical," or "useful for the purpose at hand" (χρειώδεις). This detail seems to be recorded nowhere else, but on the other hand it is hardly the sort of thing that Zeno would admit in the course of presenting his *Forty Logoi*, so I would not wish to claim it as a further testimonium to that work.

THIS seems to complete the references to Zeno's work which are not clearly derivable from the text of Plato. What are we to make of them? And how is this work that Proclus talks of to be related to that which was available later to Simplicius? I see no reason that the arguments should not come from the same work as was available to Simplicius, at least in respect of the arguments he quotes against Plurality (there seems to have been a separate treatise against the possibility of motion, cf. Zeno A15 D-K). If these seem puerile in comparison to those, then we may perhaps take refuge in Zeno's own reported distinction, just mentioned above, between *Logoi* that are ἀληθεῖς and those that are χρειώδεις. To quote Jonathan Barnes (*The Presocratic Philosophers*, I, pp. 236-237): "Many modern interpreters of Zeno have argued that such and such an account of a paradox is wrong because it attributes such a silly fallacy to a profound mind. Zeno was not profound: he was clever. Some profundities fall from his pen; but so too did some trifling fallacies. And that is what we should expect from an eristic disputant. If we meet a deep argument, we are not bound to search for a nugget of philosophical gold. Fair metal and base, in roughly equal proportions, make the Zenonian alloy."

I quote this eloquent passage with a certain relish, since Barnes does not accept the genuineness of (6) and (7) above (*loc. cit.* supra p. 336, n. 8). He may be right, but he is also right to suggest that philosophical naiveté need not be a bar to genuineness. Furthermore, all Greek thinkers were prepared to throw bad arguments as well as good at a thesis in the hope that something would stick. It did not necessarily mean that they were persuaded by the arguments themselves.

Barnes states just below (*ibid.*, p. 237): "We do not know how Zeno argued for the proposition (a) 'If *P*, then everything is alike, and (b) if

P, then everything is unlike.' " I suggest that we do, and that it is contained in passage (5) above.

My conclusion is that Proclus certainly had a document in his possession called the *Forty Logoi of Zeno*, or something such—probably, though not certainly, the same document that was available to Simplicius a century later—and it seems possible to me that it at least contained genuine material, though perhaps worked over at a later date, or even incorporated from another, genuine source into a pseudepigraphic work.

E. PREVIOUS EDITIONS AND TRANSLATIONS

There have been five editions of the Greek text of the *Commentary on the Parmenides*: two by Victor Cousin, in 1821-1827[30] and 1864, the latter of which I have used as the basis for this translation (with its pagination in the margin); and three by G. Stallbaum, which are based upon those of Cousin, though Stallbaum on occasion wisely rejects conjectures of Cousin in favour of the manuscript.

Cousin's edition is a considerable achievement, but it does not attain modern standards of reliability. He based himself on only four manuscripts, all in the Biblothèque Nationale, with some reference to a fragmentary Latin translation in a 16th-century MS in Vienna, which he attributed to the Dutch scholar Anton-Hermann Gogava, but which Klibansky has subsequently shown to be by Nicolo Scutelli (and furthermore to be a translation, or rather paraphrase, of an existing Greek manuscript, and thus useless for establishing the text). In his second edition Cousin was also able to profit from a host of emendations, many brilliant, from the English Neoplatonist Thomas Taylor, in a review of the first edition in the *Classical Journal*, in which Taylor made use of a manuscript in the British Museum, *Harleiensis* 5671, which is of the same family as two of Cousin's MSS (CD) but has some independent readings. Admittedly, Cousin did have access, in *Bibl. Nat. gr.* 1810 (A), to the best surviving Greek manuscript, but when we reflect that there exist 28 complete MSS of the *In Parm.*, as well as six mutilated ones, one can see that he had an inadequate basis for a scientific edition.

However, the most useful new source for establishing the text has turned out to be, not any Greek manuscript unused by Cousin, but rather a medieval Latin translation by the Flemish Dominican William

---

[30] It is worth noting, perhaps, from the point of view of the continuity of the Neoplatonic tradition, that Cousin dedicated this first edition to Hegel and Schelling.

of Moerbeke, who went out in the wake of the Latin conquest of Greece to become Bishop of Corinth from 1277 to 1281. While there he discovered and translated into Latin a number of works of Proclus, including his commentaries on the *Timaeus* and the *Parmenides*, the latter around 1285, near the end of his life. William's style of translation is highly literal, which frequently makes for near-nonsense, but has the advantage of enabling one to discern fairly clearly the original Greek from which he was working. The manuscript he was using is probably of the 12th century, at least two centuries older than all the extant Greek MSS except *Bibl. Nat. gr.* 1810 (which is 13th-century), and it differs significantly from all of them in its readings, generally for the better. Most importantly, it contains the end of Book VII, which completes the commentary on the First Hypothesis—while the Greek MSS break off before the commentary on 141e10-142a8—and thus adds 21 pages (in Klibansky's edition) to the text.

Raymond Klibansky rediscovered this translation in the 1920s, announcing it in his 1929 article "Ein Proklos-Fund und seine Bedeutung." The most important section of it, the commentary on the final section, was not published by Klibansky until 1953, and the full text is only being published now, in two volumes (vol. I, 1982; vol. II, 1985), by Dr. Carlos Steel.

Eventually, perhaps before the end of the decade, we may, as I mentioned in the Preface, have a modern edition of the whole text, by Steel and Alain Segonds, in the Budé series, but until then we are dependent on Cousin.

The only translation of the *Parmenides Commentary* into any modern language is that of A. E. Chaignet in 1900, reprinted by Minerva of Frankfurt in 1962. I have naturally found this repeatedly helpful, though Chaignet did not, of course, have the benefit of the Latin translation. Nevertheless, he frequently makes useful emendations. Chaignet also provides a translation of some sections of the *Platonic Theology*, then of the sections of a later commentary on the rest of *Parmenides* which Cousin appended to his edition of Proclus, and lastly some sections of Damascius' commentary. I have not felt it necessary to follow him in this.

NOTE ON THE PRESENT
TRANSLATION

GLENN MORROW reached as far as page 880, line 39, almost half way through Book IV, before he died, so that, although I have ventured to alter his terminology to a certain extent, I naturally sought to adapt my translation to his. The main difficulty has been in trying to maintain consistency in rendering Proclus' technical terminology, and it is inevitable that over such a vast extent of text, inconsistencies have gone unmarked.

One device I have adopted which I hope will clarify rather than obscure, and that involves the use of capital letters. When referring to the hypostases of Intellect and Soul, as well as to the Forms in their transcendent aspect, I have used capital initials, while referring to individual intellects and souls, and forms at any lower level, such as forms-in-matter, with lower-case initials.

In general, I have tried to translate each technical term of Proclus' metaphysics by the same English word, but in a number of cases this has meant rather a limited set of equivalent terms. Since all these terms are in regular use among modern students of Neoplatonism, no confusion should result. To assist in clarification, however, I append a list of common technical terms, with my accustomed translations:

αἰτία, cause, causal principle
κατ᾽ αἰτίαν, causally, on the level of cause
γένος, genus
γενικός, generic
γνῶσις, knowledge
δημιουργός, demiurge
δημιουργικός, demiurgic
διάνοια, discursive knowledge
διανοητικός, discursive
δόξα, opinion
δύναμις, power, potentiality
εἶδος, form, species
εἰδικός, specific
εἰδοποιός, formal, specificatory
ἕν, τό, the One
ἐνιαῖος, unitary, proper to the One
ἐνοειδής, unitary

ἑνάς, henad,
ἑναδικός, henadic
ἑνόω, unify
ἡνωμένος, unified
ἐνέργεια, activity, actuality
ἐπιστήμη, knowledge, scientific knowledge, science
ἑτερότης, otherness
ἰδέα, idea
καθόλου, general, universal
καθ᾽ ἕκαστον, particular
κόσμος, cosmos, world
κοσμικός, cosmic
ἐγ (κόσμιος) encosmic
ὑπερκόσμιος, supra-cosmic
λόγος, reason-principle, rational discourse
λογικός, rational, logical

xlv

ἄλογος, irrational
λογισμός, reasoning, ratiocination
μέθεξις, participation
κατὰ μέθεξιν, by participation
μερικός, particular, partial (opp.
  ὁλικός)
νοῦς, Intellect, intellect
νοερός, intellectual, intuitive (opp.
  διανοητικός)
νοητός, intelligible
νοεῖν, know, cognise
νόησις, intellection, cognition
ὄν, Being
ὄντως, essentially, really
οὐσία, substance, essence

οὐσιώδης, really-existent, substantial
κατ᾽οὐσίαν, essentially, on the level
  of essence
παράδειγμα, paradigm, example
παραδειγματικός, paradigmatic
ταυτότης, sameness, identity
ὕλη, Matter
ὑλικός, material
ἔνυλος, material, in matter (of
  forms)
ὑστερογενής, derived, 'later-born'
φύσις, Nature, nature
φυσικός, natural, in nature
ψυχή, Soul, soul
ψυχικός, psychic, in soul

No power on earth could make Proclus into a great stylist in any language. I have striven at all times for passable English, as far as was consistent with preserving accuracy. In some cases, I have divided up a long lemma into its constituent parts by subheadings, where it is plain that what we have is a short treatise on some philosophical point, e.g. at the beginning of Book III, on the Ideas, or the beginning of Book VI, on the number and subject matters of the hypotheses. I have also subdivided the Preface. It will be understood that these headings are not in the original.

A further element of inconsistency arises in my references in the notes to emendations from the Latin translation. At first, these seemed worth noting, but, on further reflection, I decided that since the coming Budé edition would incorporate them they would be superfluous. On the other hand, to cut out all such references would necessitate renumbering all the notes of the earlier books. The result is that some emendations from the Latin are noted, and some are not. Emendations due to Westerink are acknowledged by the abbreviation (West.). A considerable number of misprints and obvious errors in Cousin's edition are corrected silently.

PROCLUS,
THE PLATONIC SUCCESSOR
SEVEN BOOKS ON THE
PARMENIDES OF PLATO

BOOK I

◻

INTRODUCTION

▣ ▣ ▣

BOOK I of the Commentary carries us no further than 128e, a space of three Stephanus pages, in 104 columns of Cousin's edition. However, more than a third of the book (pp. 617-660) is a general introduction to the dialogue, so there are only 82 columns of commentary proper. I will deal first with this general introduction, and then touch on details of special interest arising in the commentary.

Proclus follows in his introduction the same general format as he follows in his other commentaries (*In Alc., In Remp., In Tim.*), a format going back, to some extent at least, to the Middle Platonic tradition and more immediately to Porphyry and Iamblichus, but fully developed only in the Athenian School, probably by Syrianus. Proclus himself seems to have written a treatise on the nature of the Platonic dialogue to which he refers in his *Commentary on the Alcibiades* (10.3ff.):

> As we have said elsewhere about the dialogues, each one must possess what the whole cosmos possesses; and an analogous part must be assigned therein to the Good, part to the Intellect, part to the Soul, and part to the underlying nature itself (sc. Matter).

This concept is formalised in the *Anonymous Prolegomena to Platonic Philosophy*—a product of the 6th-century Alexandrian School, but much dependent on Proclus—as follows:

> As we have seen, then, that the dialogue is a cosmos and the cosmos a dialogue, we may expect to find all the components of the universe in the dialogue. The constituents of the universe are these: Matter, Form, Nature (which unites Form with Matter), Soul, Intellect, and Divinity. In the dialogue we have, corresponding to Matter, the characters, the time, and the place in which Plato represents his dialogue as happening.

The author emphasises that in none of these areas is Plato's choice random, but always made with an eye to the fostering of philosophic truth. He continues (17.1ff.):

3

The part of Form is filled by the style (χαρακτήρ), which can be "rich" (ἁδρός), or "lean" (ἰσχνός), or "mixed," and if mixed, then either by blending (κρᾶσις), or juxtaposition (παράθεσις). Plato uses the "rich" style in his theological dialogues, the "lean" in his other dialogues, adapting his expression to the subject matter.

In view of this judgement of the Anonymous, it is interesting that Proclus, in discussing the style of the *Parmenides* (645.9ff.), is at pains to explain why we must not expect to find an elevated and "rich" style in the dialogue, but rather a "lean" one. This "befits its dialectical procedure." The *Timaeus* one would be inclined to take as an example of the "rich" style, but Proclus does not say so in the introduction to that dialogue. The only passage I find Proclus describing as "rich" is the address of the Demiurge to the Young Gods (41aff., *In Tim.* III, 200.1 Diehl), though he seems to imply the comparative *hadrotēs* of the *Timaeus* at I, 7.26ff., where he characterises the dialogue as borrowing, among other things, "loftiness of thought" (τὸ ὑψηλόνουν) from the Pythagorean tradition, and loftiness of thought may be taken to involve loftiness of diction (τὸ ὑψηλόν) with which *to hadron* is habitually linked. At all events, the *Parmenides* is agreed to be *ischnos* in style.

The equivalent of Nature in a dialogue is the method of procedure (τρόπος τῆς συνουσίας), whether expository (ὑφηγηματικός), or investigatory (ζητητικός), or a mixture of the two (*ibid.* 17.16ff.). Proclus does not deal with this in the *Alcibiades Commentary* passage, and the Anonymous does not here characterise the *Parmenides*, but it may be taken as investigatory, or, perhaps, mixed, if the second half be taken as virtually expository.

The 'soul' of a dialogue is contained in its arguments or proofs (ἀποδείξεις), and its 'intellect' is its *problēma*, which is best rendered, perhaps, as 'topic,' since the *apodeixeis* are described as surrounding it as the circumference surrounds the centre of a circle. Finally, the analogue to God in a dialogue is its 'good' or purpose (τέλος), which is another way of saying its *skopos*, or 'aim.' In the present commentary (630.25ff.), Proclus identifies the two, though in the *Alcibiades Commentary (loc. cit.)* he tries to make a distinction: "It is one thing to know the aim of a dialogue, and another the good that derives from such a purpose." This seems, however, a distinction without a difference.

This highly articulated procedure is, as I have said, only a development of Middle Platonic procedure, of which we can see something from the remains of the *Anonymous Theaetetus Commentary*,[1] probably

---

[1] Published in 1905 by Diels and Schubart in *Berliner Klassikertexte*, Heft II.

of the 2nd century A.D.[2] At the beginning of the papyrus, the author is discussing the characters and the setting; then, at 2.11, we turn to a consideration of the *skopos*; and lastly, at 3.37, the mode of the dialogue is discussed—it is *dramatikos*, presented directly, like a play, rather than reported.

In the present instance, Proclus only comes to the *skopos* after dealing with the allegorical interpretation of both the sequence of reported conversations and the individual characters—a procedure which corresponds to the traditional Middle Platonic one, with the addition, of course, of allegory.

He starts the whole work, however, with an invocation, a sort of preface-*cum*-dedication, which is not without interest. First of all, he manages to run through his whole divine hierarchy, from the intelligible gods down to angels, daemons, and heroes (618.13-23), attributing to each certain salient characteristics, which they are to bestow upon him. Secondly, he acknowledges what we shall observe to be his pervasive debt to his master, Syrianus, to whom the basic scheme of interpretation of the dialogue presented here must surely be credited. And lastly, he dedicates the work to his pupil Asclepiodotus, a circumstance which, as I have suggested in note 6 below, makes it clear that the Commentary cannot be an early work.

This done, he turns to the treatment of the various introductory topics, beginning with a discussion of the dramatic setting (δραματικὴ διασκευή), which runs from 519.21 to 625.36. He gives us here a summary account, not only of the setting, but of the whole plot of the dialogue, without allegorising or much interpretation, but previewing various major topics of discussion later, such as unity and plurality, of what things there are Ideas, and the Parmenidean dialectical method. He ends by noting that we have four distinct layers of reporting in the original conversation, a point from which he derives proper significance in the next section.

He turns next (625.37-630.14) to the allegorical interpretation, first, of the four conversations, and then of the characters in them. He sees each of the four conversations as representing a distinct level of being. The last is the lowest, representing the 'informing' (εἰδοποιία) of sense-objects; the indefiniteness of Cephalus' audience represents the formlessness of the receptacle (the *hypodochē* of the *Timaeus*). The previous conversation, that of Antiphon to the philosophers of Clazomenae (including Cephalus), represents the entry of forms into *physikai ousiai*, by which is meant natural genera and species, which receive

[2] An argument has recently been made by Harold Tarrant (*CQ* XXXIII (1983): 161-187) to date it back to the first century B.C., and indeed to connect it with Eudorus of Alexandria. The date is fortunately not relevant to my present point, however.

form prior to the information of sensible particulars. The second conversation, that of Pythodorus to Antiphon and his friends, continuing up the scale of being, represents the progression of Forms into souls. Proclus (or Syrianus) ingeniously connects Antiphon with Soul by reason of the fact that he is horsy, and Soul, as we know from the *Phaedrus* myth, may be represented as a charioteer and horses. Finally, the original conversation represents the structure of Nous itself, and true home of the Forms, each of the three original main characters—Parmenides, Zeno, and Socrates—representing one facet of that world, as we shall see. Thus the frame-narrative can be shown by allegory to represent the various stages of the progression of Form into Matter, and to mirror accurately the relation of each lower level to what is above it (626.34ff.).

To turn to the characters of the original dialogue (628.1ff.), we find an interesting set of alternatives presented to us by Proclus, each, it seems, of equal validity. Either we may take Parmenides, Zeno, and Socrates as representing, respectively, unparticipated (ἀμέθεκτος) Intellect, Intellect participated in (μετεχόμενος) by Soul, and individual (μερικός) intellect—one of the individual intellects within Nous; or we may take them as representing the three 'moments' of the hypostasis of Nous—Being, Life, and Intellect proper. Either interpretation seems to Proclus to "preserve the analogy" (διασῴζειν τὴν ἀναλογίαν, 628.30-31)—a key term in Proclus' allegorical exegesis.

To continue down the scale of being, Pythodorus represents divine Soul, receiving the *logoi* from the intellectual realm—or, alternatively, the angelic order, seeing as he performs the role of "publicising," or manifesting, the activities of the intellectual realm. Antiphon is given one identification only, with "daemonic soul," his horsemanship once again brought into play, as evidence of a desire to guide and manage the physical world, as daemons do. Cephalus and the men of Clazomenae are individual souls in the realm of Nature, filled with *logoi* from above, and themselves embedded in the physical world.

One may note, throughout this exegesis, that the metaphysical scheme presupposed is very much simpler than that of the Athenian School in its full development, or even than that of Iamblichus. This is not an entirely compelling argument, admittedly, since there are only, after all, a limited number of figures to play around with, but it might be an indication that the original allegorisation was propounded already by Porphyry, with whose metaphysics a scheme of Being, Life, and Intellect, within the hypostasis of Nous, would fit very well. If this were Porphyry's original suggestion, then the scheme of unparticipated, participated, and particular intellect might be taken as an alternative suggestion of Iamblichus, whose innovation the participated-unparticipated contrast appears to be (cf. *In Tim.* fr. 54 Dillon, and pp. 33-34 of the Intro. to my edition). In that case, Syrianus and Proclus could be seen as simply preserving the earlier allegorisations, by combining them as alternatives. The same would go for the characters further down the scale. Such "portmanteau solutions" are quite characteristic of Syrianus' treatment of disputes between his two predecessors, as we can see from the *Timaeus Commentary*, and also, as I think it will emerge, from this one.

At any rate, having identified the characters, we are now ready to approach the question of the subject matter, or *skopos*, of the dialogue. The discussion of the various views on this becomes a most useful survey of previous opinion on this most baffling of Plato's dialogues, going back well into the Middle Platonic period.

Proclus follows an order of exposition which, while taking the various theories in ascending order of worthiness, also seems to proceed in chronological sequence. The first view (630.37-633.12) is that the dialogue is a dialectical exercise, with a polemical purpose. It is an *antirrhesis* (631.22) against Zeno, using Zenonian methods to arrive at absurd and self-contradictory conclusions (even as the *Menexenus* is an attack on Thucydides[!], and Socrates' speech for the non-lover in the *Phaedrus* a satire against Lysias). The dialogue therefore contains no positive doctrine, but is simply a destructive tour-de-force. Such a view may have been put about by the New Academy, as constituting a justification for their own methods of argumentation, but we have no positive evidence of this.

A second view (633.12-635.27) holds that the dialogue is indeed an exercise in logical method, but that its purpose is not polemical (such an interpretation does violence, it argues, to the structure of the dialogue), but expository. Its purpose is to show that only rigorous training in logical method will enable one to avoid the various pitfalls into which unsophisticated "friends of the Forms," like the young Socrates, are shown falling.

With one aspect of this Proclus is not in disagreement: Parmenides is indeed concerned to educate Socrates. But that the subject matter of the second part of the dialogue is simply logical he cannot accept. He next, therefore, embarks on a survey of those views which postulate that the second part has a metaphysical purpose. Again, there is a chronological sequence observable here. The first school of thought (635.31-638.2) considers that the subject of the dialogue is Being—the same subject, in fact, as that of Parmenides' Poem. These critics make the good point that no dialogue of Plato's appears to have been composed purely to illustrate a method, but always the method is introduced as a means to some substantial end—for instance, the purpose of the *Sophist* is not to introduce *diairesis* but *diairesis* is introduced as a means to defining and exposing the Sophist (a view we would not, I think, agree with!). Since Parmenides says he is going to exercise his method on his own first principle, that must surely be taken to be the subject of the dialogue.

If we search for a possible champion of this view of the dialogue, the best candidate is probably Origen the Platonist, whom we shall meet repeatedly in this connexion later, in Books VI and VII. This theory demands that the First Hypothesis have a purely negative role, with no proper subject matter, and that the real subject of the dialogue be dealt with positively only in the Second Hypothesis (what role the later ones play is not in question at the moment). This we know to have been the view of Origen (cf. below, VI, 1064.21ff. and note *ad loc.*), and it would seem to accord with the position held here. Certainly no one later than Plotinus can have held that the subject of the dialogue was Being.

We move on from this to a second group of critics (638.2-640.16) who prefer to take the subject of the dialogue as "all things that derive their reality from the One" (638.18-19). If we are to take the previous critic as Origen, then this next school of thought should comprise some or all of a group comprising Plotinus, Porphyry, and Iamblichus. The idea that the dialogue is really a panoramic survey of the universe, as it derives from the One, would seem to cover all of their views, as outlined at the beginning of Book VI. The various affirmations and negations, the argument goes, must refer to different levels of entity. They cannot all be about Being, in an undifferentiated sense. The only problem with this view is that Parmenides does declare at the outset (137b) that he will start from his own doctrine of the One, which, as we know from his Poem, is a One that *is*, but this problem can be overcome by assuming that he takes his own One as a point of departure (640.2ff.), and uses it to set forth the whole nature of beings, beginning with the One above Being. (This problem will be raised again in Book VI, 1077.19ff.)

It is interesting that all these previous commentators, from the earliest Middle Platonists to (probably) Iamblichus, are lumped together as "the ancients" (οἱ παλαιοί), over against whom is now set the doctrine of Syrianus, but we must remember that even Iamblichus died about a hundred and fifty years (c. A.D. 325) before Proclus is writing. Syrianus (640.17-645.8) may seem to be doing no more than elaborating and further articulating the views of his predecessors in declaring that the subject of the dialogue is "all things, in so far as they are the offspring of one cause and are dependent on this universal cause" (641.3-6). To this Proclus adds: "and in so far as they are *deified*." However, Syrianus' account of the *skopos* obviously involved a preview of his remarkable views as to the various grades of being which are being symbolically represented in the second part, together with a comparison and contrast with the *Timaeus*. Basically, though, Syrianus and Proclus accept the view of the last set of commentators.

The next topic for discussion (645.9-647.24) is the style (χαρακτήρ) of the dialogue, which I have discussed already. The style is appropriate to the subject matter, that is to say, "lean" and unadorned, to reflect the "unadorned beauty" of divinity (645.13). However, though Proclus agrees with this view (possibly that of Iamblichus, cf. his remarks on the *Timaeus* quoted at *In Tim.* I, 87.6ff. = Iambl. *In Tim.* fr. 9 Dillon), he feels obliged to point out that this is not the only way one may talk of divine matters—the inspired poets may use mythical language, and others may use a hieratic or elevated mode, or images and symbols, with mathematical terminology, as would the Pythagoreans. This austere, dialectical mode, however, is proper to the Eleatic tradition, which is eminently well suited to discussing the One.

This leads us to the next topic (648.1-658.31), the relationship between Parmenides' dialectical method, as here set out, and that of Plato himself, a question of some importance for ancient commentators. Many would seek to distinguish the two, Proclus tells us (648.2ff.), on the basis of various passages in the Platonic corpus—three in particular: (1) at *Rep.* VII, 537e-539d, Socrates says that the young should not be allowed to practise dialectic; yet here is Parmenides recommending it to the young Socrates; (2) also in *Rep.* VII, and in the *Phaedo*, dialectic is presented as leading to the highest and purest level of knowledge, but Parmenides presents it here as *gymnasia* (135d), which implies that it is a preliminary skill, on the level of Aristotelian logic (cf. e.g. *Topics* VIII, 14); (3) again in *Rep.* VII, 534e, dialectic is described as "the capstone of knowledge" (θριγκὸς τῶν μαθημάτων), and in the *Sophist*, 253e, the Stranger declares that dialectic should not be communicated to any but "him who philosophises with purity and justice," while Parmenides here describes it as "babbling" (ἀδολεσχία, 135d).

These nitpicking difficulties would not have been raised, had there not been some embarrassment among the majority of Platonists who practised what they regarded as Platonic dialectic (diaeresis, definition, demonstration, and analysis), but had never found any use for this extraordinary "Parmenidean" method, and yet saw it apparently commended in *Parm.* 135-136 as "dialectic." So they tried to downgrade it. From the circumstantial way in which Proclus presents the case for the defence, it would seem that everyone before Syrianus had maintained the distinction between the two dialectics, and that this upgrading of the Parmenidean method is another Syrianic innovation. That this is so is indicated also by the fact that later, in Book V, when the question arises again, Proclus not only defends Parmenides' method, but sets out to illustrate its workings, prefacing this with the announcement that no one has ever attempted this before, except an unknown individual named Ammikartos (1020.31ff.).

Proclus, then, must set out to demolish the difficulties raised. This he does as follows (651.16ff.). Firstly, there is no contradiction between Parmenides commending the method here to Socrates, and Socrates in the *Republic* forbidding the method to the young in general, since Socrates here is a special case, and does not invalidate the general rule that the young should not be introduced to dialectic before they are ready. Legislation, Proclus reminds us, is aimed at the normal case, not the rare birds; these latter must be a law unto themselves.

Secondly, it is not true that Socrates does not describe dialectic in *Rep.* VII as a *gymnasia* (652.29ff.). He does so, in fact, at 526b6 (ἄν ἐν τούτῳ παιδευθῶσι καὶ γυμνάσωνται). Therefore the mere use of the term 'exercise' cannot be held to reduce the method to an 'exercise' on the basis of *endoxa*, such as Aristotle presents in the *Topics*. Why, then, do both Socrates and Parmenides describe their dialectical methods as *gymnasia*? The answer to this leads Proclus to distinguish three aspects of any proper educational system (653.3-654.14). The first involves stirring up in the young the desire for knowledge, "the turning of the eye of the soul." This involves not a simple leading of the pupil straight towards the truth, but also an exploration of byways, ultimately to be rejected (that is why it may be termed *plane*, "wandering"). A second form of dialectic confronts the mind directly with the world of Forms, and leads it from Form to Form, using analysis, definition, demonstration, and division, until it reaches the first Form of all, the Good beyond Being. The third type is a method of attack, designed to "purge sophists and others of their double ignorance," which Proclus, self-consciously borrowing a term from Aristotle (cf. *SE* 169b25, *Met.* Γ 2, 1004b25), calls *peirastikē*, "tentative" or "probing." This serves as a sort of purgative for those "obsessed by their conceit of wisdom." It is the first of these, and not the third, that is termed *gymnasia* by both philosophers. Other instances of it are to be found, he says, in the *Theaetetus* and the *Lysis*.

This distinguishing of types of dialectic recurs in Book V at 988.6-992.28, when the question arises again. It is a useful piece of Platonic lore.

The last problem is why Parmenides describes his method as *adoleschia*, "babbling." Once again, Proclus shows that Plato elsewhere allows Socrates to describe *his* dialectic method thus (ironically), as for instance at *Phaedo* 70b, *Theaetetus* 195b, and, above all, in the Stranger's classification in *Sophist* 219b-225d. And anyhow, Parmenides does *not* describe his own method as "babbling" at 135d; he only says it is called so by the many.

The upshot of this laborious refutation of tendentious objections is that Parmenides' dialectic method can be claimed as Platonically approved after all, and, as I have said, later, in Book V, Proclus sets out to atone for a millennium of neglect by giving the method a thorough workout.

The last topic dealt with in the Preface (658.32-659.24) is that of the significance of Plato's *prooimia* in general. Once again, we have an historical summary. The earlier commentators (before Porphyry, in this case) did not regard the prefatory portions of the dialogues as being of any metaphysical significance. Others (Porphyry, in fact) see their use as being the presentation of moral lessons (καθήκοντα), but not as being germane to the subject matter (though Porphyry does seem to have indulged in a certain amount of allegorisation). Only with Iamblichus (for it is he, 659.6ff.) are the prologues brought into relation, by systematic allegorisation, with the overall *skopos*, and it is his lead that the Athenian School is following. Only so, says Proclus, does the dialogue become an organic whole in the sense called for by Plato in *Phaedrus* 264c.

WE TURN NOW to the exegesis of the text, taking in, as I have said, just the opening section of the dialogue up to 128e6. The first part of this may be seen as extending to 127a7, comprising the preliminaries to Antiphon's telling of the story. Proclus divides this into nine lemmata, all fairly short (659.30-681.30).

The first lemma, 128a1-2, covers just the opening statement. This gives occasion for renewed discussion of the contrast between Italian (Eleatic) and Ionian philosophy, and the position of Platonism as halfway between them, a synthesis of both. This is the "literal" interpretation, though not explicitly presented as such. An ethical interpretation, probably due ultimately to Porphyry (660.39-661.9), follows, to the effect that Cephalus' departure from his homeland and arrival in Athens reminds us that we must be prepared to leave our "home" (the body), and head for the homeland of Athena, the symbol of Intellect, if we wish to obtain a vision of the truth.

There is also, however, a metaphysical (or "physical") interpretation, probably originally advanced by Iamblichus (661.10-662.33), according to which "all the individual and perceptible reason-principles (the visitors from Clazomenae) are dependent on the primary cause (Parmenides?), and being illumined by Athena to turn their attention towards the intelligible world, abstract themselves from the cosmic system, . . . and advance to the monad that contains the primary plu-

11

rality (Antiphon)." Glaucon and Adeimantus serve as a dyad prior to this monad.

Proclus goes on to a further metaphysical exegesis, the essence of which we have seen earlier, in the preface. He does not disavow the first one, but feels that this one, presumably that of Syrianus, adds a further dimension of significance to the passage. There is no need, I think, to dwell on the details of it. Those interested may read the text (662.33-665.10). Suffice it to say that Antiphon and Pythodorus are demoted to the status of daemons, as set out in the preface.

We may note in this passage the use of certain technical terms of allegorical exegesis—*symbolon, eikōn* and *analogia*.[3] Ionia is a *symbolon* of Nature, and Italy of intellectual being (660.27); the text "presents an *eikōn*" of the individual *logoi* being united with their monad (661.21, cf. 662.10); Parmenides, Zeno, and Socrates "preserve the *analogia*" with the whole divine order (663.1, cf. 664.2 and 665.12). These are the basic terms with which Proclus operates, and they will recur frequently in the exegesis of the *prooimion* of the dialogue. Elsewhere (*In Tim.* I, 29.31ff.; *PT* I, 4), he seeks to make a distinction between *eikōn* and *symbolon*, attributing this to "the Pythagoreans," an *eikōn* being an image of reality which has a one-to-one correspondence with what it represents, while a *symbolon* is a more indirect representation of reality. However, in most cases, as here, Proclus seems to observe no clear distinction between the two terms. As for *analogia*, if one could master the mysteries of that, one would have the key to Neoplatonic allegorical exegesis, but rules for the "preserving" of *analogia* are lacking.

Lastly, we must note the normal term for the metaphysical realities revealed by allegorical exegesis—*ta pragmata* (e.g. 664.2, 665.12), normally translated as "the facts," or "the subject matter" (as opposed to the *lexis*, or details of the text).

Proclus ends the lemma with a further short comment on the "leanness" of the dialogue's style, noting that Parmenides employs the same style in his Poem.

The second lemma (126a2-4) begins with an ethical comment to the effect that one should welcome strangers, the stronger should be the first to offer aid, and that one should keep one's promises (666.4-20)—all this provoked by Adeimantus' greeting of Cephalus. We move then to metaphysical exegesis (*ta pragmata*). Antiphon, Glaucon, and Adeimantus represent three grades of daemon (ἡ δαιμόνια τάξις εἰς τρία διῃρημένη), performing their roles in elevating souls towards their divine causal principles. The details of the text are ingeniously employed

---

[3] I have discussed this matter elsewhere, in "Image, Symbol and Analogy: Three Basic Concepts of Neoplatonic Allegorical Exegesis," in *The Significance of Neoplatonism*, ed. R. B. Harris, SUNY Press, Albany, N.Y., 1976, pp. 247-262.

to represent the different roles of the three daemonic figures (666.20-667.32).

The next lemma (126a5-7, 667.36-668.28) is devoted to discussing the corresponding concept of the 'receptivity' (ἐπιτηδειότης) of inferior beings to the benefits flowing from above. In the Neoplatonic universe, receptivity is all; it answers to the Christian concept of grace. The gods cannot confer gifts upon us unless and until we are ready to receive them.

The fourth lemma (126b1-3, 668.34-670.29) begins with some historical facts about Plato's family and concludes, with a slightly unexpected concern for chronology (though he speaks of Plato as being 24, not 28, when Socrates died!), that the present conversation must have taken place after Socrates' death, since Antiphon, who is considerably younger than Plato, must be given time to have grown up. But the absence of any mention of Socrates being still alive makes this fairly obvious in any case.

Then, after a brief appreciation of Plato's dramatic technique here, he makes an 'ethical' comment (669.16ff.) to the effect that Cephalus' enquiry presents the three stages of prayer in the Chaldaean tradition—knowledge, approach, and union (see n. 46 *ad loc.*)—and finally turns to *ta pragmata* proper, with the reflection that souls must be linked with the objects of their striving through knowledge and 'attention' (ἐπιβολή, a technical term originally Epicurean, but long since common philosophical property; see below, n. 116 to Book VII), and of this the *name* is the proper symbol.

To show how every detail can be made to contribute to the total picture, Proclus notes, albeit tentatively, that the fact of Antiphon being a *maternal* brother of Glaucon and Adeimantus could symbolise the fact that the whole class of daemons is presided over by a female principle (presumably Hecate). The significance of each detail of the text is plainly a principle of post-Iamblichean allegorising (as it was in the system of Philo of Alexandria), and we shall see many examples of this as we go along.

It will be unnecessary, I think, to dwell in detail on all of the subsequent lemmata. They exemplify all of the features outlined above. Every detail of the text is pressed into service as an inspired illustration of metaphysical reality. Much is made, in particular, as has been mentioned already, of the "horsiness" of Antiphon, against the background of the Phaedrus myth. We may note, however, the particularly clear sequence of literal (stylistic), ethical and 'physical' exegesis in the lemma 127a1-5 (676.39-679.38). Once again, one may be permitted, I think with probability (though not certainty—Proclus is of course quite capable of doing this on his own), to discern here the hands of

Porphyry and Iamblichus respectively. We find here, indeed, as not infrequently elsewhere, a distinction between a first level of 'physical' exegesis (678.22ff.) and a still 'deeper' (βαθύτερα) one (678.22ff.), which one might term (though it is not so termed here) 'theological.' It reads here as if Proclus (or Syrianus) is adding a rather more elaborate metaphysical interpretation to the simpler one propounded by Iamblichus.

A feature of allegorical exegesis that may be noted, and illustrated, at this stage is the utilising of an apparent contradiction in the text to reveal a higher truth (another characteristic procedure of Philo's). Proclus notes, at 680.35ff. (οὐ χρὴ θαυμάζειν is a very characteristic way of introducing such a problem), that here (127a6) Antiphon declares the task of recounting the discussion to be "very difficult," whereas earlier Adeimantus had assured the visitors that there would be no difficulty (126c6). The solution is that it is not, indeed, a difficult task for Antiphon, as a superior daemonic power, to communicate enlightenment, but it is a difficult task for inferior entities, in this case individual souls, to receive his gifts.

With the beginning of Antiphon's narrative, we reach the second stage of the frame-story, coming a stage closer to the subject matter proper. This section may in turn be divided into two (unequal) parts, the background to the session at Pythodorus' house (127a7-d5, 681.35-693.23), and Zeno's actual reading of the first hypothesis of his first argument, with the conversation between him and Socrates that ensues upon that (127d6-128e6, 694.3-722.24).

The first part is divided into six lemmata, again all quite short. Proclus begins by defending Antiphon against a suggestion made by some previous commentator that he is simply here repeating, parrot-like, material that he does not understand. No one, Proclus argues, could present so vividly what he does not himself understand—and Plato has indicated to us in the *Timaeus* (19d) that a successful narrator of the speeches of learned men must be similar in character to those he represents.

So much, then, for the vindication of Antiphon. Various indications are then produced that Parmenides is a henad presiding over a chain of causes, and a monad uniting a multiplicity—not least the circumstance that he and Zeno have come to Athens for the Panathenaea, since the Panathenaea was established as a result of the synoecism of Attica, the uniting of a group of villages round one centre, presided over by Athena!

Allegorical interpretation of details continues to add to our understanding of "the realities." Zeno's having been the *paidika* of Parmenides simply means (684.28ff.) that they used the same path of ascent to one and the same god (on the human level), and on the paradigmatic

14

level, that "secondary beings are contained in the primary, and all are united to Being" (Parmenides being a symbol of the One Being, the monad of the noetic world). Again, the lodging with Pythodorus, in the next lemma (685.8ff.) gives Pythodorus the rank of an angel, and the fact that they are "outside the city walls" represents the transcendent nature of the gods.

The rest of this section is taken up with the further elaboration of the allegory. In the process certain important principles of Procline metaphysics are referred to. One is that formally stated in the *Elements of Theology* as proposition 57: "Every cause both operates prior to its consequent and gives rise to a greater number of posterior terms." Here (689.26ff.), Parmenides, as the supreme element in the noetic realm, extends his influence further than do Zeno or Socrates, down to the most junior principle, Aristoteles, who represents the rank of individual soul (his later joining the tyranny of the Thirty symbolises the capacity of the individual soul to fall from intellectual life to the tyranny of the passions, 693.2ff.).

At the end of this section there occurs, in some manuscripts (see n. 62 below) a curious passage which is a sort of summary of the allegorical exegesis that has gone before. It sounds rather as if it is composed by a reader who was trying to sort things out in his own mind, and it is useful for that very reason; but it could conceivably emanate from Proclus himself. I have included it in square brackets.

We now arrive at Zeno's reading of his treatise against plurality, and Socrates' comments upon it. It is divided into thirteen lemmata, and covers the remaining 28 pages of Book I (694.3-722.24).

The character of the commentary now changes somewhat. Allegory and 'ethical' comment is not abandoned, but more attention is naturally paid to the subject matter in its literal meaning, since philosophical arguments have to be analysed. Proclus' concern is always to show the syllogistic form (either categorical or hypothetical) of Plato's argument, and much space is accordingly devoted to that. All through this section there are indications, it seems to me, that Proclus has before him a separate document, the *Logoi* of Zeno, against which he is checking what Plato reports in the *Parmenides*; but I have discussed this question fully in the General Introduction (sect. D).

At 696.21ff. (a passage which is curiously abbreviated in all the Greek manuscripts, see n. 64 below), we seem to have a record of an *aporia* raised against Zeno's argument by someone making an appeal to a principle of Stoic logic, that an impossible conclusion may follow from a possible premise (e.g. "If Dion is dead, this man is dead," where "this man" can only refer to a living person, making the conclusion impossible; but the premise remains possible, since "Dion," as a proper

15

name, can refer to someone living, dead, or imaginary). Proclus declares that such an argument has been long since refuted by the Peripatetic rule about hypotheticals (enunciated, among others, by Alexander of Aphrodisias, see n. 65 below) that only those hypotheticals are true in which, when the antecedent is the case, the consequent follows necessarily.

The point of this is presumably to argue that the necessity of the proposition that the same thing cannot be both like and unlike does not imply the necessity of the proposition that things are not many. The passage is useful evidence of the history of logical comment on the dialogue. As for Proclus, he draws from Zeno's argument no more than the conclusion that the many cannot exist without the One (696.29ff.), and this leads him to the series of principles with which he begins the *Elements of Theology* (1-5: "Every multiplicity in some way participates in the One," and so on), which lead in turn to the principle that the first principle of all things must be a One without plurality.

We may note in passing, under the heading of ethical comment, a series of Procline rules of etiquette for both teacher and pupil. At 695.26ff. we are told that the true philosopher, exemplified here by Zeno, will not mind repeating himself twice or three times for the sake of clarity, and welcomes interruptions, whereas the sophist will baulk at either. At 697.32ff., Socrates provides a good example for those who question the views of their elders: one should first ascertain their meaning as accurately as possible, lest we miss their true sense, and so fall into sophistry. At 701.15ff., he even derives from Zeno's behaviour the precept that if the young wish to support their elders in a controversy, they should approach the topic under discussion from a different perspective.

The allegorical interpretation, as I say, is not forgotten. Nothing new is added to what has been said in the preface, but new details bring, for Proclus, further confirmation of the correctness of the basic scheme. For instance, the fact that Socrates turns from Zeno to Parmenides (who has appeared, suitably to a monad, only at the *end* of Zeno's exposition) shows how divinities of the third order (such as Nous proper) turn towards the primary gods (such as Being) first through intermediaries (Zeno = Life), but ultimately unite themselves to the primary principles directly (700.8ff.).

In connection with the lemma 128a8-b6 (703.6-706.18), Proclus discourses at some length on Parmenides' own concept of the One in his Poem. Parmenides is primarily concerned, he says, with the unity or monad which makes each being and class of beings one, with unity in the world, rather than with the transcendent cause of unity:

It is to this unity of all beings that Parmenides was looking when he demanded that we call the All "one," primarily and most truly the All which is united with the One, but also the All generally; for all things, in so far as they participate in the One Being, are in a sense the same as one another and one. (704.12-18)

An important principle of Procline metaphysics is propounded at 707.9-11: "Every plurality has a twofold henad, one that is immanent in it (συντεταγμένη), and one that transcends it (ἐξῃρημένη)." This is laid down in slightly different terms at *ET*, prop. 67: "Every whole is either a whole before the parts, or a whole of parts, or a whole in the parts." The principle goes back at least to Iamblichus (cf. *In Tim.* fr. 54 Dillon: "Every order is presided over by its unparticipated monad, prior to the participated entities"). Proclus proceeds to develop this for a while, in support of the point that Parmenides is dealing with the un-participated henad *prior* to the plurality (the One Being itself), and thus is not obliged to discuss its relations with the plurality of beings, whereas Zeno is actually speaking of the One immanent in the Many, which he terms 'Not-Many' (711.22ff.). As an exegesis of Plato's text this leaves much to be desired, but it is a useful exposition of later Neo-platonic metaphysics. For Proclus it explains Zeno's comment that Socrates "has not altogether sensed the truth" about his treatise.

An *aporia* of some interest is raised at 711.28ff., to the effect that the dyad would constitute a counter-example to the assumption that say-ing 'not-many' is the same as saying 'only one.' Whoever raised this difficulty must either be thinking of the Dyad as a cosmological prin-ciple which is neither one nor a proper plurality, or must be taking the number two as a dual entity. In either case, the objection seems most suitable to a Pythagorean, or Pythagoreanising Platonist. Proclus dis-misses the objection by declaring the dyad to be *both* unitary *and* plural.

An interesting problem in interpretation arises as regards the sym-bolic meaning of *youth* in various connections. In Socrates' case (686.35ff.), his youth "symbolises the youthfulness ascribed to the gods," though most properly to the intellectual order of gods, by con-trast with the intelligible. In the case of Aristoteles (692.2ff.) however, and the young Zeno, 719.3ff.), it is a sign of imperfection and unripe-ness. In order "correctly to preserve the analogy," one must presum-ably take thought for the overall context.

Book I, then, brings us to the threshold of Socrates' objections to Zeno's argument. In the next passage, Proclus warns us, "we must proceed with great circumspection," in order to judge correctly how far Socrates' objections are valid, and how far Zeno remains unrefuted.

But Socrates is younger (in the second, and more obvious sense of the word!), and if anyone is in error, it is more likely to be he. Proclus speaks here (as in his other remarks on the proper behaviour of master and pupil) with a distinctly middle-aged tone, which constitutes further evidence for the relative lateness of the work.

COMMENTARY

□ □ □

PREFACE

(i) Introductory Invocation[1]

I pray to all the gods and goddesses to guide my mind in this study that I have undertaken—to kindle in me a shining light of truth and enlarge my understanding for the genuine science of being; to open the gates of my soul to receive the inspired guidance of Plato; and in anchoring[2] my thought in the full splendour of reality to hold me back from too much conceit of wisdom and from the paths of error by keeping me in intellectual converse with those realities from which alone the eye[3] of the soul is refreshed and nourished, as Plato says in the *Phaedrus* (246e-251b). I ask from the intelligible gods[4] fullness of wisdom, from the intellectual gods the power to rise aloft, from the supercelestial gods guiding the universe an activity free and unconcerned with material inquiries, from the gods to whom the cosmos is assigned a winged life, from the angelic choruses a true revelation of the divine, from the good daemons an abundant filling of divine inspiration, and from the heroes a generous, solemn, and lofty disposition. So may all the orders of divine beings help to prepare me fully to share in this most illuminating and mystical vision that Plato reveals to us in the *Parmenides* with a profundity appropriate to its subject; and which has been unfolded to us, with his own very lucid applications, by one who was in very truth a fellow Bacchant with Plato and filled entirely with di-

618

---

[1] The only other work of Proclus' to begin with a comparable dedicatory preface (with prayer) is the *Platonic Theology*, though he does invoke divine help elsewhere on occasion (e.g. *PT* III, 1; *Dub.* 10.1-2), following Plato's example at *Tim.* 27c (cf. *In Tim.* I, 214.26ff.).

[2] Reading ὁρμίσαντες for ὁρμήσαντες, as suggested by Chaignet (no help from Latin).

[3] Plato actually says πτέρωμα, not ὄμμα, at *Phaedr.* 246e2, but all MSS of Proclus have ὄμμα, and it is not an exact quotation (ἄρδεται from 251b3 for αὔξεται), so ὄμμα may stand.

[4] We find here a complete Procline hierarchy set out, νοητοὶ θεοί, νοεροί, ἀπόλυτοι, ἐγκόσμιοι, and then angels, daemons and heroes, each bestowing gifts appropriate to their natures.

19

vine truth and who, by leading us to the understanding of this vision has become a true hierophant of these divine doctrines.[5] Of him I would say that he came to men as the exact image of philosophy for the benefit of souls here below, in recompense for the statues, the temples, and the whole ritual of worship, and as the chief author of salvation for men who now live and for those to come hereafter. So may all the higher powers be propitious to us and be ready with their gifts to illuminate us also with the light that comes from them and leads us upwards. And you, Asclepiodotus,[6] who have a mind worthy of philosophy and are my very dear friend, receive these gifts that come from that worthy man, all of them in full measure, and store them in the most intimate folds of your mind.

(ii) Dramatic Setting

But before beginning the consideration of this vision I will set forth the dramatic setting of this dialogue, for the sake of those who are interested in such things. It was the festival of the Great Panathenaea, cel-
619 ebrated by the Athenians of that time with more elaborate preparations than the Lesser, which they called by the same name in honour of the goddess, thus celebrating her both with longer and shorter processions. It was while this festival was being observed, as I said, that Parmenides and Zeno had come to Athens, Parmenides being a teacher and Zeno his disciple. Both were citizens of Elea and, what is more, had been members of the school of Pythagoras, as Nicomachus somewhere relates.[7] They had come then from Elea in Italy to honour the goddess and help any at Athens who were interested in knowledge of divine things. They lodged outside the Ceramicus,[8] inviting anybody to come and converse with them. Among those who came to see them

[5] This fulsome praise of Syrianus recurs frequently in Proclus' writings, and acknowledges a very real dependence. Cf. *PT* I, 1, pp. 7-8 S-W; *In Remp.* I, 71.21ff. Kroll.

[6] A pupil of Proclus, born in Alexandria, sometime resident of Aphrodisias in Caria (presumably after Proclus' death). Damascius has many waspish things to say of him in the *Life of Isidore* (cf. esp. *Epit. Phot.* 126-128). He seems to have been chiefly renowned as a doctor, and professor of music and physics, with a special interest in theurgy and lower forms of magic. Simplicius (*In Phys.* 795.20 Diels) praises him for his grasp of physics. On the whole, hardly a suitable recipient, one would think, of a commentary on the *Parmenides* (he himself, more suitably, wrote a commentary on the *Timaeus*, which has not survived, Olymp. *In Meteor.* 321.26 Ideler); but perhaps Proclus hoped to turn him to higher things! At any rate, this dedication to a pupil who survived well into the next century indicates that the *Parmenides Commentary* is a relatively mature work.

[7] Nicomachus of Gerasa, in his *Life of Pythagoras*, now lost, but drawn on copiously by both Prophyry and Iamblichus in their extant *Lives*.

[8] Or rather "outside the walls, in the Ceramicus," to accord with the text of Plato (127c1). But it is not clear that the MS reading should be changed. Latin is no help (*extra hospitium!*).

20

was Socrates, who was then a young man, but of outstanding natural abilities. On one occasion Zeno was reading to the assembled visitors a book in which he tried to show the numerous difficulties that are encountered by those who maintain a plurality of things as primary. For Parmenides put forward as his peculiar teaching, it is said, that Being is one; and those who took these words in a rather irreverent sense assailed the doctrine with witticisms, such as that if Being is one, then Parmenides and Zeno do not both exist at the same time, but if Parmenides, then not Zeno, and if Zeno, then not Parmenides; and on these and other similar grounds they tore his doctrine apart, seeing nothing of its truth. Now Zeno, Parmenides' disciple, did not care to plead directly for his master's doctrine, since he thought it needed no additional confirmation, but attempted to give it secret aid by writing a book in which he ingeniously showed that those who suppose that beings are many encounter no fewer difficulties than were alleged against those who say Being is one. For he showed that the same thing 620 will be both like and unlike, both equal and unequal, and in general that there will result the abolition of all order in the world, and everything will be thrown into confusion.

And if I may interpolate my opinion, I think he did so plausibly. For Being must be both one and many; every monad has a plurality correlative with it, and every plurality is comprehended under some appropriate monad. But since in every case the ground of plurality is tied up with the monad and cannot exist without it, these men of Elea were focussing their attention upon the incomprehensible unifying causality of the monad when they made the "One Being" primary. Seeing that every plurality exists in unity, they declared that the "One Being" is prior to the many; for what primarily is, is one, and from it the plurality of beings proceeds. Now Parmenides did not see fit to descend to plurality, having anchored himself in the contemplation of the One Being and ignoring everything that would direct his thought to particulars. But Zeno was not his equal. Although he too made the One Being the goal of his thinking, he still wished to separate himself from plurality and gather himself into that One that is, as it were, the center of all things; so he refuted the proponents of the view that Being is many in order to purge their understanding of its propensity towards plurality. For refutation is purification, i.e. a removal of ignorance, and a way towards truth. Thus he showed that when the One is taken away there is complete confusion and disorder among the Many. For what is without a share in unity cannot possibly be a whole, or a totality, or endowed with form; all of these characters depend surely upon participation in unity, but when form and wholeness are taken away all order and arrangement depart, and nothing is left but disorderly and discord-

21

621 ant movement. He who removes the One is unwittingly doing the same as one who removes God from things, for with unity absent things will be "as it is probable they are when God is absent," as is said somewhere in the *Timaeus* (53b). It is God that provides unity to things separated, order to the disordered, wholeness to the parts, form to material things, and perfection to the imperfect; and in each of these cases unity is unquestionably conferred. This, then, is the way in which Zeno refuted the proponents of the Many and brought himself to the conception of the One Being. Hence the necessary consequence: if Being is not a many, either nothing at all exists or Being must be one. Thus in the end Zeno espoused the teaching of his father Parmenides, seeing that plurality exists in the One as in its centre, and that the One cannot be preserved in mere plurality; for this exists in itself prior to plurality, and plurality is what it is entirely from the One.

These are the contents of the book which he read to the company. When Socrates had listened to the reading of it and to all the absurdities that Zeno said result for those who posit that Being is many, he shifted the discussion from the examination of unity and plurality in things to that of the unity and diversity of Forms. There is nothing remarkable, he said, in showing that the same thing is both like and unlike, both equal and unequal; for the same thing is both right and left, and there are many things in this condition in the sensible world, that is, together with their plurality they possess also unifying Forms by which each thing is at the same time many and one. Rather, he said, it ought to be shown that among intelligible species the same is equal and unequal, like and unlike; for he saw there the unmixed purity of the Forms and thought that plurality as thus distinguished was being maintained. Hence he thought it necessary to shift the inquiry from sensible to in-
622 telligible things and look there for mingling and separation in each case, since in sensible things these characteristics are abundantly evident because of the nature which is their substratum. These are the same questions that he discusses in later life in the *Philebus* (14d), where he says that to affirm the same thing to be one and many is a commonplace when applied to composite things, but the sight of this among the monadic Forms would be something to marvel at.

At these words of Socrates Parmenides takes over the discussion and asks Socrates whether he really believes there are intelligible Forms and what are his reasons for this belief. When Socrates replies that he holds firmly to this hypothesis of Ideas, Parmenides raises difficulties about them. Are there, or are there not, Ideas of all things? How do sensible things participate in Ideas? How are the Ideas related to us? Thus the fundamental difficulties connected with the Ideas are brought up by Parmenides. When Socrates shows his bewilderment in the face of these problems, Parmenides advises him, if he is really enamoured of the truth about Being, to exercise himself in dialectic before undertaking this larger inquiry—meaning by dialectic that method that Socrates himself teaches us in other works, such as the *Republic*, the *Sophist*, the *Philebus*. When Socrates asks what this method is and shows himself ready to accept these visitors' teaching, Parmenides expounds the method whose praises Socrates also has sung on many occasions. In the *Phaedo* (101d), for example, in distinguishing the function of dialectic from that of eristic, he says that one must at every step assume an hypothesis and continue an inquiry in this way until from many hypotheses we come up to "something adequate," which he calls "the unhypothetical" (*Rep.* VI, 510b). As Parmenides recommends, we must first posit the object of our inquiry and then divide this hypothesis by the employment of antitheses (*antiphasis*). That is, we assert that the 623 object exists or that it does not exist; and assuming its existence we inquire what follows from this assumption, what is excluded by it, and what neither follows from it nor is excluded by it. For in each case some attributes are completely alien to the object under inquiry, some necessarily belong to it, and some may or may not be present in it. And then we must divide each of these three classes into four. For we must inquire, assuming its existence, what consequences are implied for it, both with reference to itself and with reference to other things, and what are implied for the other things with respect to one another and with respect to our subject; and again we must ask what is excluded from it with respect to itself and with respect to other things, and for other things with respect to one another and with respect to it. Thus our inquiry must proceed through these twelve modes, and through an equal number more when the non-existence of our subject is assumed. So that from one hypothesis two arise at first, then for each of them three other hypotheses, and for each of the three four more, making twelve hypotheses in all for each of the initial alternatives. And if you like, you could divide each of them again and thus obtain a great many others, indefinite in number. It is through these hypotheses that we must make our way in accordance with the numbers mentioned—by twos, threes, fours, twelves, until we come to the unhypothetical principle itself which is prior to all hypotheses.

When this method has been described, Socrates expresses his admiration for its scientific precision and for the intellectual quality of the visitors' teaching. (This is said to be a special feature of the Eleatic School, just as another trait, discipline through mathematics, is characteristic of the Pythagorean, and another of the Heraclitean, viz. the 624 use of names for obtaining knowledge of things.) After expressing his admiration, Socrates demands to have the method fixed in his mind by an example of its use, by Zeno's taking one of his hypotheses and showing how it works in this particular case, as is done in the *Sophist* when the Stranger in that dialogue explains the method of Division by using it to find the angler and the sophist. But Zeno says the task is beyond his powers; it requires Parmenides himself, and he invites the leader of the discussion to make such an exposition. Parmenides then takes the floor and asks upon what hypothesis he shall exercise his method. "Shall we," he says, "take my hypothesis of the One, asking what consequences for it follow respectively from its being and its not being, what consequences do not follow, and what consequences may or may not follow, both for itself with respect to itself and with respect to other things, and to other things with respect to one another and to it?" This is agreed upon, and so he examines each of his alternative hypotheses following the twelve modes. In view of these, some persons have thought that the sum total of the hypotheses is twenty-four, but we shall dispute their interpretation when we come to speak of the hypotheses,[9] where we shall make a distinction between the dialectical modes and the hypotheses that are called such. Now, however, let us proceed with matters immediately before us.

Such was the teaching given, as I have said, by Parmenides and Zeno to the young and gifted Socrates and certain others. Pythodorus, the son of Isolochus (a pupil of Zeno, as we have learned from the *Alcibiades* [119a]), was one of those present at this conversation, but he was 625 silent throughout and made no contribution to the discussion, as was done by Socrates, in part asking questions and in part serving as respondent. But he (Pythodorus) heard what was said and, like Aristodemus who recalled the discourses about Eros in the *Symposium*, reported the discussion to Antiphon and his friends. This Antiphon was an Athenian, one who prided himself on his noble ancestry (this is why he was interested in horses, a tradition of long standing among wellborn Athenians) and a brother of Plato by the same mother, as Plato himself tells us. Antiphon took in these arguments and himself recounted them to another group, certain Clazomenaeans who cultivated philosophy and who had come to Athens from the School of Anaxagoras; and this is obviously the third account of this conversation. On this occasion a certain Cephalus was present, himself a citizen of Clazomenae; and hearing the discussion from Antiphon, he arranged it in narrative form for some future persons not identified, transmitting a fourth account of the meeting. It is not even said who the persons are to whom Cephalus communicated his narrative; he simply recounts

[9] He does not, in fact, deal with these critics in his survey of previous views in Book VI.

24

the arguments he has heard from Antiphon, who has got them from the Pythodorus mentioned above, who had listened to the words of Parmenides. We have then, first, the original conversation between the principal personages at the scene where it took place; second, the account of Pythodorus recalling the original conversation and presumably narrating everything as it had occurred; third, the account given by Antiphon of the arguments that Pythodorus had expounded to him and which he transmitted, as we have said, to Cephalus and the philosophers from Clazomenae; and fourth, the account by Cephalus of the arguments transmitted to him by Antiphon, ending up with an indeterminate audience.

(iii) Allegorical Interpretation of the Conversations

Of these four conversations—for we must speak now of the analogies to reality[10] which this series presents, taking our point of departure for the present from the inquiry about Ideas, which is so prominent in the dialogue that some persons have entitled it "On Ideas"[11]—of these four conversations the last is analogous to the procession of Forms into sense-objects. For Cephalus is presenting his narrative to no determinate person, for the reason that the receptacle of sensible reason-principles (*logoi*) is indeterminate, unknown, and formless. The preceding conversation resembles the establishing of the Forms in natural essences; for prior to sensible things all natures, both general and particular, have received from the intelligible world the reason-principles by which they guide sensible things, generating them endlessly and preserving them as living beings. Analogous to them are the visiting nature-philosophers, the followers of the teaching of Anaxagoras. The still earlier conversation resembles the procession into souls of the varied world of Forms from the Demiurge, for the reason-principles exist psychically in souls and it is these with which the Demiurge fills up their essence, as the *Timaeus* (41aff.) teaches us. To them we may plausibly liken the words that go forth into Antiphon; for souls are likened to the winged pairs of horses and charioteers (*Phaedr.* 246a). And the

[10] Translating τὰ πράγματα, an expression of central importance in Procline exegesis, which will recur very frequently in this dialogue. Cf. the useful discussion of the term by A. J. Festugière, in his article "Modes de composition des commentaires de Proclus," in *Museum Helveticum* XX (1963): 77-100. Normally, τὰ πράγματα refers to metaphysical or theological truths.

[11] It seems to have been Thrasyllus who gave subtitles to the dialogues, in his edition of them (Diog. Laert. III, 56-61). Proclus, below (630.37), distinguishes "others" who disregard this subtitle, in taking the dialogue as simply an exercise in logic—perhaps referring here to Albinus—but it is not clear that they were in fact at variance with Thrasyllus' interpretation.

first of all the conversations represents the organisation of the Forms in the realm of the truly real, for there reside the primary tetractys and all the number of the divine Forms, intelligible and intellectual. These are the ultimate source from which souls receive their complement of appropriate reason-principles, the source from which also the natures are supplied with active forms, and from which corporeal bodies are supplied with sensible forms. Just as the same arguments are present in all four conversations, but in a special way in each—primarily in the first conversation, for there we have the original discussion; secondarily in the second, for here their transmission is accompanied by memory and imagination; in a tertiary way in the third, for here there is memory of memory; and in the lowest fashion in the fourth, which is the lowest stage of memory—so likewise the Forms are everywhere, but in a special way in each grade of being.[12] Those which exist primarily exist in and for themselves, Socrates says, and are in the rank of intelligibles, at which level there is no imaging of anything higher, just as in the original conversation the argument (*logoi*) was not transmitted through imagination or memory (memory is a likenesses of things remembered). The forms in souls have their being in a secondary way, in respect of perfection; and thus are likenesses of the intelligibles, even as the second exposition is secondary because it uses memory and imagination. The forms in nature are likenesses even more, i.e. they are likenesses of likenesses; for it is through the forms in souls that the reason-principles in nature come to be and are. The forms in sensible things are last of all and they are images only, for the Forms end their procession at what is unknowable and indeterminate. There is nothing after them, for all the reason-principles reach their final term in sensible things. And this is the remarkable thing: the author of the second account gives us not only the bare discourse, but also brings in the persons and the actions; the author of the third rehearses all the details of the first as well as those of the second; and the author of the fourth gives us what is in the first, as well as what is in the second and what is in the third, both the persons and the actions. So the primary realities are present at all stages, down to the last; the realities of secondary rank have their causal ground in the former and in turn pervade all the ranks below them (here it is Pythodorus who edited the second conversation); and likewise the third version (of which Antiphon is the author) has its causal ground in the second, and in turn passes on the activity of the primary realities to the very last. So much, then, as a preliminary statement about these likenesses, as we begin our study of the dialogue.

627

---

[12] Application of a basic Neoplatonic principle, πάντα ἐν πᾶσιν, ἀλλ' οἰκείως τῇ ἑκάστου οὐσίᾳ, going back at least to Numenius (fr. 41 DP). Found in Plotinus, *Enn.* IV, 9.5, Porphyry, *Sent.* 10, Iamblichus, *In Phileb.* fr. 5 Dillon, and Proclus, *ET*, prop. 103, etc.

628 (iv) Allegorical Interpretation of the Characters

If we should be required to give a likely analogy for the characters involved, it seems to me that Parmenides himself should be ranked as an analogue to the unparticipated and divine Intellect which is united to Real Being in respect of its intellection, or perhaps to Being itself, which was his special concern and which he declared to be one. Zeno is an analogue to the Intellect which is participated in by the divine Soul, filled with all the intellectual Forms which he has received into his essence from the immaterial and unparticipated Intellect; this is why he too strives to "snatch himself away" (*Chald. Or.* fr. 3.1) from plurality towards the One Being, imitating the Intellect above him, to which he refers his own perfecting. Or, if you wish, we may liken him to Life, I mean Life that is immediately subsequent to Being, for he delights in assembling contradictions and arguing both for and against a thesis, just as the Life that comes after Being is the first to furnish an expression of contraries, of rest and motion together. And Socrates could be compared to the particular intellect, or absolutely to Intellect, whereas of the other two, the former (Parmenides) is ranked analogically with Being, the latter (Zeno) with Life. This is why he is associated so closely with Parmenides and Zeno, and together with them makes up the first conversation, which we said bears the likeness of genuine being, as Intellect is itself the fullness of indivisible being. Socrates is also portrayed as especially confident of the theory of Ideas; and what other role is more fitting for the particular intellect than to see the divine Forms and declare them to others? So these three personages seem to me to satisfy the analogy, the first to Being, the second to Life, the third to Intellect; or the first to complete and unparticipated intellect, the second to intellect that is participated, the third to the individual and participated intellect. Indivisible nature stops with these grades of being; for intellect is either universal and unparticipated, or universal and participated, or particular and participated. For there is no intellect that is particular and unparticipated.

Of the three narrators of the conversation, Pythodorus is analogous

629 to the divine Soul, for he is present at the original meeting and is filled with blessed words (*logoi*), just as the divine Soul is filled with intellectual forms (for the divine Soul, as Plato tells us in the *Phaedrus* (247a) goes up to "banquet and festival" in the train of great Zeus); but he is a silent member of the group, for that kind of discussion belongs to beings with indivisible nature. But he might also be likened to the angelic order, as being the first to expound the whole theory of those divine beings. Antiphon resembles the daemonic soul, which lays hold of nature and spurs it to action; hence he wants to be a horseman, as the

27

daemonic soul wants to guide and lead according to its will the irrational steed. But he is filled with words (*logoi*) from Pythodorus in the second conversation and with them he fills the men who have come from Clazomenae, since this kind of soul occupies a middle position, being filled from the higher powers and filling nature with its own forms. Cephalus and the philosophers from Clazomenae are like individual souls which are conversant with Nature; and they have a similar role in this work because the philosophers from Clazomenae are themselves students of Nature. This interest in Nature is characteristic of the whole Ionian School as contrasted with the Italian; for the latter was always striving to apprehend the being of intelligibles, in which[13] it saw all other things causally, whereas the Ionian school occupied itself with Nature, i.e. with physical actions and effects, and regarded this study as being the whole of philosophy. The Attic school, being midway between the two, corrected the Ionian philosophy and developed the views of the Italians. Thus Socrates in the *Phaedo* (98c) charges Anaxagoras with making no use of Intellect and invoking airs and dispositions and various other like things as causes of natural events, and in the *Sophist* (217c) he invites the wise man from Elea to impart to him the philosophy cultivated there. But in those dialogues, as I have said, he brings in both schools, keeping their roles distinct, whereas in this case the plot involves bringing to Athens the men from Italy to impart to the Athenians their traditional doctrines, and bringing the men from Ionia, that they may share in the Italian teachings. Clazomenae is in Ionia and Elea in Italy. Just as all events in nature share in intelligibles through the mediation of the forms in souls, so this setting shows how the Italian philosophy was imparted to the Ionians; it brings them to Athens and through the Attic philosophers enables them to share in these esoteric doctrines.

630

(v) The Subject of the Dialogue

But we have said enough about the setting of the action—about the four conversations, the rank of the personages involved and their analogy to the grades of things in the universe—to satisfy those with the desire and the ability to contemplate the realm of beings, each in its proper place, from the perspective of the theory of Ideas. After these preliminaries there remains for us the necessity of finding the subject of the dialogue, and of seeing how all these elements are related to that single subject, as revealed by our argument. For all that we have said

---

[13] Reading ἐν ᾗ καὶ for καὶ ἐν ᾗ ᾗ of MSS. No help from Latin: *et unum erat qua* (καὶ ἓν ἦν ᾗ).

was said by way of preface to the dialogue and from the perspective of the theory of Ideas, from which some of our predecessors, as I have said, have given it its title. For just as we must proceed upwards from sensible appearances to the intelligible cause, so we must ascend from the circumstances presupposed in this dialogue to the single purpose and the single end of the whole treatise, and relate to this, so far as we can, the other details—the persons, the occasion, the setting—that we have previously considered on their own account.

An exercise in logical method: aporetic

Some of our contemporaries and predecessors have referred the purpose of this dialogue to logical exercise.[14] In doing so they discount the 631 title "About Ideas," though it is very ancient, for they say it is relevant to only a small part of the dialogue, and to the aporetic, not the expository part of it. There are some, then, who say the purpose of the dialogue is argumentative (*logikos*)—as in the *Theaetetus* (152a), where Plato writes against Protagoras, quoting "man is the measure of all things" and showing that man is no more the measure of all things than a pig or a dog-faced baboon; and they disregard its theory of reality, seeing that the arguments from the implications of saying that the One is and those that follow from asserting that it is not are mutually destructive. And of these interpreters (I mean those who say the purpose is argumentative) some suppose that Plato wrote it against Zeno, to put to the test the working of his subtle new methods of argument on a more difficult theme, that of the intelligibles; for Zeno had been occupied with applying these techniques to the sense-world and showing the clash of antithetical arguments about sense-objects.

For it is Plato's custom, these interpreters say, when he writes a controversial dialogue to do it in one of three ways. Sometimes he composes an imitation of what his rival has written, but carries the imitation to greater perfection by adding what his rival's discourse omits. For instance in the *Menexenus*, which he composed in rivalry with Thucydides, the oration written for a public funeral has the same purpose as his rival's, but in the arrangement of its main points, in its invention of supporting reasons, and in the clarity of its exposition, he constructs a much nobler discourse than that of Thucydides. Sometimes he composes arguments counter to those of his rival, as he does here against Zeno. For while Zeno produced a rich and varied show of arguments 632 aimed at catching out the partisans of the Many, and brought forth in his refutation not less than forty arguments revealing contradictions in

[14] E.g. Albinus, who in the *Isagoge* (ch. 3) presents it as elenctic, while in *Didaskalikos* (ch. 6) he treats it as a logical exercise, thus falling under Proclus' second category (see below).

their position,[15] Plato himself, they say, in rivalry with this energetic opponent of plurality, produced this varied show of arguments with reference to the One, showing in the same way as he contradictions about the same subject. As Zeno refuted the many by showing that they are both alike and unlike, the same and different, equal and unequal, so in the same way Plato shows that the One is like and unlike, not like and not unlike, the same and not the same, different and not different, and so for all the other contradictory predicates, both affirming and denying the contradictory propositions, and not, like Zeno, simply affirming them. In this way he exhibits a far more varied wealth of arguments than Zeno, who had so amazed the world that the Sillographer called him "double-tongued," and in admiration of his ability spoke of "the great and unwearied force of Zeno."[16] If he called Zeno double-tongued, what could he have called the man who increased many fold Zeno's inventions in method?

Thirdly, they say, Plato sometimes constructs a controversial piece by using both imitation and antithesis (the remaining alternative). Thus in his discourse against Lysias, the sophist (*Phaedr.* 243dff.), he takes for demonstration the same theme as Lysias, but instead of throwing his thoughts together pell-mell, as Lysias does, he introduces the logical order necessary to make the discourse like a living being; instead of beginning without method, he shows the scientific way of starting from definitions and proceeding in his inquiry from qualities to essence; and instead of ornamenting the discourse with a multitude of phrases that mean the same thing, he adds all sorts of color and variety of thought. All this shows how the sophist should have handled 633 his discourse on behalf of the non-lover. And when Plato goes over to the contrary task and enters into competition with him in pleading for the lover, he leaves his competitor far behind. He uses definitions, divisions, demonstrations, and every sort of means in his rival discourse, going even beyond the customary bounds of exposition, so that by the grandeur of his words he overwhelms the leanness of his opponent's style, and by attributing the difference to divine inspiration he conceals the cause from the ordinary hearer.

An exercise in logical method: gymnastic

Such are the contentions of this group of interpreters. But there are some[17] who say that the polemic alleged is inconsistent both with the

[15] On the vexed question of the "Forty Arguments" of Zeno, and Proclus' knowledge of them, see *General Introduction*, sect. D.

[16] Timon, *Silloi*, fr. 45D.

[17] Perhaps Albinus again, among others. Cf. n. 14 above, Thrasyllus (*ap.* Diog. Laert. III, 58) classifies it as λογικός, but without indicating whether he regards it as destructive or constructive.

contents and with the persons in the dialogue. It is inconsistent with the contents because Zeno has the same purpose as Parmenides in confuting those who, while positing that there are pluralities of beings, have no conception of that unity in virtue of which the many are many and from which they derive their being and have this designation. It is as if someone, seeing the multiplicity of men and saying that they are men, should overlook the one Form, Man, through which these beings are men and are called such; for if he had noted this, he would have said that the men as men are not many but one, as being of the same species. And it is inconsistent with the persons, for it is most incongruous to describe Parmenides and Zeno as lover and beloved, one the teacher and the other a disciple trained by him, and then make the lover and teacher swim through such a sea of controversy with his beloved, the

634 person whom he has trained. And it is also most discordant (as one can truly call it) to say that the one (Zeno) had prepared the book he wrote as an aid to Parmenides' doctrine, while the other (Plato) is arguing against this aid that Zeno had given by working out these numerous arguments.

Although discounting, then, the interpretation of the dialogue as polemic, some say that its purpose is logical exercise. For there are three main parts, speaking generally, of the dialogue, as these interpreters analyse it: one part puts forward the difficulties in the doctrine of Ideas, another contains a concise statement of the method in which it is thought lovers of truth must practise themselves, and the third works out an example of this same method as applied to the One of Parmenides. All these parts have one end, to afford practice in the exercise of logical disputation. For the first shows that such a study is necessary, by demonstrating that for those who turn to the study of being without having mastered it, even true hypotheses are overturned, since Socrates, through his lack of practice in this method, is presented as helpless to defend the theory of Ideas, and that, although he has a "divine impulse," as Parmenides says (135d), and the hypothesis is of the truest. . . .[18] And the third part is nothing else but an example, as is plainly stated (137b), to illustrate how this method works so that we may be able to exercise ourselves in this way in all our inquiries. It does somewhat the same thing as the example of division in the *Sophist* (221b); as the *Sophist* makes known the method of division by using it to find the definition of *angler*, so here dialectic is explained by applying it to the One of Parmenides. From all this they conclude that dialectic is the aim

---

[18] There appears to be a lacuna here, containing Proclus' remarks on the second part of the dialogue. These are summarised below, at 635.24-25, in the phrase, "another serves to clarify its general rules," referring to the bridge-passage 135b3-137c3, the subject of Book V of the Commentary.

31

635 of the dialogue throughout. They say it differs, however, from the method in Aristotle's *Topics*,[19] in that the latter divides problems into four kinds and devises methods of attack for each kind, even though Theophrastus condenses this fourfold division and restates the method, dealing with two species of problems, one concerned with definition, the other with accident, counting problems about genus with those concerned with definition, and problems about property with those about accident. But the method described here is a brilliant invention for examining any problem in a variety of ways and bringing the truth to light, since possible conclusions follow as necessary consequences from possible premises, and impossible from impossible. So that a method of this sort does not fall outside the compass of philosophy, as does the method of the *Topics*, which is suitable for those who are seeking only probable conclusions, but it contributes to the quest for truth itself; nor on the other hand does it allow us to speculate about any more esoteric doctrine beyond itself, seeing that one part of the dialogue shows dialectic to be necessary, another serves to clarify its general rules, and another illuminates the working of the method itself through these rules. These are the objections brought by interpreters who agree that the purpose of the dialogue is logical, but discount as implausible the views of those who look for an explanation in personal references.

Metaphysical: A study of Being

Some say, however, that the intent of the dialogue is directed towards matters of substance, and that the logical exercise is introduced for the sake of these substantive questions, although these interpreters do not import the more recondite doctrines to explain the method.
636 Some of them have said that the inquiry is about Being:[20] Plato proposes to confirm through the agency of these persons themselves how they asserted Being to be one, and by means of the methods they were accustomed to use, Zeno vigorously criticising the many and Parmenides expounding the One Being; for cathartic discourses must precede perfective ones. They say that Plato himself lauds Parmenides and testifies of the arguments here that they have a most noble depth in them. At least in the *Theaetetus* (183e) Socrates says that when he was very young he met Parmenides, then quite an old man, and heard him philosophizing about Being—not logical gymnastics, but profound con-

[19] *Topics* I, 4.101b11ff., where Aristotle makes a division into "property, definition, genus and accident." Theophrastus, perhaps in his *Topics*, reduces these to Definition and Accident. Cf. A. Graeser, *Die logischen Fragmente des Theophrast*, Berlin 1973, pp. 107-111.
[20] Possibly Origen the Platonist. See Intro. to Book I, p. 8.

ceptions—and he fears that they will not understand his words and will fail completely to grasp what he means. By all this he shows that the purpose of the inquiry now under way is an important one, and that the method introduced serves that important purpose and is understood as a necessary preliminary to the inquiry about Being, and that the difficulties connected with the Ideas are additional incitements to us to apprehend the One Being, for the plurality of Ideas has its foundation in the One Being, as the corresponding number does in its monad. Consequently, if we analyze the dialogue and range in order its various segments, we would say that what is most aimed at is its final end, viz. to expound the truth about Being in the Parmenidean sense. And since this had to be established by the use of these visitors' favourite method, the method of logical gymnastics, it was necessary beforehand to understand what this method is and by what rules it proceeds. And since the method could not otherwise be introduced than by showing the need for it, and this in turn could not be shown except by impressing upon those who embark on the study of things without it the unavoidable difficulties involved in their opinions—for this reason the dis-
637 cussion of the doctrine of Ideas is taken up first, together with the difficulties whose consideration, by the use of the method, would introduce the discussion of the knowledge we were wanting, viz. the knowledge of Being as Parmenides conceived it.

Nowhere do we find Plato producing a work which is principally a study of method; but rather we find him employing different methods at different times according to what each subject requires, and always adopting his method for the sake of the object of his inquiry. Thus in the *Sophist* he brings in the method of Division not in order to teach his hearers Division (though this is an incidental result), but in order to catch and bind the many-headed sophist. This procedure is in accordance with the nature of things, for it is nature's way to adopt means for the sake of ends, not ends for the sake of the means necessary to bring them about. A method is a necessary means when we want to exercise it in gaining knowledge of things, but not worthy of earnest attention for its own sake. An attentive look at the arrangement of the set of hypotheses would clearly confirm that Plato did not introduce the theory of being for the sake of the gymnastic method that is proposed before it. For that method requires that we posit both the existence and the non-existence of our subject, then consider what follows and what does not follow for the subject, whether posited as existing or not existing, both in relation to itself and in relation to other things, and for the other things likewise both in relation to themselves and in relation to the subject of the hypothesis. But in developing the hypotheses he does not always follow the patterns of his method, but omits some and alters others. Yet if he introduced the doctrine of One Being as an example of the method, would it not have been ridiculous not to follow the method and handle his example according to its announced rules, and say at every stage what inferences do not follow? As we make our 638 way through the so-called hypotheses we shall see that he does not altogether follow his method as he goes through them, but takes away some, adds others, and alters still others.

Metaphysical: A study of all things which derive from the One

What has been said should convince us that we ought not to say the aim of the dialogue is logical exercise; we must look for a substantive theme. Some interpreters contend, as we have said, that the theme is Being, and they cite the declaration of Parmenides at the beginning that he will take for argument his own One, and this is, they say, Being. Such is the common interpretation of Parmenides' doctrine; and the Stranger in the *Sophist* (245a) makes this clear, they say, when he criticizes Parmenides as not meaning the genuine One when he speaks of Being. Others,[21] agreeing with them in supposing that the aim of the dialogue is metaphysical, say that we should regard him as examining not merely the One Being, as the others affirm, but all things that get their reality from the One. Indeed, although the hypotheses do actually take their departure from Parmenides' One, which is identical with the One Being of the dialogue, yet as they proceed from this point they sometimes fix upon the notion of One apart from Being and develop the implications of genuine unity, purged of all plurality and therefore as transcending Being and repudiating that predicate. At other times the hypotheses apply to both One and Being alike and bring into view the whole intellectual cosmos, containing both Being, in its genuine sense, and the One, self-sufficiently participating in Being. Then again, taking being and attaching to it alone essential oneness, they show there is a Nature that exists through the One but is third in rank from the genuine One. Then, shifting to the examination of what is other than the One,[21a] they show that these things by participating in the One posit all other things along with themselves, and by not participating in it are deprived of all qualities. Since all these results cannot 639 be applied to the One Being, they conclude with plausibility that the discussion is not only about it but about all things from the primary cause down to the lowest, in which there is privation of all things. (These are thus likened to the primary cause by dissimilarity,[22] for that

---

[21] Perhaps a group comprising Plotinus, Porphyry, and Iamblichus. See Intro. to Book I, p. xx.

[21a] Reading 'τῶν ἄλλων' τοῦ ἑνὸς, with the Latin of Moerbeke.

[22] On ἀνόμοιος ὁμοιότης, cf. *PT* I, 12, p. 57.20 S-W, and the note on p. 144. Also below 695.6-7.

34

which is deprived of all qualities by its non-participation in the One is in a sense like that which transcends all things but its non-participation in Being.) Or can we reconcile with the One Being things that are so at odds with one another? For if the hypothesis is true—i.e. that the One Being is—and expresses exactly what Parmenides meant then, and he proves that the consequences are necessary consequences of the true hypothesis, according to him everything demonstrated from the hypothesis that the One Being is would be true; so that all negative and all positive consequences would be truly affirmed of the same thing, the One Being, and this is of all things the most impossible. And if all the consequences of positing that the One Being is not are in any way true (i.e. valid), they also will be predicates of the One Being. Not to mention that, as the argument shows, all the properties uniquely predicated of the One cannot belong to this same thing, i.e. the One Being. For how can the One Being be infinite plurality when the One itself, according to him—I mean Parmenides—repudiates infinity in number? How can there even be infinite number, the very thing he is always so eager to unify that he appears to eliminate every plurality of beings? How can the eternal participate in time? For such is the One Being according to Parmenides, which, as he says "remains in the same state" (fr. 8.29 D-K).

Hence, if our remarks are true, we clearly cannot say that the purpose is to inquire simply about Being in the Parmenidean sense (for not all that he affirms, and still less all that he denies, as well as everything that he both affirms and denies, is consistent with this interpretation), 640 but about all beings, some of which will accept the affirmations and the denials. So that it was both reasonable and accurate for Parmenides to say that he would start from his own doctrine of the One (137b); for he did make this his point of departure, but in revealing its consequences he set forth the whole nature of beings. Suppose someone wished to apply the same procedure to the soul, saying that he was going to start from the One Soul (i.e. the primary soul), and then from this hypothesis showed the plurality of souls and all things that participate in them: we should not say that though he began with the One Soul he was discoursing about that alone, but both about that hypothesis and all the consequences that follow from it. In general, when anyone lays down an hypothesis, the hypothesis has the status of a starting-point; but the inquiry is not about it but about its consequences, according as it remains fixed or is modified.

Metaphysical: Doctrine of Syrianus

These are the differences of opinion among the ancients with respect to the purpose of the *Parmenides*. Now we must say what our master has added to their interpretations. He agrees with those of our predecessors who thought the aim of the dialogue is metaphysics, and dismisses the idea that it is a polemic as implausible. That Zeno should ask Parmenides to practise his method before the company and that Parmenides in exhibiting it should defend himself against the treatise of Zeno is altogether incredible in the light of what has been said; and to make its purpose an exposition of method is as silly as the idea that it is a polemic. For if he had to have an example in order to make his method clear, he would have taken some other readily available topic as an illustration, instead of making the most august of all his doctrines incidental to the teaching of method, though he considered this method appropriate only to young men. To understand that august doctrine requires the intellect of an older man, and indeed an intellect more than human, as he says in his poem, and rather that of a nymph, Hypsipyle.[23]

641 Considering such to be the dialogue's purpose, our master denied that it was about Being, or about real beings alone; he admitted that it was about all things, but insisted on adding "in so far as all things are the offspring of one cause and are dependent on this universal cause," and indeed, if we may express our own opinion, in so far as all things are deified; for each thing, even the lowest grade of being you could mention, becomes god by participating in unity according to its rank. For if God and One are the same because there is nothing greater than God and nothing greater than the One, then to be unified is the same as to be deified. Just as, if the Sun and God were the same, to be illumined would be the same as to be deified; for the One gives unity, the Sun light. So, as Timaeus does not simply inquire about nature in the usual manner of the natural scientist, but in so far as all things get their cosmic ordering from the one Demiurge, so also Parmenides, we may say, in conducting an inquiry about beings, is himself examining these beings in so far as they are derived from the One.

Now this One, we may say, exists otherwise in the gods than in the beings that come after the gods; in the one case, it is self-sufficient, not like something existing in a substratum (for every god is god by virtue 642 of the One, though the supreme God is one purely and simply, having no multiple aspect, while each of the others is more than unity, one thing because it has these entities dependent on it, another those; the beings that are nearer the pure One are fewer in number, those further away are more numerous, just as those nearer have a nature more akin to it and those further away are less akin; addition[24] and plurality come

---

[23] It is not quite clear from Proclus' phraseology, 'νύμφης Ύψιπύλης τινός,' whether he is giving this as the name for Parmenides' divine guide in his Poem. The goddess's name is not elsewhere mentioned.
[24] Reading πρόσθεσιν for πρόθεσιν.

about because of their descent in the scale of being). So in the former case the One truly is, while in the latter case it exists as a character in something. For every form, every soul, every body participates in some unity, but this unity is no longer a god, although, if I may say so, it is an image of god, a divine seed—as form is a likeness of Being, knowledge a likeness of Intellect, even in the lowest of things, and as self-motion is an image of Soul. Then just as every self-moving thing is Soul, or ensouled; as every knowing thing is Intellect, or possessed by Intellect; as every form is either essence, or possessed by Essence, so every unity is either a god, or possessed by God. Hence Timaeus traces all things back to the Demiurge, Parmenides traces them to the One, and there is an analogous relation between the Demiurge and the contents of the cosmos, and the One and all things whatsoever, ⟨the Demiurge being a kind of one⟩[25] but not One in the absolute sense; for he is a god, not God, and the god that is the One is not a god, but God simply. So the Demiurge is a god, since demiurgy is a property of a god, and there are other divine properties that are not demiurgic.

As there is this analogy between the dialogues in respect of their purposes, so they agree in the temporal settings of the actions they portray. One presupposes the Lesser Panathenaea, the other the Greater, as I said before;[26] and in the latter the Athenians would carry the peplos of the goddess that pictured her victory over the giants. As a background for the presentation of the unity pervading all things, this scene of the giants is highly appropriate. For Athena is said to prevail over the giants by bringing knowledge and unity to the divisible and material regions of her administration, making the intelligent elements prevail over the irrational, the immaterial over the material, and the unified over the pluralized. This peplos, then, was the symbol of the power of Athena transcendent over cosmic things, by virtue of which she is one with her father and with him overcomes the giants. And the so-called Lesser Panathenaea exalted her rank in the cosmos, making it coordinate with the period of the Moon;[27] for which reason it seems fitting to a dialogue revealing to us the whole of the cosmic genesis.

The time is thus in agreement with the purpose of the *Parmenides*; and this conversation which Cephalos narrates, being the fourth from the original one (whoever his audience may be), is in harmony with the procession of all things from the One down to the last. For the things that proceed from that source are either henads, which have their reality immediately from the One, or essences that proceed from the One through these henads, or intermediates between these essences and the

---

[25] Accepting T. Taylor's supplement for a lacuna in the MSS.
[26] Above, 618.24ff. Cousin. But cf. also *In Tim.* I, 84.12ff.
[27] Cf. *In Tim.* II, 289.10ff.

generations produced by them (and before them by the henads and the One), or the generated beings that proceed from all the foregoing. If, therefore, the procession of all the beings that are in diminishing degrees of perfection and likeness to the supreme goal ends at the fourth stage of descent, is not this account of the descent of all things from the One, being fourth, in perfect agreement with the theory presupposed in the dialogue? And if in generated beings there exists a formless receptive capacity, the persons who receive the words uttered in this fourth account would bear a likeness to this capacity, being themselves 645 nameless in accordance with their analogy to the indeterminate; for a name is the sign of a form. We could summarize all this by saying that every existence is either essence or generation, or neither essence nor generation; and in the last case is either prior to essence and generation, or subsequent to them; for all the material element is neither of the two and resembles (unresemblingly, as they say)[28] the beings that are prior to generation and essence.

(vi) Style of the Dialogue

We must remark further that the style of the dialogue is most appropriate to the subject it treats of and to its method of inquiry. Its subjects are divine beings that have their foundation in the simplicity of the One, who fervently rejoice in "unadorned beauty" (as one of the experts in divine matters says)[29] and extend it to those capable of looking at the divine. The method proceeds by using the most exacting capacities of reason, careless of adornment, abjuring all artifices extrinsic to its subject, and intent only on finding with accuracy the objects it is looking for and tying them fast by geometrical necessity. So that to both the subject and the method its form is well and nicely adapted; the leanness of its style befits its dialectical procedure, and its naturalness and lack of exaggeration and adornment go with the divine matters it expounds. So that any trace of Socratic charm, or of any middle style of discourse appropriate to median forms of life, or any rich and elevated 646 invention suited to and arising from the fancy of divinely possessed en-

---

[28] Cf. n. 22 above.

[29] Ἀκαλλώπιστος εὐμορφία. One would assume the authority to be either Orpheus or the *Oracles*, but the phrase cannot be fitted into an hexameter as it stands, so it may come from some prose work, perhaps of Iamblichus. Philo of Alexandria is the first recorded author to use both of these words, but he does not use them together. Origen the Platonist is credited at *In Tim.* I, 86.25ff. with talking of the ἀκαλλώπιστος πιθανότης of Plato's style in the *Timaeus*, for what that is worth. The reading of one MS, (the *Harleianensis*), ἀμορφία, is a possibility, but it is not confirmed by the Latin, so is more likely to be a conjecture.

thusiasts—all this is naturally alien to the style adopted here and nothing of that sort should be expected in this dialogue.

For my part, while I admire those who have allied themselves to the critical acumen of their predecessors,[30] which has led them to applaud the entire type of diction of this dialogue, which in its sparseness marvellously preserves the character of true Being, which adequately mingles fullness with restraint and weaves harmoniously together intensity with precision, still more do I admire those who in their instructions regarding the correct mode of theological discourse have pointed out that many parts of the *Sophist* are phrased in this way and that the whole of the *Parmenides* falls into this class. Except that to what they have said this much should be added: when we say this style befits theology, we do not mean that it alone is suitable for discussing divine matters, but that these terms and this style are especially adapted to teaching divine truth dialectically, as is done in a discourse of this nature. Divine truth can be expounded in a variety of ways.[31] The poets under the inspiration of Phoebus will use a richer style, filled with terms from mythology; others, abstaining from dramatic or mythical garb but otherwise speaking in inspired language, will express themselves in an elevated style and priestly terms; others aim at presenting divine matters through images, using mathematical terms, those used either in arithmetic or in geometry.

Quite different from all these is the exposition through dialectical 647 terms, a method especially suitable for members of the Eleatic School, even as of the former, the one is specifically Pythagorean, as Philolaus reveals[32] in his use of numbers to expound the existence and the genealogy of the gods, while another is the priestly style, which gives the names of the gods according to the secret doctrines of their sect, such as those current among the Assyrians[33]—Zonai and Azonoi, Pēgai, Ameiliktoi, Synocheis—for interpreting the divine hierarchy; and yet another is the Orphic style, characteristic of Hellenic theology, which assigns the names Cronos, Zeus, Ouranos, Nyx, Cyclopes, and Hekatoncheirs to the highest principles of the world. But instead of all these the dialectical exegesis of the divine employs, as I said, such dialectical

---

[30] This sounds like a backhanded compliment to Porphyry; those with whom he is contrasted just below would then be Iamblichus and Syrianus. Cf. the discussion of the style of the *Timaeus* at *In Tim.* I, 7.17-18, 29, and the remarks about Longinus *ibid.* 86.19-25.

[31] Cf. *PT* I, 4, where the various modes of theological discourse found in Plato are set out, and Saffrey and Westerink's notes, p. 136.

[32] Probably in his *Peri Physios*. Cf. frs. 44B1-16 D-K.

[33] I.e. the Chaldaean Oracles. Again, this is possibly Iamblichus, the previous category referring to Porphyry, and the following (Orphic) to Syrianus (cf. Hermeias, *In Phaedr.* 148.17ff. Couvreur, presenting Syrianus' exegesis).

terms as One and Being, whole and parts, same and other, like and un-like—the terms with which dialectic mostly operates and here uses for interpreting divine things. This, therefore, is the kind of discourse that Parmenides follows here, a style appropriate to such terms as these and taken from ordinary speech, not grandiloquent but restrained, not overly contrived but natural.

(vii) Parmenidean Dialectic and Platonic Dialectic

648   So much we had to say regarding the expository style of the dialogue. But since I have heard many interpreters of Plato's doctrine attempt to distinguish the method that Parmenides presents here from the dialectical method so highly prized by Plato, I think it desirable to state my opinions on this point. According to some, there are three statements made by Parmenides himself that show this method is different from Plato's. Socrates says in the *Republic* (VII, 537e-539d) that dialectic ought not to be given to young men, lest they acquire a bent towards lawlessness through using their skill in argument to upset the unperverted[34] concepts in us; but Parmenides urges Socrates, a young man, to use this method and exhorts him to do so for this reason especially, that he is young; for he says, the cultivation of this method is appropriate for the young, yet Plato's legislation excludes them from dialectic. Secondly, this method is called by Parmenides an exercise, which implies that it uses arguments both for and against a thesis, like
649   Aristotle's dialectic, which Aristotle in teaching it says contributes to logical exercise. But Plato's dialectic is described in the dialogues as leading to the highest and purest stage of knowledge and insight, since its activity is based on intelligible Forms, through which it advances to the very first member of the intelligible world, paying no attention to human opinion but using irrefutable knowledge at every step. A third point, in addition to these two, is that the method of reasoning here is explicitly called "babbling" (135d5) by Parmenides himself, whereas dialectic is called by Socrates "the capstone of knowledge" (*Rep.* VII, 534e) and indeed is said by the Eleatic Stranger to be suitable only for genuine philosophers (*Soph.* 253e); and clearly we would not venture to rank among the babblers those who are striving to apprehend being.

So say those who think that this method is different from dialectic. And indeed Socrates never appears to have adopted it in his own philosophy, although as a young man he practised it on the advice of Parmenides; but he is always using dialectic, following it by preference on

---

[34] Reading ἀδιαστρόφων for εὐδιαστρόφων of MSS (West.). The latter word would make some sense, but it is otherwise unattested, while ἀδιάστροφος has a well-known technical sense in this context.

all occasions, and saying that he would "follow in his footsteps as if he were a god"[35] any man who is able to divide one into many and collect many into one. For this is the real function of dialectic, he says in the *Phaedrus* (266b)—not, as the method here prescribes, to make an hypothesis and discover what follows from affirming it and from denying it, nor to find hypotheses for hypotheses and the positive and negative implications of their consequences. But why speak of Socrates and argue that what he describes as appropriate to the dialectician is quite dif-
650 ferent from the method that Parmenides presents in this dialogue? Even the Eleatic wise man, though himself a member of the group around Parmenides and Zeno, nevertheless, when expounding the procedure of dialectic in the *Sophist*—see what he says (253c): "He then who is capable of this"—he means capable of not mistaking the same kind to be other or the other the same—"perceives distinctly a single idea pervading many, each of them posited as distinct, and many ideas different from one another included under one embracing idea, and again a single idea pervading many others but united into one, and many ideas altogether distinct in every way." Can he be saying here that the dialectician's task is to make his way through such hypotheses as Parmenides' method goes through? To hunt for the consequences, positive and negative, both for itself and for other things, of affirming a hypothesis and the corresponding consequences of denying? And yet the four parts in the above statement are consonant with the two aspects of dialectic mentioned in the *Phaedrus*. One of them was to divide the one into many; this is the property of diaeresis, to separate a genus into its species. The genus is the "single idea" spread through many separate things and existing in each of them; for the genus is not an assemblage of species, like a whole of parts, but is present in each of the species as existing before them and participated in both by each of the separate species and by the genus itself. The species are the many ideas different from one another but comprehended by one single embracing idea, which is the genus; though it is outside them, as transcending the species, yet it contains the causes of the species; for to all those who posit Ideas, real genera are thought to be both older and more essential than the species ranged under them; the realities existing prior to species are not identical with the characters that exist in the species by participation. Thus we see that to distinguish between these two kinds is the task of the diaeretic part of dialectic; the distinction between the remaining two belongs to the definitional aspect. This art (1) perceives a single unified idea pervading many wholes—collecting the many ideas,
651 each of which is a whole, into a single definition, weaving them to-

[35] *Od.* 5.193, quoted at *Phaedr.* 266b.

41

gether, and from all these apprehended wholes bringing about a single idea by grasping the many as one; and further (2) it looks upon the many ideas it has collected as distinct both from one another and from the whole which arises from them. This is what we should expect; for how could it make one out of many if it had not previously seen the many as separate from one another?

Since Parmenides makes no mention of such functions of dialectic when outlining to us his method of hypotheses, and since Socrates almost everywhere hotly pursues them but does not mention the method of Parmenides, how could one accept the view that they are the same as each other?

The answer is, to begin with, that the first point mentioned (that Parmenides recommends his method to the young, and Socrates forbids young men to practise his) is not sufficient to differentiate them; to give advice in a personal instance is not the same as to formulate a general rule. The latter envisages a variety of unruly natures and in view of them necessarily puts the general requirements of what is proper ahead of advice to individuals; for the legislator is giving guidance not to one man, but to many, and therefore considers not what is fitting for the best of natures, but what is incumbent alike upon the best, the middling, and the worst; so that he takes cognisance of reversals of fortune and takes care not to prescribe what would injure any of the persons whom he is educating. Even if he selects to the greatest extent possible the class of superior individuals, he knows that even in them there is a great deal of irregularity, as is to be expected in human beings. But if he is advising an individual on his occupation, he looks at the special character of the man whom he is counselling, especially if he is himself such a man as to be able to discern the fitness of the recipient to receive his advice, and in this case he advises him to select or
652 ignore some particular of his occupation. Hence this manner of legislation regarding dialectic was appropriate to be given to Socrates; and it also goes with the character of Parmenides, who was looking only at the divine impulse towards philosophy which, as he says (130b1), he observed in Socrates and knew that no damage would be done to any youth who practised this method if he had a character like that of Socrates. Socrates himself, after all, if he knew that all the natures for whom he was giving advice were of the highest type, would not have hesitated to give his dialectic to young men, knowing they would get no harm from it nor suffer any of the consequences which led to his withholding it from all for fear that some, whose bent for such dialectic he was not sure of, would be injured. In general we observe that all legislation is aimed at what is usual, not at the rare occurrences; it considers the general nature of the kind, not the particular individual,

whether it be laws about the gods to be honoured, or the studies and occupations to be chosen, or the selection of duties to be observed. These prescriptions are not necessarily incumbent on those who fall outside the legislation, i.e. who are endowed with a different nature higher than the common. So that there is no reason why Socrates and Parmenides, in laying down prescriptions about one and the same occupation, should not say different things about its use and both be speaking truly, the one having in mind the common human nature, the other the individual.

Nor is it true that when Parmenides calls his method an "exercise" he is using a different term from those that Socrates uses. This is evident to any one who has followed carefully the laws that Socrates lays down for dialectic. He says that his young citizens who have gone through the studies prescribed in mathematics must exercise themselves (this is the expression he uses, *Rep. VII*, 526b) in dialectic, and appoints a definite limit of time for such exercise. Either, then, his dialectic must be regarded as identical with the exercise on probable premises (*endoxa*), or it cannot be reduced to dialectic merely because 653 of the word *exercise*, although Parmenides declares that his "exercises" will "with difficulty" enable one to see the truth—which is *not*[36] the purpose of the arguments in the so-called *Topics*.

Why then did both these men call the primary use of this method 'exercise'? I shall tell you. This method of trying to attain genuine knowledge, looked at as a whole, contains three sorts of activities. One, which is suitable for young men, is useful for awakening the reason that is, as it were, asleep in them and provoking it to inquire into itself. This is actually an exercise in training the eye of the soul for seeing its objects and for taking possession of its essential ideas by confronting them with their contradictories. It explores not only the path that leads, as we may say, in a straight line towards the truth, but also the bypaths that lie alongside it, trying them also to see if they reveal anything trustworthy; and thus it brings all the soul's varied conceptions to the test. In another form of its activity dialectic places the mind at the outset in the region of thought where it is most at home, looking at truth itself, "sitting on a sacred pedestal" (*Phaedr.* 254b), which Socrates says unfolds before the mind the whole intelligible world, making its way from Form to Form until it reaches the very first Form of all, sometimes using analysis, sometimes definition, now demonstrating, now dividing, both moving downwards from above and upwards from below until, having examined in every way the whole nature of the in-

---

[36] Reading ⟨οὔκ⟩ ἐστι τέλος, with Latin translation. Proclus' whole purpose is to differentiate the Parmenidean method from the Aristotelian.

telligible, it climbs aloft to that which is beyond all being. When it has safely anchored the soul there, it has reached its goal and there will no longer be anything greater to be desired. You could say these are the functions of dialectic spoken of in the *Phaedrus* and in the *Sophist*, the former dividing dialectical procedures into two, the latter into four parts; and this is why the method is referred to the genuine philoso-
654 pher, who no longer has need of mental gymnastics but nourishes the reason in his soul on pure cognitions. There is another and third kind of dialectic, that which is 'tentative'[37] in the proper sense, which purges of "double ignorance" when directed against men falsely confident of their opinions. The *Sophist* also speaks of this kind of dialectic (231a); for as the philosopher is compelled to use refutation as a method of catharsis on men obsessed by their conceit of wisdom, so also the sophist, when engaged in refutation, was thought to assume the guise of the philosopher, like a wolf pretending to be a dog, as the dialogue puts it. For he who truly refutes another and not merely appears to do so, since he is truly a purger of false opinion, is a philosopher; for how could one purge another's soul if his own is unpurged?

Of these three kinds of dialectical activity—arguing on both sides, expounding truth, and exposing error—it is the first alone that is called gymnastics by our two philosophers. This is the method by which Socrates trains his young men, as for instance Theaetetus, by examining both sides of the question—e.g. whether what a man thinks is true for him or not, whether or not knowledge is perception—and then in turn examining the difficulties in true beliefs, or rapping them against one another and showing up any that give a hollow ring; or young Lysis, who is another of these, by enquiring: "What is a friend? Can only persons who are alike be friends? Or is friendship a relation between opposites? And is it the lover, or the beloved, who is a friend to the other?"—in this way constantly exposing him to the difficulties latent in his opinions. Such exercise is a good thing for young and ambitious persons enamoured of knowledge, to strengthen them against weariness in enquiry and giving up through not having the initial . . .[38]
655 since when he (sc. Socrates) is contending with sophists masquerading, as they always do, as experts and masters of wisdom, all the methods of dialectic are ready to his hand to show his adversaries where they contradict themselves, and since these dialectical methods are in some way cathartic of overweening self-opinion, his adversaries may eventually, after being pounded from all sides, be brought to a recognition

---

[37] Reading πειραστική (West.) for παραστατική of MSS. A reference to Aristotle's use of the term, e.g. at *Soph. El.* 169b25, *Met.* 52.1004b25.

[38] There is a lacuna here, unnoticed by Cousin. When the text resumes, the subject is Socrates.

of their own false pretenses. Many examples of this kind of Socratic dialectic are found in the *Gorgias* and the *Protagoras* and in other dialogues that attack the theses of the sophists, for example the arguments Socrates puts together in the *Republic* against the ingenious Thrasymachus.

But obviously if the dialectician is reasoning with himself, having to do with men who are neither adversaries needing to be trounced nor pupils needing to be exercised, he employs the highest form of dialectic, that which reveals the truth in its purity. Thus Socrates in the *Phaedo* lays down certain hypotheses, deduces their consequences, and shows that the soul is incapable of receiving the opposite of the quality that it confers on that in which it is present, and after proving this, he once again demands that we examine whether the initial hypotheses themselves are true, and he outlines certain rules of procedure agreeing with the method of the *Parmenides*: at each hypothesis you should look only at the consequences that follow from it, but make no defence of the hypothesis itself until you have adequately gone over its implications; then give a reason for the hypothesis itself, conducting your search in due order by assuming another hypothesis, the best of those above, until going upward step by step you come to "something adequate"—meaning by this obviously the unhypothetical principle, that which is, not by hypothesis but in fact, the first principle of what has been demonstrated. And when the Eleatic sage uses diaeresis to make many out of one and definition for getting one from many, he too is employing the highest form of dialectic, as if to show that he divides and defines by himself, as well as when reasoning in the presence of others. For in this dialogue he is not holding forth before unpractised novices—his hearers have already been exercised through arguments with Socrates, have been trained in mathematics, and thus been prepared for the theory of Being—nor before sophists hampered by their double ignorance and incapable of receiving scientific reasoning because of their self-conceit.

This, then, is why he called training in dialectic "gymnastics." That dialectic was commonly called "babbling" and those who practised it "babblers" hardly requires illustration, seeing that the comic poets called Socrates a "beggarly babbler" and gave the same name to all others who presumed to be dialecticians.

> I despise Socrates also, that beggarly babbler.

> Either Prodicus, or one or other of those babblers."[39]

---

[39] The former of these quotations is from Eupolis (fr. 352 Kock), the latter from Aristophanes, *Tagenistai* (fr. 490 Kock). In both cases, Proclus is doubtless dependent on an intermediate source, perhaps an earlier commentary on the *Phaedo* (70b).

This is why Parmenides does not simply call his method "babbling," but adds "what the many call babbling." Furthermore, Socrates himself in the *Phaedo* implies that in his earlier life the name had been applied to him in comedy (70b): "Now at least I don't think any comic poet would say that I am babbling and talking about what does not concern me when, being about to go to dwell in Hades, I discourse about my transfer of residence thither." And in the *Theaetetus*, when he has examined the Protagorean thesis from all sides and thinks he has proved the point at issue, then it is that he prepares to raise objections to what he has concluded. "A babbling man," he says, "is surely a terrible thing" (195b). When Theaetetus asks the reason for this preamble, he replies, "Because I am about to dispute with myself." Clearly what he here calls babbling is this very characteristic of dialectic, the practice of raising difficulties, of turning the same propositions this way and that and not being able to leave them alone. In short, those who were derisively called babblers are those men who do not find it easy to stop going over the same arguments.

It was, then, as I said, the multitude who gave this name to dialectic, and that is why Parmenides says it is what "the many" call the method he is going to expound. But if we look at the classification of arts in the *Sophist* (219b–225d) we shall find that even the Eleatic Stranger there puts dialectic under the rubric of babbling. He divides sciences into two classes, one creative, the other acquisitive; and of the latter, one part acquires by combat, the other by other means; and of the combative class one part is competitive, the other pugnacious; and of pugnacious acquisition, one species uses violent and bodily conflict, the other verbal controversy; and under this clearly we must place dialectic. For it is not creative, but acquisitive, like mathematics, and acquisitive in no other way than through competition. And when the art of disputation is divided into the kind that makes long speeches and that which proceeds privately by questions and answers, it is clear that dialectic would belong under the latter. This art of "antilogy," as it is called here, is again divided into a species that is concerned with particulars of contracts and another that inquires into general principles that admit of controversy (as he says, about the just and the noble and their opposites); and clearly dialectic will find its place here. He calls it eristic, not meaning that it is disreputable strife or antilogy, but indicating only its activity of controverting and raising objections. For there is a correct way of carrying on controversy, just as there is good and bad strife, if, as the poet says, there are two forms of strife (Hesiod *WD* 11): "There is, then, more than one species of strife." And so of eristic there is one species that makes money (this brings in our ingenious sophist) and another species that wastes money, which neglects private affairs for its insatiable interest in discussion. Under this we shall obviously place the dialectician, for he clearly does not belong in the other class, since that is sophistry. And when he gives a name to this money-wasting eristic he says it can be called nothing else than babbling. If then Plato himself gives this name to dialectic, how can it be maintained that the method in the *Parmenides* differs from dialectic because it is called babbling, and dialectic cannot possibly deserve this appellation.

(viii) The Significance of Plato's Preludes

But we have said more than was necessary on this point. Let us return to the project we have undertaken, with only this additional observation. The ancient commentators have held varying opinions regarding the preludes to Plato's dialogues. Some have not condescended to examine them at all, saying that hearers who are genuinely interested in the doctrines must come with a previous knowledge of these preliminaries. Others do not take them as being irrelevant, but see their use as being for the presentation of moral attitudes (*kathēkonta*), and present their relevance to the central problems addressed in the dialogues on this basis. Others demand that the interpreter bring the matter of the prologue into relation with the nature of the dialogue's subject.[40] We agree with the last group and shall begin by showing how the subject of the dialogue relates to the matter in the introduction. Not that we shall neglect the moral stances represented in the dialogue, but in studying any Platonic dialogue we must look especially at the matters that are its subject and see how the details of the prologue prefigure them. In this way we should show that each of them is perfectly worked out, a living being harmonious in all its parts, as Plato says in the *Phaedrus* (264c), and bring into harmony with this also what belongs to the outlining of moral attitudes. When the preludes are completely irrelevant to what follows, as in the dialogues of Heraclides of Pontus and Theophrastus, it offends every critical ear.[41]

[40] From parallels in the *Timaeus* commentary (cf. *In Tim.* I, 87.6ff.), it is plain that Iamblichus is the protagonist of this last view, at least in its developed form. The second view is that of Porphyry, the first that of Middle Platonic commentators, such as Severus (cf. *In Tim.* I, 204.16ff.). Porphyry's tendency to refer the contents of the preludes to *ta kathēkonta* is mentioned at *In Tim.* I, 19.24ff.

[41] For a discussion of the dialogues of these two, cf. Hirzel, *Der Dialog*, I, pp. 321-331 and 317. It sounds from this remark as if Proclus had access to them.

BOOK I

PARMENIDES
or
ABOUT IDEAS

When we arrived in Athens from our home in Clazomenae, we encoun-
tered Adeimantus and Glaucon in the agora. (126a)

The philosophers of Italy, as I have often said, concerned themselves
with the study of the really existent Forms and touched but slightly on
the study of the objects of opinion, while those in Ionia gave less attention to studying the intelligible world but examined nature and nature's works with great thoroughness. Socrates and Plato shared the
660 interests of both groups, perfecting the lower philosophy, and expounding the higher. This is clear from what Socrates says in the
Phaedo (96aff.), that he had formerly been enamoured of the study of
nature, but later had advanced to Forms and the divine causes of things.
This is precisely what Plato indicates, it seems to me, by the setting
presupposed for this dialogue, that in their philosophies he and Socrates took over the good elements from both groups and brought them
together into one complete truth. What is remarkable here and thoroughly revelatory of the matters with which the dialogue is concerned,
is that the men from Ionia present themselves at Athens to learn something of the fuller doctrine, while the men at Athens have not corre-
spondingly gone to Italy to get acquainted with Italian philosophy;
rather it is the Italians who have come to Athens to impart their special
teachings. This is also the case with reality itself, for those capable of
observing it: the presence of the higher realities extends without hin-
drance, through the middle orders, down to the lowest orders of being;
the lowest are perfected through the middle; and the middle beings receive the gift of the higher for transmission to the lowest and stimulate
the lowest to move towards themselves to receive it, and so become as
it were the center and dynamic force between the two extremes, being
filled from the more perfect and filling the inferior.

Let us take Ionia then as a symbol of nature, Italy as a symbol of intellectual being, and Athens as the intermediary that provides a way up
for the souls who are aroused to move from nature to Intellect. This is
what Cephalus says straightway in the prelude: he had come from Clazomenae to Athens to hear the discourse of Parmenides, arriving there
had encountered Adeimantus and Glaucon in the agora, and being introduced by them to Antiphon had heard him deliver the discourse
661 which he had learned from Pythodorus and which Pythodorus had
heard from Parmenides. In these details he indicates what kind of person he must be who is to be led upwards. He must first have been
awakened to leave his association with the body ("home" for the soul

48

is the body), then must join himself to Athena's domain in the universe, by residence in which the soul becomes, not surprisingly, the spectator of the primary realities themselves and through them can obtain a mystical vision of the very henads of Being.[42]

Or, if you like, we can express the analogy on a still more universal level. The gods who guide nature and comprise the various powers of enmattered forms, i.e. all the individual and perceptible reason-principles, are dependent on the primary cause; and being illumined by Athena to turn their attention towards the intelligible world, abstract themselves from the cosmic system (for this also is called the home of the gods that are in it), are lifted up to see the unified plurality in things, and there by divine power advance to the monad that contains the primary plurality. Of all these things the words quoted contain a likeness, for those not altogether unacquainted with such matters. For each of the forms in nature is inferior to the plurality of them; the plurality that participates in the one which is coordinate with the many; and prior to this is the transcendent unity of the One before the many, to which one ascends through the intermediary dyad; for the dyad is the first reality that proceeds from the One, as the *Philebus* teaches us (16e).

Hence the departure from Clazomenae expresses the activity of the gods which transcends the reason-principles in nature, the encounter with Glaucon and Adeimantus in the agora indicates the sovereignty of the dyad in the unified plurality, and the conversation through them with Antiphon shows their being led to the One, from which they receive perfection and the fullness of the divine goods. For in each rank of the gods there is the monad, the sovereignty of the dyad, and the number appropriate to it. And all that which has been differentiated is attached to the monad by means of the unified plurality and the dyad in it which is its mother and its root, so to say. But these things, as I said, bear the likeness of the gods themselves and make it very easy for those who wish to follow the analogy. For observe: the Clazomenaeans are many, Adeimantus and Glaucon are two, and through them the meeting is brought about between the Clazomenaeans and Antiphon, who is one. It is clear that everywhere the multiple gets the benefit of the monad through the dyad; that the men of Clazomenae, being students of nature, make their way through things naturally akin to each other to gain participation in the more complete doctrines; that the beings of second rank are always dependent on beings prior to them; and that all things strain to reach the one Intellect which is Parmenides. The men from Clazomenae make their appeal to Adeimantus and

662

---

[42] This sound very like a Porphyrian "ethical" exegesis, followed by an Iamblichian "physical" one.

49

Glaucon, the latter lead them to Antiphon, Antiphon fills them with the discourses (*logoi*) of Pythodorus, and Pythodorus is the messenger carrying the words that passed between Parmenides, Zeno, and Socrates. The last two in turn are one with Parmenides, placing themselves willingly at his side, Socrates looking at the plurality of ideas, Zeno unifying plurality and striving towards the One itself.[43] Let them, then, be ranked thus.

Not only can you look at it in the way indicated above, but you can also view it as follows: since Parmenides, Zeno, and Socrates preserve 663 the analogy with the whole divine order, those that are next are like the secondary kinds. And if you will take this point of view, you will rank Pythodorus with the highest of the daemonic powers that announces and transmits messages from the primary to the secondary beings. Both these roles are appropriate to him, for on the one hand he is being filled, and on the other hand he is filling, by his own powers adapting his hearing of the original words to the hearing of others. Antiphon we should rank as that daemonic power that operates with desire and impulse and, in short, since he is supposed to be a horseman, takes on the character of the second level of life; hence he is filled from the primary daemons and fills those below him with the elevating discourse that he has received from the higher powers. Finally, the men from Clazomenae are analogous to souls in the world of generation who require the help of the daemons immediately above them and are eager, all of them, to move upwards and share in the divine words. This is why they leave their homes (that is, the body) and transport themselves to Athens; for they revert upon themselves on encountering the providence of Athena and proceed from ignorance to knowledge, for that is what Athens stands for. And having thus reverted, first they attach themselves to the daemons above them, who are associated with the agora (for they are "guardians of mortal men") and with the Dyad (for they issue from the One) and with conversion, through the Dyad, to the One. Next they are presented by these daemons to certain angels and gods, for it is through the daemons, as Diotima tells us (*Symp.* 203a), that all the fellowship and converse takes place between men, whether awake or sleeping, and the gods.

Thus we have found another approach for drawing analogies be- 664 tween the contents of the dialogue and the personages in it; and it is necessary that we exercise our understanding on these details as likenesses before we enter on the mysteries of the doctrines themselves. Even the statement that when these men arrived at Athens they im-

---

[43] This seems to describe the Chaldaean dyad attached to the Father, referred to in *Or. Chald.* fr. 8 DP, and is very possibly Iamblichean doctrine.

mediately encountered (*entychein*) in the agora Adeimantus and Glaucon, the brothers of Antiphon, is an expression of another theological
reflection, namely, that the souls being led upwards are greatly helped
by good fortune (*agathē tychē*), which arranges where and how and
whom they should meet for laying hold on the truth that will save
them; and that it is not by external goods only that the gifts of good
fortune serve our needs, but also in those uplifting powers within our
own souls. As Socrates says somewhere in the *Phaedrus* (245b), the
gods' gift of madness to the lover about his beloved is the greatest of
good fortunes (*eutychia*); and in the soul's descent from the intelligible
world, he says, they suffer various vicissitudes (*syntychiai*, 248c), from
which we infer that even before their bodily contacts they are aware of
the gifts of fortune and are governed by her and led to their proper
place. So it is natural here that as the souls are being led upwards they
by chance (*tychē*) are joined by causes that make for their own perfection. We shall not argue whether "encounter" (*entychein*) may mean the
same thing as "happen upon" (*peritychein*); if we say that happening
upon occurs without choice, but encountering is the result of the
agent's own impulse, in either case we need the working of the cause
that assembles the separate circumstances, since the will of an individual can accomplish nothing without the cooperation of all things. By
chance, then, the souls being led upwards encounter and are joined
with the natures that are more perfect than themselves. They need not
665 only good fortune but destiny before they can be sufficiently perfected.
Observe again how the ranks of the personages are preserved here: they
encounter Adeimantus and Glaucon, and of these men Socrates makes
it clear in the *Republic* that Glaucon is the superior, for he says repeatedly that he admires the nature of Glaucon; so that if Adeimantus is the
inferior, it is natural that Plato should say "they encountered Adeimantus and Glaucon"; for the imperfect being first attaches itself to the less
perfect and through it to the more perfect.

So much for the analogies suggested by these facts. The first sentence
reveals the character of the dialogue in its artless precision and simplicity; for artlessness, conciseness, and simplicity of language are appropriate for expressing intellectual notions. Plato was not alone in practising this style, for Parmenides also does so in his poetry; although
supposedly, the poetic style would require him to use metaphorical
terms and picturesque figures of speech, yet he has adopted the lean and
the simple unadorned utterance, as is evident in the following:

> For being is close to being;

> (fr. 8.25 D-K)

and this:

> Since now all is together;
>
> (fr. 8.5)

and this:

> nor can any part be greater
> Nor any part less here than there;
>
> (fr. 8.44-45)

and in other similar passages. So that it seems more like prose than poetry. Note also in the first place that Plato, in this introductory section, has chosen the oratorical style called 'vehemence' (*gorgotēs*), for its vigor is suited to his subject; and secondly, that in using the form of summary report, which compresses language and rounds off a thought quickly, he shows his concern for conciseness and proceeds by using only the most necessary terms, cutting out all the ornaments of exposition that a sophist would have added.

666   *And taking me by the hand Adeimantus said, "Good cheer, Cephalus. If you wish anything of us here which we can do for you, tell us." (126a)*

You see how the men from Clazomenae become attached at once to Adeimantus, who holds out his hand to them. Glaucon is present, but silent; while it is the other who greets and welcomes the visitors. What do these circumstances symbolize? It could be said that there are many lessons in propriety here: for example, that one should be ready with help for strangers, out of respect for the daemon and god of hospitality; that the citizen should anticipate the visitor in expressions of goodwill, and in general that the stronger should be first to run to the aid of his acquaintances; and that a man should keep a promise to the best of his ability, which is what Adeimantus seems to intend here when he announces that he will do whatever he can for the Clazomenaeans. In short, we could mention many such things if we were to scrutinize the text closely.[44]

But what we should speak of are the things that lead us to insight into the larger matters which are the proper subject of this dialogue: that Antiphon, Glaucon, and Adeimantus are ranked as three grades of daemons; that souls being led upwards need the help of attendant daemons for their ascent; that by this help they are brought in contact with the highest degree of their rank and through it are lifted up to more divine causes which are completely separate from body, and move themselves spatially, so to speak, assembling their forces and rallying themselves

---

[44] This discussion of *ta kathēkonta*, once again, is reminiscent of Porphyry.

from bodily limitations; and when cooperating with certain orders of daemons, bring about now by a vital motion advancement to the higher ranks of being. Naturally, then, Adeimantus, being nearer to them, stretches out his hand and shares his goodwill with them in imitation of that order of divinity that confers power on souls that wish 667 to move upwards by attaching to itself the upward-moving capacities in them; for hands are symbols of power. And in giving them his hand he also wishes them "good cheer" (*chairein*), since for souls seeking salvation, gladness and freedom from care are gifts of the higher, not the lower, powers. For how could anyone share freedom from care with another when he is himself full of anxiety? Or how share gladness and good cheer when he is himself in despair? Therefore, it is only the gods and after them the divine classes of being, and after them good men, who are the sources of gladness and good cheer; for it is primarily the gods whose life is free of care, and secondarily the divine classes of being and, when they participate in that blessedness, temperate souls, who always manifest good humour, joy, and contentment with their fate. Souls moving upwards then receive from their attendant daemons first of all the power to ascend, next cheerfulness and freedom from care, and thirdly, a promise of good things to be obtained from their daemons. For the daemons incite them to share with them, bestow upon them bountifully everything that it is in their nature to give, and prepare them to receive even more perfect gifts from higher beings. Thus Adeimantus' readiness to promise aid, his beneficence, and his exhortation to the imperfect to become perfect (for every need renders him who feels it imperfect)—all this imitates the beneficent activity of good daemons towards souls.

"But that is exactly what I am here for," I replied, "to make a request of you." "Tell me your request," he said. (126a)

Of such a character as this must the souls be who are to be led upwards, showing by their actions their readiness to participate in the divine; they leave their ancestral and familiar ways and greedily lay hold on the more perfect goods, not regarding it as a minor matter, but their 668 first and chiefest task, to occupy themselves with the divine. For this is the way they can obtain the help of the higher powers, by laying themselves open to the boundless benefits that come from them. Everywhere what is imperfect joins itself to the perfect through its fitness for such gifts,[45] just as the perfect joins itself to the imperfect because of its perfecting power. These are the two intermediaries between the im-

---

[45] For the doctrine of *epitēdeiotēs*, "fitness," see *ET*, props. 39, 71, 79; *In Tim.* I, 25.24-30; 51.25-30.

perfect and the perfect, between what participates and what is participated—eagerness for perfection on the part of the imperfect, and on the
part of the higher powers capacity to confer it. Thus the imperfect
being undergoes perfecting and what participates acquires in a secondary degree the characters possessed primarily by that in which it participates. How necessary this fitness to receive is for those who must participate is shown by Cephalus here; it becomes them to cling greedily
to beings more perfect than themselves. We see this in an even more
authoritative fashion when we look at the nature of souls. For how
could they participate in divine favours if they were not fit to receive
them? In short, the phrase "I am here" is the proper expression. For
they must first of their own volition have aroused themselves to depart
from the body and then eagerly seek help from their superiors. When
they are thus disposed the gift of the higher powers is ready for them,
and this is shown in an image by Adeimantus' remark "Please tell me
your request," which is a promise to do anything he can for them.

And I replied, "Your maternal brother, what was his name? For I don't
remember. He was a child when I was here from Clazomenae before, and
it has been a long time since then." (126b)

The historical facts, for anyone who is interested in them, are these.
To Ariston Perictione bore three sons: Plato, Adeimantus, and Glaucon; and when her husband died, she married another man whose
name was Pyrilampes. Socrates mentions him in the *Gorgias* (481d)
when he says to Callicles that while he himself was in love with the son
669 of Clinias and with philosophy, he (Callicles), was in love with the
Athenian demos and with the son of Pyrilampes; for Demos was the
name of this son born of a former wife of Pyrilampes. Perictione, then,
married Pyrilampes and bore him a son, this Antiphon whom Cephalus here calls the maternal brother of Glaucon and Adeimantus.
From this record you can see that the meeting between Cephalus and
Antiphon probably took place after the death of Socrates; for Plato was
in his twenty-fourth year when Socrates died, and Perictione had produced three boys when she married again and gave birth to Antiphon,
who is now a grown man so that it is possible for his chief occupation
to be horsemanship.

But this is enough about these matters. I admire Plato's style of narrative for the simplicity with which it is arranged, and for the remarkable beauty, so to speak, that comes to light when it departs from simplicity. For Cephalus does not immediately state his request as
Adeimantus has invited him to do—for instance, by saying, "We want
Antiphon to recount to us the words which he heard from Pythodorus"; instead of this request he makes an inquiry about Antiphon him-

self. How much this increases its beauty the connoisseurs of such discourse will appreciate. But I admire even more Plato's skill in preserving throughout the likeness between his narrative and realities. For souls that are going to someone to be improved by him must first be linked with him through knowledge and reflection. For knowledge comes first, then the approach, and then the union.[46] For no one can be united with another whom he cannot approach, nor can he draw near to that which he does not know. It is a reflection of these realities when Cephalus asks Adeimantus, "What is the name of your brother?" for the purpose of learning about Antiphon. He does not remember him because he was a child when Cephalus was in Athens before and therefore is less known to him. For usually we remember well the name of people who are notable by their position in life whether by chance or some quality of mind or the like.

670

But to return again to the realities: the souls that are being led must first of all be linked with the objects of their desire through knowledge and attention, of which the learning of the name is an image (for names are the product of the cognitive part of the soul); and it sometimes happens that souls which are still imperfect do not lay hold on the thing they know but see it partially and incompletely, and at other times they see it as a whole, when they grasp it perfectly and through it know also other matters that are higher than it. The name, then, which the Clazomenaean asks to know is a symbol of the thing's being, and the reference to "not remembering" symbolises the forgetfulness which souls have from their birth. "For he was a child when I was here before" is a symbol of that imperfect thought which brings it about that the thing known to the soul is not seen wholly or exactly. And "for that was a long time ago" indicates that the preparation for knowledge began at a time long past. And if these three men are called "maternal brothers" because they are analogous to the class of daemons (for all the daemons come from one mother, that is, they have a common daemon-comprehending source),[47] then perhaps by this feature also the dialogue may be connected to the truths of metaphysics.

> "The name of his father, I think, was Pyrilampes." "Quite right," he said, "and his is Antiphon. But what is it you particularly want to know?" (126b)

Cephalus knows the father's name accurately but does not know the name of the son and seeks to learn it. This is the way in which self-moving beings act; some thing they know of themselves, but of others

---

[46] Γνῶσις, πέλασις, ἕνωσις. Cf. the three stages of prayer described at *In Tim.* I, 211.8-28, γνῶσις, οἰκείωσις, ἕνωσις, which is based on the *Chaldaean Oracles*.

[47] Δαιμονιοῦχος. Presumably this refers to Rhea (the term is found nowhere else). Cf. *In Alc.* 68.5.

they get knowledge from their superiors, who are ready for the giving when these have prepared themselves to receive it. This is why Adei-
671 mantus, seeing that the knowledge Cephalus has is accurate, straight-way adds what he does not know, and when he has done this asks the reason for his question. This shows that one should receive the gifts of the higher powers and, after receiving them, should desire even more of them than before. Don't be surprised that someone who knows the more important thing, the cause, should be ignorant of the lesser; for very often souls, either from a good natural disposition or from experience, have notions of the primary causes but lack knowledge of the inferior ones.

> "These men," I said, "are fellow-citizens of mine and true philosophers. They have heard that this Antiphon has been much in company with a certain Pythodorus, one of Zeno's associates, and has often heard him recount the conversation that took place between Socrates, Zeno, and Parmenides, and can retell it." (126b)

In one sense Cephalus might seem to be the most important of these Clazomenaean visitors, but from another point of view their inferior. Inasmuch as the philosophers have come to hear the conversation and he has come for their sake, he is decidedly their inferior, for in the order of things the end is superior to the means that bring it about; but he has a name and they appear anonymously, and on this account, it seems, he has the highest rank among them. (At least it is Plato's custom to introduce minor characters without names, like the (missing) fourth person in the *Timaeus* (17a), or the father of Critobulus, or the man who brings up the faulty objection in the *Phaedo* [103a].) And not only for this reason is he the more considerable, but also because he is the person who introduces them to Adeimantus and his friends. And no doubt he could be regarded as the most commanding part of the souls being led upwards, their charioteer, so to speak, whereas they are called
672 "true philosophers" as representing the powers secondary to them that attain to participation in primary realities through the action of their charioteer. Hence they are called "fellow-citizens" of Cephalus as well as "true philosophers"; for all the faculties in the soul have their source in the same hearth and fatherland, since the entire soul comes forth from the intelligible realm. Furthermore, the disposition to search and inquire into things is a property of such faculties, since the charioteer wishes rather to be united with the higher powers than to engage in inquiries about them from a perspective of separation. Thus these several faculties depend on their own summit, as the soul as a whole depends on the attendant daemons that lead it upwards, and the daemons on the primary and genuinely divine causes.

Observe again how Plato assigns their appropriate ranks to these personages. He places Antiphon under Pythodorus, and him under Zeno; and again of the triad above them, he puts Socrates nearest to Cephalus and his friends, next Zeno, and third Parmenides. How these rankings are to be related to reality is obvious from what I have said earlier. We should not be surprised that the philosophers from Clazomenae, though only natural scientists, are called true philosophers, for Plato is accustomed so to designate persons who speculate about divine matters, like the Eleatic Stranger in the *Sophist*; for he described him as a member of the group about Parmenides and Zeno and a "truly philosophical man" (216a). These men, then, because they are not content with assertions about nature but are pushing forward to knowledge of true being from what is[48] apprehended by opinion and perception, and because they have the highest aptitude for laying hold on the more perfect realities, he calls true philosophers. For he is said to be a true philosopher who is such by disposition and aptitude.

673 But so much for that. Observe once more how Plato is referring to the paradigms, when he says that Pythodorus had many contacts with Zeno, and Antiphon had heard Pythodorus many times; for the divine words exist as a unity in the gods but as a plurality in the daemons, and the further they are removed from the gods, the greater is their extension and the lower their descent into plurality. Hence the word *this* is attached to Antiphon, and *one of* to Pythodorus, for they are representations of more particular levels of being, which is different from that of Socrates, Zeno, and Parmenides himself, whom he introduces without any such addition whatever.

> *"What you say is correct," he said. "Then it is this," I said, "that we want to hear." "That will not be difficult," he said. "When he was a youth he practised the conversation very diligently; but now, like his grandfather for whom he is named, he devotes most of his attention to horses. If you wish, let us go to him. He has just left here to go to his home, and he lives nearby in Melite." (126c)*

In some of the things that Adeimantus says, he is teaching the Clazomenaeans what they do not know, and in others he is confirming by his assent what they previously knew. Thus when Cephalus gave the name of Antiphon's father, Adeimantus said, "Quite right." And now when Cephalus had said that Antiphon had heard through Pythodorus the conversation between Socrates, Zeno, and Parmenides, he replies, "What you say is correct." These remarks, then, confirm what Cephalus has previously known. But who this son of Pyrilampes is, what

---

[48] Reading $\langle \dot{\alpha}\pi\dot{o} \ \tau\tilde{\omega}\nu \rangle$ before δόξῃ μετ᾽ αἰσθήσεως.

674 kind of life he leads, and where he lives, Cephalus does not know and Adeimantus teaches him, and afterwards becomes his guide on the walk to this house, shows him the establishment, introduces the visitors to his brother, and begins the conversation.

Observe now these same elements in the nature of the universe. These souls that are leaving their native and customary occupations are moving towards a higher and more intellectual life, directing their minds from nature to Intellect, and from sense-perception to pure intellection. As I said before, they are helped by the daemons just above them, who direct their life in the world of generation. Some things they know of themselves, others under the inspiration of the daemons; and what they see of themselves they see more firmly because the daemons inspire them; and when they have adapted themselves to these daemons they become, so to speak, daemons themselves through their likeness to them, and by their aid behold the higher and more divine ranks of daemons through whom their later ascent to the gods takes place. For the agencies that order the life of souls in the world of generation are other than those that bring them into contact with the gods and fill them with divine blessings; these we ordinarily call divine daemons. The occupation of horsemanship is a fitting symbol of their activity, in that they look after secondary matters, holding nature together by serving as front-runners or bodyguards or followers of the gods. For they are in a way charioteers, and in them there are "horses," as there are among the gods.[49] This is in Plato's mind when he says that Antiphon takes after the grandfather for whom he is named. For above the daemons are the angels, and they are, so to speak, fathers of the daemons, and the gods their forefathers, bearing the same names, since daemons are often addressed as gods, on the daemonic level—but this is an homonymous designation derived from the daemons' participation in the gods' nature. Just as Antiphon was given his name in memory of his grandfather, so also the daemons, as established in the like-

675 ness of gods, are often called "gods" by those who are competent to discriminate the properties of the higher powers. There are, then, "horses" among the gods as well, and the art of horsemanship in the primary sense. But on that level the horses are to an extreme degree united with the charioteer, while on the daemonic level they are distinct, and there is a greater degree of otherness, so that the directing element appears and is one thing, and the "horses" another. Nay even the place Melite is appropriate to the rank of daemons, for the deme Melite got its name, they say, from Melite the girlfriend of Poseidon

[49] Cf. Hermeias' remarks, In Phaedr. 127.8ff. Couvreur (on Phaedr. 246a). The problem of what exactly the "horses" of divine souls represented was one that exercised the Neoplatonists.

(one of the poets mentions "Melite, the companion of Poseidon").[50]
The daemons are at home in the rank of the gods because of the intermediate station they occupy; for Poseidon occupies an intermediate
rank among the Fathers, even as daemons do among the classes superior to us. Indeed the phrase "he lives nearby" is not unconnected with
what has been said. For daemons are neighbours of daemons; they all
occupy the same rank and, with appropriate variations, preserve one
and the same daemonic property.

So much may be gleaned from these details. Their progress from
particulars to wholes is analogous to their progress from the visible to
the invisible. The fact that Antiphon learned the conversation when a
boy is proper to those entities, who, after their procession, straightway
turn back to their own causal principles and become joined to them.
For it is a characteristic of particular souls to proceed in an indefinite
manner and to move towards a lightless and murky destination, turning away from the divine.

In general these analogies should not be taken as unimportant, especially if we believe Plato, who said that nothing else is so beneficial
to the soul as what draws it from phenomena to being, freeing us from
the former and making it easy for us to imagine immaterial nature with
the help of these. Such an influence is the lover, and the philosopher,
and everyone who is moving upwards. So that even if Plato himself did
not formulate these matters in this way, it would be beneficial for us to
do so, for it is a good exercise for a well-endowed soul which is capable
676 of moving from images to their archetypes and delights in observing
these all-pervading analogies.

But I beg expositors of Plato not to exert themselves in lengthy arguments to show from this dialogue that Plato approved of beginning
the education of youth with dialectic, that he recommended the teaching of logical arguments, abstracted from subject-matter, as suitable
beginning material for young men if they are sufficiently acute to be
able to follow their subtleties. For the conversation that he says Antiphon "practised when he was a youth" contains not only the description of a logical method, but also a discussion of the most profound difficulties connected with the Ideas, not to mention the other matters
examined in the Hypotheses, which are visions of the highest principles. Remember also that in the *Republic* (VII, 537e–539d) Socrates dep-
recates the imparting of dialectical arguments to young men, lest they
be inadvertently bent towards lawlessness, as usually happens with
young men who have just acquired a taste of dialectical methods. Rare

[50] Perhaps Hesiod, in the *Catalogue of Women*. He mentions Melite, calling her daugh-
ter of Myrmex, in fr. 225 Merkelbach-West (from Philochorus, who is discussing the
deme of Melite); or possibly Pisander, cf. *Dam. In Phaed.* I, 378.3.

are the persons who do not fall a prey to this distraction and who are endowed with natures like that of Socrates, who has such a divine impulse towards philosophy that Parmenides, noting it, urges him to cultivate the whole of dialectic. Hence we should not make a common rule for the education of all young men, since the same methods are not suitable for the rare individuals as for the common run of students, for whom a prudent scholarship is sufficient, as I have said earlier. But let us go on to what follows:

> "Having said this, we set out to walk there. We found Antiphon at home, giving a bridle to a smith to be fitted. And when he was free of him, his brothers told him why we had come. He recognised me from my former visit and bade me welcome." (127a)

677   Conciseness of language, and clarity and simplicity, are evident in this passage. Plato does not strive for beauty or elegance, as is customary, by saying "having spoken and heard these words" (*Prot.* 362a), nor does he add anything unnecessary, but says directly, "having said this." For they have both spoken and heard. And the structure of his sentence is the most appropriate to the clear and simple style, for connecting phrases that distinguish what precedes from what follows make a sentence clear. The structure, then, contributes to its simplicity, and its simplicity helps out its narrative intentions, so that here also the parts are subordinate to the whole and the many to the one. So much we get from examining the stylistic character of the passage.

As to its ethical import, we can learn that good men should always make their actions consonant with their words, not speak the language of nobility and virtue and postpone the deeds that go with it—hence Cephalus says, "Having said this, we set out to walk"; and that actions should be preceded by judgements, and these by the Good—in this spirit Adeimantus says "If you wish, let us go to him," and Cephalus says, "Having said this, we set out to walk there." Again we learn that souls are perfected by friendship and worthy associations. This was the rule of the Pythagoreans especially, who made the most sincere friendship the end of life for themselves. Also we learn that we must curtail practical activities for the pursuit of virtue. This is what Antiphon does when, "giving the bridle to the smith," he gives himself immediately to his visitors. So Cephalus says, "when he was free of him," indicating that Antiphon most gladly abandons this kind of conversation for a more educated and more congenial fellowship. Furthermore, we can learn from this passage that the skill which uses the craftsman's art is superior to the product of that craftsmanship, for Antiphon who will use the bridle is set over the workman who fits it and gives him direc-
678 tions for making it suitable. We see also that in all cases extremes are

brought together by an intermediary which is akin to both; for Adeimantus and his brother are responsible for the encounter and the conversation between the Clazomenaeans and Antiphon, and they are his brothers, and friends and acquaintances of the others. Also that the extremes stand further apart from one another than the intermediary does from either, but are nevertheless not incapable of being brought together. This is shown by their mutual recognition and in general by the fellowship that is established between Antiphon and the Clazomenaeans.

Next, after the discussion of the text from the ethical perspective, let us look at the text before us from the physical point of view. We should observe that these men, as students of nature and analogues of natural forces, partake of the dyad in the soul—call it opinion or whatever you like—and by it are joined with the powers that move nature, whether they be daemons or gods, which have their own art of metal-working and hammer and anvil. How else, indeed, does the third manifestation of forms come about, if not by the reason-principles of soul being poured out, as it were, into natural forces? These, in turn, are obviously perfected by the agencies that superintend nature and make use of natural forces.

But if, abandoning this theme, we are to attain a more profound interpretation, let us return to the analogies we have mentioned before. We have seen that souls who are moving upwards attach themselves to the daemons allotted to supervise their life here; and thus the Clazomenaeans encounter Adeimantus and his friends in the agora and by their aid attain to the divine daemons whom they join in moving to the intellectual realm, and thus[51] they see how the daemons regulate the inferior levels of their lives which are bodily and derivative. We must think of the bridle as the means appointed by the higher powers for regulating these dependent faculties. For the daemons have powers that regulate the things below them, ordering alike their bodily forms and their powers of judging, and the smith who works on the bridle is their analogue. Like Antiphon, they also have powers that use this faculty of judgement and all the other results of their ordering; and it is these powers, which we can call the skill of the charioteer or whatever else you like, that define their being. For the charioteer, the horses, the bridle-maker, and all these factors are, so to speak, internal to the daemons—as is indicated by the "at home" after "Antiphon"; it is by looking to the daemons that these agencies do their work. Then when they have brought order into their own affairs, they are participated in

679

[51] Reading οὕτω for οὐ of MSS (West.). Cephalus, etc., *do* witness Antiphon's dealings with the smith.

by inferior beings, by other daemons who are, as it were, their brothers, and also by individual souls below who are aspiring to them. This participation takes place imperfectly at first, later perfectly. Imperfect participation is illustrated, as we have said, by the earlier visit to Athens, the perfect by the renewal of that visit, the recognition, and the final welcome, which signifies the union, the indivisible contact and fellowship in the divine joy. All compounds in nature, all living things with souls, are little by little and according to a well-regulated ascent allotted shares in the higher goods; at first they participate imperfectly, feebly, and subject to the pull of pleasure in the goods above them; later they lay hold of their shares firmly and completely. Thus it is that in the process of creation there first appears only an outline of species in matter, then masses and informing material powers, then figured masses with individual shapes, and then, to crown it all, the complete organisation and gift of life, the sharing in Intellect and the illumination of divinity. So it is that souls are initiated into the lesser mysteries before the greater ones, the imperfect before the perfect, and at the end of all are joined with the truly perfect realities, and when they are firmly grounded in them, their participation is an indivisible and indissoluble union. But the contact and the union come about through intermediate beings that are, so to speak, akin to the species with which they produce the contact.

680   *When we asked him to repeat the conversation, he at first was reluctant, saying that it was a very difficult task; but he then gave a full rehearsal of it.* (127a)

The request of the Clazomenaeans expresses the importunate attachment of souls to their proper guides; for in no other way can their contact and company with the gods occur than by means of these daemons; for the daemons attach themselves to the cosmic gods, as Socrates says in the *Phaedrus* (247a), and souls attach themselves to the daemons. There precedes this request, first, their knowledge of the daemons, for how would they request anything of them if they did not know who they are nor what goods they have it in their power to bestow? And then, love of converse with them, for we must desire what we ask for, since if we did not desire, we would not be in the position of petitioners. The reluctance of Antiphon is an image of the secret and inexpressive power of these divine causes; for the divine, wherever it is, is hard to lay hold of and to know, revealing itself sparingly to souls, even when they greedily aspire to conversation and communion with it. They need to get accustomed to the divine splendour in which the divine daemons show themselves to the eager souls who aspire to associate with them and behold the whole divine world. But to the souls that firmly and steadfastly cling to them they unfold and explain the divine truth. This is the "rehearsal," an unfolding and explanation of matters concealed, the training and perfecting given to souls by these divine daemons. All this you will find in the universe of things if you look; this is the way things are.

We must not be surprised that Antiphon's visitors hear him say that the task is very difficult, when previously they had heard Adeimantus 681 say that there was no difficulty in the case. Adeimantus was referring to the ability of Antiphon and his memory of the conversation, whereas Antiphon was wondering whether his hearers were competent to receive this theory. For they are men from Ionia and unaccustomed to doctrines of a mystical character. It seems to me also that Antiphon, in imitation of the Eleatic wise men, is exalting his topic in calling the task very difficult. Zeno will do the same thing, in the course of the dialogue, and the great Parmenides himself. Even the Stranger in the *Sophist* and the *Statesman*, an associate in their school, says at first that the answer to the question of Socrates is very difficult and hard to make intelligible (*Soph.* 217b). And it is not as if Eleatics acted thus and Plato recommended acting differently; he too advises us to declare the difficulty of the matter to those who come with a request of this nature. Indeed this becomes for him a reliable touchstone of the fitness or unfitness of someone who approaches him. The man who genuinely loves knowledge does not shrink from the labour involved; the more difficult a matter is to learn, so much the more eagerly does he pursue it, not trying to evade hardships. But an inferior and unqualified student, when he hears that a task is difficult, takes his leave of an inquiry that is not for him. And there in truth "both the coward cometh to light and the man of valour" (*Iliad* 13.278), and this becomes a criterion for distinguishing the well-endowed person from his opposite.

According to Antiphon, Pythodorus said that on one occasion Zeno and Parmenides came to the Great Panathenaea. (127a)

Some say that Antiphon delivers this discourse not as a man who knows and understands it, but only from memory and the tip of his 682 tongue, as if he had learned this dialogue by heart and could repeat it automatically, though ignorant of the secret thought it contains. In my opinion, however, neither the order of events nor the character of the personages would have been so well preserved, together with the appropriate setting, by one who was ignorant of the deeper meaning of the words and the purposes of the questions and answers. It is very difficult to imitate in discourse the speeches of learned men, as Timaeus (*Tim.* 19d) teaches us. An imitator must be similar in character to the

63

original speaker if his imitation of a noble discourse is to be a worthy one. I do not need to establish this, since such is the rule that Plato gives us for testing such matters. Parmenides will be the one who primarily has knowledge of the matters spoken of; next is Zeno; Socrates is third in order (for he is implicated with them in the structure of the argument); Pythodorus is fourth, for he is a pupil of Zeno and has himself heard the speakers of the argument; fifth is Antiphon who, since he gets the speech from Pythodorus, is the immediate recipient of the words that are to be spoken by them, and thus brings us up so close to the original speakers that it seems we have heard them ourselves, have been present at the original scene, and have taken part in the conversation. This plainly is the result of Plato's handling and arrangement of his theme, which all but brings the action before our eyes—the occasion, the persons, the setting, the actions and attitudes of the characters, and their words. And it seems to me that the focussing of all the characters upon one person, Parmenides, shows a profound truth about things. All pluralities, all the ranks of being, are unified about the

683 divine cause; and this truth is indicated to the intelligent reader by his mention successively of Antiphon, Pythodorus, Zeno, and Parmenides.

Again, the mention of the Panathenaea contributes to the larger aim of the dialogue. History tells us that this festival was established when the synoecism of the Athenians took place. Here, then, is another example of unification, a plurality of villages organized around their city-protecting goddess. And this is the aim of the dialogue, to show clearly how all things are fastened to the One and how each thing has its origin in it. It is no little tribute to these men that the dialogue says they came, not to Athens, but to the Panathenaea; that is, their visit was undertaken for the sake of the goddess and her festival, not in order to make a public display of their philosophy. Such a practice was disdained among the Pythagoreans, for it is what sophists and traders do.

Parmenides was already quite an elderly man, with very grey hair, but handsome and good to look upon. His age was probably about five and sixty. (127b)

Let us understand this first as applying to his appearance. He was an elderly man, and somewhat advanced in age. Among the Greeks a man was an "elder" until his seventieth year, and after that, an "old man." Parmenides was then an elder, but not an old man. His countenance was pleasing, a consequence of his manner of life, for with good men something of the comeliness and majesty of soul is reflected down into the body. But it is much more appropriate to take these terms as applying to the soul itself and say, for example, that he was venerable for his

store of knowledge and wisdom. The intellectual sciences, those that are concerned with the whole of nature, he is accustomed to call venerable, as he has shown in the *Timaeus* (22b) when he calls "young" the people who have no ancient knowledge.[52] Again "grey-haired" is a fit-
684 ting designation for souls whose highest part shares in the light of intellect, for "dark" belongs to the inferior of the two columns of opposites, "light" to the superior.[53] And "handsome and good to look upon" suggests that the eye of his soul is directed towards intelligible beauty and the good that is the foundation of all things and which makes good everything that partakes of it. Even better is it, following our analogy, to look at these qualities in the gods themselves. For where is the character of being an elder and grey-haired so evident as in the gods, or so much praised by the theologians as in the ancestral deities? Where are beauty and goodness so present as in those beings with whom reside beauty itself and the paradigm of goodness? Especially, since the compound expression "beautiful and good" is most appropriately used of them, in whom unity and goodness are the same.

And Zeno was nearing forty at the time, tall and graceful in appearance; and it is said that he had been the favourite of Parmenides. (127b)

Such was Zeno, perhaps, in bodily appearance, "tall and graceful in appearance," but far more so in respect of his discourse. For what Parmenides had uttered in an intricate and concentrated style, Zeno unfolds and transmits to us in extended discourse.[54] This is why the Sillographer[55] calls him "double-tongued," as being at the same time a refuter and an expositor. If he had been "the favourite of Parmenides," clearly it is because they used the same path of ascent to one and the same god, since this is characteristic of the genuine art of love. So, again, this erotic tie is given a mention because it accords with the purpose of love to unify plurality about participation in the divine. And if you wished to take things on a still more comprehensive level, you could say that even in the gods themselves the inferior beings are con-
685 tained in the primary and that all of them are absolutely united to Being[56] from which they all get their origin and extension, and you

---

[52] Cf. the discussion of this point at *In Tim.* I, 102.3ff.

[53] That is, the Pythagorean *systoichia*, as set out by Aristotle at *Met.* A, 986a22ff. There, however, "light" and "dark" are listed, but not "black" and "white."

[54] A possible indication that Proclus has before him a document purporting to be the *Forty Logoi* of Zeno. See Intro., p. xx.

[55] Timon, fr. 45D; cf. note 16 above.

[56] Cousin's reading ἕν for the MS ὄν (Latin *ens*) is misguided. Parmenides in analogous, not to the One, but to the One Being, the monad of the noetic realm (cf. above, 628.2ff. and below, 689.26ff.).

would not, I think, be going beyond the truth with respect to them. But what comes next?

He said they lodged with Pythodorus outside the city wall in the Cerameicus. (127b)

Their lodging with Pythodorus should be taken as a symbol, for those who pay attention to the paradigms, of the fact that the gods primarily reveal themselves through angels and in the rank of angels. A man's house is an indication of his rank, and "outside the city wall" expresses the transcendent and incomprehensible nature of the gods. As, then, in the house of Pythodorus they all appear gathered together, some from the city and others from abroad, so also among the angels both the gods that govern the cosmos and the intellectual gods reveal themselves and become known to us through their essence.

So much for the substance of this passage. As to its language, the phrase "with Pythodorus" is quite Attic. He could have said, "He lodged with me," for Pythodorus who says it is speaking about himself; but it may be that Antiphon is sometimes quoting Pythodorus and sometimes speaking in his own person, and "with Pythodorus" could be something he put in from his own perspective. "Outside the city-wall in the Cerameicus" is a clear reflection of history, for the Cerameicus was divided into two parts, one outside and one inside the wall. The men coming to Athens were avoiding the crowd and hence lodged outside the wall. Nor is this surprising, for they are there not to be with a crowd of people but to participate in a festival. Naturally then, they lodged outside the city because of the crowd inside. The Pythagoreans deprecated the use of the high roads and thought it honourable and dig-686 nified not to mix with the multitude. That the men from Elea are outside the city where those who want to see them must come to them, while the men from Clazomenae are inside conferring in Melite with the man who is imparting to them the wisdom of the other groups— this could symbolize the transcendence of the primary powers to their intermediaries, whereas the lower agencies are surrounded by them; and these circumstances, when joined with all that we have said earlier, would reveal not a little similarity to the reality of things.

Socrates and many others with him came there desiring to hear the work of Zeno, for these visitors had brought it to Athens for the first time. Socrates was quite young. (127c)

We can see here with what extraordinary intelligence and zeal Socrates seeks out these inspired men, and how different are his reasons for going to meet wise men than those that take him to the Sophists. He goes to the Sophists to convict them of ignorance and vanity, but comes to these men to elicit their wisdom and knowledge. It is with such a disposition that he meets Timaeus; and so also he appears here, leading, as it were, a troop of lovers of philosophy. Desire brings them all, but it is through him and his company that their desire is fulfilled. These details, like the foregoing, are likenesses of divine things. The young Socrates leading the young—this is almost what Plato proclaims in the *Phaedrus* (246e): the great leader Zeus heads the procession and is followed by a train of gods and daemons. Intellect everywhere has the office of turning back and leading upwards to the source of things, and it draws back along with itself the multitude of its dependents. Socrates' being young is a symbol of the youthfulness ascribed to the gods. Zeus and Dionysus are called by the theologians "boys" and "young men" ("although you are both young," says Orpheus)[57], and in general the intellectual order, when compared with the intelligible and the paternal, is called "young."

687

Their desire to hear the reading of Zeno's composition indicates symbolically that the third order of beings up there participates first in the intermediary powers and later joins the upper extremes and keeps company with the same intelligibles. Written works occupy a rank several degrees removed from knowledge. Hence Socrates makes his ascent in due order; first he listens to the reading of the treatise, next takes part in the discussion, and thirdly grows into unity with them in knowledge. For discourse proceeds from knowledge, and writings are the images of discourse.

That this is the first appearance of these writings shows that they contain something sacred and divine, for being published at the feast of the Panathenaea they become an ornament corresponding to the Panathenaic Robe in the spectacle. These writings in fact have somewhat the same aim as the Robe; as the Robe portrayed the victory of Athena over the Giants, by which she subdued the separate cosmic powers and made them all dependent on her father, so the discourse aims at attaching the entire multitude of beings to the One Being, showing how when devoid of unity the universe fills with disorder and truly Gigantic confusion. Socrates is established as being a young man, so that he may be easily moved to remembrance of the divine, but well-endowed, so as to be keen-witted in raising objections. Pythodorus says (130a) that Socrates surprised him by his objections to the arguments of Zeno, and that he easily and without affectation partook of the truth they professed. And if Zeno is the one who reads the treatise—does this not show both his benevolent disposition and the powers of those inter-

---

[57] Fr. 207 Kern, which is, however, quoted at *In Tim.* III, 311.3 of Dionysus alone, in the form καίπερ ἐόντι νέῳ καὶ νηπίῳ εἰλαπιναστῇ. Here we have a dual, referring to both Zeus and Dionysus.

mediaries among the gods through which they reveal themselves to those immediately dependent upon themselves? For they reveal them-
688 selves at the lowest, as well as at the middle and highest levels of understanding, and these levels are symbolically represented by the writings, the discourse, and the thoughts.

At this point in the narrative some persons ask whether philosophers should read their compositions to others, as Zeno does here, and if they do so on occasion, they want them to restrict their reading to what their hearers can understand, to avoid what Plato experienced, it is said, when he announced a lecture on the Good.[58] A large and miscellaneous crowd gathered to hear him; but as he read, they did not understand what he was saying and left him, a few at a time, until eventually almost all had left the hall. But Plato knew this would happen and forbade his associates to prevent anyone from leaving, for thus only those who understood would hear the reading. But the hearers of Zeno's words were qualified, especially Socrates, as is shown by his being the only one of them that raised questions after the reading was ended.

> Zeno himself read it to them (Parmenides happened to be out), and had almost completed the reading of the arguments when Pythodorus, as he said, came in and joined them, accompanied by Parmenides and Aristotle, the man who later was one of the Thirty; and they listened to the remaining part of the composition, though Pythodorus had himself heard Zeno read it before. (127c)

In these words also Plato has given us a marvellous picture of divine matters, and anyone who is not blind to analogies can see the images of a lofty doctrine here. In the first place, that Parmenides was not present
689 at the reading of the arguments themselves from the beginning, but only as they were being completed and rounded out, is a symbol of the fact that the superior divine causes reveal themselves to the beings below them at the moment when their participation in the beings next above them is complete, and not before. For how could beings unable to participate in the intermediaries ascend to communion with the primary? As Zeno's arguments are being completed, the great Parmenides appears. With him are Pythodorus and Aristotle. Pythodorus is a disciple of Zeno, and Aristotle is in a sense ranged with Parmenides, for he (later) helps him manage the hypotheses by playing the part of respondent only. For Parmenides will select him, as the youngest of those present, for this conference on lofty matters so that, as he himself

[58] The story is relayed, from Aristotle, by Aristoxenus, *Harm. Elem.* II, 30-31 Meibom. Proclus' version, however, makes Plato look a good deal less foolish than was Aristotle's intention in originally telling it.

will say, he will not obstruct the enquiry by raising difficulties but will submit to the role of mere respondent in the dialectic.

What then does this indicate, and why is Aristotle ranged by the side of Parmenides as his assistant, and Pythodorus with Zeno (ahead of Socrates, for he has heard the reading before), while Socrates is ranked with the two wise men to elicit the wisdom of Parmenides and raise objections to Zeno's arguments?

Parmenides is an analogue, as I have frequently said, to that principle which is everywhere first in the divine realm (whether it is the One Being, or the Intelligible, or whatever else you please to call it), and is present in all the orders of deity and in each of the gods. Thus Parmenides, as he fills all of them with his inspired thoughts, is acting in imitation of that order which has structured everything, from the highest to the lowest. Acting from such a summit, or mean, or totality, he himself perfects Zeno in knowledge, and Socrates also, through the combined influence of himself and Zeno, just as in that upper region the third level of being proceeds both from the highest and the middle 690 levels. And Pythodorus he perfects also, though no longer through himself alone; for his power of giving extends beyond the reach of Zeno's power and activity, down to the very lowest type of disposition; just as the generative function of Being is more extensive than that of Life.[59]

Zeno, then, is directly filled from Parmenides and provides filling to Pythodorus, as his disciple, and in a different way to Socrates, as his fellow inquirer, the first prior to Socrates and the latter after him, when he can participate not only in Zeno, but also in Socrates. For in the divine realm the intermediate level functions before its successor and moves through all things, giving a bare capacity to even the lowest of the beings that participate in itself; and it perfects this capacity after it has perfected the capacity of beings immediately dependent on itself. Hence the "earlier participation" indicates the imperfect impression of the first principles made when they are acting before the secondary order of beings, and the "second participation" indicates the perfection of the impressions which is brought about through the secondary and adjacent beings. Socrates is the third member that completes the triad pervading all the numbers, and he corresponds to Intellect, or whatever you choose to call it.[60] This is why he first learns from Zeno and through him is brought into contact with Parmenides himself, just as among the gods the Intellect in each is directly filled with a divine Life

[59] An application of the principle that the influence of higher entities extends further down the scale of being than that of those inferior to them. Cf. ET, prop. 57, and Dodds' note ad loc.

[60] That is, Intellect as the third moment in the noetic triad of Being, Life, and Intellect.

by which it is unified with the intelligible principle itself and with its own foundation in Being. Pythodorus, a disciple of Zeno and also a participant in the productive difficulties raised by Socrates, corresponds to the revelatory class of divinities; for the gods make angels lower than the intermediate and tertiary powers, not just than the primary, for these are the progenitors of gods.

691 Aristotle is ranked as analogous to the souls which are often led by enthusiasm to join with the higher beings but later fall away from such blessed associations. (For it is not unusual that a soul which at one time is inspired by the gods should later choose a life that is "dark and godless" [cf. *Alc.* I, 134e]). But he gets his filling from Parmenides alone, since even among the gods it is characteristic of the higher beings, through their superfluity of power, to give even to such souls as these some share of divine light. Thus the theologians[61] call the intellectual life Cronian, not Jovian, although the access to it is through mighty Zeus. For just as Zeus, being filled from his own father, is drawn to him as to his own intellectual principle, and also draws those beings that are below him, so also is it that, although souls make their ascent in company with Zeus, yet that higher life of the gods fills both the intermediate and the tertiary orders of being and eventually even the souls that are inspired by it. Don't marvel that divine beings stand in this relation to one another. Among philosophers themselves you can observe, if you like, how the more perfect and competent are productive of benefit to more people. For Cebes, or Simmias, benefits himself alone, or at most another who is like him, but Socrates does good both to himself and to them and to Thrasymachus. Cebes would not be able to cure the madness and effrontery of that Sophist, but Socrates restores his mind to order and persuades him that justice is more powerful than injustice. So therefore Parmenides, being the most competent, helps even that member of the company who has the least

692 aptitude. Plato indicates the weakness of his capacity by calling him the youngest of the group, which is a symbol of his undeveloped nature, and by adding to the words about him that he later became one of the Thirty. From this we draw the plausible analogy between him and souls who are at one time inspired and live with the angels (just as Aristotle here made his entrance with Pythodorus), but later lose the capacity to do so. Pythodorus adheres to his own principles and communicates the conversation to others, just as the whole class of angels always remains beneficent, filling even secondary beings with a share

---

[61] Probably an interpretation of an Orphic utterance, but its exact provenance is not obvious to me. Cousin's reference to *In Tim.* III, 262.9ff. (319d) is quite inapposite. There Κρόνιον means "proper to Saturn" (the planet).

of the divine. But Aristotle, from being a philosopher, becomes a tyrant. For souls that follow the life of philosophy through some accidental relationship, not from their intrinsic nature, sometimes desert their post and are borne towards the place of generation. Tyranny is taken as a symbol of the life of becoming, for it is brought under "the throne of Necessity" (*Rep.* X, 621a), agitated by passion and unstable discordant impulses. The rule of the Thirty Tyrants over Athens is itself a representation of the dominance of the earth-born or Gigantic life over the goods of Athena and the Olympians. The true warfare with the Giants takes place in souls: whenever reason and intellect rule in them, the goods of the Olympians and Athena prevail, and the entire life is kingly and philosophical; but whenever the passions reign, or in 693 general the worse and earth-born elements, then the constitution within them is tyranny. When then Plato says that this man was one of the Thirty Tyrants, he would appear to be saying the same, in fact, as that he is an analogue to souls which are at one time inspired and at another time join the earth-born and subject their lives to the meanest of tyrants, their passions, and thus become their own tyrants. Perhaps the philosopher also intends to show by these words that it is possible for the same soul to display a variety of lives, that a soul at one time philosophical may become at another time tyrannical, and again may change back from the tyrannical to the philosophical life. In general the tyrannical element is characteristic of souls that aim at greatness, or dignity, or power. So Socrates in the *Republic* (X, 619b) describes the souls that return from heaven as choosing, for the most part, the life of a tyrant; for when they were up there they traversed the whole of things in their revolutions, and of this they retain a memory when in their choices they go after power and tyranny. But so much for that.

[Let us now summarise briefly the theory contained in the preceding pages and then undertake the exposition of it.[62] We said that the men who have come to Athens from Clazomenae are souls who have been stirred up to move from Nature to Intellect. They need to be united with genuine reality and make the ascent up to the gods. For there is the harbour of souls, and from thence comes the fullness of benefits, descending in an appropriate manner upon all the classes of divine beings and upon all souls that are striving to attain to Intellect. Before making contact with the divine beings themselves, they encounter the

---

[62] This passage is something of a mystery. It occurs in the Σ tradition and in the Latin translation, but not in the Φ tradition (in Klibansky's terminology, *In Parm.* VII, pp. xxxxxxix). It does not sound like a later interpolation, so there seem to be two possibilities: (1) that Φ has been abridged and rewritten (because of poor legibility of the exemplar?); or (2) there was a double tradition in the archetype (going back to Proclus himself?). But in the latter case, one would expect more similar passages. Support for the former possibility is afforded by the text of 661.9-23, where the Φ text is plainly abridged and lacunose.

agencies that are near to them, for their ascent must take place through intermediaries. They are said to encounter these before they have reached their perfection and before they have all escaped from the plurified way of life, but
while still "in the market-place." Then through these intermediaries they come
in contact with certain good daemons through whom their restoration to the
intellectual realm is brought about. But this meeting takes place no longer "in
the market-place," but "at home," since it results from their more perfect fellowship. Once arrived at this point, they cling eagerly to their proper guides
and are filled with intellectual power from them; and being filled, they behold
the ranks of the angels, which receive their filling from the gods and in turn fill
the daemons with divine Forms and intellectual reason-principles; and being
further strengthened by them they behold the threefold, all-perfect orders of
the gods; and then, in company with the angels, they behold the inspired souls
that are engaged in the dance about reality. Hence they become imitators themselves, to the extent of their ability, and are attached to the gods.

This is, in brief, what may be got from the matters in the prologue, if we
undertake an examination of it by means of analogical interpretation. But now
let us consider the significance of the words that follow.]

694 *When Socrates had heard it all he asked that the first hypothesis of the first
argument be read again; and when it had been read, said, "Zeno, what do
you mean by this?"* (127d)

You see how elaborate is the order of ascent. First, Socrates examines
Zeno's thought in the composition, then tests the force of his arguments, and thirdly advances to the knowledge itself which he has in his
mind. After the reading, he stirs him up to discussion, and he does so
by showing that he himself has sufficiently understood the composition, for it is absurd to rush on to higher matters before one has fully
understood the lower ones. He shows this by viewing the whole composition as a unity. But when he has seen it thus, he does not react im-
pulsively or precipitately as a young man might, nor does he immediately advance objections. He begins by asking the author of the work
what is the first hypothesis of the first argument, both in order that he
may know more precisely what its purpose is and not appear guilty of
impetuosity in objecting to it, and also so that the absence of difficulties
at the start and the existence of agreement before the apparent refutation begins may put the whole conference on a basis of concord. Zeno
has put forth many arguments, forty in all. Socrates takes up one of the
first of them and objects to Zeno that it is propounded too eristically
695 and too much in the context of natural science. The argument was this:
If things are many, the same thing will be like and unlike; but it is impossible that the same thing should be both like and unlike; and therefore things are not many. This first argument as a whole consists of

72

two hypothetical propositions[63] with a minor premises and a conclusion. Socrates asks to hear the first hypothesis of the first argument,
namely this: "If things are many, the same thing will be like and unlike." For this is one of the three hypotheses. The second is, "If the
same thing is not like and unlike, things are not many." The third is the
minor premise, "It is impossible that the same thing should be like and
unlike." Both the two hypothetical propositions and the minor premise are called hypotheses, and from them the asserted conclusion follows. Socrates, as we said, asks to hear again the first of the three hypotheses; and Zeno, being a philosopher, reads it, undoubtedly with
some elaborations, and thus provides the starting point for the ensuing
discussion. When Sophists read a composition in public they are annoyed with any who attempt to test it; if the crowd at first oppose
them, they are unwilling to give a justification of what they have said.
This is not the way of the true philosopher; he will gladly repeat the
same words two or three times, and he allows anyone who is able and
willing to raise objections to what he has said. So when the first hypothesis has been read, Socrates summarises the entire argument,
showing Zeno the comprehensiveness of his mind, his acuteness and
capacity for clarifying obscure statements, and in general his fitness for
further instruction, that is, his ability to hold together a plurality of
ideas, to grasp the truth firmly, and to expound the hidden meaning of
the higher doctrines.

696
*"If beings are many, they must be both like and unlike; but this is clearly
impossible; for it is impossible that unlike should be like or like unlike. Is
this not what you say?" "It is," said Zeno. "Therefore if it is impossible
for unlike to be like and like things to be unlike, it is impossible that being
is many; for if it is many it would have impossible characteristics."*
(127d)

Socrates has set forth the whole argument quite clearly and succinctly, having accurately identified this hypothesis and seen the purpose of the argument as a whole. You can see each of its parts. We have
the first hypothesis at the very beginning, the second after Zeno's assent, the minor premise in "but this is impossible," and the conclusion
in "it is impossible that being is many." Zeno develops each of these
parts at length, but Socrates analyzes the syllogism as the logical experts do, taking the premises in their technical form and forming them
into a figure.

Now there may be some who would apply Stoic pedantry to so im-

---

[63] Συνημμένον, the normal term, originally Stoic, for a premise in a hypothetical syllogism.

portant an argument as this,[64] and ask whether an impossible conclusion can follow from a possible premise, dragging into the discussion the premise "if Dion is dead" and the conclusion "this man is dead" and say that the premise is possible because our inner representation is indeterminate where names are concerned, since names refer alike to an existent and a non-existent subject. But the conclusion, they would say, is impossible, because our inner representation uses the demonstrative pronoun to denote a definite subject. According to these people, therefore, the premise "if Dion is dead" is possible (for it comes true), but the conclusion "this man is dead" is impossible, for it can never be true, the demonstrative pronoun being used only to point to a definite existing person.

Now if anybody mentions such puzzles, which have already been dealt with sufficiently by the Peripatetics,[65] it will be easy to refute him. One only has to explain the ancient rule about hypotheticals, according to which only those hypotheticals are true in which when the antecedent is, the consequent must of necessity be, as has been laid down by Aristotle.[66] If this rule is kept in mind it is clear that the hypothetical which runs "if Dion is dead, this man is dead" is not true; for the first part is indeterminate and true of a dead person, the second part, however, determinate and only true of a living and indicable person. These matters, however, really belong rather to Logic.

For the present we only assume this much (as is proved both by this and by Zeno's other arguments): that it is impossible for the many to exist without the One. Starting from here, we find a short way to the first principle.[67] It is necessary either that the first principles are many, without participation in any unity whatsoever, or that they are one without plurality, or that they are many participating in unity, or that they are one containing a plurality in itself. Now if they are many devoid of unity, all the absurdities follow that Zeno's arguments allege against those that say beings are many without unity. If they are many

[64] This whole passage, down to "These matters, however, belong rather to Logic," is given in its full form only in Moerbeke's translation, the Greek MSS in both traditions (Σ and Φ) preserving only an extremely truncated and elliptical version. See on this Klibansky, *In Parm.* VII, pp. 80-81, (with xi and 99). The Greek is not obviously lacunose, however, and it is possible that Moerbeke is amplifying here, in order to clarify an obscure reference, but it seemed best to include the fuller version in the text. For the passage I borrow, with permission, from the translation of Elizabeth Anscombe (ap. Klibansky, p. 81).

[65] Cf. Alexander of Aphrodisias *In An. Pr.* 177. 19-180.12 CAG, a text that Proclus almost certainly was familiar with. Chrysippus is the author of the problem discussed here. See M. Frede, *Die stoische Logik*, 87–88.

[66] For Aristotle's doctrine, see *An. Pr.* I, 15.34a5ff.

[67] The following argument is found more formally in the opening propositions of *ET* (props. 1-6).

but participate in some unity, then that unity, being participated in, has
697 come to these principles from some other entity existing prior to itself,
for every particular unity is derived from the absolute unity. And if the
principle is one that contains a plurality in itself, it will be a whole composed of the many parts contained in it, or of elements. But this is not
truly one, but has only an accidental unity, as we learn from the *Sophist*
(245a); it is not yet simple nor self-sufficient, as a principle should be.
Therefore the principle of all things must be one without plurality.
This is the conclusion of all Zeno's arguments; but we will expound his
first argument more precisely when Socrates moves his objections to
it. For the present let us say only that Socrates is the copy of the paradigm he imitates, revealing himself and his thought to Zeno and appealing to his knowledge. For in the divine world the inferior principles
depend on the intermediates for their entire activity, and by unfolding
their own powers are filled from above with the more complete goods.

*"Then is this the aim of your arguments, none other than to maintain val-
iantly, against everything that is said, that things are not many? And you
think that each of your arguments is a proof of this, so that you consider
you have as many proofs that things are not many as the number of the
arguments in your book? Is this what you say, or have I misunderstood
you?" "No," said Zeno, "you have correctly understood the aim of the
entire composition."* (127e)

Socrates continually asks the author of the arguments whether he has
given a fair and acceptable account of his thought. Incidentally this
gives a good rule for the guidance of those who undertake to question
the views of their elders—that before doing this we should ascertain
698 their meaning as accurately as possible, lest we inadvertently meet their
arguments with empty words, in the sophistic manner, and miss the
sense of the elders' opinions. Socrates observes the proper measure
with respect to both the person and his arguments, for he praises the
arguments in a friendly way and their author as a doughty combatant.
This is shown by "maintain valiantly," a phrase most appropriate to
Zeno's hypothesis. Parmenides had already installed himself in the
One, and in contemplating the monad of all things paid no attention to
the plurality and its dispersedness. Zeno, on the other hand, was escap-
ing from plurality to the One. The former, then, is like one who has
been purified and raised up and has put away the plurality in himself,
the latter like one who is being raised up and is in process of putting
away plurality. Of him it is true that he has not been completely separated from plurality and thus "combat" is a fitting term. For what is
still extricating itself from obstacles has not attained to the quiet life,
nor what is fighting plurality to the perfect rest in the One. This com-

75

bat against plurality makes the combatant himself a plurality because he touches plurality in his thoughts. It appears also that the phrase "maintain valiantly" means to Socrates to arrive through a number of arguments at the same negative conclusion, namely that plurality is not possible apart from unity. For he likens the path through negations to a combat. It is thus that he exhorts us in the *Republic* (VII, 534c) to make our argument for the good, "as in a battle," meaning that we can only grasp it through negative conclusions. Likewise here "valiant combat" is significant; it shows that the One also is known through such negative methods, since battle to him indicates negations, both there and here.

That each of the several arguments is complete in itself and is demonstrative of the conclusion is a property of scientific reason. Often we arrive at a single conclusion from several arguments, and then none of them is sufficient by itself. This is illustrated by what Socrates says in the *Phaedo* (77c): "If we put these two arguments together, the pres-
699 ent one and the earlier, the argument from opposites and that from reminiscence, they demonstrate that the soul remains after the death of the body, and also necessarily exists before entering into it." Thus they divide between them the two parts of the conclusion demonstrated, for neither of the arguments by itself is sufficient to establish what is demonstrated when they are combined. But it sometimes happens that a particular argument is complete; for example the demonstrations of immortality in the *Republic*, the *Phaedrus*, and the *Phaedo*—each of them is adequate and they do not complete each other. Socrates means then that the forty *logoi* of Zeno are of this character, each of them alone being sufficient to establish the conclusion, and hence the arguments are equal in number to the proofs.

If I may express my opinion, it appears to me that these circumstances also preserve the analogy with the divine order. For Being abides there in union with the One; and from it the life-giving Intellect and the intellectual power of souls proceed forth into plurality; and plurality is summoned back to unity and in the intermediate order there is more plurality than in the primary. For all things there exist as unities; for all reason-principles and powers are self-sufficient, each being head of its own plurality which it attaches to and unifies with the One, referring them up to the fundamental monad of all things. The same thing could be said of the intellect which is participated but universal; it assembles each particular intellect in the universal and unparticipated Intellect, being of many species as compared with the unparticipated, but differing from particular intellect in that it is more universal. It is to these levels that we found our personages to be analogous, one of them to the One Being, another to the order of Life, and the other to the order of Intelligence. And of those in the intelligible order, one is analogous to the universal and unparticipated Intellect, another to the universal and participated and another to the particular intellect.

700   *"I see, Parmenides," said Socrates, "that Zeno here aspires to be one with you not only in personal affection, but also in his writing; for in a sense he has written the same thing as you, but he has changed it and is trying to deceive us into thinking he is saying something different."* (128a)

Again we should note the order of ascent; Socrates, having associated himself as closely as possible with Zeno, directs the argument to Parmenides and joins himself to him through the medium of Zeno, using Zeno as a pretext for his approach. These relations have been clearly shown by the theologians to exist among the gods. Are not divinities in the third level attached to the primary gods, through intermediaries, however, and because of them? For it is from the middle agencies that they acquire the power to comprehend the first principles. We should note not only that he joins the more perfect by means of what is less perfect but nearer to him, but also that above all he wants to see their unity. For it is thus that Intellect looks at Life and Being as one; and attaching itself to Life, when it sees the unity of Life and Being, it attaches itself also to Being. So it is that every individual intellect, when it sees the unity of participated Intellect with the unparticipated, turns through the one to the other; and it is clear which is the one through which it moves to the other. How then does Socrates perceive this unity? First of all by observing their way of life, for Zeno was the favourite of Parmenides, as was said earlier; and secondly, their doctrines. For similarity begins with life and ends in doctrine, and it is logical, then, that he should indicate their fellowship on the basis of both similarities. For the faculties of the soul are twofold, those of living and those of knowing. When there is similarity of beliefs, it is pos-

701 sible that there should not be similarity of life; and when there is similarity of life, not similarity of belief; but among men of science there is always similarity in both respects. Their common life provides the basis for fellowship in affection, but the profession of a common doctrine results from an agreement in beliefs. Hence Socrates' encomium of the two men is properly based upon both their lives and their doctrines. This similarity of doctrine and unity of life belong most to the divine beings, of whom these men are likenesses; and this unity of the gods is hidden and escapes attention, and only intellect sees it. Hence Socrates says that Zeno is trying to deceive everybody into thinking they are not saying the same things, but he sees the identity of their doctrines. Perhaps this also would be a fitting rule for younger men to follow, that if they wish to support their elders in a controversy they should go at the

topic in a different way. As Plato says in the *Laws* (II 661c; cf. VII, 812bff.)[68], poets must always preserve the metres of virtue that move the soul to action but change their harmonies and rhythms;

> for the song
> Wins ever from the hearers most applause
> That has been least in use, . . .

as the poem says (Homer, *Od.* I, 351-352). So these arguments must be presented in another framework and under a different arrangement, in order to divert the attacks of the more contentious critics without departing from the truth of the doctrines. For this reason, then, when Parmenides says that Being is one, Zeno shows that it is not many, employing a variety of arguments, but chiefly that the consequences of plurality are self-contradictory, i.e. the same thing will be both like and unlike.

Parmenides remained on the plane of intelligible dialectic by using, "as was his custom" (*Tim.* 42e), intuitions about the intelligible world. Zeno, however, began his hunt for the One Being by a secondary kind of dialectic, more eristic in character. Its function is to discover what hypotheses destroy themselves—for example, the assertion that no statement is true, or that every assumption is false—and what hypotheses are refuted by others, either by their consequences, or by their not agreeing with hypotheses previously accepted, as a geometer refutes this or that statement because it does not agree with its first principles, or because it is refuted by its consequences. For some hypotheses are refuted because they lead to contradictory consequences, such as that the same thing is both like and unlike; and some only by another proposition, for example that the same thing is a horse and a man. Zeno constructed his arguments by this sort of dialectic, which combines propositions and notes consequences and contradictions; but Parmenides directly perceived the unity of Being by using Intellect alone, i.e, that intelligible dialectic which has its authority in simple intuitions. Hence Zeno descends to a plurality of arguments; Parmenides relies upon an intelligible intuition of reality, ever the same in kind. Socrates therefore naturally says that in a sense the two men are saying the same things and doing so undetected. For the unity among the gods is not to be expressed in words and is hard for lesser beings to grasp; likewise the community of thought among good men escapes those not acquainted with them. Indeed the affection that unites them has a

---

[68] This is unexpected. The reference seems to be to this passage of *Laws* II, not VII 812b as Cousin suggests, but it is no part of Plato's purpose there to advocate change or innovation in musical matters, though he might in fact tolerate variation, if the subject matter remained strictly the same.

great affinity with the Pythagorean life (for the Pythagoreans made friendship the end of their life together and directed all their efforts to this end) and with the whole subject of this dialogue. For unity and fellowship come to all things from the One, the inferior beings ever united with their superiors, being grouped together around their henads, and these around the One.

703

"For you say in your poems that the All is One and for this you advance proofs in beautiful and goodly fashion; but he on the other hand says it is not many, and himself brings forward many and lengthy proofs. For one of you to say it is one, and the other that it is not many, and for each of you to speak so as to seem not to be saying the same things, although what you say is almost the same, this way of speaking of yours appears to be above us hearers." (128ab)

To say simply that being is both one and many is the safer procedure. For everything after the One has at once the mark of plurality. But sometimes it has a hidden unity of kind, sometimes it reveals a glimpse of its own plurality, sometimes the plurality has already gone forth, and its going forth is now in one way, now in another, with not the same kind of differentiation in all cases. But since the monad is everywhere prior to plurality, all beings must be attached to their particular monads. In the case of bodies, the whole that precedes the parts is the whole that embraces all separate beings in the cosmos, although itself one and continuous. Among natures there is one universal nature that exists prior to the many, and it is through this that the particular natures, though contrary to one another, are often converted to unity and sympathy by the effect of the whole. With souls the monad of souls is elder in rank to the many; and all converge upon it as to a center, the divine souls coming first, next their followers, with the attendants of these followers coming in third, as Socrates has portrayed it for us in the *Phaedrus* (247a). Likewise among the intellects, the one universal unparticipated Intellect, emerging first from the beings that exist in unity together, generates after itself the entire intellectual plurality and every indivisible being. There must exist, then, prior to all beings the Monad of Being, through which all beings *qua* beings are ordered with respect to one another—intellects, souls, natures, bodies, and everything else that in any sense whatever can be said to exist. Let the transcendent cause of unity, then, be the One; nevertheless each thing, in so far as it is one, is unified by that. And we seek to know of them, in so far as they are beings, what sort of monad they have which embraces and unifies them; for every number is connected with its correlative monad, from which it has its being and its designation, not synonymously nor by chance and at random, but as derived from a unity and

704

79

related to a unity; so that all beings are actually derived from a single monad which is and is called primarily Being, by which they exist and are named beings according to their respective ranks; and from this monad all beings are sympathetic with one another and are in a sense the same, as holding existence from the One Being.

It is to this unity of all beings that Parmenides was looking when he demanded that we call the All "one," primarily and most truly the All which is united with the One, but also the All generally; for all things, in so far as they participate in the One Being, are in a sense the same as one another and one. And Zeno was looking to the same hearth and source of beings, and it was while looking towards it that he constructed these lengthy arguments of his. Not that he explicitly posited the One Being, nor that his main purpose was to demonstrate it through his composition; his destruction of the many was only a kind of preliminary initiation into his master's teaching, although in positing that things are not many he directs his argument towards the One.

Again in "what you say is almost the same" the reservation in "almost" is justified; for the one wrote in verse, the other in prose; the one spoke to the thesis proposed, the other to the denial of its contradictory; and the one used the highest form of dialectic, that which examines realities by simple intuitions, the other an inferior form that proceeds by synthesis and arguments. The one is like intellect, for it belongs to intellect to contemplate Being since primary being is the object of the highest intellect; the other is like science, for it is its function 705 to consider contradictories together and to admit the true and reject the false. One of them has "advanced proofs in beautiful and goodly fashion," and he who has been led up to real Being itself necessarily has his soul filled with the beauty and goodness there; and this is the "beautiful and goodly fashion." For the proofs of his thesis were intellectual, in accordance with their inherent character, "whole, simple, and unshakeable," as Socrates says (*Phaedr.* 250c). The other used "many and lengthy proofs," for he moved forward into developments of arguments, into combinations and differentiations, expounding and unfolding the unitary and compact insight of his master. It is therefore fitting that somewhat earlier, when describing the physical appearance of the two men, we spoke of Parmenides as "handsome and good to look upon," and Zeno as "tall," and "nearing forty," for these are also symbols of their words. "Handsome and good to look upon" is changed here to "in beautiful and goodly fashion," and "tall" to "lengthy," almost as if Plato were proclaiming that among the gods all things are in harmonious symphony—their form of life, their doctrines, their visible forms. For each of these imitates the All, and in the All, appearances are images of invisible qualities, and there is nothing in them which is not a likeness and symbol of the intelligibles.

It is natural that the unity of these inspired men escaped the notice of the multitude. For in the first place, they cultivated to an extreme the obscure and esoteric style, like the riddling responses of the Pythian oracle to its inquirers; and in the second place their different methods of teaching concealed their inner unity and agreement, and this again is a likeness of divine things. If we look at the partibility of enmattered forms, at their divisions and masses and oppositions to one another, we might think the invisible divine kinds also have a similar extensibility and an equally great divisibility. So it belongs to the higher and more intuitive soul to see that indivisible being is the foundation of the divisible and that extensions all come from the unextended. The eyes of the multitude are not naturally made to endure looking at the divine unity (cf. *Soph.* 254a-b). If one looks at the provinces assigned to the gods, through which the beings in the cosmos participate in them, seeing the sun in one place, the moon in another, the earth here, he would surely think, unless he were expert in knowledge of the divine, that the gods themselves are separated in this way from one another. But it is not so. The gods are set over extended things in an unextended fashion and over pluralized beings in a unitary fashion. As, then, in the case of the gods their unity is unapparent and incomprehensible, so also with these inspired men; the unity and identity of their thoughts is "above us hearers," as Socrates says. But see now what Zeno replies to these remarks.

706

"Yes, Socrates," said Zeno; "but you have not altogether sensed the truth about this composition." (128b)

Neither is plurality anywhere uncoordinated with the One, nor is it divided from itself, nor is the One without offspring and devoid of the plurality belonging to it; the One is the leader of secondary monads, and every plurality has the unity appropriate to it. For all the pluralities, intelligible and intellectual as well as those in or above the cosmos, are attached to their own monads and ordered with respect to one another. And the monads in their turn are derived from the one monad, so that the plurality of monads is not divided from itself, nor a mere plurality devoid of unity. For it would not be right that the causes that unify other things should themselves be divided from one another. The life-giving agencies are not lifeless, nor the intellectualizing agencies without intellect, nor the beautifying ones ugly; they have life, and intellect, and beauty, or some quality even higher or more divine. So that the monads that unify other things must themselves have unity with one another, or something superior to unity. But there is nothing more di-

707 vine than unity except the One itself. If the One is prior to them, then they themselves are necessarily unified, for things participating in the One acquire unity. And if they are unified, whence comes their unity? From nowhere else than from the One. Thus all the many henads must be derived from the One, and from them the pluralities are derived, both the primary pluralities and the ones that succeed them; and always those that are further away from the One are more pluralized than those that precede them, but even so every plurality has a twofold henad, one that is immanent in it and one that transcends it.

Look at this first in the case of the Ideas; see how Man, for example, is double, one transcendent and one participated; how Beauty is twofold, a beauty before the many and a beauty in the many; and likewise Equality, or Justice. Hence the sun, the moon, and each of the other forms in nature has a part that is outside and a part that is in itself. For the things that exist in others, i.e. the common terms and the forms that are participated, must have prior to them that which belongs to itself—in a word, the unparticipated. On the other hand the transcendent form which exists in itself, because it is the cause of many things, unites and binds together the plurality; and again the common character in the many is a bond of union among them. This is why Man himself is one thing, another is the man in the particulars; the former is eternal, but the latter in part mortal and in part not. The former is an object of intellection, the latter an object of perception. Therefore as each of the kinds is double, so also every whole is double. For the kinds are parts of wholes, and the unparticipated whole is distinct from the participated. The unparticipated soul is one thing, the participated another, the former tying together the plurality of souls, the latter generating the plurality. And the unparticipated intellect is distinct from the participated, the latter introducing the intelligible plurality, the former holding it together. Hence the unparticipated being from which all beings come, including the whole number of them, is different from the participated, which also is one being; the former is elevated above beings, the latter is participated in by beings.[69]

708 Hence at every level of things we must think of a transcendent henad and another henad accompanying the plurality; and then, after doing this, think of plurality as such, not participating in its own henad (not that there is anything of this sort in reality, but because this notion also must be entertained for the moment because of Zeno's doctrine). For Parmenides was looking at Being itself, as we said earlier, the transcendent summit above all things in which being is primarily revealed.

[69] The principle that "at the head of every order of beings is the unparticipated monad, before the participated" is basic to Proclus' metaphysics (cf. *ET*, props. 21, 23, 67–69, 101), but seems to originate with Iamblichus (cf. *In Tim.* fr. 54 Dillon).

Not that Parmenides ignored plurality in the intelligible world; for it is he who says "being is nigh unto being" (fr. 8.25); and again, "It is all one to me / Where I shall begin, for I shall come back to it again (fr. 5); and elsewhere, "Equal in weight from the center" (fr. 8.44). All these phrases show that he posits many intellectual beings and an order among them of first, middle, and last, and an inexpressible unity. He is not unaware of the plurality of beings, but sees that all this manifold proceeds from the One Being, for that is the source and the hearth of all, the secret center from which things are derived and on which their unity depends. Just as the divinely inspired Plato himself knew the many intelligible living kinds and supposed that their unity and inconceivable compass lay in the Animal Itself, monadic and unique of its kind, and did not think that its unity annihilates the plurality of animal kinds, nor again, because there is plurality, that there is no being prior to the plurality; so also Parmenides knows that intelligible plurality proceeds from the One Being, that prior to the many beings there is this fundamental One Being in which the plurality of the intelligibles has its unity. It is therefore far from true that he had to deny plurality because he posited the One Being—he who in the passages above supposes that beings are many; rather in saying that the many get their being, whatever it is, from the One Being, he rightly regards this cause as sufficient and so declares that Being is One.

709   That the One being must be prior to plurality you can grasp by a logical procedure, as follows. "Being" is used either homonymously in all its applications, or synonymously, or as indicating predicates derived from and relative to one thing. But it is impossible that it is used homonymously, when we say that one thing "is" more and another less; for more and less are not applicable to things that are named homonymously. And if "One Being" is used synonymously of each of the things there are, or if it is used as derived from and relative to one thing, it necessarily follows that there is some being prior to the many beings. Or we may follow another procedure, more scientific, such as that introduced by the Eleatic Stranger in the *Sophist* (243bff.) when contending against those who asserted that beings are many. If beings were many, they would necessarily be different from one another, as many; but as beings they would be the same. And this sameness of being must be present in all of them from something else, or from one of them transmitted to the others. If one of them transmits it to the others, this one would be primarily being, and the others would have being because of it; and if it comes from something outside, this would be the prior being which gives to all of them their participation in being. There is still a third, more theological starting-point, as follows. Everything that is participated and exists in others, its participants, has

its access to being from the unparticipated. What is participated becomes pluralized along with the things under it, becoming a part of
each of them and sharing its own essence with the realities that participate in it. But the pure and unmixed beings that exist in themselves are
fundamentally prior to particulars that exist in things other than themselves.

If all this is true, the One Being necessarily exists prior to the many;
710 and from this, Being in the many has its reality, in which they participate. And as the unparticipated exists prior to both what participates
and what is participated, so what is participated is the necessary intermediary between the unparticipated and the things that participate.
How otherwise could the beings that participate be what they are
called, if they have nothing in which they participate and which is a
part of them? Therefore, that which is participated by the many beings
is not the only Being, but prior to it is the unparticipated; neither is
there only the unparticipated, but after it comes what is participated
and distributed among the many beings. Now Parmenides, as I have
often said before, seeing this monad of being transcending the plurality
of beings, calls being one, separating from it the plurality of things that
proceed from it. But the multitude, contrariwise, seeing only the many
separated things, made fun of his doctrine, bringing up sticks and
stones and diverse animals and plants, even things that are contrary to
one another, such as heat, cold, black, white, dry, moist (cf. *Soph.*
246aff.). They did not see how these are one, but looking only at their
differences and their plurality without unity, they ridiculed the man
who championed their unity. For since each of them was himself a
multitude, they delighted in plurality, but he, being one, was at home
with the henad of being. Zeno did not have to look directly at the Parmenidean thesis. He refuted the doctrine of the many which sees only
the multitude of scattered particulars, and by refuting it led them to the
one in the many by showing them that if they separated the many from
unity, a host of absurd consequences logically follow. But if, on the
other hand, they called "many" these things that participate in the one
being that is in them, they would respect the Parmenidean doctrine that
introduces the transcendent One Being, since the participated gets its
711 reality from the unparticipated, the immanent from the transcendent.
This was what set the multitude against Parmenides, their not being
able to observe this intermediary, I mean the one in the many. When
this middle term in things is seen, it is sufficient to persuade us that Parmenides' doctrine is true. For participated realities are second in rank to
the unparticipated, as we said, and things that exist in others are subordinate to things that have their reality in themselves. It is in this manner that Socrates usually leads us to the hypothesis of Ideas, arguing

from the common characters existing in the many to the primary efficient causes that are prior both to the many themselves and to their
common characters. Hence the people who reject Parmenides' doctrine
are subjecting themselves to infinity and dispersedness in things; and
Zeno, in showing up this illogical move, refers them back to the one in
the many, to that one in which the many directly participate, and thus
shows the way to Parmenides' thought, for the way upward to the
transcendent causes leads from the unities in the many.

So Socrates was right in thinking that Zeno had the same purpose as
Parmenides, both in his life and in his writings, but not right in thinking that Zeno meant the same thing by "not many" as Parmenides
meant by "one." For Zeno's "not many" leads us to the one in the
many, not to the one that is prior to the many; so that he was demonstrating the immanent one, the other the transcendent one. "Not
many," then, is not identical with the One itself, but with the one in
the many. He showed that when this is taken away, to say "many" is
absurd; therefore in saying "not many" he is adding the factor whose
absence enables him to refute the hypothesis of the many. This is the
meaning of Zeno's admirably perspicacious statement that Socrates has
not altogether sensed the truth about his composition. Those who
think they have demolished Socrates' remark by adducing the dyad,
712 which they say is not many and not one, are really out of their minds;[70]
for the dyad everywhere—among the gods, among the intellects, in
souls, in natures—is the principle and mother of plurality; and the cause
of plurality is itself, in a way, causally[71] plurality, just as the one, the
cause of unity, is causally one. In general the dyad is exactly what it is
called, a dyad; but it does not exist when deprived of unity, for everything that comes after the One participates in the One, so that the dyad
itself is also in a sense one, and therefore both unity and plurality. But
it is a unity as participating in the One, and plural as the cause of plurality. These critics, then, assert that it is neither plurality nor unity,
but we say it is both unity and plurality; its plurality is one in form, and
its unity is productive of duality.

*"Although you are as keen as a Laconian dog in picking up the scent and
following the track of my arguments, . . ."* (128c)

In the *Republic* (II, 376a), too, Socrates, mentioning the dog, says this
animal deserves to be called philosophic. Here Zeno adds "Laconian,"
which gives Socrates the character of a hunter, clearly a symbol of "the

---

[70] It is hard to see who could seriously produce this objection except a hostile Neopythagorean commentator, of the type of Moderatus, unless perhaps the objection is simply that 'two' is neither a unity nor a plurality, in which case the field is far wider.

[71] Κατ' αἰτίαν. A technical term for Proclus, cf. *ET*, prop. 65, and Dodds' note *ad loc.*

hunt for being" (*Phaed.* 66b). Symbolical also is "following the track," i.e. following Zeno's writings. These writings being, so to speak, the traces of the writer's thought, Socrates pursues and hunts down the precise meaning of what the writer says. And "picking up the scent" appropriately expresses the acuteness of the thinker in discovering the path of the argument. From all this it is clear that Zeno admires Socrates' keenness and ability, is stirring it to activity, and correcting it as it misses the truth. You see also how relevant these details are to the paradigms of these personages. Parmenides abides in the transcendent One, Zeno projects the many on the One, and Socrates turns back even these many to the Parmenidean One, since the first member in the every triad is an analogue of rest, the second of procession, and the third of reversion, and the reversion rounds out a kind of circular path 713 connecting the end with the beginning. So Socrates, with his "not many," ascends to the Parmenidean One; while Zeno, guarding his own middle position, both respects the thesis of Parmenides and perfects the opinion of Socrates. He makes these relations clear in his ensuing words, as follows.

> *"Nevertheless you are first of all mistaken in thinking that my writing, whose purpose was exactly what you say it was, made any lofty pretension of deceiving the public into thinking that something great was being worked out. What you mentioned is one of the incidental consequences."*
> (128c)

Loftiness, grandeur, and secrecy he in fact assigns to the argument of Parmenides, with respect to the matter with which it is concerned. For the transcendent One Being is truly an august object, as ensconced in unity; it is great, as possessing an incomprehensible power, and secret, as remaining inexpressible and inscrutable at the summit of existence. These are characters that the object itself has primarily, and the discourse about it secondarily; the discourse is lofty, and for this reason, it is great; it goes beyond the usual vein and is therefore august; it is enigmatical and therefore secret. But it is the discourse of Parmenides that has these characters; that of Zeno, as its author himself says, is not in any way as august as the other, for its solemnity is derivative, just as the "one" about which it teaches us is secondary to the transcendent One. Nor is its author, as he says, working at anything as great as Parmenides' enterprise; for the latter is aiming at the most causal of all causes, at the most ancestral of causes, if you will. Nor was it its intention, he says, to deceive the multitude; for he wished to lead people from the fragmented plurality to the immanent unity in pluralities. 714 From all this it is clear that Zeno's composition is not as inspired as that of Parmenides, nor so recondite and august as to lead the hearer from the Many up to the transcendent One Being. In a way it reveals this One Being, but its immediate purpose is to effect the transition from plurality to the One Being immanent in the Many, but since in a way it also reveals that Parmenidean One Being, it is natural that he should add: "What you mentioned is one of its incidental consequences." "For I am not discoursing," he says, "about the One as such; but it happens that to those who reflect upon my thesis that other reality, which is inaccessible to the multitude, makes its appearance." This is why it is Socrates' custom, as we said a little earlier (711), to busy himself with the definitions of things, asking, "What is Justice?" "What is Beauty?" "What is Holiness?" For definitions are of the common characters in particulars and of the henads in which the particulars participate. When we have occupied ourselves with these henads we can easily proceed to the transcendent causes themselves of these common characters; hence it happens that those who have studied these common characters find the transition from them an easy one. For everyone would be constrained to ask, "Whence come these common characters? Whence come the natures of these universals (for what is in this particular is not also in another)? And what then makes it the same in each, and what is the unity in which it participates?" So that as they continue to inquire, they get sight of the monads that exist of themselves.

So much for these matters. If it is clear that Zeno distinguishes in this passage between what is *per se* and what is incidental, what room is left for the comment, "But Parmenides did not yet see this distinction," which a crude critic has directed against him.[72]

"It is indeed true that these writings are a kind of aid to Parmenides' discourse against those who try to make fun of it by saying that if it is One, many ridiculous and self-contradictory consequences follow for his doctrine." (128c)

715   These phrases come from a philosophic soul; they are utterances of an understanding accustomed to honour things higher than itself. Is there any mark of gratitude that he has omitted, or any due measure of honour that he has not fulfilled? First he calls Parmenides' Poem "discourse" (*logos*) but his own teaching "writings." The discourse is a unity, the writings are a plurality; and the former is paradigm, the latter images. Inasmuch, then, as the one is greater than plurality, and the paradigm superior to the copy, so Parmenides' Poem is shown to be greater than Zeno's teaching. Next, he says of those who set themselves against his teacher not that they refuted his word but that they

[72] This is a quotation of Aristotle *Phys.* I, 3.186a32, the conclusion of an objection begun at 186a23. Proclus uses against Aristotle the epithet φορτικῶς, a favourite of Aristotle himself.

ridiculed it, which is the worst of villainies. As Socrates says in the *Republic* (X, 606c), "you will end up by becoming a comedian." For, in general, comedians attacked those who were more venerable and distinguished than themselves, such as generals, philosophers, or orators. This again shows how majestic and superior are the words of Parmenides. In the *Philebus* (49c), too, he says that to ridicule is shameful and springs from weakness. Thus the shamefulness and weakness that are comic are characteristics of those who see plurality, abandon unity, and are simply swept away by the divisions and separations in things. Zeno is not even satisfied with "make fun of," but adds "try to," thus doubling their weakness; this also goes with men whose minds are enslaved to plurality. So that if being a comedian is the mark of a feeble soul, to try to be one and to fail is a double weakness in him, since his failure comes about through a defect both in intention and in skill. But Zeno exalts his teacher, and to the description of his works as an aid, he adds "a kind of"; and he says that it is an aid to Parmenides' words, not to Parmenides himself (for what need had he of an additional support? the writings of Zeno are a way towards clarifying his discourse), like one who says "aid the altars of the gods," not the gods themselves. Then, not even this does he add without qualification, as I said before, but by inserting "a kind of" he shows that the discourse of Parmenides gets its perfect aid from itself in possessing the irrefutability of knowledge; Zeno's writings contribute a kind of aid to it in so far as they lead us to a clear understanding of it. Just as one might say the lesser Mysteries are a kind of aid to the greater ones, not implying that the greater are defective, but that they are revealed more fully because of the others. It seems even that Zeno's composition is not really an aid to Parmenides' discourse, but rather to the people who come to it, the very multitude whom he tries to refute. For refutation is a method of healing and a way that leads to truth, and Zeno's writings help them by purifying them of their irrational bent towards dispersedness and plurality.

So much, then, about these two discourses. What the ridiculous objections are that the fun-makers have brought against Parmenides' argument is clear to anyone who has listened to the Peripatetics: dog and man are the same; heaven, earth, and all things are simply one—white, black, cold, heavy, light, mortal, immortal, rational, irrational. And at the same time they declare one and not-one to be the same. If a thing is one because continuous, this same thing will be many because divisible; if it is one thing with many names, again it will be many because names are a kind of thing. In general, all their crude arguments were intended to show Parmenides' discourse contradicting itself and were brought up to upset their interlocutor and reduce him to apparent con-traditions. These things arouse laughter, as Zeno says, but are not worthy of the purity of Parmenides' thought.

"This writing is directed against those who affirm the many, and it more than repays their attacks; its purpose is to show that the hypothesis of the many has even more ridiculous consequences than the hypothesis of the one, if we examine it thoroughly." (128d)

As the gods have a guardian class, as the intelligences have the "undefiled form,"[73] and living beings their means of defence, so Parmenides' discourse[74] has its protective part, the power of dialectic such as Zeno here exhibits. This defensive power is present in all the levels of being mentioned, beginning with the gods and extending down to the lowest kinds. And as these powers of the gods emitted from the primary realities reveal to the beings below them the unitary and uniform and inexpressible existence of those primary beings, so also Zeno with his refutations leads the multitude up to the one in the many and thence opens a way to the transcendent itself. Such is Zeno's aim. Clearly, they who assume plurality in itself are likely to suffer "even more ridiculous consequences," for they are swept away to the region of the indefinite and the unordered; they are compelled to admit that the same is like and unlike and neither like nor unlike, the acme of absurdity, and that contraries and conflicting treatises coincide with one another. This, then, was required to give support to the discourse of Parmenides and as a dynamic projection of him and a mediation between him and the multitude, analogous to similar offices in the divine hierarchy.

718   *"In this controversial spirit I wrote it when a young man; and someone stole a copy of it, so that it was no longer open to me to consider whether or not it should be published."* (128d)

The ethical interpretation, as far as that goes, is as follows. Writings of a genuinely profound and theoretical character ought not to be communicated except with the greatest caution and considered judgement, lest we inadvertently expose to the slovenly hearing and neglect of the public the inexpressible thoughts of god-like souls. The human mind cannot receive all the contents of Intellect, for there are some things known to Intellect but inconceivable by us. Nor do we think it proper to put in speech all that we think of, for there are many matters that we keep secret and unexpressed, preferring to guard them in the enclosures of our minds. Nor do we put in writing all that we express in speech; we want to keep some things in our memory unwritten, or de-

---

[73] Ἄχραντον εἶδος, a reference presumably to the ἄχραντοι θεοί.

[74] Here, *logos* must also be given its sense "reason-principle." Indeed, throughout this passage there is a systematic ambiguity in Proclus' use of *logos*, which is impossible to render in translation.

posit them in the imaginations and thoughts of friends, not in lifeless things. Nor do we publish indiscriminately to all the world everything that we commit to writing, but only to those who are worthy of sharing them, indulging with discrimination our eagerness to make our treasures common property with others.

If you wish also to connect the details of this passage with the divine order and speculate on the analogies there, compare the theft of Zeno's manuscript with the theft that Plato tells us of in the *Protagoras* (321c); recall how among the gods gifts are delivered without deliberate intention from the higher to the lower orders of being—for example, immortality to the mortal, reason to the irrational—and since theft is a secret appropriation of another's goods, how that secret and unintended participation in divine goods by inferior beings is called, even by the gods, divine theft, since it brings to light things that had been hidden among the gods.

719 This, then, may serve as an interpretation of these matters. But of Zeno's "youth" and of his "controversial spirit," what shall we say if we want to relate these details also to the paradigms of our personages? Perhaps that youth, being an inferior condition, is comparable to the descent from the universal, transcendent, and primarily real Intellect to that which is secondary and participated. Of this inferiority youth can be taken as a symbol, for in general inferior beings always have the rank of juniors as compared to the things above them. Since Time is the king of kings, what is causally elder in the divine order becomes identified with what is older in time, and that which is secondary in rank with what is younger in time. The spirit of controversy is not to be interpreted as the eristic temper or as shabby and vulgar contentiousness, but as an indomitable power that stands guard with acuteness and vigour over divine thoughts and, holding fast to the Olympian and divine goods, puts down all the earthborn opinions that spring up from below. And even the opportune imparting (of Zeno's writing) has a likeness to the appearance on appropriate occasions in the world's history of some divine gift, such as fertility, or the medical art, or prophecy, or initiation into the mysteries; or if you wish to look higher, it is an image of the transmission of benefits among the gods themselves, bringing them from secrecy to the light of day in accordance with Time, that beneficent cause that affects all things.

> *"This is where you are mistaken, Socrates; you did not see that it was written in a youthful spirit of controversy, not in the emulous ambition of an older man. And yet, as I said, your likening of it[75] (to Parmenides' discourse) is not ill-taken."* (128e)

[75] This rendering of ἀπῆκασας is required by Proclus' interpretation of it below. The real meaning is, presumably, simply "characterise" or "describe."

Zeno contrasts "young" with "old," the spirit of controversy with the passion of rivalry. How, then, and in what manner? "If, as you say, I had the same purpose as Parmenides, to expound the One Being from which all things are, and I, Zeno, had been already advanced in age, my motive for writing the book would have been the ambitious rivalry of an older man. For why would it have been necessary for me to write a book on this subject when my master had already completed such a finely reasoned account of it? To have done so would have been an act of jealous ambition. This feeling is always shameful. But since I wrote on another topic[76] as a young man defending the doctrine of my father against those who were trying to ridicule it, you could say that I wrote the book in a youthful spirit of controversy. I wrote as a young man defending my master against the multitude, not as an older man in jealous rivalry of him, as you think, Socrates." This is what Zeno would say. "To speak and write about the same things as one's elders without adding anything is the mark of an envious man. He who does this wants to wear another man's laurels in order to win praise from those who know." This is the whole thought of the passage quoted.

In this passage Plato indicates that the powers attached to the primary realities know many things that the beings below the gods cannot grasp, and also that many of the things they know they apprehend through other beings who are intermediaries, those other beings serving as curtains by which the most unitary causes are concealed. And Socrates' mention of the likeness in their themes is correct, inasmuch as the discourse of Zeno aimed at being assimilated to the Parmenidean discourse, but being unable to be that discourse itself, becomes like it, just as, I think, the one in the many is an image of the one prior to the many. So then, Socrates' likening the discourse of Zeno to that of Parmenides is not ill-taken, for there is a likeness between them. But Zeno does not say "well-taken," but "not ill-taken," because Socrates did not also see the unlikeness between them, the superiority of the one and the inferiority of the other. The relations of these discourses to their paradigms are appropriately presented. Among the paradigms the middle terms have a likeness to the firsts, but also a certain unlikeness, inasmuch as they have proceeded from them. But the tertiary beings contemplate their likeness and their unity, for the beings prior to themselves become for them one intelligible order. At the moment of their knowing and understanding them, the differentiation among the divine causes and the diversity of their rank appear to them as a unity owing to their benevolent purpose.

---

[76] Omitting οὐδὲ after ἄλλου (West.). Otherwise one must translate "since I wrote about no other topic," but οὐδὲ ἐγὼ is curiously phrased. The "other topic" would be the impossibility of plurality.

"I accept your explanation," said Socrates, "and believe that it is as you say." (128e)

Socrates accepts what Zeno says about the likeness and unlikeness of the two discourses; he sees that Zeno's "not many" does not quite bring the argument to Parmenides' transcendent One, but to the secondary one participated in by the many which is a likeness of that other One. For everywhere what is participated has its being from the unparticipated, the mixed from the unmixed, the one seen in the many from the One established above the many, and generally what is in something other, from what is eternally in itself. And he believes what Zeno says regarding the time and manner of the book's composition and how it was published, viz. that he wrote it when a young man in the spirit of controversy, not as an older man seeking fame, and that it 722 was by a theft that it got out of his hands and was made public (to those in Italy, obviously); and now it has been brought for the first time to Greece.

About the relation of these details to the paradigms among the gods we have already said enough. Socrates is now about to proceed to the objections he has to Zeno's discourse. In the words that follow we must obviously proceed with great circumspection through the objections brought up by Socrates. Since Socrates claims to be refuting Zeno, we must be especially attentive, on the one hand, to the degree to which Socrates' objections are correct (for it is presupposed that he is naturally gifted and comparable in keenness to a hunting dog), and on the other hand, to how far Zeno remains unrefuted. And in so far as it is necessary that one be mistaken as compared with the other, Socrates is presumed to be still young and in process of being developed by these (older) men, while Zeno is already forty years old and engaged in educating Socrates up to the insight of Parmenides; so that if one of them must be in error, it is better to make the error proceed from the youth and undeveloped mind of the one and not from the other's greater maturity and perfection. Socrates, then, begins the statement of his difficulties at this point.

BOOK II

◻

INTRODUCTION

◻ ◻ ◻

BOOK II, which runs from page 721 to page 782 Cousin, covers the section of the dialogue from 128e6 (τόδε δέ μοι εἰπέ) to 130b1 (. . . ἐπὶ τοὺς λόγους). It is divided into ten lemmata, most of them quite long, and the first one, from 721.29 to 742.15, constituting a sort of introduction. I have divided it by subheadings. This section of the dialogue comprises Socrates' initial statement of the Theory of Ideas as a solution to Zeno's puzzle about likeness and unlikeness, and the coexistence of opposites in general. This provides an occasion for Proclus to discuss, first, Zeno's own theory, and then, drawing on the *Sophist, Philebus*, and *Timaeus*, a series of questions connected with the Theory of Ideas, specifically the function or status of the Forms of Likeness and Unlikeness, which he makes into basic structural principles of the noetic world.

First, though, Zeno's own theory, which Proclus discusses from 721.19 to 729.38. Zeno, says Proclus, is concerned, as was Empedocles before him, to try to lead the mass of men, who were completely dominated by multiplicity and the illusions which this fosters, to a sense of the unity of things, the monads which preside over all multiplicities (724.13ff.). The most interesting aspect of Proclus' exposition of Zeno's doctrine is that he seems here definitely to be using the document to which he has referred in Book I as "the *Forty Logoi* of Zeno" (694.23ff.). Certainly his account of Zeno's argument on likeness and unlikeness is not derivable from the text of the *Parmenides*. (I have discussed this question in a special section of the Introduction, pp. xxxviii-xliii).

Proclus goes on (727.10ff.) to improve on Zeno's argument by showing that a multiplicity of things, as well as being both like and unlike, can be demonstrated to be neither like nor unlike. Plurality devoid of unity is therefore impossible.

The fact that Socrates demands that Zeno apply his method to the world of Forms has led some critics, says Proclus (727.26ff.), to suppose that Zeno's argument contains a fallacy. Others defend Zeno, and claim that Socrates is misunderstanding him. Someone (probably Syrianus, but see n. 4 below) then comes along and provides a compromise solution, arguing that both sides are right up to a point. Socrates does not attack Zeno's argument that a sheer plurality without unity cannot exist (taking his assent at 128e5-6 as referring to that!), but merely goes on to raise an ingenious question, starting an inquiry into something other than what Zeno has demonstrated.

This brings us to the Theory of Ideas (729.29ff.). After crediting the Pythagoreans with the initial development of the theory, Proclus turns to analyzing Socrates' technical term for an Idea or Form, "itself by itself" (αὐτὸ καθ᾽ αὐτό). The 'itself,' he says, expresses the unmixed simplicity and purity of the Ideas, while the 'by itself' serves to distinguish them from attributes predicated of particular things (τὰ ἐπὶ τοῖς πολλοῖς κατηγορούμενα). One may say 'itself' distinguishes the Idea from mental concepts (ἐννοήματα), while 'by itself' distinguishes it from that common element which is in something other, that is to say, in a particular object. Both parts of the expression are therefore necessary (731.13-14).

He goes on now (731.14ff.) to distinguish the Platonic Idea from various "inferior imitations," Epicurean, Aristotelian and Stoic (presumably in ascending order of acceptability). All these come into the category of "later-born" concepts, derivative from particulars, whereas the Ideas are prior to, and generative of, particulars. However, we may borrow some terminology, especially from the Stoics, to produce a definition of Ideas (732.2-6) as "the demiurgic and intelligent causes of all things that come into existence naturally, being established as unchangeable and prior to the changing, simple and prior to the composite, separable and prior to the things that are inseparable from Matter."

He turns from the nature of Ideas in general to the question of the particular role of the Ideas of Likeness and Unlikeness in the structure of the intelligible realm (732.25-734.20). Proclus takes his start from *Timaeus* 29e, where it is stated that the Demiurge wished all things to be as like him as possible. Likeness, therefore, is a formal aspect of the Demiurge; but if so, Unlikeness must be as well, because his creations, while being like, must also be unlike himself and each other. So Likeness and Unlikeness are not only Forms; they are cardinal elements of the world of Forms. Ultimately they descend from Limit and Unlimitedness at the henadic level, the former bringing things together, the latter presiding over separation and variety. Thus Proclus manages to introduce into the realm of Forms an entity, Unlikeness, which might be reckoned a Form of a negativity, but which can be viewed as an aspect of *apeiria*, which is a basic constituent of the noetic realm.

What, then, is the rank (τάξις) of these two (734.32ff.)? In this connection, Proclus sets out a hierarchy of Forms, with at least three levels: (1) the most general, such as the *megista genē* of the *Sophist*; (2) the most particular, such as Man or Dog, which are participated in by sensible individuals; and (3) intermediate Forms, such as Justice, which are participated in by certain classes, such as souls, but not by others (in this case, inanimate objects). It is into this third class that Likeness and Unlikeness fit. These are participated in by most classes, but not by all—not, Proclus says, by "the qualityless substratum of bodies, which is between Matter and the numerous proximate forms" (735.33-36), secondary matter, we may term it. Such stuff participates in the *megista genē*, such as Being, Motion, or Rest, but having no qualities, does not participate in Likeness or Unlikeness. Sameness (or Identity) and Otherness it will have, but these are more general than Likeness and Unlikeness, being in fact the heads of the *seirai* of which the latter two are members.

It next occurs to him to raise the query whether, as some authorities maintain (and as would seem superficially plausible), Likeness is superior to Unlikeness, or perhaps the reverse (737.34ff.). There is something to be said for the latter view, he concedes, but the weight of Platonic authority, especially that of the *Philebus* (23c) and the *Timaeus* (29e, 33b), makes it clear that Likeness is superior.

The next question that arises (739.14ff.) is the sense in which Unlikeness is the 'contrary' of Likeness, since there cannot be contraries, in the normal sense, in the world of Forms. The answer is that the 'normal' sense, which implies the enmity and mutual destructiveness of contraries, is applicable only to the sense-world; in the noetic world, contraries are complementary. Even in the heavenly realm, indeed, the motion of the Same and the motion of the Other are complementary, as also in souls. Limit and Unlimitedness, after all, are the ultimate contraries, and they form the basic combination that produces all else. The contrariety of Likeness and Unlikeness, similarly, is complementary and creative.

He brings the prefatory portion of Book II to an end with a brief summing up (742.3-15), and turns to the next lemma. This is 129a2-6, and the commentary on it runs from 742.24 to 747.38. He begins by giving various reasons why Likeness and Unlikeness are eminently suitable examples to pick, since the very process of participation, which is what is under discussion in this passage, involves both likeness and unlikeness of image to model. This leads to the question, a lively topic of dispute in Neoplatonic circles (see n. 20 below), whether only sense-objects participate in Forms, or whether there is participation also in the intelligible realm. "Those for whom Intellect is one"—a reference, it would seem from other evidence (cf. *In Tim.* III, 32.32ff.), to

Porphyry and Plotinus— hold that only sense-objects participate; but "those who hold to a plurality of Intellects" (that is, unparticipated as well as participated Intellect)—a reference to Amelius and Iamblichus—raise the question whether lower entities in the noetic world might not participate in higher ones. Why should this be? Proclus begins by saying that it might seem that no intelligible entity could be both an image and a model (which latter it inevitably is), since intelligibles are indivisible, and this would imply a division of it. But if one separates off the intellectual realm proper, the realm of Time (the image of Eternity) and of Soul, which has aspects both of model and of image, we must recognise that at this level there is participation (744.34ff.). The "you and I" of the lemma, therefore, may be taken to refer to our *souls*, relying on Socrates' assertion in *Alc. I*, 130c that each individual is most properly his soul (746.27-9), while "other things" may be taken to refer to sense-objects, of which Otherness is an appropriate designation—a nice piece of creative exegesis!

The next lemma, 129a6-b4, the commentary on which runs from 748.9 to 760.18, concerns mainly the problem of connexions and distinctions between entities in the intelligible world, and the question of the individuality of the Forms *versus* the unity of Nous, which constituted a problem within Platonism from the time that Plato first raised it in the *Sophist*. The general discussion on this extends to 757.12, the last three pages being commentary on the *lexis*.

First, an interesting doxography of interpretations of Socrates' remark that in his opinion "it would be a monstrosity" ($\tau\acute{\epsilon}\rho\alpha\varsigma$ $\mathring{\alpha}\nu$ $\mathring{\mathring{\eta}}\nu$) if like things themselves ($\alpha\mathring{v}\tau\grave{\alpha}$ $\tau\grave{\alpha}$ $\mathring{o}\mu o\iota\alpha$) were to be shown to be unlike. The first set of people Proclus portrays (with what justification we cannot know) as taking encouragement from this passage to propound a doctrine that all things were all things, opposites the same as opposites, and parts as wholes (749.41ff.). The only class of people known to have propounded anything like this who were to any extent followers of Socrates were Eucleides and the Megarians, who seem to have been prepared to employ the verb *to be* to express identity in order to press their claim that all being is one, but it is unlikely that they paid much attention to Plato's *Parmenides*. On the other hand, a later Platonist, such as Porphyry, might have chosen to fit them in here, perhaps merely to satirise them as foolishly taking Socrates' use of *teras* as complimentary, and his expression of admiration as serious.

A second group of people (750,16-35), who assert the unmixed purity of the Forms (like the "friends of the Forms" of *Sophist* 248aff., but perhaps not identical with these) maintain, reasonably, that Socrates is indeed being sarcastic here; while a third group (750.35-751.6) suggests

that he is only expressing his doubts on the subject, and neither rejecting nor affirming mixture among the Forms.

Proclus is surprisingly polite to all these points of view (οἱ κλεινοὶ
καὶ μακάριοι ἐκεῖνοι)—unless, of course, he is being ironic—but feels
that they have not penetrated the full depth of Plato's thought here.
Plainly in the noetic world we have the problem, one that Plotinus
wrestles with so productively (especially in such a treatise as *Enn.* VI,
7), of how we are to imagine the unity, the all-togetherness of Nous,
while preserving the distinctness of each of the Forms. There is also the
problem of the connection of Forms, such as opposites, or genera and
species, with one another.

It is not clear that Proclus solves these problems, but he gives them
a good airing, and presents a useful statement of Neoplatonic doctrine
on the subject. He summarises this doctrine at 755.5-14:

> Consequently we must not suppose that the Forms are altogether
> unmixed and without community with one another, nor must we
> say, on the other hand, that each one is all of them, as has been
> demonstrated. How, then, and in what way are we to deal logi-
> cally with this question? We must say that each of them is precisely
> what it is and preserves its specific nature (ἰδιότης) undefiled, but
> also partakes of the others without confusion, not by becoming
> one of them, but by participating in the specific nature of that
> other and sharing its own nature with it.

It is best, perhaps, to see the Platonic Forms as distinct "points of view"
within an integrated system, each containing the whole, but from a
unique perspective. If that makes no sense, then it is doubtful if any attempt to analyse their relationship will.

When he turns to the details of the text, at 757.13ff., we find a remarkable interpretation of the three statements of Socrates: (1) ". . .
that, I think, would be a monstrosity"; (2) (in the next lemma, at
129c1) ". . . at this I should be amazed"; and (3) (at 129e3) "that, Zeno,
I should remarkably admire." These seem to Proclus to represent three
stages in Socrates' realisation that Forms are indeed involved in mixture, as well as remaining purely what they are—another striking piece
of creative exegesis.

He next notes (758.32ff.) the peculiarity that Socrates, in apparently
referring to the Form Likeness, speaks of it as "the like themselves"
(αὐτὰ τὰ ὅμοια, 129b1). Modern critics would connect this with the
expression *auta ta isa* in *Phaedo* 74c and understand it as a studiously
vague description of "things viewed purely in their aspect of being
like," but no such solution is possible for an ancient Platonist. Proclus'
explanation is that Likeness is both one and many, since it is composed

of "parts," all of which are like, even as Intellect itself is composed of intellects (759.1ff.). This is an interesting concept, considering that Forms are meant to be simple, but what he means by "parts" appears to be the elements of likeness to be found in all the other Forms, and/ or the various "powers" (δυνάμεις) of the Form which produce various kinds of likeness at lower levels.

All in all, the present lemma is an important passage for Proclus' doctrine on the Forms.

The commentary on the next lemma (129b6–c1) runs from 760.25 to 765.27. Proclus, as suggested above, sees this passage as containing an exhortation from Socrates to Zeno to raise the level of his argument to deal with the intellectual realm, and at the same time indicating progress in Socrates' mind: "for 'I should be amazed' is the expression of a mind that, though suspecting the truth, is not yet in secure possession of it, as it will be when it has gone further in the study of the question and can speak as one who is committed to the doctrine and has seen the mode of mixture involved" (761.14–19).

He actually begins with another reference to Zeno's original arguments, not derivable from the text of the dialogue (see Intro., p. xl). This, and the present lemma, lead him to discuss what is the 'one' and 'many' that Socrates mentions here, and what is their relation to each other and to the likeness and unlikeness mentioned previously. The cause of Proclus' concern is that 'one' here might be taken to refer to the One itself, which could not in any way be many, nor can it ever be said to exist. He must therefore specify that the 'one' here is the monad, and the unifying power, of the Demiurgic Intellect, and the 'many' its diversifying and protective power. This in turn provokes the problem as to why 'one' and 'many' are not mentioned among the greatest genera of the *Sophist* (764.3ff.). The answer is that Plato there was searching for the highest of the many genera and species in Intellect; 'one' and 'many,' however, are not genera in Intellect, they *are* Intellect, in the sense of being its wholeness and its particularity. They are therefore on a higher level than Sameness and Otherness, since the latter are relative terms, while they are absolute (765.6ff.).

Proclus' interpretation of the next lemma, 129c1–d6, is dependent upon his interpretation of Socrates' phrase *axion thaumazein* at 129c3. He passes over this long passage briefly, in just three pages (766.9–768.24), concentrating mainly on details of the text. Socrates at this stage has an intuition that there is communion among Forms, but is still in doubt, and the next lemma will indicate the lightening of this doubt to hope. His comments on individual phrases are good examples of his method, but need no further remark here.

The commentary on the next lemma, 129d6–e4 (768.34–777.30),

concerns mainly the status of Rest and Motion in the intelligible world. We begin with a further reference to Zeno's own work (769.23-770.1) and it is noted that "I should remarkably admire" denotes a further stage in Socrates' appreciation of the complexity of the question of mixture in the intelligible world.

The questions he raises about Rest and Motion are what is their rank in the intelligible world, and do they participate in one another? The answer to the first is that these are both essential properties of the demiurgic intellect, 'rest' representing the eternal immutability of the demiurgic thought, and 'motion' representing "the continuous uniformity of the demiurgic activity, guarding its creative power" (772.11-13). They are, therefore, thoroughly pervasive forces in the realm of Forms.

But do they combine with one another? The view of the Eleatic Stranger in the *Sophist* (255a) is that they do not. Nevertheless, he says (773.6ff.), we cannot conceive that Rest could be bereft of that aspect of Motion which constitutes activity and life, nor Motion bereft of stability and permanence, so that they *must* participate in each other. All the Stranger can mean is that "there is more otherness and differentiation in them than there is in Sameness and Otherness" (773.29-32)—that is, presumably, they are more extreme opposites. He proceeds to an enthusiastic discourse on the various types of communion that there can be between Forms, symbolised by the sacred marriages between the gods described by the theologians—equals with equals, and superiors reciprocally with inferiors.

He turns from this to the *lexis* (776.1ff.) and here discerns in the word *diairetai* a reference to the "undefiled power" (ἄχραντος δύναμις) of Intellect while *auta kath' auta* he sees as referring to its "implacable power" (ἀμείλικτος δύναμις), these latter being Chaldaean terms for orders of gods, adapted to the economy of the noetic realm. He sees significance also in the listing of *pairs* of Forms, and in the fact that there is a *triad* of pairs. Their order, too, is carefully chosen. I mention all this only to give a flavour of his method, not for any light it throws on the meaning of the text.

The commentary on the last three lemmata (129e4-130a2; 130a3-8; 130a8-b1) adds nothing of consequence, being mainly concerned with reinforcing details of the allegory. It is amusing, however, to note Proclus' view that Pythodorus misunderstands the tenor of Socrates' remarks and is thus surprised, in 130a3ff., that Zeno and Parmenides are not annoyed, because Pythodorus is an inferior entity and thus takes Socrates' comments on Zeno as criticism and irony. We are all inferior beings now, I fear.

Another interesting detail is a reference to theurgic practice at 781.7ff.:

> "And thus Parmenides is moved to address Socrates "when he had finished." In this phrase also Plato has given us a divine symbol. When a man is anticipating the appearance of the divine, he must exert himself to stir up the divine spark within him in preparation for participation in higher beings"—by uttering incantations and performing theurgic rites, I would suggest; "but when the illumination from above is at hand, he must be silent, and this is what Socrates does."

All this is in accord with magical practice as revealed in the treatises of the *Papyri Magicae Graecae*, and is evidence of what we know otherwise from Marinus' biography (and from many other passages scattered through this and other works) that Proclus practised theurgy.

The book ends on the encouraging note of Parmenides' commendation of Socrates' acuteness and zeal. Book III will begin with the process of the questioning Socrates' assumptions, which forms the substance of the first part of the dialogue.

COMMENTARY

□ □ □

*"But tell me this. Do you not think that there exists a form, Likeness,
itself by itself, and another form contrary to it which is Unlikeness?"*
(128e)

(i) The Nature and Purpose of Zeno's Treatise

We must begin by stating again what Zeno's argument was, how it
went, and what truth there was in it; and then give the manner and
starting-point of the objections that Socrates raises. Consequently it
must once more be recalled that while Parmenides was elevating all
beings to the transcendent One Being, withdrawing his thought from
plurality and dividedness to the monad of the entire plurality of things,
most people were turned in the opposite direction, being carried away
by the unruly steed (*Phaedr.* 247b), and preferred their own plurality to
intellect and unity. They did not recognise the existence of the One
Being for a start, but thought that the many separated things simply
exist and get their access to being without the One; and because they
thought this, they were of course contemptuous of Parmenides' doctrine. Supposing that he had posited that Being is one only and had denied plurality, they took the opposite course of positing plurality devoid of unity, despite the impossibility of there being plurality without
unity. Every plurality comes from a unity, a different one for each; and
all pluralities and bodily masses are held together by the One. Since,
then, plurality needs the One, and the One has no need of plurality, it
is better to say that Being is one than that it is only many things existing
in and by themselves without a share in unity. Parmenides, then, in
showing that Being is one, also set up the plurality that his critics saw,
not only perceptible plurality (he gave us this in the section of his poem
called *The Way of Opinion*; for this is what he called sense-objects, as
did also another Pythagorean, Timaeus), but also intelligible plurality;
for in the intelligible world all the things unified with one another make
up a divine number. This is what Empedocles saw later, being a

101

Pythagorean himself, when he called the whole intelligible reality a sphere (frs. 27.16, 28.2) and says that it converges upon itself by virtue of the goddess of love who beautifies and unifies. For, as he says, all things, in their love and desire for one another, are unified with one another for eternity (fr. 17.14ff.); and their love is an intelligible love, and their communion and mingling are ineffable.[1] But the mass of men have deserted unity and the monad of things; and their own intrinsi-

724 cally divided and unorganised life carries them down into plurality, to opinions of all sorts, to vague fancies, to feelings and sensations, to physical desires. They accepted pluralities by themselves without their inherent unities, not seeing how these "manys" are dominated, each of them, by the monad immanent in them, nor how indeterminate things are subject to definite measures, nor how things that are dispersed exist fundamentally as sympathetic with one another and unified through participation in common qualities. Failing to see this, they missed the truth and consequently ridiculed the Parmenidean discourse and rudely dismembered it.

It is persons in this state of mind that Zeno confronts, as a monitor of the multitude to lead them from folly to reason, and as an ally of his master's teaching. He urges them primarily to rise above these pluralities to the henads that are in them, to see how plurality itself, though it has set out into infinity, is nevertheless under the control of the monad of all beings, and each plurality is held together by a henad that has come to be in it. His method of persuasion is to take an hypothesis that is to their liking, that of the many without unity, for in this form their theory is easily refuted; if they had assumed plurality with unity, he could not have refuted them. So assuming plurality devoid of unity, he constructs his refutations in direct confrontation with their own opinion. Parmenides himself makes this clear in the hypotheses, by the fact that only by assuming the many as separated from the One is he

725 able to show that the same thing is like and unlike; but this will be made evident in that portion of our commentary. Let us assume not merely sensible pluralities, nor merely intelligible ones, but all things without exception that are called "many," existing as such anywhere in the intelligible or sensible orders of reality. For we must not understand the argument only as limited to a part of reality, as has sometimes occurred, some persons asserting that Zeno's questions are asked with reference to intelligibles, others that they apply to the sensible world. Nor should we consider only a few of the relevant common characters

---

[1] For a good discussion of Proclus' doctrine of Eros, see Gersh, ΚΙΝΗΣΙΣ ΑΚΙΝΗΤΟΣ, app. 1, 123-127. As for Empedocles, cf. In Tim. II, 69.23ff., where Proclus presents the theory that Empedocles' Sphere of Love is actually a description of the intelligible world! Admittedly, Empedocles does say of it, at fr. 17.21, 'τὴν σὺ νόῳ δέρκευ.'

present in all pluralities, however constituted. An inquiry such as Zeno's is part of a more complete and authoritative science; it applies the same method to all things of like species and sees analogies everywhere. Whether, then, it be a plurality of intelligibles, or of sensibles, or of intellectual objects, or of objects studied by discursive understanding, let them all be included for the present. We have, then, to find how it is that the many everywhere are also one and do not exist when deprived of a unity above them; for if that is so, the same thing will be both like and unlike. How, then, and in what way are these pluralities, if they are devoid of unity, and by the very fact that they have no share in unity, both like and unlike? It is because things that have no share in unity and sameness are unlike one another; and again they have a common character by this very fact of not participating in a "one," and things that have something identical in common are like. So that the same things are both like and unlike. Consequently, if the many have no share in unity, by this very fact (I mean their lack of participation in unity) they will be both like and unlike—like, as having this common character, and unlike, as not having a common character. They are unlike because they are so characterized as not to share in a "one"; so that the same things are both like and unlike. In short, their having nothing in common is common to them, so that the thesis refutes itself.[2]

Do we need to say that the things that have been shown to be like and unlike are shown by the same procedure to be neither like nor unlike? If they do not share in a one, they are quite simply not like, for like things are like by sharing in some one character, since likeness is unity. And again, if they do not share in unity, this itself will be a common character; and things that have a common character are not unlike in this respect. So that the many are neither like nor unlike. Consequently, the same fact, i.e. non-participation in unity, will make them both like and unlike and neither like nor unlike. Plurality devoid of unity is therefore impossible, since it involves so many absurdities for those who posit it. It is a serious thing when contradictories coincide, more serious when contraries do, and most serious of all when both contraries and contradictories follow from a thesis. When we showed that the same thing is like and unlike, we were establishing contraries; when we showed that it is like and unlike and neither, we were adducing contradictories, since like and not-like, unlike and not-unlike are contradictories. And if you would like to use the dialectic method to be expounded later, you could say that likeness follows from saying that the many are without a share in unity, and then again it does not fol-

726

---

[2] This argument seems to be derived from the *Forty Logoi* of Zeno, rather than from Plato's *Parmenides*. See Intro., sec. D.

low, when we say it is not-like; and again it follows and does not follow when we argue that the many are at the same time like and not like, and also unlike and not unlike.

But this is a method that we shall practise later.[3] For the present, now that we have learned the movement of Zeno's thought, we shall remind ourselves of what was said earlier, that by this method of attack we can also show that first principles cannot be many. For assuming these principles are many, will they share in some "one" or not? If they do, what they have in common will be prior to them, and the principles will not longer be many, but one; and if they do not share, this very fact that they do not share in unity will make them like one another as having a character in common, and unlike inasmuch as they have no common character in which they share. And it is impossible that the same things should be both like and unlike in the same respect. Likewise we can prove that the same things are neither like nor unlike. But if they are participating in some "one," it would not have been possible to conclude that they are unlike in respect of their participation in the one, but only that they are like; and in this way we will refute the thesis that first principles are more than one. This result is something like a porism in geometry that is afforded by this argument, as we said earlier.

In this fashion and with this method of argument Zeno showed, as has been said, that it is impossible to separate the many from the one; he raised up plurality from plurality to the unities of the pluralities, and through them was going on, as we have indicated previously, to examine the nature of the transcendent henads of all things; for the immanent monads are images of the transcendent ones. Socrates, having introduced the doctrine of Ideas, positing that common characters exist in and for themselves and, having postulated a different plurality in them, now demands that Zeno apply his method to the Ideas and make it clear that among them the like is also unlike and the unlike like. This demand has led some persons to suppose that Zeno's argument contains a fallacy and that Socrates is exposing it. They say Zeno argues that if beings are many, then in being called many, they differ from one another, and so far are unlike; but inasmuch as they are beings, they are like, for being is common to them, and things that have a common character it is appropriate to call like. Consequently (they say), Zeno uses different criteria for inferring respectively likeness and unlikeness. Hence Socrates is justified in objecting and saying that there would be nothing remarkable in showing that from different points of view things may be both like and unlike, but only if, taking kinds them-

727

[3] That is, in Book V, 1000.34ff.

728 selves, he had shown that likeness itself is also unlike, or that unlikeness is like. Others, however, maintain that Zeno's argument is scientific and free of fallacy and that Socrates has taken it too narrowly. For Zeno's refutation is designed quite generally for intelligibles and sensibles alike, and it shows that in neither the intelligible nor the sensible order is there a plurality devoid of unity; but Socrates, while accepting the argument so far as sensibles are concerned, asks that it be shown that among intelligibles themselves the same is both like and unlike, for Zeno had said that any plurality not participating in unity exhibits the self-contradiction mentioned.

But recently someone[4] has said that both of them are right. Zeno reasons correctly and Socrates perceives his intention, viz. that he was trying to bring the multitude around from indefinite pluralities to the monads inherent in them, and approves of it ("I accept your explanation," he says, "and believe that it is as you say"); but he raises another ingenious and acute question. If we go above the many immanent forms to monads of a different sort, existing of themselves and transcendently, he wonders how unity of species can be seen also in them, and if so what is its source and cause. And on this point it remains for Parmenides to be induced to expound the One itself as the cause of unity, both in the Forms and in everything without exception that in any way has access to being. And what part of Zeno's doctrine does Socrates attack, he asks. Socrates does not deny that if intelligibles are a mere plurality, the same must be both like and unlike, nor assert the falsity of the assumption that declares this to be impossible. Anyone disputing Zeno would have had to contest either the main hypothesis,

729 or the minor premise. But Socrates admits that all things in this world consist of contrary forms, but it is about the Forms themselves that he wants to know the mode and manner of their combination and separation. This is not to dispute Zeno and his contention that a sheer plurality without unity does not exist; rather it comes from one who accepts these arguments of Zeno and starts an inquiry into something other than what Zeno has demonstrated. Granted that all men participate in the Form Man which is in them, and horses in the Form that is in them, and that all things that are like have in common the Form of Likeness and those that are unlike the Form of Unlikeness. Let it stand as a noble discovery that the many must have community with one another through the monad immanent in them. But let us lift our thoughts from them to the transcendent realities that are causes of these common characters and (endeavour to) see in turn whether or not they

---

[4] This reconciling of conflicting exegeses is characteristic of Syrianus (cf. *In Tim.* I, 441.15ff.; III, 174.13ff), but this seems a rather dismissive way for Proclus to refer to him (normally "our master").

participate in one another, and whether they are unified by participation with one another or by there being another unifying cause prior to them. Let us then adopt this interpretation as we approach the words of Socrates, saying that neither Socrates nor Zeno is in error, but that both of them are right; Zeno in his demonstration and Socrates in his question; and that the argument has been transferred from the immanent monads to the transcendent ones, since it is among them that Socrates wishes to observe Zeno's skill in demonstration.

(ii) Brief Survey of the Theory of Ideas

Such is the purpose of this reasoning. But before touching on the difficulties concerning the being of Ideas, Socrates asks Zeno whether he assumes that there are Ideas and whether he is one of those who like himself recognise this cause; in short, what opinion he has of them. The theory of Ideas existed even among the Pythagoreans; Plato himself shows this in the *Sophist* (248a) when he calls the wise men from Italy "friends of the Ideas."[5] But the man who was most eminent and specific in positing Ideas was Socrates. From his inquiry into definitions Socrates discovered what things are objects of definition, and advanced from them as images to their ideal causes. Consequently, he first asks Zeno if he himself posits that the Ideas exist, and regards as primary this kind of being that is in and of itself without any other foundation. He indicates this character by the phrase "itself by itself," which he thinks particularly appropriate since it expresses the unmixed simplicity and purity of the Ideas—"itself" their unmixed purity as compared with inferior beings, and "by itself" serves to distinguish Ideas from attributes predicated of particular things. For how could an attribute be "by itself" when it has its reality in relation to its subject, when it exists as a product of opinion derived from a number of like sensations, when it is mixed with secondary notions derived from imagination? And "itself" distinguishes the common element in particulars, which is the object of definition. This common character is in something other and subsists along with Matter, whence it is highly changeable and in a way mortal because of its association with what is enmattered; and yet to them he often applies the designation "itself" to discriminate a particular kind from the many instances that come under it. But whenever he wants to distinguish it not from the individual instances under it but from the primary Ideas above it, he uses "itself" of these latter. It may even be that here also "itself" belongs to them as separable Ideas, not

730

---

[5] This identification is by no means so clear to modern interpreters. The present consensus seems to be that Plato is simply referring to his own earlier theory of Ideas (Cornford, pp. 242ff.; Bluck, p. 94; Crombie, *Examination of Plato's Doctrines* II, pp. 419ff.)

as expressing a character peculiar to this rank but as indicating also kinds that are participated; while the addition of "by itself" makes clear their difference from the kinds that are participated. We must therefore refrain from regarding defining concepts or attributes as identical with Ideas that exist in themselves, and from speaking of the immaterial and eternal Ideas "standing on the sacred pedestal" (*Phaedr.* 254b) as the 731 same with material concepts of later origin that are filled with diversity and relativity. For the former are unmixed, undefiled, and simple, having their foundation eternally in the Demiurge and deriving their purity and sanctity from the "implacable divinity"[6] that has gone forth with the Demiurge; while their simplicity comes from the intelligent essence of the Demiurge, which is unifying, indivisible, and as the barbarians would say, "the source." You could then say that "itself" distinguishes the Idea from mental concepts (for no concept is an "itself" since it connotes the things of which it is the concept, belonging to and derivative from things other than itself), and "by itself" distinguishes it from that common element which is in something other, viz. the particulars, so that the two phrases together distinguish the genuine Idea from both the others.

In discussing this point Aristotle sometimes says that "animal" is either nothing or a concept of later origin, and sometimes that it is either nothing or it exists in the particular animals.[7] From these alternatives we must exempt the Idea, for the two reasons mentioned. Consequently, we cannot accept the doctrine of those who say that the Ideas are "summaries of pervasive common characters in particulars,"[8] for they exist before the common characters in perceptible things, and these (perceptible things) get their common characters from the Ideas. Nor can we agree with those who suppose that they are notions in our minds, and who therefore raise the question why there are no Ideas of individuals or of things contrary to nature;[9] for our notions about these objects are secondary to what gives rise to them, and are in us, not in him who ordered the Universe and in whom we assert the Ideas exist. Nor do we agree with those who attach them to the "seminal reason-principles,"[10] for the "reason-principles" in the seeds are imperfect,

---

[6] Ἀμείλικτος, πηγαῖος, Chaldaean terms. Cf. *Or. Chald.*, frs. 30, 35, 36, 37, 42, and above, 647.6ff. Here both epithets are used to characterise aspects of the Demiurge, but there are also classes of intellectual divinity with these titles.

[7] E.g. *Met.* Z, 3.1028a30-32; *Cat.* 5.2a11ff.

[8] Possibly the Epicureans, 'Κεφαλαιώματα τοῦ ἐντρέχοντος κοινοῦ τοῖς πολλοῖς' sounds like technical language. Ἐντρέχω, at least, is used in this sense by Philodemus, *De Diis* 3.8; *De Ira*, p. 75 Wilke.

[9] This corresponds to criticisms levelled against the Theory of Ideas by Aristotle in *Met.* A, 9.990b8ff.

[10] Plainly the Stoics, though Proclus' criticism of the concept of *spermatikoi logoi* is ill-founded.

and those that are in the "Nature" that generates the seeds are devoid of knowledge and below even the level of imagination; whereas the Ideas manifest the same actuality eternally, for they are in their essence intellectual.

But if we want to define their special nature in terms more easily understood, let us take from the "reason-principles" in nature the character that their very existence makes them creative of what they produce, and from the "reason-principles" in the arts the character of 732 knowing what they produce, even though their mere existence does not lead to production; and putting these two traits together let us say that *Ideas are at once the demiurgic and the intelligent causes of all things that naturally come into existence—being established as unchangeable and prior to the changing, simple and prior to compounds, separable and prior to the things that are inseparable from Matter.* This is why Parmenides continues to discourse about them, until at the end of his arguments (134ce), he calls them gods,[11] thereby indicating all that we have just said. And here Socrates, with his "itself" and "by itself," has presented succinctly their common character; and the various ways in which I have expounded these two terms are only the numerous ways in which he presents this common character. So much, then, let us say about Ideas in general apropos the question that Socrates raises. But let us add this: the word "deem" (*nomizeis*) is properly chosen with reference to the Ideas; for it is appropriate that pronouncements about Ideas and doctrines regarding the immovables be something like laws (*nomoi*), not opinions or empty notions. Such realities are not matters of opinion, but have their foundation in a higher form of knowledge. It is by intellection that we apprehend intelligible objects, but opinable things by opinion.

(iii) Are There Ideas of Likeness and Unlikeness?

Next it is fitting for us to discuss Likeness and Unlikeness. We must first inquire whether there are Ideas of Likeness and Unlikeness, and if so, what is their force. In approaching the question of their reality, we shall start from the very words of Plato, spoken by Timaeus, who, choosing to speak of the cause of the cosmos, refers it to the goodness of the Demiurge (*Tim.* 29e). "He was good," he says, "and the good can never be envious of anything—being without envy, he desired that all things be as nearly like himself as possible." If then, as Timaeus says, he desired and was able to make everything like himself, he clearly has within him the power to bring this about. For what he wishes to do he 733 can, and of what he can do he possesses the potency in advance, for the

---

[11] Cf. below 830.18-19, and *In Remp.* I, 32.19-20.

capable is capable by its potency. There is, then, in the Demiurge a potency and cause able to liken to himself the things that he creates.[12] If this is so, there is in him an idea of likeness by which he makes his creations like himself and one another. But if so, he must also provide the cause of unlikeness to himself on the part of the things created; for it is not possible for a likeness to be brought into being unless there is also a notion of unlikeness; for without this, Plato says (*Crat.* 432c), there would be two Cratyluses, Cratylus and a likeness of Cratylus. Consequently, the things brought into being are unlike him, being perceptible, instead of intelligible; and they must also possess unlikeness to one another along with their likeness. And this, furthermore, accords with the will of the "Father." For the cosmos necessarily comes to be a cosmos from things harmonized with one another; and every harmony is a conjunction of things unlike and different, a proportion which is, as it were, a likeness among the unlike. Necessarily, then, the Demiurge has also the Idea of Unlikeness; for he who generated things that are subordinate to one another and that consequently differ from one another also harmonized the whole cosmos by means of Likeness.

Likeness and Unlikeness, then, are primarily in the Demiurge, or to speak more clearly, they have their source in him.[13] This, however, is more obvious among the assimilative gods and particularly among the "Fathers" in that order of being, as we shall see when we discuss the Second Hypothesis. But since the Demiurge is also the unique source of their being, obviously the form of Likeness preexists in him, the primary unity of the Ideas. For the Demiurge is the monad that embraces the many divine monads, and the many monads share their properties with each other, one giving purity, another likeness, another some other character according to the special reality that has been allotted it. We must not suppose that, whereas the Forms preexist as causes of the things that come into being in accordance with them, there is no distinct Idea that causes things to become like and unlike one another, but that these are accidents in generated beings, whose essences are constituted by Forms. For while, on the one hand, the accidental has no place among the realities that create or come to be by virtue of their own being, neither, on the other hand, does anything common to particulars exist without a single cause pervading them all, the cause of which each Idea creates of itself the likeness or unlikeness that is produced. Consequently the power of producing both like and unlike things must belong to all the Ideas. But if this identical power is common to them all, likeness and unlikeness cannot be identical with anything in the uni-

734

---

[12] For this assimilative power of the Demiurge, cf. *In Tim.* III, 1.10-2.11, where his other powers are also listed.

[13] πηγαίως, a Chaldaean term.

verse; there are separate causes of all these accidents, causes common to all the Ideas in which each of them, according to its special kind of existence, participates and thus possesses their power.

There is then a demiurgic Likeness and Unlikeness, the former analogous to the cause of the Limit, the other correlative with the Unlimited. The former brings things together (which is why he says [132d], "The like is like to the like"); the latter is separative, delighting in procession and variety and movement, and at the extreme is responsible even for contrariety. The essence of each of them is immaterial, pure, simple, uniform, and eternal; and their powers correspond to their respective essences, those of the former, as we have said, being aggregative, unifying, limiting, and tending to uniformity; those of the latter are discriminating, diversifying, leading to indefiniteness and duality.

(iv) The Rank of Likeness and Unlikeness

As to their rank, they belong neither among the most general nor among the most specific Ideas. By the most general I mean those that are participated in by all beings, so that nothing at all exists without a share in them—for example, Being, Identity, and Otherness, for these

735 extend to all things. For what is there without being, or otherness, or identity? Do not all things have a certain existence, are they not distinguished from others by this very being, and do they not have traits in common with other things? Then the common cause of all things is this triad, or rather the one monad, as will be clear as we proceed. By the most specific I mean those Ideas that are participated by individuals, such as Man, Dog, and others of the sort. Their "makings" have as their immediate result the generation of individual unities—Man of individual men, Dog of particular dogs, and Horse and each of the rest in like manner. I call intermediate those ideas that have wider application than these, but are not active in all things. Justice, for example, belongs to souls; but how could it be an attribute of bodies, or soulless beings in general? What justice is there in the stone, or the piece of wood? And yet the activity of Dikē extends even here, since she is a goddess and contains the cause of these things also; but Justice in itself, apart from all other ideas, illuminates only the beings that are capable of receiving it, and that is not all things in general. Since, then, there are these Forms of intermediate rank between the most universal and the most specific, let us put with them Likeness and Unlikeness, which are the subject of our present consideration. For they are not restricted to one species only, such as man or horse, but have a place in all created things; but they are not found in all beings whatsoever. Consider that qualityless

substratum of bodies which is between matter and the numerous prox-
736 imate forms; you will find that it also has being and form and otherness
and identity. How could it be, without being? How could it have three
dimensions without diversity? And how could it hold together without
identity? But Likeness and Unlikeness are not in it, for it is without
qualities; these are found in things already qualified.[14] It is true that it
has Motion and Rest—Motion because it is in constant change, and
Rest since it never goes outside its appropriate receptacle—but has no
differentiating qualities or powers. It has sameness, but this is irrelevant, for we do not regard likeness and sameness as the same thing
(Plato distinguishes them, assigning one place to likeness and unlikeness, another to sameness and otherness, as will be clear in the hypotheses), for sameness unites the essences of things, likeness their
powers; and likewise their activities are united by equality and inequality; for that in the[15] world of pure number there are differences of
swiftness and slowness and equality of velocity, we learn from the *Republic* (VII, 529d), and there can be intellectual operations of equal
speed whose type of thinking makes them unifying rather than plurifying, and operations of unequal speed which are plurifying more than
unifying. But these are, as we said, differences in activities, whereas
those are differences in substance and potency. Things are identical
when they have a common substance, similar when they have common powers.

If Likeness is not the same as Sameness, it is clear that Unlikeness is
distinct from Otherness; and these two powers, Likeness and Unlikeness, are at the head of the procession[16] of the two genera of being,
namely Sameness and Otherness; they accompany them in their
procession as far as they can, but cease at some point and are unable to
go with them into all kinds of being. But then if Likeness is not the
same as Sameness, is it superior to it? For we posit likeness among the
737 gods and often speak or write of approaching them through likeness to
them; but sameness we ascribe to beings as beings, so that, if it exists
among the gods, it belongs to them by virtue of their substances, not
by virtue of the henads of their substances. Or else we assume likeness
in them to be other and different in kind from that which now concerns
us; and being unable to make clear the unity of the gods and their community with one another because of the incomprehensible and inex-

[14] Reading πεποιωμένοις for πεποιημένοις (West.).

[15] Reading ἡ ἰσότης καὶ ἀνισό⟨της· ὅτι γὰρ⟩ τάχος . . . (West.). Cf. *In Remp.* II, 18.1-
4.

[16] The verb used here, προπομπεύω, is generally used by Proclus of daemons in attend-
ance on their respective gods (e.g. *In Tim.* I, 34.9; 369.27), but with the implication of
leading a procession out and downward from their essences.

pressible mode of their existence, we take the likeness found in secondary things and apply it to them. But not sameness, and that for good
reason, for the term 'sameness' is, we say, a term of essence, whereas
likeness does not apply to essence. For this reason we thought it appropriate to superessential being, since it does not convey to us of itself the
notion of essence. But in general, if likeness is superior to sameness,
everything that partakes of sameness would have to partake of likeness
also, but things that share in likeness would not all partake of sameness.
For the powers of the higher and more universal beings extend further
than those of inferior beings. We see this with especial clarity in the species here below; for the more general terms are predicated of more subjects, in imitation of the superior rank of the primary creative and demiurgic classes of being. But all things in the cosmos have sameness, but
not all have likeness; for where is likeness in the things devoid of quality? Consequently likeness is not superior to sameness; on the contrary,
sameness is more of a cause and more powerful than likeness, just as,
by the same reasoning, otherness is superior to unlikeness. This could
not be otherwise.

We must further ask about these Ideas whether Likeness is superior
to Unlikeness, as some persons have decided, or on the contrary Unlikeness superior to Likeness. It would seem that we see likeness in the
cyclical regressions of things, unlikeness in their progressions. Hence
738 as progression is better than regression, so Unlikeness is better than
Likeness; and if this is so, Otherness is superior to Sameness. Now if
the first principle were a plurality, it would obviously be necessary to
assign the primacy to Otherness, for plurality and differentiation are
akin to otherness. But if the cause of all things is one, clearly the more
unifying principles will be more akin to the first principle; and those
causes more akin to the first principle are superior and more honourable. So the more unifying principles will be superior and more honourable than their opposites. If, then, Sameness is a unifying cause,
while Otherness is diversifying and a cause of plurality in the things in
which it appears, it is abundantly clear that Sameness is superior to
Otherness. And if so, Likeness is superior to Unlikeness. For by analogy, as Sameness is to Otherness, so is Likeness to Unlikeness; and
Likeness is certainly similar to Sameness, as a kind of unity and making
for unity, and Unlikeness is discriminative and similar to Otherness.
Furthermore, we can confirm this result in short order from the principles that follow after the One. Socrates in the *Philebus* (23c) says that
what comes after the One is the Limit and the Unlimited; that the Limit
defines and measures and holds everything together, the Unlimited di-
versifies and leads to the More-and-Less; and that the Limit is more divine than the Unlimited. For thus it is, he says, that intellect gains the

victory over pleasure, for the former is defined in terms of Limit, while pleasure moves in the way of the Unlimited. If, then, Likeness is in the column (*systoichia*) of Limit and Unlikeness in that of the Unlimited (and Plato shows that the More-and-Less belongs to the Unlimited), it is clear that Likeness necessarily is superior to Unlikeness, for the reason that led Socrates to place intellect ahead of pleasure. Furthermore, and thirdly, we say that progression itself occurs more through likeness than through unlikeness; otherwise that which proceeds would not revert to its generating cause, if it is unlike it and simply other, but in some way it makes its procession while being connected with and established in its cause. This is why Timaeus made likeness to the Demiurge responsible for the whole cosmic creation (*Tim.* 29e). For since it was not possible nor lawful for the thing produced to be identical with what produced it, progression comes about in accordance with likeness, which is the next dependent on sameness. Why need we say more, when Plato has declared this to be the Creator's judgement, that the like is ten thousand times better than the unlike (*Tim.* 33b), as much as what is self-sufficient is superior to what needs the support of another. And if in the intelligent judgement of the Demiurge the like prevails over the unlike as being the better, it is clear at once that in the Forms themselves, which the Demiurge comprehends in himself, the former is better, the latter inferior.

739

(v) How Is Unlikeness the Contrary of Likeness?

From this it is clear that Likeness is superior to Unlikeness. But we must next consider how it is that Plato calls Unlikeness the contrary of Likeness; for it would seem impossible that, being intelligibles, they should be contrary to one another. Perhaps, then, we must call contraries not only those that occur in Matter, fighting against and destroying one another, for these are the lowest and weakest of the contraries; and obviously the nature of contraries should not be determined from imperfect examples of them. In general the purity of things is distinct from their strength;[17] the property of strength is striking power, that of purity is perfection and competence. It must needs happen, then, that contraries are sometimes—in Matter, say—violently associated with one another, while elsewhere pure contraries come together. In the latter case they will not destroy nor injure each other, but both of them will remain in their specific purity. Contraries in Matter, therefore, are quite different from immaterial contraries; the

---

[17] σφοδρότης, "strength," in the sense of the strength of an alcoholic drink, for example, or of a fever. The translation "violence" will be required just below.

former strike and injure each other, the latter are intangible, pure, and conspire together. Again, if you will, think of the successive stages of contrariety as four in number; suppose one stage in Intellect, another in souls, another in the heavens, and another in Matter. The contraries in

740 Matter are destructive and yield to each other out of their common receptacle, and what is occupied by the one cannot participate in the other. A white object does not become black except by the destruction of the white, nor is the cold made warm without the disappearance of heat. But contraries in the heavens naturally coexist. The motion of the Same is contrary to the motion of the Other, but the same thing (the heavens) is moved in both ways, and when it is moving in one way, it does not abandon the other motion. From this you can infer that the ether is immaterial in nature, for in Matter the contrary that formerly was there retires at the entrance of the other. As we said, then, the contraries in the heavenly motions—such as their opposite revolutions, their centres, and whatever other contrarieties there are in the powers of the heavenly bodies—these naturally exist together, but have been allotted existence in an extended subject. But in souls the contraries— i.e. the circle of the Same and the circle of the Other, the pair of horses—are unextended, yet they are multiple and separate and exhibit excursions and gyrations in performing their functions. But the contraries in Intellect, being unified to the highest degree, partless and immaterial, and constituted as a single form, are creative in company with one another; for Sameness creates together with Otherness, and Otherness with Sameness. In sum, the contraries in Matter flee one another; those in the heavens coexist, but by accident of the fact that their common subject is receptive of both; the contraries in souls exist with one another as such, for their essences are in contact; and those in Intellect even participate in one another. That is, the procession of the contraries begins with participation, moves through contact and coexistence in the same subject, and ends in mutual avoidance.

This shows that we must suppose contraries to exist in the intelligible world, and how they can exist, and that contrariety is an imitation

741 of the two principles that come after the One; and just as Limit and the Unlimited are united with one another, so also, by participation in them, the contraries in the Ideas imitate their transcendent unity. For this reason contraries everywhere depend from a single summit (cf. *Phaedo* 60b); just as the Dyad there springs from the One and has its being about it. The better of two contraries is an imitation of Limit, while the inferior imitates the Unlimited, which is the reason why the physicists say that the worse of two contraries is a deprivation of Limit. The Likeness is the contrary of Unlikeness, we must establish by recalling, in the first place, that Likeness as such never participates in Un-

likeness, nor Unlikeness as such in Likeness. But you could say this of other things that are not contraries; for example, man does not participate in the Idea of horse, nor horse in that of man; hence to what has been said we should add that whatever is receptive of both is unlike when it is not like, and like when it is not unlike. This cannot happen in the case of things that belong to a different species; for what is not-man is not a horse, nor the not-horse a man. But you could say that the principle asserted does apply to privations. Everything capable of receiving a state or its privation is deprived if it does not have the state, and if it is not deprived, it has the state. So we must add a third point, that it is the nature of this pair to change into each other. This, however, could be said to hold of likeness and unlikeness here; let us reply to this that also Likeness and Unlikeness there in the intelligible world, inasmuch as they are the foundation of all contraries, are themselves contraries. For if of two contraries one comes to be from one of the primal pair, and the other from the other, and neither from the remaining one, it is evident that in their causes too, though in a different way, the antithesis exists nevertheless. Inasmuch, then, as the unifying cause is the antithesis of the separating cause, the aggregative of the discriminating cause, by so much also is Likeness the antithesis of Unlikeness. For if their functions are always and essentially contrary, they clearly
742 have a certain contrariety in their essence as well; for they act because of their very being and have been allotted activities concurrent with their essences. And we have said before how there are contraries in the intelligible world.

Thus we have shown what Likeness and Unlikeness are in the realm of Intellect,[18] their essences and their powers; what their rank is, namely that they are intermediate among the Ideas, ranking below Sameness and Otherness, neither superior to them nor identical with them (for the like is unlike the same and the different);[18a] what is their relation to each other, i.e. likeness is more divine than unlikeness; that contrariety exists among the intelligibles and how it does so; how many levels of contrariety there are and their causes; and finally in what sense the like and the unlike are said to be contraries. With these matters explained we may proceed to what follows.

"And that of these two Forms you and I and the other things which we call "many" partake? Also that things which partake of Likeness come to be alike in that respect and just in so far as they partake of it, and those that partake of Unlikeness come to be unlike, while those that partake of both come to be both?" (129a)

[18] Reading ἐν νῷ for ἐν ᾧ of MSS (West.).
[18a] This phrase is omitted in the Latin translation.

115

Socrates' intention, as we interpret it, was to lead the inquiry from the immanent monads to the transcendent and indivisible causes themselves of these Ideas that are immanent in other things, and to see with Zeno how these indivisible beings are united together, whether by participation in one another or by unity brought to them in some other way. Such being his intention, he first asks Zeno if he himself is a friend of the Ideas, and (as if having answered to himself that no wise man would rightly refuse assent to this hypothesis) fixes the discussion upon Likeness and Unlikeness because Zeno too, in the first of his arguments, had proved these to be the same things which he had earlier called contraries (and Socrates agrees). And also because these are intermediate among the Ideas, as was recalled thirdly;[19] because a discussion of Likeness is appropriate for persons who are being led upwards; and for many other reasons, of which the most decisive is that all the Ideas require these two, inasmuch as the Ideas are causes of likenesses, that is, of all things that come into being in accordance with them. Now he proceeds to discuss the participation of Ideas on the assumption that Ideas are participated in and that things here participate in them and through this participation come to resemble them. (From this you can understand why I said that this is the most decisive reason for speaking of these Ideas first.) For if in general Ideas are patterns and things here are copies of them, obviously the latter are both like and unlike the former. This is the nature of a copy, that together with likeness to its pattern it reveals also its unlikeness to it. Likeness alone makes another pattern, not a copy, and unlikeness alone, in removing likeness, does away with the copy's likeness. It is therefore necessary, if anything is to be a copy of something else, that there be both likeness and unlikeness. The Forms of Likeness and Unlikeness must then be presupposed by anyone who is going to discourse about Forms; for if they do not exist, there could hardly be any other Form. For first a copy must come into being, and then in this way a copy of something.

But since our present inquiry is about participation in Forms, we must deal with the question whether only perceptible objects participate in Forms as their patterns, or perceptibles and intellectual entities as well, or both these and also intelligibles, such as are secondary to the ones above them.[20] Those for whom Intellect is one would not say that intelligibles themselves are patterns of intelligibles; and those who hold

743

---

[19] ἐν τρίτῳ, i.e. in the third of the sections of the discussion of Likeness and Unlikeness in the introduction to this book; see above 734.20-737.33 (actually my *fourth* section).

[20] This was a subject of dispute in later Neoplatonism, as we learn from *In Tim.* III, 32.32ff. (= Iambl. *In Tim.* fr. 64 Dillon). Porphyry held that only perceptible things participated, whereas Amelius and Iamblichus, followed by Syrianus, held that there was participation also in the noetic realm.

to a plurality of Intellects could surely consider if we should say that the intelligibles in the upper ranks are patterns for those in the lower, that is, that the intelligibles in the unparticipated Intellect are patterns of Ideas in a participated mind that are of secondary reality and derived from the former, or that the contents of universal Intellect are patterns of those in particular intellects. These matters are worth pausing over, for they involve the justifiable inquiry what sorts of beings should be called patterns and what copies. Now if, as I have said, pattern and copy are so related to one another that the copy reveals in itself equally likeness and unlikeness to its pattern, or it would not be recognised as a copy (for a perfect likeness, as Plato says [*Crat.* 432c], makes it impossible to see the copy as a copy and leads to the conclusion that pattern and copy are the same)—if, then, we have been correct in saying this, obviously we must never make an intelligible a copy of an intelligible. For all intelligible being is, as Timaeus says (*Tim.* 35a), indivisible; and if it is indivisible it is not possible to say that it is part pattern and part copy, so extreme is the interval between these things. For the copy, Plato says, in so far as it is a copy, is not in itself, but belongs, as it were, to something else and is therefore in something else. Rather we should say that cause and effect are in the intelligibles, and monads and numbers, but not pattern and copy. The One is the cause of Intelligibles, but not their pattern; and it is not lawful to speak thus of the things in that world. Hence intelligible substance proceeds towards itself, in the way in which the intelligible proceeds from the One. And in general every image, according to the *Timaeus* (39e), must partake of generation, so that by this process of coming into being it may be likened to genuinely real being. For if the image itself is one of the eternally real beings, it will no longer be an image; as Plato says in the *Sophist* (240b), the genuinely real ⟨is true being⟩,[21] but the image, in so far as it is an image, exists neither in truth nor in reality, but rather it is "not-really existent."

What then? Should we call only these sensible appearances images? But Plato himself said that time is an image of eternity (*Tim.* 37d); and time is to eternity as Soul is to Intellect, time being a psychical measure, eternity an intellectual one. So that the Soul will have the relation of image to Intellect, and becoming in general will not be restricted to perceptibles, but will be found also in souls. For Soul is the best both of the things that are generated and those that are eternal,[22] as the *Timaeus* says (35a), and it is both divisible and indivisible, whereas Intellect is indivisible only. Hence we are not told of the generation of In-

---

[21] Adding, with Cousin, ἀληθινόν, following the text of Plato.
[22] Omitting μή before ὄντων (not represented in Latin).

tellect as of Soul. Intellect, then, is not an image of the Father, but a procession from him that arises by way of Identity, whereas Soul is an image of primary rank, since it is the first of the things generated, and bodies, as images, come after Soul. And indivisible nature has the characteristics of a pattern only, but Soul, being both indivisible and divisible, is both like a pattern and like an image, thus maintaining the intermediate status appropriate to it. In general, procession occurs either by way of unity, or by way of likeness, or by way of identity—by way of unity, as in the supercelestial henads, for there is no identity among them, nor specific likeness, but unity only; by way of identity, as in the indivisible substances, where that which proceeds is somehow the same as what it came from, for being all safeguarded and held together by eternity, they manifest in a sense the identity of part to whole; and by way of likeness, as in the beings of the intermediate and lowest levels, which, though intermediate, are the first to welcome procession by way of likeness, whether in some cases it be identity and difference or likeness and unlikeness that is their cause. And clearly there are other causes involved in the production of things differing from one another in sameness or otherness, likeness or unlikeness; for example, like things are produced through whiteness or blackness, unlike things through both of them. Things related to one another are like hybrids, in which different species grow together, and the causes that produce them work always in conjunction with other Ideas, so that it is useless to look for some of them that act by themselves, apart from other Ideas. And we must remember also that monads of all things whatever

746 that are said to exist produce some of them as if from the entirety of their natures but diminished for particular instances, their specific character being preserved but becoming more partial in them; while others they produce by a change in essence, as in the case of the production of the procession of images from paradigms. For all images will naturally deviate in their essence from their paradigms—not to have the same formula, but one similar to that from which they came. Thus Intellect in its entirety produces particular intellects by diminution of its being,[23] but it produces souls by procession, the former being partial expressions of its whole nature, the latter being images of itself as their paradigm. And Soul in its entirety produces particular souls by declension, the latter being in a partial way all that the former is in its entirety, but produces the divisible natures in body by procession, they being images of itself and no longer having the same formula as Soul, but only a characteristic similar to Soul in their life-giving power.

---

[23] καθ᾽ ὑπόβασιν, more literally, "by declension." Ὑπόβασις is the technical term for derivation within a level of being, πρόοδος, "procession," being the term for "vertical" derivation. Cf. ET, prop. 21, and Dodds' note ad loc.

From this it is clear that we must suppose that images begin with the beings of intermediate rank and extend down to the lowest; so that we speak of intellectual entities as participated, and the beings that participate primarily as souls, while those that participate secondarily are the whole region of divisible being. If these views are accepted, we can say that "you and I" in Plato's text, said to partake of Likeness and Unlikeness are the souls; for each individual is his soul, as Socrates says in the *Alcibiades* (130c); but that the "other things" are sense-objects,[24] for it is to these that these terms are most appropriate, as will be clear to us later from Plato's own words. The intellectual Ideas he labelled "themselves by themselves" but perceptible things he calls "other" and "many," since simplicity and substantiality unmixed with Matter are appropriate to the former, and otherness and plurality to the latter.

So much, then, may be said about things that participate in the Ideas. In immediate connection with this our text speaks of participation itself. Since the Ideas are indivisible and united with each other, and since 747 they are measures that do not admit of more-and-less—for things that are established eternally in their purity are far removed from such indeterminateness—since the Ideas are of such a nature, the things here participate in them partially and separately and subject to the qualification "more-and-less." The words "in that respect and in so far as they partake of it" express all this. "In that respect" indicates that the participation is partial, for it is not in every respect that each of them is like or unlike, and in a way they are both like and unlike. And "in so far as they partake of it" suggests the going beyond or the falling short of the mark, i.e. the more-and-less. Likeness itself, if you examine the intellectual Idea, is as a whole homogeneous with respect to itself; the part, so to speak, is like the whole of it, as among things here where a portion of fire is fire. And Unlikeness is equally homogeneous, being such as it is throughout the whole of itself, not unlike in one part and like in another, for it is a simple Idea, having the same nature as a whole and throughout the whole of itself. But likeness here is not in every way like, nor unlikeness unlike. On the other hand what participates in Likeness does not participate in similar fashion all over, but a part of itself does so more, another part less; and what participates in Unlikeness is not unlike in the same way all over. Rather each of them is said to be like or unlike in so far as it participates in Likeness Itself and in Unlikeness Itself, sometimes more, sometimes less. The paradox is that, through this interposition of the more-and-less, like things are by that fact also unlike; whereas unlike things, by the very fact that they

---

[24] The word παραδείγματα after αἰσθητά seems meaningless, and is not represented in the Latin translation.

have in common this idea of unlikeness, are like. So extensive is this conspiring of the Ideas; for Identity and Otherness are similarly related, and also Equality and Inequality. For all the highest Ideas are unified with one another and create in common, even those that would seem to be antithesis of each other.

748 *"Even if all things partake of both, contrary as they are, and by having a share in both are at once like and unlike one another, what is there surprising in that? If someone were proving that like things themselves become unlike, or unlike things themselves like, that, I think, would be a monstrosity; but if things which partake of both are shown to have both characters, it does not seem to me strange, Zeno."* (129ab)

Things here partake of both Likeness and Unlikeness and so are called like and unlike by participation in them. Each of them, Likeness and Unlikeness, is a simple Idea there, one being on the side of Limit, the other on that of Unlimitedness. But here Likeness is monadic and Unlikeness dyadic, the former deriving its character from above, the latter springing from Matter and indefiniteness. For there are two ways in which a thing may be unlike itself or something else, either by nature or contrary to nature. Thus Theaetetus is unlike Socrates by nature, since nature has made him so. Call this ideal unlikeness and put it down as an image of that Unlikeness above, for it is the product of nature. But if you see something becoming unlike itself or another thing because of a tendency contrary to nature, say that this unlikeness comes upon it from "the sea of unlikeness" (*Pol.* 273e), i.e. from the indeterminateness of Matter. Those who say that likeness is ideal and unlikeness material should have seen this and not mingled God with Matter, making him produce likeness among created things by himself and unlikeness through Matter. Rather they should have said that he does both himself by having in him the ideas of both; but that in what happens contrary to nature, unlikeness occurs because of Matter only, for nothing unnatural or evil in general has its origin from above or is modelled upon the intelligibles there. For it is not possible for what is
749 likened to the intelligibles to be contrary to nature, and it is unlawful that anything corrupted by the unseemliness of Matter should move towards likeness to intelligible Ideas. Consequently, the unlikeness which springs from contrariety to nature should be called earthborn, not Olympian, whereas the unlikeness that springs from nature and is seen in wholes and parts, in genera and individuals, comes from above to all the things in which it is present. Likeness, however, we should think of as one; for everything has likeness from nature both to itself and to other things, and it cannot be attributed to anything from what is contrary to nature, neither to itself nor to anything else, because what

is contrary to nature is indefinite, i.e. it goes beyond the bounds of the unity appropriate to it. Our statement therefore was a fitting characterization of these genera; to Likeness belong uniformity and unchanging identity, to Unlikeness the double aspect mentioned and heterogeneity. Likeness, as we said before, is in the column of Limit, Unlikeness in that of the Unlimited; and Socrates regards this distinction and proceeds in accordance with these columns of contraries.

These things have been said to bring out the analogy just mentioned. But let us go back to the thought of Socrates and repeat that he proposes to change the direction of the conversation away from the many immanent monads towards which Zeno was trying to lead the multitude, to certain monads intermediate between the doctrine of Parmenides and Zeno's exposition. And he summons to his aid the intellectual power of Zeno, in which Zeno is completely at one with Parmenides, since the object of his thought is the same and has the same end. With this purpose in mind he remarks that there is nothing strange in there seeming to be a mixture of kinds in the world of sensible things, for the same subject can partake of contrary attributes in different respects, but that it becomes a great puzzle to him how things in the intelligible world can be united without confusion, and again how they can be discriminated without being divided. This problem so greatly puzzled others who came after him that some of them,[25] following up difficulties proper to their own thought, declared that everything is everything, that likeness itself is unlikeness, motion rest, and each part no whit less than the whole, i.e. that the being of the parts is homogeneous with that of the whole. And in fact they think they are accomplishing something that Socrates would have admired. At any rate he will himself say, as he comes to the end of his speech, that if anyone should prove to him that all things are mixed with one another he would greatly admire such a demonstration, implying that he desired to have this shown. And they will even interpret the words at the beginning of Socrates' speech, "that would be a monstrosity," as denoting something supernatural and transcending natural distinctions, and so say that Socrates is in agreement with himself in calling the same thing a "monstrosity" and "admirable." But others,[26] considering the unmixed purity of the Ideas, say that they are all of them separated from one another; neither is likeness filled with unlikeness and so divisible with respect to unlikeness, nor unlikeness with likeness, but each of

[25] This may refer to arguments with Pyrrhonian or Academic sceptics, but I can find no other evidence for it. Possibly it may refer to the position of Euclides of Megara and his immediate followers, and his assertion that "the Good is One" (Diog. Laert. 2.106). Cf. W. K. Guthrie, *A History of Greek Philosophy* III, Cambridge, 1975, p. 500.

[26] This group sounds like the "Friends of Forms" of *Sophist* 248aff.

them is pure and simple and uniform. This is why Socrates says at the beginning of his speech that if anyone can prove that the Ideas, including Likeness and Unlikeness themselves, partake of one another, it would be a monstrosity, for we must maintain each of them in its own peculiar character unconfused with other things. And at the end, when he says that he would greatly admire it if anyone should show him that these Ideas are mingled, he was not praising the man who tried to prove this, but condemning the uselessness of his effort; for we marvel at those who attempt the impossible, they say, in that they do not sense their own inability nor the nature of things that surpass their understanding. Still others,[27] taking a position between these two groups, said that Socrates neither assents to the mixture of the Ideas in this passage nor rejects it, but only expresses doubts and raises questions, summoning Zeno to help in their solution. Thus "it would be a monstrosity" and "I wonder" and "I should admire" are the words of a man in doubt, neither approving nor disapproving of the mixture of Ideas, neither simply affirming nor simply denying. We often use such terms to our teachers to challenge them to prove their worth.

751

Such are the things that these illustrious men of blessed memory have said on this topic, and they have all, I think, spoken correctly;[28] though Plato has acted more divinely than they suppose. He has arranged his materials in the fashion before us, assigning the fitting role to Socrates who, though a young man, is yet gifted and subtle in intellectual inquiry, and furnishing him in due measure with the method and the reasonings required to reach the very truth of the matter. For a fuller understanding of what is said, let us, if you please, first think through these questions in the following way. Should we say that Likeness itself is Unlikeness, and Unlikeness likewise Likeness, and Sameness Difference, and Many One and One itself Many? And will we be correct in saying that each thing is all other things, and so make the part no whit less than the whole? But then should we say only that each thing is all things, or say also that each of the many parts in this is likewise all things, and again that each part of these parts is all things, and proceed thus to infinity? If, on the one hand, we say that only each of the totality of things present in this is all things, and not every part of this "each" likewise all things, what is the reason for this? And how will we be consistent with ourselves in saying that some Ideas partake of each other and others are unmixed, no longer making the parts of the parts the same as the wholes? On the other hand, if every "part" in

[27] This group, at least, sounds like a commentator or commentators on the *Parmenides*, whatever doubts one may have about the first two.

[28] It sounds from this as if Proclus is commending even the first group, and he speaks of them all in terms which he normally uses of his Neoplatonic predecessors.

succession partakes of other things, the Ideas will be infinite in number and each of them infinitely so, for it is not "all things" alone that will have this infinity, but each of them as well. But how can things near to the One be infinite in number: For things that are nearer unity, being contracted in quantity, have infinity in potency.[29] And how can there be an infinity of paradigms in Intellect for one perceptible kind (Man, for instance, corresponding to the infinity of existing men)? On the contrary, there must be one Idea of the infinite number of instances. For this reason we revert to the hypothesis of Ideas, in order to contain in Intellect the monads of the many separate individuals, since unity essentially precedes plurality, not plurality the One Idea. In short, if the one Idea posited in Intellect will produce the same results, what need have we of an infinity of them? It is better to work from finites than from infinites, for what is finite is more akin to the First Principle and more suitable for knowledge. All knowledge is of finite things, and finite things are not known by things infinite; on the contrary the finite is always known by the finite. Consequently, we should by no means think that Intellect knows, or creates, finite things by means of an infinite number of Ideas—Intellect which is so much more unified than knowledge that it embraces all varieties of it and comprehends, indivisibly and in advance, its entire development.

In the second place, turning our attention to Likeness and Unlikeness themselves, when we refer to them, are we referring to one thing, though called by two names, as we frequently do when speaking of something that has more than one name, or are we indicating a separate thing by each name? And in the latter case, is it the result merely of our reflection or is it in accord with the nature of things? If they are two names applied to one object, the terms are not contrary to one another, for contraries are things, not mere names. Nor will things originating from unlikeness be different from those originating from likeness, but one and the same; for we are supposing that the object is one, and what comes into being has its genesis from the object and is assimilated to the object, not to the name. Nor in general will the Ideas be many, but only one something called, it seems, by many names. Nor even will there be the five genera of being, since one is essentially all of them, sameness exactly like otherness, otherness like sameness, and each of them all things. So that if all things are in all things, then all things are all things, and nothing is in anything, for there will be only one thing, and other things will be names only. On the other hand, when we say that Likeness is one Idea and add that Unlikeness also is likewise one Idea, we are indicating different things by these names; or why do we

[29] A general principle of Procline metaphysics; cf. *ET*, props. 13, 62, 86, 177.

say that one is superior and the other inferior, if we do not also see the distinction between them? Then shall we say that the things indicated are different in our thought only, or different by their very nature? If they are different only by our thought, the distinction between the Ideas will go away when our thought is removed, and so when the soul is not thinking there will be one intelligible Idea, not many; for things that possess distinctness by our thought are naturally annihilated together with our thought. The totality of things that comes to be from our thought and is founded on that alone departs and is gone when our thought is ended because nothing at all can remain in existence when the primary cause that produces it does not exist. But if, then, they differ by their very essence, Likeness and Unlikeness are distinct from one another, and Sameness and Otherness, and all the Ideas; and Likeness itself is not Unlikeness, nor Sameness itself Otherness, nor everything all things.

From this it should be evident and taken as proved that each of the Ideas is not all of them, nor the part, as they say, identical with the whole. Rather the part is both a whole and not a whole, and the whole 754 is essentially superior to the parts. Shall we then say that the Ideas are all unmixed and do not partake of one another? But this also is absurd, for we see that even the parts of sensible things are in sympathy and continuity with one another, serving to constitute and to complete one single Form. Much more, then, must the Ideas above, being parts of the One Intellect, move through one another and be in each other. Sensible things, that need extension, welcome continuity as a substitute for unity; but intelligible things have the unity that befits them and penetrate one another without confusion. They are in an indivisible subject, and the attributes of indivisibles coexist with one another without separation—not some of them in this portion and others in that, for what they are in is in no way divisible. Indeed we see this kind of thing even in seeds, for each seed contains all the reason-principles, and whatever part of a seed you take you will find all the reason-principles in it. Now the seed, which has the reason-principles potentially, has them all potentially in each part; and there must be, prior to the seed, that which actually has everything in each part. For nature nowhere starts from the imperfect, nor would imperfect beings even proceed to their full development if there were not perfect beings existing before them, to which they bear a dim likeness, having received an imperfect image. What else is it than Intellect, then, in which all things partake of all things, and in which anything whatever that you take will be found to have community with other things? And if we say that that higher being is indivisible, how can it have parts that are divided so as to be unmixed and without community with each other? Things that are unmixed with one another and without community have no sympathy whatever with each other. It is not their nature to desire one another nor to contribute to making a unity. On the contrary they are divided and estranged from one another; for if each part preserves its own nature by being unmixed with the others, it will avoid community with 755 them in order to survive. Where, then, will what is indivisible find a place among the divine Ideas? Where will be that friendship among the intelligibles and that love which we are in the habit of praising? Where is the unity that comes upon them from the One, and all the other traits that we speak of in hymning that divine nature?

Consequently, we must not suppose that the Ideas are altogether unmixed and without community with one another, nor must we say, on the other hand, that each one is all of them, as has been demonstrated. How, then, and in what way are we to deal logically with this question? We must say that each of them is precisely what it is and preserves its specific nature undefiled, but also partakes of the others without confusion, not by becoming one of them, but by participating in the specific nature of that other and sharing its own nature with it, just as we say that Identity partakes in a way of Difference without being Difference (for there is a plurality in it: not only is it different from Unlikeness but also different from itself), and that Difference likewise partakes of Identity inasmuch as it is common to all other things and in another way is the same as itself; Identity is not Difference, nor Difference Identity; this has been refuted by what we said earlier; and again we say that Unlikeness partakes of Likeness (for inasmuch as all Ideas have a character in common they are like one another), and Likeness of Unlikeness, for if Likeness, like all Ideas, contributes something of itself to others, it is unlike them, for otherwise[30] in so doing it would not be the contributor, and the others partakers, and if Unlikeness contributes something of itself to others, it becomes like them, more than that, itself and Likeness become like; and that Likeness is not Unlikeness, nor Unlikeness itself Likeness. Likeness as likeness is not unlike, nor Unlikeness as unlikeness like. For the term *as* has a double usage. We may use it to express the idea that as one thing is present, then another thing is also, as when we say, for instance, "as this is air, so also is it 756 light, and as it is light, so also is it air." Suppose that a volume of air is lighted, and that air is not light nor light air; yet here air is in light and light is in air because, since the parts of air and the parts of light are together, there is no part of either that we can take in which the other is not also seen. Or we can use the term in another way as meaning what we customarily express by *qua* (*hēi*); for example, man *qua* man is re-

---

[30] Maintaining the οὐ of the MSS against Cousin's emendation οὕτω.

ceptive of knowledge. It is not true that air *qua* air contains light in this meaning of *as*, since *air* does not necessarily imply *light*, as we say *man* implies *receptive of knowledge*. For air is one being, light another. It is in this sense that Likeness, as Likeness, partakes also of Unlikeness, for there is no part of it which does not partake of the other, and the being of one is different from the being of the other. So also, Unlikeness, as Unlikeness, partakes of Likeness. It is not true that a part of it partakes of the other and a part remains non-partaking. Nobody prevents its penetrating that, nor does its indivisibility permit it to partake here and to remain unmixed with it there. Consequently, Likeness as a whole pervades Unlikeness as a whole, and Unlikeness Likeness. Not however *qua* either one of the two does it partake of the other; it partakes of it while preserving its own being undefiled. And Likeness is not Unlikeness, neither in itself *qua* Likeness, nor as being primarily Likeness and by implication Unlikeness; nor is it wholly Unlikeness, though it partakes of Unlikeness throughout all of itself. It is unlike, but not Unlikeness, being unlike by participation.

Thus when Plato in the *Sophist* (256a) demonstrated the community of Identity and Difference he did not call Identity also Difference, but different, and hence "not-x."[31] For it became different by participation,[32] while remaining Identity in essence. In the same way Difference is in essence Difference, but the same by participation. In short, each 757 Idea is what it is in essence, but by participation enjoys the others. So all the Ideas are beautiful by partaking of Beauty and are just by partaking of Justice, but none of them is Beauty itself or Justice itself. Consequently, the Ideas are unified with one another and also distinct from each other. This is the peculiar property of the bodiless Ideas. They penetrate one another without being confused and are distinguished from one another without being separated. Because of their indivisible nature they are more unified than the things that perish into each other, and because of their unmixed purity are more distinct than the things in this world that are separated in space.

Now that we have clarified these introductory principles, let us proceed to the inspection of the text before us and say that Socrates sees a part of the arguments above when he rejects mixture in the case of the Ideas, and expresses his amazement at any argument leading to it. That Likeness itself is unlike he calls "a monstrosity." Then reviewing the question from another angle, he has a suspicion of the truth, but says he would be "amazed" (129c1) if this could in any way be proved; and at the third stage he has an intuition of the veritable doctrine and de-

---

[31] The correct rendering of μὴ ὄν poses a problem here.

[32] ἀλλ᾽ ἕτερον after this omitted by ABD and Latin translation, though retained by Cousin. It seems unnecessary to the sense.

clares that anyone capable of proving it would be "worthy of admiration" (129c3). To repeat, then, in his perplexity whether the Ideas are
associated with one another he summons Zeno to help in the solution
of the question; and when it occurs to him to wonder if perhaps Forms
are so mixed that Likeness itself is unlike, he rejects mixture of that sort
and calls this doctrine a "monstrosity"; but again suspecting that because of the unity of the intelligible world the Ideas may somehow partake of one another, he says he would be amazed if anyone could prove
it, using the word *prove* as if already suspecting the truth; and finally,
apprehending that they may be both unified and distinct, he calls "worthy of admiration" any man who could demonstrate it. You see
through what stages he advances. First he rejects, next gets a suspicion
758 of the truth, and finally arrives at the doctrine itself firmly established
by proofs. His rejection of mixture is not mistaken, for the Ideas are
not mixed in the fashion he supposed. Nor is his suspicion faulty, for
in a sense they can partake and in a sense are without community with
one another; and his ultimate judgement is truest of all, for they are
both unified and discriminated, as has been shown by what we have
said above. And Socrates' judgements are all in harmony with one another: "It would be a monstrosity," "I would be amazed," and "I
would admire"—these are expressions respectively of rejection, suspicion, and rational belief. This shows how fully Plato portrays the nature of a well-endowed soul. It is characteristic of those who are being
led upward first to reject, then to suspect the truth, and then to grasp
at it and move always onward. This also is a trait of the well-endowed
soul, that its rejection of a doctrine is not vacuous, nor its suspicion of
the truth illusory, because it is noting the respects in which a statement
is not true or considering in what sense it is true and in what sense not.

We shall take up the other stages for consideration later, but now let
us say something about the passage cited. Socrates agrees that in sensible things the same thing can be both like and unlike, like in one respect and unlike in another; but he doubts whether among the Forms
themselves the like is unlike and the unlike like, and in his doubt calls
that statement a monstrosity, for this is not the mode of mixture that
makes each Form precisely what it is, as shown by the reasons set forth
above. You should not be surprised that in speaking of the Form itself
he presents it again in the plural when he says, "if someone were proving that they are 'likes'," for Likeness is one and many, so that it is both
"like" and "likes." As the arithmeticians say the parts of an even-times-
even number are themselves even, so also must we speak here: the parts
759 of the like are likes and those of the unlike are unlikes. Intellect as a
whole, after all, consists of intellects, not of unintelligent beings; and
similarly the like does not consist of unlikes. If likeness is a plurality

127

and not essentially one, it is not only likeness, but likenesses, for it contains many, or rather all the powers that make for likeness, those that make images like their patterns, or images like one another, or parts like wholes, or parts like one another; and the likeness corresponding to each of these powers makes Likeness itself a plurality of likes. Unless perhaps the question that Socrates seeks to answer is not whether the like and the unlike partake of one another, but whether even if all the intelligible Forms are like one another, they are all of them also unlike, through partaking of both Likeness and Unlikeness, even as the things in this world, by partaking of the likeness and unlikeness in them, are like and unlike one another. But let us, if you please, look in another way at the cause of his speaking of likes and unlikes in the plural. This Likeness, the Form itself, exists in the Maker of the whole, and it exists also in the other intelligences, both those above the cosmos and those that are within it. Suppose that our argument, then, is to find whether all these essential Likenesses are the same as Unlikenesses, and there is nothing so remarkable in his using the plural, not the singular. For Likeness is not singular in its action, but as numerous as are the ranks of intelligent beings proceeding from the Demiurge, so numerous may be regarded as being the workings of this Form, when we consider that it is active in each intellect in its appropriate fashion, supracosmically in the intelligibles above the cosmos, and encosmically in the ones contained in the cosmos.

But is this doctrine then totally false, and are likeness and unlikeness nowhere the same? Yes, perhaps even this is true in a sense. Obviously, before the actual duality there must be a unity which brings together the duality of these terms. For every duality comes forth from a unity 760 which has a prior and unitary grasp of the power of duality; and if this is true, there must be a single unity of them which is the unitary cause of both likeness and unlikeness. If, then, you say that in this unity their causes are secretly contained, completely at one and unseparated, so that Likeness is Unlikeness there and Unlikeness Likeness, with no discrimination but only unity, you would perhaps not be far from the truth. For all differentiations come from unities. All things are at first one, existing ineffably and inexpressibly in their own causes, and are later discriminated and separated from one another, resulting in a certain order of procession. After that which is one only comes that which is a hidden unity, in which everything is everything; and after that the differentiated unity, in which all things partake of one another, but in which each of them is not the others but maintains its freedom from mixture in community with them.

" . . . nor if somebody should prove that all things are one because partaking of unity and the same things many because partaking of plurality. But

128

*if he could show that the one itself is many and the many themselves one,
at this I should be amazed.''* (129b)

After the words about likeness and unlikeness he shifts back to unity
and plurality, drawing here again upon Zeno's own discourse. For just
as Zeno had refuted those who separate the many from the One by
showing that likeness and unlikeness become the same, so likewise he
argues against them by starting from the One and from plurality, and
shows that apart from the One the same thing will be many and the
many one.[33] For a plurality apart from the One is a many by the very
fact that it does not partake of unity, for what is not controlled by unity
is many; and since they have in common their not being one, they will
be one by this very fact, for things that share a character in common are
one by virtue of this common character. So that if not being one is
common to them, the many will be one by virtue of not being one; and
inversely their not being one will be one because it is present in them
all.

In some such way as this and from such premises Zeno conducted his
argument. Socrates admits that Zeno has adequately argued his case
before the multitude and has not neglected the monads in sensible
things, but demands that he go on to other monads of an intellectual
sort and look at the unity and plurality there and show how there also
unity and plurality are unified, and whether it is by way of participation, and, if so, what sort of participation it is. At this point you can
clearly find Socrates coming to suspect the community of the Ideas. For
"I should be amazed" is the expression of a mind that, though suspecting the truth, is not yet in secure possession of it, as it will be when it
has gone further in the study of the question and can speak as one who
is committed to the doctrine and has seen the mode of mixture involved.

Such then is the direction of the argument. But at this point in our
progress we must consider what this *one* is and this *many*, and how they
are related to each other and to the genera mentioned previously. We
should note that each of us individuals is one and many—one in essence
and many in capabilities, or one in substance and many in attributes, or
one as a whole being and many in our parts, or one in form and many
in the matter that embodies it. For it is possible to conceive of our unity
and our plurality in diverse ways, and in every case unity is seen to be
better than plurality; for the whole is superior to the parts, the form to
the matter, the substance to its attributes, and the essence to capacities.

[33] Since this argument cannot be derived from the text of the *Parmenides*, it must be
taken from the *Forty Logoi* of Zeno which Proclus claims to have at his disposal. This
document may not be genuine, but it is none the less of some historical interest. See my
note "More Evidence on Zeno at Elea?" in *AGPh.* 58 (1976): 221-222, and Intro., p. xl.

Each of us, then, is both one and many. But clearly it is by virtue of our likeness to the whole of things that this character belongs to each individual and to the parts of him. For long before us this great cosmos is both one and many. It is many not only in its bodily expanse—containing, as it does, such contrasts as that between the eternal and the perishable, the immaterial and the material, the essentially living and that which is lifeless by its native constitution—but also in the incorporeal lives it contains. For there are gods in it, and daemons; men, animals, and plants; and the world of (real) life is full of variety, even prior to the visible world. On the other hand the cosmos is one because of the harmony of its bodily structure, because of the mutual sympathy of its natural processes, because of the supply of unitary life emanating from the soul of the whole, because of the single intellectual bond that holds it together. From all these causes a single life and breath inspires the whole; it is one indissoluble arrangement, brought into being by Intellect.

Whence, then, has this cosmos such a character, such a character, I mean, as to be both one and many? Does it not come from the god who fashioned and fitted it together? But from what sources did he fashion it or whence did he provide it with its unity and multiplicity? Was it not from his own essence? Indeed we must say this, and this is how it is. For he creates by his very being; and that which creates by its very being acts in this way and bestows on what it makes this character that it possesses, this character that is in itself, or rather this character that itself preeminently is. If, then, the demiurgic intellect has established the cosmos as one and many, the plurality and the unity would be in him; and just as the cosmos is not a unity here and a plurality there, but a unity and a plurality at the same time throughout its whole being (for whatever part of it you take partakes of unity and plurality), so also the demiurgic intellect is both one and many through the whole of itself. Its plurality is a unity of kind, its unity is multiple, and there is nothing you can take within it that is not both one and many. Each of the Forms, then, is both a unity and a multiplicity. Besides, it was not possible that the Intellect should be a plurality only (for it would not, then, be a unity, nor could it be an indivisible unity—there is no possibility of there being a multiplicity that is not a unity), nor yet a unity only (for it would not in that case be a demiurge, nor an intellect at all, but would lie beyond that order of being).

From this it is clear that there is unity and plurality there. But what it is we must next inquire. In the first place, the one there must not be understood as the primary One, for that is transcendent over all things. That One is neither a genus nor a species; for a genus is a genus of something, but the One is relative to nothing; and a species is always essence and plurality and secondary to its genus, but that unity is above essence, above all plurality, and second to nothing at all. Nor can it be understood as the divine character of Intellect, by which Intellect is both father and maker of all things. For this divinity cannot partake of plurality; it is the generator of all the plurality it contains, and it is not lawful that what is generated should be participated in by its generator. But neither can we take it to be the one that is, as it were, the entirety of the Forms. For again we seriously restrict its power when we speak thus; although this one and many are the full complement of the Forms, yet this character does not embrace the whole nature of the Demiurge. The one, then, must be said to be that character which is the wholeness of the entire demiurgic intellect, that to which the theologian is looking when he says, "One came to be."[34] For it itself contains all things on an intellectual level; it is a single intellect embracing many intellects, and an intellectual cosmos which is a monad of fully perfected intellects. For not only does it contain the whole compass of the Ideas but also many other wholes, as the theologians have taught us. We must then call that single wholeness the unity that pervades all wholeness, if we are to preserve its character as being (for wholeness is a real being); and on the other hand by the plurality we must understand the more specific ranks of beings that are comprehended by this wholeness, and none of which appears without a share in wholeness; for anything whatever that you might take participates in the whole and in its intellectual character, if this language be permitted. Unity and plurality are the most general of all kinds of beings whatever, and it is through them that the demiurgic Intellect himself is the cause of all Forms.

If in the *Sophist* (254d) Plato calls the five kinds[35] of being the greatest kinds, we should not be surprised. He was searching for the highest of the many genera and species in the Demiurge; but this one and many are not *in* Intellect, they are Intellect itself. For unity is its wholeness, and the idea by which it takes thought for its proper parts is an inseparable character; and plurality is its many specific properties and its particular forms of unity. Consequently each of the demiurgic ideas is one and many, just as is the entire demiurgic intellect. It is for this reason that this unity is the Form that unifies the whole and its varied Forms, and the plurality is one prior to everything, in virtue of which Intellect as a whole becomes many, and each of the intellectual forms is in itself many. So that One and Many are the most general of the kinds, the

764

---

[34] A reference to the Orphic verse: "ἓν κράτος, εἷς δαίμων γένετο, μέγας ἀρχὸς ἁπάντων" (fr. 168.6 Kern).

[35] Reading πέντε (with Latin) for πάντα of Greek MSS.

source of each Form's being both one and many, being[36] analogous to the primary Limit and the primary Unlimited. For what unifies plurality is a limit, ⟨and what pluralizes makes for the unlimited⟩.[37] But the converse is not true; for suppose it makes an infinite in magnitude or in power? Anything that pluralizes, as such, makes for the unlimited; but not every factor making for the unlimited is a pluralizing factor. And if, as we said, Plato in the *Sophist* failed to list the One and the Many among the greatest kinds, what is there surprising in this? May it not be that since plurality and unity exist not only at the level of being but also in the region beyond being, whereas sameness and difference belong among beings, when he was dealing with kinds of beings he duly mentioned sameness and difference as two of them, but left unmentioned the cause that makes plurality one and the cause that pluralizes unities because in this passage he had posited Being as the greatest and most sovereign of the kinds? For to Being, sameness and difference was appropriate, but not pure unity and pure plurality, whose level of existence was prior to being. At any rate, of all the questions that Plato raises in that passage and all the problems he discusses in the context of Being, each in fact receives the appropriate treatment to Being, whether extended or brief.

765

If you inquire how these Ideas—I mean unity and plurality—differ from sameness and difference, you will find that the former belong among the beings that exist in themselves, and the latter belong among things relative to something. Neither one nor many is called such relatively to another being; but same and other, whether in themselves or in something else, are used relatively, never absolutely. Therefore one and many are by nature prior to sameness and difference, as absolute terms naturally precede relatives. And it appears that one and plurality in this passage, whether considered in the demiurgic intellect or in each of the Ideas, are thought to depend rather upon Limit and the Unlimited as their primary causes; for the Limit unifies, and the Unlimited produces the plurality in each thing. Hence clearly we should not understand the superessential One here, but the one on the level of being, as the unity and integrity of Intellect. This is what Plato shows when he says "if he could show that the one itself is many," for the one about which he inquires whether it partakes of plurality is that to which we connect the verb *is*, not that which is greater than being.

"And likewise in all other cases. If he shows that genera and species themselves have in them these contrary attributes, that would be worthy of ad-

---

[36] Reading ὑποστᾶσι for Cousin's ὑποστάσεσι (MS ὑποστάσι, misinterpreted by Moerbeke as *ypostasim*).
[37] Accepting Taylor's addition here.

miration; but what is there astonishing in showing that I am both one and many? When he wants to show that I am many, he would say that my right side is different from my left, that my front is other than my back, and so also my upper and lower parts; for I do partake of plurality, I think. And when he wants to show that I am one, he will say that I, as one person among the seven of us, also partake of unity; and so he shows that both statements are true. Consequently, if someone undertakes to prove that things like these—stones and sticks and the like—are many and one, we shall say that he is showing that such things are many and one, but not that one is many nor that many is one; and that he is not saying anything remarkable, but only what we would all agree to be true." (129cd)

766

This passage gives us a general rule about the communion of Ideas, admonishing us to rise above sensible things and the intermixture of contradictory genera and species in them to the preeminent intellectual realities themselves, declaring that it is not surprising to observe among divisible and extended beings that the same thing appears to be one and many, and introducing us to unified and indivisible substance and to the recognition of timeless pure Ideas which exist in and by themselves, without need of foundation or receptacle such as we require. We see that perceptible things are both one and many—one in essence, in wholeness, in substratum, in form; but many in their accidents, their parts, their powers, their matter and generally in all those respects by which we are accustomed to expose the divisibility and plurality of sensible things. Are these not the beings that have various shapes, that are separated by intervals of space, and in which, in general, unity is apparent, that, in short, present an appearance of unity, while plurality dominates their whole being? For their nature is divisible and enmattered. Well then, it is not surprising, as Socrates says, if the same thing in the realm of sense is both unity and plurality—in one sense a unity, in another a plurality; but in the intelligible world it is astonishing if the same single thing partakes of plurality and the plurality partakes of unity, something which Socrates suspects but doubts whether it can be proved. We have said that this suspicion of Socrates' is sound, for the community of kinds does not come about in every way, but in the manner appropriate to them; and what this is, we have said above.

767

But let us return to the text and examine each of the phrases we have quoted. By saying "likewise in all cases" he indicates the completely ordered arrangement of the divine Ideas, their unity and sympathy with one another; but by adding *other* he shows that their plurality is not a homogeneous one, but contains distinctions within it. By the

133

words *genera and species* he teaches us that this plurality contains simpler
and more general causes as well as more particular and relatively more
composite realities. For, the more comprehensive and uniform Ideas,
those that are more of the nature of causes, he calls genera, saying, obviously, that they are other and different from what they call 'later-
born' kinds, immanent in individual things. These latter are images of
the former, and it is the function of division to discern primarily the
intellectual plurality of genera and species, i.e. the order of procession
among them, and the intellectual series that they form. The phrase "in
them" shows what kind of communion he is seeking in the Ideas, a
communion not acquired, nor existing in them from any external
source, but from their very substance and nature itself. And surely in
the oppositions he adduces in demonstrating the plurality of sensible
things he has adequately shown, I think, their divisible character. For
their relations are infinitely numerous and, being of all things the least
substantial, are dissipated to the limit of divisibility and to infinity.
And the numbers six and seven—are they brought in without a purpose? Or because six was appropriate for exhibiting plurality (since six
is an even number and above all a perfect number, and a plurality that
is to partake of unity must not be imperfect), and seven for showing
unity, since it is a monadic number, the product of the monad alone,
and odd numbers generally are on the side of unity? And if you will
mount up to the gods corresponding to these numbers, you will see
768   there also the cause of the communion and separation of the Ideas; for
the hexad is sacred to Aphrodite, as the Pythagoreans maintain, and the
heptad to our mistress Athena.[38] The latter brings a plurality to unity,
and the former provides communion in plurality for the intelligibles
and all other beings. If, then, you say that the heptad of Athena is
unifying, and Aphrodite's hexad safeguards plurality in company with
communion, you will find that each is aptly introduced, the one to
demonstrate plurality, the other unity. Again "showing that stones and
sticks and the like are one *and* many" is a marvellous way of showing
how one unity and plurality exist here, i.e. they are divided from each
other and require a conjunction to bind them. For how is the form,
which is one, joined with matter? Evidently through nature, for she is
what brings them together. But among Ideas we have "the one many"
and "the many one" without conjunction. The whole Intellect itself is
one-many; and the many specific unitary forms within it are not simply
others alongside it, for they form together its single wholeness.

*"But if someone of those I was talking of just now would first distinguish
Ideas as they are by themselves—such as Likeness and Unlikeness, Plu-*

[38] Proclus had a personal devotion to Athena (Marinus, *VP* 6).

rality and Unity, Rest and Motion, and all the like—and then would show that these Ideas in themselves are capable of blending and separating, that, Zeno," he said, "I should remarkably admire." (129de)

Socrates has reached the final hypothesis regarding communion of ideas in saying that they all undergo ⟨separation⟩[39] and combination. For the joint presence of these characteristics in them provides both unconfused unity and inseparable distinctness to these divine objects, so 769 that while they are in one another each may preserve its purity. Consequently, he admires the man who can show that the intelligible Ideas can be both unified and distinct, that they do not lose their unmixed purity through union nor their divine communion through separation, but are both distinguished and combined simultaneously by the bond of "that wonderful god, Eros," who, according to the Oracle:

> sprang forth first out of Intellect,
> His unifying fire clothed with fire, to mix the mixing-bowls
> From the Source, directing towards them the bloom of his fire.
> (*Or. Chald.* fr. 42, DP)[40]

It is, then, this joint mingling and distinctness that Socrates wants to see among the partless intelligible realities; to this he invites his companions' attention, applauding this insight which unites while it distinguishes the intellectual powers governing the sense world[41]—ideal Likeness and Unlikeness, Plurality of that realm and Unity, divine Rest and Motion. These last two he has added to the pairs previously mentioned, since Zeno also had used them as well as the former ones to prove the absurdity of separating the many from the one. Zeno's refutation had been based not only on Likeness and Unlikeness, Unity and Plurality, but also on Rest and Motion.[42] He showed that if the many is without unity, it follows that the same thing in the same respect is both at rest and in motion. Everything at rest is in a one something, and everything that is in motion is departing from some one [position]; so that if the many do not share in a unity, they will be unresting; and again, if they have in common the character of not sharing in some unity, they will be in some one [state] and hence will be in this respect unmoving. The same things, therefore, will be moving and sta-770 tionary, so that the many are not altogether devoid of unity. Such was Zeno's argument. But Socrates, considering that it has already been sufficiently demonstrated that these things must always partake of

---

[39] Accepting Taylor's addition of διακρίνεσθαι.
[40] Quoted also below, 777.9.
[41] Cousin's reading νοητῶν for αἰσθητῶν here is misguided.
[42] A further argument of Zeno's not derivable from the text of Plato; cf. above 760-761, n. 29, and Intro., p. xli.

unity, demands that Zeno, who has left aside the proof that sensible
pluralities are not merely separate from but united with one another,
not show how the same thing in the sense world is both moving and at
rest, but that he proceed to the intellectual monads and show how they
also are unified and partake of one another. It has been adequately
shown that the pluralities in this world partake of certain monads
through which their divided and separate existences are brought under
uniting bonds; yet before we can rise to that highest Parmenidean unity
we must see how the many invisible and transcendent monads exist in
one another—how homogeneous their community is, how unmingled
their purity, how likeness is mingled with unlikeness, how unity and
plurality interpenetrate one another, and how rest and motion partake
of one another. He who apprehends this kind of mixture and inter-
weaving of the ideas is the one whom Socrates really admires—and not
as an ordinary object of admiration, for the term "remarkably" (*thau-
mastōs*) adds emphasis to his praise, indicating that this is what is really
and truly an object worthy of remark (*thauma*). We see then how relevant are all the reactions of Socrates, his (initial) rejection, his suspicion, and his hope, the first when he contemplates the confusion and
intermingling of the divine Ideas, the second when he envisages merely
their union, and the last when he sees their joint unity and distinctness.
This came last, like a flame lighted from fire-sticks, as the consequence
of his attentive scrutiny of the problem and his prolonged attention to
the Ideas themselves (cf. Plato *Ep*. VII, 341cd).

So much, then, may be said regarding the character of the discussion
and its purpose in general. But now let us go back and look at the prob-
771 lems themselves. What are Rest and Motion in the intelligible world?
What is their rank there? Do they participate in one another? Anyone
can see, I think, that the demiurgic intellect, constituted of pure and
immaterial notions, being the supracosmic creator of all things together, must be unchangeable in essence and in activity. For every indivisible Idea is eternal, and what is eternal has its nature in rest. For,
everything that changes either in essence or in activity, becoming or
acting at one time in this way and at another time in that, is originally
or eventually divisible; but every intellect is indivisible, being simple
and ungenerated. If then every intellect is indivisible, and every indivisible thing eternal, and every eternal thing is immutably at rest, it is
clear that every intellect is at rest, and especially the demiurgic intellect;
for by so much as it is mightier than the things that come after it, by so
much the more does it guard its own station unmoved. And if in its
entirety it establishes the whole cosmos, both its general form and the
poles within it and their centres and axes, and gives to each of them an
abiding power, whence could it confer this gift if not from its own na-

ture? For it gives by virtue of its very being, and there is rest within it which is the cause of all things that are at rest. But there is also movement in it. For if it is a demiurge and thinks itself, clearly it does so by energizing. Energizing is said to be perfect motion, and such is the demiurgic making and thinking. Furthermore if, as Plato says (*Tim.* 37c), motion is, as it were, the life of bodily things, with much greater reason must we call motion that life-giving cause that is in the Demiurge, for life itself is to be possessed of motion. And if it gives motion to the heavens and the world of generation, and gives it from its own nature, there must obviously be motion primordially in it. For whatever creates by virtue of its being transmits to other things from the being that it has. Fire does not give coolness to other things, but heat; for it creates not by choice but by its being, and it has no coolness in its being. Likewise the sun gives light, and the soul life. So that if the Demiurge gives motion to the things below it, he has the cause of motion, together with rest, in his constitution. These considerations show that rest and motion both exist in the intelligible world, the latter as the eternity of the demiurgic thought and the agent of its providence, the former as the continuous uniformity of its demiurgic energy guarding its creative power. How can the providence of the Demiurge of the universe be alert and at its prime of effectiveness except through motion? And how can it be steadfast, undeviating, and unchangeable except through rest?

772

These two kinds, therefore, Rest and Motion, we must posit as existing in the Demiurge. But do these two kinds participate in one another or not? Now the Eleatic Stranger in the *Sophist* appears to deny mixture in their case (255a); for it is not fitting, he says, that all things be unmixed, nor again that all be mixed with one another; Sameness and Otherness mingle with one another, but Rest and Motion do not. Perhaps when Socrates in the present dialogue says he would admire anyone who is able to show that these Forms can be mingled, he is leaving room for the arguments in the *Sophist* that distinguish between the Forms that mingle and those that do not; and Socrates himself affects to be in doubt about these matters and aims at learning something; whereas the Sage in the other dialogue gives a scientific exposition and proves that some kinds are separate and some are mingled with one another, for having the capability of experiencing the same things does not necessarily involve reciprocal participation ("being open to" is the same as "having the capability"). Or perhaps the measures of separation and combination are not the same for all Forms. For there is both unity and differentiation in the genera of being, and there is no one of them that does not mingle with the rest. But as in these genera some are more unified and others more disparate, so also some are more ac-

773

tive in participation, others more effective in preserving their purity. Consequently, when in comparing Rest and Motion with the others we said they do not participate in one another, we did not mean that they are altogether unsociable and unmixed. For how, being correlative in a single system, can they fail to be friends of one another and partake, in a sense, of each other's natures—Rest deriving effective energy from Motion and Motion enduring power from Rest? Shall we make Rest ineffective and lifeless, or give it a share of life and energy? But if it is ineffective and lifeless, it will not be generative, nor an intellectual form. Every part of Intellect has Life, since it is not lawful to constitute Intellect of unthinking nor Life of lifeless parts. But if Rest is to have both life and energy, it will also have motion. In the same way shall we not also say that Motion energizes in a stable and unvarying fashion? How otherwise would one of the intellectual Forms act? This is why we call them unmoving causes. And if they have unchanging power, they partake in a sense of Rest. Consequently these Forms participate in each other. Nevertheless we often say they are unmixed, because there is more otherness and differentiation in them than in Identity and Difference; the latter are more unified than differentiated, but Rest and Motion more differentiated than unified.

Perhaps again each of the Ideas aims at being both unified and separated, just as was said earlier about the things in this world, that each of them is both one and many, and perhaps this is what Socrates meant 774 in saying that he would admire one who could demonstrate that each of the intelligible Ideas is both differentiated and unified. This would seem to be shown by the added phrase "in themselves." He does not say "with each other," which would have set us to searching for their mixture with one another, but "in themselves," as if asking how each of them is at the same time differentiated and unified—so that Rest is one and many, and Motion too, like you and me and every sensible thing, the unity in the intelligible world being pluralized and the many there unified. If this view is accepted, the unmixedness here is quite different from that of Rest and Motion in the *Sophist* (255a); and it accords more with what is written in the *Philebus* (15d), that to say the same thing is one and many is a commonplace about sensible things, but that it is worth investigating how each of the intelligible monads is one and many. For this is the same as to show that each of the intelligible Ideas is differentiated and unified, as is said in the present passage.

So much, then, let us say in general about the communion of Ideas, as they are unified and differentiated, each of them in itself, and all of them in relation to one another. But for a thorough understanding of their mingling and their failure to mingle, we would perhaps be better to refer to our exegesis of the *Sophist*, where Plato's primary subject is the participation and non-participation of the kinds of being.[43] Do Likeness and Unlikeness mingle not only with one another but also with others, such as Rest and Motion? In general, do the genera of being mingle not only with themselves but also with the species of being? Or do some of them only partake of one another and others not? This is matter for a later inquiry. At any rate it seems absurd that causes partake of their effects, yet the five genera are the cause of the being of all the species. Perhaps, then, we should say that mixture occurs in several ways; beings of the same rank will mingle with each other in one 775 fashion, superiors with inferiors in another, and the inferior with their superiors in still another. Beings of equal rank circulate freely with one another and share their peculiar powers; the superiors move among their inferiors and give of their specific properties to them, and exist in them through participation; the inferiors have their ground in their superiors, they become their table-companions[44] and enjoy the same intelligible fare, since they are in them causally. If this interpretation is true, the species mingle variously with one another, and so do the genera, in accordance with the first kind of mingling, for such fellowship is appropriate to beings of equal rank; the genera with their species in the second way, for they give something of themselves to their species; and species with their genera in the third way, for they have their foundation, their unity, and their being in them, nay rather, they are already causally in them from aforetime because of the constitution of all things in the indivisible.[45]

These are not distinctions that we have invented; the theologians have expressed them symbolically in the doctrine of the "sacred marriages."[46] In general they call a "marriage," in their mystical language, a homogeneous union and community between two divine causes. Such a union they sometimes find between beings of the same rank, and so speak of the marriages of Zeus and Hera, of Ouranos and Ge, of Cronos and Rhea; sometimes of the marriage of an inferior and a superior, as in the marriage of Zeus and Demeter; and sometimes, conversely, of superiors with inferiors, as when they talk of the marriage of Zeus and Kore; since some of the divine marriages are with equals, some with beings above them, and others with beings below them; and we must recognise the special character of each such union and transfer from the gods to the Ideas the type of intermingling involved.

776 Now that we have spoken in proper order of the subjects it deals

---

[43] This would seem to indicate the priority of a commentary on the *Sophist* which does not survive.

[44] This rather striking image is possibly a reminiscence of Empedocles, fr. 147.1 D-K.

[45] For the theoretical background to this passage, cf. *ET*, prop. 23.

[46] Cf. *In Tim.* III, 176.10ff. Diehl = *Orph.* fr. 112 Kern.

with, let us consider the text itself. First of all then, in "distinguishing" the beings that participate from those in which they participate, the intelligibles from the sensibles, and by elevating the higher over the lower, the text expresses the "undefiled"[47] power of Intellect, which cuts off all that is enmattered, composite, and alien from the intellectual and divine beings. Placing the intelligible Forms "apart by themselves" is an image of the "implacable" power that stands unremitting guard over their purity. By taking them up in pairs it exhibits their generative and infinitely productive powers, and the triadic presentation of the antithesis within them reveals their completeness and self-sufficiency and their whole power of producing perfection. And further, the order in which they are enumerated expresses their continuity and unity; for after Likeness and Unlikeness come Plurality and Unity, and after them Rest and Motion; thus Plurality is appropriately joined to Likeness and Unlikeness, and Rest to Unity. If then, as we have said, unity and plurality are seen throughout the whole of Intellect, motion and rest in the primary genera, and likeness and unlikeness in the secondary ones, then perhaps the first pair are most in evidence in the part of Intellect which rests (for that also is many and one), the second pair in the part which goes forth (for what goes forth from it is stable in its movement), and the third pair in that which reverts, for every such being is both like and unlike that to which it returns; so that it is reasonable that he should be content with these three antitheses. In any case, these too are genera, and more universal than the other kinds, their species, and it is they with which Socrates begins, following the course of Zeno's

777 arguments. For that he is following those in raising these points will be evident from what Parmenides later says to him: "And do you think there is a form of Likeness and of the One and Many which you heard Zeno expound?" The term "blending" (*synkrasis*) expresses the inseparable community among the kinds and the immaterial bond of their unity; and perhaps also the source-like nature of their primal efficacy. "Mixing-bowls filled from the source" we frequently meet in other writers,[48] and the *Timaeus* (41d) calls a "mixing-bowl" (*kratēr*) the cause in which the kinds of being are mixed. It is, then, in conformity with these ideas that he calls the mixture a blending. The philosopher knows many kinds of blending; there is the blending of Zeus in the *Timaeus*, and in the *Philebus* (61c) those of Dionysus and Hephaestus.

Finally, the salutation "Zeno" is addressed to the wisdom of the man and his arguments and expresses adherence to his doctrine as a whole.

---

[47] The ἄχραντος δύναμις, and the ἀμείλικτος δύναμις below, are Chaldaean terms, normally referring in Neoplatonic theology to classes of gods, but here taken as powers of Intellect. Cf. Psellus, *Hypot. ap.* Des Places, pp. 198-199.

[48] *Or. Chald.* fr. 42.3 D.P.

Socrates all but presents himself as uniting with Zeno and through this fellowship turning towards the one intellect of Parmenides. This is why in the ensuing conversation Parmenides responds to him, who has furnished such proofs of his acuteness, his sureness of judgement, and his enthusiasm for divine things so far as was reasonable for one so young; and also because, of all those present, he is the most fitted to be a receptacle of this mystical doctrine of things divine.

> "You have dealt with this subject very valiantly, I think; but as I say, my admiration would be much greater if anyone could show that these same perplexities are everywhere involved in the Forms themselves, among the objects we apprehend by reasoning, just as you have shown them to be involved in the things we see." (129e-130a)

778 Socrates' whole purpose and the purpose of the whole discussion are contained in these words. He praises the discourse of Zeno as valiantly done, because it uncovers and refutes the foolishness of the multitude, and stands to Parmenides' Being as the Auxiliaries do to the Guardians.[49] But Zeno has said that he wrote his book in a spirit of controversy, and Socrates changes *controversially* to *valiantly*, making the passion into a virtue. How else would it have been fitting for a young man to converse with his superior? He praises, then, as I said, the work of Zeno with striking alertness, but diverts the inquiry from the seen to the unseen world. Let it be taken as proved that there are unities in this world of visible things. For even if Zeno was saying of every plurality, whether it be supposed to be an object of intuitive or discursive intellection or of sense-perception, that it was not devoid of unity (for he did not attach any qualification to his "many," but demonstrated his absurd consequences by postulating simple plurality), nevertheless the multitude to whom the argument was directed thought it was concerned in each case only with visible pluralities. Let it be taken, then, as proved to the multitude that in visible pluralities there are certain monads and ties binding multiplicity together. In the same way show me, says Socrates, that communion of Ideas in the intelligible world; so that as you have shown the multitude that visible things are both many and one, in the same way you may show that all things in the higher world are mingled with and separated from one another. Socrates seems to say that he was persuaded that all beings in that other world are united with one another, even as are the visible things of this world;[50] but he wants to know how they are united. Their simplicity leads him to doubt whether they can be both unified and differentiated, whereas the

---

[49] A reference to the political scheme of the *Republic*.
[50] Reading τὰ ὁρατά for ἀόριστα of MSS (West.). Cf. below, 1.36-37.

141

composite character of visible things makes it easy to recognize that they have both characteristics. It is not, then, whether they are unified
779 and differentiated, he would say, but how these assertions about them can be made acceptable, as they are about visible things. For there are many things that we know are possible, but want to know how they are so. For instance, we know that the gods foreknow even contingent events, yet we want to know how they do so. Likewise, though we know there is unity and distinctness among the Forms, we seek to know how this is, for it is by searching for it that we will discover the unifying cause of the intelligibles. In fact there must be a single cause of the mixture, like the intelligibles that are the causes of the community between sensible things, since the pervading monads in the latter come from the higher unities.

This, then, is the whole sense of this text. About the variety in this intermingling we have already spoken; the beings of equal rank mingle with one another, the inferior have communion with those above them, the superiors give of themselves to those below, and each of them is differentiated and combined within itself. These links we may call, in philosophical language, interweavings; but the theologians speak of them as "sacred marriages" and of the entities generated in common by them as "offspring." (This is the way Plato proceeds in the *Sophist*, and so also the Socrates of the *Philebus* ([15b]) says he would greatly admire it if anyone could ascend from sensible things to the monads in the Ideas and show that each of them is both one and many.)[51]

> While Socrates was speaking, Pythodorus said he was expecting that Parmenides and Zeno would both of them be annoyed; but, he says, they gave him their close attention and frequently looked at each other and smiled, as if in admiration of Socrates. And this indeed is what Parmenides said when Socrates had finished. (130a)

These words make it plain, to anyone willing to notice it, that Pythodorus is Socrates' inferior in disposition. For, first, he has not understood the tenor of Socrates' remarks, that they were an attempt
780 to elicit these men's wisdom by shifting the discussion to a problem of a higher order; instead he supposes that Socrates' reply was made for the sake of controversy and refutation. Furthermore, he has not yet grasped the greatness of these men, even though he is on most familiar terms with them, but thinks they will react in a boorishly sophistic way and be annoyed by objections. He is moved to this, first, by Zeno's saying, "You think my book was written from motives of ambition,"

---

[51] This last passage seems out of place. A comment on ἀγασθείην of lemma?

and then by Socrates' words, "You are trying to deceive us into thinking that you are saying different things" and "It would be a monstrosity if a man should prove that likeness itself is unlikeness" and "There
is nothing wonderful in showing that they run together in sensible
things." From these and other such remarks he takes Socrates to be
ruder than he should have been and them to be more boorish than befits
the philosophic temper. In any case it is clear that he is their inferior,
that he is disturbed by Socrates' difficulties, and has not grasped either
the purpose of Socrates or the high-minded intentions of his eminent
companions. But he is not lacking in philosophical disposition, nor is
he a mere sophist, since it is he, after all, who reports the conversation,
and he makes no secret of his own reaction, in order to give to the
world a faithful report and a vivid picture of the life of those who took
part in the first conversation. In so doing he reveals to the second audience both his own imperfection and the superabundant wisdom in
the thought of his teachers. First of all he says that they gave their attention to Socrates, recognising the inspired excitement in him and his
drive towards knowledge of the immaterial realm. Then, he says, they
looked at each other, as if they thought Socrates of himself was ex-
781 pounding their own mystical doctrine, for what they had said to one
another in secret they heard Socrates express by virtue of his native genius. And then they smiled, as if in admiration of Socrates. This action
is a symbol of their goodness, for they were not dispirited by Socrates'
objections, but rejoiced at finding a worthy recipient of their doctrines.
And thus Parmenides is moved to address Socrates "when he had finished." In this phrase also Plato has given us a divine symbol. When a
man is anticipating the appearance of the divine, he must exert himself
to stir up the divine spark within him in preparation for participating
in higher beings; but when the illumination from above is at hand he
must be silent, and this is what Socrates does. Having aroused himself
for the reception of these men's insight, having by his words unfolded
and exhibited his fitness for partaking of it, he stops speaking and begins to receive the midwifely instruction that they give him.

"Socrates," he said, "your urge for discussion is worthy of admiration."
(130a)

Parmenides has been moved to speak, as he himself, says, by observing the astuteness and the eagerness of Socrates, who is not content to
remain longer in the sensible world busying himself with the monads
there, but has raised his thought to the intellectual monads themselves,
immaterial and partless, thus completing a kind of circle and working
his way back from progression into plurality to unity itself, ⟨thus imi-

tating)[52] the divine realm, which, following upon the power that generates the secondary orders, turns back the completed term of the
procession to its own beginning. For, as we have said, while Zeno was
782 mainly contending against the multitude, Socrates was withdrawing
from plurality and ascending to the One; as Zeno was uniting plurality,
he himself was fleeing upwards from it and returning to the Parmenidean unity. ⟨Rest⟩[53] is appropriate for beings of a paternal and unitary
nature; to beings of the second order belongs the generative power that
leads to plurality; and to those after them, in the third rank, the power
of reverting and leading back to the abiding cause the things that have
proceeded from it. This, then, is what Socrates has done, as his rank
requires, and Parmenides is therefore moved to converse with him. For
the gifts of the first causes are not conferred upon beings of the third
rank before they have been converted, but after the complete juncture
with them which is brought about through conversion. Moved, then,
as I said, to discuss with Socrates, Parmenides begins with a salutation
which summons him to himself. For *Socrates* is not an empty word
here, but signifies a unification of his soul with Parmenides. For it is
this that is the veritable Socrates, and in addressing him he appears to
be doing nothing less than summoning the young man's soul and uniting it with his own intellect. To the salutation he joins praise, which is
an imparting of additional power; for praise coming from inspired men
renders a well-endowed youth stronger for the reception of greater
goods. Hence in praising his divine impulse towards the intellectual
world he is also endowing him with greater competence. And in the
third place he interrogates him about the constitution of the Ideas,
arousing his mind to activity; for to what else does it belong to inquire
into intelligibles than to Intellect and the life of intelligence? If, then, in
saluting him he gives him unity with himself, and with praise power,
and with his questioning stirs up his intellectual insight, from all this it
is clear once more that it is the first causes, among the gods too, that
bring into play unity, power, and thought among their successors.
And what the question is, we will next see.

[52] Adding ⟨καὶ οὕτω μιμουμένου⟩ before τὰ θεῖα, as seems necessary for the sense
(West.).
[53] Accepting Taylor's supplement.

BOOK III

◙

INTRODUCTION

▣ ▣ ▣

LIKE BOOK II, Book III is comparatively short. It covers something less than a Stephanus page of the text, 130b1–e4, in a little over 50 columns of Cousin's edition, and concerns Parmenides' initial probing of Socrates' belief in Forms. (Parmenides is actually probing the validity of the doctrine of Forms as set out in the *Phaedo*; that Proclus and his predecessors view the doctrine of the *Phaedo* from the perspective of the *Timaeus, Sophist,* and *Philebus* makes for distortions in their exegesis, but we must accept that.) Parmenides asks first whether Socrates believes in Forms separate from particulars, and then tries to make him specify of what things, or sorts of things, he postulates Forms. These are the first two of the traditional set of four questions about Forms ("Are there Forms?" "Of what things are there Forms?" "How do particulars participate in Forms?" and "Where are the Forms situated?") which Proclus discerns as being raised by Parmenides in this part of the dialogue. The last two are dealt with in Book IV of the *Commentary*, as we shall see.

The first lemma, 130b1–6, which runs from 783.10 all the way to 807.23, gives Proclus the opportunity for an extended discussion of the existence of Forms, from both the philosophical and the theological perspectives. He begins, methodically, at 785.4, with a set of six traditional arguments for their existence. The first may be termed the argument from the nature of the cosmos, and, though traditional, it is couched in distinctively Neoplatonic terms. The cosmos is not self-constituted (αὐθυπόστατος), and consequently, not self-activating (αὐτενέργητος). Whatever is self-constituted must be without parts, for the creative element is partless, and if creator and created are the same, the whole must be without parts, which is not the case with the cosmos. Nor is it self-activating, because nothing corporeal is self-activating, and the cosmos has a corporeal element (the fact that it also has a soul does not count, since its soul is not the whole of itself). So the cosmos has a cause outside of itself.

We therefore turn our attention to this cause (786.17ff.). This cause

145

must either create by choice and reasoning, or by its very being. But things that create by choice are intermittent in their creations—they can change their minds—and would thus produce a perishable product, whereas things that produce essentially create eternal products, and the cosmos is one of the latter. Since the power of creating essentially extends lower down the scale of creation than creation by choice and reasoning (e.g. fire heats without deliberation), it follows, according to a principle of Procline metaphysics enunciated most clearly at *ET*, prop. 57, that it is also ontologically prior to it (787.16-19). Therefore the causal principle of the cosmos is something that transcends deliberation.

It is also that primarily which its product is derivatively (*ET*, prop. 18). The cosmos is agreed to be filled with immanent forms, so that its archetypal cause must be a plenum of transcendent Forms, and that is what we wanted to arrive at—the realm of Nous. Forms must therefore exist.

Having established this, he turns to criticise Aristotle's doctrine in *Met.* XII, 10, which grants the universe a final cause, but not an efficient one. But, says Proclus, if the cosmos receives nothing from this Cause that it strives towards, its striving is in vain, whereas if it receives something, then the cause is its efficient cause also; and we cannot suppose that the cosmos strives eternally towards a Good from which it receives nothing.

The subsequent arguments we may deal with more briefly. The second (788.29-790.4) is that from our intuition of perfection. There are no perfect specimens of anything, such as a circle or a straight line, in the physical universe, and yet we conceive of these and have some sort of acquaintance with them. If we can conceive of these entities, how much more so can the Demiurge, in his creation of the world? These he contemplates within himself. This argument derives ultimately from the *Phaedo*, overlayed with centuries of scholasticism, and should be thoroughly familiar to us.

The third argument is that from the order of the universe (790.5-791.28). How could this come about, if it all came together by chance? If this is impossible, then the universe must be given structure by a causal principle and this principle must know itself (otherwise it would be inferior to beings in the universe of its own creation which know themselves), and the objects of its self-knowledge will be the Forms. He ends this argument by enunciating a principle which he also produces elsewhere (cf. *In Alc.* 132.11ff., *In Tim.* III, 25.11ff.), to the effect that the external *energeia* of an entity is only a reflection of its inner *energeia*, and that thus the cosmos as a whole is a reflection of the "all-complete monad of the Forms," and its individual parts of the particular monads (791.22-28).

The fourth argument (791.29-795.8) is based on the regularity of genera and species. The individual man, for instance, may indeed come from seed, but the genus Man must preexist any potentiality such as a seed, and exists eternally. It is Nature as a whole which regulates the production of individuals according to their species, according to the *logoi* inherent in it. But prior to the immanent *logoi* are the transcendent Forms, to which Nature looks, and so we are once again back where we want to be.

The fifth argument (795.9-796.14) puts the case that there must be unmoving causes of the permanent genera and species, the heavenly bodies, and the cosmos itself, and these cannot be bodily, or even in Nature, since Nature is unreasoning, and these causes must be intelligent (since they produce intelligent things). So once again we are brought back to the Forms. At 795.39ff., we find a Procline hierarchy of levels of being, presented as follows:

> All things exist either visibly or invisibly, either inseparable from bodies or separately; and if separate, unmoving in both being and activity, or unmoving in their being but mobile in activity. The genuine unmoving beings, consequently, are those that are unchangeable both in their being and in their activity. Such are the intelligences. Second come those that are unmoving in being but mobile in activity, such as souls. Third are those that are invisible, but inseparable from visible things, like the natural forms (τὰ φυσικά); and last are the visible forms that exist distributively, in sensible objects. Thus far extends the procession of the Forms, and with them the descent comes to an end.

The sixth and final argument (796.14-797.3) is based on logic. "Demonstration," says Proclus, "proceeds from premises that are prior and more authoritative" (he appeals here, with mild irony, to the authority of Aristotle, *An. Post.* II, 5). These premises are universals (τὰ καθόλου), and may be regarded as *causes* of the propositions demonstrated from them. These universals cannot be found in bodies, and so must be ontologically prior to them—a conclusion by no means Aristotelian from Aristotelian doctrines.

He ends this section of the commentary, the philosophical discussion of the existence of Forms, with a sort of coda (797.4-798.26), showing that only a man like Socrates, who has in his own life separated off his soul, and his consciousness of himself as soul, from his bodily concerns, can really understand the Theory of Ideas. He then gives a summary of the six arguments. As Proclus presents them, they bear a notable similarity to Stoic arguments for the existence of God (particularly those from the order and regularity of the universe), but that is perhaps not surprising, since the Stoics were the great formulators of arguments, and many of their reasonings serve a Platonist purpose just as well.

We pass on now (799.23–804.37) to a rather more exotic mode of argument, which Proclus denominates "theological," being based on the doctrines of the theologians (Orpheus), and of the gods themselves (the Chaldaean Oracles). In view of the traditional antithesis of later times between Philosophy and Theology, it is interesting to note the relations between the two in Proclus' system. Theology is given superficially a more honoured place, but in fact the doctrines of the theologians (and of the gods) must concord with those of Plato (as understood by Proclus) in order to be acceptable, though this is tactfully disguised by claiming Plato to be in accord with them.

This section, for the length of which Proclus ends by (almost) apologising ("I have dwelt at length on this subject because of my own interest in it," 805.1–2), is most useful as a survey of his doctrine on the various levels of Form, and what they each contribute to sensible particulars, but it cannot be said to advance our comprehension of the text, so it may, I think, be passed over lightly. At 805.1, however, he turns back to the text, to discuss the Forms which Parmenides mentions; first Likeness, and then Unity and Plurality.

What is Likeness in the intelligible realm, first of all? It is "the power that assimilates all secondary things to the intelligible causes, and brings the two extremes together," performing thus the role taken on by the assimilative order of gods in the henadic realm. It is of interest here that Proclus shows mild embarrassment in explaining that of course we should not be surprised to find the expression *aphomoiōtikē taxis* referring also to Likeness itself, in the noetic realm, as in fact it is later, in Book VII, when we come to discuss *Parm.* 139e7–140b5 (1191.13ff.), since "these names are used both in a general and a particular sense, as referring to henads or to Forms" (805.15–17).

In situating Likeness in the noetic realm, he takes the opportunity to reject three false views, the first and third terminological, the middle one more substantial. First (805.33ff.), he condemns one thinker for terming likeness and unlikeness "slack" (ἀνειμέναι) forms of sameness and otherness. He condemns the same view in Book VII, at 1193.16–24, when the subject of Likeness comes round again. There I suggest Iamblichus as the culprit, on somewhat slender grounds, but there is really no compelling evidence.

The second heresy (and quite a plausible one) is that only Likeness is proper to God, while Unlikeness is characteristic of Matter (806.44ff.).

Plotinus, for one, does refer to Matter as "the place of Unlikeness" at *Enn.* I, 8.13.16, actually quoting the *Politicus* (273d6)—where some secondary authorities (Simplicius, for example) read *ponton* for *topon*, a reading which Proclus appears to be following here—and it could well be he whose interpretation of Plato Proclus is "correcting" here. If so, it will serve as another of the small, but significant, number of places where Proclus criticises his great predecessor.

The third position to be condemned is one which places likeness and unlikeness in the category of relation (σχέσις). They may preside over the relations of secondary entities to primary, says Proclus, but they themselves must be regarded as absolutes, as must all Forms. Who would have claimed this, among Proclus' immediate predecessors, is unclear, but it seems hardly worth his while to criticise ancient Stoics at this point.

The other Forms mentioned in the lemma are Unity and Plurality. These Proclus places at a level below the basic principles of Limit and Unlimitedness, which are manifested primarily in the henadic realm, but also are basic constituents of the intellectual realm. Unity and Plurality perform the same role at the intelligible-and-intellectual level (as we shall learn more fully, he promises [806.40-41], when we come to the Second Hypothesis). Below that again, we will find Same and Other, as structural principles at the intellectual level. Thus Proclus disposes of the possible embarrassment of Parmenides' producing *hen* and *polla* as representative Forms.

In the next lemma (130b7-10), Parmenides adduces the Forms of Justice, Beauty, and Goodness, in that order, and this leads Proclus to a brief discussion of each of them. At each stage, he has to exert his ingenuity to explain why Parmenides mentions just the Forms he does mention and not others, and why in that particular order—problems very much the product of the demands of Neoplatonic exegesis. He begins with a reminder that it is only at the level of Soul, and so of dialectical discourse, that Forms are distinguished from one another. In Intellect they are all together: "So it is that the Forms that we have considered hitherto have been the most general and universal—unity, plurality, likeness, unlikeness, rest, motion—whereas the ones now presented are, in a sense, secondary to them, and in another sense not" (809.19-24). These latter, "ethical" Forms are concerned, not with conferring being on things, but rather with their perfecting (τελείωσις), and in this way they are secondary. But even among these three there is a distinction in the extent of their influence. Justice imposes order on souls, but does not concern itself with bodies as such; Beauty confers lustre on bodies, and the Good gives all things the cohesion and symmetry which allows Beauty to shine out in them (things, it seems, can be informed by the Good without exemplifying Beauty), and thus, by the principle that higher entities extend their influence further down the scale of being than lower ones (cf. *ET*, prop. 57), we observe a hierarchical order—Good, Beauty, Justice.

Proclus here takes the occasion to note that Parmenides does not mention the opposites of these Forms, whereas he has previously talked of Likeness and Unlikeness, One and Many, and Rest and Motion. This is because there *are* no Forms of the opposites to moral or aesthetic qualities. The issue had been a live one in Neoplatonic circles ever since Amelius had asserted the existence of such Forms, and Proclus will, as he promises, return to this question below (829.22ff.).

Finally (811.4ff.), Proclus points out that each of these Forms exist also on a higher level, as a henad. This point is probably brought in to solve a potential embarrassment about the status of Goodness (or the Good), which is plainly, in *Rep.* VI, 506aff., situated at a level above the Forms. This passage, Proclus assures us, refers to the henad of Goodness, and so once again, as in the case of Unity, mentioned by Parmenides previously, there is no contradiction.

The next lemma (130c1-2) brings in the Forms of Man, Fire and Water, about which Socrates is more doubtful. Proclus takes this as an opportunity to set out the whole *seira* or causal chain of a form like Man. Remarkably, he postulates a form of man proper to every level of the physical cosmos—a heavenly, a fiery, an airy and a watery man, all prior to ourselves, the chthonic species (812.10-16), and the same in the case of Horse or Lion. As to what these entities might be, we are given no clue. They are introduced here abruptly and unexpectedly, where one might have expected a series of intelligible, intelligible-intellectual, and intellectual forms. In the case of Fire, one can more easily comprehend a distinction between, at least, heavenly and sublunar fire, but what the watery level of fire would consist in I find it hard to imagine. Perhaps the superior classes of Man and Horse are not individuals at all, but simply transitional levels of Form, mediating between the intelligible Form and the material individual, but this is not made clear. In any case, they cannot be regarded as types of daemon or other superior being, because these entities, on Proclus' theory, already inhabit, as such, the spheres of fire, air and water.

At any rate, such Forms as those of natural genera and species are more particular than those mentioned previously, and Proclus wisely declines to go into their exact status in the realm of Forms, as being a subject "surpassing human intelligence" (813.19-20). To do so would invite, as it has in the past, refutation and ridicule.

There follows a short, transitional lemma (130c3-4), in which Proclus first praises Plato's dramatic portrayal of Socrates' gradual development from certainty, through doubt, to (negative) certainty, and secondly reminds us that, although all Forms are together in Intellect, they do vary in dignity (even as a statesman holds in his mind simultaneously conceptions of officials of very varying rank!). This leads up to the second main excursus of the book, provoked by the lemma 130c5-d2, on the old question in Platonism, "Of what things are there Ideas?" This continues for most of the rest of the book (815.14-833.23) and is of considerable importance as a statement of Neoplatonic doctrine. For the Middle Platonic doctrine on this subject one may turn to Albinus' *Didaskalikos*, ch. 9 (163.20ff. Hermann). There, after giving Xenocrates' definition of an Idea as an "eternal paradigm of natural things," Albinus goes on to list those things of which "most Platonists" would deny that there were Ideas—artificial objects (such as "shield" or "lyre"), unnatural conditions (fever, cholera), individuals (Socrates, Plato), trivial or worthless (εὐτελῆ) things (dirt, chaff), or relative concepts ("greater," "prevailing" [ὑπερέχων]). Against this background, we may examine Proclus' account.

He begins by posing eleven questions which one may ask about the range of things of which they are Forms. They represent a certain elaboration of Albinus' list, but we do not know how comprehensive, or representative of Middle Platonism as a whole that really was. I will run through these questions briefly. What we will discover, I think, is that developed Neoplatonic metaphysics puts the original Theory of Ideas (if we can speak of such a thing!) under considerable strain.

1. *Is there a Form of Intellect*—or, as Proclus puts it, a paradigm of *noera ousia* in the Demiurge? To postulate a Form of Intellect in Intellect, among all the other Forms, which are themselves intellects, would seem eminently superfluous, if not absurd, but the question has to be faced by a consistent Platonist. Proclus' argument (816.1ff.) is that anything that has a paradigm must be a copy, and to call intellectual being a copy of anything would be absurd, since being a copy involves partial not-being (*Soph.* 240b), and an element of unlikeness to its model, and neither of these conditions holds for the individual intellect. The intellect has a cause, then, but no paradigmatic Form. This argument may not be convincing, but it is interesting as showing a Neoplatonist attempt to avoid an awkward anomaly in the Theory of Ideas.

2. *Is there a Form of Soul* (817.3-820.37)? This Proclus finds more complicated, since there is agreed to be a monad of Soul in the Demiurge, but we have the problems (a) that there are many grades of soul in the universe, and (b) that individual divine souls are immortal, and should have Forms of their own (the question of Forms of individuals

will be taken up later, as Question 8). There is also the awkward point that Soul might be described as an "image" of Intellect, even as Time is an image of Eternity.

It is divine souls that Proclus deals with first. The problem there is that Neoplatonic metaphysics, partly based on the "sowing" of the souls described in *Timaeus* 41de, demands a separate paradigmatic soul associated at least with each of the heavenly bodies (or rather with their intellectual archetypes), each with a "chain" of souls dependent upon it (as envisaged in the *Phaedrus* myth). These must have some relation to the basic monad of Soul, but they cannot just be subsumed into it. He concludes (819.17ff.): "We must therefore posit an order among the Ideas: there is an Idea of Soul in general; yet each soul, being monadic, is constituted by its specific formula (*logos*). . . . And necessarily it must be Intellect that produces the Idea that produces each of these souls; hence an intelligible Idea of each must be present in the producer." There are in fact, then, Forms of these divine souls. (For a more comprehensive statement of Proclus' theory of souls, see props. 184–211 of *ET*.)

Irrational souls also have an intelligible paradigm (819.30ff.). This apparently paradoxical claim was made already by Plotinus, in *Enn*. VI, 7.9, where he points out that the Form of an irrational entity need not itself be irrational—the Form of Horse, for example, will be an intellect. If we are to try and identify this paradigm more closely, Proclus suggests (820.1ff.) that we might consider either the archetypal faculty of sense-perception present in the Demiurge (another remarkable entity proposed by Plotinus in *Enn*. VI, 7), or perhaps the archetype of Nature, the "fount" of all natures—the use of the adjective *pēgaios* in this connexion suggests Chaldaean theologising, and specifically the Chaldaean Hecate (cf. *Or. Chald.* fr.54 DP). That irrational souls are immortal is a doctrine attributed even to some Middle Platonists (Numenius, Harpocration of Argos, cf. Olymp. 'B' *In Phaed.* 124.13ff. Norvin; Hermeias, *In Phaedr.* 102.10ff. Couvreur), but whether they postulated any sort of noetic archetype of irrational soul is quite uncertain.

3. This curious doctrine on irrational soul leads to his third query (820.38-821.33), *whether there is a Form of Nature*. Proclus comes down in favour of this, relying both on Chaldaean doctrine and on *Timaeus* 41e, where the Demiurge exhibits to souls "the nature of the universe," which Proclus understands to be the paradigm of Nature in his mind (cf. his comments at *In Tim.* III, 270.16ff. on this passage). He ends with what he declares to be a personal opinion (inadvertently, perhaps, revealing how much of his doctrine is *not* personal but derived from his

predecessors, especially Syrianus), to the effect that the Form of Nature contains all those souls which partake in eternity, while irrational souls, or "natures," are comprehended in the god who presides over the creation of body, the sublunary Demiurge—or Hephaestus, in mythological terms.

4. Whatever the merit of this personal contribution, it leads him to his next problem, *is there a Form of Body?* (821.34-822.38). Again, the body-creating (σωματουργός) god is brought in, to contain the intellectual and formal causes of bodies. It becomes apparent, though, that what Proclus is primarily concerned with are the *heavenly* bodies, e.g. the body of the Sun. If *our* bodies have a paradigmatic cause, it would be only at many removes.

5. Fifthly, *is there a Form of Matter?* Even here, Proclus is unwilling absolutely to give up on the notion, bizarre as it might seem. Of course, matter as such is the antithesis of Form, but in the case of the "matter" of the heavenly bodies, one *might* postulate a paradigm of that in the mind of the Demiurge.

6. *Are there Forms of animals and plants* (823.16-824.12)? This is straightforward enough, since *Timaeus* 30d guarantees that the Essential Living Being contains the concepts of all living beings, and it was always part of the Platonic tradition that there were Forms of all natural objects, though there were inevitably difficulties about the relations between genera and species.

7. The next question, however, is a very vexed one, that concerning *Forms of individuals* (824.13-825.35). The general Platonic view on this, expressed, as we have seen, by Albinus, was that there were not, and with this position Proclus is in agreement. The notion of Forms of individuals, however, had tempted Plotinus, who wrote a treatise on the subject (*Enn.* V, 7), though what his final view on the question was is a matter of controversy into which we do not need to go now (see n. 28 below). The causes of individuals, says Proclus, are not intelligible paradigms, but rather causes within the cosmos, such as differences of season or region.

8. A similar situation obtains with *parts of animals*, such as finger or eye, which is the eighth question. It would be absurd, says Proclus, to postulate Forms of these, but there are causes of them in Nature, and even at the level of Soul (826.13ff.). This again relates to the interesting theorising of Plotinus, at the beginning of *Enn.* VI, 7, where he raises

the question whether souls receive their lower faculties (including the power to shape parts of the body) on entry into the body, or whether they possess them originally. Either way there are difficulties, but Plotinus prefers the latter alternative, and so does Proclus. Once again, though, he appends a "personal" view, revealing his theurgic interests (826.21ff.): "And if I may give my own opinion, we ought not to dismiss the view that daemons are separate causes of the parts, as is shown by the invocations of those who are assigned to the finger, eye, and heart, although gods are the causes of the wholes that contain them." The *Papyri Magicae Graecae* are full of such invocations, together with the sacred names of the daemons concerned.

9. We move next to *accidents* (συμβεβηκότα), or qualities 826.27ff.). Are there Forms of these? In answer, Proclus makes a distinction between qualities which are "perfective and completive" (τελειωτικὰ καὶ συμπληρωτικά) of their substances, such as likeness, beauty, health, or virtue, and those that are not, such as whiteness, blackness, or sweetness. Of the former there are Forms; the latter are present in bodies by virtue of *logoi* emanating from Nature. This is not a distinction between primary and secondary qualities in the accepted sense, but something more peculiar. The difference between beauty, say, and whiteness is perhaps that beauty concerns the whole essence of a thing, while whiteness only concerns one aspect of it. But where, one might ask, would such qualities as roundness or softness fit in? There is a Form of Circularity, but not, I think, of Softness; yet both might be seen as "completive and perfective" of a peach. But we must not get into an argument with Proclus.

10. Next, we turn to *artificial objects* (827.26ff.). Traditionally, as we have seen, Forms of these were not admitted, but Proclus cannot ignore certain troublesome Platonic passages, such as *Republic* X, 497b, with its Idea of Bed, and the Idea of Shuttle in the *Cratylus*. He disposes of the Ideal Bed, however, by suggesting that the "form" of bed is simply the reason-principle in the mind of the artisan, the overall skill of whom is conferred upon him by the Demiurge, who in that sense could be spoken of as having an archetype of bed in his mind. There are in fact, then, no Forms of artificial objects. However, Proclus does wish to make a distinction (828.20ff.) between arts and sciences which are "anagogic," leading us to a vision of reality, and those which are not. Of the former, such as arithmetic or astronomy (in their higher forms, as described in *Rep.* VII), there are Forms; of the lower, purely material or recreational arts, there are not.

11. We come, lastly, to the vexed question of *Ideas of Evils* (829.22ff.), a matter which had been raised by Amelius, as we have seen, and which was still to some extent a live issue. Amelius' argument, it seems (see n. 31 below), was that if there were not, then God could have no knowledge of evils. Proclus refers us at the outset to a special essay he has written on the subject (preserved only in a Latin translation), *On the Existence of Evils*, but he repeats the arguments here. His basic point is that, if one accepts (as all Platonists did) that Forms themselves are good, then we are in an insoluble difficulty. Are Ideas of evils good? If so, how can their manifestations be evil? On the other hand, if they were evil, then the Demiurge would have evil in him as well as good, and would be the cause of evils as well as goods, which would conflict with the well-known testimony of the *Timaeus* (29a–e) that the Demiurge is good, and that he wishes the cosmos to be as like himself as possible. The argument reported by Asclepius as being that of Amelius Proclus does not address here at all. He views evils as having only a derivative existence (παρυφιστάμενα, 829.26), being perversions of Forms or reason-principles caused by Matter.

In his summary (831.25ff.), Proclus specifies three basic attributes of Forms—Goodness, Essentiality, Eternity, deriving respectively from the One (the First Cause), the One Being, and Aeon. All paradigmatic Forms derive their being from these three. Having asserted this, he adds a sort of coda about "things of no account," such as hair, mud, and dirt, since they were mentioned in the text. Hair is a part, not a whole, so it is disqualified by that alone; mud is an indeterminate mixture of elements, so it does not count as a definite thing; and dirt is simply a by-product of other processes.

Apparently, some witty or malignant person (832.12ff.) had attempted to argue that there was a Form of Dirt, as follows: *katharsis* (cleansing or purification) is a virtue, and there are Forms of virtues; but *katharsis* is cleansing of *dirt*; therefore there must be a Form of Dirt. The basis of this argument, such as it is, must be that cleansing is a relative term, and if there is a paradigm of it in the noetic world, then there must be a paradigmatic correlative of it for it to cleanse. The argument is patently sophistic, but Proclus is sufficiently bothered by it to devote half a page to its refutation, though he seems rather to miss the point. He accepts that there is a Form of Purification, but denies that that implies a Form of Dirt. However, Light and Intellect, the counter-examples he produces, are not relative to anything in the way that Purification is. He would have done better, one would think, to deny that Purification, in the sense in which it is a Form, is a relative term.

Since this curious argument is brought into relation with Amelius' argument about Forms of Evils, through the argument that Intellect, if it knows good, must know evil also, one might suppose that Amelius is the author of this argument also, but the thoroughly frivolous and anti-Platonic tendency of it seems characteristic rather of a sophist like Lucian.

Proclus recalls himself from this major excursus to the text (833.19ff.), by making a point which he will maintain throughout the exegesis of the first part of the dialogue, that all the difficulties raised by Parmenides are "maieutic," have a positive purpose, that of deepening Socrates' understanding of dialectic and of the Theory of Ideas, and not simply of refuting him.

The next eleven lines of text (130d3-e4) Proclus dismisses in two lemmata and a little over three Cousin columns. His chief concern here is that Parmenides might seem to be suggesting (as indeed, on an impartial view, he *does*) that when Socrates becomes more mature, he will see that there must be Forms of all things to which we attach a common name, even mud and hair, and that one should not import normative criteria into the Theory of Ideas. That he could be saying this, though, Proclus cannot accept. What he must be saying, he feels (835.4ff.), is that we must not think that such things as mud or hair are devoid of *any* higher causes. All things, even Matter itself, depend, at some remove, on the One, but the causes of trivial, material things will be, not intelligible Forms directly, but rather reason-principles in Nature (φυσικοὶ λόγοι). Alternatively, or in addition, Parmenides is also looking to the causal principle above the Forms, the One Being, the creative power of which, being superior to the particular Forms, extends further than they do, down to the creation, by means of *physikoi logoi*, of such things of hair and mud. All things have their cause in the One Being.

And on that note we then turn to Book IV, which takes us through Parmenides' ever more troublesome objections to the "classical" Theory of Ideas, which, on Proclus' interpretation, has the purpose of providing us with a panorama of the full range of levels of form, and a proper discerning of their characteristics.

COMMENTARY

▢ ▢ ▢

783   *"Tell me. Do you yourself make this distinction you mention and separate*
       the Forms themselves from the things that participate in them? And do you
       think that there is a Likeness itself separate from the likeness which we
       have, and a One and a Many and all the other things in Zeno's argument
       that you have just been listening to?" "I think so," said Socrates. (130b)

Parmenides questions him first about the reality of the Ideas,
whether he thinks there are things that are separate from the many and
are their causes, and whether he had come upon the reality of these objects himself, or had heard it from someone else. This is not an idle
question that he is asking; he wants to know, above all, whether Socrates merely has an opinion about them "drawn from other sources"
(*Phaedr.* 235c) or whether it is his own intelligence that has aroused him
to this insight and enabled him to see the transcendent monads above
the immanent ones, the unparticipated prior to those that are participated. For the disciples of Parmenides held some such opinion, and it
was likely that this doctrine had come to Socrates' attention and that he
speaks as he does from accepting it as a dogma, and not as a result of
his own inquiry. This, then, and nothing else is the purpose of Parmenides' question, to arouse Socrates' intuitive reason and prepare it
for the sight of the intelligibles; he is appealing to the intellect in him,
784 not to his opinions. For it is visions of Intellect that Parmenides is going
to reveal in the discourse that will follow. And we must infer from
these assurances (of Socrates) that he had the notion, not only of objects
of definition, but also of separable Ideas, and had not been led to posit
Ideas, as Aristotle said,[1] from his great concern with definitions, but
that a genuinely divine instinct led him to them also, since he was only
a young man when he was clearly roused to see these Ideas by his own
efforts. This is just what Parmenides wants to know about him.

Enough about the language of the text. Let us now turn our attention
to its substance. There are four problems involved in discussions about
the Ideas. First, are there Ideas? For what could anyone say about them

[1] *Met.* A, 6.987b3-4; M, 4.1078b27-30.

157

unless their existence has been previously agreed upon? Second, of what things are there Ideas and of what things not? (There are many differences of opinion on this point also.) Third, what sort of realities are Ideas, and what is their peculiar property? And fourth, how do things in this world participate in them and what is the manner of this participation? The three last-mentioned problems are brought up in the dialogue and receive considerable attention; but the first is not developed, doubtless because Plato left it for us to explore. Since we must reach agreement on this before we take up the other questions, let us 785 examine it on our own and see what arguments can establish the hypothesis of Ideas and demonstrate that they exist to those who want to learn it.

1. Let us begin with the following point. Is this visible cosmos—by cosmos I mean the corporeal cosmos as such—self-constituted, ⟨or must we suppose that it depends upon a cause outside itself?⟩[2] This is the first question to be examined. Now if this cosmos is self-constituted, many absurd consequences result. For whatever is self-constituted must be without parts, since everything that creates and everything that generates is altogether bodiless. Even bodies create by means of bodiless powers, fire by heat, and snow by cold. And if whatever creates must be bodiless, and in a self-constituted thing it is the same thing that creates and is created, that generates and is generated, the self-constituted must be altogether without parts. But the cosmos is not of that sort, for every body is divisible in every way; thus the cosmos is not self-constituted.

Again, from another point of view, whatever is self-constituted is self-activating; *a fortiori* whatever generates itself is naturally able to act upon itself, since to make and to generate are to act; but this cosmos is not self-moving, since it is corporeal. Certainly no bodily thing is formed by nature to move and be moved simultaneously as a whole, any more than it can heat itself and be heated by itself at the same time as a whole, since when being heated it is not yet hot, and when it heats 786 it has heat; thus the same thing will be, and will not be, hot. Hence just as it is impossible that anything bodily can change itself, so also it is impossible that it should move in any other way. In general every form of bodily movement resembles rather an effect, whereas self-moving activity is bodiless and partless; so that if the cosmos is corporeal, it cannot be self-moving, and if not self-moving not self-constituted.

[2] Accepting Cousin's filling in of the lacuna here. On the doctrine of self-constituted entities (αὐθυπόστατα), see *ET*, props. 40-51; Gersh, *ΚΙΝΗΣΙΣ ΑΚΙΝΗΤΟΣ*, App. II, pp. 128-135; and John Whittaker, "The Historical Background of Proclus' Doctrine of the *Authupostata*," in *De Iamblique à Proclus*, Entretiens Fondation Hardt XXI, 1975.

And if it is not self-constituted, clearly it has its being from some other cause. For whatever is not self-constituted is such in one of two ways, either as superior to a cause, or as inferior. The sort which is superior to a cause has a successor which is such as to be self-constituted; the inferior type is altogether dependent upon another cause which is self-constituted.[3] Consequently, the cosmos must be dependent upon another and higher cause.

Let it, then, be taken as demonstrated that the cosmos depends upon some higher cause. Now does this cause act by choice and reasoning, or does it produce the universe by its very being? If it acts by deliberate choice, its action will be unstable and variable, now in this way and now in that, and the cosmos then will be perishable; for what comes into being from a cause that acts differently at different times is changeable and perishable. But if the cosmos is eternal (a point which is not under inquiry at present), what creates it must create by its very being. In fact, everything that acts by deliberate choice necessarily has some creative activity that it exercises by its very being. Our soul, for example, does many things by deliberate choice, but nevertheless gives life to the body by its very being; while its substratum is serviceable, it necessarily lives its own life, even without the soul exercising a choice.[4] For if the life of our body were dependent upon our deliberate choice, the living thing might easily be dissolved as a result of any turn of events, the soul on such occasions deciding not to cooperate with the body. Not everything that creates by its very being has another power of creating by deliberate choice. For example, fire heats by its presence only and does no action by deliberate choice; nor does snow, nor any other bodily thing *qua* body. If, then, the power of creating by its very being extends more widely than creation by deliberate choice, clearly it comes from some higher and more august cause.[5] And this is to be expected; for the creative activity of those beings that make what they do by their very being is effortless, and we must concede that effortlessness belongs primarily to the divine, since we also live most easily and with least effort when our life is god-like and in the path of virtue. If, then, the cause of the All is one that creates by its very being, and what creates by its very being does so from its own essence, this creator is primarily what its product is derivatively, and gives to it in a lesser degree the character that it has eminently; just as fire both gives heat to something else and is itself hot, and the soul gives life and has life. You will find this statement true of all things that create by their very being.

787

---

[3] The unexpressed minor premise: the cosmos obviously has no self-constituted successor.

[4] Reading καὶ μὴ προελομένης (sc. τῆς ψυχῆς). Latin: *et non electionaliter*.

[5] A general principle of Procline metaphysics. Cf. *ET*, prop. 57.

788 Therefore the cause that makes the All by its very being is primarily what the cosmos is derivatively. If, then, the cosmos is a plenum of Forms of all sorts, these forms will exist also primarily in the cause of the cosmos. It is the same cause that gives substance to sun and moon and man and horse and in general all the Forms in the universe. These, therefore, are in an eminent degree in the cause of the universe, another Sun besides the one we see, and another Man, and likewise for each of the Forms. Consequently, the Forms exist prior to sensible things and are their demiurgic causes, preexisting, according to the argument just given, in the single cause of the entire cosmos.

If someone should say[6] that the cosmos indeed has a cause, not, however, an efficient but a final cause, and that all things are thus related to that cause, he is right in making the good preside as cause over the whole. But let him say whether the cosmos receives anything from that good or receives nothing from it that corresponds to its desire. If it gets nothing, its striving would be in vain for a being that never enjoys at all the object of its desire. But if it receives something from it, that cause is surely and eminently the good which it bestows upon the cosmos, particularly if it not only gives good to the cosmos but also does so in virtue of its essence. And if this is true, it will be what establishes the universe, since it will first be the cause of its being if it is to give it its good in virtue of its essence. And so we arrive at the same doctrine as before; that cause will be not only a final, but also an efficient, cause of the All.

2. Secondly, let us consider the argument which asserts that things in the world of appearance are both equal and unequal, like and unlike, 789 and that in general nothing that is perceptible is at all capable of being truly designated. What sort of equality can there be in these things that are mixed with inequality? Or what sort of genuine likeness in things filled with unlikeness? Where is there real beauty in things whose substratum is ugly? And where is the good in things characterised by potentiality and imperfection? None of these objects of perception is truly what it is called; so that even if you consider the heavenly bodies, though they are more exact than enmattered things, you will not find perfect precision in them. Neither circle, nor centre, nor pole can exist precisely in extended things. How could these realities, whose nature exists in the partless and unextended, be perfectly present in what is extended and divisible? But our soul can conceive and generate things far purer and more precise than sensible appearances; it corrects the sensible circle and says by how much it falls short of the exact circle; and

---

[6] Aristotle *Met.* Λ 10.1075a10ff.

clearly this is because it sees something else, a form more beautiful and more perfect than the sensible object. For if it were not in touch with, nor looking at, something purer, could it say that this object is not really beautiful, or those things not perfectly equal? These very assertions show that it sees what is completely beautiful and perfectly equal. Then if our individual soul can conceive something more beautiful and more exact than the things that appear to our senses, and can see in itself, by bringing forth its ideas, an exact sphere and circle, and perfect beauty and equality, can't the soul of the whole cosmos conceive and contemplate what is more beautiful than sensible appearances? If not, how can the one be the demiurge of the whole and the other of the part? For the greater power is productive of more perfect effects, and a movement more immaterial can envisage superior conceptions. Therefore the maker of the cosmos can certainly engender and conceive far superior, more accurate, and more perfect forms than sense appearances. Where, then, does he engender and contemplate them? Obviously in himself; for he looks towards himself and, in thus contemplating and engendering, he simultaneously brings to birth within 790 himself, and hypostasises, forms more immaterial and more perfect than phenomenal things.

3. And thirdly, if there is no cause of the universe, but all things come about spontaneously, how is it that they are all ordered with respect to one another? Why are there always beings, and how do events in nature happen in accordance with general laws, when things that arise by accident occur only rarely? And if there is a single cause that orders all things, and it does not know itself, must there not be something other prior to it which knows itself and is the cause of that thing's being a cause? If it does not know itself, it will be inferior to the beings in the universe that know themselves, and at the same time superior, which is impossible. But if it knows itself—that is, knows itself as a cause—then it knows also the things of which it is the cause, and will therefore also contain the things which it knows. Then, if Intellect is the cause, it will also regulate all things with respect to one another; for the demiurge of the world is one, and the whole is multifarious, not all its parts possessing the same dignity and rank. Who is it that measures out their ranks, if not he who established them all? Who is it that has set each thing in its proper station, as was required—in this place the sun, in that the moon, in another the earth, and in still another the mighty heaven—if not he who produced them? Who is it that has brought about a single harmonious ordering of them all, if not he who gave each of them its existence and nature? If, then, he put them all in order and determined its rank for each, he was evidently not ignorant

161

of order and disorder in things, for otherwise his action would be that of an irrational being and not of a divine cause, characteristic of necessity, not of intelligent forethought. And if in thinking himself he knows himself, and in knowing himself knows also the essence that he possesses—that he is an immovable cause and the goal of desire for all things—he knows also those beings for which he is an object of desire, for his being an object of desire is not accidental, but his very essence.

791 Either, then, he will be ignorant of his very essence, or in knowing this he will also know that he is an object of desire, and in consequence will know that all things are relative to each other, to know one of them with precision and the other vaguely is not characteristic of scientific knowledge, still less of intellection. Knowing determinately the things that desire him, he knows their causes, since he is looking at himself and not at the things dependent on him. And if his knowledge of the causes of all things is not to be irrelevant, he necessarily determines the order of all things in accordance with these causes; thus he is the unmoving cause of all things, as determining their order by his very being. Is it because he is going to create all things that he thinks them, or does he create them all because he thinks them? But if he thinks all things because he is going to create them, his inner activity—that which is directed toward himself—will be inferior to that which goes outside himself; it will be for the sake of something other than himself that he knows beings, that is, he will know them for the sake of something inferior to him. And if this is absurd, he is the maker of all things by his knowledge of himself. And if this is true, he will make external things to resemble what he has in himself. Such is the natural order of things: the activity that goes forth is dependent upon its inner source,[7] the whole cosmos upon the all-complete monad of the Ideas, and the parts of the universe here upon the separate monads.

4. Fourthly, in addition to these arguments, let us consider another. We say that man comes from man, and from each species its like. How and in what way does this occur? For you cannot say that their generation is a matter of chance. Neither nature nor God does anything in vain, and in general all such production comes about for the most part, whereas the accidental occurs rarely. So if it is not by chance that man is born, whence does he come? You will of course say that he comes

792 from seed. The grain of corn, when it is sown, produces the ear, and the fig seed the fig tree, and so man comes from human seed. But I did not ask whence comes a particular man; what comes from the seed is not man unqualified, but an individual man, whereas man exists al-

---

[7] For other formulations of this principle, cf. *In Alc.* 132.11ff.; *In Tim.* III, 25.11-16. Cf. also C. Rutten, "La doctrine des deux actes dans la philosophie de Plotin," *Revue Philosophique* 146 (1956): 100-106.

ways; and this seed itself comes from man. Granted then that man comes from seed; still the seed has its reason-principles potentially, not actually; for being body, it cannot have the reason-principles undividedly and actually. What, then, is it which has the reason-principles in actuality? For everywhere actuality precedes potentiality, and the sperm, being undeveloped, requires something else that will develop it. You will say it is the nature of the mother that does this; this nature is what actualizes the reason-principles and moulds the creature coming to birth. It is not, of course, the visible form of the mother that makes the babe in the womb, but Nature, which is a bodiless power and a source of motion, as we say. If, then, it is Nature that changes the reason-principles of the sperm from potentiality to the fully formed actuality, it is Nature that has the reason-principles in actuality; therefore, although without reason or imagination, it is nevertheless the cause of the reason-principles in natural things. Shall we say, then, that the nature of man contains the seminal reasons of human beings, but the nature of the lion not those of the lion—i.e. the head, the mane, the feet, and all the other parts of a lion? How does it happen that when a tooth is lost another grows, if there is no inner capacity of making teeth? And how does their nature at the same time make bone and flesh and each of the other parts of the animal? Nature could not by itself fashion the same replacement over such a variety of organic parts, especially since it is essentially devoid of reason. But shall we say that Nature has the reason-principles of animals and not of plants? But no, there too their orderly generation and growth shows that plants also are developed by assigned causes. Then the same argument shows that their natures contain in advance the reason-principles that are manifest later. And finally let us ascend to that single nature that is in the earth, which generates alike "All things that breathe or creep upon the earth" (Hom. *Od.* 18.131). Must we not say that this nature contains in advance the reason-principles of the creatures that grow upon it? Or how explain the cases that we see of generation coming about other than from like, such as the creatures produced by putrefaction? What is the source of the generation in these cases? And how is it that in the same region sometimes certain plants grow and at other times others, without human design? Clearly because Nature as a whole has in herself the reason-principles and capacities for creating them all. Why say more? For as we mount upwards in this way we shall find the nature of every stage contains the living beings that are in that rank, and the nature in the moon the species of all these ranks, for from there the whole of generation is guided, and in her the transcendent monad of embodied natures is preestablished. And so making our progress upwards through the spheres we shall come finally to the nature of the whole; and we

793

163

shall ask about it whether it possesses or does not possess the Ideas, and we shall compel our respondent to admit that the reason-principles, i.e. the creative and moving powers, of all things are contained in it. For all things that are perfected through inferior powers are established more firmly and perfectly by more universal beings. Being, then, the mother of all things, the Nature of the All would include the reason-principles of all things. Otherwise it would be absurd that art, which imitates the reason-principles in nature, should proceed in accordance with reason-

794 principles and Nature herself be without reason-principles and internal measures. But if Nature has the reason-principles, there must be some other cause prior to it that contains the Ideas. For Nature, when she enters into bodies, acts as you might imagine a carpenter descending into his pieces of wood, hollowing them out inside, straightening, drilling, and shaping them. Such is the way of Nature, infusing herself into bodies, dwelling in their solid masses, and breathing her movement and her reason-principles into them from inside. A cause like this was necessary for things that are moved from outside themselves, a cause which had to be without reason lest it separate itself from the bodies that continually require an indwelling cause, but also had to possess their reason-principles so that it could guard them within their own bounds and move them all appropriately. Nature then belongs to other things, not to itself, because it has been rendered non-rational in accordance with its rank. The most genuine cause must then be transcendent over the things that are made. The more the maker transcends his product, the purer and more perfect is what he makes; and in short if Nature is devoid of reason, it needs a cause to guide it. There is therefore something prior to Nature which contains the reason-principles upon which all things in the cosmos must depend. To entrust the All to non-rational reason-principles would, I fear, be really irrational and not correct. It is then necessary to put the reason-principles in some other being that will know what is within him and whose action will be knowing as well as creative. It would be absurd that we should know the All and the causes of what comes to be, and the maker himself be ignorant both of himself and of the things he makes. A knowledge, then, greater than our own will reside in the cause of the cosmos,

795 inasmuch as it not only knows but gives reality to all things, whereas we only know them. And if the demiurgic cause of the All knows all things but looks to the outside, again he will be ignorant of himself and be inferior to a particular soul. But if it is to himself that he looks, all the Ideas are in him, intellectual and knowing, not outside in phenomena only.

5. Fifthly, we must consider the following argument. It is said that all things produced by an unmoving cause are unmoving and un-

changeable, but those that come about from a variable cause are, on the contrary, mobile and changeable, being sometimes in one state and sometimes in another. And if this is true, all things that are eternal in essence and unchangeable are produced by an unmoving cause. For if they come from a mobile cause, they will be changeable, which is impossible. All unmoving things, therefore, come from an unmoving cause, that is, if they come into being at all. Then shall we not say that Man, in the unqualified sense (I mean the Idea itself), and Horse (the Idea itself) come from a cause, seeing that the whole cosmos depends upon a cause? Upon what kind of cause, then? An unmoving or a mobile one? If from a mobile one, the human species will some time disappear; for everything established by a mobile cause is naturally liable to disappear. I will ask the same questions about the sun, moon, and the other stars: do these also come to be from an unmoving or a mobile cause? If their cause is mobile, their existence is also subject to change. But if it is from an unmoving cause that these and all the other forms that are eternal in the cosmos are derived, where are their unmoving causes? Clearly not in bodies, for it is the nature of every physical body to move. In Nature, then, as their immediate cause? But Nature is without reason, and genuine causes must be intelligent and divine. Consequently, the unmoving causes of these forms are in Intellect primarily, secondarily in souls, thirdly in Nature, and last of all in bodies.

796 All things exist either visibly, or invisibly, either inseparable from bodies or separately; and if separate, unmoving in both being and activity, or unmoving in their being but mobile in activity. The genuinely unmoving beings, consequently, are those that are unchangeable both in their being and in their activity. Such are the intelligences; second come those that are unmoving in being but mobile in activity, such as souls; third are those that are invisible, but inseparable from visible things, like the natural forms; and last are the visible forms that exist distributively in sensible objects. Thus far extends the procession of the Ideas, and with them their descent comes to an end.

6. Sixthly, let us look at the existence of the Ideas in another way, taking our departure from the nature of demonstration itself. It is generally agreed that demonstration proceeds from premises that are prior and more authoritative, and demonstration has been thought by some persons to be so august and noble a thing[8] that it has been assumed to be superior even to the method of division. Let us, then, grant this generally accepted doctrine that a demonstrated conclusion depends upon causes that are by nature more authoritative. Now the premises of demonstration are universals, for every demonstration proceeds from

---

[8] Aristotle *An. Post.* II, 5.91b12ff.

them; these, then, are causes for those things demonstrated from them.[9] When the astronomer says that the circles in the heavens bisect one another because every greatest circle bisects its like, is he demonstrating or not? And yet he has based his assertion upon a universal. But where shall we find these causes of the bisection of circles in the heavens, causes more universal than the circles? They will not be found in bodies, but must be in an incorporeal substance, for everything bodily is particular. It is necessary, therefore, that Ideas have a prior existence to the phenomena and are causes of their being, as being more universal and authoritative than they. From this also it is clear, as we said before, that since science requires us to posit universals as more substantial and more of the nature of causes than particulars, the Ideas are prior in being, and it is from them, being separate, that particulars derive their reality.

797

And consider, on its own account, if you will, how Socrates—or anyone else who has applied himself to the Ideas—arrived at the conception of their reality. A man who has already reverted to Intellect, who has observed the distinction between his soul and his bodily life and has separated himself from his composite nature, and who sees nothing strange in assuming that the bodily substrate is one thing, the participated form in this substrate another thing, and still another the transcendent and imparticipable Form—this is a man who will become excited about the hypothesis of these divine monads. The common man, who has confused his own life with the life of his composite nature, cannot distinguish between the participated form and what is unparticipated; for anyone who has seen this distinction should himself become, as far as possible, the kind of person who has risen above his body because he has seen that separable part of himself. And the man of superior character, who has seen the distinction between these moments in himself, investigates it universally and conceives of the transcendent and immaterial monads prior to all participated Forms. And not with respect to Forms only does he proceed thus, but he advances in the same way when he considers Motion. He sees that all this body by its own nature is not self-moving but needs some outside source of motion if it is to move, and that the primary and most authoritative source resides in that which moves all things. For that possesses the motion of a moving agent, but body the motion of a thing that is moved, and the latter is an image of the previous motion in that first mover. For that motion is perfect, since it is actuality; the motion in body is imperfect actualisation, and the imperfect gets its reality and

---

[9] *Ibid.* I, 11.77a5ff., where, however, Aristotle denies that Forms are required.

perfection from the perfect. And again when we consider Knowledge,
798 we see that knowledge of bodies is the lowest form, whether you call
it perception or imagination. All such knowledge is devoid of truth and
fails to touch the reality of things; it sees nothing general or universal,
but everything in particular shapes and forms. More perfect is the
knowledge that is without shape or form, immaterial, existing in and
of itself, and of this sense-perception is an image, an imperfect form of
knowledge, not springing from itself but conditioned by other things.
If then in the cases of Motion, of Knowledge, and of our own lives we
find the threefold distinction between the participant, the participated,
and the imparticipable, the same principle holds also for all the species
of things; matter is one thing, the form-in-matter another, and another
the separate Form. You cannot think that God and Nature make the
imperfect things, beings whose nature is shadowy and dependent on
something other than themselves, and failed to produce perfect things,
completely real and independent. Rather he established these far in advance of the others, and from them are derived the more obscure realities, the forms that are participated and immanent in Matter. It is
through such thoughts that Socrates, and all others like him, were led
to posit Ideas and to distinguish between forms participated in by particular things and others that exist in and for themselves. This separateness is what most of all belongs to Ideas.

To summarise the reasons that made them adopt the hypothesis of
Ideas, let us say that all visible things, both heavenly and sublunary,
exist either by chance or by a cause. But that it should be by chance is
impossible, for in that case superiors and inferiors will be classed together—intellect, reason-principle, and cause along with things derived from causes—and thus products will be superior to principles.
Besides, as Aristotle says,[10] essential causes must be prior to accidental
ones, for the accidental cause is a by-product of essential causes—so
that what comes about causally would be prior to the accidental if even
the divinest parts of the visible world have come about by accident.
799 And if there are causes of all things, they will be either many and unconnected, or one. But if they are many, we shall be unable to say what
makes the universe one; and yet the one is superior to the many, and
the whole to the parts. But if there is one cause of the unitary universe
with respect to which all things are ordered, it will be absurd if this
cause is without reason; for again there will be something superior to
the universal cause among its effects, viz. whatever being acts according to reason and knowledge, which will be within the All and a part
of it and be the kind of thing it is from an irrational cause. But if this

[10] *Met.* K, 8.1064b15ff.

cause has reason and knows itself, it obviously knows itself as the cause of all things; otherwise, being ignorant of this, it would be ignorant of its own nature. And if it knows that it is by its own essence the cause of the All, it knows also the effect of which it is the cause. For what knows the cause determinately, necessarily knows also the effect. Therefore it knows also determinately the effect which it causes. Consequently it knows both the All and everything of which the All consists and of which it is also the cause. And if this is true, it is by looking to itself and knowing itself that it knows what comes after it. Hence it is by immaterial reason-principles and forms that it knows the reason-principles in the cosmos and the Ideas of which the All consists; and the All is in it as in a cause separate from Matter.

This is the reasoning that satisfied Zeno and those who posited the existence of Ideas. Nor is it the case that while these men supposed Ideas to exist in this way, the experts in divine matters thought differently; the theologians also have been a part of this tradition. Orpheus tells us[11] that all things came to be in Zeus, after the swallowing of

800 Phanes, because, although the causes of all things in the cosmos appeared primarily and in a unified form in him (sc. Phanes), they appear secondarily and in a distinct form in the Demiurge. The sun, the moon, the heaven itself, the elements, and Eros the unifier—all came into being as a unity "mixed together in the belly of Zeus" (*Orph.* fr. 167b.7 Kern). And he was not satisfied to tell us this only; he gives the list of the demiurgic forms through which sensible things have received the order and arrangement that they have. And the Gods have thought it well to reveal the truth about these matters to men, and have told us what is the unique source of the Ideas in which the full company of them is primordially established, and how they go forth and assimilate to the Father of the cosmos all things that are in it, both the wholes and the parts. Considering the interest of our hearers in this doctrine, we may profitably recall the very words of the *Chaldaean Oracles* (fr. 37 Des Places):

> The Intellect of the Father whirred, conceiving with his
>   unwearying will
> Ideas of every form; and they leapt out in flight from this single
>   source
> For this was the Father's counsel and achievement.
> But they were divided by the fire of intelligence
> and distributed among other intelligent beings. For their lord had
>   placed

---

[11] Cf. *In Tim.* I, 312.26ff., and 324.14ff., where the Orphic passage is quoted at greater length.

Before this multiform cosmos an eternal intelligible model;
And the cosmos strove modestly to follow its traces,
And appeared in the form it has and graced with all sorts of
    Ideas.
Of these there was one source, but as they burst forth
    innumerable others were broken off and scattered
Through the bodies of the cosmos, swarming like bees
About the mighty hollows of the world,
801   And whirling about in various directions—
These intelligent Ideas, issued from the paternal source,
Laying hold on the mighty bloom of fire.
At the prime moment of unsleeping time
This primary and self-sufficient source of the Father
Has spouted forth these primally-generative Ideas.

In these words the gods have clearly revealed where the Ideas have their foundation, in what god their single source is contained, how their plurality proceeds from this source, and how the cosmos is constituted in accordance with them; and also that they are moving agents in all the cosmic systems, all intelligent in essence and exceedingly diverse in their properties.

We could see much else if we went deeper into the interpretation of these divine thoughts. But for the present, it is enough to understand that the gods bear witness to Plato's doctrines in calling Ideas these intelligent causes and in saying that the cosmos is moulded in accordance with them. So if arguments persuade us to the hypothesis of Ideas, if wise men—Plato, Pythagoras, Orpheus—are agreed about them, and if the gods clearly confirm their opinions, then we ought to regard as of little worth the arguments of Sophists, which refute themselves and have nothing sound or scientific in them. For the gods have clearly said that they are ideas of the Father (for their residence is in the Father's thoughts), that they go forth for the making of the cosmos (for the "launching forth" is their procession), that they have all sorts of forms as containing the causes of all particular things, that from the primal
802 Ideas others have gone forth, like swarms of bees, to their allotted roles in the framing of the cosmos, and that they generate the second order of beings. So then, the *Timaeus* places the single primary productive cause of all the Ideas among the intelligibles (for that is the location of the Living Being Itself, as we have shown elsewhere)[12] and the *Oracles* say the source of the Ideas preexists in the Demiurge. These two accounts do not disagree with one another, as some might think, for it is

[12] Cf. *In Tim.* I, 418.30ff. From *ibid.* 324.19-22, it can be seen that this is the doctrine of Syrianus.

not the same thing to seek the single universal cause of the cosmic ideas and to contemplate the primary manifestation of the whole series of them. But we should refer the content of the one class to the Demiurge, and of the others to the intelligibles in the divine hierarchy, from which both the Demiurge and all the orders of being are filled with ideal substance. And this is why, I think, the *Oracles* speak of the Ideas as being "launched" from their intelligent source and being "scattered through" the bodies in the cosmos and distributed "in various directions," implying that this source contains the cause of the cosmic structures, and through it are formed all the compounds that arise in the cosmos by the will of the Demiurge. But the Forms in the Living Being Itself, which are established within the bounds of the intelligible, are not said by Plato to move or to "leap" in among bodies, but to give being to all things by their existence alone. If, then, to create through activity and motion is secondary to the creation that is prior to action and motion, it is clear that what is established intelligibly and immovably in the Living Being Itself has a higher rank than the demiurgic ideas. And the Demiurge is form-giving in two ways, both by virtue of the source in himself, and by virtue of the intelligible[13] Ideas; for among the latter are the universal causes of all things, i.e. the four monads.[14] From that intelligible realm they move downwards through all the divine orders to the last, so that even the lowest—the sensible images—have some likeness to them, in some cases relatively clear, and in others more obscure.

Anyone of us who is capable of following the divine processions can see, even if he examines the perceptible forms of enmattered things, that every perceptible form has received properties from all the ranks of being. Self-motion itself and eternity are present in sensible forms from no other source than the primary Ideas. These are what is eternal in the primary sense, and they pass on their properties to the things in the next and each succeeding rank. Again, each form exists as a plurality, but is constituted in accordance with its own peculiar number and filled with the numbers appropriate to it, and hence the forms are variously derived, in a way unknown to us, and ineffable, from different divine ranks. This feature comes from the summit of the intelligibles-and-intellectuals, from the forms established there in a secret and ineffable manner. Likewise the power of unifying separate things and bounding an infinity of generated beings within common limits comes from the ranks of the unifying deities and the forms there. And the gen-

---

[13] Emending νοερὰς to νοητάς. The "source in himself" is the intellectual Ideas, with which these must be contrasted.

[14] *Tim.* 39e-40a. Cf. *PT* III, 27, pp. 96-97 S-W. The four monads are in the intelligible realm.

eral capacity of perfecting imperfect nature and developing the aptitudes of their subjects into actuality, by shaping the shapeless and correcting the imperfect, demonstrably comes from no other source than
the divinity who perfects and from the forms that are manifested with
it. Again, to the extent that each form strives to converge upon itself
and comprehend its parts as a unity, to that extent it carries the likeness
of the summit of the intellectual realm and of the undivided constitu-
804 tion of the forms established at that rank of being. But the more it goes
forth in company with life and subsists through motion and is presented as a motionless image in moving things, the more does it participate in the chain of life-generation and express the powers of the life-
generating forms. But in so far as it shapes matter and is filled with the
technical skill that pervades nature herself, exhibiting refinement of
workmanship and rational construction, in this way and by so much
does it carry the mark of the demiurgic ideas. And in assimilating sensible things to intelligibles and distinguishing their essences by differences related to reason-principles, it is clear that it resembles the assimilative orders of Forms, from which comes the particular processions
of the cosmic forms that envelop sensible things in outward appearances of the intelligibles. And if each form, moreover, penetrates many
things, even if it be a material form and bounds their plurality by its
special shape, is it not through this power related to that rank of the
gods who exercise free and independent authority over the allotments
in the cosmos and draw up to themselves large portions of the divine
allotments in the All? So then, as we proceed downwards from the intelligible Ideas to the lowest orders of being, we shall observe the continuity of the whole series and can distinguish intelligently what pecu-
liarities sensible things have drawn from each rank. For all secondary
things must participate in the beings that precede them, and thus each
of them, according to the rank assigned it, enjoys each of its predecessors. This is in perfect accord with the divine processions themselves;
for the sequence of the secondaries parallels the particular organization
in each of the divine series, whether intelligible, intellectual, or supra-
cosmic, and again whether functioning as cohesive, or generative, or
creative, or in accord with some other divine attribute.

805   I have dwelt at length on this subject because of my own interest in
it. But now we must turn to the text of Plato and recall his teachings
with respect to Likeness, since the text reminds us at this very point
that this is the power that assimilates all secondary things to the intelligible causes and brings the two terms together. For the movement of
procession must always revert back to its own causes. Among the gods
themselves the Assimilative Order accomplishes this by turning the
plurality of the divine henads back to their unitary causes, and Likeness

has the same function among the forms. We must not be surprised that the same words are used to indicate both forms and divine orders, for these names are used both in a general and a particular sense, as referring to henads or to forms. Since it is the property of Likeness to make the Father's productions resemble him, it is reasonable that Unlikeness be yoked congenitally with it, so that the products may be discriminated as images of patterns. For things that are only alike are not images, since without unlikeness a likeness is an original and not a copy; nor are things that are only unlike, for the word *images* itself indicates that its form resembles something else. We need, then, both Likeness and Unlikeness in order that the image may be a likeness or something other. For this reason these have a middle rank among the Ideas, just as the Assimilative Order of the gods is intermediary between the unitary gods and those that have gone forth into their numerous channels. For the factor that assimilates is a bridge between that to which there is likeness and that which is likened to it. If someone should call Likeness a loose form of Identity and Unlikeness a loose form of Difference, we reject that statement by saying that Ideas are not constituted by more and less (for the principle of the more-and-less characterises the indeterminateness of the forms in matter), but each of them is a measure and has its own essence and determinate power. Besides, some char-
806 acters belong to essences *qua* essences, other are qualities and powers connected with them, just as others are quantities, as equal and unequal are said to be. And if some say that Likeness comes from God and Unlikeness from Matter, we will not accept this doctrine either.[15] Even if there really is a "sea of unlikeness," (*Pol.* 273d) yet Plato is addressing himself to the form of Unlikeness here, i.e. the paradigm of the unlikeness in this world, so that they would be speaking of some other kind of unlikeness, not that which is given us here. Nor do we agree with those who put Likeness and Unlikeness in the category of relation (for the demiurgic forms are not constituted by bare relations), unless they mean that these forms give to secondary things their relation to primary beings and to copies their relation to their patterns, thus confirming their status as assimilative. For the most distinctive character of this pair is that they both join and distinguish pluralities from their proper monads, and copies from their particular patterns.

We have said earlier what unity and plurality are, but let us now repeat more clearly that for Plato there are two principles of being after the One,[16] viz. the Limit and the Unlimited, (*Phil.* 23c); and every Intellect, both intelligible and intellectual, assimilative, absolute and en-

[15] Plotinus may be the culprit here. Cf. *Enn.* I,8.13.15ff.
[16] For the background to the doctrine set out here, cf. *PT* III, 6.

cosmic, universal and particular, is composed of them. Since, then, the demiurgic Intellect is mixed, possessing in itself both the Limit and the Unlimited, because of this it could be called both one and many—the essential one being its limit and its plurality the essential indefiniteness of its contents (form in bodies also is ⟨mixed⟩,[17] its oneness being its essential limit, and its plurality the indeterminateness in it). Intellect is therefore one and many, since it too is derived from the Limit and the Unlimited. And as those principles, I mean the Limit and the Unlimited, are primarily in the intelligible realm, so the One and the Many in

807 the intelligible-and-intellectual realm are primarily in the number there, as the Second Hypothesis will fully teach us. One is the limit of number, and the Many is number, Limit and the Unlimited being seen both in plurality and in the continuous, and thus being more comprehensive than the One and the Many; for these exist in number only, since number is nothing other than One-together-with-Many. The Many without the One is indefinite plurality, the One without the Many is only the beginning of number; when separated, the One is not yet number, and the Many are no longer number. As, then, the Limit and the Unlimited are primarily in the intelligible realm, so the One and the Many belong to the next rank, to the beings both intelligible and intellectual, and the Same and the Other to the third rank, that of the intellectual realm. One and Many come before them, for they are absolutely what they are, whereas these are relative to something. What is other must be other than something, and what is the same must be the same as something; but every one is by itself a unity, and every many is what it is numbered as. Everything that is numbered is by itself such as it is, or rather so much as it is, and we do not say that it is numbered with respect to something else. Now that we have analyzed these terms sufficiently, let us turn our attention to what follows in Plato.

"And of things like these," said Parmenides, "is there a form of Justice in and by itself, and of Beauty and Goodness and all such things?" "Yes," said Socrates. (130b)

808   The divine and demiurgic Intellect contains pluralities in unity, divisible things undivided and distinguishables undiscriminated. Soul is what first separates these contents that exist previously in perfect unity in that Intellect—not our soul only, but the divine Soul too. For Soul has not been granted thoughts that are established on the level of eternity, but she aims at grasping the full actuality of Intellect; and in her striving for this perfection and for the form of comprehension that belongs to that one and simple being she circles around Intellect as in a

---

[17] Adding μικτόν, as seems required by the sense (as against Cousin's μεριστόν).

dance, and as she shifts her attention from point to point divides the undivided mass of the Ideas, looking separately at the Idea of Beauty, and separately at the Idea of Justice, and separately at each of the others, thinking of them individually and not all together. For, to put it briefly, Soul is third in rank from the One and is naturally actualised in this way. For the One is one only and precedes thought, Intellect thinks all Ideas as one, and Soul sees them all one by one. So division is the peculiar function of Soul, since she lacks the power of thinking all things simultaneously in unity and has been allotted the thinking of them all separately—all, because she imitates Intellect, and separately, for this is her peculiar property; for the power to divine and define appears first in Soul.

This is why the theologians[18] say that at the dismemberment of Dionysus his intellect was preserved undivided through the foresight of Athena and that his soul was the first to be divided, and certainly the division into seven is proper primarily to Soul. It is therefore appropriate that Soul should have the function of division and of seeing things discursively. It is no wonder, then, that whereas the divine Forms exist primordially together and unified in the demiurgic intellect, our soul attacks them separately, at one time contemplating the first and most universal Forms, at another time those that have a middle station, and again the most particular and, so to speak, the most atomic. For when we have said that the divine Soul divides their undivided mass by successive touchings and contacts, what could we say of the particular soul but that *a fortiori* she also apprehends separately the Ideas that are all together in and with each other? And so it is no wonder, as I said, that dialectic questions and answers approach different Forms at different times, and that each inquiry is, as it were, a contact with one of their ranks; for spoken discourse breaks apart the single unitary thought and traverses in temporal succession the parts of the unified conceptions in the mind; and so it is that the Forms that we have considered hitherto have been the most general and universal—unity, plurality, likeness, unlikeness, rest, motion—whereas the ones now presented are, in a sense, secondary to them, and in another sense not. Just as we say virtue is in a way subordinate to the soul and in another way superior to it—authoritative in that its function is to improve the soul, and inferior in that it is lodged in the soul as a part of it—so also Goodness, Beauty, and Justice are in one sense superior, and in another sense inferior to the existence-giving Forms. In so far as those others are the most universal, these too partake of them, but the higher ones

809

---

[18] *Orphic.* fr. 25, Kern. Cf. *In Tim.* II, 145.18ff = fr. 210 Kern. It is actually his heart which was said to have been preserved, but Proclus interprets that as signifying the intellect.

174

give existence to things by their being, and as such are the primary ar-
tificers of the being of things here, whereas these later Forms are concerned with their perfecting, Justice reaching down to souls and regulating and improving them, Beauty giving lustre even to bodies (for
810 Beauty, as Socrates says in the *Phaedrus* [250d], has been given the role
of being the most visible and enticing of all the Forms, whereas there is
no light of Justice in its likenesses here below), and the Good perfects
all things according to the specific essence of each. It is because of the
symmetry it introduces between the form and the matter (there is symmetry whenever the naturally better dominates the worse) that beauty
shines out in bodies, and the good is manifest through the perfection
that appears in every product of the forms when it has its natural completion. Hence in this triad the Good comes first, Beauty second, and
Justice third. These forms Plato no longer lists with their contraries—
good-evil, beautiful-ugly, just-unjust—clearly indicating by this, I
think, that he altogether rejects Ideas of the contraries. For why does he
bring in the former ones with their opposites—like-unlike, one-many,
rest-motion—but these by themselves without their opposites, if he is
not recognising Ideas of the good ones, even though they have contraries, but rejecting ideal causes of the evil ones?

This question, however, we must examine later (cf. 829.22ff.). But
that there are Forms of these concepts—I mean the just, the beautiful,
the good and, as he says, all other such things, i.e. temperance, courage, wisdom—you can convince yourself if you reflect that every virtue, and every perfection in accordance with virtue, makes us like the
divine, and the more fully we possess it, the nearer we are to the life of
intelligence. If, then, beauty and goodness and each of the virtues make
us more like Intellect, Intellect must certainly possess their intellectual
paradigms. For whenever we speak of something as like a superior,
then the superior possesses in a higher degree that quality by which the
inferior, when he acquires it, becomes his like. That is, if one thing is
like another, either it partakes of a common form with it, whence the
811 proverb "like to like" (cf. *Parm.* 132d), or it possesses in an inferior degree what the other has eminently, and is called like as being an image
of it. We must then conclude that the Ideas of the virtues and of Beauty
and Good exist in Intellect prior to Soul.

But again, we must look at each of these from two different points
of view, first of all, in one way as a divine henad, and in another as an
intellectual Idea, for these do not belong to the same rank of being. The
Just, for example, exists otherwise among the Forms than among the
gods. In the former case it is one Idea among others, distinct from all
of them; it is a character in something other than itself, and the intellection it carries it imparts only as far as souls. But among the gods, Dikē

175

is all in a manner peculiar to itself, and its providence goes forth to the lowest grades of being, beginning with the primary intellectual deities, for there is where it first becomes manifest; whereas the Just is an Idea in the intellect of the Demiurge, as we said. Likewise the Idea of Beauty is a different thing from the henad of divine Beauty. The latter acts upon the gods *qua* gods, beginning with the highest intelligible being; but Beauty, on the other hand, is one of the Ideas and its relations are with them. As for the Good, do we need to say that essential Good is one thing and another is the Good beyond Being? For this has been clearly said by the ancients (e.g. *Rep.* VI, 506aff.). Hence we must not confuse the doctrine about Forms with those about the gods, nor regard the organisation of the particular Forms as identical with that of the divine henads, but study the gods in themselves, distinct from essences and multiplicity.

"*And a form of Man separate from us and from all beings like us—a separate form of Man, and of Fire, and of Water?*" (130c)

The Forms that exist everlastingly in the universe must have unchanging causes preexisting, for changelessness belongs to a thing through the character of eternity in its cause; so that the eternal causes of man 812 *qua* man and of each atomic species of animal or plant are in the intellectual world. They all come from that source, but their procession does not immediately produce these generated material things. For it is not according to divine law that intellectual and immaterial beings should generate the multitude of senseless enmattered individuals whose character is ever changing, since procession takes place through likeness, and so before things in every way different from their cause, there arise beings that are close to it and more clearly like it. From Man Himself, then, comes a heavenly man, then a fiery man, an airy man, a watery man, and last of all this earthy man. All this series that comes to be as the Form proceeds through successive downward steps is dependent upon the intelligible henad that we have called Man Himself. And similarly there is another series dependent upon the Horse Itself, the Lion Itself, and another for each species of animal and plant. Before species that are eternal only in kind the unchangeable causes generate beings that are eternal as to number; likewise before the species embodied in matter and mixed with ugliness, they produce those dominated by beauty and symmetry. Thus also intellectual fire, water, earth, and air do not at once give existence to the enmattered kinds of them in this world, but before them to the heavenly and immaterial elements. This is why in another work[19] we have said that the heaven is composed of

[19] The reference is probably to the *Timaeus Commentary*. Cf. *In Tim.* II, 44-45.

the four elements, not however of the most material, but of the more immaterial kinds; these are the first manifestations of the Ideas. Just as every intellect comprehends all things, so in general each cosmic sphere contains everything in its own fashion, in the fashion of the sun here, in the fashion of the moon elsewhere, in another sphere after the way of fire, and in an earthy way on the earth. We may infer that this is why Plato, after saying "and a form of Man separate from us" adds "and from all beings like us"; for we must set apart the intellectual Idea from all things in the cosmos, whether it be the heavenly or the fiery or the earthy man that we may be speaking of. The whole number of men in this world, descended through many processions and ranks, depends upon that intellectual henad that we have called Man Himself, since that is the primary cause and source of the series of men. And just as this is the source of the series of men, there is another source and henad for fire everywhere, and another for all the water in the cosmos.

813

It is evident that these monads are more particular than those discussed earlier, and clear also that of all the forms mentioned in this text the most particular and, so to speak, atomic is the monad of man; thus the argument, as it proceeded, has made its way from the more general to the more specific. But what each of these is, it is dangerous to construct in those cases. Indeed, of all who have said anything about these questions, some have been refuted by their successors, and the others have added nothing of importance to what their predecessors have said. Do not wonder that in general we confine our remarks to the properties of the more universal Forms, touching but little on the more particular ones in our inquiries. For to go into the minute and peculiar differences among them all is something that surpasses human intelligence, and it is more feasible for us to study what applies everywhere or to the greatest number of things.

"I have often been in doubt, Parmenides," said Socrates, "whether or not we should say the same of them as of the others." (130c)

Let us state, on the literary level, as some commentators have suggested, that the author out of consideration for Socrates has imagined, before his denial, this state of doubt between full denial and positive assent. For it would be strange, and in no way characteristic of a careful thinker, for him to bring in denials immediately after his previous affirmations. So before he denies Ideas of any objects, he first says he is puzzled about these that have just been put before him. Consequently, here again Socrates meets the issue fully, assenting, doubting, or denying, according to the measure of the reality of the things under consideration. He confidently asserts that there are Ideas of all things that appear both among the immaterial gods and in bodies and in all visible things—such as likeness and unlikeness, motion and rest, unity and plurality, justice, beauty, and goodness. But about the characters he sees in material and perishable things, constantly fluctuating from one state to another—about these he is in doubt. On the one hand he looks at their perishableness and questions whether they are products of a form, for forms are causes of eternal things; and on the other hand he observes their stability as to species and wonders whether the Ideas may not be the cause of this stability in them. But of the most unseemly and trivial members of this second class—such as hair, mud, and dirt—of these he denies that there is any ideal cause at all. Once more, then, we see that Socrates' assent, hesitation, and denial are fully based on reason.

But you may ask why, since the Forms are originally united with one another, there should be such a difference among the things that have proceeded from them as to raise the problem whether or not to posit Forms of some things, when all of them have their Forms and intelligent causes? Is not the answer that there is a difference among them even up there? For not all things there are of equal rank. Things that are completely unified in their causes are pluralized and separated as they proceed from them. The difference among them when they are inside their primal causes is no measure of the difference that appears when they are outside, but the relations of superiority and inferiority are more numerous and greater. For an analogy, the mind of the statesman contains notions of all the officers under him—the general, the orator, the taxiarch, or the public executioner; and there is little difference between these notions when compared with one another, for they are all alive and subsist together at the same time in the stateman's mind; but outside there is the utmost difference between the general and the executioner. Inside there were only species of officials, and their substratum, so to speak, was indivisible. So it is, then, that although all Ideas are contemporaneous[20] in the divine mind, in the cosmos we see very great contrast among them—between mortal and immortal beings, between lifeless and living things, between irrational and rational—although all of them up there are eternal, living, and thinking. It happens, moreover, that in some cases our sense-perception can see the primary members of their series, in other cases only the last, and because of this finds the greatest difference here between Ideas. We do not see the first participant of the Idea "Man," but the last; and comparing this with the best examples of divine beings in the sense-world, we naturally perceive as very great the difference between them.

But enough on this point. Plato's text goes on as follows:

[20] Taylor's suggestion ὁμοχρόων ("of one hue") for MS ὁμοχρόνων is ingenious, but not absolutely necessary. Proclus may be using this "temporal" expression metaphorically.

"And of things that might seem ridiculous, Socrates, such as hair, mud, dirt, or some other unseemly or trivial thing, are you in doubt whether or not we ought to say there is an Idea of each of these, separate and other than the things that we handle?" (130cd)

What things have Ideas and what things do not? We ought to consider this question first, so as to have a general theory of Ideas from which to follow Plato's thought in this passage. And it is no slight matter to deal with these hackneyed topics, as they have been called (*Phileb.* 14d), especially if one does it in the following way: (1) Is there a paradigm of intelligent being in the Demiurge? (2) Are there Ideas of Soul, and are they one or many? Are there paradigms of irrational life, and if so, how? (3) And of the Natures, and how many? (4) and of Body *qua* Body, and if so, is it one or many? (5) And of Matter? And if so, is it of the matter of perishable things only, or of the heavenly bodies as well? (6) If there are Ideas of animals, are they generic only or do they include the atomic species? And of plants likewise? (7) Are there Ideas of individuals along with these? (8) Or Ideas of the parts of animals, such as the eye, the finger, or the like? (9) And Ideas of attributes, or of some and not of others? (10) Are there also Ideas of the products of art and of the arts themselves? (11) And finally, Ideas of evil things? If we take these questions in turn, we will be in possession of the complete teaching on this subject, from which we shall be enabled also to discover Plato's thought.

816   Necessarily, then, there are Ideas of natural beings only, or Ideas of things contrary to these as well, and if of natural beings only, either of eternals only or also of things not eternal; and if of eternals only, either of substances only or of unsubstantial beings also; and if of substances, of wholes alone or also of their parts; and if of wholes, either of simple beings or also of compounds derived from them.

Having made these distinctions, let us take up each of the questions in order.

1. First, then, about intelligent being, let us say that the existence of more than one intellect derived from a single intelligence does not require us to posit a paradigm for them, as I have said somewhere above. For whatever has a paradigm must be a copy; and to call an intelligent being a copy is the extreme of absurdity. Every copy is a likeness of what it copies, and the Eleatic Stranger in *Sophist* (240b) explicitly says that a likeness is "not really not real." If then all intelligent being belongs to what is really real, it would not do to call it either a copy or a likeness. Besides, every intelligent nature is indivisible, and procession from it occurs through identity; hence its derivations are inseparable from their origin; they are in part what the whole is entirely. But a

179

copy, on the other hand, must always have unlikeness mixed with likeness, and indeed through it[21] be known (as a copy) and revert through
its likeness back to its paradigm. Consequently, there is no relation of
likeness to paradigm among the intelligent beings, but that of cause and
its products. This is why the theologians,[22] while positing many
"sources" in the demiurgic Intellect, make one of those many the
source of the Ideas. Consequently, not everything that proceeds from
the Demiurge comes forth through the causation of Ideas; only those
that proceed comparatively further and contain divisible being are pro-
817 duced by the causation of Ideas. The other sources are generators of intellectual and divine realities. For intellectual being, then, in its entirety, we must not suppose a paradigm of Intellect, but only a unitary
and divine cause.

2. This question, then, we have summarily disposed of. The next
question to be considered is whether there are efficient causes of souls
among the Ideas, and whether they are one or many.[23] That there is a
monad of Soul in the Demiurge that contains in prior unity the whole
number of souls is evident both from the nature of things and from
what Plato has taught us. For if Soul is the first thing to be generated
and the first thing to be divided, necessarily the indivisible Idea must
precede the divisions and the eternal everything whatever that was
generated. And if soul is to intellect as time is to eternity, as we said
above, and time is an image of eternity, then soul must be a likeness of
intellect. And if reality contains not only life but soul, as Socrates declares in the *Philebus* (30a), we must suppose that Soul is the paradigmatic cause of the plurality of souls that proceed from Intellect and that
it contains in unity their order and number.

Whether these demiurgic souls are caused by one Idea only or by
many is the next point to consider. Since they are all immortal, each of
them must have its paradigm, but on the other hand it is impossible
that those that have come forth should be the same in number as those
that remain. To say explicitly what I think, we must posit for all the
divine souls other distinct causes after the single Idea and say that from
these causes souls proceed in the well-ordered downward procession

[21] Reading δι' αὐτῆς for αὐτῆς of MSS (West.).

[22] Perhaps a combination of *Or. Chald.* fr. 37 DP, where there is talk of one "source"
from which all the Ideas come, with a passage like fr. 49, where there is mention of many
"sources." Cf. also Psellus, *Exeg.* 1136a, p. 173 DP, *Expos.* 1152a, p. 189 DP, and *Hypot.*
12, p. 199 DP, where the πηγὴ τῶν ἰδεῶν is mentioned as belonging to the demiurgic order.

[23] A question discussed by Plotinus in *Enn.* V, 9.13 and VI, 7.2-7. Proclus' fullest discussion of the theory of Soul is to be found in the last section of *ET* (props. 184-211).

from the divine through the daemonic souls, the process[24] ending with
the particular souls. What I mean is this. In the divine Intellect there is
a paradigmatic monad from which all the multitude of souls emerge
and which contains in unitary form the measure that determines the
number of them. Attached to this monad, and congenital with it, is a
second number, discrete, which provides the paradigms of the divine
818 souls, for each of them is a single idea and a special paradigm from
which proceeds the divine soul first and after it the plurality of souls
that belong in its series. Thus from the paradigm of the soul of Helios
the divine soul of the sun first proceeds and, after it, all the angelic souls
in his train, then the souls of daemons associated with the sun, and
lastly the particular souls in this procession. All of them are generated
on the model of a single Idea, and so exist as orderly arrays of parts to
wholes and of followers to leaders, while the one intelligent cause fur-
nishes unity and continuity to their procession. Similarly, the paradigm of the soul of Selene first generates the divine soul belonging to
the moon, then the angelic, the daemonic, and the participated souls;
and the intellectual monad contains the whole number of them. Likewise, the Idea of the soul of Chthōn first produces the divine soul of
earth, and then all the souls—angelic, daemonic, and particular—that
belong to this monad. And all of them are produced by one Idea when
the succession by descent is maintained. The same is true of all other
divine souls; each has its determinate Idea, and the ranks of the angelic,
daemonic, and particular souls that follow it partake of that single Idea.
And just as the single monad of the paradigmatic soul-monads in the
intellectual world produces the single world-soul, so do the many monads produce the many souls that follow them. The supreme monad
embraces in unity the whole number of them, but they contain the
measures of their own series, one measure that determines the series of
Helios, another that of Kronos, and another that of some other series.
These cosmic souls, which are the first manifestations of the measures
established on high, extend this one form down to the lowest souls in
their respective series. Consequently, the intellect in the Demiurge is
the primal possessor of the Ideas of the divine souls, and these souls are
the first which he generates. Each of them is both a unity and a plural-
819 ity, for each contains the entire plurality of the souls subordinate to it,
by virtue of being their cause. Thus each soul exists in accordance with
its specific paradigm, and above them all are the paradigms of the divine souls, among which are contained the Ideas of the more particular
souls.

This is why, I think, when Timaeus has set up the divine souls and

[24] Reading ὑφέσεως for φύσεως of MSS (West.).

is then generating the particular ones, he calls the genera he uses to complete them the "remainders" of the higher ones (*Tim.* 39e, 41d)[25] and why when he has formed them he distributes them one to each star (41de), for the demiurgic intellect makes their distribution in accordance with the Ideas and the numbers in himself. Why did he attach some to the sun, others to the moon, and others to some other star? Is it not because he had generated some after the Idea of the sun, others according to the Idea of the moon? And although all of them are generated in accordance with and in respect to a single Idea, they do not all participate in the Idea in the same way. We must therefore posit an order among the Ideas: there is an Idea of Soul in general; yet each soul, being monadic, is constituted by its specific formula (for one soul does not differ from another by reason of matter; therefore either by nothing at all, or by virtue of its form). And necessarily it must be Intellect that produces the Form that produces each of these souls; hence, an intelligible Form of each must be present in the producer. This is what the theologians have in mind when they say that the universal causes of souls—i.e. those that produce entire series—are different from the particular causes, from which comes their distinction according to species and their division into the so-called atomic souls.

This is what we have to say about these souls. And of irrational souls it is also clear that there is an intelligible paradigm.[26] For there are immortals among them, as among other genera of being. I call irrational all the secondary vital forces that are parcelled out among bodies. From what source is their eternity derived? It must be some unchangeable and intellectual cause, and how this is we must now say. Once more we must posit as prior to them a single monad and a single Idea. Call 820 this whatever you please, a "spring-like" nature, or a nature endowed with perception. For from their cognitive properties you could say that these irrational souls are derived from the primary faculty of sense-perception in the Demiurge, and from their appetition, that they come from the sovereign Nature that is the prime source of the many natures. From these causes, in any case, come the multitude of souls in this world—eternal, indeed, but naturally devoid of reason, and distributed among the everlasting vehicles in accordance with the number that is preestablished in them, viz. the measure contained in the Idea. For every eternal plurality is bounded, and for every bounded plurality there must previously exist the principle that bounds and numbers them. And not only this; they proceed also from the rational souls, or rather from the paradigms in them. This is why they are dependent on

---

[25] The word Plato uses at 41d is ὑπόλοιπα, rather than Proclus' κατάλοιπα (which he used, however, at 39e). Cf. the exegesis of this passage at *In Tim.* III, 244.12ff. (esp. 257.5-29.)

[26] Cf. Plotinus' discussion of this question at *Enn.* VI, 7.9.

rational souls here—that is, because their number has been generated from the one measure in that higher world, together with the many species of rational souls. But the divine souls, and all that are pure, preserve their reason uncorrupted here, whereas the individual souls that make use of irrational souls have a life intertwined with theirs, and sometimes the better member of a pair prevails, but often is subservient to the inferior. From these eternal irrational souls the souls that are mortal are descended, but even these survive as species because of the intelligible paradigm in them, though they perish as individuals because they have been brought into being by the "younger gods" (*Tim.* 42e). The irrational souls above them, however, have been generated from the higher souls, and their making has intertwined them with the monads of the entire series to which they severally belong. There is a certain analogy, then, between the relation of perishable souls to the divine causes from which they are derived in this world and the relation of the immortal souls to their ideal causes in that higher world.

821 3. In the third place, we must see in what sense we need to posit a paradigm for Nature. For surely, as Plato says (130c2), we are not going to suppose an Idea of fire and water and motion and deny an intellectual cause of Nature, which is their cause. The theologians have supposed the source of Nature to be the zoogonic goddess: "On the back of the goddess infinite nature is suspended" (*Or. Chald.* fr. 54 DP).

But we will follow Plato and say that her Idea in the mind of the Demiurge is what established the entire vehicle of nature, which Timaeus says the Demiurge exhibited to souls, revealing to them the nature of the whole and proclaiming the laws of destiny (*Tim.* 41e); for his mind contains this nature entire and all the encompassing foreordained laws by which he ordered and divided the universe. In short, if it is the Demiurge who speaks, he is turning the souls towards himself, and this means he is showing that the nature of the whole and its foreordained laws exist in him. In him, therefore, is the one Idea. The souls which make use of bodies bring into being the natures into which they have breathed life; and these, in turn, being everlasting, produce the particular souls that live in time. And if I may give my own opinion, I consider that the paradigm of the natures unified in the demiurgic intellect includes the roll of the souls that have been accorded eternity, but only the god who generates the Idea of Body, whoever the theologians may say he is,[27] contains specific causes of the everlasting na-

---

[27] At *In Tim.* II, 70.6-31 this god is identified as Hephaestus, and *Or. Chald.* fr. 68 (quoted at II, 50.25-27) is alluded to in this connection. For Hephaestus as a secondary demiurge, cf. *In Tim.* I, 142.14ff.

tures, for it is this god that directly imparts existence and the fire of life to the order of nature and the plurality of the natures.

4. Now that we have come to bodies in our account, shall we not say
822 that for them also there is a single universal cause in the primal Demiurge that contains the entire number of whole bodies, but that, after the monad, the separate causes of their parts are also in the body-making god? This is indeed the necessary conclusion. For he who contains the one Idea of the cosmos is himself the first Father of the All, but the things that come about by necessity, the parts, are what is left, and these need the providence of the body-making god. And this additional point is clear: as we said in the case of souls, we must assert that there are causes here also, intelligent and ideal causes of the divine bodies. For the vehicles of the daemonic and particular souls participate, at a second and third remove, in these causes—for example, the Idea of the sun's body also generates the vehicles of the daemonic and the particular souls in the sun's train. Thus it is brought about that as soul is related to soul, so its vehicle is related to its particular sphere.[28] In general, since there is a plurality of divine causes, we must suppose that the causes of the same things will reside differently in different gods; that is, the particular causes of bodies *qua* bodies will reside in the divine maker of bodies, their causes as souls in the principles that generate souls, and their causes as living beings in the Demiurge who generates wholes, which receive from that higher source their existence both as souls and as bodies.

5. It remains for us to enquire about Matter itself. Is there also a Form of Matter? As a matter of fact, the answer is not the same for all matter. For if we say that the matter of the heavenly bodies is formless and shapeless, there would not be a Form of it. Yet if it exists, it will be
823 either a Form or fashioned in accordance with a Form, and it is impossible that what is without proportion or shape be similar to a Form. But if we say that the matter in the heavens has been formed by its own reason-principle (and perhaps it is necessary here, as in the case of souls and natures and bodies, that the work of the Demiurge not begin with imperfect beings, and so in the case of Matter there must be, prior to that which is shapeless and has only a fleeting being, a matter that is somehow a form and is grasped in a single definition and determination), there would be a paradigm of it. This matter would have a twofold genesis, from its paradigm and from the divine cause acting alone. For every intellectual agency creates in company with the divine, and

[28] Cf. *ET*, prop. 205.

the divine also goes forth alone and reaches even those things that do not have an origin in it.

6. From the simple hypotheses of being, let us carry our discussion forward to their compounds, that is, animals and plants. All of these likewise are generated from intelligible paradigms, since in each case both the genus and the species help to fill up the universe and make it more like its paradigm. The *Timaeus* (30d) tells us that the intellectual cosmos contains the concepts of all living beings, as the visible one contains all creatures. Hence, they are all individually made in the likeness of an intellectual form. The Living Being Itself, however, contains the causes of souls as well as the causes of bodies and living beings, all of them together in the unity of intelligibility. For just as in the tetrad[29] it holds together the entire number of the Ideas, so in its intelligent causes it anticipates in unity the separate causes both of the so-called simple beings and of the compound. In general, the being and the universality of the cosmos come from above, else why does the succession of its generations never cease, unless their cause is eternal? And from what source do they possess the common character that pervades their many particulars? Things produced by the revolution of the heavens 824 are all particular, since this movement itself is a particular character; and for a universal to be generated from a particular counts as impossible. Consequently, each species of animal and plant is constituted in accordance with an intellectual paradigm above. For everything that exists or comes to be in any way, unless it is one, without sign of plurality, owes its being to a cause. From what source, then, are these species derived, and from what kind of cause? From a changeable one? But that is impossible. Therefore, from an unchangeable one, since they are eternal; and such we declare the intellectual cause to be, for it resides complete in eternity.

7. Then shall we suppose there are not only Ideas of species but also Ideas of particulars[30]—such as an Idea of Socrates or any other individual, not as members of the species Man, but as manifesting, each of them, its individual property? Yet would not this argument compel us to say that the mortal is deathless? For if everything that comes to be by virtue of an Idea comes to be from an unchangeable cause, and if everything that exists through an unchangeable cause is unchangeable

---

[29] That is, the quartet of basic Ideas, Fire, Air, Water, Earth, or rather, the classes of living beings corresponding to them. Cf. Proclus' exposition at *PT* III, 19.

[30] A question addressed by Plotinus in *Enn.* V, 7. For a good discussion of Plotinus' doctrine on this knotty point, see H. J. Blumenthal, *Plotinus' Psychology*, The Hague, 1971, ch. 9.

in its being, Socrates and every other individual thing is the same at every moment of its being and established in eternity. But this is impossible. Furthermore, it is absurd that the Idea should be at one time a paradigm of something and at another time not, for what eternally is has eternally what it has; hence the Idea either does not have the character of a paradigm or it has it always, for it is absurd to speak of accidental characters in the intelligible world. If, then, the Idea is to be a paradigm, there must be a likeness of it, for every paradigm is the paradigm of a likeness. Now if the thing that is an image of it exists at some times and not at others, the paradigm will at times be a paradigm and at others not; it will exist for a period, and be non-existent through infinite time. But certainly to exist and not to exist in turn is absolutely alien to the being of an Idea. Why should we not listen to Socrates when he says that our reason for positing the theory of Ideas is that we 825 may have a one prior to the many? But if there are Ideas of individuals, there will be a one before the one, nay rather, an infinity of things prior to the finite, for there will be an unlimited number of Ideas, although things in the sense-world are limited. What could be more absurd than this? For things nearer to the One are more limited in number than those further away because number is more akin to the one.

These considerations show that it is absurd to admit Ideas of individuals. But since everything that comes to be comes to be from a cause, we must also posit causes of individuals: if you want a single cause, it could be the order of the universe; or if several, you could name the motion of the heavens, the particular natures, the properties of the seasons, or the various regions, or the gods that superintend these causes, for all of these are involved in the making of individuals. And for these reasons the changes of the seasons also play a part, for a cause, once moved, carries its effects along with it. And likewise the special properties of the superintending gods, who differ from one another in the shapes, colours, speech, and motion peculiar to them; and the differences between regions, for the processes of generation and the particular natures involved vary greatly in different places. The natures have not only proceeded from Nature in general, but have taken on something additional from the character of their seeds, being shaped to conform to that character by descending into bodies and becoming, as it were, properties of the bodies rather then of themselves. Thus we can understand how individuals are not brought into being by a paradigmatic cause. To exist by virtue of a cause is not the same thing as to have been brought into being by a paradigm. For while the paradigm is a cause, we have become accustomed to use the term *cause* in various sense, the paradigmatic cause being one among many.

8. So much about these matters. As for the parts of animals, shall we say that there are also Ideas of them, so as to make a paradigm not only of man but also of the finger, the eye, and every other part? Since in
826 general each of them is clearly a substance, let us admit that they exist by virtue of a cause, but since they are parts, not wholes, they are inferior to indivisible intellectual being. Things that are not only parts, but also wholes, may without absurdity be said to exist by virtue of that higher reality, but it is absurd to say this of parts only. Wholes are descended from that higher source, since the unity that precedes plurality, and the wholeness that is prior to the part come from there. Perhaps, then, it would be correct to say that of all such things as are parts, there are no intellectual causes (for every intellect is indivisible; hence we must posit in intellect only the wholes prior to the parts, and indivisible things prior to the divided), but only psychic and natural causes, for division takes place first in souls, next in natures. Here then, in souls at least, there is a reason-principle or form of finger, tooth, and every other part. The wholeness that they presuppose preexists in intellect, the wholeness that comprehends plurality in unity is in souls, the wholeness that distinguishes, as do living beings, their unity from their many parts lies in the natures, and finally the wholeness that makes this distinction spatial lies in bodies. And if I may give my own opinion, we ought not to dismiss the view that daemons are separate causes of the parts, as is shown by the invocations of those who are assigned to finger, eye, and heart, although gods are the causes of the wholes that contain them.

9. Let this be our summary treatment of the parts. And now we must examine their accidents. Are these also to have Ideas? In fact, our account of them falls into two parts. Some qualities, such as likeness, beauty, health, and virtue, complete and perfect their subjects; others, like whiteness, blackness, and the like, exist in substances but do not complete or perfect them. Now those qualities that primarily add perfection and completeness to their subjects have paradigmatic causes; but those that are otherwise present in bodies come to be there by virtue of a reason-principle. The temperament of bodies is not enough to explain their genesis; a form enters into them from nature, not, however, through a distinct intelligent cause. It belongs to Ideas to give
827 being, perfection, and universality, but characters devoid of these qualities come from elsewhere and have not their foundation in the primal Ideas. Nature, when she receives the ordered system of Ideas as they proceed into bodily masses, distinguishes parts from wholes and accidents from substances, and uses her powers of division to unfold the Ideas that come to her unified and undivided. Since it is not possible for

187

beings that are divisible through and through to be constituted directly from the unified realities nor for the most particular beings to come immediately from the most universal, their differentiation must occur in the intermediary natures as they descend into plurality. We must therefore posit a cause that confers figure upon all figures, and for numbers a single monad that generates them all. When it has been proved that the monad here is both odd and even and in its unity contains all species of number, can we not say of that intelligible monad that it is the unitary cause of all things and that it is its infinite power that generates infinite number in us also? Are we not compelled to say this, if unity here has come forth from that unity as its likeness?

10. So much is to be said about accidents. Of artificial objects shall we say there are Ideas too? Socrates in the *Republic* (X, 597b), they say, did not hesitate to speak of an Idea of bed and of table. Or rather, did he not in that passage call "idea" the reason-principle in the mind of the artisan and say that this reason-principle is produced by God, because he thought the skill itself is conferred upon souls from above? Evidence for this interpretation is that he calls the poet third in rank from the truth by analogy with the painter, who does not make a bed but a picture of it; whereas if the divine Idea is distinct from the reason-principle in the thing being made (since God is the demiurge of the form of the bed as the carpenter is the maker of the particular bed), the painter would be fourth, not third. And consider the question by a look at the facts themselves. If Intellect has Ideas of artefacts, will they proceed directly to the sense-world or through the medium of nature? To say they proceed directly is absurd, for nowhere else does procession take place in this way; the first partakers of the Ideas are things nearer to Intellect. And if it is through the intermediacy of Nature, Nature will be the cause of the artefacts. (Art is said to imitate Nature, for Nature will have Ideas of artefacts, if Intellect has them, much sooner than the arts.) But all things produced by Nature, since they are embodied in matter, are alive and undergo birth and growth, for Nature is life and the cause of living things. But it is impossible that the bed or any other artefact should live and grow. Consequently the products of art do not have a preexisting Form or an intelligible paradigm of their existence.

But if one wants to classify sciences among the arts, we must make the following distinction.[31] Of all the arts that elevate the soul and make it like Intellect we shall posit Forms to which they make us like. For there is likeness between figure and the conception of figure, and between number and the conception of number. So we will postulate

[31] Cf. Plotinus *Enn.* V, 9.11.

forms of arithmetic and geometry and astronomy, if we mean, in each case, not the vulgar kinds but the intellectual arts that are makers of divine Forms. For these arts clearly join us with Intellect, as when we pursue astronomy beyond the heavens and contemplate the intellectual harmony according to which the Father of all things generated souls and the cosmos, or that divine Number that exists secretly and distinctly in all Forms, or that intellectual Figure that generates all figures and according to which the Demiurge caused the cosmos to revolve and established each of the elements in accordance with its own figure. Of these arts, then, we must posit Forms, and of all others that lead the

829 soul upwards and that we require as we move towards the intelligible world. But all those that the soul uses when it is at play, or occupied with mortal things, or ministering to the needs of human life—of none of these is there an intellectual Form. The soul, however, has a power residing in its opinative faculty of bringing forward theorems that it is by nature able to produce and to judge; but there are no distinct Ideas at all of the arts or of their products. It is not surprising that their causes are thought to reside among the daemons, who are said to have given them to men, as their patrons and overseers, some of one, some of another, and among the gods only in a symbolic manner.[32] For example, the art of bronze-working may be said to have its patron in the daemon Hephaestus who possesses the Idea of the art, while the great Hephaestus could be said only symbolically to have forged the vault of heaven. Likewise the art of weaving has as its patron some demi-goddess in the train of Athena, while Athena herself is celebrated as weaving, in a different and demiurgic fashion, the fabric of the intelligible Ideas.

11. These are the views we had to express with regard to intellectual Ideas. About the question of evils, it remains for us to say summarily that evils too are without any divine paradigm, since they have come about incidentally from certain other causes, as I have said in another work.[33] Should we speak of the idea of evils as being itself evil, or can

830 we say that just as the idea of divisible is indivisible and the idea of plurality monadic, so the paradigm of evil is good? The former assertion, in positing evil itself as among the paradigms, is by no means in accordance with piety; in saying that there are paradigms of evil in God, we should be compelled to say that he is the cause of evils, since he has established their paradigms. And yet, when we look towards the par-

[32] συμβολικῶς, here must be taken to mean something like "archetypally."
[33] *De Mal. Subst.*, pp. 245-247. The only Platonist known to have posited Ideas of evils was Amelius (Asclep. *In Nic. Ar.* p. 44, 3-5, p. 32 Tarán), his argument being that otherwise evils must remain unknown to God. He probably quoted *Phaedo* 97d and *Timaeus* 41b in support of his position (cf. below, 832-833).

adigms, we are made better. If we say that the idea of evil is good, do we mean it is good in essence only or in function as well? If in essence only, it will be a worker of evil, which it is impious to say; and if in function also, clearly what it produces will be good. For the product of any beneficent power and activity is good, no less so than the product of fire is hot. So evil *qua* evil does not come about by virtue of a paradigm. And if, as Parmenides himself will say,[34] every Idea is a god and no god can be charged with responsibility for evil, as we learn from the *Republic* (II, 379c), then Ideas, being gods, cannot be held responsible for evils.[35] But the paradigms are causes of the things of which they are the paradigms. Consequently, no Idea can be a paradigm of evil. In addition to this, the Demiurge, who desires that all things come into being like himself and that all things in the intelligible world be brought into being in the sense world, desires that there be no evil at all if he can prevent it. All these things are said in the *Timaeus* (29e). If there had been in him a paradigm of evil, in wishing to make all things like himself he would have introduced evil as being like himself. But in fact he does not wish evil to be; this would be wishing that this very paradigm, one of the paradigms in him, should not be. Thus the argument will continue to be an impiety to the Father of the universe until we renounce this hypothesis and are willing to recognise that the causes and patterns of evil are somewhere in this world, since the rule laid down in the *Timaeus* is that everything made in the likeness of an eternal model is beautiful (28a). Hence, if evil comes about with reference to such a model, it would no longer be altogether ugly, but beautiful; and clearly everything beautiful is good, so that the evil would be good. Furthermore, who is it that would create evil by looking to the paradigm? For a paradigm requires that someone be creating with reference to it. If the creator is Intellect, he would be himself the cause of evils; and if it is someone in this world who creates evil things knowingly, he would have to do so by knowing the paradigm. But if neither of these suppositions is possible, there would be no paradigm, since there is no maker who makes by looking to it.

But enough about evils. Let us summarise the foregoing demonstrations by saying that the Forms are of universal substances and of their perfections; for these are the most characteristic attributes of Forms: goodness, essentiality, eternity—the first being derived from the primary cause, the second from the One Being, and the third from Eternity. They descend into the first order of Forms, a rank, however,

831

---

[34] The reference is probably to *Parm.* 134cd, in which case it is a considerable distortion of what Plato intended. Cf. above, 732.8-9.

[35] Cf. *In Remp.* I, 32.15ff. Kroll.

which is second to Eternity and third from the One Being but dependent, like all beings, on the cause of all good. Hence from these three
elements we must determine what things are produced by an intellec-
832 tual paradigmatic cause and what owe their existence to other causes,
without reference to an intellectual paradigm. Hair, for example,
though a basic part of the body, would not be derived from above, for
we have shown that wholes, not parts, have their origin there. Mud is
an indeterminate mixture of two elements, not the product of a natural
reason-principle. Indeed we are used to making hundreds of other mix-
tures to meet our needs, but none of them do we refer to an Idea. They
are the products of art or choice. Dirt does not even come about by
anyone's choice, but is an incidental product. Yet one of our predecessors has quite earnestly attempted to establish that there is a paradigm
of dirt:[36] if, he says, there is a paradigm of virtue, there is a paradigm
of cleansing, and if so, also of dirt, for all cleansing is a removal of some
kind of dirt. I admit that there is a Form of cleansing, but do not for
that reason admit an intellectual Form of dirt. For cleansing is a removal of evil, and it has been shown that no evil has an origin there.
Every instance of dirt is necessarily a defect in that of which it is an incidental product. For this very reason these things have not an origin
above, since they are departures from or privations of things that do
have an existence from above. Darkness is a privation of light, but the
sun, the cause of light, is not itself the cause of the absence of light. So,
too, Intellect, though the cause of knowledge, still is not responsible
for ignorance, which is the absence of knowledge. And Soul, the dis-
penser of life, is not also the giver of lifelessness. For those beings that
receive gifts from the powers above, privations are incidental by-products of the gifts, not preexisting traits in the beings that confer the positive states so as to have an origin from above like the states of which
they are privations. If someone should say that Intellect, in knowing
some good thing, knows evil also, and for this reason posits evil in In-
833 tellect (so in the *Phaedo* [97d] it is said that there is a single knowledge
of the better and the worse; so also in the *Timaeus* [41b] the Demiurge
is pictured as saying "Only an evil being would wish to undo that
which is harmonious and happy," showing by this that he knows evil),
we must reply that although there is no paradigm of evil in him, there
is knowledge of evil, and this is the paradigm of all knowledge of evil,
which makes better whoever acquires it. For ignorance is evil, not the
knowledge of ignorance, which refers both to itself and to ignorance;
so that once again, it is not the paradigm of an evil, but of a good, the

[36] It is hard to imagine who this might be, unless it is another eccentricity of Amelius,
like the Ideas of evils.

knowledge of evil. If we say this, we shall neither be bringing in Ideas of evils, as some Platonists do,[37] nor saying that Intellect knows only the better, as others think. We take a position between the two, granting that there is knowledge of evils, but not that there is a paradigmatic cause of them, itself evil.

Now Parmenides in asking these questions has been practising the art of midwifery on Socrates, and drawing out his opinions about the objects mentioned, and so Socrates, at this juncture, is about to say that he rejects vigorously Ideas of such objects.

"By no means," replied Socrates, "these things are exactly what we see them to be. To think there is any Idea of them would, I fear, be altogether ridiculous. And yet sometimes I have been seized by the disturbing thought that the same thing may be true of them as of the others. Then when I reach this point I retreat in haste, fearing that I may fall into bottomless nonsense[38] and perish; and so, coming back to the things which we said just now to have Ideas, I spend my time working with them." (130d)

This is Socrates' answer. Looking at the lifelessness, the triviality, and the corporeality of the things that he is being questioned about, he thinks it improper to say that they have Ideas and allows them an existence only among visible things. But when he considers the common element revealed by later reflection in these particular instances of them, he reasons that there may be Ideas of them also. For as in the many examples of mud there is a common feature, mud, which later thought brings to light, and in the many individual hairs a common form, hair, by which we characterise the many instances, one could say that there is prior to all pluralities a single such factor constitutive of the many individuals. This is the thought that disturbs Socrates. For since in other cases Socrates advances from a determinate group of objects to the formulation of their common characters, and from these to the reason-principles in them, and then from these reason-principles to the intelligible Ideas themselves—a process described in the *Phaedrus* (251bff.)—he reasons that it may be possible also in the case of the things he has rejected. As we can proceed from the consideration of particulars to the one in them and then to the one over them, so also it may be possible to advance in this case to something else, the one prior to them all. But then he sees that if he allows Ideas of these things, he will be compelled, proceeding on the *sorites* model, to posit Ideas of everything, including Matter itself. Well, this is the "bottomless nonsense" into which whoever falls will perish in lifeless incompetence. So

---

[37] I.e. Amelius. Cf. n. 26 above.

[38] Proclus read here εἰς τιν᾽ ἄβυθον φλυαρίαν, as is apparent from 834.21 below.

he turns back to the universals and substances that have a preeminent standing and provide the essential components of the universe. With these he spends his time, as with realities that have come about through ideal causes, while other things exist here only and not beyond the world of the senses.

"That is because you are still young, Socrates," said Parmenides, "and philosophy has not taken hold of you as it will, in my opinion, when you have learned not to despise any of these things. As it is, your youth still causes you to defer to the opinions of men." (130e)

In thus rebuking Socrates' expression of bewilderment Parmenides
835 may appear to some persons to be himself positing Ideas of everything, including the trivial, the most material, and the unnatural. For why would he rebuke Socrates, if he does not himself attribute the existence of these things to an ideal cause? But I think his rebuke was addressed not to Socrates, but to those who consider that the generation of things so trivial and insignificant is uncaused. Parmenides himself corrects this opinion in refusing to admit that there is anything uncaused. "Anything that comes to be, necessarily comes to be from a cause," the *Timaeus* (28c) says, "for nothing can have an origin without a cause." Hence nothing is so unseemly or trivial as not to share in the Good and draw its origin from above. Even Matter, if you consider it, you will find to be good, and evil itself turns out to have good in it, to be incapable of existing otherwise than by carrying a tinge of the Good and partaking of it in some way. But popular opinion is ashamed to ascribe the existence of cheap and insignificant things to the divine cause, for it looks at their nature, not at the power of that cause, and does not consider that a cause capable of creating the greater things is *a fortiori* able to bring lesser things into being, as the Athenian Stranger somewhere says (*Laws* X, 902e). But genuine philosophers regard all things in the cosmos, great and small, as dependent on providence; they see nothing dishonourable or worthless in the house of Zeus, but regard all things as good, in so far as they arise from providence, and beautiful, as having come to be in accordance with a divine cause.

That Socrates, in denying an ideal cause of these trivial and particularly material things, also denies that they have any cause—this Parmenides infers from Socrates' declaration that these things are only "what we see"; for if he had seen that nothing is uncaused he would not have uttered this phrase. For instance, hair may not have an intelligible paradigm, but it still has a natural reason-principle as its cause. Then is it not necessary that this hair be not only what we see, but also that hair which is in the reason-principle of Nature? For Nature does not create even hair in vain; she is working for the good in furnishing animals

193

with it, and its absence is contrary to nature, who equips the creatures that need the aid of hair. And again clay, if it comes about by art, has its form in the mind of the workman[39] and if this clay or dirt is pleasing to certain spirits for whose aid sorcerers look when they use such things in their operations[40]—the art of sorcery we owe to the daemons, as we learn in the *Symposium* (203d)—what is strange in supposing that the daemons who delight in them know their kinds, just as we say the overseers of the various parts of the cosmos comprehend the boundaries of their particular provinces? And if you are in doubt about the proximate causes, raise your thought to that single cause of being from which everything proceeds, and say that it produces them so that of none of them is its existence uncaused.

Or perhaps Parmenides, looking at the One Being prior to the Ideas, thinks it proper to place existence on the causal level before existence on the level of Idea; and he therefore rebukes Socrates when, in denying Ideas, he denies all other causes. He should have supposed their origin to lie not in the intellectual Form, but in a cause older than Forms, since when we make objects by human art, the Intellect also makes them. For everything that comes to be by secondary causes is brought about in a more fundamental sense by the primary causes, not, however, through Forms, but by Being itself alone. It is true that when we make, we make in accordance with certain reason-principles that we have in us, but it is the Forms that we make in our products, while Intellect is creator of their substance. And of the things to which Intellect gives form, it is the monad of Beings that gives the substance. For that cause is greater than any ideal cause. Thus Socrates, intent on the form-giving cause, naturally supposes the origin of these things to be uncaused, while Parmenides advances to the cause above Ideas and sees that their substance is derived from that cause. For all things have their sources in it.

836

838

[39] Here Proclus is making πηλός mean "potter's clay."
[40] Further evidence of Proclus' abiding interest in magical practices.

BOOK IV

◘

INTRODUCTION

▣ ▣ ▣

BOOK IV covers almost five Stephanus pages, from 130e4 to 135b2, and thus most of the vexatious problems about the relations of Forms to particulars raised by Parmenides in the dialogue. It is a long book, unlike its two predecessors, and falls into various sections, which I shall indicate as we go along. Before, however, we examine Proclus' solutions to the problems raised by Parmenides, we may recall what I said in the General Introduction (p. xxxiii), that for Proclus there are no insoluble problems in the *Parmenides*, since Parmenides' purpose is for him not eristic but maieutic, and all his puzzles are simply designed to lead the young Socrates to a higher level of sophistication in his view of the structure of reality.

The book begins with an excursus on the question of the way in which particulars participate in Forms (837.8-853.12), which, like the previous ones, is a most useful account of Platonic theorising and Neoplatonic doctrine on the subject. He begins by refuting the notion that Parmenides is concerned to demolish the Theory of Ideas, as some authorities have supposed. His purpose is in fact to provoke Socrates to articulate the theory more perfectly. He does this by moving downwards from the most universal through the more particular and atomic kinds of being, and coming finally to those that are not constituted in accordance with a Form at all, but still are derived from the monad of all existent things, the One Being. Only after setting out this hierarchy clearly are we in a position to consider properly the problem of participation (μετοχή).

There are various processes, says Proclus (839.20ff.), to which participation may be likened. First, to reflection in a mirror:

> Just as in this case the shape and relative positions of its parts cause an image of the countenance to be seen on the surface of the mirror, so receptive matter, holding itself up, so to speak, before the Demiurge and the artifice (πόρος) of his mind, is filled with Ideas from him.

Plotinus makes this comparison in *Enn.* III, 6.7-9, a passage which Proclus plainly has in mind here.

The second analogy frequently presented to the participation in Forms is that of a seal in wax (841.1ff.). This seems to have been the dominant one in Middle Platonism (see references in n. 7 below). Proclus regards this as too crudely physical, in its imagery of pressing down by the Form and resistance by Matter—more suitable to Stoic theory.

Lastly, the analogy of *eikones* (841.18ff.), which must here mean both "portraits" and "statuettes," is unsatisfactory, since these only reproduce a surface likeness to their model, while the Forms "shape their substrates in their entirety and from within." This analogy too seems to have been a Middle Platonic one. It is criticised as too crude also by Plotinus in *Enn.* III, 8.2, where he mentions *kēroplastai*, "makers of wax dolls," as here.

Proclus does not go so far as to reject these analogies outright (841.30ff.). Rather, he recognises in them all some vestige of the truth, and commends them as useful aids for less advanced students; but the true Platonist must transcend them. The correct element in them is their isolation of *likeness* (841.34) as the feature that unites individuals to Forms, and Plato does admittedly use all these types of imagery in speaking of the process of participation, but we must treat them as no more than images.

For participation to take place (842.15ff.), there is needed not only the "efficacious power" ($\delta\rho\alpha\sigma\tau\acute{\eta}\rho\iota\sigma\varsigma\ \delta\acute{\upsilon}\nu\alpha\mu\iota\varsigma$) of the Forms, but also the appetition ($\acute{\sigma}\rho\varepsilon\xi\iota\varsigma$) of the beings to be informed and, ultimately, of Matter. The Peripatetics and the Stoics have presented inadequate accounts of this process, by disregarding respectively the efficacity of the Forms and the appetitiveness of Matter. Proclus now gives a discourse on the mystery of the variety of levels of being in this world by virtue of the varying degrees of receptivity of Matter.

His solution to this problem is stated in terms of the metaphysics he has inherited from Syrianus, but it is possible, I think, to restate it in terms more acceptable to modern sensibilities. He distinguishes *four* levels of demiurgic agent—Father, Father-Creator, Creator-Father, and Creator—each of whom performs a different role (844.11ff.). However, this can be seen as merely a way of distinguishing four stages of creation. First, Matter itself is dependent for its existence on the Father or Primal Cause, prior to any imposition of Form on it. The second stage in the process of creation is the introduction into Matter of the "traces" of the Forms (cf. *Tim.* 52b), that is, inchoate tendencies to receive ordered Form. As a third stage, we must postulate the imposition on Matter in general of the Form of the Cosmos, or perhaps the

Idea of an ordered universe in general, as a condition of the creation of all particular ordered things. And lastly, the formation of ordered things themselves, in their genera and species. So Matter is subject to various degrees of informing, and this can be taken to account for the variety in Nature.

This setting out of a multi-staged process of creation is only a formalisation of the doctrine of the *Timaeus*, which has been gradually worked out in the Platonic tradition. It does not, of course, explain the basic "mystery" of the imposition of Form on Matter, but it provides an elaborate conceptual framework within which it may be discussed. We are left, then (845.25ff.), with three causes of participation in Form: the Good, towards which all things strive; the creative power of the Forms themselves; and the receptivity of individual material receptacles.

Before he leaves the discussion of *metochē*, Proclus turns to the critique of a predecessor (846.22ff.), whom he refers to only as τὶς τῶν πάνυ γενναίων, and who may be either Amelius (who liked triads) or Iamblichus—probably not Porphyry. This theorist, like Syrianus, would like to preserve a role for all three Middle Platonist analogies to participation (the seal in wax, the reflection in water, the statuette), but, unlike Syrianus and Proclus, who would regard all three as imperfect statements of a higher truth, he would see them as descriptions of the mode of participation in different levels of form. Sense-objects participate *by way of impression* (τυπωτικῶς) in the forms-in-matter (φυσικὰ εἴδη): they receive *reflections* of the forms at the level of Soul, and they are *images* of the intellectual forms. Proclus commends the ingenuity of this thesis, but rejects it in favour of the Syrianic one (847.30ff.).

> But perhaps it is better and more in accord with theology not to make these distinctions, but to say that sense-objects simultaneously (1) partake of intellectual forms as present to them (2) receive reflections from them, and (3) resemble them as images. For Plato in this very passage says simply that things here "participate in the Forms," as if the primary Forms were participated in in all these ways by sense-objects.

He turns now, at last (848.21ff.), to a study of the *lexis*, but even this produces another excursus on the theory of names, arising out of τὰς ἐπωνυμίας αὐτῶν of the lemma (849.16-853.12). His basic point is that properly given names are primarily of Forms, and only secondarily of the individuals which participate in them. It is interesting here, I think, for the chronology of Proclus' works that, though he refers us to the *Cratylus* at various points, he does not refer us to his commentary on the dialogue, which might suggest that it was not yet composed; but this is hardly conclusive (see also the General Introduction, p. xxxiv).

After this introduction, the first section of the book covers Parmenides' problems about participation in Forms as wholes or as parts. This extends from 853.18 to 877.31, covering *Parm.* 130e6 to 131e7, and it is divided into 11 lemmata, all short. I shall not comment on them all individually.

In the first of these (130e6-131a3; 853.18-856.3), Proclus addresses himself to some concepts—Likeness, Greatness, Beauty and Justice—mentioned in the text, the definition of which as Forms posed problems for later Platonists. 'Equal' and 'big', after all, are spatial concepts, and 'beautiful' and 'just' seem to involve possession of, and interaction with, material attributes. At the level of Form, they must mean something else. In fact Proclus identifies Likeness as the force which renders secondary things like primary ones, perfecting them and bringing them to completion. Greatness he presents (853.34ff.) as "that which gives preeminence to anything in its particular class" (adducing a number of Platonic passages to support his interpretation, in particular *Phaedo* 100e). Beauty (855.6ff.) is what dispenses symmetry, unity, and the charm of perfection to the Forms, and Justice is the cause of the Forms' performing their proper functions.

What we seem to have here in each case is not so much a Form in the traditional sense (if we can speak of such a thing), as rather a series of organising principles of the intelligible world—second-level Forms, one might term them—giving order and coherence to the primary Forms, in the way that the five *megista genê* of the *Sophist* might be supposed to do.

The next lemma (131a4-7; 856.9-858.40) leads Proclus to reveal a controversy among previous Platonists arising out of both the previous argument (130a-e) as to whether there are Forms of all things, and the present one about the mode of participation (130e-131e). Even as some, he says, approached Parmenides' problem by asserting that there are Forms of all things and that Socrates should not have been embarrassed by the question of the existence of Forms of mud or hair, while others accepted that there were not Forms of all things, but denied that that was destructive of the theory, so here one party accepts the major premise, that if a sensible object participates in a Form, it must participate in either the whole or a part of it, and asserts that in fact each participates in the whole of a Form, while another school of thought disposes of the problem by accepting that participation in Form is of another type than that in whole or part, since such an antithesis is really only appropriate to participation of one body in another. It is with these latter that Proclus agrees, though with certain refinements. It is quite clear to him (858.29ff.) that when Parmenides adds "Or could there be some other way of participation than this?" he is actually rousing Socrates up to consider what this other way might be.

The subject of comment on the next lemma (131a8-b2; 859.7-861.37) is the sense in which 'whole' and 'part' are to be understood in relation to participation in immaterial Forms. Once again, Proclus' conviction that Parmenides' purpose is maieutic comes to his aid. On the one hand, a material object cannot participate in the whole of the Form, say, of Beauty, "since nowhere do caused objects absorb the whole power of their causes" (cf. *ET*, prop. 75). But on the other hand, "since these things possess the property, say justice or beauty, by which ideal Justice and Beauty are characterised in their own nature, for this reason things could be said to partake of the whole, not the part." For Proclus, the paradox is resolved by specifying that participation in an immaterial entity is quite different from participation in a material one, and so "secondary things partake both of the whole and a part of their corresponding Forms" (860.3-4).

The next lemma (131b3-6; 862.4-864.3), in commenting on Socrates' choice of the example of daylight as something that can be present as a whole to many individuals simultaneously, brings in further interesting evidence of the *Forty Logoi* of Zeno (see the General Introduction, sect. D). This document, as I have said, may be spurious, but the two arguments that Proclus reports from it in detail are sufficiently primitive in their logical form to suggest that, if spurious, it was quite a good forgery. Zeno seems to have presented, as an argument for the one-ness of apparent multiplicities, the example of people here and in the Antipodes both being white, and thus "one." Apparently, some previous commentator had suggested that Plato makes Parmenides attack this argument in the form presented by Socrates to avoid the unsuitability of having the master publicly correct the pupil (evidence that Proclus was not the first to make use of the *Forty Logoi* in the exegesis of the dialogue). Proclus refutes this suggestion by asserting that Zeno's argument is valid, as it relates to the *immanent* form, while the invalidity of Socrates' arises from the fact that he is referring to the transcendent Form.

The comments on the next two lemmata (864.12-866.24), both very short, contribute little except a reinforcement of Proclus' view that Parmenides' purpose is not destructive, but maieutic. He amusingly takes Parmenides' ironic ἡδέως γε (131b7) as straight commendation; it is a recognition of the spontaneity (τὸ αὐτοφυές) of Socrates' thought: "This is why Parmenides remarks 'how readily' he makes the one whole in many things, meaning by 'readily,' not naively or ridiculously, but *naturally*." Socrates' intuitions are correct, but still insufficiently articulated (865.7).

We come now to a series of lemmata (131c12-e7), running from 866.31 to 877.31, which concern Parmenides' problem about participation in Greatness, Equality, and Smallness, in which he compounds Socrates' difficulties about part and whole. For Proclus, Parmenides is only teaching here that participation in immaterial Forms must be conceived differently, and that these concepts have a different force in the intelligible world from what they have in this. Among intelligibles, Greatness is "what confers upon anything its superiority and transcendent perfection, whether intellectual or vital or physical," Equality is "the cause of harmony and proportion in all things," and Smallness is "the cause of essential inferiority" (868.24ff.). These Forms thus become, like Beauty and Justice, structural principles of the realm of Forms. As he says a little farther on (869.14ff.):

> And it seems that all things get their ordering from this triad of Forms, since they furnish to superior beings their very superiority, to the secondary ones their inferiority, and fellowship to those that are parallel in rank. . . . Every series needs these three moments—excess, deficiency and parity; so that if every Form has its procession that preserves the distinction between secondary and primary beings, together with community among them all, it is this triad that brings it about.

Proclus thus finds a use for these rather troublesome Forms which Plato produced in the *Phaedo*, such as Large, Small, and Equal, by making them principles of organisation for the others. How else, after all, is Largeness to coexist with Dog or Tree, or even Triangle? And in this way one can explain the relationship between Animal and Dog or Cat, and between Dog and Cat. Proclus is able to tidy up thus many loose ends in the realm of Forms.

Some interesting points arise in connexion with the argument about Smallness, which seems to have given particular trouble to previous commentators (872.33-36). Proclus, though he is rendered impervious to the logical difficulties presented here by his conviction that all this concerns only the fallacious assumption that participation is bodily, does report an argument of his friend Pericles (872.18)—whether oral or in a written commentary is not clear—designed to show that the very notion of subtracting a part from Smallness is incoherent, since the same part, if added to a particular, makes it bigger, while, if returned to the remainder from which it was subtracted, it would make it smaller. The cogency of this escapes me, and Proclus does not seem too sure about it either. Particulars, then, for Proclus, participate in their Forms in a sense as wholes, and in another sense as parts (875.7ff.):

> They participate in them as wholes in that the activity of a Form is indivisible, and thus is present as a whole in all its participants, being in itself first and then filling up the being of its participants with its own character. But they participate in part in so far as they participate not in the Forms themselves, but in images (εἴδωλα) of them, and these images are parts of their own paradigms; for thus the likeness stands to its pattern as part to whole.

We come now to the "Third Man" Argument (131e8–132b2), which constitutes the next section of the book (878.1–890.38), divided into just two lemmata. In Proclus' view, even as the previous argument is designed to show that participation in the Forms is not of a bodily nature, so this argument, advancing a stage further, demonstrates that participation in transcendent Forms is distinct from participation in immanent forms, or forms-in-matter (ἔνυλα εἴδη or φυσικοὶ λόγοι), which do have an element in common with their participants (878.17ff.). Once again, therefore, Parmenides' purpose is maieutic.

In this connection Proclus adduces Socrates' admission of uncertainty at *Phaedo* 100d as to whether one should call the mode of participation in the Forms "presence" (παρουσία) or "communion" (κοινωνία), or perhaps something else (881.39ff.). For Proclus, what Plato is telling us here is that neither *parousia* nor *koinōnia* is a suitable term for participation in transcendent Forms. The *Phaedo* passage, he feels, is good to juxtapose with this passage in the *Parmenides*, as it shows Socrates still professing doubt at the end of his life about a question raised here at the outset of his career (883.9ff.), thus indicating that any terminology of participation based on material analogies is bound to be inadequate. This leads Proclus to a commendation of Plato for refuting in advance the views of all later schools on the question of the creation of the world.

Aristotle's Third Man Argument (and the "No-man" Argument, whatever that was) do not disturb him (889.6ff.), as being only valid against forms which would coordinate with their participants, as are the forms-in-matter. For the transcendent Forms, Proclus postulates a relationship with particulars which one might term "non-reciprocal communion." As he says at 890.2ff.:

> The Forms both commune with their participants and do not commune with them. To the extent that they illuminate them from their own essence, they commune with them, but to the extent that they are unmixed with what they illuminate, they do not

commune; so that it is not for themselves, but for the things derived from them, that they have generated a certain degree of likeness. For this reason, indeed, it may be said that they commune in
some way through these means with those entities with receive
them, but the communion is not that of synonyms, but rather of
primary and secondary participants in a term (ἀλλ᾽ ὡς δευτέροις
καὶ πρώτοις).

Proclus here makes use of Aristotle's distinction between *prōtōs* and
deuterōs legesthai (e.g. *Met. Δ*, 18.1022a18; *EN* VIII, 9.1158b31-33; *EN*
X, 5.1176a29) in an attempt to formulate what we might express by
using subscripts, e.g. just$_1$ and just$_2$, Justice itself being just$_1$ and just
actions or individuals being just$_2$. It is clear to him that Plato intends the
infinite regress to be patently absurd, and that his purpose is to lead us
to a better perception of the nature of particpation.

We turn now to the suggestion of Socrates that the Forms may be
thoughts in a mind (132b3-c12; 891.4-906.2). Proclus sees the preceding two *aporiai* as concerning the mode of participation in Forms,
which is the third of the four problems about Forms which Parmenides
sets out to address, while we turn in the next two to the fourth problem, "Where are they situated? Are they in souls, or prior to souls?"
(891.4-21).

He begins with an attack on the Peripatetic view of general concepts
as simply abstractions from sense-perceptions—"later-born entities"
(ὑστερογενεῖς). This term must have been adopted by later Peripatetics to describe general concepts. Aristotle himself uses the term only (in
a philosophical sense) at *Met.* N,4.1091a33, in connection with asking
whether the Good is an *archē*, or *hysterogenes* (as was the doctrine of
Speusippus), and so not directly in connection with a discussion of
Forms or concepts. However, it seems likely from Simplicius *In Cat.*
82.22-83.20 (esp. 83.8) that Alexander of Aphrodisias used the term to
describe the status of *ta katholou* (though he *may* have simply spoken of
them as ὕστερα τῇ φύσει). How, Proclus asks, could a concept of a
Form arise out of the contemplation of the limited number of members
of any class with which we are likely to come into contact? We could
not arrive at the notion of a class except by virtue of *anamnēsis*.

A true Form, then, is a thought (νόημα), "but primarily in the sense
of a thought-process (νόησις) of Intellect in the true sense, in fact of the
Paternal Intellect, in which both true beings are thoughts and thoughts
true beings" (893.3ff.). These "thoughts" come to be, at a lower level,
in the Soul (896.22ff.), and must not be confused with "what is produced in the soul as a result of projections from individual sense-objects."

For Proclus, then, Socrates has arrived at a truth about the nature of Forms, but only at the level of Soul. Parmenides now proposes to lead him a stage higher, by raising a difficulty about this (896.29ff.), which Proclus deals with in the next lemma (898.12-906.2). Thought must be "of" an object of thought, and this object of thought, rather than the thought, would be the Form. This, again, Proclus does not see as a problem, but as the revelation of a truth about Forms at the intelligible level:

If, then, thought is of the object of thought, not only in us, but also in the divine and veritable Intellect, it is plain that the object of thought is prior to the thought, and it is by virtue of its striving towards this that the reason-principle in the soul is a thought. (899.23-27)

We are thus led up to the level of *ta ontōs onta* (901.24ff.), where Intellect and the objects of intellection are united, but yet the objects of intellection, the Forms proper, are logically and ontologically prior.

He now, however, has to deal with Parmenides' objection in 132c, that all things which participated in Forms would be thinking entities, since they would partake in thought. In answer to this, he specifies (902.16f.) that Forms are *noēmata* only in the sense of being objects of thought, not as being thought-processes themselves. Indeed, as he says, "Things must take their start, not from thinking agents, but rather from elements which are objects of thought, in order that there may be causes of both things that have mind and things that have not" (902.35-38). Nous contains within itself the triad of causal principles—Being, Life and Intellect proper—which among them produce all things in the cosmos.

This provokes him to a brief disquisition on the subject of *seirai* (903.2-904.34), on which he has already spoken at pp. 874-875, in order to explain the different degrees of participation in Forms. He ends the lemma with a recapitulation of the stages of understanding through which Socrates has been led by Parmenides' midwifery.

He turns next (906.3-918.35, on 132c12-133b3) to the discussion of Socrates' suggestion that Forms are "like patterns fixed in the nature of things" (ὥσπερ παραδείγματα ἐν τῇ φύσει), of which things here are "likenesses" (ὁμοιώματα or εἰκόνες). Proclus' only criticism of this formulation is that it appears to neglect the creative and preservative aspects of the Forms, in favour of the assimilative—unless, perhaps, he suggests (910.1ff.), we regard him as including these other aspects in assimilation, "for things that are assimilated to what 'stands fixed' are necessarily indissoluble, and are held together by their own reason-principles, and are conserved in their essence by them." These things will not be sensible particulars, but rather the immanent forms of genera and species, which do enjoy a kind of eternity.

He correctly draws attention to Socrates' use of *hōsper* with *paradeigmata*, as making clear that the term is not to be taken in any restrictively literal sense. The Forms are living and active principles, not just inert exemplars.

This brings us to the next lemma (132d5-e5), and to Parmenides' objection that, if the image is like the exemplar, then the exemplar must be like the image, and in virtue of this "likeness" the Third Man Argument once again raises its head. "To this," says Proclus (912.31ff.), "Socrates should have replied that 'like' has two senses—one, the likeness of coordinate entities, the other, the likeness which involves subordination to an archetype—and the one is to be seen as consisting in the identity of some one reason-principle, while the other involves not only identity but at the same time otherness, whenever something is 'like', as having the same Form derived from the other, but not along with it."

Proclus here seems to have exposed the flaw in Parmenides' argument (as Cornford points out in his commentary *ad loc.*): the relation of a photograph to its original is not the same as that of one photograph of the same original to another. The photographs resemble each other through having the common quality of being images of the same original, but it is absurd to say that the original and the photograph have any quality in common by virtue of which they resemble some third thing.

Once again, therefore, Parmenides is just provoking Socrates to deeper understanding, when he asks, "Or is there any way that what is like can avoid being like what is like it?" (914.41-42).

This lemma is a good example of Proclus' exegetical method. He approaches the problem first *logikōs kai aporētikōs* (911.33ff.); then *philosophikōs* (912.38ff.); and lastly, *theologikōs* (913.14ff.)—which in this case involves the distinguishing of Forms at various divine levels, at some of which there is reciprocal likeness with particulars, but at the highest level, that of the unparticipated Intellect, only non-reciprocal likeness.

Arising out of the question of likeness to the Forms, some commentators raised the interesting problem as to whether each Form confers not only existence on the particulars, but also likeness to itself (916.14ff.). If so, what then is the role of the Form of Likeness? If not, and it is in virtue of Likeness that particulars resemble their Forms, then how can the Form be said to make an "image" of itself? Proclus gets out of this quandary by reminding us that all Forms cooperate with one another, and indeed are *in* one another, but it does bring us up against the curious role of these "meta-forms," such as Largeness, Equality and Likeness, which we have discussed earlier. In fact, as we see again, they function as organising principles, and are not to be viewed as being on the same level as, say, Forms of natural objects.

We come now to the relatively lengthy argument about the lack of communication between ourselves and the realm of Forms (133a8–134e8), the commentary on which takes up most of the rest of the book (919.1–971.9). It is divided into 13 lemmata, which we need not deal with individually. The second, however, is of considerable length (919.30–928.27) and constitutes a sort of introduction to the topic.

For Proclus, this final difficulty raised by Parmenides is really designed to expose inadequate conceptions of the relationship of Forms to particulars, both that later taken up by the Stoics, that Form is immanent in Matter, and that of the Peripatetics, that the divine is not providentially concerned with the sense-world (921.10ff.). Parmenides continues to lead Socrates on the upward path of understanding of the Forms at every level.

The real question is, in what sense do we *not* know the Forms, or what levels of Form are superior to our understanding? First, on the philosophical level (924.1ff.), we must distinguish between apprehension of "coordinate" objects, objects on the same level of reality as ourselves, and that of objects on a superior level. If we decide that we can have *knowledge* of coordinate objects, that is, of the sense-world, then the apprehension which we have of superior levels of being must be something other than knowledge. Looking at the question "theologically" (924.41ff.), we realise that what Plato is doing is distinguishing the "intellectual" level of Forms, the forms in the Soul, which we *can* know, from higher levels (the intelligible-intellectual and the intelligible) which transcend our powers of understanding.

The notion that the highest level of reality, the One, or even the summit of the intelligible world, can only be apprehended, if at all, by some faculty in us superior to intellect, and analogous to the One (the "One of the Soul") is adumbrated by Plotinus (e.g. *Enn.* III, 8.9; VI, 9.3), but formalised only by Iamblichus (e.g. *In Phaedr.* fr. 6 Dillon = Hermeias, *In Phaedr.* 150.24ff. Couvreur), and elaborated further by Syrianus and Proclus. Here even the intelligible-intellectual level (that of the median moment of the realm of Nous, Life) is superior to our individual understanding, so that *a fortiori* so are the intelligible and the henadic realms. All this is an excellent example of Proclus' ability creatively to derive positive doctrine from a passage of essentially negative argument.

Under the rubric of *lexis*, Proclus now indulges in a homily on the nature of the ideal student (926–927), making use of the ancient Platonic triad of qualities required for success in study—good natural parts, love of learning, and willingness to do one's homework (φύσις, μάθησις, ἄσκησις, or, as Proclus lists them, εὐφυία, ἐμπειρία, προθυμία)—this being provoked by Parmenides' remarks in 138b. He then gives a sketch of the ideal teacher (927.31ff.), of whom Parmenides provides a good example. When, however, he declares that one chief characteristic of such a teacher is that "he will not want to expound the divine truth with elaborate verbosity, but rather to reveal much through few words", one can only wish that he had practised what he preached.

Proclus, then, sees the argument for the unknowability of the Forms as teaching that we need to postulate intermediate levels between the totally transcendent, noetic forms and ourselves, to wit, the forms in soul and the reason-principles in Nature. Parmenides' commendation (καλῶς λέγεις, 133c7) of Socrates' admission that no being which is *autē kath' hautēn* could exist in our world, Proclus declares to be, not ironic, but quite serious (932.16ff.); it is true that no transcendent Form can be present in our world, nor be directly cognised from it, but this simply teaches us that there is another level of Form which *is*.

At 934.38ff., Proclus gives us a useful summary of the nature of a Form in the primal sense, as derived from the six arguments which have been produced by Parmenides: "The Idea in the truest sense is an incorporeal cause, transcending its participants, a motionless being, exclusively and really a model, intelligible to souls through images, and intelligising causally the existents modelled upon it."

The next topic of interest (935-939) is a discussion of the nature of relativity in the realm of Forms. There is, for instance, he maintains, such a thing even in this realm as natural righthandedness and lefthandedness, as of the left or right hands of an animal, as opposed to mere accidental right and left. There will therefore be Right and Left in the intelligible realm. Each of these is a substantial Form, existing "for itself," primarily, but producing a relation in this world. Certain Forms, such as these, and such others as Mastership and Slavery, have special reciprocal relations in the noetic realm, but are nevertheless substantive entities "in themselves," whereas "master" or "father" here is not a description of a substance, but only of a relation.

If this sounds dangerously close to nonsense, one can only say in Proclus' defence that later Platonists were faced with an inheritance from Plato of what appeared to be Forms of relatives, and they had to come to terms with them somehow. What we get is a series of interesting attempts to work out a structure of the realm of Forms. Mastership and Slavery, for instance, as we learn a little later (941-943), are the structures which enable the more generic Forms to dominate the more particular.

In an interesting note (939.19ff.) on Plato's use of *homōnymos* to describe the relationship between Forms and particulars at 133d3, Proclus appeals to Aristotle's formulation of τὰ ἀφ᾽ ἑνὸς καὶ πρὸς ἕν λεγόμενα (*EN* I, 4.1096b27; *Met.* Γ, 2.1003a33; *Met.* Z, 4.1030b2) to clarify the sense of *homōnymos*—a use of the formula which Aristotle, of course, would have vigorously repudiated. One would have liked him to have given a reference for his statement that Aristotle "sometimes classes (these) as homonyms," since in the passages above he is careful to distinguish them, but he is probably thinking of *Met.* A, 6.987b9, where Aristotle speaks of sensible particulars in Platonic theory as being κατὰ μέθεξιν ὁμώνυμα τοῖς εἴδεσιν where, on his own terms, he should have said συνώνυμα. At any rate, *mutatis mutandis*, this Aristotelian formulation is very much what he wants, and indeed very much what Plato means.

The Forms of Knowledge and Truth (134a), like those of Mastership and Slavery, Proclus presents as structuring principles (944-946):

> Knowledge makes all things There intellectual, for this Knowledge is the eternal and uniform intelligising of the eternal; (Truth) makes them intelligible, for the light of Truth, being intelligible, gives them a share of its intelligible power. (944.24-29)

In the course of discussing the nature of knowledge at our level (the problem of the connection of the two levels of knowledge and truth he does not regard as a question worth dwelling on), he makes the interesting point (947.21ff.) that, while there is a Form of Knowledge in general, we must not postulate Forms of particular branches of knowledge (ἐπιστῆμαι) or skills (τέχναι), such as cookery, perhaps, or carpentry, since they concern themselves with products of this world, and are thus in the position of accidental attributes (συμβεβηκότα), of which there can be no ideal archetype. The Form of Knowledge, then, as operating in this realm, is really the *concept* of Knowledge or Skill, that characteristic which makes it an *epistēmē* or *technē*. This, again, clears some of the undergrowth from the realm of Forms.

Under the lemma 134bc, we learn (950.39ff.) that Beauty and Goodness are also to be seen as structuring principles of the various levels of Form. Goodness confers perfection and self-sufficiency on each Form, while Beauty ensures that they are objects of love to the entities below them (on the same "chain"), and thus provokes *epistrophē*. Proclus regards us, we must remember, as having ascended, in this last Parmenidean argument, to the contemplation of the intelligible-intellectual, or median, level of Forms, which is still above the range of our knowledge in any direct sense. We now, with the next lemma, 134c, ascend to the intelligible Forms proper, and the arguments of Parmenides which are false and aporetic at lower levels now become true at this highest level. We cannot know the intelligible Forms, and they do not *directly* take cognisance of us, though the physical universe is still indirectly the product of their providence (952.26ff.). However, Parmenides' apparent assault here on the concept of Providence leads Proclus to a discourse on that subject (953–960).

First, he sees Parmenides' argument as an attack on the two false positions concerning the relationship of the divine to the physical world, represented respectively by the Stoics and the Peripatetics (954.20ff.), the former making God immanent in his creation, the latter exempting him from any active care for it, on the grounds that his only proper object of knowledge is himself, and that it would be unseemly for God to be bothered with the flux of sensible particulars, and impossible for him to have knowledge of contingent events.

The various problems about Providence Proclus dealt with later in his career in a special monograph *On the Ten Problems about Providence* (presumably later, or he would have referred us to it here), but he gives us a brief account of his position now. God can know inferior levels of creation in a manner proper to himself (957.18ff.):

> What is there astonishing, then, in the fact that God knows everything according to his nature, divided things in an undivided way, things that come into being eternally, and partial things universally, and, in a word, in a different manner than is the nature of each of the things in question, and along with such knowledge he has control over the production of all things, and by the very fact of knowing all things with simple and unified knowledge, he bestows upon each their existence and their coming into existence. (cf. *ET*, prop. 124)

In this connection, Proclus produces a theory of cognition which is an interesting development on Aristotle's doctrine of the 'common sense' in *De Anima* III. He postulates as prior to the *koinē aisthēsis*, which compares the evidence of the individual senses, and apprehends properties common to more than one sense, a unitary principle of the soul (ἕν τῆς ψυχῆς, 958.1), which can be conscious of its various intellectual activities as well as of its sense-perceptions, and say "It is *I* who am doing this." This is not at all the mystical faculty of the soul which is elsewhere termed the One of the Soul, but simply consciousness as a synoptic principle. He only introduces it to illustrate the possibility of the unitary knowledge of God, which can have consciousness of the physical world without having sense-organs, or being spatially extended itself.

We may note also, at 966.10ff., a criticism of Aristotle's doctrine of

God's self-knowledge which seems well taken: if God knows himself, he must know himself as object of desire for all things; if he knows that, he must have knowledge of all the things which desire him, "since someone who knows definitely one side of a relation cannot not also know the other side." Aristotle would presumably deny that God *knows* that he is an object of desire; he just contemplates himself, and *is* an object of desire. But Proclus has a point: must not God know everything about himself, and does not everything include, in a way, the whole universe?

He ends the whole section on the difficulties about the Forms with a triumphant recapitulation of the various levels of Form (969–970), listing eight different levels, from the primal, intelligible Forms down to the forms-in-matter, each of which, he declares, contributes some characteristic to all the lower forms which proceed from it, down to the lowest form in the sense-world. It is a suitable climax to an intellectual *tour de force* which has transformed Parmenides' series of destructive arguments into a maieutic revelation of the truth about the whole structure of the realm of Forms, at every level.

The passage 134e8–135b2 Proclus takes as a suitable conclusion to Book IV, since here Parmenides appears to indicate to Socrates that he has been trying to educate him to the true nature of the Forms, and warning him against overhasty conclusions about them, and his exegesis of the four lemmata into which he divides this section brings this out, with his usual attention to telltale details of the text. Most remarkable, perhaps, is his discerning of *three* stages of uncertainty adumbrated by Parmenides in the passage 135a3–5 (see n. 111 below). The general message, for Proclus, is that "it is not possible for the comprehension of intelligible things to arise in natures not suited to it, nor will it ever be the case that those things which have their being and their seat in pure Intellect will become manifest to those who have not purified their minds, if indeed it is true that in all cases like is comprehensible by like" (975.31–37).

COMMENTARY

□ □ □

"Then tell me this: you say you think there exist certain Forms in which these other things here participate and so carry their designations?" (130e)

Since Socrates in his discussion with Zeno has said that Forms exist and that things here participate in them, and has advanced to the concept of the community of Forms through their participation with things here, some persons have at once concluded that Parmenides, as if warding off Socrates and his criticism of Zeno, takes a stand against both these notions of Socrates, that is, against the existence of Forms and against the process of participation. For in the preceding discussions Parmenides has contested the assertion that there are Forms, and in what follows will contend that sense objects do not participate in them, almost saying in plain words that even if we grant the existence and being of Forms, participation in them is impossible. Consequently, it is neither true that Forms exist nor, if they did, that sensible things participate in them. This is what they have thought: that is, in the preceding discussion Parmenides has at least shown that Forms do not exist; ⟨if there are Forms, there must be Forms of all things⟩[1] but there are not Forms of all things, as Socrates himself admits; hence there are no Forms. This, they say,[2] is the point of the reproof that Parmenides addresses to Socrates, when he shows that we cannot allow some things to be produced from above and others by chance, but must derive them all from the Forms, if they exist. But about this reproof we have expressed our opinion in the preceding comment; and as to the handling of the argument as a whole all we have to say is[3] that Parmenides' words are designed to develop Socrates' notions, to organise and push them further, praising the natural soundness of his convictions, while perfecting what is incomplete in them and articulating what is confused. Of the four problems connected with the theory of Forms, as we have distinguished them, he has not dealt with the question of

838

[1] Added from Latin translation.   [2] Reading τοῦτό φασι for τοῦτο πᾶσι of MSS.
[3] Reading τοσοῦτον for τοσούτων.

210

their existence, since he accepts this hypothesis; but regarding the range of things that have Forms he questions him judicially, trying to learn whether he makes all things depend on ideal causes, or whether he realizes there is another cause superior to the Forms; and the reproof, as we said, looks to this first cause. What he does, then, is to move downwards from the most universal through the more particular and atomic kinds of being, and finally coming to those that are not constituted in accordance with an intellectual Form, but are still derived from the monad of all things existent. Having thus gone from the highest to the lowest class of beings and made them all dependent upon the paternal cause, thus perfecting Socrates' notion about them, he goes on to the third problem, the problem of participation, using now the method of midwifery in an opposite way; for while his argument throughout is maieutic, not contentious, paternal,[4] not defensive, yet it differs in that at first it proceeds downwards to the lowest ranks of being, while later it advances from below to the arguments appropriate to divine causes, in both of these ways bringing Socrates to perfect understanding and leading him upwards by articulating the notions he has of them.

839   Such, then, as I have said, is this method of argument, eliciting our spontaneous ideas and making them articulate when they are incomplete. It educates those who are capable of following its leading, truly imitating the paternal cause which, from the summit of the constitution of things, preserves, perfects, and draws upwards all things by means of its unknowable powers.

We must now turn once again to look at the subject matter of the text, and say what we think this participation is and how it comes about, and afterwards examine the words of Plato. But first I will say by way of preface, that here too, as when we discussed the unity and differentiation of the Forms, we are investigating the manner of its occurrence. That there is participation in the Ideas, if they exist, we should all admit, but we are in doubt how things participate in them. This is what Parmenides is investigating here, just as Socrates in the preceding passage was puzzled to know how Ideas can be separated and at the same time joined together, if they are indeed simple and not like visible things, in which union and differentiation are easily accepted by everyone. Now after these preliminaries, let us turn to the problem before us.

Let us say, then, that participation in intellectual Ideas is like reflection in a mirror. Just as in this case the shape and relative positions of its parts cause an image of the countenance to be seen on the surface of

---

[4] The reading πειραστικός (Cod. Harl.), rather than πατρικός, is tempting, but not attested in Latin (paternalis), and is not necessary.

the mirror, so receptive matter, holding itself up, so to speak, before the Demiurge and the artifice[5] of his mind, is filled with Ideas from him. Again let us say that participation is like an impression made by a seal upon wax; for the seal, I mean the Idea, leaves a trace and an impression of itself; and this impression is not the same as the seal that made it, just as the enmattered species is not identical with the divine and immaterial Idea. This analogy differs from the preceding one in that it implies a certain passive modification in the recipient of the impression; the mirror in the other example suffers no perceptible effect, as the wax does in this. Hence those who wish to keep matter impassive as it participates in the Forms[6] liken it to a mirror and call the

840 forms in it images or reflections, while those who think matter is affected in the process[7] say it is shaped like a wax under a seal, and call the forms states of the matter. The former look to prime matter when keeping it impassive. Since prime matter is simple, it would disappear if it suffered an effect, for what is simple cannot have one part of itself affected and a different part remain unchanged. The others look to its bodily character, for this is moulded by the qualities which are bodily. But we might also say that the products of participation are somewhat like the images (eikones) made by the art of painting, or sculpture, or some other technique. For it is by divine craftsmanship that things here are shaped into likenesses of the divine Ideas, and this is why the whole sensible cosmos is called a likeness (eikōn) of the intelligible (Tim. 92c). This analogy is superior to the former kinds in that it distinguishes the maker from the pattern, whereas they take these two factors as one.

But those who are lovers of the vision of reality must recognise that each of these descriptions is imperfect by itself and taken alone is incapable of presenting to our thoughts the whole truth about participation. In the first place, you see that the action of the mirror requires an extended surface in which the image is produced, hence a reflection of this sort cannot appear in an unextended medium. Again, the subject itself faces the mirror, whereas the intelligible cause turns upon itself and does not look outwards. And even if the mirror receives only an apparent, not a real, transmission of something (for the reflections of the rays of light come back to the subject himself, as those would say who believe that no image is emitted by those who look into a mirror),[8] is is surely clear that this type of occurrence is quite different from participation in the Forms, for even if an image is really in the

---

[5] Πόρος, with reference, presumably, to Symp. 203b-d.

[6] E.g. Plotinus Enn. III, 6.7-13.

[7] E.g. Plutarch De Is. 373ab (seal on wax); Arius Didymus, ap. Euseb. PE XI, 23.2-6 (Fr. 1 Diels); Albinus, Did., ch. 12.

[8] Cf. perhaps Plotinus Enn. IV, 5.7.44-46.

mirror, yet effluences from the face come onto the mirror, which is not proper for the Forms, since no part of them is parcelled off to proceed to things here, nor do they emit effluences, since they are bodiless and indivisible.

841   The second analogy, the impression produced by a seal, fits the Stoic hypotheses asserting that the maker acts and the recipient is affected in a bodily way; they require pushing, resistance, and reaction, otherwise an impression does not occur. The agent must press, the wax must resist, and this is how the mark of the seal is produced. Furthermore, the agent is external and the wax suffers an effect produced from without, whereas the Form enters into the whole of its subject and acts upon it from within (for nature shapes the body internally, not externally as an artisan does). And, finally, the factor that is participated comes into contact with the thing that participates, whereas the Forms must be independent of everything and be mixed with nothing else. Also, if the seal should receive a trace from the wax, it would be far from resembling the Forms, whose being is undefiled by taking on anything alien.

Thirdly, as regards the analogy drawn from images, surely we see that it, too, operates only on the surface, whereas Forms shape their substrata in their entirety and from within; and prior to these considerations, it has the pattern and the maker existing separately. The model does not generate its own likeness, nor the maker produce a product like himself, whereas the divine Forms are at once patterns and creators of their likenesses. They are not like the makers of wax dolls,[9] they have a being that is efficacious and a power that likens secondary things to themselves.

As I said, then, all of these—reflections, impressions, replicas—are to be mentioned primarily as aids to the less advanced students, in order to indicate through them all that it is through likeness to the Forms that specific kinds are constituted (for there is one feature that appears in them all, the operation of likeness). But we must realize that none of
842 these analogies has any scientific value, nor do all of them together adequately grasp the true nature of participation in the divine Forms. This seems to be the reason why Plato sometimes calls the products of Ideas portraits and likens them to paintings, sometimes impressions, and sometimes images. In the *Timaeus* he says that God "painted" the universe in the shape of a dodecahedron (55c), and that the Receptacle receives "impressions" from the Ideas (52b), and in the *Sophist* that the not-really real is an "image" (240b). This suggests that none of these analogies is capable of catching the real nature of the process of partic-

[9] Cf. Plotinus *Enn.* III, 8.2.

ipation, though each expresses a different aspect of it.[10] But perhaps if we could discover the authentic manner in which participation occurs, we should see how each of these analogies approaches the truth, though failing to convey its full character.

Accordingly we must affirm that the cause of this participation is, on the one hand, the efficacious power of the primordial divine Forms themselves, and on the other hand the appetency of the beings that are shaped in accordance with them and that participate in the formative activity that proceeds from them. For the creative action of the Forms is not alone sufficient to bring about participation; at all events, though these Forms are everywhere to the same degree, not all things participate alike in them; nor is the appetency of the beings that participate adequate without their creative activity. For desire by itself is imperfect; it is the perfect generating factors that lead in the form-giving process. Those, then, who make Intellect a final but not an efficient cause[11] possess only half the truth; for they give appetency to sensible things, but have deprived the divine factor of its creative power and left the production of sense objects to chance. Whence do these sensibles get their appetency if not from the source of their being and existence? And how could they have a desire for an uncreative principle that neither gives nor is capable of giving them anything. And those who make the divine principle generative but leave objects without a desire for it,[12] have a doctrine that is incomplete and absurd in another way. First of all, every creative agent works upon what is by nature susceptible to 843 its action, that is, upon what is capable of receiving its action, so that when the Demiurge will create something of a given character, the subject that is fitted to receive it, whatever the character may be, by its very aptitude presents itself as a collaborator with the agent that can create; and it does so through its desire, for its approach is caused by desire for what it is moving towards. Furthermore, all things would be alike if each thing came to be according to the divine creativity alone. For since that creativity is always the same and present to all things, unless there were a difference in the aptitudes of the subjects how could we explain their variety and the fact that some things always participate in the same way and others sometimes in one way, sometimes in another? It must be that some things possess a substratum such that it always holds the Forms and is susceptible to its creative action, and others sometimes an aptitude for participating in the Form and at other times for participating in its contrary. For since it is potentially everything, but actually nothing, and since it is filled with the indefiniteness

---

[10] Reading ἄλλου δὲ ἄλλο τι παριστάντος αὐτῆς.

[11] The Peripatetics. Cf. *In Tim.* I, 266.28ff.

[12] Presumably the Stoics, Matter for them being purely passive.

of the more-or-less, it accepts different reason-principles at different times, for although it desires to enjoy them all, it is not able to partake of them all at the same time. Consequently, we must affirm that the cause of the form-giving activity is not only the generating power of the demiurgic intellect, but also the appetency of its substrata and their varying aptitudes. The former is the active cause, the substratum-nature the passive; and the former acts not by physical impact, for it is bodiless, nor by unbounded impulses like us, for it is impassive, nor by acts of deliberation,[13] for it is perfect, but by its very being itself. So the thing that comes to be is a likeness of its creator, thinking in that realm being bound up with essence; hence as he thinks he makes, and as he makes he thinks, and he is always doing both. For this reason the thing that comes to be always comes to be from thought, for the being being made is everywhere together with its maker. Hence even in things that come to be in time the Form appears instantaneously, the creative actions preceding its appearance serving only to remove the obstacles to its appearance. For the removal of obstacles ⟨takes time, but the appearance ⟨of Form⟩ occurs⟩[14] in an instant, imitating in this the eternal genesis of all things at once through the principle of aptitude for reception.[15]

844

What is the source of this receptivity and how does it come about? This is the next question to be considered. Shall we not say that it comes from the paternal and creative cause? The whole of nature that is subject to the work of the Demiurge was produced, if we may rely upon those who are expert in divine matters,[16] by the intelligible Father, whoever this is. Upon this nature another Father who is also Creator cast reflections of himself; and the Creator who is also a Father ordered it as a whole; and the Creator alone filled it up with particulars by means of his craftsmanship. From these four causes appears first the matter which is prior to all form-giving activity, described in the *Timaeus* (51a) as a shapeless kind which is a universal receptacle; second, something that has received traces of the Forms but is disordered and inharmonious; third, the cosmos as a whole, composed of wholes in accordance with the unique and universal paradigm; and last the cosmos provided with all the living beings—the different causes produc-

[13] Reading βουλαῖς, with MSS B and C, for Cousin's βολαῖς (Latin *consiliis*).
[14] Postulating a lacuna after ἐξαίρεσις, e.g. ⟨κατὰ χρόνον, ἡ δὲ παρουσία⟩ κατὰ τὸ νῦν (West.).
[15] For the principle of *epitēdeiotēs pros hypodochēn*, cf. *ET*, props. 39, 71; *In Tim.* I, 51.25ff., 139.20ff., 163.27ff., etc.
[16] What follows reproduces Syrianus, who is no doubt himself influenced by Numenius' distinction (fr. 21) between the πατήρ and ποιητής of *Tim.* 28c. Cf. *In Tim.* I, 310.3ff.

ing all these creatures, ⟨both immortal⟩ and mortal,[17] prior to the cos-
845 mos as a whole. But what these causes are we must learn from the
family of the theologians. We ought not then to wonder whence come
these various aptitudes. For the things in this world that seem to be relatively permanent are the products of more sovereign powers in the intellectual world that because of their indescribable plenitude of being
are able to penetrate to the lowest grades of existence,[18] and the things
here imitate in the indefiniteness of their own nature the ineffable being
of those higher powers. The substratum therefore possesses their reflections, I mean the one substratum as well as the many and diverse
kinds of receptivity by which the things here are disposed towards desire of the Forms, and of the rich plenitude of the demiurgic reason-
principles and their texture. Being endowed with these aptitudes, the
substratum supports the visible cosmos and participates in the whole
process of creation.

If, again, we ask to know the principle that unites the power of the
Demiurge and the aptitude of the things subject to it, we shall find that
the Good itself is the cause of all unification. It is through desire for the
Good that the recipients advance to receive the cosmic causes, and it is
the good that causes the demiurgic forms to make their procession into
secondary things, imitating the source of all good which gave existence
to all the ranks of divine beings because of its own goodness, if this language be permitted. Thus we have three causes of participation in
forms:[19] the unitary Goodness, the demiurgic power of the Forms, and
the aptitude of the beings that receive illuminations from above.

Now since participation is brought about by these three causes, we
see how it is possible to liken it to reflections in a mirror; for the fitness
and the appetency that things derive from above cause them to turn
back to those higher realities. Again in another way it is like the
impression made by a seal, for the effective power of the causes endows
things with traces of the Forms, visible impressions of the invisible
846 causes. And thirdly, in turn, it resembles the making of replicas, for we
said that the demiurgic cause binds together the invisible and the visible
elements.[20] This is what the maker of a likeness does, i.e. he brings the
material and the pattern together. And in actualising the material he
places in it the figure that resembles the Form. These analogies, therefore, touch the truth in part. But it is not surprising that no one of them

---

[17] Reading πάντα ⟨ἀθάνατά⟩ τε καὶ θνητά. But the word order is still strange. ταῦτα
(1.29) seems out of place.
[18] For a statement of the principle of the greater extent of superior powers, cf. *ET*,
prop. 57.
[19] Putting a comma after τῶν εἰδῶν. Cousin's supplement ⟨τῆς τῶν ἀγαθῶν πάντων
πηγῆς⟩ seems unnecessary.
[20] Cf. 840 above.

is capable of apprehending all that is involved in participation, for the things described are divisible and perceptible and the peculiar character of the invisible and divine causes is beyond their grasp. We must be content if we can even indicate how it is through the power of description. Since, as we have often reminded ourselves, secondary things are always dependent on the beings above them, it is clear that we shall make the heavenly bodies dependent on the divine Forms and say they receive the whole of their formation from that source, whereas mortal beings are dependent also upon the heavenly bodies and receive thence much variety in their modes of generation. Thus the cosmos as a whole has received its entire visible order from the Forms as a whole and the single Form that holds together all things in it.

So much for this. But since it has become customary to speak of three modes of participation, by impression, by reflection, and by likeness (the wax, for example, partakes of the form impressed on it by the seal; water receives reflections from visible things, images that appear to be some particular thing but have no being at all; and thirdly the waxen figure or the painting is a likeness of Socrates), and since it is obvious how these modes differ from one another, a very ingenious person[21] has said that participation occurs in all these ways. Sense-objects participate in forms by way of impression, but only in the forms presented by nature, for these reason-principles act somewhat like seals when they descend into things. And they receive reflections of the 847 Forms, but only of the forms on the level of Soul, so that they become semblances of souls animated by them with clearer living powers. And they are likenesses when they are made to resemble intellectual Forms, as in the *Timaeus* (92c) the visible animal is said to be a likeness of the intelligible. Hence, he says, things are likenesses of intellectual Forms, reflections of the soul-forms, and imprints of the physical forms.

These distinctions seem to me ingenious, especially since we can often observe the three kinds of participation interwoven with each other. The body of a good and wise man, for example, appears itself handsome and attractive because it participates directly in the beauty of nature and has its bodily shape moulded by it, and by receiving reflections from the beauty of soul it carries a trace of ideal beauty, the soul serving as connecting term between his own lowest beauty and Beauty Itself. So that the reflection reveals this species of soul as being wise, or courageous, or noble or a likeness of some other virtue. And the animated statue, for example, participates by way of impression in the art which turns it on a lathe and polishes and shapes it in such and such a

---

[21] Since Amelius is referred to at *In Tim.* 76.26 as ὁ γενναῖος Ἀμέλιος, Cousin, with some plausibility, suggests him. Certainly the tone of the reference is mildly ironic, which would accord with Proclus' general attitude to Amelius.

fashion; while from the universe it has received reflections of vitality which even cause us to say that it is alive; and as a whole it has been made like the god whose image it is. For a theurgist who sets up a statue as a likeness of a certain divine order fabricates the tokens of its identity with reference to that order, acting as does the craftsman when he makes a likeness by looking to its proper model.[22]

But perhaps it is better and more in accord with theology not to make these distinctions, but to say that sense objects simultaneously partake of intellectual Forms as present to them, receive reflections of 848 them, and resemble them as images. For Plato in this very passage says simply that things here "participate in the Forms," as if the primary Forms were participated in all these ways by sense-objects. There are three intermediate ranks of gods, the cosmic gods, the gods independent of the cosmos, and the leader-gods.[23] Through the rank of the cosmic gods things in this world partake of the Forms by way of impression, for these gods are most directly their supervisors. Through the independent gods they get reflections of the Forms, for these gods are in some respects in contact with things here and in some respects not,[24] but because of their transcendent powers they can provide sensible things with appearances of the primary Forms. And through the assimilative gods (these are what I have called the leader-gods) sensibles are made like the intellectual realm. Consequently, it is through the single demiurgic source and cause that impressions, reflections, and likenesses come to be, and through its all-perfecting goodness.

So much for a summary statement on these matters. Now we must return to the text, and by the aid of what we have said try to bring each part of it into accord with what we have just said.[25] Let us begin, then, as follows. The phrase "you think" calls forth Socrates' opinion and stirs him up to have a look at it himself; for by concentrating more closely on this hypothesis of Ideas, he has made his grasp of it more perfect. "As you say" are the words of one who is arguing from a common ground with his adversary; his purpose here is not to dislodge 849 Socrates from his theoretical positions, but to find proofs consistent with their common starting points. It is midwifery, not refutation, as

---

[22] For other references to theurgic consecration of statues, cf. *In Tim.* III, 6.8ff., and 155.18ff.

[23] For the class of θεοὶ ἡγεμόνες or ἡγεμονικοί, see *In Tim.* I, 114.13, 141.1; III, 262.6ff. and *PT* VI, 1-14. For the ἀφομοιωτικὴ δύναμις of these gods, cf. *In Tim.* III, 1.14ff., 227.6ff. For the ἀπόλυτοι θεοί see *PT* VI, 15-24.

[24] Cf. *Parm.* 148d5-149d7, and *PT* VI, 24, where these gods are discussed as "hypercosmic-encosmic".

[25] Reading προσβιβάζειν ⟨τοῖς⟩ εἰρημένοις.

we have frequently mentioned before.[26] "There exist certain Ideas" repeats what they had said before, meaning that there are Ideas of some
things and not of others, and not of everything that is caused by the
One; for the One is cause of more things than Being is. In the phrase
"these other things," "these things" indicates that sensible particulars
are meant, and "other" that they are distinct from the Forms; for they
have descended far from the principles from which they started. From
the universality of these principles they have ended in particularity, and
from the unity of the Forms they have reached the extreme of diversity
and dispersion. For in this world we have Empedocles' Strife and the
war of gods and giants; but up there are Friendship and unity and the
goddess that unifies all things.

Finally, the statement that the Forms have given their names as well
as their being to the things in this world is a remark of genius and well
worthy of Platonic principles. Those who think that names exist only
by convention make the multitude responsible for conventional usage
and assert that names have their origin in perceptible things; for these,
being before everybody's eyes, are the first to have received specific
names, and from them, by the use of certain analogies, the wiser men
set names for invisible realities. Thus if they should call God an eternal
living being, and "living being" denotes the perceptible being, then
this sensible thing will have the name primarily, and God will have it
derivatively, as a result of our transferring the name to him by analogy,
and it will not matter whether we call God "living being" or by any
other name that we choose to put upon him, even as a certain man once
imposed upon his slaves the names of certain conjunctions. But those
who think that names have a natural origin[27] say some names are suited
850 for some things, and others for others. Each name carries a likeness of
the object to which it is applied; i.e. the properties of its component
parts and their number and particular combination, they think, make
the name an image of the "accident," that is, the object.[28] They therefore would entrust the finding of names to the wise, as Socrates says in
the *Cratylus* (390d) when he puts names under the authority of the dialectician, and makes each name refer primarily to an immaterial form
and secondarily to sensible things. Since they are presumed to be wise
and to enjoy the benefits of dialectic, they must know that immaterial
forms are more precisely what they are than enmattered and visible

---

[26] E.g. 838.25.

[27] A large lacuna here in the Greek MSS, filled from the Latin translation. The man
referred to as giving his slaves the names of conjunctions is the philosopher Diodorus
Cronus, cf. *Megarica*, frs. 111-113 Döring.

[28] τὸ τυγχάνον is the Stoic term for the external object denominated by the name, *SVF*
II, 166. The Stoics, therefore, are the school of thought here referred to, but later Platonists generally are in agreement with them.

things, and that it is more possible to know and name them than these. For example, what is here called "equal" is full of its contrary; so, not being purely equal, how could it legitimately carry the designation "equal"? As if one called something fiery "fire," when it does not retain the property of fire. Furthermore, even if you say "man," the word does not strictly apply to the perceptible man. For the visible man is in many respects also not man. Obviously the parts in him of which he is composed are not each of them men. Therefore, although he is a man in one sense, there are many senses in which he is not man. The Form 'man' on the other hand, is not in one sense man and in another not-man, but has that character through and through; whatever part of it you take is man, just as every part of beauty is beautiful and every part of motion is motion. In short, none of the Forms is made up of its own opposite; Intellect is not composed of elements lacking intellect, nor Life of lifeless, nor Motion of motionless parts, nor Beauty of things

851 not beautiful; so that neither is Man composed of not-men, nor any other Form of what is not such as it is. For it would be a compound with its character added from without if it were made from things that are not of the sort that it itself is said to be and is. Thus we see that the term "man" is correctly applied to the intelligible Form, but not correctly nor quite truly to the visible man.

Consequently, if names are images in words of the objects to which they apply, they refer primarily to immaterial Forms, and derivatively to sensible things, so that things in this world derive both their being and their designation from that world. This is what Plato says elsewhere as well as here, at the same time by using the term "designations" (*epōnymiai*) indicating that the names given to them are epithets, even as their being is a later attribution. Just as when one tries to give a dignified name to a humble object, the name does not mean the same thing to him when he applies it to an undignified object. For example, when we speak of man, i.e. use the term "man," we use it in one sense as an image of the divine Form and in another sense when we refer to a visible man. Some persons have thought that Plato is using his terms synonymously, and others that he is using them homonymously,[29] when he uses the same names for intelligibles as for sensibles. My opinion is that he is using them homonymously, though in a different way from that which they presuppose. For "man" is not an ambiguous term in the sense of a bare name applied to two different things, but as being primarily a likeness of the intelligible reality, and secondarily of the sensible thing; for this reason man is not the same thing when we are speaking of the intelligible as when we refer to the sensible man. In the

[29] I.e. "homonymously" and "synonymously" in the Aristotelian sense (*Cat.*, ch. 1).

one case it is a likeness of the divine object, in the other the likeness of the sensible individual. Suppose someone had seen Athena herself such as she is portrayed by Homer:

> . . . the child of aegis-bearing Zeus
> Within her father's threshold dropped her veil
> Of airy texture, work of her own hands,
> The cuirass donned of cloud-compelling Zeus
> And stood accoutred for the bloody fray.
>
> (*Iliad* V, 754-758)

If, after encountering this vision, a man should wish to paint a picture of the Athena he had seen and should do so; and another man who had 852 seen the Athena of Phidias, presumably in the same posture, should also want to put her figure into a picture and should do so, their pictures would seem to superficial observers to differ not at all; but the one made by the artist who had seen the goddess will make a special impression, whereas that which copies the mental statue will carry only a frigid likeness, since it is the picture of a lifeless object. In the same way the word *man*, though applied to the two objects, is not in the same way a likeness of both; in the one case it is the likeness of a paradigm, in the other case the likeness of a likeness, the image of an image. Likewise Socrates in the *Phaedrus* expounds the meaning of the name *love* in one sense when he is looking at the divine Eros and calls him a winged being (*pterōton*, 252b), and in another sense when he is looking at his likeness and says it is called *erōs* because of the strength (*rhōmē*) of its desire (238c). As their being is not the same, so also their names are different; and as being belongs to the less authentic by derivation from the more genuine instance, so also the names of secondary things come from the beings prior to them. For in general, since we use names because we want to indicate distinctions in thought between things, and distinction and unmixed purity are proper to the higher realm,[30] the names we use will be suitable primarily to Forms, not to things that contain a considerable mixture of opposite qualities, such as white with black, equal with unequal, and the like. And if we suppose that the multitude, and not the wise, are the legislators of names, Plato would say of them as of those persons in the *Gorgias* (467aff.) who "do what they like," that they assign names as seems best to them, not as they really wish. For when, having in mind simply the notion of equality, they call this particular thing equal in the primary sense, and apply this designation to it, they may think they are naming it, but are really being diverted to the primary equality, for that alone is equal, while the

---

[30] Reading ⟨ἐκεῖ⟩, ἐκείνοις (West.).

particular thing here is both equal and unequal.[31] It is clear from all this that names refer primarily to intelligible Ideas, and that sense-objects get their names, together with their being, from that source. But we must recognise that what has been said is about the names that our
853 mind is able to consider. There are many grades of names, as of knowledge. Some are called divine, the names by which the inferior gods designate the beings above them; some angelic, the names by which the angels designate themselves and the gods; some are demonic, and some human. And some are names we too can utter, others are unutterable. In short, as the *Cratylus* has taught us (391e), and before it divinely inspired tradition, both knowledge and name-giving among the gods transcends ours.

> *"For example, things become like by partaking of Likeness, and great by partaking of Greatness, and just or beautiful by partaking of Justice or Beauty?" "Exactly," said Socrates.* (131a)

Of Likeness we said earlier (848 above) that its peculiar function is to render secondary things like primary ones and to be the single tie that holds all things together. Hence it is not simply an accidental attribute of things here, but the factor that perfects the being of each, for perfection comes to each when it becomes like its intelligible Form. As the aim of Soul is likeness to Intellect, so the good for all things sensible is likeness to the intelligible and divine Forms. Whence, then, comes this common and perfecting element if not from intelligible Likeness? Or, if you prefer, whence comes the factor that fills up their being? For the being of each thing is defined by this, I mean by its likeness to intelligibles, and it is through being like its Idea that each thing is what it really is.

About Greatness all lovers of truth should know that it is not merely
854 the cause of extendedness. It is not magnitude in the sense in which the geometers use the term, for they call magnitude whatever is extended in any way, whether we take a line, or a plane, or a solid. But it is not Plato's custom to call Greatness the cause of magnitude in general; rather it is what gives preeminence to anything in its particular class. So in the *Phaedo* he calls a thing great by reason of greatness (100e), and says it is by greatness that a thing becomes greater than another, while a thing becomes less than another by smallness. Yet what is less has a certain extension and would possess magnitude in the geometrical sense. But Greatness is not a principle of this sort; rather it is such a principle as causes excellence and superior quality in all grades of being, from the gods to the lowest. Thus in the *Phaedrus* he calls Zeus a "great

---

[31] Reading ἐκεῖνο δὲ μόνως ἴσον, ⟨τοῦτο δὲ καὶ ἴσον⟩ καὶ ἄνισον (West.).

leader" (246e), meaning that he excels other leaders, as being preeminent over them in the qualities of leadership. And in the *Symposium* he calls Eros a "great daemon" (202d), as possessing the height of daemonic qualities. And if we are used to calling some people great-souled or great-minded, greatness must be in souls in a manner appropriate to them; and also, in another sense, whenever applied to persons of superior accomplishments (*megalourgoi*) or style (*megaloprepeis*). This is why in the *Republic* (VI, 487a) Socrates ascribes the quality of grandeur (*megaloprepes*) to the philosophic nature, since it is striving for elevation and greatness. And if, as Socrates says in the *Phaedo*, one body is greater or excels another because of greatness, in such a case "great" is relative to the quality characteristic of that grade of being. The range of Greatness therefore extends from the highest to the lowest beings. Among the gods it is unitary greatness, that is, it is considered as preeminence in unity; among the daemons it is dynamic greatness, that is, as superiority in power, for power is characteristic of daemons and the great among them are the more powerful; in souls it is vital greatness, for in them the greater is what represents the higher type of life; and in 855 bodies it is superiority in extension. Thus whether it is preeminence in unity, or in power, or in level of life, or only in quantity and extension, Greatness everywhere presents the same character. If, then, this is common and universal, it has a predominant cause which is intellectual.

Similarly Beauty dispenses symmetry, unity, and the charm of perfection to the Forms. It is what gives to souls the beauty they have, and casts a splendour upon bodies from its beautifying power, making them to bloom, as it were, imposed upon the various species, making the rational element dominant over the material causes. For the dominance of reason and Form is a condition of the presence of beauty, which is why the heavenly bodies are more beautiful than things here, for up there the Form perfectly controls the underlying nature. And intelligible things are more beautiful than the heavenly bodies, for they are purely Forms. That, then, is the primary Beauty "gleaming most brightly" (*Phaedr.* 250d), and Beauty in the true sense. For beauty here is mixed with ugliness. As Matter partakes of beauty through the Form, so Form is filled with ugliness through Matter, which is ugly and lacking in beauty.

Of Justice, finally, let us say that it is the cause of the Forms performing their proper functions; for by justice each remains in its own station and does what is incumbent upon it. Greatness does not make small, nor smallness confer preeminence, nor does likeness separate derivatives from primary beings, nor unlikeness bring together and unite; but each of the Forms discharges its own function, carries on its own activity, reflects upon itself, and belongs to itself. Not only among the in-

223

telligibles is this the case; in the heavens also each of the powers does its appointed task, as Socrates says in the *Phaedrus* (247a). And in ourselves justice is present when each part of us maintains the activity and the
856 form appropriate to it, and likewise in the state. Justice, therefore, which brings life and the Forms to perfection, is common and universal. Consequently above justice here there is a single intellectual image according to which all just things are said to be and are just.

> *"Therefore does not every thing that participates participate in either the whole or a part of the Form? Or could there be some way of participation other than these?" "How could there be?" he replied.* (131a)

About both the previous argument and this one now before us I observe the same difference of opinion among the interpreters. In each case those who accept the major premise attack the minor, and those who accept the minor reject the major.[32] The earlier argument they state somewhat as follows: if there are Forms, there are Forms of all things; but there are not Forms of all things, as you (Socrates), admit, hence there are no Forms. Those who suppose there are Forms of all things accept the major, but reject the minor premise, and therefore say that Socrates is justly rebuked for not positing Forms of all things. They accept Parmenides and regard Socrates' caution as invalid. The others take the opposite position; they welcome the minor premise, and discredit the major as incorrect. That is, it is false to say that if Forms exist there are Forms of all things; but the minor premise, that there are not Forms of all things, is true. They accept quite readily the denial of Socrates and reject Parmenides' reproof. We have explained above, however (838-839), how both Socrates' denial is justified and Parmenides' reproof inspired; and that the argument is not aimed at the refutation of Forms, but only at the explication of that second problem. Similarly in the present argument, which is concerned with the third problem—if a sensible thing participates in a Form, it participates either in the whole or a part of it, but it cannot participate either in the whole or in the part, hence it does not participate—in this argument the one
857 party accepts the major and denies the minor premise, while the other party does the reverse. The former say it is true that if something here participates in a Form it participates either in the whole or in a part of it (there is no middle ground between whole and part, since what is a part is for them not the whole); but the statement that it participates in neither way is false, for it participates in the whole of it. How could the whole idea of Man fail to be present in each individual man? And the

---

[32] Proclus here uses the Stoic terms συνημμένον and πρόσληψις, which it seemed best to render thus for the present purpose.

whole idea of Swan in swans, and similarly for all other Forms? The other party rejects the major but accepts the minor premise. That is, if a thing here participates in a form, it is either the whole Form or a part of it that is participated in—this is not sound, they say, for there is an alternative way of participation. But they regard as sound the premise that Forms are participated neither as wholes nor as parts, for they participate in neither of these, but in a different way. If this is the correct statement of their positions, both parties are alike opposed to Socrates and to Parmenides himself, the latter as being sophistical and the former as being misled. And yet Parmenides admonishes Socrates not to look to the opinions of men but to the nature of things, so he obviously is not immediately thereafter going to lead Socrates astray from the truth by plausible arguments. Perhaps, then, it is better to say that the dialectic exercise connected with the second problem proceeds downwards from the most universal Forms through the intermediate and divine atomic kinds, to end with the things whose nature is so weak and degenerate that they do not have a formal cause and are wrongly classed with the products of the Forms. So that in the third problem—how participation occurs—Parmenides is working back upwards from below, showing in what manner participation in the Forms comes about, and that we ought not to think of this participation as bodily or material or as taking place in any other way characteristic of realities of the second, third, or lower levels, but in a manner superior to them and appropriate to demiurgic and primary and immaterial Forms. For the

858 modes of participation, I think, are many. Gods are said to participate in gods in one way, angels in gods in a different way, daemons in angels or gods in a third way, souls in daemons or angels or gods in still another way, and still otherwise do sense-objects participate in souls or higher beings and the gods themselves, and bodies in bodies. We must obviously, then, examine carefully in what way we should speak of participation in the case of Forms, if we are fully to solve the third problem. Above all we must consider whether participation in Ideas is bodily, that is, whether things here participate in Forms in the way that body participates in body. Bodily participation is naturally of two kinds: the body incorporates either the whole or a part of the body in which it participates. For example, when we are hungry we partake of the whole of the food we eat, for since it is the lesser quantity it can pass into the greater. And since we are formed from the elements as totalities, we partake of each of them in part. The fire in us comes from the universal fire, the water in us likewise from the universal water, and so with each of the other two elements. As Socrates says in the *Philebus* (29e), we share in the universal elements, not they in us. So it is true that in bodily participation, the participant takes either the whole or a

part of what is participated; and if participation in Forms is neither in the wholes nor in the parts, participation in Forms is not bodily in character. So the examination will shift to another kind of participation, and again to another, until we have disqualified all those that do not fit the participation in Forms that we are concerned with. This is why Parmenides here, to incite Socrates to a more adequate attack on the problem, adds, "or whether there could be any way of participation other than these." He is acting like a midwife, provoking him to a consideration of non-bodily participation; and Socrates, seeing the possibility of non-bodily participation, submits to the questioning and goes along with the refutation of the hypotheses. For it is shown that things here cannot participate in Forms either wholly or partially, as bodies participate in other bodies. Participation is possible in another way, which will be made clear as we proceed.

859

"Then do you think that the Form, being one, is as a whole in each of its many particulars, or what?" "What is to prevent it from being in them,[33] *Parmenides?" said Socrates. "Then, while remaining one and the same, it will be, as a whole, in many separate things at the same time, and thus will be separate from itself." (131a-b)*

Anyone who is not examining whole and part in the sense of bodily unity, but in a way appropriate to intelligible and immaterial Forms, will see that things here participate, each of them, in both the whole and a part of its Form. For since the relation of Forms to things is that of causes to their effects, and since nowhere do caused objects absorb the whole power of their causes, things do not partake of the whole of their Forms. For how could a thing of sense receive the intelligible life and power of a Form? And how could the unity and indivisibility of a Form come to be in Matter? On the other hand, since these things possess the property, say justice or beauty, by which ideal Justice and Beauty are characterized in their own nature, for this reason things could be said to partake of the whole, not the part. The specific character of beauty is everywhere and in all beautiful things, but sometimes it is present in an intellectual and sometimes in a material fashion. And clearly the more perfect beings participate more fully than those that are more distant from perfection, the former by virtue of their more numerous and others by virtue of their fewer capacities. Beauty itself is an intellectual Form, possessed of life, and a cause of symmetry. Thus this Form that is productive of symmetry is present to every thing of beauty; for this is the property of Beauty itself, so that each beautiful

---

[33] Proclus reads ἐνεῖναι here, for the ἓν εἶναι of the Plato MSS, so that this is not just a conjecture of Schleiermacher, as is commonly stated.

thing partakes in the whole of the property itself. Intelligence, however, is not present to everything that is beautiful, but only to ensouled things, for the beauty in soul is intellectual[34] in nature, nor is life present to every beautiful thing, but only to the heavenly bodies and to any others of similar character in the world of generation. But the light of beauty is present also in gold and in certain stones. Thus some things
860 partake of both intelligence and life, others of life without intelligence, still others of the property of bare beauty—the more immaterial being receiving more of its powers than do material things. Consequently, secondary things partake both of the whole and a part of their corresponding Forms.

This is the proper answer for persons who are capable of seeing the bodiless being of Forms. But to those who think of participation as bodily, we can say that things here cannot partake of Forms either wholly or in part. This is what Parmenides proves to Socrates as he leads him to the discovery of the authentic mode of participation in Forms. And he shows first that things cannot partake of the whole of their Forms. Socrates himself first implies this, when he asks what is to prevent us from assuming it. But Parmenides refutes the assumption by pointing out that one and the same thing will be wholly in many separate things, and this is the extreme of absurdity. At the least there will be a separation of itself from itself. Consider this finger, for example, or anything else that is in something, whether as a bodily part or as a power: if it could be at the same time in several separate things, it would be separate from itself. A power, which resides in a subject, will belong to different subjects and thus be separate from itself; it will be in two bodies, yet unable to exist apart from either of them. And a body which is wholly in this place cannot be in another. It cannot be denied that more than one body may be in the same place, but for the same body to be in more than one place is impossible. Therefore it is impossible that a bodily whole be in more than one underlying substratum.

Notice the precision of his terms. He is not content to say "(everywhere) one," but adds "and the same"; and that it "will be in many," and also "in many separate things"; that it will be in them "as a whole," and also "at the same time." For it could be in one thing in one respect and in another in a different respect, but not in an identical respect. Or it could be identical in them if they are implicated in each other (as immaterial and divine light may be both in air and in the place occupied
861 by the air). Or again a part of itself, not the whole, could be in one thing and another part in another, these two parts being separate. Or

---

[34] Reading νοοειδές, with Latin translation, for ἐνοειδές of Greek MSS.

again it is possible that it be in different things at different times, but not simultaneously. He says also that it is "one," for it would be possible for it to be in something not in this way, though if it is in itself, it can be everywhere and in all its particulars, alike. If you wish to see more esoterically the precise point here, examine Plato's language and put the matter to yourself as follows. Since Forms exist primarily, as we learn from the *Timaeus* (31a), at the inferior limit among the intelligibles, clearly each of the primary forms is "one," "being," and a "whole," and as such can be identically present to many different things at the same time, but transcendently; so that a Form is both everywhere and nowhere, and being present to all its instances in a non-temporal fashion is unmixed with them. Consequently, the addition of the phrase "will be in them," which places the Form in a foundation alien to itself, makes nonsense of the whole doctrine, and so he adds "and thus it will be separated from itself." For this cannot be said of the primary hypostases, since every divine being is in itself and present to other beings. And this is why they cannot be in many things, viz. that they are not in themselves; for what is a part of one thing cannot become a part of another. Such is what Parmenides is saying.

Socrates' contribution is to try to resolve these difficulties; whether he does so rightly or wrongly will become clear as the argument proceeds. Socrates will not object to the mode of participation, but will defend this same hypothesis, despite Parmenides' frequent suggestions that he go further. In fact he has made such a suggestion earlier when he asks, "or is there some other way of participation?" and in this later passage he adds "or how?" Such additions are not made idly, merely from dialectical custom, but are intended to move the thought of his patient in labour to a more satisfactory position.

862   *"Not," he said, "at least if it is like day, which being one and the same, is in many places at once, but is not for that reason separated from itself— if, I say, it is like this, then each Form is the same and simultaneously present to all things."* (131b)

Socrates here thinks he has found something that can be present to many separate things at the same time, viz. the day, which is present to all things under the same meridian, the same day, but simultaneously present to many different things. If you say further that the Good is analogous to the Sun, and the forms analogous to the day and its light (for they illuminate the darkness of Matter, and each of them is light, just as Matter is darkness) and its dependence on its own principle (even as they are dependent on the One), you could say that the likeness is very apt. But Parmenides is going to correct him, since Socrates has not noticed that he has not adhered to his premise that it is one and the

same thing that is present to the many. For if you think of the day as an interval of time, it is not present as a whole to the many. For the precise zenith point varies for different places, and as this varies, so do the points from which the lines to the zenith are drawn, and all the places are defined by their relation to the zenith. And if you think of day as the illuminated air, it will be even less present as a whole to all these places, for its different parts are adjacent here to these and there to other things. But this, nevertheless, is Socrates' objection to the statement of Parmenides. It is clear that he has taken his example from the discourse of Zeno;[35] for Zeno, in his endeavour to show that the many participate in some one, and are not devoid of one, even though greatly separated from each other, has said in his discourse that whiteness is present both to us and to the antipodes, just as night and day are. The reason why Socrates is portrayed as using this example is not, as some have supposed, that Zeno should not be refuted by his master for having taken an example unsuited to the hypothesis of Forms, and that Socrates should be refuted in his stead. For if Parmenides did not approve of the
863 example, what was to prevent his pointing out to Zeno and correcting this oversight before his reading of his discourse? I think the reason rather is that Zeno had applied the example to the enmattered form, which in truth is both one and not one, and is only partly participated, since it is distributed among its particulars and does not exist in itself. So Zeno had correctly and irrefutably applied the example of night and day to the form conceived in this fashion. But Socrates had incorrectly applied the example to the veritable Form which is indivisibly one and at the same time present to its many particulars. And so Parmenides corrects Socrates for no longer maintaining the unity and identity of the Form in using the example of the day; he had brought up the divisible instead of the indivisible Form, and instead of the one, something that is both one and not one, like the whiteness that is present both to us and to the antipodes. Indeed we said earlier that the purpose of Zeno's argument, in his polemic against the many, was not to lead us up to the unitary Form that is separate from the many, but was directed toward the form that exists along with the many and is inseparable from them. But Socrates had posited the Form as being different from the form in us, i.e. a Form that does not exist in the way of the whiteness that is both in us and in the antipodes, and the latter is obviously what Zeno had likened to day and night.

But enough of this. We must return to examine the text, which contains a certain irregularity. First we must link the whole thought to-

---

[35] This appears to be a further reference to the *Forty Logoi* of Zeno. Cf. Book I, n. 31, and J. M. Dillon, "New Evidence on Zeno of Elea?" *AGPh*. 56 (1974): 129-131.

gether by assuming an hyperbaton. Socrates says the absurdity mentioned by Parmenides would not follow; "if a Form were like the day, each of them would then be present simultaneously the same to all things." Next we must suppose the phrase "if in this way" to be resumptive (*epanalēpsis*) and to mean "if this proposition is laid down." For in a statement of more than a certain length, resumptions are useful. Thirdly, the intermediate clause, "being one and the same, is in many places at once," must be read as a detached element (*kat' apostasin*) and interpreted as indicating the way in which the one Form is present

864 at the same time to many things. If you read the text thus, you will see how its beauty results from the intermediate detached clause and its resumption in the apodosis that follows.

> *"How readily, Socrates," he said, "You make one and and the same thing present in many places at the same time. It is as if you spread a sail over a number of men and say that it is a single whole over many. Is not this the sort of thing you are saying?" "Perhaps," said Socrates. "Then would the whole sail be over each man, or a part of it over him and another part over another?" "A part."* (131b-c)

Parmenides recognizes the spontaneity of Socrates' thought, though he sees it is imperfect as yet and in need of correction. He welcomes and applauds its inner source, but corrects and develops it. Socrates' imagination was picturing to him the extension of the single Form to all its particulars and its undivided presence to them all, and this is why Parmenides remarks how readily he makes the one whole in many things, meaning by "readily" not naively or ridiculously, but naturally. Socrates' picture of the transcendent cause as present at once in all its particulars is the product of a mind that is imaginative, and also attentive to reason and to intellect. For the faculty of the mind that is operating determines the particular way in which the nature of things is apprehended. If it is sense-perception, things will be apprehended in the way of sense, as divisible and enmattered only; if it is reason alone, they will be understood as both indivisible and divisible; and if it is intellect, they will be indivisible only. So then, since Socrates was expressing his native convictions, he divines the unitary and universal presence of the intellectual forms; but since he has not articulated his notion but conceived this presence as extended in space, Parmenides confronts him with the sail, and shows him that it is not a single whole over many, but that its parts correspond to different units of the many. And he does not ask, "Is not this the sort of thing you are thinking?" for he knows the "birth-pangs" Socrates is undergoing in bringing to birth his spontaneous notion about the matter. Instead he asks, "Is not this the sort of

865 thing you are saying?" as if Socrates, led astray by his imagination, and

unable as yet to formulate the thought within him, were thinking one thing and saying another. Socrates, pressed from two sides, from his natural convictions and from the suggestions of his imagination, utters a word of doubt, for "perhaps" expresses something of this kind. He cannot think that his present statement is entirely satisfactory, since he is stirred up by his own inarticulate[36] intuition of the subject, nor can he abandon his view based on imagination with its inclination towards viewing things as extended; and so his answer shows his divided mind. Consequently he is induced to say that things participate in parts, not the wholes, of their Forms. Parmenides, on the other hand, by the illustration of the sail, has "with soundless tread"[37] contrived to effect the transition to the other half of his disjunction, and so draws the following conclusion.

> "Consequently, Socrates," he said, "the Forms themselves are divided, and the things that participate in them will participate in a part of them. No longer will the whole of a Form be in each thing, but a part of it." "So it appears." "Then, Socrates," he said, "will you allow that our one Form is really divided? And will it still be one?" "By no means," Socrates replied. (131c)

This is the second half of the disjunction, showing that things here cannot participate in parts of the Forms either. It invokes their indivisibility to demolish the proposed suggestion. For if the Forms are indivisible monads, how could some parts of them be shared by some things and others by others? For example, if Man is a unity, how can it be divided into many? If each of us has a part and not the whole, how could he be called a man and not a part of man? And if we are separate from one another and a part of the Form is in me, a part in you, and a part in someone else, then, if participation is again being conceived as extended, how can the Form remain one when it is divided among us who are physically separated from one another? In this sense fire also is
866 not one, since a part of it is here and a part in another place; and likewise also water and air. But though fire here is by its own nature divisible, its Form is indivisible. Fire here is a plurality that has an adventitious unity; the Form, however, is a unity that embraces plurality in its unity. For in the divine world procession begins with unity and existence, and if we posit plurality as prior to unity, unity will be adventitious. Hence when he says "consequently the Forms themselves will be divisible," and adds "will you allow that the Form is really divided?"

[36] Reading ἀδιαρθρώτον (Latin *indearticulato*) for ἀδιαστρόφου of Greek MSS.
[37] Euripides *Tro.* 887-888 (Hecuba's description of Zeus, emphasising Parmenides' demiurgic role). Cf. *In Tim.* I, 398.18, where Amelius is quoted as using the expression of Plato.

he is shocking us into an awareness of the absurdity of this supposition. For though we say that the visible man and every other material form is divisible, still it is absurd to say that the immaterial Forms themselves are divisible; even if we say that the Form itself is divided in being participated in partially by things in this world, we are not saying that it is in truth divided. You can understand from this in what sense the myths speak of dividings and dismemberings of the gods, when secondary beings participate partially in them by dividing up among themselves the preexisting indivisible causes of divisible things. It is not really a division of the gods, but of themselves with respect to the gods.

> *"For consider," he said, "if you divide Greatness itself, and if each of the many great things is great by a part of Greatness smaller than Greatness itself, does that not appear illogical?" "Very much so," Socrates replied.* (131cd)

To show that it is absurd to suppose ideal being as divisible, he builds his argument upon Greatness, Equality, and Smallness, since each of these is manifestly concerned with magnitude. Magnitude does not have any part of itself the same as the whole, in the way in which a part of a quality appears to retain the character of the whole. Thus a portion of fire, looked at quantitatively, is less than the whole, but qualitatively it preserves the character of fire. Naturally, then, he uses Greatness, Equality, and Smallness to refute those who say that Forms are divisible, for this will enable him to use the argument *a fortiori*. If things that are most thought to be divisible because involving the notion of quantity—if these prove not to be divisible in their function as Forms, much more will other things that do not involve the notion of quantity, such as Justice, Beauty, or Likeness and Unlikeness, assuredly be indivisible. Putting these in the same class with Greatness, he asks how sensible things participate in them, and so naturally he focusses his demonstration on terms that appear to be quantitative, not on the others.

First, then, on Greatness. Let us suppose Greatness is divisible physically; then a part of it is less than the whole, and if this is so, the whole is greater than the part; so that if any great thing here becomes great because it participates in the Form "Great," this sensible great is called "great" by virtue of participating in the Smaller, for its part of Greatness is less and smaller. But this is not as it should be, for we have posited that great things are great by participating in Greatness and small things small by participating in Smallness; and we said that the names of things come from the Forms in which they participate. Such, then, is his argument.

But we who conceive of Greatness in itself apart from corporeal division, should we not say that it itself has plurality and is not merely

867

232

unity? And if it has plurality, shall we say that each part of it is Greatness, or that though each is less than the whole, it is in no wise small? If we say that the part is Greatness, and in no respect less than the whole, we have an infinite series; for this part will itself have parts that are the same as itself, and again these parts will have like parts, and the parts of these parts likewise, in each successive case the parts being the same as their wholes. On the other hand, if Greatness is to have parts that are magnitudes, its unity will be adventitious and the whole will consist of parts that do not belong to it. Hence it is necessary that the supposed parts of Greatness be great and homogeneous with the
868 whole, but not identical with the whole. For example, the part of fire is fire, but the potency of the whole is greater; and neither is the whole composed of parts that are cold, nor is each part equal in strength to the whole. Now suppose, if Greatness has a plurality of powers, that one of them is the power of conferring superiority upon bodiless things with respect to other bodiless things (for these also have a kind of magnitude), and another that of giving superiority to a body over another body, and that there is a different measure of superiority in the latter. It is not necessary, when one Form has this twofold power following from a single reason–principle, that one of them be less than the other. Its being less than the whole does not make its power small; rather, it reveals this power, too, as Greatness in itself having the same potency in other and less things. Thus even if the Form is polydynamic, it does not abandon its own distinguishing property in the plurality of powers it contains. This is the conclusion, if we intelligently conceive parts and wholes in the ideal world; whereas if we consider the separation of part from whole to be bodily in character, we will fall into the absurdities that Parmenides alleges.

"Or again, if each thing that participates in Equality will take off a small part of it, will it, by having something less than Equality itself, be equal to anything?" "Impossible." (131d)

We have remarked in the preceding comments what power Greatness has in immaterial and material realities; that is, it is what confers upon any thing its superiority and transcendent perfection, whether intellectual or vital or physical. Of Equality, which is now mentioned for the first time, let us say that it is the cause of harmony and proportion in all things; for it is Equality that reveals the mean term in any proportion, whether in souls or in nature, and its end is friendship and unity. Then since the Demiurge, in constructing the universe, used all the means—arithmetical, geometrical, and harmonic—and the uniting bonds based upon them, you would hit the truth about it, I think, if
869 you say that this Equality used by the Demiurge is the one intellectual

233

cause that generates and organises the cosmos. For as ideal Unity is the foundation of every number in nature, so ideal Equality generates all the proportions here below. At least in our world it is Equality that generates the middle terms; and if this is the case among likenesses, much more will Equality in the intellectual world be the parent of all the variety of middle terms that proceed into the cosmos. Equality, then, is the cause also of all these proportions in the cosmos. Moreover it is the source of all parity of rank and order among things, just as the Greater is the cause of transcendent excellence and the Lesser the cause of essential inferiority. And it seems that all things get their ordering from this triad of Forms, since they furnish to superior beings their very superiority, to the secondary ones their inferiority, and fellowship to those that are parallel in rank. And clearly the serial orderings of universal beings have been engendered eternally indissoluble according to this triad. Every series needs these three moments—excess, deficiency and parity—so that if every Form has its procession of members extending downwards to the lowest, a procession that preserves the distinction between secondary and primary beings together with community among them all, it is this triad that brings it about. It is they that make possible for every Form the procession from its summit to the lowest term in each series. Assuredly Beauty, Justice, and each other Form is the leading member in its own series, and is present in all the intellectual, ensouled, and even bodily beings below it, though present in a different fashion in the various kinds of souls—divine, daemonic, and human—and differently also in the different sorts of bodies. Beauty, as an example, appears differently in divine souls, in daemonic souls, and in souls subordinate to them.

From this it is evident what Equality is. Now consider, in this context, how Parmenides refutes those who think equal things here participate bodily in parts of Equality. Suppose this particular sense object, taken separately, has a part of Equality. Now if it has a part, clearly it has something less than the whole; and if so, what participates in the less is not less, but equal. But this is not as it should be, for it is presupposed that Forms give their names to sensibles. Hence something participating in the Less ought not to be called equal, but less; nor something participating in the Equal less, but equal; nor anything participating in the Greater be equal or less, but greater. Again, you see, the argument proceeds on the assumption that participation is physical. The phrase "taking off a small part" shows by "taking off" that participation is thought of as physical, and attributes division to the indivisible and bodiless Forms themselves. For, if you consider Equality in itself, any part of it will also be an equality; for Equality is not made up of unequals, ⟨even as Greatness itself is not made up of non-greats,

870

234

since then the thing-in-itself would have something comprising it which is not itself equal)[38] (the superimposed form is a different matter; it will be a compound, not simple, like Equality Itself). It is therefore necessary that any part of Equality Itself be itself equal. For the Form Equality contains in its unity the causes of all equalities—equality of weight, of mass, of number, of worth, of birth—so that each of these different equalities is a particular equality, having a power and value inferior to the whole. At any rate, it is quite possible that though the one Form produces every property of the powers it contains, yet it generates this one of such a kind and in such kinds of substrates, that one of another kind, and that thus there should be a whole range of equalities, multiple in subordination to the one. And we should not be surprised that they should be all equalities and yet subordinate to the Henad in their series, and should owe this subordinate status to participation in Smallness, since all Forms participate in all others. Even Greatness itself, inasmuch as it is less than some other Forms, participates in Smallness; and Smallness itself, in so far as it surpasses others, participates in Greatness. But things here participate in each of them in its essential nature, not in its nature relative to the others.

871   *"But suppose one of us has a portion of Smallness. Smallness itself will be greater than this, since this is a part of it, and so Smallness itself will be greater; and when this part that is taken off is added to anything, that thing will be smaller, not greater, than it was before." "That certainly cannot be," said Socrates.* (131de)

Again we must first ascertain what Smallness is and what power it has. As we said that Greatness is the cause of excess, or superior worth, or preeminent power alike in all things that are, and that Equality is the parent of all analogy and parity of rank, so also we may say that Smallness is the source of all declension among the Forms, and, if you like, of indivisibility and contraction and power of self-concentration wherever it exists. It is Smallness that enables souls to retreat from externals to the indivisible inner life, and bodies to be constricted and held together by the partless causes within them, and the entire cosmos to be a unity and have its whole life converging upon a single center. From Smallness also come poles and centres, sections without thickness, the tangent points of cycles, the boundaries of the signs of the Zodiac, and all the indivisible measuring points that the demiurgic Intellect has fixed in the divisible world. Such is the power of Smallness.

The present argument shows that in the case of Smallness also it is impossible that things should participate bodily in a part of the Form.

---

[38] Added from the Latin translation.

For if Smallness has any part at all, Smallness will be greater than the part of itself, since the part of the Small, *qua* part, is smaller than the whole; so that Smallness will clearly be greater than its own part, which is smaller. But it is impossible for the Small, *qua* small, to be great; for here we are examining Smallness by itself, without touching on its relation with Greatness. This, then, shows one absurd consequence for those who divide Smallness itself, considered as a Form.

872 Another is revealed when we examine things that participate in the part, as follows. Since we have divided Smallness itself, and have shown that this part of it is smaller than the whole, clearly whatever takes on the part that has been subtracted from the whole will be smaller, and not greater, than it was formerly. For that which participates in the smaller must become smaller; and yet we see that anything, even if it be smaller, when added to a given magnitude makes the whole greater. Consequently you must not divide Smallness; for if you keep it indivisible, you cannot add the whole to something, as you would the part, and thus make the recipient greater instead of small. For the previous argument has shown that for a whole Form to exist in many things is impossible.

This, then, is one way to interpret the passage before us. It is also possible, however, as our colleague Pericles has maintained,[39] to consider the whole matter in reference to the Form itself. For whatever takes on a part subtracted from the Small must necessarily become bigger; but that which is subtracted, if added to the remainder left after the subtraction, nevertheless makes the whole small, not greater than it was before; for the Form was small to begin with. It is therefore absurd to suppose that Smallness is divisible, because any part subtracted from it would be less than the whole and reveal the whole to be greater, and because when added to the remainder it makes what took on this addition greater. And in neither of these cases is the whole small. This had to be said about the second of the alleged absurdities, a passage that has seemed to some commentators so difficult to construe that they have regarded the text as spurious and denied that it was Plato's words.

But enough on this point. It is easy to see that the argument itself, by
873 bringing in subtractions and additions, shows that bodily participation is what is being refuted, and no further comment on this point is necessary, I believe. But let us say about all these three Forms—Greatness, Smallness, Equality—and indeed about all Forms alike, that they are without parts and have a bodiless nature. For nothing that is bodily and

---

[39] One of Proclus' very rare allusions to the process of debate within the school, or perhaps just to discussions in Syrianus' class. Cf. Hermeias' occasional references to Proclus in the *In Phaedrum*, e.g. 92.6 Couvreur. Pericles is the dedicatee of the *Platonic Theology*, and one of Proclus' closest associates.

is bounded in extension can be present in the same way to greater and lesser things; whereas Equality, the Greater, the Less, and each of the other Forms can be present alike to all things that participate in them, whatever their extension. The Forms, therefore, are all unextended. For the same reason their foundation transcends all place; they are present without difficulty in all things everywhere that participate in them. Things that are dominated by their position lack this capacity of unrestricted presence, for it is impossible that they should be participated in by things in different places. Likewise the Forms transcend all time; they are present non-temporally and immediately to all their participants. Although, as we have said before, comings-into-being are conditions preparatory to participation in the Forms, and these are of course temporal events; nevertheless the Forms permit things in the world of generation to participate in them without any lapse of time at all, indivisibly in an indivisible instant, which is a reflection of their eternal reality. Let no one, then, transfer from the things that participate to the Forms participated either the notion of time, or of spatial position, or of physical divisibility, nor suppose there are bodily combinations and divisions in their world. These conditions are completely inconsistent with the simplicity of the Forms, with their immaterial purity, and their continuous and partless existence in eternity.

"In what way, then, Socrates," he said, "will other things participate in your Forms if they can participate in them neither in part nor as wholes?" (131e)

874   The whole of this conversation is hortatory in character, intended to bring out Socrates' thoughts; hence it is not as a contestant eager for victory that Parmenides adds that things here consequently do not participate in the Forms. Rather he is stimulating Socrates, inviting his intelligence to discover the authentic way of participation; that is, by leading him round through the more spurious modes, he will leave it to his intelligence to discern that manner that is truly appropriate to the creative activity of the divine Forms. We said earlier that those who understand whole and part not in a bodily sense, but in a way appropriate to immaterial and intellectual beings, will see that things here participate in Forms both in part and as wholes. In that the special property of the Forms extends down to the very lowest of its participants, the participation is in the Forms as wholes; but since secondary things do not receive the full force of their causes, the participation is partial. Hence the higher among the participants receive more of the powers of their paradigm and those that are further down fewer. So that if there exist men in other parts of the universe who are superior to us, they too, being nearer to the Form of man, share in more of its powers. This is

237

why the lion in the heavens is intelligent,[40] while that in the sublunary world is without reason; the former is nearer the Form of Lion. But the property descends into mortal realms; hence the sympathy between things here and heavenly things, brought about by the single Form and the community it produces. But I need hardly expand on this point. If you take the Moon, for instance, while you will see that the heavenly moon is a goddess, you will also see the moon-form here, preserving in stones the power appropriate to its rank, waxing and waning regularly as its nature prescribes.[41] In this way the single property comes down from above to the lowest members of the series, and obviously passes also through the intervening species. For if this one form is present in both gods and stones, far more so, surely, will it appear in the intermediate classes, such as daemons and other forms of life. There are

875 series that descend from the intellectual gods to the heavens, and from there again to the realm of generation, suffering alteration in each of the elements, and finally settling down upon the earth. The higher members of these series have a greater share of their paradigms, while those nearer to earth share less in the common property which, however, extends to every member and makes the whole series a unity.

But there is another way, I should like to note, in which things here participate in Forms both wholly and partially. They participate in them as wholes in that the activity of a Form is indivisible, and thus is present as a whole identically in all its participants, being in itself first and then filling up the being of its participants with its own character. But they participate in part in so far as they participate not in the Forms themselves, but in images of them, and these images are parts of their own paradigms; for thus the likeness stands to its pattern as part to whole. Now if anyone, relying on this interpretation, works through the preceding dialectical arguments, he will see nothing impossible in the things that we formerly rejected as being so. For where is the impossibility of a whole's being the same in all its participants, if you think with me that that immaterial and intellectual Form, being in itself and requiring neither seat nor place, is present equally to all things capable of participating in it? How is it impossible that the preexisting Form, in itself indivisible and one, should be divided among its participants and undergo a sort of Titanic dismemberment? Is it not the very truth that what participates in Greatness itself participates in what is less than Greatness? For the greatness in the participant, being extended, is an image of Greatness itself, and the image is less than the paradigm by a part of it. Would you not say likewise that the sensible

[40] I.e. the Zodiacal sign Leo.
[41] The moonstone, selenite, was so called because it was supposed to wax and wane with the moon. Cf. Diosc. 5.141.

equal is called equal because it participates in what is less than Equality itself? And what is called equal here is less than the power of the Equal itself. And how can the likeness of the Small fail to be smaller than Smallness, in so far as it falls short of its perfection? Smallness is greater than this small thing in that it is more perfect in power. And all of the three Forms together, since they transcend their participants and take the measure of their being, furnish the cause for their differences in rank; Greatness is needed for marking exceptional superiority, Equality for the capacity of measuring, and Smallness for the assignment of inferiority. All of them, then, work together in the making of derivative beings.

In fact, although Greatness contributes the capacity for universal extension, and Smallness gives partlessness, yet these two are inseparable, since partlessness that extends to more things is greater partlessness; and both of them are preeminently equal, since they are distinguished as measures, both of themselves and of other things. There is therefore nothing absurd here if you understand whole and part in the appropriate way, but everything follows properly from the hypotheses. This is why, I think, Parmenides persists in asking how things participate in Forms and how we are to envision whole and part in that world, endeavouring to bring Socrates to the most correct conception.

"In the name of Zeus," he said, "there is no easy way that I see of determining such a question." (131e)

On the first problem, the one concerning the reality of Forms, Parmenides did not attack the opinion of Socrates as incorrect, nor did Socrates himself have any doubt of their reality. In the ensuing questioning he was puzzled to say what things have Forms, but his perplexity was minor and not deeply disturbing. But on this third issue he is very much at a loss because the inquiry is a profound one. And not in this passage only is the profundity of the problem expressed, but also in the *Timaeus* (51a), where Timaeus himself says that Matter participates in Being in a most mysterious way. Naturally, then, the question appears difficult of resolution to Socrates; and it appears to have seemed so not merely in his youth, but even near the end of his life. At least he says in the *Phaedo* (100d) that he is not sure of the way in which participation in Forms occurs, and he mentions the Great and the Small in that passage. And here is something that, as I have said before, both in this and in many other contexts, is very important: the investigation of the "how." It is the sort of inquiry we said Socrates was pursuing when he asked how the Forms themselves are separated and combined. Granting that, though many in number, they are necessarily united,

239

and they are both divided and yet not devoid of unity, he sought to know how the Forms, being simple, can show both these characteristics. Are they united in the same way as visible pluralities are? For these are compounds, and it is not difficult to see their unity and distinctness as resulting from their various aspects in relation to others, since they are compound; but in the case of simple beings it is extremely difficult to see these differences of aspect. He inquires, then, how separation and union are possible in their case—not whether there is such union and separation, but how it can be. Likewise in the present passage the argument asks not whether there is participation, but how it is possible. This is what Socrates says is difficult to comprehend, since he has been brought by these counter-arguments to a recognition of the difficulty of the problem. And if the addition of the oath is not irrelevant but is intended to put him somehow in the hands of the god in whose name he swears and from that position make the inquiry easy, you will discover, when you reflect, that even this is not extraneous to the inquiry about Forms. For in Zeus is first revealed the unitary source of the demiurgic Ideas and the whole number of them. Thus in calling upon Zeus and making him a witness of his perplexity, he shows himself apt for receiving the full vision, by rising to the cause that is separate from the realm of appearance.

> *"Well, what do you say to the following problem?" "What is it?" "I believe your reason for thinking each Form is one is the following. When you observe that several things are large, then no doubt you conjecture a single character that is the same when you look at them all; hence you consider largeness to be a single thing." "That's true," he replied.* (131e–132a)

878   Why we ought not to think of participation in Forms as bodily has been sufficiently demonstrated in the foregoing comments, from which you can understand that the activity of the Forms is not by means of bodily thrusts and levers,[42] like the moving forces in bodies. If this is so, the cosmos of Forms is bodiless. The argument in the *Sophist* (245a) shows that the One is without body; for bodily being itself needs a unifying factor; and here it is shown that true Being and the intellectual Forms are indivisibly established in their being. And the *Laws* (X, 895a) shows that souls are bodiless because of their self-moving reality. These are the three orders of being prior to sensibles—the order of souls, the order of intellectual beings, and that of the henads—

---

[42] Both ὦσις and μοχλεία are terms that Aristotle uses in the *Physics* (VII, 243a16ff., and VIII, 259b20, respectively). Proclus employs this slightly disdainful collocation again at *In Tim.* I, 297.28.

and to all of these bodilessness has been assigned by ineluctable arguments.

But enough of this. From this point Parmenides advances to a more perfect hypothesis. May it not be that things here participate in Forms as they do in the reason-principles in nature which, though bodiless, are in the same rank of being and have a common origin with the things that participate in them? The preceding difficulty took participation in Forms as bodily, the Forms being other than the forms in us, but nevertheless bodily, and in this fashion present to them, being able to be present as bodies to other bodies. Now he advances to an immaterial concept which, if we want to define it with reference to the facts, we shall call physical; viz. that there is a mode of participation which, though immaterial, nevertheless has a common element with the (material) participants. For if besides immaterial participation we understand the participated beings as altogether outside the participants, no longer will there be any difficulty about participation. Two things give rise to the difficulty: the bodily mode of presence, and their community with the participants. It is these that Socrates has in mind when he says in the *Phaedo* (100d) that he is in doubt whether he should assume the presence of Forms in their participants (just as the preceding inquiry was whether things here partake of the Forms as wholes or in part), or not their presence, but as when, the strings of a lyre being tuned to the same pitch, a man can by plucking one string produce vibrations in another. At any rate this second inquiry posits the Forms as in their participants and in the same rank with them; and therefore in their case, as in that of the similar things mentioned, it is necessary to posit some other thing identical with both. Hence he ascends to the natures; for the reason-principles in Nature and the natures are in a rank above bodies and the visible order of the species; they descend into bodies and hold them together, acting immanently, not transcendentally. Hence the reason-principles in Nature are ranged in the same rank with the sensible species. How we advance to the reason-principles in Nature Parmenides tells us clearly; we proceed upwards from the common element in particulars to their immediate cause, which of course is the natural species. For when we see a multiplicity of large things and perceive a single character pervading them all, we hold that there is one Largeness common to all the instances of largeness in the individual things. That the argument is about the natural species and the transition to it from sensible things he makes clear by the insertion of such terms as *thinking, it seems to you, you consider*; none of these is a term that can be used with respect to objects of scientific knowledge, but only about the realm of nature. Similarly we should say that we see many men and a single character extending to every man exhibited in the particular

879

241

cases; and from this we consider that a single man, generative of the visible man, exists previously in the reason-principles of nature, and that in this way the many men participate in the one man, as a natural reason-principle proceeding into Matter, the reason-principles not being separate from Matter, but, as we have said above, resembling the seal which descends into the wax, impressing its form upon it and harmonizing this with the whole Form which is impressed upon it.

Now this immediate transition from bodies to natures shows that the reason-principles in the natures fall short of the primary creative 880 perfection of the Forms unmixed with their participants. From this we should infer that the community between the one Form and its many instances should be not merely nominal, lest we should have to seek next, because of the common name, for some single element common to the one and the many, as unity is the common element in plurality; nor that we should consider the single Form to be synonymous with those of the particulars coming under it, or we shall have to ask what is the common element present in both kinds of being that are covered by the same term; but rather, as has often been said, the common element in the many instances is that of being derived from and having reference to a single source. For what the one Form is primarily, the many grouped under it are derivatively. And we should not seek for some further community in their case. For although community belongs to things coordinate in rank, yet it is not coordinate with the things that have community. And the One itself, when we apprehend its presence in each of the Forms, ought not to be viewed by the faculty of opinion, nor by discursive reason, for these kinds of knowledge are not cognate with intellectual monads, which are neither objects of opinion nor of discursive reason, as we learn from the *Republic* (VI, 511a). Rather it is proper to see by intuitive apprehension that simple and unitary existence of the Forms. Nor must we think that unity belongs to them by synthesis from the many, nor as a secondary conception abstracted from them, but rather, since the intellectual number of the Forms proceeds from the One, it has its foundation also preeminently in the One, and does not stand outside its native and congenital unity with the cause that supports its being.

This is why Socrates in the *Philebus* (15ab) sometimes calls the Forms henads and sometimes monads: for with respect to the One they are monads because each of them is a plurality and a single being and a life-principle and an intellectual Form, but with respect to the things produced from them and the series which they establish, they are henads. For the divisible things that come after them derive multiplicity from them, though they themselves remain indivisible. If, then, the uniting element in them transcends the many, it is plain, surely, that the uni-

881 tary knowledge of the intellect is sufficient also to grasp the unitary principle of the Forms. Even if there is a multiplicity of participants, that does not multiply the unitariness of what is participated in; if there are differences in the parts, yet the undivided element in the Forms is preserved unchanged; even if there are compound products, yet the simplicity of the intellectual Forms stands always the same; for it is not counted with its own products, nor does it form part of their substance; for if it were in any of those things which come to be, it could no longer be viewed as a first principle and generative cause of them; for it is in general impossible that anything that comes to belong to something else should be a cause in the absolute sense, because that which is in the true sense a cause transcends its products, and is established in itself and by itself separate from the things that participate in it. If, then, one cares to transfer his attention to the Forms from these things of sense and spatial distinction, let him establish intellect instead of opinion (*doxa*) as his guide on the road, and let him contemplate each Form unconnected and unmixed with the things of this realm; and let him not conceive of any relationship in connection with them, nor any account of essence which is common to them and to the many particulars, nor let him see any linkage at all between the participated and what participates in them, ordered and preserved though they are by virtue of their connection with them. But if anyone employs opinion in making the transference, and fastens upon Forms which are mingled with things of this realm and counted with the reason-principles in Matter, he will have a hard time ascending to the nature and natural structure of the Forms. And from there in turn he will see other more comprehensive unities, and he will be chasing after unities of unity, and his problems will extend to infinity, until, coming up against the very boundaries of Intellect, he will behold in them the distinctive creation of the Forms, in the self-created, the supremely simple, the eternal. Therefore it is that Parmenides in demonstrating the superior simplicity of the primal and complete Forms to the particular ones, straightforwardly shows them as transcending with remarkable superiority those mixed entities which are counted with them.

882   Having got this far, it is worth while pausing to admire the hesitation of Socrates in the *Phaedo* about the mode of participation of the Forms; for he says (100d), "I would not be dogmatic as to whether one should call it 'presence' or 'communion', or any other term besides these."

    As a result of the first question raised it is possible to demonstrate that 'presence' is impossible, since neither wholes nor parts (of Forms) as such can 'be present' to the things that participate in them; and as a result of the second question one can refute those who uphold the 'communion' theory. For if there is anything in common between

243

Forms and the things which participate in them, the infinite regress will emerge as between those things participating in the common property and the common property itself. For this reason this distinction is reasonably made between this question and the one preceding it; the former postulated the Form as present to the participants and being itself the thing participated, while the present one treats it as separate from the entity participated in, though having much in common with it. So in the former case there was a valid refutation in the fact that it could not be present either as a whole or as bestowing a part of itself, while in this case the refutation is no longer of the same type, but arises from the fact that from the common element in both one would proceed upwards to another entity common to the one Form and the many particulars. And thus the argument for participation and for 'presence' is refuted, and the one from 'communion' also in a different way, since the former based itself on the principle that the Form is present to the participants, the latter on the principle that, though it is not *in* them, yet it is in communion with them. The only way, then, in which one could give an account of participation conformable to true knowledge would be if one first removed all notion of materiality from the concept of presence and any idea of common quality from that of immaterial association, and so laid down that things of this realm participate in the Forms through their being present to the things participating in them immaterially, but not controlled by them according to any one formula, in order that the same Forms may be both everywhere by virtue of their immateriality, and at the same time nowhere in virtue of their transcendence over their participants; for any 'community' with the participating entities destroys their transcendent superiority. There must, then, be 'community', but not as between entities of the same rank, only to the extent that the participants are dependent upon the Forms, while the latter are completely transcendent over them; bodily 883 'presence' eliminates the possibility of undivided omnipresence. It is a characteristic of bodies, after all, to be incapable of being present as wholes in many different places, whereas things essentially incorporeal are able to be present as wholes to all those things which are capable of participating in them, that is to say, they are not present to the participants, so much as the participants are present to them. This, indeed, is what Socrates in the *Phaedo* (100d) was hinting at when he said, "Whether 'presence,' or 'communion'," or whatever other cause there might be of the participation of the Forms, that we may remove from these terms their problematic overtones. We should admire all the more this caution of Socrates in the *Phaedo*, since it arises from these two problems which he had learned in his youth from Parmenides; and we should admire also the divine inspiration of Plato, which led him to refute in anticipation all the deviations from the truest theory about the Forms which later arose. For even as the divine Intellect comprehends all future events in a single causal principle, so also Plato's knowledge, it would seem, anticipates and provides antidotes for all deviant versions of divine teachings, portraying as he does a young and intelligent man being baffled in each case by questions about which later theorists caused difficulties. For many attributed the creation of the world to material forces,[43] although it has been shown that it is impossible for the Forms to be material and to be participated in in any material way. One must, therefore, neither postulate the Forms to be products and offshoots of Matter, as some assert, nor can we agree that they come to be out of the mingling together of the basic elements; nor again, can we grant that they have the same essence as the (so-called) seminal principles,[44] for all these are corporeal and imperfect and reveal themselves as having a divisible existence. How, then, can perfection be present to things that are imperfect, unity to things that are totally scattered, unfailing existence to things that are constantly coming into being, if there is not preexisting all these things the incorporeal and perfect system of Forms?

Others again have attributed the permanence of the Forms to the 884 common element in individual phenomena (for man begets man,[45] and like in general springs from like), but these people must first address themselves to the problem as to whence the common element in individuals takes its origin. For this could not be the genus, being immanent in Matter and divisible and not absolutely eternal, nor, if it comes from another causal principle, could this be one that is subject to motion and change; for in that case it itself would be totally changeable.[46] But in fact inasmuch as it is a Form, it remains always the same, like one identical seal impressed upon many pieces of wax. They may change, but it remains uninterruptedly the same in all the instances of wax. What, then, is the immediate cause of the imposition of the seal? Matter is in the place of the wax, and the individual man is to be identified with the imprint, so what are we to identify with the signet-ring that descends upon objects, if not Nature that permeates Matter and thus moulds the sense-realm with its reason-principles? With the hand that wields the signet-ring we may identify the Soul, which directs Nature, Soul as a whole directing Nature as a whole, and individual souls directing individual natures; and with that soul that does the impressing of the seal by means of the hand and the signet-ring may we not

---

[43] The Epicureans seem to be the object of criticism here.
[44] The object of criticism now becomes the Stoics.
[45] Aristotle *Met.* XII, 3.1070a8.
[46] Cf. 786 above, and Proclus *In Tim.* I, 267.4ff.

identify the Intellect, which through Soul and Nature fills the sense-realm with Forms, that which we may truly characterise as Resource (*Poros, Symp.* 203b), the begetter of those reason-principles which flow forth as far as Matter?

One should not, then, rest content at the level of the individual common properties, but rather seek out the causes of them. For what other reason is there that men partake of this common property, and other animals partake of another, than these invisible reason-principles? Nature is the one mother of all. But what are the causes of the various patterns of likeness, and why do we say that the generation of species follows nature, when man arises from man, if not because there is a reason-principle of Man in nature, in accordance with which all men in this realm come to be? For it is not enough that the entity born should be an animal, since even if it were a lion, it would still have been a natural animal, but yet it would not have been "according to nature," because it would no longer be following its proper reason-principle. There must therefore be prior to entities which are similar something which is the cause of their similarity, and one must for this reason ascend from the particular common features to this principle of unity, the immediate cause of the existence of sense-objects, to which Parmenides has actually led us. That he will not permit us to remain at the level of this cause, he will make clear in what follows; for if we are going seriously to contemplate these common elements as a basis for the fabrication of Ideas, we will find that we have inadvertently formed Ideas equally on the basis of all common elements, not only from existent ones but also from non-existent ones, as for instance mistakes of nature or art or reason, things without existence, things even without substances, such as goat-stags or hippocentaurs—for these too have common properties—and hence we will be in the position of postulating Ideas of non-existent entities, and also of concepts involving infinity, such as irrational lines, and of ratios among numbers. For both irrational lines and ratios in numbers involve the concept of infinity, and yet there are properties common to these. If then, we fabricate Ideas from these entities, we will often be involved in creating infinite concepts, whereas the Ideas ought to be less than the individuals that participate in them, those entities participating in each being more numerous than the Idea in question. Parmenides, then, is right to correct this manner of ascending to the Ideas, as not being scientific if it is based on common properties observed in particulars, and he starts out from enquiries into the mode of participation; for it is possible to conceive of ever more common properties, and thus proceed to infinity—as indeed he proceeds to show in what follows.

885

246

"But now take Largeness itself and the many large particulars. Suppose you contemplate all these in the same way in your soul, will not yet another unity make its appearance, by virtue of which all these appear large?" "So it would seem." "If so, a third Form of Largeness will present itself, over and above Largeness itself and the things that share in it;
886 *and again, covering both of these[47] yet another, which will make all of them large. So each of your Forms will no longer be one, but infinite in number." (132ab).*

The purpose here is to show that the transition from common properties to Ideas, as we said earlier, is not envisaged correctly, but results in an endless ascent from one common property to another. For this very reason, as I have said, Socrates did not consider 'communion' to be the causal principle of participation; for if there were some property in common between the participant and what is participated in, we will have to make a transition again from these to something which would be the cause of the communion of both of them, and so one would proceed to infinity; for in the case of any things which have a property in common, there must be something prior to them which is the cause of their community. If we wish to derive some profit from this problem, in the way of speculation leading to the Ideas, let us reflect that there could be demonstrated by this approach, as I have said, the essential nature of the Idea, which is not the same as the seminal reason-principles, nor as reason-principles of nature in general, which are on the same level of being as material things, but rather something different in nature prior to these, unconnected with all that is divided about the many particulars. For that principle of unity in nature which generates all forms in sense-objects is not of such a kind as to transcend the objects of sense, but it has a great measure of community with them, and very little distinction from them. Indeed the degree of its community is such as to seem in no way to differ from forms in matter, but to be itself something material and divisible. As, then, this nature is not separate from the things it administers, so the reason-principles of nature are inseparable from the things to which they give form—as if you were to conceive of an art itself with instruments proper to it descending into the products of the art, and producing from the inside what it now makes by external application. So the reason-principle of the Large in Nature, inasmuch as it is not separate from the large objects of this realm, but plunged into Matter along with them and ranked with them, feels the need of some other nature prior to itself, which can
887 stand as cause both of itself and of the visible large objects; for the cause

---

[47] Reading καὶ ἐπὶ τούτοις ἀμφοῖν ἕτερον, with Proclus.

in the true sense in all cases utterly transcends its products, and it is this towards which Parmenides is in fact leading Socrates.

Thus far, then, his statements are valid; but what he adds to this as an absurd consequence, the phrases "and another again on top of this, and another," and "infinite in number," are no longer valid. For this reason he said earlier, "by virtue of which all these things must appear large"; for there must be some separate and invisible reason-principle as cause of visible things. In adding the reduction to absurdity, he says, "and so each of *your* Forms will no longer be one." He adds the "your" not simply as a stylistic adornment but in order to show that anyone who is not yet able to discern where the Forms are primarily must fall victim to this infinite progression, since there must be, prior to the Form in Nature, another one at the level of Soul, and prior to this another one in Intellect, but this is not an infinite progression. For there is one henad of the Ideas, from which all proceed, and beyond which there is no question of taking one's enquiry, for what could proceed higher than its own proper henad? For even as there is no body outside the universe, nor ⟨any soul⟩[48] prior to its own monad, so there is no Idea prior to the henad of the Ideas. You see, then, how he has led us up to the reason-principles of the soul-realm from those of the realm of nature, and has exhorted us not to proceed to infinity, but to seek for the single monad of the Ideas; in order that there may be something that is the same in the many particulars and diffused over all of them in their separateness, there is a place for the natural reason-principle, as being an immediate bond for the multiplicity of individuals; in order that those things participating in the Idea may persist and never be exhausted, there is need of some other causal principle, which would not be present in them nor in motion, but established on its own, motionless prior to things in motion, and through its own stability providing to what is in motion an uninterrupted condition for participation.

All thinkers are in fact working towards this type of cause. Some, like the Stoics, considered the seminal reason-principles to be of this nature and declared them to be indestructible. Others, as for instance 888 the Peripatetics, established the unmoving objects of desire prior to all things which are in constant motion, as being the occasion of motion for those things that move. Plato, however, producing what is a combination of both theories, postulated the Ideas to be reason-principles of the intellectual realm and made all creation dependent on these. For neither were the seminal reason-principles sufficient to preserve in being things subject to generation, since they are not able to converge upon themselves nor to hold themselves together nor in general to

---

[48] Supplying ψυχή (from Latin trans.) after οὔτε.

bring themselves to completion, but remain incomplete (for they all exist in potentiality and in a subject); nor yet are the unmoving objects of desire, being solely objects of desire, causes of the generic variations of generated things. But the Ideas enjoy both these characteristics, being both intellectual and motionless in their essence, "established," as they are, "upon the holy foundation" (*Phaedr.* 254b) of the pure Intellect, having the power of bringing to completion things potentially existent and being the cause of their acquiring form. For this reason he ascended to these as first principles and made the whole of creation depend on them, in accord with what Xenocrates says, who defines the Ideas as the paradigmatic cause of whatever is composed continually in accordance with nature (fr. 30 Heinze). For one should not situate it among the contributory causes, by which I mean the instrumental, material, or specifying (*eidika*), because it is a cause in the fullest sense; nor, among types of cause proper, among the final or the creative, for even if we say that it creates by reason of its very essence, and that becoming like to it is an end for all generated things, nevertheless the final cause of all things in the strict sense and that for the sake of which all things are is superior to the Ideas, and the creative cause in the strict sense is inferior to them, looking to the Paradigm as a criterion and rule of procedure. The Idea, then, is median between both these, striving towards the one, and being striven towards by the other. If it is indeed the paradigmatic cause of whatever is composed in accordance with nature, there are no Ideas of things contrary to nature, nor of things made by art; and if it is of those things only which come into existence *continually (aei)*, there would be no Ideas of individuals, since these come to be and pass away.

Now Xenocrates propounded this definition of an Idea as being in accord with the views of his master, laying it down as a transcendent and divine causal principle, while Socrates in the present work, on
889 hearing Parmenides say, "If you contemplate in your soul both Largeness itself and the many large particulars, yet another unity will appear to you over and above these and different from them, which will be common to both the One and the Many," was provoked by this to the conclusion that the Forms are not, then, primarily in the Soul, and thus that the objects of sense participate in the Forms as they do in Soul. When, therefore, some try to discredit the theory of Ideas, either by the Third Man Argument or by the one about the No-man (*Outis*) emptily fabricated from the many particular no-men,[49] the one being conceived

[49] The Third Man Argument is known to us from Aristotle, *De Ideis*, fr. 4 Ross (*ap.* Alex. Aphr. *In Met.* 84.21-85.11 Hayduck), and *Met.* I, 9.990b17. It had various forms; see Ross's note *ad loc.* in his edition. As for the "Outis" argument, Chrysippus wrote a book with this title (Diog. Laert. VII, 198), but from *ibid.* 82 it seems that it had nothing

of on the basis of the single form of Man and the many particulars, the other on the basis of the many particular no-men, these and all similar objections we shall refute, admitting the force of the infinite progression of similarities against those who hold that the Forms are coordinate with their participants, and that the common qualities are to be counted as inherent in the many particulars, but not against those who say that they are productive of particulars from a transcendent and separate level, maintaining that the progression from distinct particulars to primary and self-substantiating entities develops not through negation of qualities but through Forms and in Forms. For how could we attain to form and limit and bound through things boundless and formless? If we ascend from forms in matter to seminal reason-principles, we will find an element common to both of them—incompleteness; if we ascend further to natural reason-principles, we will find as the common element the fact of their having their activity based in body; and if we ascend from these to the reason-principles on the level of soul, we find a common element in the temporal nature of their creation. But if we ascend as far as the Forms proper, we will not find anything in common between these and all those other things; for they are perfect, and their activity is entirely incorporeal and eternal and transcending all generation. For these are the characteristics of all generation, incompleteness in oneself, divisibility, temporality, from all of which the Forms are free, and thus transcend all things of this realm, having nothing in common with them, so that it is no longer possible to make the transition to any further common entity. It is because he realised this that Parmenides introduced the problem arising from the 'communion,' which caused Socrates also to admit a difficulty concerning the mode of participation in the Forms.

As we said, then, in connection with the previous problem that the 890 Forms both are present to their participants through imparting a share in themselves, and are not present by reason of their transcendent essence, even so in the case of the second problem we shall say that the Forms both commune with their participants and do not commune with them; to the extent that they illuminate them from their own essence, they commune with them, but to the extent that they are unmixed with what they illuminate, they do not commune; so that it is not for themselves, but for the things derived from them, that they have generated a certain degree of likeness. For this reason, indeed, it

---

to do with an argument against the Ideas. It may, however, serve as testimony to an earlier form of the argument in the Peripatetic School. Presumably, the argument consists in claiming that, since *no one* (*outis* or *oudeis*) can serve as a general term in statements ("no one came," "no one is here"), on Platonic principles there must be a Form of it. The *outis* form will be a reference to Odysseus' trick against the Cyclops.

250

may be said that they commune in some way through these means with those entities which receive them, but this communion is not that of synonyms, but rather of primary and secondary participants in a term.

So much, then, for that. That Plato also considers absurd this procession to infinite multiplicity he makes clear in the present passage. Therefore there are according to him no Forms of particulars, since that would involve an infinite number; nor is the part the same as the whole, for there would follow from this a multiplicity defying distinct divisions, since all parts would have equal status with the whole. It must therefore be in some other manner that infinity must be understood in the realm of Forms, an infinity of power rather than an infinity of number.[50] It is not proper, either, that one should have unlimited Multiplicity following directly upon the One, for the Limited is nearer to the One (Cf. *Phileb.* 16ce). In the realm of numbers, furthermore, the numbers contained in the Decad are nearer to the Monad than those outside it. For where would the four among the tens derive from, if not from the four among the units? And whence the five, or any other number among the tens, if not from the unitary numbers? So then those entities which are nearer to the first principle have their multiplicity compressed, but their power more developed than those more remote from it.[51] They are limited in respect of quantity, but are incomprehensible to the secondary entities by reason of the presence of the generative causal principle, being dominated, indeed each by its own henad, but dominating in turn all of the numbers subsequent to them.

891 *"But Parmenides," said Socrates, "may it not be that each of these Forms is a thought, which cannot properly come into being anywhere but in souls. In that way each of them would be one, and would thus not be liable to the difficulties which have just been described." (132b)*

That the problems about the Ideas are four in number we have said at the beginning of our discussion. Of these four, then, the first was laid down as being as to the bare existence of the Ideas (Bk. III, 784ff.), and whether they are distinct from things of this realm, the second question asked was simply of what things there were Ideas (Bk. III, 815ff.), without raising any difficulties, except to the extent that at the end of the passage he rebuked Socrates for hesitating to attribute them to some objects on the visible plane; the third problem, which concerned the mode of participation (Bk. IV, 837ff.), he faced in the aforementioned two enquiries, on the clearing up of which, in the manner just

[50] Cf. *ET*, prop. 86.
[51] Cf. *ET*, props. 61-62.

described, we will be in possession of the manner in which the Ideas are participated in by those things which bear their names. The fourth problem, to wit, where they are situated, is examined in the two questions put next, whether they are in souls or rather prior to souls, and it will be stated what are the difficulties consequent upon either alternative. It is quite evident, surely, that there follows upon the second problem, which is concerned with the realm of Nature, this third one which transfers itself to Soul, so that on the heels of the last statement of Parmenides, he came straightway to this hypothesis. When Parmenides, then, separates the Idea from the forms in nature, and says "If you contemplate all these in your soul, the many large things and the one thing that generates them, there will appear to you prior to these another one thing," Socrates situates this "one" in the Soul, and calls the Idea a thought in the soul, and defines its place as the soul; for the form in the soul is both one and incorporeal and is not subject to the difficulties raised in respect of the previously mentioned entities. This transcends the many particulars, not being on the same level as the many, since the latter subsist in Matter, while the former subsist in Soul. For there is no common ground between Form and the many particulars, as the argument which led to the difficulty was trying to force us to admit; neither as a whole nor in respect of any of its parts is it in those
892 things which participate in it, so that it might be shown either to be apart from itself or to have a divided existence. It thus avoids the aforementioned difficulties, and for this reason does not suffer the same fate as the previous hypotheses, as Socrates says, the argument being that each of the Forms is a thought, and remains a single thing external to the many particulars. And this has a very compulsive force, which leads Socrates to assume that the Ideas have their essence in some kind of thought. When one says "thought," let us not think that what is meant is the object of thought, even as we call "sensation" what is perceived by the sense, but rather the actual thought-process which thinks the Form is what we are calling the "thought," the word being used in the sense that we call "theorem" or "doctrine" that which arises in souls concerning facts which are objects of doctrine or theory.[52] For which reason Parmenides will compel him to admit that it is the objects of thought that are more properly Ideas. This "thought," then, he describes as "coming into being in souls," by "coming into being" making it clear that it does not exist essentially in them. It is this that the Peripatetics have in their heads when they go on about the "later-born"

---

[52] Reading θεωρητῶν (with Latin trans.) for Greek MSS. θεοειδῶν, to preserve the point of Proclus' remark.

form,[53] which is meant to be quite different from the reason-principle in soul; by "reason-principle in soul" I mean that which resides essentially in souls, from contemplating which we say that the Soul is the totality of the Forms, and that the Soul is the place of the Forms, these being present in it not only potentially, in Aristotle's words (*De An.* III, 4.429a27ff.) but in actuality, according to the first meaning of actuality, as he defines it (*De An.* II, 5.417a22ff.). This, "later-born" entity, then, which is called a "thought" is obviously different from the reason-principle in the real sense. For the "later-born" is a dimmer entity than the many, inasmuch as it arises from them and is not prior to them, whereas the real reason-principle is more perfect than they. Whence the former is less substantial than the many particulars, whereas the latter is more substantial, and inexpressibly more perfect than objects of sense.

That one should not rest content with these "later-born" entities, but should proceed onwards to the real reason-principles which have been allotted their existence from within themselves from eternity, is obvious, then, to anyone who looks to the real nature of things. For
893 whence has a man the power to do this, I mean "to gather together into one in thought what proceeds from a multiplicity of sense-perceptions" (*Phaedr.* 247b7-c1), and to postulate as prior to the visible and separate individuals the one, identical, and invisible Form, whereas none of the other mortal animals, so far as we know, has formed the concept of any such common entity? For none of them has a rational essence, but employs only sensation and impulses and sense-images. Whence, then, do rational souls produce these general notions and make the progression from perceptible objects to the formation of opinions, if they do not possess in their essence the reason-principles of things? For even as Nature possesses the power of creation of things of sense by having reason-principles within it, and thus moulds and holds together the objects of sense—by the power of the inner eye the outer eye, and the finger likewise and all other parts of the body—so also that which possesses the power of knowing them on the general level, by possessing beforehand the appropriate reason-principles contemplates their common properties. And it does not derive these common properties from the objects of sense themselves; for that which is derived from sense-objects is an impression (*phantasma*) and not an object of opinion, and must remain the same, when taken within, as when it was originally apprehended, in order that it may not become false or "non-existent," but it may not become anything more perfect or noble; nor

---

[53] ὑστερογενής, a word used by Aristotle (e.g. *Met.* N, 4.1091a33), but in somewhat different contexts, mainly biological. Probably Alexander Aphr. used the word in the present context (cf. Simpl. *In Cat.* 83.9, an Alexandrian passage).

is it produced from any other source than the soul itself. It is not the case, after all, that Nature, in producing, produces by means of physical reason-principles and norms, while Soul, in producing, will not produce by means of psychic[54] reason-principles and causes. Further, if Matter possesses the common element in the many individual entities in its essential state, and is thus essence more truly than individuals (for it is eternal, while each of them is subject to destruction, and takes its individuality from it; for it is through the form in it that each thing participates in essence), while the Soul possesses only the "later-born" common properties, how can we avoid making the Soul of lesser account than Matter, if the form residing in Matter is more perfect and more of an essence than that in the Soul? For this latter is what is most properly termed "later-born," while the former is eternal; and the latter arises from the many particulars, while the former is the principle of coherence for the many, and so the latter is an offspring of the former. For the impression of the common quality present to us takes its existence from beholding the common quality in individual objects, for which very reason it directs its reference to that quality (for everything directs itself towards its own first principle), and is said to be nothing other than a predicate, precisely by the fact of being predicated of the many individuals. Furthermore, the general concept in the many is narrower in range than each of them; for each of the individual entities is amplified by additions and accidental accretions, and the "later-born" concept comprehends each of the many; for which reason it serves as a predicate for each of these, and the individual is in any one of the general concepts as a whole; for this common quality is predicated not only of the general concept mentioned above, but of every individual subject as a whole. How, then, could it be composed from that source, and out of the common quality in the many? For if on the one hand it arises out of the many themselves, where are we to see that infinite number of men, to all of which we apply the same predicate? Or if it arises out of the common quality in the many, how can this be more comprehensive than its own cause? It must therefore take its origin from somewhere else, and receive from some other source this power of comprehending each form. Of this source, indeed, it is an image, coming into existence in a way contrary to what one would expect, by virtue of reminiscence, on the basis of sense-objects, of the causal principle aroused within us.

I would go so far as to add this, that every proof is made on the basis of concepts prior and more august and more universal than itself;[55]

[54] Reading ψυχικαῖς (with Latin trans.) for φυσικαῖς of Greek MSS.

[55] An application of Aristotle's principle in *An. Post.* I, 11.77a5ff, where in fact Aristotle is denying the necessity for Platonic Forms in this connection.

how then can the universal concept be worthy of honour, if it is "later-born"? For in "later-born" entities the more universal a concept is, the less substance it has; which leads to the species having more substance than the genus. Our rules about the truest type of proof would then have to be abandoned, if we lay down that only "later-born" universals reside in soul; for these are certainly not more powerful than, nor causative of, nor prior in nature to, more particular concepts.[56]

895 If these results are absurd, it must then follow that prior to the "later-born" concepts there exist essential reason-principles, which are always present and active in the divine souls and those of the classes of being superior to us, but which in us are sometimes obscured and sometimes operative, and that sometimes on the theoretical level only and sometimes on the providential level, when we, in union with the gods, take a hand in administering the whole world (cf. *Phaedr.* 246c2).

Let it be said, however—to return to our original subject, that being that the true Form is a thought—let it be said, then, that the true Form is a thought, but primarily in the sense of a thought-process of Intellect in the true sense, in fact of the Paternal Intellect, in which both true beings are thoughts and thoughts true beings. At any rate, the Oracles, in explaining to us the Ideas as they exist primarily in that entity, have called them "paternal concepts" (*ennoiai*), as being creative thoughts by virtue of the unity in substance of the thoughts with their objects:

"These are the concepts of the Father, after which my coiling Fire . . ."[57]

For the thoughts there are not distinct from their objects, but are rather thoughts of themselves; for which reason they are truly essences and truly thoughts and are both of these together, and for this reason are "concepts of the Father." Following on the paternal Ideas, in all the intellectual entities subsequent to the Father, each Idea is again an object of thought by virtue of its likeness to Him; nor in the case of these is either their activity devoid of essential being or their essence devoid of activity, since their thought is co-extensive with their essence—with the qualification that they are in each case co-extensive with the objects of thought on their own level of being, while being thoughts only of the objects of thought on higher levels, but not being identical with those objects, inasmuch as they are superior to the agent thinking them. On the level below all the intellectual levels of being, there are

---

[56] A critique of Aristotle's discussion of knowledge of first principles at *An. Post.* II, 19?

[57] Fr. 38 DP (emended by H. Lewy to read Ἔννοιαι πατρὸς αἵδε, μεθ᾽ἃς ἐμὸν εἰλυμέ-νον πῦρ, for Ἔννοιαι πατρὸς, αἰδεύμεθα σ᾽, εἰλυμένον πῦρ of the Greek MSS. Confirmed by Latin trans.: "post quos meus εἰλίμενον (sic) ignis."

thoughts and objects of thought distinct from one another in souls that are constantly intelligising, in such a way that one element in them is thinking, the other being thought; the thoughts here are transitive, while the essential reason-principles inherent in the souls remain always the same.

Lastly, in individual souls thoughts are of two types. The one has as its object essential reason-principles; the other results from the assembling together, by means of ratiocination, of a multiplicity of sense-impressions (cf. *Phaedr.* 249b7-c1). It is actually through these that Socrates says that they "come into being in souls." That which "comes to be," after all, plainly is not present essentially. This, then, is the ultimate echo of the primal level of thought, in so far as it is both universal and resides substantially in the intelligising soul. When we give the title of "thoughts" to the projections of the essential reason-principles, by virtue of which we understand how the Soul is in a way the totality of all the Forms, we must be understood to use the term "thoughts" in a different sense from that which we use to describe what is produced in the soul as a result of projections from individual sense-objects; for the former are thoughts of things substantially existent and always present in us, constituting images of the realm of true existence, and when we come up against these, at that point we become filled with thoughts in the true sense, which do not "come into being," but are projections of things we did not know we possessed. We should not, therefore, equate these thoughts arising from essential reason-principles with what are called by some "notions,"[58] even though the terms are almost identical (*noēmata-ennoēmata*); for these latter are objects stimulated by sense-impressions. Nor should we equate them with the incorporeal "expressions" (*lekta*); for their existence is seen as insubstantial and dim even to those who postulate it. Nor, in general, should we equate them with the insubstantial forms in souls, but rather with those that exist in them essentially, and which serve as constituent components of their life.

We must, then, as I have said, ascend from the reason-principles in Nature to those in Soul, and not only to the "later-born," but also to the essential ones. The "later-born," after all, are images of these latter, not sprung from the sensible particulars. For it is not the case that there is a common principle of all multiplicities (we do not, after all, postulate universal principles of evil things); nor yet in the case of unique things[59] do we decline to conceive of a common property because of their uniqueness. It is from within, then, and from our essential nature,

---

[58] The Stoics, cf. *SVF* II, 83.

[59] As, for instance, the Sun and Moon, and other heavenly bodies, or the Cosmos itself.

that the projections of the Forms arise, and not from sense-objects; for in that case objects of knowledge would be far fainter than objects of sensation. As it is, however, even as knowledge is stronger than sense-perception, so the objects of knowledge are stronger than those of sensation. Universal concepts are objects of knowledge, and knowledge concerns them. These are therefore stronger and more worthy of respect than objects of sense; for it is repugnant to reason that causal principles should be inferior to the things they cause; it is internally, then, 897 as has been said, and essentially that we possess the Forms.

These are, then, "thoughts" in another sense, and not in the sense of "thought-processes"; for since they are productions of the Intellect (*nous*) one might reasonably call them "intellections" (*noēmata*) as being results of the Intellect's activity, even as we call "art" the results of Art, and "nature" the form that arises from Nature; and because all the psychic reason-principles are dependent upon the divine Forms and strive towards intelligising them, they might be called "intellections" for this reason also. For one can describe as "thought" both the intelligible object as a thing intelligised, and the activity of intelligising— the knowing function of the intelligising agent—even as the activity of the thing moved is a motion. But in the Intellect, as has been said, both these elements are co-extensive with each other; as for the objects of intellection in the Soul, in relation to the thoughts in the Soul, one might call them objects of intellection[60] as being thought by them, while in relation to the Forms which are the true objects of intellection, they have the rank of intelligising elements, inasmuch as they become objects of intellection for them; for in all cases intelligising elements must have a secondary relation to objects of intellection.

The nature of Intellect is naturally disposed towards the contemplation of the Forms; for even on the universal level the Intellect is a creator of Form, and the whole creation and the beauty of the sense-realm and its order is brought about through the sovereignty of Intellect; and neither, if one were to abandon Intellect as a cause, could one comprehend how the essential nature of the Forms can serve as origin for the substance of the universe, nor, if one were to disregard the hypothesis of the Ideas, could one maintain the creative activity of Intellect upon this realm. Intellect and the Forms are therefore mutually entailed; and it is in view of this relationship, it seems to me, that Socrates defined the Forms as "thoughts"; and it is obvious that this definition must be modified according to the type of Intellect concerned, either universal or particular, on the level of Soul or of Intellect itself. He was in fact striving towards an intuition of the essence of Intellect, but he fastened

---

[60] Adding ⟨νοητὰ⟩ after νοήματα in 897.15 (West.).

on the intellect of the soul level as the place where these "thoughts" should be constantly coming into existence, ascending as he was from below through the levels of being contiguous to himself. For Soul, after all, is Intellect in extension, and the intellections in it are images of 898 the primal ones. Parmenides now leads Socrates from these soul–intellections onward to the actual Forms at the level of Intellect, in the following words:

> "Then, is each Form one of these thoughts, and yet a thought of nothing?" "No, that is impossible." "So it is a thought of something?" "Yes." "Of something that is, or of something that is not?" "Of something that is." "In fact, of some one thing which that thought understands to preside over all the cases, as being some one single idea?" "Yes." "Then will not this thing that is thought of as being one and always the same in all cases be a form?" "That again seems necessary." (132bc)

From the common elements in particular things he ascended to something other than them but immediately proximate to them, to wit, the form in Nature, and then on from this to the reason-principle in soul, which is of the nature of a thought of some existent thing, such as we gave the epithet of "later-born," which is a true description of what arises in souls. But he must proceed onward from here also to the actual thought of the essential reason-principle, and from this again he must make the transition to Being itself, towards which Socrates is now being led through the midwifely arguments of Parmenides.

For since we accept that the reason-principle in the soul is either a thought of something or of nothing—but a thought of nothing is empty and fictional, as when one tries to form a concept of a hippocentaur or a goat-stag, or, rather, of a "thingumabob" (*skindapsos*)[61] or something else quite without substance, for of the first-mentioned we form at least some conception—the alternative is, then, that the reason-principle in the soul is a thought of something. If it is of something, we must then ask is it of something that is or something that is not. It is plain, surely, that the reason-principle in the soul is a thought of what is. In that case is it not far rather of that Form that "presides over" all those at the level of Soul or of Nature, that Form which we say that thought apprehends, "being some one single idea"? For that is far more really existent than the thought which corresponds to it. Besides, how can both the Form and the thought, being two different kinds, preside over one and the same thing? If we must make one or the other of these 899 the Form, it is plain that the more dominant should be the Form; and

---

[61] A common school example of a meaningless word, like *blityri*, cf. Sextus Empiricus, *Adv. Math.* 8.133.

of such a nature we have declared the object of thought to be, which presides over all those things of the same type of which are apprehended by the thought; for this is the cause of existence for similar things, and not the thought that thinks it. For even as it is not the thought that my father is my father that is the cause of me, but my father himself, so in the case of all causal agencies, it is not the thoughts about their existence that the causes of the things dependent on them, but they themselves, prior to the thoughts about them, which are indeed the causes of the truth of the thoughts which declare that they are the causes of whatever they are causes of. Those who hold Ideas to be mere thoughts mean by saying that every thought is "of something" that the thought is *of* the thinking agent, as if one were to say that there were no such thing as an object of sense perception, understanding "perception" as being merely a function of the perceiving agent; and for this reason they say that Parmenides is guilty of a logical fallacy. But those who hold that thoughts are mutually implied by objects of thought define thought (*noēma*) as being both *of* the thinker and *of* the entity thought, all three elements being united with each other, the thinker, the process of thought, and the object of thought; and that is not to be wondered at, seeing that in the case of objects of sense-perception they say that the process of perceiving is the same as the object perceived, calling both "perception" (*aisthēma*).

If then, the thought is of the object of thought, not only in us, but also in the divine and veritable Intellect, it is plain that the object of thought is prior to the thought, and it is by virtue of its striving towards this that the reason-principle in the soul is a thought. For the discursive and spatially distinct and transitive aspect of the reason-principles in the soul manifests sufficiently in its activities that the intelligible Form is something else again, that which unitarily and indivisibly contains the cause of all the reason-principles. That is the "one thing" to which he is referring in the present passage, "presiding over all," by taking in all the systems of Forms, and which he says is understood by the thought as being "some one single idea." From this you may gather that the intelligising of the universal Intellect also has intelligible objects existent prior to it; and neither is intelligising simply knowledge, but knowledge of something, nor are objects of thought secondary to thinking agents; for in this case acts of thinking would be prior to these and they would not yet exist. Either, then, the objects of thought are prior to the thinking agents, and hence prior to the acts of thought (for the acts of thought are of necessity in the thinking agents, even as acts of sense-perception are in the perceiving agents, and all acts of knowledge in general are in the knowers, and not external to the knowers); or at least they are in the thinking agents. For at least they cannot be

259

posterior to them, lest, before they come into becoming, these exist as actualised thoughts of nothing. But if the objects of thoughts are prior to the thinking agents, there must also be another object of thought in them, because every thinking entity thinks itself, and everything that thinks itself thinks by means of its own faculty of thought, not looking outside itself. This is what one must gather from Plato's saying that "the thought exists," and not adding that being is external to thought, because mind may be distinguished into that which simply thinks itself, and that which thinks both itself and the things prior to it, but no mind thinks the things posterior to it except in the sense of containing their causes. For the term "object of thought" has three senses, participatively at the level of that which thinks what is prior to itself, substantively at the level of that which thinks itself, causally at the level of that which thinks what is posterior to itself.[62] And when the participative level is operative, then so also is the substantive; for what thinks those things prior to itself must also think itself. But where the substantive level is operative, it does not always follow that the participative is also; for the primal Intellect thinks itself only, since it has no object of thought prior to it. And where the causal level is operative, there the substantive must be also; for in the process of thinking itself, a mind can also think objects of thought posterior to itself. But when the substantive level is operative, it does not follow that the causal level is operative—if there were some lowest mind, which would have nothing secondary to itself that it could think causally, but which would simply think itself and be an object of thought to itself.

These reflections might occur to you, as I have said, as a consequence of Parmenides' statement that the thought must be "of something that is." He also in the *Theaetetus* (167a) spoke of opinion (*doxa*) as being "of something"; from which it is deduced that what is not cannot be the object of opinion, and all knowledge is of something, and never of nothing. And because unity is more especially present in things that are, thoughts are dependent upon it;[63] the phrase "the one presiding over all the cases" indicates this.

901   We shall not therefore stay our course, as we ascend from one level of forms to another, until we arrive at the level of real existence (*ta ontōs onta*). For even if we find the Intellect and the objects of intellection united together in one nature, the Intellect there will be a plenum of forms by virtue of the object of intellection within it; and as we unite Intellect and the object of intellection to one another, so also we bring together intellections with existence; for the Intellect, being in itself

---

[62] For the distinction κατ᾽ αἰτίαν – καθ᾽ ὕπαρξιν – κατὰ μέθεξιν, cf. *ET*, prop. 65.
[63] Reading αὐτὸ (= τὸ ἕν) for αὐτὰ of MSS (West).

and thinking itself, is at the same time full of objects of thought. And even as in the realm of things of sense, whatever appears as a unity is in reality a multiplicity, even so in the intelligible realm the dual nature of thought and being is substantiated as a unity. Soul, then, in passing from its own thoughts to real beings, transfers itself as it were from one set of things to another; but the thoughts of Intellect are identical with the real beings through the process of intellectual self-intention and the sameness that prevails in things at that level.

"And besides," said Parmenides, "according to the way in which you assert that the other things have a share in the Forms, must you not hold either that each of those things consists of thoughts, so that all things think, or else that they are thoughts which nevertheless do not think?" "That too is unreasonable, said Socrates." (132c)

He uses two arguments to bring the discussion from the subject of thoughts in the soul to that of the intelligible Forms, which are the objects of thought for these thoughts, and are for this reason called thoughts. The first argument is based on the thought itself; for Real Being is essentially such as to be an object of thought (*noēmatikon*);[64] that Real Being therefore is the Form properly so-called, and that which is over all the Forms eternally existent and identical and one and already being thought, not just thinking, as is the case with the thought in the soul; that there is a difference between a thought as thinking and as being thought, is obvious; therefore either both are Forms, and primary being will be double and there will not be just one Idea of each thing; or else the dominant part of the thought is the object of thought, so that this would be the Form, and not the thought.

The second argument is as follows: everything that partakes of thought *qua* thought must think, and things of this realm partake of the Forms, so that if the primary Forms were thoughts and the things of 902 this realm partake of Forms as thoughts, all things would be intelligent (*noētika*); for that which partakes of thinking (which, as we say, is thought) thinks; that which partakes in life, lives; and that which partakes in being, exists. So then, the Forms are not just objects of thought, but thoughts of the class of things that are involved in thought-processes, and there is nothing strange in the fact that that which participates in thoughts should not think. If, then, all things participate in Forms, and not all things participate in thoughts, the Forms cannot then be thoughts. One of three consequences would then fol-

[64] This term is of interest, as being attested elsewhere only in the Hermetic Corpus (XVIII, 4).

low—either that those things participating in thought would not think, or that the Forms would not be thoughts, or that things that do not think do not participate in Forms. Of these, two are plainly absurd; for everything participating in thought thinks, since thought is a manifestation of the thinking process; and things that do not think participate in Forms, as for instance lifeless things participate in the Equal and the Less and the Greater, which are Forms. So then, Forms are not thoughts, nor are thoughts a substantial element in them, but rather objects of thought.

Let us ascend now from particular entities to the undivided reason-principles of Nature, which does not have the characteristic of thinking what is prior to it (for Nature is not only mindless, but also lacks reason and even imagination); and from these to the objects of thought which preside over the forms in Nature, and which are activities of the intelligent soul, according to the definition of them given by Socrates; for he says that they come to be in the soul (132b), and are thoughts of the soul in the sense of thought-processes. From these we ascend to the true objects of thought; for one may call these causes of all things that have acquired form, but not simply thoughts in the strict sense. So that even if the demiurgic Intellect should be termed world-creator and cause of all things, it is by virtue of the intelligible element in it that it is the cause of the existence of everything, by virtue of its life the cause only of things being alive, and by virtue of its mind only of their thinking. Things must take their start, therefore, not from thinking agents, but rather from elements which are objects of thought, in order that there may be causes of both things that have mind and things that have not. For existence is common to all things, but mental activity is not. Thoughts at the soul level are not therefore the primal level of Forms, but rather what are the objects of the thought of these, the elements 903 that are primally creative and causes to all things of being and unity and perfection.

At this point it is worth raising the question as to why, although all things in Intellect exist in an intellectual mode, not all things of this realm that participate in the Forms think, and why, when everything on that plane is alive, yet not all the things that are assimilated to those things have life. The answer to that is that the decline in levels of being, which declines from the primal causes right down to the lowest ones, obscures the participation of lower elements in the universal and perfect essences. The process of creation, proceeding throughout all levels, brings into existence all things according to different measures of being, and it is not even the case that all things participate in the same Form in the same way, but some to a greater extent and others to a lesser, and some are assimilated to the Form by virtue of one potency, others of two, and others of more than that. And hence it is that so-called "chains" appear,[65] stretching from the top to the bottom of the scale of being; as for instance the Form of the Moon—let us take that as an example. At the divine level it appears as the "One" and the "good" of the Form; for all things are divinised by virtue of the Good, as Socrates says in the *Republic* (508d), through the light of truth. It appears also at the angelic level by virtue of its intellectual phase, and on the daemonic level, to continue, in the living beings that image that Form in thought and are intellectual—not able yet to imitate it in thinking, but rather in living. And many examples of animals in the moon chain will occur to you, such as the Egyptian Apis-bull, and the fish known as the moon-fish, and many other animals which imitate the heavenly form of the moon in one way or another. It appears finally also in stones, so that there is a certain stone also connected with that Form, which undergoes waxings and wanings along with the moon in the heavens, although it has no share in life. In every case you may observe the same situation, and you should not imagine that all things receive all the faculties of their respective Forms, but only in accord with their rank on the scale of being, some more, some less.[66] So it is not the case that all the qualities that are present in the Forms also inhere in all their images. All that there is of each Form which necessarily appears at all levels is that essential characteristics of each Form by which it differs from all others; for even though all the Forms are a unity, yet there is always one element more prominent in each which marks off its distinctive essence, in which all things participate which take their origin from it; and this quality it is which makes one "chain," whereas participation in greater or lesser potencies within the Form produces the first, middle, and last elements on the chain, the same thing participated in at various levels in different degrees. The one Paternal Intellect defines for all other entities the measures of their participation and the contributions of each to the cosmos, assuming in advance the beginnings and middles and ends of each chain of Forms, and decrees how far the characteristic quality descending from each must reach.

We must add to this that, there being different degrees of participation, the first to leave the participating entities are the lowest characteristics of the Forms, second are the more universal ones, and appearing in all the end-products equally are the primarily creative ones which are most closely akin to the One; for each Form is both a unity and a multiplicity, the multiplicity not filling out the unity by means of addition, but rather the unity giving substantial existence to the many character-

904

[65] For other discussions of this important concept, cf. *ET*, props. 21, 97-102, 110-112.
[66] He has said much of this earlier, at 874, including the remark about the moonstone.

istics contained within it. For it has existence and life and intellect on the unitary level, while of the things produced in accordance with it some participate in all of these, others in existence alone; since in the Forms themselves the intellectual element derives from the one ⟨Intellect⟩,[67] life from the unparticipated Life, and being from the One Being, as indeed their unity springs from the henad beyond beings.

Enough has now been said about the underlying doctrines. As for the two arguments by means of which he ascended from Soul to Being itself, one of them he has concluded in the passage quoted just previously, saying that "the Form itself as object of thought will be always existent and self-identical in the case of all the Forms," and that this is prior to the thought in the soul. For the object of thought is superior, as has been said, to the thinking agent. For even if the thinking element is Soul, the object of thought Intellect, still Intellect is superior; and if Intellect is the thinking element, and the Intelligible the object of thought, the Intelligible is superior.

The second argument he examined as a whole in saying that if the things of this realm participate in the Forms, and the Forms are thoughts, the things of this realm would then participate in thoughts; and what participates in thought must necessarily think; but if thoughts were to participate in them (sc. the Forms), this would not necessarily follow. Therefore, the primary Forms are not thoughts.

This argument not only shows us that the Forms are not primarily in Soul, but also that they are prior to Intellect; for Intellect, thinking itself and the objects of thought prior to it, *qua* Intellect, is appetitive, but *qua* object of thought is an object of appetition; of these two elements, one is more akin to the Good, the other less; for the Good also is an object of appetition, but is not itself appetitive. It follows necessarily, then, that, whereas the reason-principles in Nature are neither intelligible nor intellectual, it is through the medium of these that there is brought about our ascent to the intelligible Forms. There will then be, prior to unintelligent Nature, the whole intellectual order, and this of two types, transitive and intransitive. In so far as each entity intelligises, it strives towards the intelligible akin to it, as we have said. I certainly mean the intelligible to be prior to this Nature because neither Nature nor body are intelligising entities. Then prior to this we have the being that both intelligises and is intelligible, such as is the intellectual Form or Form in Soul; and above this there is the Intelligible itself. For there must also be prior to this, which shows in itself a certain duality, the Intelligible itself on the primal level, and this is participated in by Intellect and, through Intellect, by Soul. We must, then, not only transfer

905

---

[67] Adding *νοῦ*, as seems necessary (West.).

our attention from the Forms in Soul to the intellectual entities as being objects of intellection, but on from these to the intelligibles proper, from which Being is imparted to all the Forms. Thus the midwifery of Parmenides has led the argument from the lowest entities to the most primal, demonstrating that we must not think of participation in the
906 Forms as a corporeal process, nor yet a physical one, nor even as a psychic one, but one proper to intellectual and intelligible Forms.

> *"But, Parmenides, it appears to me very likely that the case is as follows: that these Forms stand fixed as patterns, as it were, in the nature of things; the other things are made in their image and are likenesses; and this participation they come to have in the Forms is nothing but their being made in their image."* (132cd)

Socrates, having been led up to a comprehension of the Forms at their intelligible level, guided by the midwifery of Parmenides, now is of the firm opinion that he has worked out the order and the manner of participation in the Forms, saying that the Forms "stand fixed in the nature of things," and the other things come to be in relation to them; what else does he mean by that than that he is allotting to the Forms motionless and unchangeable essence, and to the things that come to existence in dependence on them an essence which is tossed about in the realm of generation? For this is the distinction he makes between "standing fixed" and "coming to be," making his own distinction here between that which is always identical and in the same state, and that which is never in the same state, but only in process of generation, even as Timaeus (*Tim.* 35a) and the Eleatic Stranger in the *Sophist* (256aff.) distinguished apart Becoming and Being.

Thus he analyses, then, the distinction between these two. And he brings on at the same time the question of the method of participation, by way of solution to the difficulties introduced previously, declaring it to be an "assimilation" (*homoiōsis*), in order that he may not be forced to say the things of this realm share in the Forms either as wholes or as parts, nor that the Forms are coordinate with the things of this realm. For the pattern is not present to the image, nor is it coordinate with it. Participation, then, takes place by assimilation. He has introduced this concept by calling the Forms patterns and the things participating them likenesses, and this participation for this reason assimilation. And he has placed so much confidence in this argument, that, whereas he had
907 formerly sworn that it was no easy thing to define the nature of this participation and how the Forms come to be in sensibles, now he says that "it appears to him very likely" that this is the method of participation, and by his use of the phrases "very likely" and "plainly appears" (*kataphainesthai*) rather than simply "appears" (*phainesthai*), he

265

shows that he is especially confident about this theory. He has arrived at this position both through his own intellectual acuity, and through Parmenides' faculty for bringing to fruition his spontaneous notions about divine things. This makes it plain that the method of these discussions is midwifely, not contentious; for otherwise Parmenides would not have caused his interlocutor to make progress and to grow always more perfect in his concepts. For the end result of "midwifery" is the eliciting of the thought hidden within the interlocutor, but of a verbal contest victory over the opponent and the reduction of him to complete perplexity. If, then, Socrates rises to new heights on the head of each problem raised, and perfects and articulates his ideas about the primal Forms, it must be said that he is having his ideas brought to birth by Parmenides rather than being overthrown, and that this action is performed for his improvement rather than his defeat.

This, at any rate, as has often been said before, is the form of the discussion. Let us consider now in what way Socrates' present hypothesis constitutes an advance, without constituting a complete solution. He is correct in so far as he has grasped the notion of intellectual and real patterns, and in that he has defined their characteristic, declaring that they "stand fixed," and, further, that the other things are assimilated to them; for being stable[68] and being always in the same state is characteristic of the Forms, which are eternally both existent and active. For that being always the same and in the same state is proper only for the most divine of things is said by the Eleatic Stranger; and "standing fixed" is nothing else than "being always the same and in the same state," as he lays down respectively in the *Sophist* (249b) ⟨and in the *Statesman* (269d)⟩.[69] If, then, Socrates says that the Forms "stand fixed," and what stand fixed are stated to be "always the same and in the same state" in the *Sophist*, and what are "always the same and in the same state" are defined in the *Statesman* as the most divine of all things, it is plain that the Forms would then be the most divine of all things, and no longer thoughts of souls, but transcendent over all such things.

In these assertions, then, he was correct, and also in that he postulated as prior to the multiplicity in them a unity; for by the phrase "in the nature of things" he indicates the single henad of all of them. Plato, after all, was accustomed to apply this term "nature" also to the intelligible realm. At any rate, Socrates in the *Philebus* (30d) talks of a royal mind and a royal soul existing in the *nature* of Zeus. And Timaeus says (*Tim.* 37d), "It happened that the *nature* of the living being was eter-

908

---

[68] Reading μόνιμον for γόνιμον of MSS, since the idea of productivity seems irrelevant here (West.).

[69] The τὸ μὲν earlier in this sentence seems to require a balancing clause such as that provided (West.).

nal," referring here the term "nature" to the mould of the intelligible
Ideas, and by saying that it is eternal asserting that it "stands fixed"; to
prove its "standing fixed," he says that Eternity remains in one state,
whereas Time is in motion and has its existence involved with generation (*Tim.* 38b); just as now Socrates has allotted the quality of generation to those things that participate in the Ideas. Such, then, is the "nature" mentioned here, the single henad, and such is the transcendent
status of the intelligible Forms.

So much, then, as I said, of Socrates' statement is correct. But in so
far as he allots only the quality of being a pattern to the Forms and not
also the qualities of bringing to fruition and preserving things, in this
he would seem still to have an incomplete grasp of the correct doctrine
about them. Each Form is not only a pattern to sensible objects, but is
also the cause of their being; for they do not require any other force to
produce things in their own image and to assimilate to themselves the
things of this realm, while remaining themselves inactive and motion-
909 less and without any productive capacity, like wax moulds in this
realm, but rather they themselves produce and generate their own images. It would be absurd, after all, if the reason-principles in Nature
were to possess a certain creative power, while the intelligible Forms
should be devoid of any causal role in creation. So then, every divine
Form has not only a paradigmatic aspect, but a paternal one as well, and
by virtue of its very being is a generative cause of the many particulars;
and not only this, but is a cause of completion to them; for it possesses
the faculty of leading the things of this realm from an incomplete state
to completion and of conferring goodness upon them, and of filling out
their lack, and leading Matter, which is all things potentially, to being
actually all that it was potentially before the creative onset of the
Forms. The Forms, you see, have also this perfective faculty within
them.

But have they not also the faculty of preservation? And where would
the indissoluble creation of the universe come from if not from the
Forms? And whence arise the reason-principles that stand fixed and
preserve unbroken the single sympathy of all things, those reason-
principles through which the cosmos remains complete, no Form
being absent from it, other than from the steadfast causes, even as
change arises from moving causes? The divisible and dispersible quality of bodies, after all, is compressed and held together by no other
agency than the indivisible power of the Forms; in and of itself, body
is prone to division, and it requires the cohesive force of the reason-
principles. And if it is the case that unity is the prior condition of this
cohesion (for everything that causes cohesion in others should itself
first be one and indivisible), the Form would then be not only genera-

267

tive, as we said, and conservative and perfective, but also cohesive and unificatory of all secondary entities.

Socrates should then, one might say, not have concentrated only on the assimilative power of the Forms, but should also have examined their other powers, and on that basis have defined the mode of participation in them, calling this participation assimilation, certainly, but also declaring it to be cohesive and conservative and perfective of what is assimilated. This is indeed what Timaeus (*Tim.* 32c) is teaching us 910 when he declares that the cosmos is perfect and indissoluble by reason of its assimilation to the perfect Living Being.

We might reply that Socrates, in calling participation an assimilation, has included all these concepts. For things that are assimilated to what "stands fixed" are necessarily indissoluble, and are held together by their own reason-principles, and are conserved in their essence by them; otherwise they would not be "similar" to the things that "stand fixed," being borne along on the restless flow of generation and scattered in all directions from their original state; nor would those others be immovably patterns if they were not patterns of things that resembled themselves, so as to be "like" the immovable essences. This is the reason why we say that there are no Ideas of particulars, but only of those things that are eternal in the sphere of generated and unstable things. Let no one, then, criticise our term "pattern" (*paradeigma*) as being a metaphor taken from patterns in this realm, which are perceptible by sense and inactive and requiring other agents to act on them. Socrates, after all, did not actually call the Forms patterns, but "patterns, *as it were*"; this qualification serves both to remove from the patterns familiar to us their sterile and lifeless aspect, and to reveal the primally active and image-generative principle within the Forms. And let us not separate apart the pattern and the creative principle, but rather combine them in one and contemplate both together; for the paradigm by virtue of its very essence brings into being that which is modelled upon it, and the creative principle, in creating by virtue of its very existence and in making like to itself whatever comes into being, and providing to it secondarily whatever is within itself primally, also establishes itself in the rank of paradigm, so that the one entity is creative as a paradigm, while the other is a paradigm in a creative manner; for it is proper to a paradigm to be capable of creating something like itself, and to a creative principle to produce Becoming rather than Being. For this reason in the *Philebus* (26dff.) he says that everything that creates pre-911 sides over what comes to be, and whatever comes to be comes to be through some cause; and in the *Timaeus* (31a) he says that the paradigm is a paradigm of an image, for each of them is a relative term; the one is spoken of in relation to generation, the other in relation to image.

Nevertheless each is implied in the other, the creative principle in the paradigm under its aspect of paradigm, and the pattern in the creative principle under its creative aspect.

There is, then, one unifying principle that brings together in those entities both the paradigmatic cause and the creative, except that there are creative principles of many things in so far as they are generated, whereas there is no paradigmatic cause of them; these are individual entities, which come to be as individuals, but yet do not have paradigms as such. So let us then not make an absolute distinction between the paradigmatic and the creative cause, but only in the manner stated, nor let us say that the activity of the paradigms on things of this realm requires the aid of any other types of Form, such as those in Soul or in Nature. For their activity is present transcendentally everywhere to everything, and binds together secondary entities by means of the generative abundance of the divine Forms, while they give completely of themselves to all things assimilation in respect of their whole being.

"Well, if a thing is made in the image of the Form, can that Form fail to be like the image of it, in so far as the image was made in its likeness? Or is there any way that what is like can avoid being like what is like it?" "No way." "And must not the thing which is like share with the thing that is like it in one and the same Form?" "It must." "And will not that in which the like things share, so as to be alike, be just that Form itself?" "Certainly." (132de)

Socrates has defined the Forms as "patterns standing fixed," and has called the things of this realm "likenesses" of them, and for this reason has termed participation "assimilation," and in all these questions has seemed to produce imperfect theories (for the Forms are not only patterns, but also productive and perfective and conservative of sensible objects, as we have said; nor are the things of this realm simply likenesses, but also products of the former, protected by them and gaining all their completeness and coherence from that source)—unless, indeed, as we have said, under this one term of "likeness" of the things that come to be to the fixed Form, Socrates intended to include all these characteristics. At any rate, once Socrates has proposed this formulation, it is with truly divine acumen that Parmenides agrees that, as Socrates says, "these patterns stand fixed in the nature of things," as though he had quite correctly uttered their intelligible essence. But since he had undertaken to solve the first problems about participation, introducing the notion of assimilation and of participation in the mode of assimilation, designed to free us from the difficulty about whole and part, Parmenides, wishing to reveal the primal and universal causality of the paradigm, transcending all relationship of whatever kind with

269

the things assimilated to it, shows that even if the sensible object is "like" the intelligible Form, it is still not necessary that this relationship be reciprocal, and the Form be said to be "like" it, lest prior to these two "like" entities we should go in search of some further Form as cause of the likeness between these two; for things that are like one another have in every case in common some identical quality, and it is in virtue of this identical quality in them that they are said to be "like." Once this has been agreed, then, that the participated entity and the participating, the paradigm and the image, are like one another, there will be prior to these another thing that causes their likeness, and this progression will continue to infinity.

To this Socrates should have replied that "like" has two senses, one the likeness of two coordinate entities, the other the likeness which involves subordination to an archetype, and the one is to be seen as consisting in the identity of some one reason-principle, while the other involves not only identity but at the same time otherness, whenever something is "like" as having the same Form derived from the other, but not *along with* it.

These questions have been raised from a logical perspective to propound problems. If, however, you wished to transfer them to the multiple levels of the Forms, then you would discover the depth inherent in them. For the Forms in Nature are distinct from and prior to sensible objects, and the Forms in Soul are different again, and so are the Forms in Intellect, and there are no others prior to these; these latter are, then, solely patterns and in no way "like" the things below them, while the Forms in Soul are both paradigms and images, and inasmuch as both they and the entities inferior to them are images, they are "like" each other in so far as they exist in relation to the same things, the Forms in Intellect. The Forms in Nature are in the same situation; for they are intermediate between the Forms in Soul and sensible objects, and are "like" sensible objects, not as being patterns of them, but inasmuch as both are images of what is prior to them. But those things that are solely patterns are no longer "like" their images; for things are "like" that have some property in common, and they, being primal, do not have properties.

This is all on the philosophical level. One might also approach the question theologically. The Forms in the cosmic Intellect are one thing, and those in the demiurgic Intellect are another, and there are others intermediate between these, which are in the Intellect that is participated, but which is yet supracosmic and binds the Forms in the cosmic Intellect to those in the unparticipated Intellect. Since, then, the Forms exist on so many levels, in the case of some the relation of likeness is reciprocal, and in the case of others not, as in the case of the demiurgic

Forms; for they are superior to the assimilative level of Forms, which we identified as being that of the participated but supra-cosmic Intellect. The Forms on any level below this one are assimilated in one way or another both to each other and to those prior to them, but the Forms in the unparticipated Intellect are superior to the assimilative level, so that sensible objects are assimilated to them, but they are no longer assimilated to sensible objects. For if they were, we would not yet have reached a resting-place, but would have to proceed to infinity, nowhere able to discover the originating point of assimilation.

If one begins from the bottom, one can say that the Forms in the Intellect of the universe and the Forms in Soul are "like" one another, in so far as all these are secondary to the assimilative Intellects and as it were brothers to one another. To those, however, who ascend as far as the unparticipated Intellect, it is no longer possible to say this; for the assimilative order is an intermediate one and not superior to both of these; and being intermediate, it only assimilates sensible objects, which are inferior to it, to the intellectual realm, and not the other way round, the intellectual to the sensible; for it is not right for the secondary to give anything to what is prior to it, nor for the prior to receive anything from things secondary. In order, then, that Parmenides may reveal to Socrates these patterns as being intellectual, certainly, but established in the unparticipated Intellect above the assimilative intellects, he demonstrates that the relationship of the Forms with the things of this realm should not be seen as reciprocal; for this is the condition of secondary things in respect of the assimilative cause, being bound together by it as it extends its activities from above upon both classes of thing, the assimilated and those things to which they are being assimilated.

This has been on the theological level, as we have been enumerating the various orders of Forms, those in Nature, those in Intellect, and those, as we have said, situated either at the level of the participated, intracosmic Intellect, or at that of the unparticipated Intellect, and the assimilative order of Intellects situated in the supracosmic and participated Intellect, as the second Hypothesis will make clear to us,[70] and as the divine utterance of the theologians on these subjects has taught those who have correctly understood them. We may also, however, consider philosophically, in the case of Like and Unlike purely on the level of the Forms which are median between the most generic and the most particular types of Form, how they serve the most generic in the work of assimilation by acting only on the participating entities, but

914

[70] Not extant, but recoverable in part from Damascius' commentary on Proclus' commentary, *Dub.*, chs. 127-190, vol. II, pp. 5.1-67.10 Ruelle. Damascius discusses the "assimilative order," however, only at chs. 338ff.

not on the others as they are prior to themselves; and cooperating with the individual among the Forms, they give both to them and to those things which come into being in dependence upon them participation in themselves, giving them a share in Likeness and Unlikeness; so that in the case of these it is true that Likeness is reciprocal—not, however, in the case of all classes, so that it is false that reciprocity extends to all levels alike.

How, then, does he demonstrate this? If, he says, the things of this realm are "like" the Forms, the Forms will also necessarily be like them; and knowing in what way this is false, he yet persists in questioning Socrates, in order to stir him up to a proper distinguishing of the types of likeness with the words, "Or is there any way that what is like can avoid being like what is like it?" To this premise he adds the 915 next proposition, that like things participate in one and the same Form, in virtue of which their likeness exists; there is, then, prior to the Forms some further Form, which is the most dominant of all. And you see how, if this argument is taken as has been said, in referring to the Forms inferior to the assimilative order, and in respect of the most particular Forms which are ranked after the Like and the Unlike,[71] there is nothing marvellous in the fact that all the secondary entities should participate in the actual assimilative cause, as being more perfect than themselves; but if it is taken as referring to the unparticipated Forms, it is not true. And it is in that connection that Parmenides refutes Socrates; for the primal Forms must have no other Form greater than they; and if this is so, then the relationship with them is not reciprocal; and if this is so, they are not secondary to the assimilative Forms; and if this is so, being intellectual, they are also unparticipated. For these are in the category immediately superior to these gods.

We shall say, then, that the things of this realm are like the primal Forms, related to them through the assimilative causal principle, but not vice versa. For what is like is indeed sometimes like what is like it, when both participate in one principle which likens them to each other, but sometimes it is like a pattern, when one thing is likened to another as superior to inferior, the latter being "likened" to its pattern, and the former being the pattern of that which is like it. The demiurgic Ideas, then, are superior to the assimilative, being intellectual in essence, and having been allotted their existence on the level of the unparticipated Intellect and for this reason being solely patterns, and no longer "like" the things that have come into being in dependence upon them.

This, then, is clear. Well, then, must one describe each Form itself as

[71] The "like and unlike" of *Parm.* 147c1-d4 is equated with the assimilative order in *PT* VI, 14. See vol. I, p. lxix of Saffrey and Westerink's edition.

like or unlike the things that have come into being in accordance with it? Some in the past have used the term "unlike," while others have talked of "neither like nor unlike"; for "like" and "unlike" are not, after all, they say, contradictory opposites. It seems to me that one must first analyse the concept "unlike"; for one calls "unlike" both what partakes in Unlikeness, and that which is declared to be the con-
916 tradictory, which is the same as the "not-like." Then one may divide further and say that on the one hand the contradictory is proper to the Forms; for this is just what we are saying, that they are *not like* sensible objects, although these latter are likened to them; but the other meaning, inasmuch as it betokens participation in the Form of Unlikeness, is not proper; for in that case we would be in the same position as we were in the case of Likeness, and the argument would be liable to an infinite regress. We will then be enquiring about the concept of Unlikeness also, whether it is like or unlike those things which participate in it, and if it is like, then there will in turn be a Likeness prior to both; if it is unlike, and is so in such a way as not to be according to the essence of Unlikeness, then Unlikeness is prior to them, and this also involves an infinite regress; only, as is in fact true, if the Unlike is identical with the Not-Like, one may say that the patterns are unlike their images.

This problem may be solved, then, in this way; but people have commonly also raised the following problem: does the Form Man create only the man of this realm, or does it also make him like to itself; in other words, does it give to it substance only, or also assimilation to itself? For if it bestows substance only, it is not making an image of itself, since it is not making something like itself; if it also bestows assimilation, what is left to be the work of Likeness, since each of the Forms is sufficient to produce a generated entity similar to itself? In answer to this I would say that all the Forms cooperate with each other and beget together, and I would not artificially distinguish their creative activities, but take a total view of the single and undivided harmony that exists between them. Man, then, in so far as it participates in the Form of Likeness, assimilates to itself the generated entity, and so does Likeness, and their activity is unified; and Horse likewise, and every other Form operates both in accordance with itself and in cooperation with Likeness; and it operates in concert with all the Forms as something distinct from each of them, and it creates both man and horse, but not *qua* man or *qua* horse, but in so far as they have in common a likeness to their patterns, even as those Forms create each of the two solely according to its form, and in the case of the highest of the Forms, through the Forms Like and Unlike, ⟨while in the case of the lower ones, in co-

operation with them).[72] Wherefore these also extend equally throughout all, even if to some in the relationship of instrumental cause, as towards superiors, while to others in the relationship of cooperating
917 factor, as towards inferiors. And more directly still, you might say that
Man assimilates to itself the relevant generated entity, and Dog, and
each of the rest of the Forms, whereas Likeness assimilates to itself the
central likenesses; for even as men are images of Man, so all likenesses
everywhere are images of the Essential Likeness; and through the Essential Man men are assimilated to the intellectual Form of Man, while
through Likeness all the likenesses in this realm are assimilated to their
proper patterns, by which I mean that of Likeness. This is the role of
Likeness, to work both in concert with the other Forms and through
itself; for it is one distinct thing, and its role consists in the assimilation
of likenesses in this realm to itself, in accordance with which each is
said to be an image of intellectual Likeness. And the same must be said
about Unlikeness; for this in turn is responsible for the existence of all
unlikenesses among participant entities both as regards each other and
the participated entities; its unity contrasted with their multiplicity, its
transcendence with their relativity.

> *"If so, nothing can be like the Form, nor can the Form be like anything.
> Otherwise a second Form will always make its appearance over and above
> the first Form; and if that second Form is like anything, yet a third; and
> there will be no end to this emergence of fresh Forms; if the Form is to be
> like the thing that partakes of it." "Quite true." "It follows that the other
> things do not partake of Forms in virtue of likeness; we must look for some
> other means by which they partake." "So it seems."* (132e–133a)

The falsity of both parts of the statement that the Form is neither like
the participant, nor the participant like the Form, he proves by means
of the infinite regression. The proposition that the Form is not like the
participant was contained in Socrates' suggestion, which postulated
that what is like must always be like what is like it. So the composite
statement is altogether false because of the illogical consequence, and
918 the second part of it by reason of the first, in accordance with Socrates'
postulate. And thus Parmenides brings the argument round to a refutation and concludes that it is not in virtue of likeness that the things of
this realm participate in all the Forms, but in virtue of another, more
powerful cause—a more correct conclusion. The unifying cause of all
things brings together the active power of the Forms and the receptivity of the things of this realm for the unified fulfillment of creation. The
causal principles in the cosmos are able to intertwine and link up with

---

[72] Added from the Latin translation.

their participants the assimilative class of Forms; the primary intellectual Forms, however, can be joined to their participants by this class acting as a mean, providing a relationship with those former for the secondary entities; but from above and transcendently they are joined together by the entities higher than those, that is, the intelligibles and the unifying cause of all things itself. And if you wish to regard as a third cause of likeness the quality of receptivity, you would not be in error; for it is through the fact that this is potentially what the Form is in actuality that the generated thing becomes like to the Form. So there are three causes of likeness, one on the lower level, as a substratum, another on the higher level, serving to bring together the perfecting forces and the things to be perfected, and another in the middle of these two, binding the extremities together.

This, then, is the sense in which the argument is correct. For if you are looking for the single most potent cause of participation, you will not say that it is Likeness, but rather that which is superior even to the intellectual Forms themselves. These Forms, after all, are greater than those which are constituted according to Likeness and Unlikeness, so that they would not only be intellectual in so far as they exist in Intellect prior to those in Soul or Nature or the sense-realm, but are actually in the unparticipated Intellect and on the level of the intellectual gods in the strict sense. And that is as high as the argument has taken us so far.

> *"You see, then, Socrates," he said, "what great difficulties there are in asserting their existence as Forms just by themselves?" "I do indeed." "I assure you, then, you have as yet hardly grasped how great they will be, if you are going to set up a single Form for every distinction you make among things." "How so?"* (133ab)

919　　In this passage he demonstrates that the essence of the divine Forms is incomprehensible and indescribable to our mental efforts. For this argument presents an insuperable obstacle to anyone who sets out to define accurately their substance and arrangement and capacities, and to see where they are, first, and how they proceed from there, and what quality they adopt in each class of gods, and how they are participated in by the lowest entities, and what chains of being they generate, and all the other theological questions which one might investigate in their regard.

It is in the interest of demonstrating all this that Parmenides said that Socrates had not yet even grasped the difficulties concerning them; for he wants not only to define their order, starting from below, but to behold their essential property, from above. The Forms in Nature, and the intellectual Forms in the general and in the proper sense, have been dealt with; it remains now to say something about the so-called intelligible-and-intellectual Forms, and finally about the purely intelligible. How he discourses about these, and how the process of raising difficulties is used as a cover for this, will already be obvious from what has gone before to those endowed with understanding.

> *"The worst difficulty will be this, though there are plenty more. Suppose someone should say that the Forms, if they are such as we are saying they must be, cannot be known. One could not convince him that he was mistaken in that objection, unless he chanced to be a man of wide experience and natural ability, and were willing to follow one through a long and remote train of argument. Otherwise there would be no way of convincing a man who maintained that the Forms were unknowable."* (133b)

That the theory of Forms teems with very difficult problems is shown by the fact that those coming after Plato propound a vast multitude of arguments directed towards either its refutation or its confirmation, and among those who strive to confirm it, there are varying views 92 about the essential nature of the Forms, and on the questions as to of what things there are Forms, about the mode of participation, and about all sorts of other problems. Parmenides, however, is not concerned to deal with the full range of these problems, nor to descend into an endless series of investigations, but rather, by taking two main problems, to encompass the whole enquiry about them, as he does in this next passage, in which he shows that the Forms are neither apprehensible and knowable by us, nor can they have knowledge and forethought for the sense-realm. And yet it is primarily for this reason that we value the Forms, that we may exercise our intellects about them and may be able to contemplate in them the providential causes of all things. If the Forms are not knowable by us, it is going too far even to assert their existence; for we are not even in a position to know whether they exist, since we do not know their nature and are totally incapable of apprehending them, having no starting point in our nature which would lead to such understanding. For even as he who removed intellect and knowledge from the realm of existents is not to be trusted in his assertions about anything, since he is removing precisely those faculties by which alone things can be known; so also he who overturns our knowledge of the first principles does not allow us even to ascertain whether they exist at all; for we are all in the same position in their regard, if no one possesses the faculty of knowing them.

Such, then, are the problems arising. Both come about as a result of the transcendent nature of the Forms, which we consider to be so transcendent as to be without any connection with secondary entities; a thing so constituted is alien to us and cannot be known by us, nor is it such as to know us. If the transcendent nature of the Forms possessed, along with their superiority, universal omnipresence also, our knowledge of them would be preserved and their intellectual knowledge of secondary entities; for if they are present everywhere, then it is possible to come across them everywhere, if only one makes oneself ready for their reception; and if they organise all things, they anticipate on the intellectual level the causal principle of all that they organise. It is necessary, then, for those who wish to preserve these doctrines to postulate both that the Forms are motionless and transcendent and that they penetrate all things. And you see how this in turn follows on what has been said just previously in which the non-relative nature of the Forms was demonstrated. For neither is the demiurgic aspect of them such as to involve relation with secondary entities, nor is their non-relational and transcendent aspect such as to render them non-communicative and alien to things here.

921

But as we have often said, Plato's argument preserves their perfect comprehensiveness. Those who came after him, however, fastened on only half of the truth. One group was concerned to preserve the providential aspect of the divine causal principle along with its relationship with Matter, by asserting that the divinity penetrates throughout Matter.[73] Another group lays emphasis on its unrelatedness at the expense of its providence, depriving the divine both of its creative and of its providential power, stating that intelligibles are something separate from this world, and are neither creative of the secondary entities nor patterns nor causes of any other type, unless one were to describe them as objects of striving for sense-objects; for the whole heaven, they say, dances around them, and its blessedness consists in its appetition of them.[74] But the theory of Plato both preserves on a non-relational level the providential aspect of the divine Forms (or, if you prefer, the unmoving causes), and the transcendental aspect as cognisant and providential of the secondary entities; and it neither destroys their transcendental superiority in the interest of their universal omnipresence, nor their providential governance in the interest of their non-relational power. Preserving as he does, then, both these aspects simultaneously, it is natural that he should have demonstrated in the previous arguments, in the form of raising difficulties, that it is absurd to allow a relationship between the patterns and their participants; and in the present argument, that if one preserves the Forms themselves completely without relativity, without adding in what way they are both transcendent and yet penetrate through all things, and are everywhere as regards their providential aspect, while being nowhere in respect of

[73] The Stoics.
[74] The Peripatetics, cf. 788-791.

their essence, then we can neither have knowledge of them, nor can
922 they have causal and transcendental intellection of our affairs.

This is what we traditionally reply to those who do not make the intelligibles creative causes of secondary entities: how could the heaven
have appetition of the divine realm, if it be not derived from that
source? Appetition would then be a result of chance, if the one is not
the generative cause, and the other does not derive its existence from
that quarter. As things are, it is reasonable that the thing generated
should strive towards its own source and cause, and it is according to
nature that the secondary should turn towards the power that creates
and cognises it. In the case where we do not have a causal agent and a
causated entity, what is there to create appetition between one and the
other? How would it strive towards it, having received nothing from
it? For everything that strives in every case strives after something for
the sake of acquiring it. If it possessed this thing, appetition would in
the circumstances be superfluous; but if it does not, appetition arises in
all cases from the lack of what something does not have. So that if
nothing is added from the object of appetition to the appetitors, the
process of appetition once again becomes superfluous, seeing that
nothing can be acquired.

Further, how comes it that only the lowest entity imitates the primal? The lowest entity is, after all, incapable itself of generating; all the
entities, on the other hand, which are median between the highest and
the lowest strive to produce, and to produce each according to its
proper rank; for that which pertains to what is primal of its own nature
is most worthy of honour and, being most honoured, would not then
pertain to what is lowest, without at the same time pertaining to the
median entities, which are closer akin to the primal. Being an object of
appetition, in any case, pertains to the median entities, whereas it does
not pertain to the lowest.

Further, how could the divine stand inactive and ineffectual, while
this heaven, imitating it as it does, exhibits such creative power in respect of what is beneath it, so that all its movement and arrangement
acts upon the whole realm of generation, and turns it and orders it by
means of a host of immanent reason-principles, penetrating through all
the living things contained in each of the elements, down to plants and
even inanimate objects? For if it is a good thing not to cause generation,
923 why does it not imitate in this what is superior to it, being itself a god
and striving towards the imitation of that god? Or if it is not good, how
could it be that something not good pertains to the divine realm, while
something good pertains to the heaven? And how do we have knowledge of it, if we do not spring from there, nor partake of the truly existent reason-principles from which knowledge by recollection derives? We would then be without connection to it and alien, being

detached from that source of existence. Such, then, must be our reply to this sort of argument.

One must admire the divinely inspired design of Plato, which removes in advance, by means of the airing of these difficulties, the erroneous and godless view of the divine Forms, in imitation of the practice of Intellect itself, which, even before the secondary creation[75] of evils, created the powers which would eliminate them. That one should not present the generative capacity of the Forms as a relationship with the thing generated or their paradigmatic quality as involving an inclination towards the thing set in order, Parmenides has reminded us well enough in the previous arguments; for every relation requires some other cause which brings it and binds it together, so that there would be prior to the Forms another Form which would unite both sides of the relationship through assimilation. For relationship is between like and like. And that the transcendence of the Forms is not devoid of activity and providence, nor alien from secondary entities, he demonstrates by raising the present difficulties; for possibly one might say, looking to their non-relational aspect alone, that the Forms neither know their participants nor are known by them. By raising this problem, then, he leads Socrates to an understanding of the manner of the transcendental power of the divine Forms. How he concludes that the things of this realm are not known by them will become plain to us later on; he wants first to establish how we cannot know them. He establishes this very brilliantly, by taking as his premise that our knowledge is of the objects of knowledge of our realm, while divine knowledge is of things divine and has a certain validity, and not on one level

924 only, but in one way if one looks at it philosophically and in another if one looks at it theologically. For let us accept that our knowledge is of the objects of knowledge proper to our realm; what is there to hinder the objects of our knowledge being images of divine objects, and our knowing the divine realm through them? Even as the Pythagoreans saw in numbers and geometrical figures manifestations of the divine order, and by devoting themselves to the study of these tried to derive, as it were from imprints, knowledge of things divine. What is there remarkable in this, then, if knowledge on our level is said to be of the objects of knowledge on our level, and is linked to them? For what a thing is said to be relative to, it is taken to be coordinate with. But it can also be linked to the intelligibles, not as coordinate knowledge, but as subordinate. For instances of coordinate knowledge of all things must be distinguished from types of knowledge which are on a different level from the objects, and either grasp the nature of an inferior

---

[75] Παρυπόστασις, a Procline term for incidental generation, particularly of evils. Cf. *In Tim.* I, 375.14ff.; III, 303.15ff. Cf. 829, 26 above, and 987, 5 below.

level from a superior perspective, as opinion (*doxa*) grasps the objects of sense, or what is on a superior level from a secondary and inferior perspective, as opinion grasps the objects of knowledge. The man exercising knowledge and the man exercising true opinion, after all, cognise the same things, but the one from a superior perspective, the other from an inferior; there is therefore nothing peculiar in knowledge also being said to be not of an object of knowledge in that realm, but of what is within itself and linked to it, and to relate to that realm secondarily, not in virtue of the knowledge that is coordinate with it.

Plato himself, after all, in the *Letters* (VII, 342aff.), in saying that the intelligible Form is known not by knowledge (*epistēmē*) but by understanding (*gnōsis*), stimulates us to the realisation that a Form is an object of understanding and is not an object of our knowledge, but apprehensible "by intellection with the aid of reason" (*Tim.* 52a). For understanding of the knowledge-type approaches its intellectual object rather more synthetically, whereas intellect is the most proper organ to contemplate the Forms, since they themselves are intellectual in nature, and we in all cases know like by like, by intellect the intelligibles, by opinion the opinables, and by knowledge the objects of knowledge. It is therefore no wonder that there is no *knowledge* of the Forms, and that there should be rather another type of understanding of them possible, such as that which we term intellection.

925 If you wished to speak rather on the theological level, on the other hand, and were to assert that he ascends to the level of the intellectual Forms to show that the things beyond this realm, being Forms and transcendent, as indeed are the intelligible-and-intellectual entities, are superior to the reach of our understanding (at any rate he leads to the contemplation of those entities souls that have been thoroughly purified and united with and following upon the Twelve Leaders (*Phaedr.* 247a), you would not, I think, misinterpret the inspired theory of Plato. There are, as we know, three classes of Form prior to the assimilative order, the intellectual, the intelligible-intellectual, and the intelligible. Of these the intellectual are immediately contiguous to the secondary entities, and both by reason of their quality of distinctness and because the causal principle of our order is linked to the henad of this class, are more available to our understanding:

> Following upon the paternal thoughts,
> I, Soul, dwell.

as the Oracle says (fr. 53 DP). Plato knows this order of Forms, as has been shown elsewhere.[76] The intelligible-intellectual are superior to

---

[76] Cf. *In Tim.* II, 61.22ff., part of a comment on *Tim.* 32d-33a.

our individual understanding, ranged as we are beneath them, whence unknowability is proper to them by reason of their transcendent superiority; for we cannot in our present state project the understanding that would be adequate to them. So much, then, for this median class of Forms, Parmenides demonstrating to us that one must not absolutely separate the intellectual Forms from their participants—not to the same extent, certainly, as one would those of the intelligible-intellectual gods (for they are entirely superior to our understanding), but rather it is the case that the specific henads, which we have postulated, must be open even to our understanding.

It is possible, then, to approach the analysis of the present question on the level both of philosophy and of theology. On the philosophical level one may say that it does not follow that, when we dispose of the previously mentioned modes of participation, every mode of communion has then been removed between the sensible and intelligible realms. For in that case they would neither be knowable to us or know us, knowability and knowledge being somehow mutually involved. 926 On the theological level, the lesson is that one must separate the intellectual Ideas from their productions, as one must those beyond that level, which are unknowable to our mental efforts, from which these have proceeded.

This much may suffice on the general theory contained in the passage. Turning now to examine the details of the text, we may say that it gives us a picture both of what goes to make a worthy auditor of such a lesson, and what makes a competent instructor.[77] For the auditor must be of outstanding natural ability, that he may be a philosopher by nature and enthusiastic for immaterial being, always pursuing and assuming something else beyond what is visible to the senses and not resting content with what presents itself, and in general just such a person as Socrates in the *Republic* (VI, 490aff.) portrays as he who has a natural love of contemplating universal truths. Then he should have a wide range of experience, and by this I don't mean of human affairs (for these are of small importance and quite irrelevant to divinised life), but rather of logical and physical and mathematical subjects. For such things as our intellect is not capable of contemplating on the divine level it may contemplate on these levels as it were in images, and in beholding them will find repose in their contemplation and will believe also in what is said about the higher entities. I mean, for instance, if someone were to wonder how many can be in one, and all things in

[77] The formulation of three conditions for successful study of philosophy is an old one in Platonism, going back ultimately to Aristotle (*EE* I, 1.1214a16ff., *EN* X, 9.1179b20ff.), but receiving clear exposition in Philo *Abr.* 52-55, and Albinus *Did.*, ch. 28. Cf. *PT* I, 2.

something that has no parts, let him think of the number one, and how all the numbers, both even and odd, are demonstrated to be in it, and the circle and the sphere, and all the other types of number. If one were to wonder how the divine creates by virtue of its simple existence, he will recall that in the physical sphere fire heats and snow cools, and so with other entities. If one were to wonder how causes are everywhere present to their effects, he will be able to observe in logic a perfect image of this; for genera are always predicated of those things of which their species are predicated, the species along with the genera, but the genera even without the species. And so in each case where one is not able to observe something on the divine level, he will be able to observe it on one of these levels in images.

927   One must therefore first of all possess good natural tendencies, which are akin to the realm of real being, and able to "sprout wings" and grasp hold of thoughts about Being as firm cables (cf. *Laws* X, 893b). For even as for every activity we need some preparation, so also for the ascent to true Being we have need of untainted and purified knowledge, with the prerequisite of a suitable cast of mind, which one might term "good natural tendencies," inasmuch as they spring from the nature both of the universe and of so-called naturally gifted souls.

Our candidate, then, as we have said, must possess such natural ability as this. Next, as has been said, he must possess experience of many and various disciplines, by means of which he may be raised to an understanding of things intelligible. And, thirdly, he must have such intense enthusiasm towards this study that, when his instructor gives only a hint, he may be capable of following such hints by virtue of an enthusiasm which concentrates his attention.

There are three things, then, which he says are required by anyone embarking on the study of the intelligible nature—natural ability, experience, and enthusiasm. Natural ability will naturally endow him with faith in the divine, experience will enable him to hold fast to the truth of paradoxical doctrines, and his enthusiasm will stir up in him a love of this study, that in this sphere of activity also there may be Faith, Truth, and Love, those three qualities that save souls through the natural suitability which joins one to them. And, if you like, through experience he will acquire receptivity in the cognitive part of his soul, while through enthusiasm he will gain an intensification of the vital part, directed towards the intelligibles, and through natural excellence the preexisting basis for both these, since right from birth all these qualities have been granted to him. So the prospective student should be of this nature, and have a character made up of this triad of qualities.

As for the teacher, having journeyed long before along the same path, he will not want to expound the divine truth with elaborate ver-

bosity, but rather to reveal much through few words, uttering words
928 of like nature to the concepts they express; nor will he proceed from
widely acknowledged and obvious concepts, but will contemplate
reality beginning from above, from the most unitary principles, taking
a remote point of departure for his systematic treatment, inasmuch as
he has separated himself from his immediate surroundings and drawn
close to the divine; nor will he take thought so that he may seem to
speak clearly, but he will content himself with indications; for one
should convey mystical truths mystically, and not publicise secret doctrines about the gods. Such should be the nature of both the auditor and
the purveyor of such discourses.

One may take Parmenides as an ideal example of such an instructor,
whence one will be able to gather the manner in which he will deliver
his discourses, namely that he will convey much in a small compass,
that he will proceed from the top down, and that he will discourse only
in hints about the divine. As for the pupil, he will be naturally apt and
of an erotic nature, but not yet fully experienced, for this reason it is
that Parmenides urges him to become practised in dialectic, that he
may gain experience of technical argumentation. He welcomes his natural ability and enthusiasm, and adds to that the bringing up to par of
what is deficient. The object of this triple excellence he has stated himself, being proof against deception in argument about the divine. For
he who is deficient in any of these respects will be compelled to agree
to many false propositions, if he enters naively upon the contemplation
of reality.

> *"Why so, Parmenides?" said Socrates. "Because, Socrates, I imagine
> that you or anyone else who asserts that each of them has a real being 'just
> by itself,' would admit, to begin with, that no such real being exists in
> us." "True; for how could it then exist just by itself?" "Very good," said
> Parmenides.* (133c)

The argument now passes to other problems, of which one results in
the removal from our souls of the knowledge of real being, while the
929 other tries to demonstrate the impossibility of the divine realm having
knowledge of ours. Following from both of these, the concept of our
procession from and return to that realm is disposed of. Primary and
secondary entities are presented as being cleft apart from one another,
the secondary being without share in the primary, the primary incapable of producing the secondary. The truth is, however, that all things
are in all in their proper mode, the median classes in the universe and
the lowest being in the primary ones in a causal mode, which results in
their being known by the highest in the same way that they exist in
them. The primary are in the median by participation, and both of

these are in the lowest in the same mode. Hence souls have knowledge of all things in a mode proper to each—through images what is prior to them, causally what is inferior to them, and congenitally and homogeneously the reason-principles within them.

These problems, then, are brought up following upon the two which were raised before these about the order of the Ideas, because Socrates, and everyone who postulates the existence of Ideas, comes to this hypothesis for the sake of a knowledge which is on the causal level and is acquainted with everything in the cosmos; whence it is that somebody,[78] mocking them, said that they proposed to acquire knowledge of reality by doubling it, conceiving of a set of intelligible entities prior to the sensible—although even he who said that gave no other cause of the eternal motion of things that have circular motion than to postulate as many motionless entities prior to them as there were circularly moving entities (*Met.* XII, 8). So to achieve scientific knowledge of all things in the cosmos they turned to the postulation of the existence of Ideas, and to their providential administration of all the things that come to be in accordance with them. Hence those who abolish the Ideas abolish also the providential care exercised by the intelligible realm, assuming the things of this realm to turn towards these as to objects of appetition, while asserting that no influence comes from that quarter to this realm (*ibid.* XII, 7).

So, since these two problems are directed against those who postulate the existence of the Ideas for the reasons we have stated, in the investigations next following it behooves us to show, first, how the postulation of solely transcendent Ideas of existents makes them unknowable to us, on the grounds that we no longer have any communion with them, or any knowledge as to whether they exist or not, and if they are participated in or not, and what rank they have, if, that is, they are only transcendent and are not, in addition to their non-relative status, also causes of secondary entities.

To the consideration of this subject the argument first brings to bear certain axioms and common notions. The first is that if the Ideas are completely transcendent and on their own, they do not exist at all; for how could they exist completely separate both from us and from everything else. For the mind is the place of the Ideas—not "place" in the sense that they need a place to situate themselves, as do the accidents in substance, or the forms-in-matter in Matter, nor in the sense that the mind contains them like parts of itself heaped together by a process of accumulation, but rather as the centre of a circle holds within

930

---

[78] Aristotle *Met.* I, 9.990b2.

itself the many termini of the lines proceeding from it,[79] and as a branch of knowledge contains a multiplicity of theorems, not being made up of this multiplicity, but prior to it and being in its totality in each part of it; for Intellect is a one-many in just this way; partlessly, containing a multiplicity in its oneness, because it is not the One Itself subsisting prior to all multiplicity, but rather having oneness and multiplicity together. This, then, is the sense in which it is the "place" of the Ideas (Arist. *De. An.* III, 4). So if Soul and Intellect are not identical, then the Ideas whose place is the Intellect are not "in us."

It is obvious now from this how according to Plato one must separate the intelligible realm from that of souls, and how an account of the Forms becomes progressively more complete as it ascends to hypostases more unified than they; for such an account does not any longer make them material or natural or thoughts in souls, but something prior to all these; for they are not, he says, "in us," that is, on the same level as our mental activities. One might say, speaking in philosophical terms, that they are transcendent, and are not "on our level," and yet are present everywhere and are participated in by us, while not coming to be in its participants. For the Ideas, while subsisting in themselves, are yet available to those things that are able to avail of them, and that which is in any way apt to receive them comes in contact with them, since they are present everywhere; for by virtue of that which we possess[80] we also necessarily participate in them. Nor is this true only of ourselves, but the levels of being superior to us also, by having acquired within themselves substantial images of the Ideas, and confronting these, which are, as it were, traces of the patterns, with the patterns, come to know through them also those realities of which they are images; for they simultaneously cognise them both in their own essence, and as images of something else; in acquiring a notion of this latter fact they must also grasp in their thoughts a notion of the patterns.

Speaking on the theological level, on the other hand, one may say that the Forms which transcend the intellectual realm are raised completely above our level. Of the intellectual Forms themselves we see images both in ourselves and in sense-objects; the essence of the intelligible, however, completely transcends, by reason of its unitary nature, both ourselves and everything else, being unknowable in itself. Gods and Intellects it fills with itself; we must be content with participating in intellectual Forms through our souls. Plato demonstrates this truth when he presents our life as double, having both a political and a theoretical aspect (*Polit.* 272b), and happiness similarly as double, and

[79] Cf. Plotinus' images in *Enn.* VI, 5.5 (centre and radii) and III, 9.2 (knowledge and theorems).
[80] Sc. the *logoi* immanent in us.

traces the one life back to the patronymic supervision of Zeus, and the other to the order of Cronus and pure Mind. From this it is plain that he refers back our life in its entirety to the realm of the intellectual Kings; for the one of these defines the beginning, and the other the end, of this order of being. Such entities as are beyond these he declares to be objects of contemplation for souls that are divinely possessed and are being initiated into a mystical vision of these things (*Phaedr.* 249aff.); so that on this level also the foregoing axiom would be true, since it fastens upon some other of Forms.

So much may be said concerning the subject matter. As regards the details of the text, Socrates' question "Why so, Parmenides?" shows how astonished he is that the intellectual Form should be unknowable, and that he does not realise the transition that Parmenides is making, and how he is traversing the whole gamut of the Forms, until he comes to rest at the actual primary Forms.

932 The phrase "For how could it then exist just by itself" is spoken in accordance with common notions (*koinai ennoiai*); for everything that is transcendent is in itself and "just by itself," not being either in anything else or in us. Further, in these three phrases, "itself," "by itself," and "substance," he has set out the whole truth about the Forms, for these describe respectively their simplicity, their transcendent superiority, and their perfection residing in their essence alone. This being the case, let us not make a distinction in the case of the Forms between the thing itself and being that thing, as between substance and "being a substance," and between thought and "being a thought." In the case of composite entities this distinction is valid, but in the case of simple entities it makes no sense. If, then, each Form simply exists, it should also remain in the simplicity proper to its unity, and one ought not to transfer to them the properties of composite things.

It remains to consider the phrase "Very good," which Parmenides says not, as one might assume, ironically and as prefacing a refutation, but rather as recognising the natural aptitude of Socrates and his understanding of divine truths; for the axiom that has been accepted is true, a fact confirmed by Timaeus' using it to prove (52a) that real being neither receives anything into itself, as Matter does Form, nor does it itself enter into anything else, as Form does into Matter. It remains, then, separately by itself even when participated in, and it does not come to be one and with its participants, but being itself prior to its participants it bestows upon these as much as they can receive; and it neither exists in us, for we participate in it not by receiving it itself (for what proceeds from it is different from it), nor does it come to be in us, for it does not admit of any coming-to-be whatever.

"And further, those of the Ideas which are what they are with reference to one another, have their being in such references among themselves, not with reference to those likenesses (or whatever we are to call them) in our world, which we participate in and so come to be called by their several names. And, on the other hand, these things in our world which are homonymous with the Forms are related among themselves, not to the Forms; and all the names of that sort that they bear have reference to one another, not to the Forms." "How do you mean?" asked Socrates. (133cd)

933

This constitutes a second axiom, which helps Parmenides, like the former one, to the elucidation of the problem before us. The former was, we recall, that the Forms are in no way inherent in us, but are "in themselves"; this second lays it down that the things of this realm can be stated to have relationships to each other, and the things of that realm also to each other, but not to this realm, nor this realm to that. And indeed those who look at these matters from the point of view of formal logic remark very well that one should connect general relative terms with general relatives, and particular to particular, e.g. knowledge in general to the object of knowledge in general, particular knowledge to particular object of knowledge, indefinite relatives to indefinite, definite to definite, potential relatives to potential relatives, actualised to actualised. The treatises of the ancients on logic and natural philosophy are full of statements like this.[81] If, then, in the case of general and particular terms, to take these as our example, we should not allow interchange in corresponding terms, then far more strongly should we disallow it in the case of Ideas and the images of those Ideas; but we will relate things of this realm to things of this realm, and those of that to that. This principle will be absolutely true, if we consider each thing as it is in itself, and not in so far as it does something or becomes something; for in that case we might relate things of this realm to those of that realm as coming to be from them, or things of that to those of this as creators of them, these to those as images to Ideas, and the Ideas to these as models (*paradeigmata*). If, therefore, we take Mastership Itself, thought of in its essence as Mastership, it will be spoken of only in relation to Slavery Itself; whereas if we take it as a model, then we will relate to its likeness, Mastership in this realm. Admittedly, we are accustomed to call the Gods our masters, which might seem to be a relating of Mastership in that realm to our slavery in this; but this is valid, since we participate in Slavery Itself, towards which Mastership Itself has a relationship by priority. And you see how Mas-

934

---

[81] Possibly such a work as that of Theophrastus, Περὶ καταφάσεως καὶ ἀποφάσεως (fragments in edition of A. Graeser, esp. fr. 4).

tership in that realm shows the higher beings to be our masters, because we participate in Slavery Itself. On the other hand, Mastership in our realm, which is spoken of in relation to Slavery in our realm, cannot be said to be in relation to Slavery in that realm as well because Slavery there does not derive its existence from the existence of Slavery with us, but *vice versa*. For that which rules among superior levels of being must do so among inferior levels as well; but not the other way about. We must, then, as I have said, speak of things in themselves of that realm in relation to things of this.

But this question I will return to later on. Let us now deduce from all these problems the nature of the primal Idea. From the first we may gather that it is incorporeal; for if it were a body, it would not be possible to participate in it either as a whole or in a part of it. From the second, that it is not coordinate with its participants; for if it were coordinate, it would have some property in common with them, because we would have to postulate another Idea prior to it. From the third problem we gather that it is not a thought of Being, but itself Being and existent, in order that that which participates in it may not be necessarily participant in knowledge. From the fourth we gather that it is exclusively a model and not also an image, as is the case with the reason-principle at the level of Soul, lest its having some similarity to that which derives from it may involve the introduction of another Idea prior to it. For the reason-principle in Soul is a Being also, but it is not a model only, but also an image—for the Soul is not Being only, but also Becoming. From the fifth, we gather that it is not intelligible to us immediately, but only through its images, for the faculty of knowledge in us is not on the right level to grasp it. From the sixth, that it intelligises what proceeds from it not coordinately but causally; for in intelligising itself it knows itself as a paradigm, and what proceeds from it[82] in a secondary way, and by knowing itself as their cause.

In sum, then, the Idea in the truest sense is an incorporeal cause, transcending its participants, a motionless Being, exclusively and really a 935 model, intelligible to souls through images, and intelligising causally the existents modelled upon it. So that from all these problems we have ferreted out the single definition of an Idea in the true sense.

If, then, any wish to attack the concept of Ideas, let them attack this definition, and not assume them to be either corporeal images (*phantasiai*) of their own minds, or coordinate with the things of this realm, or devoid of being, or correspondent with our conceptions, or let them produce some other sophistic definition such as these, and then fabricate their arguments on that basis; but let them bear in mind that Par-

---

[82] Added from the Latin translation.

menides declared the Ideas to be gods, and that they subsist in God, as the Oracle also declares (fr. 37 DP):[83]

> The Intellect of the Father whirred, conceiving with his unwearying will
> Ideas of every form.

For the "fount of the Ideas" is God, and the God in whom it is contained is the Demiurgic Intellect; and if it is the primal Idea, then it is to this that the above definition, assembled from the problems posed by Parmenides, pertains.

Having settled this, then, we must next examine, first, whether there is relativity also in that realm; and next, in what way this account is true, and in respect of what Forms; for each of the problems must bring us near to some basic characteristic of the reality. That the term "relative" has various meanings you may gather from what we have often had occasion to say. "Relative" in one sense applies to mere accidents, in which relationship has no essential being, such as "double" and "half," and suchlike, which are the only relatives that the majority of logicians are accustomed to consider. There is another type, however, which has the nature of substance, and in which relations do involve real being, as for instance natural right and left; for the right hand of an animal is not a mere accidental attribute, but a real reason-principle, according to which the right is said to be the originator of motion, and has certain differences from the left which is acquired from Nature. It is plain, then, that "relative" has these two senses, even in 936 the case of these terms just mentioned, for accidental right and left, if interchanged artificially, accept the rearrangement, whereas the same relations in animals cannot be otherwise, since their composition is natural. It is in accordance with this distinction, certainly, that Timaeus (*Tim.* 36c) establishes right and left in the cosmic cycles, postulating real powers in them, primary and secondary, leading and following respectively.

There is yet another sense in which "relative" might be used, one more perfect and more suitable to self-substantiating entities, in reference to cases where a thing, being primarily "for itself," is also "for another," that other thing being also primarily "for itself"; as for instance the intelligible is "for itself" and the Intellect is "for itself," and through this very relation the Intellect is united with the intelligible and the intelligible with the Intellect, and the Intellect and the intelligible are one thing. Whereas a father in this realm, even though he is naturally a father, yet is not first "for himself," and only then father of

---

[83] Cf. 800.21ff., where the Oracle is quoted more extensively.

someone else, but he is what he is solely "for another." But in that realm any paternal cause is primarily "for itself," completing its own essence, and only then bestows an emanation from itself upon things secondary to it; and any offspring exists "for itself," and only then derives from something else. So when we speak of things being relative to each other in that realm, we must remove from them any notion of pure relation, devoid of essence; for nothing of that sort is proper to the Gods. Instead of relativity we must apply the concept of self-identity, and prior even to this self-identity the subsistence of each entity in itself; for each thing exists primarily "for itself," and in itself is united to everything else. For each, even of so-called relational concepts, is a single Form, as for instance Righthandedness is a substantial Form, cause of this relation, and Lefthandedness likewise; so that there is one reason-principle which provides to things of this realm the relational characteristic that appears in them.

Such an entity There, then, is non-relational, though productive of a relation; for it is not something other before it becomes "right" or "left" There; but yet it comes about There also that right and left are spoken of in relation to each other and are united together more intimately than the generality of Forms, because they operate in all cases in 937 conjunction with each other, and wherever one is the other must also; for among the Forms some necessarily operate to the exclusion of each other, as in the case of opposites, while others operate always in conjunction, as in the case of what There too are called relations; others again operate in such a way that one always accompanies the other, but not *vice versa*, as in the case of whole and part.

Connection by means of participation, then, characterises the potency of things termed relative There; and corresponding to what is relativity in the case of things Here, There we have Sameness. For if, as will be stated in what follows, everything is related to everything else either as whole or as part, or as identical or different, it is clear how Whole and Part may be viewed in the case of those Forms in which the one participates in the other, but not *vice versa*—Otherness especially in the case of opposites, the presence of one of which causes the other to disappear; and Sameness in the case of those participation in which involves the union of each to the other, there being no possibility of both not being simultaneously present to or absent from their potential participants.

One must, then, conceive of each of the things There termed relatives as being one separate Form, productive of one relation, but not itself being a relation to any subject, even though they are described as being "in relation to each other" because of their mutually implicative conceptualisation, as the argument has shown. It is clear, then, that relative entities There must be conceived of as described above, and not in the way proper to things Here; for Here like is like to its like, and equal is equal to its equal, and things like each other or equal to each other must be at least two distinct things, but There Likeness is one thing and Equality is one thing, and it exists in relation to itself and not to anything else, nor does it exist in things separate and detached, but in itself; for either of the Forms concerned is such as to have its essence fixed in itself, and one of a kind and on its own and not in other things. The first principles of the Forms and all existing things, after all, in the most proper sense, being Limit and Unlimitedness, in discrete entities, Limit generates unity, whereas Unlimitedness generates multiplicity; in continuous magnitudes, Limit generates the point, Unlimitedness extension; in ratios Limit generates equality, Unlimitedness all other ratios; and in qualities Limit generates likeness, Unlimitedness generates unlikeness. That the more and less are of the class of the Unlimited has been demonstrated to us by the Socrates of the *Philebus* (23cff.); but everywhere the image of Limit takes hold of what is presented to it of Unlimitedness and makes limited those things that had hitherto been unlimited by virtue of their own nature, the monad imposing numeration on multiplicity, the point imposing bound on extension, equality imposing measure on the ratios (for equality *is* equality of ratios), and likeness putting a check on the more and less by means of the tension and slackening of likenesses. Equality and Likeness There, then, have a monadic nature, the one being the Limit of qualities, the other the Limit of ratios, as the point is of continuous magnitudes, and the monad of discrete ones. So what Here are relative entities we must think of as There subsisting in self-identity, and what Here exist only in relation to each other as There being "of themselves" and primarily "in themselves," only secondarily communicating with the other things; and what are Here without substance and adventitious are There fully substantial; and the things that take their name from those from which they derive their contingent existence, There preexist by virtue of a single causal principle.

This, then, is the nature of relatives in the intelligible realm; that is to say, not existing in mere relativity, nor accidentally, but there exists absolutely There what exists relatively Here; "in itself" what exists in relation to others; essentially, what exists Here accidentally; and everything in general in a more powerful mode than in its products. For the inferiority of Becoming to Being reveals itself in producing relations in place of non-relatives, composites from things simple, and adventitious entities from things endowed with substantial existence. From this one can reach also the following conclusion, which we set out above, that, according to Parmenides' intention, one must posit Ideas

291

939 even of some things that seem to be accidents, inasmuch as he himself declares that there are Ideas even of relations. Except that, in the case of those which exist on the primal level as real and perfectly realised beings, but whose subsistence in other things is adventitious, he presents only this accidental aspect of theirs; for substantial relations are prior to insubstantial ones, some bringing about existence in those things that participate in the Ideas, others bringing about their perfection; for things Here must participate in Ideas both as existent and as perfect, and for this reason the order of the Ideas is double, the one producing existence, the other perfection.

So much, then, about the doctrine. As regards the details of the text, the phrase "those of the Ideas which are what they are with reference to one another," teaches that of the Ideas some are more distinct from one another, preserving their own purity, while others are rather more united to each other. These latter, however, exist in themselves and of themselves, and are not solely "of others," nor for that matter even "of each other."

The statement that sensible things are "homonymous" with intelligible ones is made according to Platonic theory, which states that the names for things Here descend to them from those entities, as in the case of things which are homonymous as deriving from and referring to a single central concept—which, indeed, Aristotle too sometimes classes as homonyms. Let no one, then, expect an identical definition of particulars and their Ideas, since the latter are unconnected and entirely superior to the former, as is proper for transcendent causes in relation to their effects—or rather let one not even expect a definition of those utterly simple and partless Forms; for definitions are of composite things and are concerned with the differentiae of immanent forms. But we entrust the comprehension of transcendent Forms to the pure and divine intuitions of the soul and say that Plato declares things Here to be homonymous with things There, and homonymous in the sense of participating in them. Wherefore he proclaimed a relation of likeness between them, which is what Socrates means when he declares that the Ideas "stand fixed as patterns in the nature of things." Bearing in mind the point of view expressed in the objections, he added "or whatever 940 we are to call them," as much as saying that one can call them likenesses and not-likenesses, "likeness" having two senses, and being either like or unlike its pattern.

> *"Suppose, for instance, one of us is master or slave of another; he is not, of course, the slave of Master itself, the essential Master, nor, if he is a master, is he master of Slave itself, the essential Slave, but, being a man, is master or slave of another man; whereas Mastership itself is what it is*

of Slavery itself, and Slavery itself is slavery to Mastership itself. The significance of things in our world is not with reference to things in that other world, nor have these their significance with reference to us; but, as I say, the things in that world are what they are with reference to one another and towards one another; and so likewise are the things in our world. You see what I mean?" "Certainly I do," said Socrates. (133d–134a)

How the concept of Relation is to be understood in the case of the Forms should now, I think, be clear from the previous discussion. You will find the concepts "master" and "slave" There too, if you attend to their essential meaning. For what else is proper to masters than absolutely to control slaves and to organise all their affairs for their own good? And what else is proper to slaves than to be controlled by others and to serve their master's will? How, then, would these characteristics not be present in a far prior way among the Forms, some being ranked beneath others, one set being more powerful and making use of its subordinates, the other set serving and cooperating with the powers of their superiors? For Mastership is a utilising power, and Slavery is a serving power, and they both exist there substantially and not by accident, as is the case with their images; for the Mastership and Slavery present in these are mere echoes of the substantial entities There.

And if you would like to consider these facts not merely on the philosophical level in the case of the Forms, but on the primary level, in the case of the divine order, turn your mind to those intellectual and intelligible orders and the Forms in them, and you will find that both characteristics pertain to those orders of Forms; for, being primarily median, they control and hold mastery over all entities secondary to them, but are dependent upon those prior to them, and act in relation to their good, and are what they are in virtue of those; for being the first manifestations from them, they are dominated by them and remain in them, but at the same time direct from above the substances and potencies inferior to them. One may observe this principle in the secondary orders also: the more comprehensive dominate the more particular, and the more unitary the more pluralised, and the transcendent the immanent; as for instance in the demiurgic classes Zeus directs now Athena and now Apollo, and then again Hermes, and Iris; and all these obey the wishes of their father, while according to the demiurgic norm directing their own providential wills towards the entities secondary to them; and further, the tribe of angels and all the superior classes of being are said to serve the gods and to do the will of their powers. And why need we say more, when the Oracles also expressly speak in relation to the gods themselves who are prior to that intelligible-and-intellectual order in the following terms (fr. 81 DP):

293

To the intellectual thunderbolts of the intellectual fire
All things yield, subserving the compelling will of the Father.

and again (fr. 80):

But also everything that serves the material connectors.[84]

These, then, are said to be in service to the entities prior to them, and they in turn to dominate them, while they rule over as slaves those entities inferior to themselves; for these, as we said, are names of primary and secondary powers respectively, transcending and being immanent in the things brought to completion by them, the one having the role of agents, the other of instruments, in their common products. And 942 that these things are according to nature and not the result of chance you may learn also from what is said in the *Phaedo* (80a); for there he says that Nature ordained the body to serve, the soul to be the master. If, then, even in this realm these relations are according to nature, it is no wonder if we postulate There Mastership Itself and Slavery Itself— since the theologians employ these terms to indicate the controlling and subservient powers among the gods; as indeed the paternal and maternal faculty appears in one form at the divine level, and in another at the level of the Forms, not being even among these a mere relationship, but rather a generative power and a substance suitable to gods.

Now it has been said[85] that the faculties of master and slave on our level too are not only a matter of chance, but prior to this there is also that which is a matter of conscious intent. Far more properly, then, there exist in the realm of universals substantial Mastership and Slavery, even as Here there exist natural varieties; and voluntary types, even as Here they exist according to choice, since There substantial power cooperates with the will of dominating and subservient entities. For it is through obedience that the dominated are dominated, and the dominant dominate; for all things, as the Oracle says, "yield to the intellectual thunderbolts, subserving the compelling will of the father."

So each exists substantially, and either is according to nature, both dominating and being dominated in obedience, down from the intelligible Father above, and possessing this Mastership and Slavery, as Parmenides says, in relation to each other. Why, then, do the gods not also exercise mastery over us, as Socrates in the *Phaedo* (62b) said that the gods are our masters, and we are their possessions? Once again let us state our views on this, namely that they *are*, but in a different way.

---

[84] The *synocheis*, a Chaldaean triad of gods, following on the *iynges* and preceding the *teletarchai*. Cf. H. Lewy, *Chaldaean Oracles and Theurgy*, pp. 129-131. For Proclus, the *synocheis* constituted the second, or median, intelligible-and-intellectual triad.

[85] Aristotle *Pol.* I, 5.

For they dominate us transcendently, whereas There the more general dominate the more particular coordinately, and, as has been said, 943 through the medium of the Slavery There, which brings us also into relation to the gods as masters. When both are acting upon both, the better, acting primarily on the better, has revealed the gods as our masters, while the worse acts on us, the worse, revealing us to be dominated by the gods. So, then, the mode of Mastership is different There, and not such as is the mode of rule over us, since the mode of Slavery also is different; for the gods themselves bring themselves near to their own causes, and if voluntary slavery has any existence anywhere, it is in that realm; for domination exercised by the more perfect is according to the will of their inferiors; in fact, the fact of belonging to the superior classes of being does not cause them to depart from their proper blessedness, and their being themselves all the more places them in the power of what is above them. Even thus does Intellect rule over Necessity in the cosmos, as we hear in the *Timaeus* (48a) persuading it for the most part to act for the best, as Socrates in the *Phaedo* also relates (97c); and taking these two as the causes of the composition of the cosmos, generation came about through Necessity, but was established in accordance with Intellect, Necessity subordinating itself to Intellect in order that the universe might stand fast, guided by Intellect. Gods, then, rule over gods, and men over men, the one essentially, the other by chance, Slavery being There subjected to the gods. For the whole chain of Slavery is subordinate to divine Mastership; for Mastership There is not coordinate with Slavery, but is superior to it, though in a manner consonant with their common level of being, and superior entities necessarily dominate all that their inferiors dominate. So, then, since the whole chain of Slavery Itself is subordinate to that of Mastership Itself, it is natural also that the gods should dominate by virtue of their mastering power; and not over the gods only, the more universal over the more particular, but over men also, who partake, to the extent they can, in Slavery Itself, which makes the worse slaves to the better.

944   *"And similarly Knowledge itself, the essence of Knowledge, will be knowledge of Truth itself, the essentially real?" "Certainly." "And again any given branch of Knowledge in itself will be knowledge of some department of real things as it is in itself, will it not?" "Yes."* (134a)

Divine Knowledge is celebrated also by the Socrates of the *Phaedrus* (247d), when he pictures the ascent of the universal souls to the intellectual and intelligible orders, and relates that they contemplate there Justice itself and Moderation itself and Knowledge itself, being joined in essence with the median rank of these gods; and there, he also declared, is Truth, which proceeds from the intelligibles and shines intelligible light upon all the median classes of gods, and he linked that Knowledge to that Truth. These things were fully discussed by my teacher and by myself in our investigations of the divine insights of Socrates in the *Phaedrus*.[86]

It is no wonder, then, if here also, in making mention of the realm of Forms, he says that Knowledge itself is of Truth itself. For There both Knowledge and Truth and all the Forms in them participate in Knowledge itself and Truth itself. The one makes all things There intellectual, for this Knowledge is the eternal and uniform intelligising of the eternal; the other makes them intelligible, for the light of Truth, being intelligible, gives them a share of its intelligible power. And since there are many orders of these intermediate Forms (for some of them are "highest," as he says,[87] and unitary and intelligible, while others have the role of linking and binding everything together, and others are concerned with bringing things to completion and turning them towards their source), for this reason after the singular knowledge he made mention of the plurality of types of knowledge, for it proceeds from above through all the classes of being accompanied by the light of truth; this is the One inherent in every order, and that to which the in-
945 telligible and intellection is linked. So, then, even as intellection in general is directed at the intelligible in general, so the many intellections are united with the many objects of intellection. These Forms, then, have their intellections united with their own intelligible elements, and totally transcend the range of our knowledge; as for the intellectual Forms, even though they transcend us, yet, since we derive immediately from them, they are somehow in us, and we have some knowledge of them, and through them of the unknowable superiority of the more divine ones. We must not, however, say, as do some of the friends of Plato,[88] that the divine Knowledge does not itself know anything, but provides this faculty to others from itself; for each of the divine beings acts upon itself first and initiates its proper characteristic from itself, as for instance the cause of Life fills itself with life, and the cause of Perfection renders itself perfect.

After all, that which provides the faculty of knowing to other things

[86] Cf. Hermeias *In Phaedr.* 152.26ff. Couvreur, another record of Syrianus' seminars on the *Phaedrus*. No commentary by Proclus survives, though *PT* IV, 4-26 constitutes a commentary on 246e-247d.

[87] Reading φησί (sc. Plato *Phaedr.* 247b7) for φασί of MSS. It is hard to see to whom the plural would refer, since the doctrine is that of Syrianus and Proclus.

[88] The reference is not clear. This is consonant with the views of Speusippus as to the propriety of attributing goodness or beauty to the first principle (*ap.* Arist. *Met.* XII, 7, 1072b30ff.), but the reference may be to someone much more recent. Of course, if the reference were to the One, this would be a criticism of Plotinus, but Proclus is talking here of the One-Being.

has itself the knowledge of existents prior to all other things, seeing that the knowledge in us, which is a mere image of Essential Knowledge, knows everything else and itself before anything else. Or what is that faculty which formulates the question "What *is* Knowledge?" And how will it not be proper to that same faculty to recognise simultaneously the simultaneity of relatives? So in knowing the objects of knowledge, it also knows itself as being the knowledge of them. Nor should we say that all other grades of knowledge are of objects of knowledge, but that divine knowledge is knowledge of knowledges, but not the cognising of objects of knowledge, and that this should be a special peculiarity of it; for if there are other grades of knowledge co-ordinate with the One Knowledge, then it should know both them and all the objects of knowledge related to them, by virtue of its knowledge of them, because they are what they are in relation to each other; but if the One transcends the many and does not extend towards them, it stands in itself in actuality, and it has coordinate with it the purest object of knowledge; and even as its mode of cognisance is pure and simple, even so its object is both unitary and such as to comprehend all those other subjects.

946   This, then, is Essential Knowledge, both cause of knowing to what participates in it, and far more basically to itself; for it is an essence through being the essentialised knowledge both of itself and of Being; for knowledge There is not a faculty nor a quality, but is an independent substance belonging to itself, and fixed in itself, and, through knowing itself, knowing also the primary object of knowledge, which is pure Being. For it is yoked in unity with this, as is pure intellect to the pure object of intellection, and as is pure sense-perception to the pure object of sense-perception. The many essential Knowledges following upon this are "processions" from the one Knowledge, linked to the multiplicity of beings which are comprised by the Being which is the object of that single knowledge; and the one Being is many, and the Knowledge likewise. The unitary aspect of it is united to the One of the realm of Being, and knows it, and its own One. The multiplicity, in turn, knows the multiplicity of beings, which that Being comprises, and also itself; and some beings are cognising essences, while others are cognisable[88a] substances, and there is one unification of these, suitable to the simple substances of the Forms.

"While the knowledge in our world will be knowledge of the truth in our world? And again it would follow that each branch of knowledge in our world must be knowledge of a class of beings in our world?" "Necessarily." (134a)

[88a] Accepting Chaignet's emendation γνωσταί for γνωστικαί of MSS.

297

We too partake to some extent of Truth, but not of that of which those Forms partake, but rather of that granted to our order by the work of creation; and knowledge in our world is of this truth. There are also branches of knowledge more particular than this, interpreting various particular departments of the knowable; some concerned with generation and its various manifestations, others investigating Nature as a whole, others contemplating the hypostases of beings superior to Nature; some employing the senses, and doing their work with the help of these, others requiring the aid of the formative conceptions of 947 imagination, others being content with accounts based on opinion, others directing the pure reason in upon itself, others again extending the reason in us to unite with Intellect. All these types have been defined also by the Socrates of the *Philebus*, who distinguishes (59c) the pure and unmixed of them from those that are not, and declares not pure those that use the senses and are filled with mere probability, whereas those that are independent of these are pure and accurate; indeed he places superior to all other arts (*ibid.*, 55e) these three—arithmetic, the art of measuring, and the art of weighing—and above these the philosophic versions of them as distinct from the popular, and above these again Dialectic itself, which is the purest type of intellect and thought. Since, then, there is such variation in the levels of knowledge, it is plain that the different types of knowledge are concerned with different subjects, and some of them with subjects which contribute to stimulating our recollection of Being, as for instance geometry deals with the description of the concept of shape inherent in us, while arithmetic by its proofs develops the single Form of numbers, and various others of the individual subject matters of knowledge do the same for the various real existents within us, through theorising about them.

We must, by the way, keep to the strict meaning of the term 'knowledge' (*epistēmē*), and not introduce here consideration of the various crafts, and postulate Ideas answering to them, since it is only our needs that produced them in our world, being as they are images of images; for they are mere images of the true sciences. So then, even as we say that there exist Ideas of those accidents which contribute to a thing's essence, but not of those things which derive from these and exist in other things purely as accidents, entering when the Forms are already complete (a distinction we have made above)[89]—for these are mere echoes of entities that draw their primary existence from Above; so also crafts, being mere images of the sciences, take their origin from this realm, whereas the real sciences derive from the varieties of Knowledge preexistently There, through which there is granted to us

[89] Cf. 826-827, in his discussion of the possibility of Ideas of accidents.

948 the possibility of ascent to them and assimilation to Intellect. And even as There the one Knowledge is necessarily prior to the many, the knowledge which is of real Truth, as the many knowledges are of the many Truths (for in the case of each their object is a Truth); even so from among the many varieties of knowledge in our realm one must discern the one complete form of knowledge by itself, neither made up from the many, nor on the same level as they, but preexistently subsisting by itself; and the many, on the other hand, dividing among themselves the single power of knowledge, and assigning themselves as different to different objects of knowledge, and referring back to it and receiving their first principles from it.

Knowledge in us, then, is different from the divine sort, but through this knowledge we ascend to that; and neither do we need to situate the intelligible realm within us, as some assert,[90] in order for us to know the intelligible objects as present within us (for they transcend us and are causes of our essence); nor should we say that some part of the soul remains above, in order that through it we should have contact with the intelligible realm (for that which remains always above could never become linked to that which has departed from its proper state of intellection, nor would it ever make up the same substance as it); nor should we postulate that it is consubstantial with the gods—for the Father who created us produced our substance at the first from secondary and tertiary materials (*Tim.* 41d). Some thinkers have been driven to propose such doctrines as this, through seeking to understand how we who are fallen into this realm can have knowledge of real Beings, when the knowledge of them is proper not to fallen entities, but to those who have been roused and sobered up from the Fall. But we must rather say that it is while remaining at our own rank, and possessing images of the essences of all Beings, that we turn to them by means of these images, and cognise the realm of Being from the tokens of it that we possess, not[91] coordinately, but on a secondary level and in a manner corresponding to our own worth, while with what is in our own realm we are coordinate, comprehending as a unity both knowledge and its objects.

949 *"But, as you admit, we do not possess the Forms themselves, nor can they exist in our world." "No." "And presumably the classes of being, just as they are in themselves, are known by the Form of Knowledge itself?" "Yes." "The Form which we do not possess." "True." "Then none of*

---

[90] Notably Plotinus (in *Enn.* IV, 8 and elsewhere) and Porphyry. Cf. *In Tim.* III, 334.3ff., where Proclus gives Iamblichus' objections to this doctrine as well as his own (= Iambl. *In Tim.* fr. 87 Dillon).

[91] Reading οὐ or οὐχί for οὖσι of MSS. (West.).

the Forms is known by us, since we do not partake of Knowledge itself."
"Apparently not." (134b)

In this passage, taking his start from the axioms laid down previously, he draws the present conclusion as follows: the transcendent Forms exist by themselves; what exists by itself and of itself is not in us; what is not in us is not on the level of our knowledge; what is not on the level of our knowledge is unknowable by our faculty of knowledge; so then the transcendent Forms are unknowable by our faculty of knowledge. They may, then, be contemplated only by the divine Intellect. This is so for all Forms, but especially for those that are beyond the intellectual gods; for neither sense-perception, nor cognition based on opinion, nor pure reason, nor intellectual cognition of our type serves to connect the soul with those Forms, but only illumination from the intellectual gods renders us capable of joining ourselves to those intelligible-and-intellectual Forms, as I recall someone saying under divine inspiration.[92] The nature of those Forms is, then, unknowable to us, as being superior to our intellection and to the partial conceptions of our souls. And it is for this reason, indeed, that the Socrates of the *Phaedrus* (249d), as we said before, compares the contemplation of them to mystic rites and initiations and visions, conducting our souls up to the vault beneath the heaven, and the heaven itself, and the place above the heaven, calling the visions of those same Forms perfect and unwavering apparitions and also "simple" and "happy." We have
950 shown long ago, I believe, with explanations of great clarity, in our commentary on the Palinode passage[93] (*Phaedr.* 243ab), that all those orders of being are intermediate between the intellectual gods and the primary intelligible ones; so that it is plain that a certain degree of truth is contained in the present passage. Knowledge of the intellectual Forms then, as has been said previously, has been instilled into us by the Demiurge and Father of souls, but as for those Forms that are above Intellect, such as are the Forms that are in the aforementioned classes, the knowledge of them is beyond our efforts to achieve and is of automatic provenance, achievable only by god-possessed souls, so that the conclusion in the present passage follows from our conceptions of the intelligible-and-intellectual Forms; and it follows also that "we do not partake of Knowledge itself, which, he says, "knows each of the classes of being in themselves."

[92] Possibly a reference to Iamblichus (cf. Procl. *In Tim*. II, 310.4ff. = Iambl. *In Tim.* fr. 59 Dillon, where Pure Soul "illuminates" the human mind with knowledge of Forms), but more probably to Syrianus, since the postulation of intelligible-intellective gods seems to be an invention of his.

[93] Cf. Hermeias *In Phaedr*. 75ff. Couvreur. A reference to Proclus' lost commentary on the *Phaedrus*.

By "classes of being"[94] we must not understand the common concepts presenting themselves to our imagination, nor yet the entities answering to any set of common definitions (for these are posterior to true beings), but rather such as possess generative power which is more universal, and causally dominate the productions of more particular Forms; for even as Here genera are either conceived of in the imagination as covering a broader range, or are predicated of a wider range of things, than species, so the entities in that higher realm are more widely dominant and more perfect and more comprehensive than the other Forms, surpassing those things that they comprehend in simplicity and generative power. These things must be declared to be known by the Form of Knowledge, as taking its origin from Above, and comprehending all pluralised entities unitarily, and all particular entities universally, in accordance with a single unitary knowledge. This is indeed what our knowledge would like to attain, always to be contemplating the processions of true beings from their causal principles, whereas knowledge in fact attains only a secondary position.

"So Beauty itself or Goodness itself and all the things we take as Forms in themselves, are unknowable to us." "That may be so." (134bc)

Beauty and Goodness proceed downwards from the highest peak of
951 the intelligible realm, upon all the secondary classes of gods; the median orders of Forms, at least, receive the procession of these in a manner fitting to them, by virtue of Goodness being full of their own perfection and self-sufficiency and freedom from lack, while by virtue of Beauty they are objects of love to their secondaries, and a force of recall for those entities that have proceeded, and a force of binding together for differentiated causes. For the turning back to Beauty brings together all things and unites them, and as it were propels them towards one centre. These entities, then—I mean Beauty and Goodness—exist covertly and unitarily in the primal levels of being, while in each of the remaining levels they manifest such permutations as are appropriate to that level; so that it is not to be wondered at if there is one beauty that is cognisable by the senses alone, another which is recognisable by opinion, another which can be contemplated by discursive reason, another by intellection with the aid of reasoning, another by pure intellection, and yet another that is unknowable, completely transcendent, on its own, and able to be beheld by its own light alone.

"Then here is a still more dreadful consequence for you to consider." "What is that?" "You will grant, I suppose, that if there is such a thing

---

[94] Proclus is provoked to these comments by Plato's use of γένη rather than εἴδη at 134b7.

301

as a Form of Knowledge, it is much more exact than the knowledge in our world; and so with Beauty and all the rest." "Yes." (134c)

The foregoing arguments, as we examined them theologically, have ascended as far as the intelligible-and-intellectual orders of Forms. For, whereas they are false and problematic at the level of the intellectual, they are revealed as all true and divinely inspired in respect of those levels of being with which we are presently concerned, and lead us up to the actual preexisting essence of the Forms in the intelligible realm, still problematic in their outward form, as proceeding from the intellectual realm, but in reality indicating the distinctive essence of the most primal Forms. This very characteristic, at all events, of not having knowledge of this realm nor exercising rule over it, the argument as it proceeds, as far as concerns the demiurgic Ideas, shows to be false; for the things of this realm actually derive their existence from these, and they control their creation and their multifarious division into individual kinds, so that they have assumed providential care and administration of them. However, as regards the most primal and unitary level of Ideas, the truly intelligible level, it is absolutely true; for these appear first from Being in the intelligible Intellect in a simple and unified and holistic mode; for, containing the paternal causes of the most general and comprehensive classes of being, they are superior to the articulated knowledge of this realm and immediate mastership over things of sense. For they, the intelligible gods, are masters of the gods who are manifested forth from them, and their type of knowledge is beyond all the other divine levels of knowledge.

It is these facts that Plato is taking into account when he concludes that the gods neither are our masters nor have knowledge of human affairs; for the causes of these, as already stated, and the powers that control them reside in the intellectual gods. The powers of the intelligible gods are superior to all such distinctions, and produce all things according to the most unitary and simple level of cause, and their creative and cognising activity is single and instantaneous and uniform. At any rate, the intelligible cause There of the heavenly race produces all the heavenly beings—gods, angels, daemons, heroes, souls—not *qua* daemons or angels (for this is the proper activity of the partial causes and the distinct Ideas of which the intellectual gods have made the division into multiplicity), but in so far as all these classes of being are in some way divine and heavenly, and in so far as they have been granted an essence united to the gods. And the same goes for each of the remaining Ideas. For instance, the intelligible Idea of the whole class of what has feet and goes on dry land (cf. *Tim.* 40a) would not be said to "be master of" those things which are distinguished according to individual spe-

952

302

cies; for this is the task of those things that are separated from it into multiplicity; its role is to preside over all as a single class. Those things nearer to the One create more generally and unitarily all those things which their inferiors create in a more particular and multiplied way. And so it is in the case of all the other intelligible Ideas, which are com-
953 prised by the intelligible Intellect.

But these matters we shall consider in more detail later on. Plato's doctrine on Providence has been most clearly expounded by the Athenian Stranger (*Laws* X, 903bff.), where his discourse declares that the gods know all things and possess the power of directing all things. Nevertheless, even in the present passage, people are accustomed, somewhat unsuitably I feel, to introduce discussions about providence into these problems about the Forms. Let us now, therefore, also say something on this question. It is plain that, even if Parmenides raises difficulties about the universal pervasiveness of divine knowledge and domination, yet right from the outset he makes plain the absurdity of such a postulate; for the fact that he declares the conclusion resulting from this difficulty to be "more dreadful" than that of the previous one is, I think, a reasonably clear indication that he disapproves of the arguments that eliminate Providence. For it is "dreadful," on the one hand, to assert that the gods are not known by us, in spite of the fact that we possess reason and intelligence and have some element of the divine in our essence, but it is "more dreadful" still to remove as well the knowledge proper to the divine realm; for the one suggests simply that we do not enjoy reversion to the divine, while the other tends to the elimination of the universal pervasiveness of the goodness of the gods; the former sins against our essence, the latter against divine causality. "More dreadful," then, is not to be taken in the sense of a "more powerful" objection, as one is accustomed to speak of someone who prevails with the power of his words as "a dreadfully clever speaker," but as meriting greater dread and caution from those of prudent mind. For it tears apart the unity of all existents and separates the divine from the cosmos; it also limits the divine power as not extending to all things, and circumscribes the knowledge of the intellectual realm as not complete. Indeed, it overturns the whole creation and the order be-
954 stowed upon the cosmos from the transcendent causes, and the goodness proceeding from a single will which unitarily fills all things with blessings. And inferior to none of these evils is the confusion which it casts upon piety. For what connection can there be between gods and men, if their knowledge of the events of this realm is done away with? Certainly this will lead to an abolition and nullification of all worship of the godhead, all traditional rules of religion, all oaths which take their validity from calling the gods to witness, all those intuitive beliefs

about them which exist without instruction in our souls. What sort of benefaction is left for the gods towards men, if there do not exist previously intellectual measures among them of the comparative worth of recipients of their benefits, if they do not have knowledge of all things that we do and suffer and contemplate doing even if we do not do them? It is with reason, then, that he calls "dreadful" an argument that puts forward such theories, not in the sense of its being powerful and difficult to face, as I said, but as worthy of every fear; for if it is unholy even to alter any of the laws of religion, on the ground that the whole belief in them will be overturned by such an action, how then would such a piece of innovation as this be free from apprehension?

No, it is clear from all this that he is accusing of such an hypothesis rather those to whom he attributes ignorance about the administration of the cosmos. Since, then, he wishes God both to know and to do everything, while some of those who came after him[95] tried utterly to overturn such arguments, we should now say about these people as much as is required by the context; for some of those who followed him are troubled lest the fact that things here are not firmly fixed and carried this way and that might be an argument against providence and the existence of God. For those things that are said to be derived from chance and the apparent inequality in the apportionment of lives and this disorganised flux of material things, has provided for them considerable argument in favor of lack of providence; and further the notion that God should not be troubled by being involved in the convolutions of various and complicated causal connections, and the desire to separate all such activity from his essential blessedness have led them to
955 such error; for the trouble to which our soul is subject and the disturbance which it undergoes when it descends to care for bodies, they concluded would also be true in the case of God if they were to attribute to him care for things of this realm; and in addition to this, due to the fact that the types of knowledge proper to different objects of knowledge are different—sense-perception to objects of the senses, opinion to things that are the objects of opinion, scientific knowledge to the objects of science, and intuitive knowledge to the objects of intellect— since they did not wish to attribute to God either sense-perception or opinion or scientific knowledge but only immaterial and intuitive intellect, they denied him knowledge of all those things which are not intelligible; for if he is external to Matter, it is necessary that he be pure

---

[95] The Epicureans, presumably (the term *apronoēsia*, indeed, is attested for Epicurus by Alexander of Aphrodisias, *De Fato* 31 = fr. 368 Usener); but Epicureans could hardly be described as τῶν ἀπ᾽ αὐτοῦ τινές (line 28), who must therefore be sceptical Academics or Peripatetics, disturbed by Epicurean arguments, such as Philo of Alexandria represents his nephew Alexander as being in his *De Providentia*.

from all those conceptions which are turned towards Matter, and being pure of these he could not know the things that are contained in Matter; and it is for this reason, as I said, that some thinkers have deprived him of the knowledge of things of sense and providential care of them, not through any weakness of his, but by reason of the superior nature of his cognitive activity; as those whose eyes are full of light are said not to be able to see the things in the cosmos, this inability of theirs being a superfluity of sight; and they say that it is better not to know many things,[96] as in the case of those who are divinely inspired not to know such things as would distract them from their inspiration, or in the case of those possessed of scientific knowledge, such things as would detract from the powers of concentration on that knowledge of theirs.

Others,[97] in granting to God the knowledge also of things of sense, in order that they may say that he has providential care of them, have turned his consciousness outside of himself and have brought it about that he penetrates throughout the perceptible world and comes into direct contact with what he administers, and gives a physical impulse to each thing and is present everywhere in a spatial sense, for they do not see that he would be able to exercise providence in this sphere in any other way.

Others[98] say that he knows himself, but that for his providential care of the sense-world there is no necessity for him to have knowledge of it, but by virtue of his very being he both produces all things and organises all things that he produces, having no knowledge of what is produced. Nor, they say, is there anything astonishing in this, since Nature does its work of creation without having knowledge or any faculty of imagination, while God differs from Nature in having knowledge of himself but not of those things which are created by him.

956   These, then, are the sorts of considerations which have persuaded some thinkers to declare that God is either not separate from things in the universe or even to do away with the knowledge that he possesses of things secondary to him, and the providential care of them that goes with that knowledge. As for ourselves, we say that there is something in what they assert that is correct, and something that is not correct. For it is true that, if there is providence, there can be nothing that is unordered, nor can God be supposed to be put to any trouble, and even more so he cannot be thought to know objects of sense by means of any sense-organ that involves feeling—so to this extent they are right. But in that they do not recognise the transcendent power and the unitary knowledge of the gods, in this respect in turn they seem to fail of the

[96] Aristotle *Met.* XII, 9.1074b32.
[97] The Stoics, cf. 921 above.
[98] The Peripatetics, cf. also 921 above.

truth. Let us question them suitably, in the following manner: Is it not the case that everything that acts, acts according to its own power and nature, and, according to the rank it has in the scale of being, such is its action, in accordance with its own rank? As for instance, Nature acts on a natural level, Intellect on an intellectual, and Soul on a psychic level; and even if the same thing is brought into being by a multiplicity of different causes, is it not the case that each thing acts according to its own power, but not according to the nature of the thing created? Or do man and the sun generate a man in the same way,[99] and what comes into being in one, and is it the case that the things creating it created in the same way and not as is the nature of each, the one partially and imperfectly and with trouble, the other without trouble and, by virtue of its very being, universally? But even to state this is ridiculous; for the divine acts in one way, and the mortal race acts in another. And if this is so, and everything that acts, acts according to its own nature and rank, the one divinely and in a way superior to nature, the other according to nature, and something else some other way, it is obvious, surely, that that also which knows, knows according to its own nature. So it will not be the case that because that which is known is one and the same, for this reason those things also which know it should be related to the objects of their knowledge in exactly the same way; for, after all, a white thing is known by sense-perception and by opinion, 957 and by our intellect, but not in the same way; for sense-perception cannot know the essential nature (*to ti ēn einai*) of the white; nor does opinion comprehend its proper objects of knowledge in the same way that intellect does; for intellect knows also the cause, while opinion knows only the fact; it is by virtue of this, indeed, that we say that correct opinion differs from knowledge, the former knowing only the fact of the thing and being weak for this reason, the latter comprehending the object of knowledge along with its cause and thus able to comprehend it more strongly. Is it not the case that that noble entity, the Intellect, knows its object of knowledge on the one hand, and we ourselves know it also, as has been said previously, but not in the same way, owing to the difference in cognitive power? So then, knowledge varies according to the nature of the knowing agent. It is not the case that it is according to the nature of the known object that it is known by everything, but it is known in a superior way by superior agents, in an inferior way by more inadequate ones. What is there astonishing, then, in the fact that God knows everything according to his nature, divided things in an undivided way, multiplied things in a unified way, things that come into being eternally, and partial things universally, and in a

---

[99] Cf. Aristotle *Met.* XII, 5.1071a13ff.

word, in a different manner than is the nature of each of the things in question, and along with such knowledge he has control over the production of all things, and by the very fact of knowing all things with simple and unified knowledge, he bestows upon each their existence and their coming into existence? For indeed hearing perceives the objects of hearing in one way, and our common sense-perception perceives prior to the individual senses all objects of sense; and above this again reason perceives in a different way both these things and all other things of which there is not sense-perception. For again we find the faculty of desire (*epithymia*) striving after one set of things, and the faculty of spiritedness (*thymos*) pursuing others, and rational choice directing itself towards others, but there is also one single life-principle which moves the soul towards all of these things, by virtue of which we say "I desire" and "I am angry" and "I make such and such a choice"; for that life-principle directs itself to these objects along with the faculties mentioned and it lives with all of them, being a power which directs an impulse towards every object of impulse. And indeed prior to both these faculties is the unitary principle of the soul, which often says, for instance, "I perceive such and such" and "I am calculating" and "I desire such and such" and "I wish such and such," and which is conscious of all these activities and works along with them; otherwise we would not have known all these activities, nor would we be able to say in what way they differed, if there were not one single unitary thing in us which knew all these, which is over and above the common sense-faculty and prior to opinion and prior to desire and prior to will, and which knows all the deliberations of those faculties and which has gathered together into itself partlessly all their impulses, saying in the case of each "It is I who am doing this, and I who am acting."

How, then, can it be right to disbelieve that the undivided knowledge of God, although it is not sense-perceptive, yet knows objects of sense, and, although not being divided, yet knows things divided, in a manner proper to itself, and that although it is not spatially present to those things that are in space, yet it knows these also, prior to any spatial presence, and gives to all as much as each of the recipients can take, even though it is transcendently separate from them? So then, the disordered aspect of divisible things is not known by God in a disordered way, but in an orderly way; nor is that which is changeable known uncertainly but entirely consistently; nor does the knowledge of the complicated and varied cause him any difficulty; for by the very fact of intelligising himself he knows all things of which he is the cause, having more accurate knowledge than if someone had apportioned to him knowledge of the objects of knowledge on the same level as them; for knowing each thing on the causal level is superior to all other types of knowledge. So then, his knowledge does not involve any trouble, because in his case the knowing element remains in itself, and by knowing itself alone knows all other things, and does not need sense-perception or opinion or knowledge for the cognising of any of the objects of sense; for he himself it is who produces all these things, and in his bottomless thoughts he contains causally and in single simplicity the unified knowledge of all these things; it is as if someone had constructed a ship and embarked men on it of whom he himself was the creator, and as if he were to launch the ship on the sea and bring to bear certain

959 winds upon it, possessing as he would some art of Aeolus, and thus he would send the ship off to be carried along, and he should be able to do all this by the very fact of conceiving of it; as if by the very fact of imagining all these things in this way, he were to produce the external existence of all the things which he possessed within himself in his imagination. It is obvious that he himself, then, would be the cause of all those things which would befall the ship by reason of the winds on the sea, and thus, by contemplating his own thoughts, he would both create and know what is external, not requiring any effort of attention towards them.

It is in this way, then, and in a more transcendent way than this, that the divine Intellect, through possessing the causes of all things simultaneously, creates them all and contemplates them, without issuing forth from its own conning-tower (*Pol.* 272e). If it is the case that there is one intellect that is more general, and another that is more particular, it is obvious that the intelligising of all things by each of them is not the same; but where the objects of intellect are more general and undivided, then also the knowledge of them is general and undivided. But where the number of Forms has proceeded into multiplicity and extension, there also the knowledge of them is one and multiple.

And we should not wonder when we hear the verses of Orpheus in which the Theologian says (fr. 169 Kern):

This is the abode of Zeus, and under the eyes of the king their father dwell the immortal gods and mortal men,
and all things that have come to be and such as will be in later time.

For he is filled with all the intelligible objects and he possesses the already distinguished causes of all things, so that he generates both men and all other things according to their particularities, not in so far as each of them partakes in divinity, as does his intelligible father before him; wherefore this latter (sc. Zeus) is called "father" of all things distinguished according to their species and is said to penetrate through all things, whereas that other (sc. Phanes) is said to be the father of all things distinguished according to genera, although he is in a far supe-

rior way father of all things, but of all things in so far as they each partake of divine power. And the one (Zeus) possesses the knowledge both of human affairs in particular, and of them in common with all other things; for there is in him the causal principle of men, both distinct from all other causes and united with all of them; whereas in the
960 mind of the other (Phanes) they are all together unitarily and undividedly, as for instance that of man, in so far as man is a footed animal; for as the concept "footed" there is cause comprehensively of everything—gods, angels, demons, heroes, souls, animals, plants—of everything on the earth, so also the knowledge of all these things together is one as being of one genus, and there is no knowledge of human affairs in a distinct way.[100] And even as on our level the more general classes of knowledge, as Aristotle says (*An. Post.* I, 24.85b14ff.), are regarded as being knowledge in a truer sense than those subordinate to them, and more akin to Intellect (for they employ more comprehensive conclusions), even so among the gods also, superior and simpler intellections have precedence over the multifarious variation of the secondary ones. So in the case of man the most primary cognition of him among the gods is that he is, and there is one cognition that knows all being as being one according to one principle of unification; the second cognition of him is that he always is; this knowledge embraces in one causal principle unitarily all of that which always is; the cognition following on this is of man as an animal; for this knowledge in its turn cognises animal in a unitary way; and the one after this is of man as belonging to this particular species, as for instance, that of footed things; for there is one intellection of this whole class as one, and division follows first upon this, bringing in variation after the simplicity. But all the same the intellection of man is not only at this level, for it is not the same thing to think of everything on earth as one thing and to think of man in this way. On the level of demiurgic and, in general, intellectual forms there is also some cognition of man as man because this form also is distinguished from others on this level of being. So it has been simultaneously demonstrated both how God has knowledge of human affairs and how he rules over all, and in what way all things are divine and in what way they partake of some divine characteristic. But all this, I think, has now been discussed adequately.

It is clear then that Mastery Itself and Knowledge Itself exist in the
961 first rank of ideas; for there is divine intellection of all things unitarily, and the power that controls all things—the one being the fount of all knowledge, the other being the primal cause of all mastery, whether it

[100] The relations between Zeus and Phanes are discussed in similar detail at *In Tim.* I, 313.2-315.4, and elsewhere in that commentary. See Diehl's index s.v.

be among the gods, or in the classes of being superior to us, or in souls. And presumably it is for this reason that he, in this passage, calls intellection the genus (*genos*) of knowledge, intending by this to indicate its quality of encompassing all the species there, and its unitary quality; further back, indeed (134b), he has called it simply specific Form (*eidos*)[101] placing it among the median Ideas; for the median realms also are filled from intelligible cognition with the intellection relevant to themselves, and so also are all the divine Intellects, and intellection in these has the same relation to intellection there as has species to genus. If the expression "much more exact" is used in respect of this knowledge, it is obvious that such an epithet conveys to us its unificatory quality; for this is what it means to be "exact," to encompass all other things and not leave anything outside of itself.

> *"And if anything has part in this Knowledge itself, you would agree that a god has a better title than anyone else to possess the most perfect knowledge?" "Undoubtedly."* (134c)

Every divine mind and every order of gods possesses within itself in a prior form both the knowledge and the causal principle of all things; for neither are their cognitions ineffective through having an indefinite element in the very act of knowledge, but they both know all things and provide all goods (for the primal good wishes to project the provisions coming from itself onto all secondary things); nor are their creations in any way irrational and devoid of knowledge; for this is the work of Nature and the lower form of life, not of the divine form, which actually produces even the class of rational beings. So then, by the same token, they both know all things and create all things, and prior to these in virtue of their will and their knowledge they have laid claim also to the *power* of creating all things; so that by virtue of their will they possess in a prior form both the knowledge and the power of creating all things, and through this triad everything receives the benefit of their forethought. And if you wish, by bringing into unity the fragmented characteristics of secondary things, to refer them back to their divine cause, perhaps you might achieve more accurate truth about this cause. At any rate, nature appears to possess creative principles, but not ones that have knowledge; discursive thought, in its turn, has cognition which has its end in itself; while rational choice, in its turn, has the good and the will towards goods. If you gather all these three into one, the faculty of willing, the faculty of knowing, the faculty of doing, and conceive of the divine henad prior to these, then you may refer this to the divinity on the ground that all these things to-

962

---

[101] It is impossible to do justice to the virtual pun here between "species" and "Form."

gether preexist unitarily on that level. But whereas all the gods possess all these faculties, it is apparent that intellection in the primary sense is proper to the intelligible level, as is the primal power of generation of all things, and the goodness of will; for inasmuch as they have come into existence immediately following on the source of all goods, they become, in the beings secondary to them, that which the Good is to all things, expressing its supra-causal rank by their paternal power, its goodness by their boniform will, and its superiority to all knowledge by their hidden and unified cognition. And it occurs to me that it is for this reason that he now first terms the forms "gods," as having referred himself back to their primal source, and on the grounds that they are uniform and nearest to the good, and that they thus have the power of knowing and ruling over all things, inasmuch as each partakes of divine power and inasmuch as all things are dependent upon the gods.

> *"Then will the god, who possesses Knowledge itself, be able to know the things in our world?" "Why not?" "Because," said Parmenides, "we have agreed that those forms have no significance with reference to things in our world, nor have things in our world any significance with reference to them. Each set has it only among themselves." "Yes, we did agree on that."* (134d)

There is no need to say how this argument would be refuted in so far as it is directed against the intellectual forms, for God knows himself; it is plain that, in so far as he is cause of all things, by virtue of his very being, he encompasses the creative cause of all things. In so far, then, as he is cause of all things and knowing himself[102] and beholding the primal causes in himself, he would also then know all things according to the divine definition and perfect intellect and the unitary comprehension of all things. And we should not wonder how he, being an intellect, should know things that are not objects of intellection, and how not being divisible he should know divided things, and how being situated above the cosmos he should yet know objects of sense, and even things ugly and in general evil; for these things are not after all completely evil, but are also good, and that not just in relation to Intellect, but they are not even evil from the point of view of the cosmos as a whole. So then, by virtue of this single knowledge of the good, he comprehends on a prior level within himself both such things as are primarily good and such things as are secondarily good, both such things as are good absolutely and such as are good in one respect but not in another, and in general he contains within himself all the processions of goods. For even as by the single knowledge of likeness he

963

---

[102] Supplying ἑαυτόν, as Cousin suggests.

knows everything that has any degree of likeness, whether it appears in immaterial things or in the realm of bodies, so his single knowledge of the good comprehends unitarily in itself all things of which the good is in any way the cause. The ones who make distinctions and see some things as evil are we ourselves, since, as far as God is concerned, knowledge is one and simple and undivided, in virtue of the monad of the good. And the same is true in the case of all the other Forms; for being indivisible in his own nature and containing the indivisible causes of divisible things, through his knowledge of these he comprehends in a prior way all divisible things also. And it is necessary that it should be thus; for which of these propositions are we prepared to demolish? Is it that according to which there are indivisible causes of divisible things? But we see that the monad is the cause of numbers, and nature which is incorporeal the cause of bodies, and the point is the cause of magnitude and everywhere the more unitary are productive of the substance of things more multiplied and more extended into distinctness. Are we then to reject the argument that Intellect has within itself indivisibly the causes of divisible things? But this was demonstrated previously, that the Demiurge, in creating things like to himself, is the producer for all

964 things of their well-being. Well then, are we to reject the thesis that he knows them by having the undivided causes of them in himself? But what is there astonishing in the idea that Intellect should know itself, seeing that in our case, even, it is possible for us to live intellectually through knowing ourselves? There is nothing strange, then, if Intellect knows undividedly things divided, and if it knows them in a more intense way than the knowledge that is on their own level; for to know something from the perspective of its cause is a much more accurate form of knowledge than that which is without an intuition of the cause.

I forebear to mention that the theologians[103] have handed down to us the doctrine of intellectual sense-perception, according to which the divine mind directs and knows the realm of sense, which would remove far from us all objections of this sort; so that he can know even things of sense in a sensory way, but these only in so far as they are intellectual; for in him even sense-perception is an intellectual form of life. For every element in intellect is intellectual by virtue of its own nature; there is nothing, then, witless, nor lifeless, nor mindless in intellect that is in act.

So then, as I said, it has been described often before how these objections may be dealt with in the case of intellectual forms. But if God, in knowing himself to be the cause of those things subsequent to him,

---

[103] Perhaps a reference to *Or. Chald.* fr. 8 DP: νῷ μὲν κατέχειν τὰ νοητά, | αἴσθησιν δ' ἐπάγειν κόσμοις. Cf. Proclus *In Crat.* 51.30 Pasquali.

knows also those things of which he is the cause, then we must take our stand also against Aristotle, and show how Intellect according to him, in knowing itself to be the object of desire for all things, also knows all things such as strive towards it, and in knowing itself definitively also knows all things that strive towards it definitively. For there is no way in which someone who knows definitely one side of a relation cannot also know the other side. He also, then, will have a definite knowledge of all things, inasmuch as he knows himself definitely. One must not then remove from the Intellect which possesses a knowledge of all things the knowledge of itself, by possession of which it knows also that it is the object of striving for all things.

In what way, then, the remarks of Parmenides are true and in respect of what sort of Forms, we must call to mind again. For the intelligible forms do not have such knowledge of our realm as do the intellectual forms, that is to say a separate knowledge of human things as human, and in general of the individual forms and of the sense-realm, but they 965 have a unitary and general and monadic knowledge of all things ranked under a single genus, I mean, for instance, the heavenly and the aerial, or the watery or the terrestrial, whether it be the whole class of gods or of superior classes of being, or of mortals, it knows them as being divine and as being living things simply, and as undivided from each other; so then the primal knowledge and intellection is not proper to[104] those things in our realm (for these are partial things, or rather the ultimate products of division), but it is knowledge of wholes in a general and uniform way, since everything exists in the intellect undividedly. And of these intelligible Forms it is true to say that they "have no significance with reference to us nor we to them"; for they are unknowable to us and are fixed above our ability to know them, being hidden in the sanctuary of the Father and, as the theologian says,[105] knowable only to the class of gods ranked directly below them; and their power is too great for it to be immediately responsible for generating us; for it produces gods, as has been said often before, and it presides over gods, but not over souls; but it is from the intellectual classes and forms that the multitude of souls and the successions of men and of other animals have come forth.

"Then, if this most perfect Mastership and most perfect Knowledge are in God's world, the gods' Mastership can never be exercised over us, nor their Knowledge know us or anything in our world. Just as we do not rule

[104] Reading ἴδιος, with Latin translation.
[105] Cf. Proclus' interpretation of Orpheus, *In Tim.* I, 312-313 Diehl = fr. 167-168 Kern. Cf. also fr. 86 (only Night can see Phanes) and 104, where ἄδυτον (sanctuary) is mentioned.

over them by virtue of rule as it exists in our world, and we know nothing
that is divine by our knowledge, so they, on the same principle, being
gods, are not our masters, nor do they know anything of human concerns."
"But surely," said Socrates, "an argument which would deprive the gods
of knowledge would be too strange." (134de)

966   He has linked together Knowledge and Mastership in order to lay
down for us starting points for showing to others, also, that the gods
have knowledge of our affairs and are masters over us on an intellectual
level, and that they therefore know us; and if they do not know us, they
do not rule over us, which then appears a supremely paradoxical consequence. For men are somehow in the habit of calling the gods their
masters without hesitation, and appealing to them in their bodily dis-
tresses, and calling upon the gods to help them in cases where their
own efforts are not sufficient to produce a result, on the assumption
that they are able to control all things without distinction. But the
question is raised by some as to whether the gods actually have knowledge of our affairs and whether there is any reasoned account among
them of things human; for they see that it is abundance of power to rule
over all things equally and dominate all things, whereas it is a mark of
excellence of knowledge to know only the best things; for, as they say,
there are many things that it is better not to know.[106] So they attribute
to the gods mastership and administration of all things, but they remove from them knowledge of all things; for that aspect of the soul
that loves God thinks it proper to attribute only that much to the divine
cause as appears to it to be noblest. And it is of course quite right to do
this; for one should not just view the surface phenomena, but also the
causes of all things which reside in God, at which stage even things
which are far different from each other on this level are united with
each other and are in some way similar; a good act, after all, differs
enormously from an evil one, more, indeed, than one can express, but
the knowledge of virtue and of vice possessed by men of knowledge is
not far different. Acting from vice is not good, but knowing vice is
perfectly good, even as is knowing virtue; for knowledge of opposites
is one and the same. So then, it is better for Intellect to know all things;
for it knows all things as being in itself; and all these things it is better
for it to know in order that it may know itself in its entirety.

For those who behold what is external to themselves, it is better not
to know many things; for that which falls in an unmeasured way towards Matter is filled with ugliness deriving from Matter, since it looks
967   toward it. But for those who are turned towards themselves, all things
are equally to be known, and the distinction is to be made on the basis

[106] Cf. Aristotle *Met.* XII, 9.1074b32 (cf. 955 above).

of the comprehensiveness of the knowledge, not as between knowing and not knowing. This phrase that he adds, "being gods," is a good indication of the nature of the problem; for all that is divine is good and wishes to fill all things with goods; how then can it either be ignorant of things of our realm, or not have mastery over things secondary to it? And how can it be that it should not rule by virtue of its own power over those things of which it is the cause? And how could it not have providential care of them according to its own knowledge? It seems to me, in fact, that Parmenides added this phrase to what he had said, intending to show that it was above all things absurd that "being gods" they should be ignorant of our affairs over which they rule, showing with deep insight that it is proper to gods as gods most of all to know all things, and that the Forms should exercise providence over all things, in so far as Forms are the causes of the being of all things. In so far as they are divine, it is proper for them to know all these by reason of the unitary principle in them; for it is a properly divine act to exercise providence, and an intellectual act to generate and preserve the whole world of Forms. Even so in the *Laws* (X, 898a) also, Plato says that universal souls exercise providence, precisely by attributing to them divine intellect, on the grounds that providence is proper to God but not to Intellect; for other things also partake in intellect, but only divine souls in divine Intellect.

So the whole syllogism of what has been said comes out like this: the gods possess Knowledge itself and Mastery itself; but those things which possess Knowledge itself and Mastery itself are not said to have knowledge and mastery in relation to us; so then, the gods do not have knowledge and mastery in relation to us—they do not know us, nor do they rule over us; for then they would have knowledge and we should be objects of knowledge for them, and they would have mastery with reference to us, and we would be their slaves, which would be the most absurd result of the preceding arguments. It seems to me that he is most of all anxious to make clear the absurdity and the conflict with our uncorrupted conceptions by referring the terms 'god' and 'the gods', the one to the Ideas themselves, the other to that which possesses the Ideas; because it is quite true that one should remove Mastery or Knowledge from the Ideas in general and from that Intellect which possesses them, if we mean both all those things which are produced by the Ideas and such things as are external to them; for Intellect *qua* Intellect does not have knowledge of all things, but only of universal things, nor are the Ideas causes of all things but only of those things which are always naturally existent. So that this argument is not entirely false in regard to this class of things, in removing from them knowledge or mastery of our affairs in so far as we are individuals and not in so far as we are men and possess a common form.

It is necessary, then, that God and the gods know all things, both the general and the particular and the eternal and the contingent; and that they rule all things, not the general classes only, but also the particular, since one providence from them permeates all things. So the Forms, then, inasmuch as they are gods, and Intellect, so far as it is a god, have knowledge of all things and mastery of all things; but Intellect is a god by reason of the One in it, and the Forms in so far as the light of the Good is present in them. In this respect, then, being superior to the essence of Form, they have established Knowledge and Providence unitarily of all things; wherefore the statement that denies these things of them, "The gods are not our masters," is even more unreasonable and conflicts more radically with common sense. And it is by way of emphasising this that Parmenides produces with great emphasis the phrase "being gods"; for in that realm each thing is rather united to its own godhead, whereas in the intellectual realm it is rather distinguished according to the various levels of descent. And Socrates calls "too strange" the argument that deprives God of knowing; though first of all he should not have talked of deprivation but rather of superiority of knowledge (for that knowledge is said to be far more exact than all others); then if he had to say deprivation, he should have attributed the deprivation to the knowledge of our affairs, not of knowledge in general; this is not what the argument concluded. But it seems that he, taking his stand at the level of intellectual forms, got an incomplete grasp of Parmenides' theory, since Parmenides was raising the hypothesis about the Forms from the sense-world up to the very peak of the intelligible world, in which are found the Forms in their primal manifestation and the unitary aspect of numbers which is deified by light from the Good, from which the ascent to the One Being and the "hearth" of real beings is easy for him.

969

For it is necessary, in order that we should make manifest the whole chain of Ideas, to establish prior to the numerical multiplicity of the Ideas the unitary cause of beings, and the "hidden" and the unitary level of Being, and that being which is above Form, from which the number of the most unified Ideas has gone forth to all the secondary levels and orders of Being; for the primal Forms are the intelligible ones, and secondary are those which are intelligible on the one hand, but in the intellectual, and the third are those which are cohesive of all things, and fourth are those which bring to completion all intellectual and supracosmic realities, and after these again are the intellectual forms, such as have this characteristic in its proper form; the sixth rank is taken up by the assimilative forms, through which all the secondaries are made like to the intellectual forms, while the seventh rank is taken up by the transcendent and supracelestial forms which have a unifying force in respect of those forms which are divided about the cosmos, and the last rank is held by the forms in the cosmos; and of these some are at the level of intellect, some at the level of soul, others at the level of nature, others at the level of sense-perception, and of these latter some are immaterial and others are material. It is down as far as these that the procession of the forms descends from the intelligible Forms on high, making their first appearance at the limit of intelligible beings, and having their final manifestation at the limit of the sense-world.

Indeed, from all the levels of forms there necessarily descends some particular characteristic to all the lower forms which proceed from them, down to the lowest of the forms in the sense-world—as, for instance, from the intelligible forms the characteristic of unchangeability, for they are primally eternal; from the primal level of intelligible-intellectual forms each bears a token, not susceptible to knowledge, of its own paradigms, according as each has been allotted one or other divine characteristic; from the middle rank the characteristic of each being a whole and holding together with its wholeness the multiplicity of its parts; from the third rank the characteristic that each form is perfective of that which previously existed only potentially; from those which are in the realm of the intellectual the characteristic of being distinguished according to all the variety of numbers, and of separating the things that participate in them; from those among the supra-cosmic the characteristic of each being assimilated to their own paradigms; from those which are simultaneously above the cosmos and in the cosmos the characteristic of each being such as to collect all those things which are in a pluralised state into the aggregates proper to each; and from those in the cosmos the characteristic of being unseparated from the nature dependent upon them and the characteristic of, with this nature, bringing to completion the generation of composite entities. From each level of forms, then, there should come some characteristic to the forms in the sense-realm, these being the ultimate limits of the chain of forms.

You will not find anything else customarily said about these, I persuade myself, except these things which we have said, such as that every sensible form requires another base and receptacle than itself, that each one is in many participant entities, and if they are eternal it is in the sense that the participants take their principle of order from one source and are directed towards one source in respect of their primary participation; and that each of them has come into being through assimilation to the transcendent Forms, and has come into being in accordance with those assimilations; that every individual form is that

317

which is immediately followed by the individual in the truest sense,
when it has proceeded down to the ultimate material division; that each
one brings to completion its substrate nature, which exists potentially,
and brings it to actuality by its presence; that every Form is a whole
experiencing as an attribute the One within it but not being that One,
but rather containing a multiplicity of essences and powers; that everything possesses some necessarily unknowable divine token, by reason
of which each thing has been allotted a different rank and place and circuit in the universe according to a particular number and shape (for
each of these things has been allotted to them by the creative agency in
virtue of a certain secret kinship towards the gods); that everything is
always the same in the same state in the cosmos and that the universe
never experiences deficiency, but that even when it has its substantiation in things of generation, yet it exists without generation.

These things, then, which are usually attributed to the forms which
go to make up the cosmos, are bestowed upon them, as has been said,
971 from all the formative realms; and we would not be able to find anything else generally said about these things by those who have looked
into things of this nature; so that it is with reason that we trace back
each thing to its proper first principle, rising from the lowest level to
the primary ones. Thus many, then, are the orders of forms, to speak
generally; and on either side of each of these there is, above them, on
the one hand, the intelligible wholeness and the monad of Being, and
below them, both the primary substrate, which is the image of that
wholeness there, and that which bears the lowest of all imprints of
being.

*"And yet Socrates," said Parmenides, "these difficulties and many more
besides are inevitably involved in the forms if these ideas belong to real
things and one is going to distinguish each form as a thing just by itself."*
(134e-135a)

It is in a thoroughly admirable way that Parmenides has by means of
these problems led the argument up from the realm of sense to the first
manifestation of the Forms, and through the pretext of objections has
revealed many orders of forms, and has demonstrated, by going more
deeply into the exposition of reality, the order that governs them; so
necessarily he now ends by persuading Socrates not to rush carelessly
or without testing into the hypothesising of Forms, but to take his
course first through a great deal of dialectical exercise, in order that he
may become equal to solving the aforementioned problems and all
others concerning Forms, and to get straight the truth about the doctrine. And there is evidence of inspiration also in the way he takes up,
in what has been said, all the topics of controversy which have been

318

used by those thinkers who have subsequently tried to deride the theory of Ideas; for if one cares to examine both those objections which have been brought against the common element in individual things, and those arguments which make use of the "later-born" concepts, and those which will not go beyond reason-principles in Soul, and those which postulate them as being in Intellect, but make them inactive and 972 motionless, not having any power of creation or of assimilating to themselves those things which come to be from them—I at least am astonished that these people think that they on each occasion have something new to say in raising difficulties against this doctrine, since none of those arguments which are capable of raising a difficulty were neglected by Plato.[107]

But this is enough about that. To turn to the details of the text, Parmenides shows how it is possible to develop other problems which arise from what has been said. For the phrase "and besides these" shows the ready supply of problems available to those who wish to search for them. And he also demonstrates that those things that have been said on the pretext of raising difficulties are from another point of view true; for it is necessary, he says, that the Forms should possess all the characteristics that we have mentioned, both unknowability and the characteristic of not knowing anything of our affairs, and in general all the above-mentioned characteristics will be proper to some level of Forms; for it is not surprising if what is true of one is false when proposed for others. So then, the text not only sets out the difficulties (for he would have said, if he had wished simply to air difficulties, that these consequences must follow on the postulation of Forms), but also the truth about the Forms hidden in all these objections; for the Forms do not contain contradictions but always truths.

And when he says "if these ideas belong to real things," it is not the things of sense that he is calling "real things," as if claiming that it was of these that the Ideas were, but he is actually demonstrating that the Ideas are ranked among the true realities, and are not just names given to empty concepts; and in saying this he has revealed that these difficulties do not operate for those who wish to make the Forms subsequent to particulars or inherent in sensible objects; but it is precisely for those who wish to number the Ideas among the true realities that the argument is difficult and challenging to belief. And in adding the phrase "one is going to distinguish each form as a thing just by itself," he has made clear to us how those who postulate Forms differ from those who do not postulate them; for other people too say that there is

---

[107] Translating Latin nullo *neglecto* a Platone for οὐδενὸς παρακειμένου τῷ Π. of the Greek MSS. This may conceal παραλελειμμένου or something such.

an intellect prior to the cosmos, and call this same intellect God, but yet they deny the existence of Ideas;[108] for they do not admit that this In-
973 tellect has the causal principles of things in the cosmos distinguished within it, for instance the Forms of Man and Horse and Lion and those other things which are among mortal entities. So in this respect those who deny and those who postulate the Ideas differ from each other in so far as the one lot preserves distinct causal principles which are intellectual and motionless and divine, whereas the others declare that there is one thing only which is an unmultiple and motionless cause as being an object of striving; and what we declare is proper to the cause which is situated above the Intellect and intelligible number, this they attach to Intellect; in so far as they consider this thing to be primary they were correct, for the realm of reality must not be governed badly,[109] nor should multiplicity have dominion over reality, but the One; but in so far as they postulate that Intellect and the One are the same thing, they are not correct.

It is, then, a particular characteristic of the formative cause to be distinguished in respect of the multiplicity of true beings; and for this reason in the realm of first principles where we have the hidden and undistinguished level of being, we do not yet have Form,[110] and where we have first distinction, there we have the primary level of Forms, as for instance there is one form for the heavenly bodies and another for land animals, and where the division is into more individuals, there arise particular entities, and finally, as the formative creation proceeds, the last among creative forms have distinguished causes even for parts and for accidents; for the reason-principles in nature contain distinct causal principles even of an eye and a foot and a heart and a finger. So that at the highest level we have principles of the most general entities and at the bottom, principles even of parts, while at the middle rankings we have a situation which is analogous; for intellectual entities are not divided to the same extent as assimilative entities, nor are these divided in the same way as detached entities are, but in so far as they are between objects of sense and intellectual entities they are more divided than the latter, but are more unified than the former, and are more general than sensible entities, but more particular than intelligible entities.

The phrase "if one is going to distinguish," as we have said, means the same as if one were to postulate distinct causes, but not by pro-

---

[108] The Peripatetics.

[109] A reference, presumably, to οὐκ ἀγαθὸν πολυκοιρανίη, εἷς κοίρανος ἔστω (*Iliad* 2.204), quoted by Aristotle at *Met.* XII, 10.1076a4.

[110] For this doctrine, cf. Iambl. *In Philebum* fr. 4 Dillon = Damascius *In Phileb.* 105 (pp. 49-51 Westerink). For Iamblichus the Forms proper come into existence only in the Intellectual realm, not in the Intelligible.

974 pounding definitions; it indicates, rather, the postulating of a multiplicity of intelligible principles of the things of this realm; for this is proper to the study of the Ideas.

The phrase "each just by itself," as has been said often, indicates the simplicity and the immateriality and the purity of the Ideas; for each just by itself is so by being of itself and not of anything else, nor being called what it is called in any borrowed sense; the addition of "something" indicates its unitary quality and the fact that it enjoys a prior existence as a causal principle; for the word *something* is not used in the case of Forms as it is in the case of material and individual things, but as a symbol of their oneness and of delimitation; and in so far as the Form is partial, if one were to confront it with the One Being, as such it is reasonably termed "something."

> *"The result is that the hearer is in doubt and in two minds whether to question their existence, or to contend that, if they do exist, they must certainly be unknowable by our human nature." (135a)*

This also is said with marvellous aptness and relevance to our nature; for neither does the brightest and wisest of us have an absolutely undeviating knowledge of divine things (for Intellect alone knows the intelligible realm without any doubt whatever, whereas our level of being, in so far as it falls short of intellectual knowledge, to that extent is deprived of the clearest level of knowledge); nor, on the other hand, is the most undeveloped and "earth-born" of us entirely without any intuition of the formal cause; for what could such person refer to when sometimes he abuses the phenomenal world as being changeable if he did not have in himself some undeviating preconception (*prolēpsis*) of true reality? And between these two extremes there is the man who is in doubt, and he who is in two minds, and he who is inclined to deny the truth;[111] the man who is in doubt has on the whole his mind secure in the belief that the Forms exist, but he is cautious also in the face of opposing arguments; he who is in two minds is carried equally to either side, both towards their existence and towards their non-existence in arguments; he who is inclined to deny them is inclined more towards their non-existence, on the one hand, internally prompted towards their existence according to his undeviating intuition (*ennoia*), but on 975 the other hand, because of the forgetfulness which has been shed about him, being inclined to do away with their existence; for if, he says, they do not exist, they do not exist; whereas even if they exist, but are unknowable to us, he who postulates them is not worthy of attention; for

---

[111] Proclus derives three classes of person from the lemma, representing three degrees of uncertainty, ὁ ἀπορῶν, ὁ ἀμφισβητῶν, and ὁ ἀρνούμενος—this last class being derived from the ἄγνωστα of the lemma.

in claiming to support what is unknowable, he invalidates his own vote. See, then, how Parmenides admits the force of the aforementioned difficulties, and how he urges us to their solution; for there is some danger that we too might fall into these difficulties which he says those suffer who hear those troublesome arguments, and we might fall into doubt, and then be of two minds, and then completely reject this hypothesis, on the grounds that even if it is the case, it is quite useless to us, as being unknowable in itself. It has been shown, then, how all these things are true, and how what falsehood lies in them may meet with suitable correction.

"Moreover, there seems to be some weight in these objections, and as we were saying, it is extraordinarily difficult to convert the objector." (135a)

It has been previously stated absolutely, that he who approaches the study of these things without sufficient ability and preparation will end up making him who wishes to assert that the Ideas are unknowable more plausible than one who tries to defend their existence; for in all cases like is wont to attach itself to like. So then, what is dark to our eyes and appreciable only by philosophy is not going to become comprehensible to those who are inadequate of soul, but only to those souls who through natural virtue and outstanding care and power of enthusiasm have applied themselves worthily to the study of this subject; for it is not possible for the comprehension of intelligible things to arise in natures not suited to it, nor will it ever be the case that those things which have their being and their seat in pure Intellect will become manifest to those who have not purified their minds, if indeed it is true that in all cases like is comprehensible by like.

976 *"Only a man of exceptional gifts will be able to see that a genus, or essence, just by itself, does exist in each case; and it will require someone still more remarkable to discover it and to instruct another who has thoroughly examined all these difficulties."* (135ab)

He teaches us again in this passage who is the most suitable auditor of these discourses, calling him a man in no casual sense but with the idea that he should be so called from his form of life, exhibiting a great deal of stoutheartedness[112] and lofty spirit; for anyone who is proposing to acquire some comprehension of the gods should have nothing in his thoughts which is small or lowly; and in calling him one of exceptional gifts, he wishes to indicate that he should be adorned with all the qualities of a philosophic nature, and in receipt of many contributions from his nature to the intellectual comprehension of things divine. And

---

[112] There seems to be a word-play intended here between *andra* and *(h)adron*.

following on this he reminds us again who should be the instructor in
knowledge on this subect, that he should be productive and inventive
in respect of his teaching; for some people make sufficient progress so
as to be sufficient for themselves, but others are able to stimulate others
also to a memory of the truth of things; and for this reason also he has
called this person "still more remarkable"; for such a person is analogous to Resource, and the learner to Poverty, and between the two of
them is Eros, who joins the less complete to the more complete.[113]
Then, third after these two things, he informs us what is the end of this
teaching, that the learner and receiver of this knowledge should sufficiently have sorted out all the classes of beings, and contemplated with
thorough accuracy the various causes of things whence they take their
start—how many ranks of them there are, how they come to be in each
level of being, how they are participated in, how they govern all
things—and in a word, all such questions which we have been discussing up to this.

But so much for that. As regards the details of the text, the expression "having thoroughly examined" indicates the unconfused and pure
intellectual apprehension of each of these truths; for thorough examination is a type of defining clarification of the properties of each thing.
977 The expression "some genus of each thing" indicates the primary
causal principle of each chain of being which preexists on the divine
level; for the Form, although being a Form in relation to some other
individual in that realm, is a genus, as being more general than the
forms in the sense-realm, and as encompassing those which are not
completely similar in form to each other; for how could the man on
earth be similar in form to that in the heavens or that which had been
allotted its being in some other element of the universe?

[113] An "ethical" allegorisation of the myth of Poros and Penia in Plato's *Symposium*,
203bff.

BOOK V

◻

INTRODUCTION

◻ ◻ ◻

BOOK V covers *Parm.* 135b3 (συγχωρῶ σοι) to 137b6 (ἡ ἐκείνου ἀπό-
κρισις), less than half the length of Book IV both in terms of text and
commentary, and similar in size to Book III. It comprises the transition
passage to the second part of the dialogue, in which Parmenides reas-
serts the necessity of postulating the existence of Forms, but asserts the
complementary necessity of submitting oneself to proper training in
dialectic in order to avoid the errors and confusion into which the
youthful Socrates has fallen. The most remarkable feature of Proclus'
commentary on this section is his attempt to exercise Parmenides' dialectic method on a number of subjects other than the One (997–1017).

The first section of the Book may be taken as covering 135b3–d6,
running from 977.5 to 992.28. It is divided into five lemmata. We begin
with Socrates' admirable welcoming of the maieutic process of refutation to which Parmenides has subjected him. Parmenides' next remark
(135bc) is for Proclus sure evidence that this is how the preceding arguments are to be taken. The second lemma (978.21–983.18) is taken
up with showing how, if one refuses to admit the existence of Forms,
"one will have no direction in which to turn his *dianoia*"—which Proclus chooses to take in the technical sense of "discursive intellect,"
being that faculty properly concerned with logical reasoning—definition, demonstration, and division. "If we are to discover the definition
which will serve as the beginning of a demonstration, the definition
must be of an entity of such a sort as to comprehend everything more
particular than itself. Such things are the forms in us, and not those inherent in particulars." (981.24ff.)

His praise of Analysis (*analytikē*) in this connection (982.21ff.) is of
some interest, as being a Neoplatonic statement of Aristotelian doctrine: "Analysis is the complement to Demonstration, inasmuch as it
leads us to analyse effects into their causes; and to Definition, inasmuch
as it proceeds from the particular to the universal." For Aristotle, *analytikē* is an instrument for analysing particulars into their basic elements; for Proclus, its purpose is to separate off the universal.

324

He takes pains to distance Plato from Aristotle also a little further down, at 984.24ff. Parmenides' dialectic must be distinguished firmly from Aristotelian "epicheirematic," as described, for instance, in *Topics* VIII, 14. The awkward thing is that Aristotle does seem, in that chapter, to be describing very much the method of the Platonic Parmenides:

> For training and practice in this kind of argument one should, in the first place, accustom oneself to converting arguments (ἀντι-στρέφειν); for thus we shall be better provided for treating the subject under discussion and obtain by a quick method a thorough knowledge of a number of arguments. For conversion is *the reversing of the conclusion*, together with the other questions raised, and the demolition of one of the points conceded; for of necessity, if the conclusion is not true, one of the premises must be demolished, since it was owing to the assumption of all of them that the conclusion necessarily followed. In dealing with any thesis, we must examine the arguments both for and against, and having discovered it, we must immediately seek the solution, for the result will be that we shall have trained ourselves at the same time both for question and for answer.

Since this is rather what Parmenides says he is going to do in the dialogue, and since it was believed at least until the end of the Middle Platonic period that that is what Plato intended, it is important for Proclus to reject the idea here. Epicheirematic, he says, is concerned with the realm of opinion, while the purpose of this method is the definition of Forms.

This leads him (985.11ff.) to raise the problem of the definition of a Form. Strictly speaking, Forms are not definable. Proclus relies here on that passage of the Seventh Letter (342ad) which declares that it is impossible for a name or a definition to comprehend adequately the essence of a Form—that is to say, Proclus specifies, Forms on the intelligible or intellectual levels. Forms at the level of Soul, and forms-in-matter, are definable. Dialectic defines, by diaeresis, these images of Forms, but the Forms themselves it can only contemplate.

On the other hand (986.36ff.), we can produce definitions of things, such as evils and artificial objects, of which there are no Forms (like the shuttle of the *Cratylus*), since our mind has the faculty of putting these concepts together on the basis of the *logoi* of positive and natural entities which it contains.

In the final lemma of this section (988.6-992.28), Proclus once again finds it necessary to refute the suggestion that the "exercise" which Parmenides recommends to Socrates at 135d4 is the epicheirematic method of the Peripatetics, recommended by Aristotle in the *Topics*. To do this, he repeats what he said in the prefatory portion of the Commentary (Book I, 653.3ff.); there are three processes of dialectic—the cathartic, used to purge Sophists and others of their "double ignorance," their conceit of knowledge; the recollective, opposite to the first, which rouses suitable candidates to the *anamnēsis* of true reality; and thirdly, a mixture of the two. Proclus picks out the *Lysis* as a particularly good example of this latter type of γυμνασία. Once again, the difference from Aristotle's epicheirematic lies in the assumption of Forms, the recollection of which one is trying to awaken in the interlocutor.

However, a difficulty has been raised (991.5ff.) as to whether this exercise can be identified with Platonic dialectic. After all, this is here described as ἀδολεσχία, and suitable to the young, whereas dialectic, in the *Philebus* (58d), and in *Republic* VII (537c-e) is spoken of as the highest intellectual activity, and not to be communicated to the young. But there is no real problem here, says Proclus; the reference to "idle talk" is ironic, and Socrates is not just *any* young man—young men as envisaged in *Republic* VII might be of uneven quality (a strange point to make, perhaps, since they would all be duly selected Guardians!).

The second main section of the Book may be taken as covering the passage 135d7 to 136e4, which contains Parmenides' description of his method. The commentary on this runs from 992.32 to 1026.39 and is divided into 13 lemmata, most of which, however, are quite short. The main feature of the section is Proclus' attempt to illustrate Parmenides' method (997.16-1007.34).

Proclus begins with a recapitulation of the plan of the dialogue, and a reminder that this sort of dialectical exercise is a necessary tool for the comprehension of the metaphysical truths of the second half. In the process, he shows (993.38ff.) that he understands dialectic already in its "Hegelian" sense, as being not concerned with argument or refutation, but rather with the logical working out of systems of opposition or "contradiction" in the world, which leads to a synthesis on a higher level. But of course we must remember that Hegel knew his Proclus.

The transfer of the subject matter from the physical realm to the intelligible is for Proclus a sure indication of the superiority of this method to any Aristotelian imitations. It is a small bother to him (995.26ff.) that Parmenides describes the method as a "wandering" (πλάνη, 135e1), but he takes this to refer to the dialectical procession from opposites to opposites which is characteristic of the method.

He begins his exposition of the method by commending the observation of "the older authorities" (οἱ πρεσβύτεροι)—possibly Middle Platonists—that Plato here brings to completion the writings of both

Parmenides and Zeno, that is, Parmenides' Poem and the *Logoi* of Zeno (to something purporting to be which, as we have seen, Proclus seems to have had access). At present it is the latter with which we are concerned. Parmenides here points out that Zeno only considers what follows and what does not follow if something exists or is the case; to get a complete picture of reality, however, we must also consider what follows (and does not follow) if it is *not* the case.

What is the importance of this? Proclus explains (998.19ff.):

> If, for instance, I were to postulate that soul exists, and then were to show that the consequence is that motion exists, and then, saying, "Let us suppose that soul does not exist," I were to demonstrate that motion no longer existed, then it will be through soul's existence that motion exists. It will therefore be the first principle and cause of motion. If, on the other hand, motion were to occur with soul not existing, then it would be plain that motion does not derive from soul.

In other words, to gain a full understanding of something's role in the universe, and thus of its essence, we must contemplate the results of its non-existence as well as of its existence. The only problem with this, as he goes on to point out (999.13ff.), is that one might wonder how anything could *follow* from the non-existence of something. Here Proclus seems to cause himself unnecessary trouble by launching into a distinction of modes and degrees of "not-being," taken from the *Sophist* (258aff.), and asserting that Parmenides means, not the *absolute* non-existence of something, but merely its *relative* non-existence. But this seems misplaced ingenuity. Parmenides surely is intending to say, "What would the world look like if *x* were *not* there?" with no reservations as to the type of non-existence involved. At any rate, we get a rapid survey of the various meanings of "not-being," up to 1000.33.

Proclus then turns to examine the logical form of Parmenides' method. Any initial hypothesis, he says, gives rise to two others, and each of these two in turn to three, thus producing a set of six. Proclus means by a simple hypothesis one that simply states a predicate of a subject (τίνι τί συμβαίνει, 1001.3). The two propositions arising from this postulate, respectively, that it is and that it is not the case, and the three hypotheses arising from each of these state what is true, not true, and both true and not true, of the subject if it exists, and again if it does not exist.

But this is not the end of the process. Each of these six hypotheses is quadrupled, by reason of the variety of possible relationships of the predicate to the subject. For we must consider what is true of a subject if it exists, not only in relation to itself, but in relation to others, and what is true of the others, in relation not only to themselves, but also to it. We get thus a set of twenty-four hypotheses in relation to any concept we propose to ourselves for examination.

To demonstrate the method in action, Proclus volunteers to take us through the postulation of the existence of Soul (1004.8-1006.17). He claims for the method that it is superior to the four traditional procedures of logic—definition, division, demonstration, and analysis—in that it comprehends all of them, and can be used for any of the purposes for which they can be used. In the case of the Soul, he sets out to provide, through the method, both a definition of it and an account of its power in the world. He does this, it seems, by hypothesising the various relationships (e.g. "If Soul exists, what is true of 'the others'—in this case, bodies—in relation to it?"), and then, by introspection, coming up with a series of predicates resulting from this, e.g. "being vivified by it," "being preserved and held together through it," "being in general dependent on it."

What sort of validity, one wonders, is this procedure meant to have? Proclus seems to think that if you pose the right questions in the right order (that is, according to this twenty-four part scheme), all the relevant truths will emerge. Having gone through the method, at any rate, he declares (1006.17ff.):

> . . . we conclude from these arguments that Soul is the cause of life and motion and interaction for bodies, and in general of their existence and preservation. For on the assumption that Soul exists these things follow, and in the case of its non-existence the negation of these follows. Only, then, from Soul and through Soul are these qualities present to bodies. This is the purpose of the whole method, to discover the properties of a thing, and of what things it is the cause both to itself and to others.

But in what sense do these various propositions "follow"? Not in any strictly logical sense, surely. If anything, they seem to follow intuitively from the positing of each hypothesis. But then this, after all, is how Platonic diaeresis operates. Intuition tells one how a given concept is to be divided, in order to reach the definition that one wants. That, however, does not make this process any more respectable, from an Aristotelian, or a modern, viewpoint.

Proclus, on the other hand, is entirely satisfied with it. He regards Aristotle as having developed his syllogistic method in imitation of this system (1007.10-11), but feels that this "Parmenidean" system "is far more complete, setting out as it does by the process of division all the modes through which one must proceed if one proposes to exercise one's intellect on each aspect of Being."

In the next four lemmata (1008.4–1017.39), Proclus takes us through the analysis of a series of concepts by means of the method, though in an abbreviated form, comprising eight hypotheses instead of twenty-four. He begins with Zeno's own hypothesis. "That there are many," and proceeds through Likeness and Unlikeness, Motion and Rest, Generation and Corruption, following Parmenides' suggestions in 136b. In each case, he feels that a true understanding of the nature and power of each entity is arrived at by this procedure. In the case of Generation and Corruption, however, he feels the need first to explain their presence in the world of Forms (1011.33ff.). He does this only by relating them respectively to Being and Not-Being—which latter, as we learn from the *Sophist* (258a), is no less real than Being. It is the property of Generation, we learn through the method, "to rouse things to existence," and of Corruption "to lead them away from existence" (1013.14–16).

The next lemma (136b6–c5) introduces the possibility of considering not only whether a given entity exists, but whether it possesses a given attributes, e.g. whether the soul is immortal. Proclus now proceeds to show that the method can tackle this form of proposition just as well (1014.7ff.), though in fact the conclusions do not differ greatly from the postulation that Soul exists. He ends his exercise of the Parmenidean dialectic by running through the twenty-four modes in the case of the proposition "that Providence exists" (1016.3– 1017.33). Once again, one gets the impression that he has simply put to himself the various hypotheses—e.g. "If Providence exists, what follows for other things, in relation to themselves?"—and finds that he can only think, "They do not suffer anything at each other's hands randomly," "They do not suffer injustice from any quarter," and that exhausts his intuitions on the subject; therefore, that is what follows. He does not summarize his findings as regards Providence, but we might hazard a conclusion as follows: "Providence is the cause of the preservation and orderly interrelationships of all things," or something to that effect.

In the next lemma, at 1020.31ff., he makes the remarkable statement: "A sign of the difficulty involved in using this method is the fact that none of those who followed Plato set out any of their own works in this form (we leave aside Ammikartos, whoever he was). It is for this reason that we have tried above to employ it by using a number of examples." One might propose other reasons why no one ever made use of the method, but it is a most interesting testimony that Proclus gives here to its total neglect by Plato's successors. He is the first since Plato himself to attempt to use it (as for Ammikartos, we can only echo Proclus' dismissal of him; he is unknown to history).

The rest of this section of the book (up to 1026.39) is occupied with

329

"ethical" interpretation of the relationship between Parmenides, Zeno, and Socrates, and "physical" interpretation of their relations as cosmic principles, as already set out in the prefatory section of Book I. An example, perhaps, will suffice, in the form of Proclus' opening comments on the lemma 136d4–6 concerning Zeno's "laughter" (1021.6ff.):

> Even so among the gods the third joins himself to the second, and strives for fulfillment from him, whereas the second, inasmuch as he is situated in the first, draws forth the benefactions deriving from him upon all [all this a description of the relations between the Chaldaean triad of πατήρ, δύναμις and νοῦς]. It is remarkable also to note in this passage that, when there was question of a smile [130a6], they both smiled, Zeno and the great Parmenides, whereas here, when there is talk no longer of smiling, only Zeno laughs, Parmenides remaining in his state of calm. . . . The smile, then, represents the invisible and hidden activity of the divine, whereas laughter is more perceptible than smiling. So the one represents the permanent and quiescent and hidden god, the other a god who remains above, but is already in the process of proceeding forth and becoming manifest.

We have already learned in Book I that Parmenides is the ἕν ὄν, or monad of the noetic world, while Zeno is his ζωή, or dynamic element, and this passage for Proclus is further confirmation of the correctness of that interpretation.

The third section of the Book (1026.40:1038.39) covers *Parm.* 136e5–137b8, the final portion of the first part of the *Parmenides*, in which Parmenides, after some modest demurral, agrees to give a demonstration of his method, on his own hypothesis, "That there is a One."

Proclus' exegesis is mainly on the allegorical level, explaining Parmenides' hesitation as the unwillingness of the One Being to descend from the level of pure intuitive thought to that of discursive reasoning. Parmenides quoting of Ibycus' comparison of himself to an old warhorse (fr. 2 Bergk) naturally puts Proclus in mind of the charioteer and pair of the *Phaedrus* myth (1029.5ff.). Parmenides does descend, however, because the higher principles are always ready to extend their benefits to those lower entities which are ready to receive them.

We may note, however, in the midst of all this, an interesting *aporia* (ultimately solved, as so often, by Syrianus) as to how Parmenides can call the postulation of the One "my own hypothesis," when what he has actually hypothesised in his poem was One Being. Some suggested that this is just another instance of Plato "correcting" the doctrine of a predecessor, as he does that of Gorgias or Protagoras. In what seems to be a second view (1033.10ff.), though it is presented as a continuation of the first, it is suggested that Parmenides may have postulated a One above Being in "unwritten discourses," which he communicated to Zeno, while he went no higher than Being in his Poem. Syrianus, however, manages to reconcile the Poem to the dialogue by arguing that the postulation of One Being naturally leads to the postulation of the One above Being, which is itself "non-hypothesised" (1034.5ff.):

> The only thing, then, which is non-hypothesised is the One, so that whatever is hypothesised is something else, and not the One, but he ascends from this to the One, as from an hypothesis to the non-hypothesised. One might thus properly admire the whole structure of Parmenides' discourse here; for if on the one hand he had assumed as an hypothesis that which was non-hypothesised, and taken what has no first principle as proceeding from one, then he would not have been following his method, which calls in every case for hypothesising something and seeing what follows from it; or, on the other hand, if he assumed what was not the non-hypothesised, but something more or less remote from the One, it would not have been easy for him to make the transition to it, nor would he have been able to reveal to us the cause of Being naturally and without strain.

This is a typically Syrianic solution to a not very real problem, to which the correct answer is presumably the first of the three mentioned above, but it is a useful example of the Neoplatonist commentators' approach to their subject matter.

The remaining portion of the book comprises an introductory discussion of why there is a plurality of hypotheses (1034.37ff.), which will be taken up again in Book VI, and a little more allegorising of the characters, which we need not dwell on further—except to note the interesting use made of the exchange between Hera and Iris in Book XXIV of the *Iliad* in order to illustrate the way in which lower entities particularise the more generic intellections of higher entities, even as Aristoteles has particularised to himself the general request of Parmenides to have the youngest present as his interlocutor (1139.19ff.). And so we pass on to the First Hypothesis itself.

COMMENTARY

□ □ □

977   *"I agree with you, Parmenides," said Socrates, "what you are saying is
very much to my mind."* (135b)

That very thing which was said in the *Gorgias* (458a) is here also, as
it seems, well demonstrated by Socrates in his actions; for there he says,
"The unexamined life is not a good thing for those who are not good,
so that I would be no more displeased to be refuted, if I were to say
something incorrect, than I would be ready to refute another." So then
having practised this habit from boyhood, it is obvious here also that
he welcomes refutation, and so far is he from being annoyed at it that
he actually says that this has all come about "to his mind." For even as
those who are contentious take arguments which refute them "to
heart," even so those who are of philosophic nature regard the problems directed at themselves as being "to their mind." And indeed it is
clear that Parmenides is doing this very thing which Plato himself in his
Letters (VII, 340bc) urges us to do, to demonstrate to those who are
pursuing some subject of study the difficulty that surrounds it and to
exaggerate remarkably the unpleasantness attendant upon that, in order that he who is apt for the comprehension of such a subject of study
should be shown to be more enthusiastic for participation in it, while
he who is unsuited should be revealed as such, through his shrinking
back from the threatened unpleasantness and becoming a fugitive from
it. This then is what Parmenides has done, in intimidating Socrates
with the problems involved in the theory of Forms, and showing him
978 that it requires much greater power to resolve them than he is in command of at present. As for Socrates, he marvels at the problems, and
gathering his mind together within him he will thus try to "join" with
Parmenides "in the ecstasy" (*Phaedr.* 234d) of contemplating divine
things; wherefore Parmenides now extends some help to him for the
comprehension of intellectual and scientific understanding of things divine.

*"But on the other hand," said Parmenides, "if, in view of all these diffi-
culties and others like them, Socrates, a man refuses to admit that Forms*

332

of things exist or to distinguish a definite Form in every case, he will have no direction in which to turn his thought, so long as he will not allow that each thing has a character which is always the same; and in so doing he will completely destroy the significance of all discourse." (135bc)

He reminds us here most concisely and thoroughly scientifically that Forms of things in fact exist. For if the knowledge proper to the discursive and intuitive intellect is superior to that derived from sense-perception, then necessarily the objects of the discursive and intuitive intellect are more divine than those things apprehended by the senses. For the objects of knowledge must have the same relation to each other as the organs coordinate with them. Discursive and intuitive intellect, then, contemplate the transcendent—immaterial Forms and those things that are universal and "in themselves"—while sense-perception deals with individuals, and with forms not separate from their substrate. The objects of the vision, therefore, of discursive and intuitive intellect must be more divine and eternal. The universal, after all, is prior to the particular, and the immaterial to the material. Whence, then, would the discursive intellect derive these? They are not always present in us on an actualised level; but necessarily what is actualised must precede what is potential both in the sphere of cognition and of existence. So then the Forms exist somewhere else, prior to us, in the realm of divine and transcendent entities, and it is from these that the forms in us are brought to completion; for if these did not exist, neither would the forms in us, nor can what is complete come from what is incomplete. From what source, then, does completion come to the forms in us? Certainly not from the realm of sense-perception, which is inferior to them. It is not right for the better to owe its creation or perfection to the worse. And whence derives the multiplicity of these forms in the multiplicity of souls? In all cases, after all, one must assume prior to a multiplicity a unity from which it derives. Even as the multiplicity of sense-objects could not have derived from anything but a single source, which is superior to the sense-objects and which produced the common element in the individual particulars, so neither would the forms in souls have come into being, since they too are many. For the Form of Justice and each of the others are present in each individual soul. These, being many, have need of a unity to give them existence, which will be on a superior level to the psychic, even as that what created the objects of sense is on a higher level than that of sense-perception, comprehending as it does unitarily all their diversity. And how can we avoid the necessity of there being prior to the self-moved forms the unmoved Form? For even as externally moved entities are outranked by self-moved reason-principles and the entities which

979

333

constantly[1] generate what is externally moved, in the same way presumably, there are established, above the self-moved, those entities which are unmoved and conduct their activities in eternity, since everywhere the stationary cause must precede the moving one. If then there are forms which are in the multiplicity of souls, there must, far more so, be prior to these ones intellectual Forms, prior to the self-moved the unmoved, prior to the pluralised the monadic, prior to the imperfect the perfect, and prior to the potential the actualised. So if the intellectual Forms were to cease to exist, the forms in the soul would no longer exist either; for nowhere does Nature begin from the imper-
980 fect and the multiple, nor is it proper for multiplicity not to exist in reference to monads, nor things imperfect to what is perfect, nor things in motion to what is motionless.

If, then, there is no such thing as forms-in-soul, "one will have no direction in which to turn ones thought (*dianoia*),"[2] as Parmenides says; for imagination and sense-perception must direct themselves to objects on their own level. With what level of reality, then, shall we say that the discursive intellect concerns itself? Of what things will there be discursive knowledge within us, if forms on this level are done away with? We will certainly not be contemplating derived concepts, for these are actually less respectable than sense-objects and the common qualities inherent in them. How then could it be that the objects of knowledge coordinate with the discursive intellect should be inferior to those things known by the senses? The only alternative would be that we know nothing else but objects of sense-perception. Whence, then, would logical proofs derive their validity? For logical proofs depend on these entities, which are also the causes of the principles of demonstration and are prior in nature and not relative to us, and more honourable than what is demonstrated by means of them. But the entities on which proofs are based are universal, not particular; the universal, then, is prior and more causative and more honourable than the particular. Thus it comes about, I suppose, that even those who do not believe in the Forms, being constrained by the force of truth, pay honour in their writings on Demonstration[3] to the universal and term it more divine than the particular; for it is this that makes logical proofs such as they declare them to be.

And whence will definitions derive—for a definition is constructed

---

[1] Reading ἀεὶ for εἴδη (West).

[2] Proclus treats this use of διάνοια as being a technical term to denote "discursive intellect," as opposed to νοῦς, "intuitive intellect." It is so translated, therefore, in what follows.

[3] Cf. Aristotle *An. Post.* I, 11.77a5ff., though the universal is not there described as θειότερον.

in virtue of the reason-principles in the soul? It is the common element in particulars that we define, having first within ourselves the Form, not the image, present in them. If, then, definition is the beginning of demonstration, there must be some other definition prior to this of the many forms and really-existent reason-principles in souls; for since the Form of Justice exists in each soul, as we have said, it is plain that instances of justice in us are manifold, but have something in common, which circumstance enables each soul, through being acquainted with the reason-principle of Justice within itself, to see equally that present in all others. If it possesses some common element, it is this common element that we define by calling it the "what it is," and this is the beginning of demonstration, not the materialised and, as it were, mortal entity inherent (in the particular). In demonstrations and definitions the particular must be subordinate to the universal and the definition. Definitions of common features in particular do not take in the particulars as a whole. How, for instance, is the whole of Socrates comprehended by the definition "rational mortal animal," when there exist in him other elements also which make up his so-called 'personal quality'?[4] The reason-principle of Man in us comprehends the whole of each particular, for the particular comprehends unitarily all those potencies which are seen as being involved in the individuals. In the case of "animal" likewise, the instance of it in particulars is less comprehensive than the particulars themselves or the species; for it does not have in actualised form all the differentiae, but only potentially, wherefore it becomes a sort of "matter" to the specificatory differentiae that superimpose themselves upon it. The "animal" inherent in us is greater and more comprehensive than "man," for it contains in unified form all the differentiae, not potentially, like the concept, but actualised. If we are, then, to discover the definition which will serve as the beginning of a demonstration, the definition must be of an entity of such a sort as to comprehend everything more particular than itself.

Such things are the forms in us, and not those inherent in particulars. Therefore, if these are abolished, definition will no longer be possible. So the science of definition will disappear, along with that of demonstration, departing from the range of human thought. Furthermore, following on these, the science of division will become a mere name; for divisions do nothing other than distinguish the many from the one, and separate off those things preexisting in a unified manner in the whole into their proper differentiae, not adding the differentiae from without, but viewing them as being within, in the genera themselves, dividing off the species from one another. Where, then, would be the

981

982

4 Ἰδίως ποιόν, an originally Stoic term

task of this science, if really-existent forms were not present in us? For to identify its business as being with these derived concepts is the approach of men who have no awareness whatever of its power. For it is proper to a division based on opinion to divide derived concepts, but to intellectual and scientific division to study the really-existent differentiae of the reason-principles in the soul, to unfold their unified potencies, and to see the more particular arising out of the more general. Far more, then, than the sciences of definition and demonstration would this science be totally without substance, if souls do not possess really-existent reason-principles. For Definition is a more august and sovereign art than Demonstration, and Division in turn than Definition. Division gives to Definition its first principles, but not vice versa. And since Demonstration does not permit itself to fool about[5] with derived concepts, Definition and Division are certainly not going to take as their subject matter such objects, and objects yet more worthless. We will then be abolishing the whole of Dialectic if we do not admit the existence of really-existent reason-principles in souls; for the ability to discuss those things which remain always the same employs these methods, since Analysis also should be included among these arts. For it serves as complement to Demonstration, inasmuch as it leads us to analyse effects into their causes; and to Definition, inasmuch as it proceeds from the composite to the more simple; and to Division, inasmuch as it proceeds from the particular to the universal (in so many ways is Analysis implicated with these other arts); so that if these were abolished, it too would suffer the same fate.

If, then, the Forms do not exist, neither will the reason-principles of things within us; and if the reason-principles of things within us do not exist, then neither will the dialectical methods by which we come to know true reality, nor "will we have any direction in which to turn our thought." For it is this faculty of the soul in particular, in its desire for the cause of things, that takes refuge with the Forms and the monads which generate the multiplicities of things, while Opinion is content 983 with derived concepts, such as are inherent in particulars. How, then, will it give an account of the causes of these things, and towards what first principles will it direct its theorising? For the true causes of existents are paradigmatic and creative and final,[6] and if the Forms did not exist, it would not be possible that paradigms could exist; for these Forms are the most powerful class of paradigms. Nor could there be a god who creates the contents of the cosmos; for it is the Forms which possess the creative capacity and the causal principles of all that comes into being. Nor could there be a final cause, for the final cause of some-

---

[5] Ἀθύρειν, perhaps a *vox Platonica* for Proclus; cf. *Laws* VII, 796b.
[6] Reading τελικὰ for τέλεια καὶ, in view of line 8 τελικὸν αἴτιον (West.).

336

thing's existence reveals the creative principle between that which exists for the sake of something and the thing itself, according to which the things which exist in reference to that thing[7] attain their proper end. It would not, then, be possible to give the reasons why each thing came to be what it is.

So then, he who does not accept this theory has succeeded in abolishing at one sweep from the sphere of existents, along with the paradigms, the demiurgic cause also, and has rendered the final cause imperfect; for he makes it the end of motion, but not of the existence of all things.

"But that consequence I think you perceive only too well." "Quite right," he said. "What are you going to do about philosophy, then? Where will you turn while the answers to these questions remain unknown?" "I can see no way out at the present moment." (135c)

He had just provided the first piece of assistance to Socrates after the confusion induced by the posing of problems, in the form of the concisest and truest demonstration of the theory of Forms, of which Parmenides says that Socrates acquired a grasp even before the presentation of his own arguments, but imperfectly; for "perceive" is the term proper to the lowest and most imperfect form of knowledge. And indeed it would not be likely that, if he did completely comprehend the existence of the Forms, he would still be disturbed by these problems. Now he provides a second piece of assistance, by sketching to him the procedure by which he can add what is lacking, and acquire a complete grasp of the theory of Forms. For let us postulate that the Forms exist. But it has been shown that, if they are knowable by us, they do not 984 exist. How then can we philosophize about them as existing, when knowledge of them cannot arise in us, as the argument presenting the problems showed? In face of this Socrates was plunged into profound bafflement. But Parmenides has discovered a second piece of assistance for him, to which he exhorts Socrates in a fatherly and solicitous spirit, that by making up what is lacking in his preparation, he may stand revealed as a worthy contemplator of the Forms.

"That is because you are undertaking to define 'beautiful', 'just', 'good', and each one of the Forms too soon, before you have had a preliminary training. I noticed that the other day when I heard you talking here with Aristotle." (135cd).

In point of good natural parts and enthusiasm Parmenides finds no need to correct any deficiency in Socrates from the proper measure; it is in respect of experience alone that he deems him deficient, for which

---

[7] Reading δι'αὐτὸ for δι'αὐτοῦ (line 10), and πρὸς αὐτὸ for πρὸς αὐτὰ (line 11) (West).

reason he urges him to become more widely skilled through extensive practice of dialectic and following out the consequences of the various hypotheses, and only then, thus fortified, to turn to the study of the Forms. For the problems that were baffling him now are easily soluble by those who are exercised in dialectic.

This, indeed, is the whole purpose of the discourse that follows. This exercise is not to be considered the sort of thing it is customary to call "the argumentative method."[8] That relates to opinion, whereas this, he says, despises the opinion of the many; it means nothing to the many and is for this reason termed by them "idle talk." The former presents many ways of dealing with one proposition, on the basis of which we can either confirm or refute what is proposed to us, making use of opinion; the latter, on the other hand, presents to us the same method applied to many different propositions, which conducts an examination of opposite statements,[9] . . . or, in other words, secures the confirmation or refutation of one of a pair of conflicting propositions. So the latter differs from the former and is so much the superior to it, as it 985 uses, from the outset, more noble methods than it for the achievement of its proper task, that is to say, divisions and definitions and demonstrations. If, then, we are trained in this method, there is good hope of our acquiring a genuine grasp of the theory of Forms, since we will have become able to articulate hidden confusions in concepts about them, and to solve apparent problems, and to demonstrate propositions hitherto unknown; but before we master this discipline, we will not be able with knowledge to define each of the Forms.

And how, someone might ask, is it possible to define the Forms? For what is simple and partless does not admit of varied and composite description. Everything that is definable is in some way an object of knowledge. But in no case is a Form an object of knowledge. Plato himself in his Letters (VII, 342c) has shown that the Form of Circle is made known to us neither by the name nor by the representation of it, nor by definition, nor by demonstration, but by direct intuition. Indeed the term 'define' here, as previously, indicates not the making of defining statements about the Forms, but states that each of them exists independently by itself, separate from all others, and distinct from its participants. But if, nevertheless, we are to enquire into this question by itself, whether or not it is possible to define the Forms, as for instance the Form of Beauty or of Justice, the situation being that, on the basis of what he says in the Letters (ibid. 342d), it is necessary to say that each Form is apprehensible by intellection alone, nor is it possible for

---

[8] Ἐπιχειρηματική, cf. Aristotle Topics VIII, 11.162a 16 and 14.163a 37ff; De Mem. 451a19.
[9] There seems to be a lacuna after ἐξεταστικήν.

either a name or a definition to comprehend it adequately, while on the basis of the fact that dialectic concerns itself with the Forms, we must say that divisions produce a kind of definition of Forms (for either of these activities is a part of this science of dialectic)—if, as I say, for these reasons we are to enquire into this by itself, whether one should say that the Forms are definable or not, we must say that Beauty itself and Justice itself and Goodness itself are not only in the intellect, but also in 986 souls and in objects of sense; and the former class are not definable, whereas the latter are. One must not, because of the addition of "itself," immediately assume that one is enquiring into the intelligible Forms in the stict sense. It is through falling into this error that certain theorists have postulated Ideas of evil things and of artificial objects because of the "shuttle itself" in the *Cratylus* and "impiety itself" in the *Euthyphro*, because all classes of Forms are given the epithet "itself" in order to distinguish them from particulars. Once this is sorted out, if I may briefly express my own opinion, the intellectual Forms, even though they be present in many particular things, are not definable by reason of their simplicity, both because they are apprehended by intuition and not by synthetic reasoning, and because all things subject to definition must participate in some common element in the role of substratum, which is something distinct from themselves. At the level of the divine Forms there is nothing like this (Being, similarly, as Timaeus says (50c), does not proceed into anything else). But, even if they are involved in some kind of procession from themselves, yet in a way such products are the Forms themselves, coming into being on a secondary level.

On the other hand, Forms at the level of the Soul and sense-perception are definable, and so in general are all those entities which come into existence according to a paradigmatic cause, and such as are said to participate in the Forms. But as for those primary Forms, which neither proceed forth according to[10] paradigms nor participate in them, they are not definable, but only apprehensible in intellect. It is the task of dialectic to contemplate those primary entities, employing itself pure conceptions, but in defining or dividing it must look to their images. For how could there be divisions of partless things, or definitions, in the real sense, of things incomposite? If, then, such knowledge is the purest element of intellect and thought, it is plain that it also uses pure intellections which relate to intelligibles, and methods of many types, with which it ties down the objects of contemplation which are in the levels of being secondary to those. In this way we can confirm the truth

---

[10] Reading κατὰ for ὡς, since to say that the primary Forms do not proceed forth as paradigms is contrary to Procline doctrine; cf. *PT* III, 14, p. 64.17-18 S-W (West.).

of the statements of Plato both about the primary Forms and about the methods of dialectic.

That is what I have to say about that subject. If there are various other things which we define of which Forms do not exist, such as ar-987 tificial objects, parts of things, and evil things, there is no cause for astonishment here; for it is by virtue of the fact that we have within us reason-principles of all natural entities and good things, that we know also such things as comprise (*qua* parts) the totality of whole entities, or imitate Nature, or arise as by-products of good things. According to the mode in which each of these things exist, so they are knowable and definable to us, and we discourse about them on the basis of the definitively established reason-principles within us. So there need be no occasion for astonishment in all this. The former point rather should be noted, and it is by reason of this that Socrates in his conversations always leads each discussion towards the question "What is X?" since he is anxious to study the reason-principles in the soul in his search for the Form of Beauty, in virtue of which all beautiful phenomena are beautiful, that is, the reason-principle of beautiful things preexisting in the soul, and Knowledge itself, which is truly existent in souls, not the intellectual, nor yet the intelligible, for it is not possible for his interlocutors to be raised to that essence, but on such occasions as he is seeking intelligible Beauty, he proceeds by inspiration rather than by midwifery or testing. For this reason it is not astonishing that whereas both the *Hippias* and the *Phaedrus* concern the subject of Beauty, the former seeks the essential Beauty in souls, whereas the latter seeks intellectual Beauty, from which all beautiful things derive their beauty; for the former is, after all, a dialogue of testing, and dialectical procedures are proper to those who concern themselves with forms in souls, that is, testings and refutations and definitions and demonstrations and divisions—synthetic and analytic procedures.

So much for that, then. But note how Plato in this passage shows how Socrates from his youth both worked to bring to perfection the less perfect than himself and associated himself with those who have a higher vision of reality. For he who was leading along the young Aristoteles and testing the reason-principles in him, now presents himself to Parmenides and demands to receive instruction from him, and he who had himself been instructing that one (Aristoteles) in definitions, now is ready himself to receive more complete rules of procedure from another.

988   *"Believe me, there is something beautiful and divine in your impulse for argument; but you must make an effort and exercise yourself more, while*

you are still young, in that activity which seems to be useless and which the many call "idle talk." Otherwise, the truth will escape you." (135d)

Some people are neither impelled towards nor are enthusiastic for the study of true reality, while others have already grasped perfection in knowledge. Others again have the impulse, but still need perfecting and testing and exercise in logic before the attainment of their goal. It is in this latter intermediate class that Socrates is situated. For this reason Parmenides acknowledges his impulse and calls it "divine" as being philosophical. For to disregard visible things and exercise one's imagination on incorporeal essence is something philosophical and divine. Everything divine is of such a nature as ⟨to transcend⟩[11] the realm of appearance, and to have its basis in immaterial intellections. He calls it "beautiful," on the other hand, as leading to the true Beauty, which is not to be found in the sphere of action, as the Stoics later thought, but in the activities of the intellect, and as being proper to true love. For the erotic form of life is most of all linked to Beauty and to the beauty in the gods themselves.

For these reasons he approves the impulse as "divine" and also as "beautiful," and reasonably so, as leading up to Intellect and the One (*qua* divine, it connects to the One; *qua* beautiful, to Intellect, which is the home of the primally beautiful), and as purifying the eye of the soul and rousing up the most divine part of it. He proffers the way through dialectic as infallible and most efficacious, being of like nature with reality and employing many powers for the apprehension of truth, imitating the Intellect and receiving its first principles from Intellect, extending itself nobly through well-ordered graduations towards Being and putting a stop to the error involved in sense-objects, testing each
989 thing by irrefutable methods until it arrives at the overview of the One and the Good.

So much may be said about the subject matter. However, since some commentators, relying on the word *exercise* would have it that this exercise is the dialectical method (*epicheirēmatikē*) of the Peripatetics (for Aristotle, in stating its usefulness (*Top.* I, 2.101a25ff.) says that it contributes to exercise), although I have said a good deal in refutation of these in the Preface (653 above), yet now I would like to say something again briefly, since I consider it of primary importance to define what is the exercising quality in this dialectic. For Socrates in the *Republic* (VII, 534e), says that those being educated should be exercised in it.

There are three processes of dialectic: (1) that of purification through

---

[11] Supplying ⟨ἐκβαίνειν τὸ⟩ after τοιοῦτον. (line 16), as seems necessary for the sense (West.).

cross-questioning, as he says himself in the *Sophist* (227cff.)—this Socrates uses a good deal against the tribe of Sophists, chastising their double ignorance; (2) the opposite of this, that which induces recollection of true reality, by means of which he used to lead on those naturally suited to contemplation, revealing to them truth unalloyed; (3) a compromise between these two, partly refuting (false opinion), partly stimulating the interlocutor towards the truth. Socrates can be seen to be exercising arguments in many dialogues, for instance in the *Lysis*. It is this testing of opposing arguments that is proper to dialectic that he seems to me in this passage to call "exercise" and "ranging" (135e2), and for this reason no longer to separate the method he is now about to impart from the dialectic that he is so impressed by.

So much for this. Turning to the details of the text, the addition of "believe me" seems to me to strengthen the praise which he bestows upon him. As for "make an effort", this contains an indication of his sympathy and enthusiasm for Being. He uses the phrase "make an effort" as with reference to things difficult to draw away from or to shift, meaning by "effort" the practice on the present occasion of dialectical theorems, and the transference of attention to these from the contemplation of true reality.

990   The phrase "exercise yourself more in that activity which seems to be useless and which the many call 'idle talk' " indicates what he considers to be dialectic of his sort. He says that it seems to be useless, but is in fact a force that leads souls upwards to the truth; that is, it is called by the many "idle talk," but in the most proper sense the true salvation of souls; from each of which considerations it is plain that it is identical with that faculty which contemplates reality and judges truth. And it does not base its existence on mere argumentation and logical procedures. For such a system as that is actually admired by the multitude, whereas the one communicated here they turn away from and declare to be unpleasant, by reason of the fact that it is unfamiliar and says nothing clear to them.

The phrase "while you are still young" is an excellent addition; for great labours are proper to the young, because it is easier when one is young to change the pattern of one's life, and because an orderly path of progress is more suitable to them, since they have time enough to traverse all the intermediate steps.

The phrase "Otherwise, the truth will escape you" makes clear the magnitude of the danger which threatens the untrained from any impulse towards untrodden areas of knowledge which is precipitate and disorganised, to wit, a falling away from all truth. For in the case both of metaphysical speculation and of theurgy it is this that makes our ascent safe and unerring, that is, an orderly scheme of progress. As the

Oracle says (fr. 136 DP): "For no other reason does God turn away from man, and with living power send him off on empty paths" than when we make the ascent to the most divine subjects of study or action in a disorganised and faulty way, and, as the saying is, with uninitiated mouths or unwashed feet. For those who approach in this way, transitions are unfulfilled, impulses are empty, the paths are blind. For this reason, in obedience to Plato and the *Oracles*, we must always make our ascents to the superior levels through what is more contiguous to us, and from the more lowly through the intermediate to the higher.

991

Basing themselves on these considerations, some commentators hold that this exercise is not a dialectic, for these two reasons. One, that this activity has been condemned as "idle talk"; the other, that whereas this exercise is spoken of as being suitable to the young, dialectic is clearly praised by Socrates himself, in the *Philebus* (58d), as "the purest part of intellect and thought," and is judged, in the *Sophist* (253e), "to belong properly to him who philosophizes purely and genuinely," and not to be communicated to the young, as he says himself in the *Republic* (VII, 537c-e), lest perhaps they may fall unawares into lawlessness, as a result of this power, from the natural concepts of goodness and justice which are in us. For it is not easy to control a power which is external for one who has not acquired the intellect which governs that power.

Now on the basis of what principles of Plato (bearing in mind that Parmenides clearly uses the term "idle talk" not as representing his own judgment, but rather the gossip of the multitude) shall we say that he distinguishes this exercise from dialectic? For this is what the multitude used to call dialecticians, as witness some of the comic poets who in jeering at Socrates himself called him "a beggarly babbler," as I recall saying prior to the Commentary proper.[12] And he himself sees fit to call him this because of the multiform testing which he is accustomed to make of questions under investigation, and of the tenacity with which he pursues arguments until the discovery of the truth, as I also said before. For "a terrible thing," as he says himself in the *Theaetetus* (195b), "is an idle talker," speaking of himself as "turning this way and that" the arguments about which he was there conducting his investigation. In the *Phaedo*, again, he says (70b), about the mockery of the

992

comic poets, that he will not then, at least, have to put up with them calling him an "idle babbler"; for he is talking about matters which concern him, since he is about to depart to Hades, and is seeking to establish whether souls survive in Hades after their separation from the body. This title, then, is conferred by the multitude upon dialecticians,

---

[12] πρό τῶν ἐξηγήσεων, in the prefatory part of Book I, 656.20ff.

and one should not produce it as an argument against the logical exercise that is in question here.

The argument that in the *Republic*, dialectic is not to be entrusted to the young is valid, but can be easily explained away, since the young being educated there have necessarily uneven natures, and not in all cases the best. For this reason there might be a fear that some of them might turn to the aforementioned lawlessness. But in the case of Socrates, who has a divine impulse and the highest degree of natural excellence, Parmenides here exhorts him to partake in dialectical discussions, having no apprehension lest he suffer any such consequences as might the majority of the young men who are undergoing communal education in the *Republic*. For it is not the same thing to lead on a single supremely excellent nature, and a multitude of talents unequal to one another, among which necessarily those that are not the best are often led astray towards the worse. So both are correct, both Socrates in the *Republic* laying down a course of education for a troop of young men, and Parmenides here taking in hand the best of young men and proposing to lead him through this training, which it was not possible to accommodate to the general run of youth.

> *"What form, then, Parmenides,"* he said, *"shall this exercise take?"*
> *"The form,"* he said, *"which you heard Zeno employing."* (135d)

From all that has been said hitherto this much may be gathered on the level of metaphysical truth—that Ideas exist, of what things there are Ideas, how they are participated in, what sort of entities they are. For it has been said that they are not corporeal, not physical, not psychical, but intellectual and paradigmatic and non-relative, and present to all things secondary to them without contamination. And further we have learned how many orders of them there are—for we also defined this—and where their bounds are placed, where they first appear, and how they make their orderly progress through the middle ranks.

We may also gather, as regards the interpretation of the characters, that Parmenides is the force bringing all to completion; and ⟨second comes Zeno, whom⟩[13] he exhorts Socrates to emulate; while Socrates is third in the group, as being led upwards by both the others. As regards the form of the teaching, we have gathered that Plato, after having by means of the Forms traversed all the divine realms and having ascended from the world of sense to that of intelligible reality, then in turn, beginning from above at the level of the One, will show how it is the cause of all existence, and how it generates the primal henads, by which all first principles of things are held together; and that the pre-

---

[13] Adding, ⟨δεύτερος δὲ ὁ Ζήνων, ὃν Παρμενίδης⟩ after Παρμενίδης (West.).

paratory rites for such a study is this exercise in the Forms. But before he begins this very mystical initiation, he wishes to communicate the method in accordance with which he will proceed, and the power which he will draw on to weave together all his hypotheses, and the manners of the lines of reasoning, by which he leads us through the truths of metaphysics, kindling in our souls this light of the whole of mysticism.

So then, Parmenides exhorts Socrates to this method and to exercise in it. When he asks, "What form should this exercise take?" he urges him to look to the arguments of Zeno, showing by this at one and the same time that this type of exercise was a particular feature of the Eleatic School (for he was not able to mention any other practitioner of this method than his own pupil Zeno), and that for the lowest levels of being the beginning of salvation is coordination with the intermediate levels (for it is through these that they enjoy the blessings of the primal goods).

So much, then, may be said about the purport of all the discourses which follow. If, once again, one terms this dialectical procedure "exercise," although it does not involve argumentation, that should not occasion surprise. The whole of the logical procedure and this unfolding of theorems, in relation to intellectual life, is a field of exercise. Even as endurance is exercise for courage, and self-control is an exercise for moderation, so we see fit to call the whole theory of logic exercise for intellectual understanding. And even as the power of opining, when exercised on conflicting propositions, exercises one on the level of opinion for the unerring grasp of demonstration, so the scientific progress of the discursive intellect is a field of exercise for the purest intuition of the soul.

> *"With this exception: there was one thing you said to him that impressed me very much; you would not allow the survey[14] to be confined to visible things or to range only over the field; it was to extend to those objects which are specially apprehended by rational discourse and can be regarded as Forms." (135e)*

Once again in this passage Parmenides reveals his admiration for Socrates' enthusiasm in respect of the intelligible and immaterial nature of the Forms. For he picks on this for approval from everything that Socrates said—the call to transfer the sphere of operations of dialectic from the sense realm to the intelligible—and he gives the reason for this: the things specially apprehensible by rational discourse are the in-

---

[14] The word here is πλάνη, more literally "wandering." It is this sense which Proclus adopts in his commentary. I have tried, but failed, to maintain consistency.

telligibles. Timaeus also says (*Tim.* 29b) that discourse about objects of sense is not stable or firmly fixed, but subject to conjecture, while that about intelligibles is unmovable and irrefutable. Sense-objects are not strictly that which they are at any given moment called, while intelligibles, since they exist in the fullest sense, are also the more truly knowable.

One might say in another way also that the intelligible Forms are most knowable by rational discourse, if one takes one's start from the faculties of knowledge. Sense-perception does not to any degree achieve knowledge of the Forms; imagination receives images of them endowed with shape; opinion grasps them through rational discourse without the aid of shape, but still has a differentiated quality about it and is in general only competent to discern the bare fact of their existence. Only, then, the faculty of reason in us is sufficiently competent to contemplate the Forms, and it is for this reason that Timaeus says (*Tim.* 27d) that true reality is to be comprehended by intellection accompanied by rational discourse. So those things which are most comprehensible by intellection are the Forms which are Forms in the strictest sense, and reasonably so. All objects of perception are particulars, since every body is a particular. No one among bodies can be all things, nor can it be one in many without being divided.[15] Forms in nature incline towards bodies, and are divided about them. Forms in soul partake in variegation, and fall short of the simplicity of the intellectual Forms. So those things that are most comprehensible by intellection are those Forms which we call intellectual and intelligible, and the further they are removed from Matter, the more properly they are Forms, preserving their own unsullied purity. There is need, then, for the dialectical "survey" (*planē*) in the study of these Forms, to give us preliminary training and instruction for the comprehension of them. And indeed the survey that is in fact instituted we declare to be not the argumentation which proceeds by means of popularly agreed notions (*endoxa*), as has often been said, but the whole science of dialectic, which he called in the *Republic* (VII, 534e) the coping-stone of the sciences, exercising us by means of logical chains of reasoning and constructions toward a more accurate understanding of immaterial and transcendent things. And do not be surprised that he calls this scientific study a "wandering" survey (*planē*). For he called it so in comparison to pure intuition and to unadulterated comprehension of the intelligibles; for a "survey" involves not only the examination of how correctly to understand the truth, but also how through refutation to circumvent falsity by the same methods. Why, then, should we be

---

[15] Reading ἀμερίστως for μεριστῶς of MSS (West.).

surprised if he termed this sort of progression a "survey," seeing that, even at the level of Intellect, some of his successors[16] did not shrink from calling the variation of intellections "an excursion" (*planē*), and this though intellection does not involve transition, through being an integrated unity and only experiencing multiplicity because of the multiplicity of its objects. And why speak of Intellect? The chief of the inspired sages[17] are wont to talk of the "wandering" undergone by the gods themselves, not only those who proceed unerringly (*aplanōs*) through the heavens, but the intellectual gods also, by this alluding to their procession and their presence to all the secondary levels of being, and their generative providence extending even to the lowest. For everything that proceeds to multiplicity they talk of as "wandering," admitting "unwanderingness" only at the stationary and henadic level.

"Excursion" or "wandering," indeed, seems to have four senses: (1) a multiplicity of activities, even if they are all integrated; (2) a multiplicity which proceeds transitively; (3) a multiplicity which goes from opposites to opposites; (4) a multiplicity of disordered motions. Of these four, dialectical training is said to be an "excursion" or "survey" in the third sense, since it proceeds by means of contrary hypotheses.

"Yes," he said, "because in the former field there seems to be no difficulty about showing that things are both like and unlike and have any other character you please." "You are right." (135e)

Socrates says here again just what he said earlier, that it is easy to see the mixture of Forms in sense-objects (often one can behold opposite qualities having different relationships at different times in one and the same subject), but difficult in the intelligible world. He says this not as an objection to Zeno's discourse (for Zeno does not say that), but casting his vote on the question of the community of Forms, which he was exhorting Zeno to clarify. Parmenides would surely not have praised him for this, if he had said what he said in refutation of Zeno. If Zeno showed that the Many were like and unlike in the same respect, and Socrates showed that they were so in different respects, and took "same" and "different" in different senses, and from this perspective attacked Zeno's discourse, how could Parmenides come to be praising Socrates? "You are right," is, after all, praise. It is better, then, to take this statement as not being a refutation of Zeno, but another form of problem raising by Socrates, who is asking to see how the Forms at the intelligible level are mixed together, and what is the method of their communion. Like and unlike exist together at the level of sense-per-

---

[16] Probably Plotinus; cf. *Enn.* VI, 7.13.28-35.

[17] This seems to refer to the wanderings of Demeter, as recorded in the Homeric Hymn to Demeter, but possibly in Orphic poems as well.

ception, but we want to see their interaction also in the intelligible world. This is the desire that Socrates is uttering, dismissing the mingling of visible things, and ascending to the communion of intelligibles, and Parmenides accepts this as expressing the sentiments of a noble and magnanimous soul.

"But there is one more thing that you must do. If you want to be thoroughly exercised, you must not merely make the supposition that such and such a thing is, and then consider the consequences; you must also make the supposition that the same thing is not." (135e)

It is well said, it seems to me, by the older commentators, that Plato has here brought to completion the writings of both Zeno and Parmenides, extending the "exercise" of the former to both sets of opposite statements, and advancing the theorising of the latter to the One in the truest sense, and doing both these things through the medium of Parmenides himself. For to be perfected by a lover and teacher holds no unpleasantness for Zeno, and to transfer oneself to the unity truer than all reality is most suitable to one who through comparative youth is able to behold metaphysical reality clearly, and who has "directed the gaze of his soul" towards the true cause of all things, as he says himself in the *Republic* (VII, 540a), to contemplate it. The bringing to completion of Parmenides' writing we will discover in what follows. Let us in the present context consider the bringing to completion of Zeno's. Zeno's discourse postulates the existence of many forms separated from unity, and then draws absurd conclusions, considering what follows and what does not follow, and what both does and does not follow. For instance, he concludes that they will be alike and that they will not be alike, both in the case of One and Many, and similarly with Motion and Rest. Parmenides is asking him now not only to postulate that something *is* in his dialectical investigations, but also that something *is not*, and consider what follows from this hypothesis also; as for instance, not only to postulate that likeness *is*, but also that likeness *is not*, and then see what follows and what does not follow, and what both follows and does not follow.

What is this addition that he is making, and what is the reason for it? The reason, I would say, is that if we only postulate that something is the case, and then find out what is the consequence of that, we will not in all cases discover what it is of which the thing postulated is the essential cause. If, however, we also demonstrate that, if it is not the case, the same result does not follow as would have followed if it had been the case, then it becomes plain that after all this is the case because that is the case; for otherwise this would follow, even if that was postulated

348

not to be the case, if[18] that were not by its own nature the cause of this.

If, for instance, I were to postulate that soul exists, and then were to show that the consequence is that motion exists, and then, saying, "Let us suppose that soul does not exist," I were to demonstrate that motion no longer existed, then it will be through soul's existence that motion exists. It will therefore be the first principle and cause of motion. If, on the other hand, motion were to occur with soul not existing, then it would be plain that motion does not derive from soul. Just so in the *Phaedrus* (245c), in order to demonstrate that self-motion is a first principle of motion for all other things, he assumed the self-moved not to exist and declared that "all heaven and all creation would fall into confusion and come to a halt." And again in the *Laws* (X,895b), after postulating that all things are at rest, he causes the self-moved to move and confers motion on all the things that are at rest. So then if the self-moved exists, motion will exist; if not, it will not. Therefore only the self-moved is the cause of motion.

It is not, then, sufficient to examine what follows if something is the case, but one must also investigate what follows if it is *not* the case, if one is going to see and understand of what the thing postulated is a cause, or what attributes belong to it in and of itself. For in the present example, if we rested content with enquiring only if it is the case, it is not yet plain whether only the self-moved is of itself the cause of motion in others. What would prevent there being another entity with the same power? On the other hand, when one has shown that if the self-moved does not exist, nothing else moves, it is not then true that there is something else that is the cause of the motion. For in that case it would cause motion without the existence of the self-moved, and it would no longer be possible to conclude that if the self-moved does not exist, nothing else moves. In view of this, then, it is necessary to examine the consequences not only of the postulation that something is the case, but also that the same thing is not the case.

One might reasonably raise the question as to how it is possible at all for anything to follow from what is not the case. What can arise on the basis of the non-existent? How can something which is not there at all be a means of demonstrating anything? Once it has been eliminated, it can neither experience any effect itself, nor can it have relations with anything else; it is simply that which is not. To this question we may reply that "that which is not," as we have learned in the *Sophist* (258e), can be taken to mean both "that which is absolutely non-existent" and the negation of something (this is in itself non-existent, but exists incidentally); it can also refer to Matter—for it "is not," by virtue of being formless of its own nature and unlimited and shapeless; and also

---

[18] Supplying ⟨εἰ⟩ before ἐκεῖνο as syntax requires (West.).

to all that is material, inasmuch as it exists on the phenomenal level, but has no true existence; also the whole world of sense, for it "comes into being and passes away, but never truly exists" (*Tim.* 28a); also, prior to these, the element of non-existence in souls, by virtue of which they are said to be the first of things that come to be, and not fully to be among those things that really exist, which are ranked among the intelligibles; and further, even prior to souls, there is the element of non-existence in the intelligibles themselves, the primary Otherness in things, as the *Sophist* teaches us (255de), which Plato says (258a) is no less real than Being itself; and even beyond these there is the non-Being prior to Being, which is the cause of all beings, transcending the multiplicity inherent in beings. Seeing, then, that "what is not" has so many senses, it is plain that we should never in fact postulate the existence of that which in no way exists at all. For that cannot even be uttered, nor thought, as the Eleatic Stranger has demonstrated in the *Sophist*, confirming the argument of Parmenides on that subject (258d). He says that that which in no way is, is unknowable and inexpressible, since all knowledge and all opinion knows and utters *something*, and that which in no way is, is nothing; for that which is not, Parmenides himself does not speak of, which indeed is an impossible thing and actually nothing. But when we say that the Many "are not," or that the One "is not," or that Soul "is not," we make this negative statement with the implication that something else exists, but Soul does not, and we enquire what follows from that. For instance, if we say, "Let us suppose that Intellect has no existence," we are not saying "Let what in no way exists exist!" but rather "Let Intellect be removed from the number of existents." This is the same as saying "Let Intellect not be one of all the things that are"; it is only in the context of one thing being in existence that another thing is said not to exist. So the hypothesis is not concerned with that which in no way is, but with what to an extent is and to an extent is not, or what is *this* and is not *that*. In general, negations are products of Otherness at the intellectual level. By reason of this, something is "not-horse" because it is something else, and "not-man" because it is something different. That is why he himself says in the *Sophist* (258e) that, when we say that something "is not," we are only uttering a denial of being, not stating the opposite of being, by "opposite" meaning that which is at the furthest remove from being and is completely devoid of it. So that we do not when saying[19] "is not" introduce the totally non-existent, nor in postulating not-being do we postulate that, but only that signification of not-being that can be known and expressed in speech.

[19] Reading εἰπόντες for εἰ πάντες with Latin translation.

So much for that, then. Next, since Plato is setting out the Eleatic method in this passage, let us examine its logical form, at least as far as is sufficient for the present context. We must conceive of one hypothesis giving rise to two others, and three arising, one out of each of these latter, so that the six hypotheses springing up, after the monad and the dyad, on being quadrupled, attain to a total of twenty-four. A unitary and simple type of hypothesis is one that states what is predicable of what. This is a common element in all hypotheses; for he who says that some predicate is or is not predicable of something in relation to itself or to something else is plainly in each case treating of something. This is clear. A dyadic hypothesis is one which provides a division into two, when one does not say simply what is true of something, but also distinguishes what the nature of that thing is of which something is true. The primary division is that by contradiction, into the propositions that the subject exists and that it does not exist.

Let these be two hypotheses, then. Each of them generates for us three further hypotheses. Previously we took being and not-being to be predicated of something, and so divided our hypothesis in two; now, if we take the predicate three ways, we shall triple each of these two hypotheses. The predicate, then, is to be taken as either being true or not being true, or as being both true and not true. For the predicate is either affirmed or denied of the subject, or partly affirmed and partly denied. For the discourse does not say this, that the pair of contradictory attributes are simultaneously true and that both opposite statements are true of it, but that the same thing is in one way true of the same thing, and in another way not. If we consider these three propositions in the context of the existence and of the non-existence of the subject, it is plain that we will have tripled[20] the original two hypotheses. There will then be six hypotheses: if the subject *is*, what is true of it, and what is not true of it, and what is both true and not true of it; and if it *is not*, similarly. The subject is in a double case, being and not being, and the predicate triple—being true of it, not being true of it, and being both true and not true of it—two by three is inevitably six.

Again, each of these six hypotheses is quadrupled by reason of the varied relationship of the predicate to the subject. Either it is predicated of its subject, or of anything else; and each of these two has two possibilities: either of its subject in relation to itself, or of its subject in relation to others; or of others either in relation to themselves, or to it. If you apply these four variations to each of the six first hypotheses, it is plain that you will create twenty-four hypotheses in all. What I am saying may be understood from the following scheme:

---

[20] Reading τριπλασιάσομεν for ἑξαπλασιάσομεν of MSS. The MS reading is perhaps provoked by the ἑξ immediately following (West.).

1. If the subject *is*, what is true of[21] it in relation to itself;
2. if it is, what is not true of it in relation to itself;
3. if it is, what is true and not true of it in relation to itself.

Again,

4. if it is, what is true of it in relation to others;
5. if it is, what is not true of it in relation to others.
6. If it is, what is true and not true of it in relation to others.

This is the first group of six. The second is as follows:

7. If it is, what is true of other things in relation to themselves;
8. if it is, what is not true of others in relation to themselves;
9. if it is, what is true and not true of others in relation to themselves.

Again,

10. if it is, what is true of others in relation to it;
11. if it is, what is not true of others in relation to it;
12. if it is, what is both true and not true of others in relation to it.

This is the second group of six. The third is as follows:

13. If the subject *is not*, what is true of it in relation to itself;
14. if it is not, what is not true of it in relation to itself;
15. if it is not, what is both true and not true of it in relation to itself.

Again,

16. if it is not, what is true of it in relation to others;
17. if it is not, what is not true of it in relation to others;
18. if it is not, what is both true and not true of it in relation to others;

This is the third group of six. The fourth is as follows:

19. If it is not, what is true of other things in relation to themselves;
20. if it is not, what is not true of others in relation to themselves;
21. if it is not, what is both true and not true of others in relation to themselves.

Again,

22. if it is not, what is true of others in relation to it;
23. if it is not, what is not true of others in relation to it;
24. if it is not, what is both true and not true of others in relation to it.

These, then, may be taken to be the four groups of six propositions which Parmenides employs in his hypotheses. He examines nine hypotheses, in view of the nature of the subject matter on the basis of which he makes his survey, and in the course of these hypotheses, in the first five he makes use of the first two groups of six, and in the four latter ones the latter two. And again, in the course of the five, he uses

---

[21] I have translated ἕπεται by "is true of," as being less clumsy on the whole than "follows."

the one group of six[22] in the first three hypotheses, the other in the lat-
1003 ter two of the five. In the course of the four, he uses one group of six in
the first two hypotheses, the second in the last two, as we shall discover
as the discourse unfolds.

The whole form of the dialectical system is as here described, being
truly intellectual and based on knowledge, not based on opinion and
completely unstable and undefined by knowledge. To this single, integrated system the four procedures of definition, division, demonstration and analysis are subordinated. Sometimes it is necessary to make a
division, either of a single genus into species, or of a whole into its different parts, or of any other type. Sometimes one must make a definition, and one must know the distinctions between the things to be
defined[23] and between definitions in every rank of being. For a definition can be made starting either from the form or from the matter or
from both. Sometimes one needs to make a demonstration, and there
too one must discern the distinguishing characteristics of various types
of cause. For causes are to be understood differently at the material
level from at the immaterial level, and differently among things subject
to motion from among things that are not. Again, sometimes one must
make an analysis of things back to their first principles. For the transition from the subject under investigation to everything that is not the
subject sometimes proceeds by analysis to the causes, sometimes to the
accessory causes (synaitia), at other times to both. These matters deserve the careful attention of the user of the system, since the subject of
analysis is either going to be at the highest level of reality, or at the lowest, or will hold an intermediary rank. This is also clear—that of all
methods, half demonstrate something true, and the rest come to an impossible conclusion, depending on the status of the subject as regards
existence or non-existence. It is clear, too, that sometimes we are making a transition from our chosen subject to some single opposite, as for
instance if we consider the proposition "If likeness exists, what is its
relation to unlikeness?"; sometimes to a multiplicity, as, for instance,
"If likeness exists, what is its relation to all the Forms?"; sometimes to
everything, as, for instance, "If Intellect exists, what is its relation to all
1004 beings, both intelligible and sensible?"—since it is the task of the man
of knowledge in all these cases to see from what starting-point he can
provide himself with that path which is easiest and best for the demonstration of the topics before him. For often it will be necessary to begin from affirmative propositions, and often from a consideration of
what follows in relation to something else or to everything else. In general he will take his beginning in each case from the most familiar ele-

---

[22] Reading ἑξάδι for τετράδι of Greek MSS both here and in line 43 below. The Latin
actually reads ternario (τριάδι).

[23] Reading ⟨τῶν⟩ ὁριστῶν for ὁριστικῶν of MSS (West.).

ments and by this means will construct all the subsequent steps, following the established divisions of modes.

Let such, then, be the general outline of this system. Perhaps though, before Parmenides begins on his own hypotheses, we should practise the system on some more familiar hypothesis. Let us take the soul, and consider it both in relation to itself and in relation to bodies, and see what is true and what is not true, and what is both true and not true, both of the soul in relation to itself and to bodies, and of bodies in relation to themselves and to the soul.

So then, if soul exists,

    1. there is true of it, in relation to itself, self-motion, essential life, and self-substantiation;

    2. not true of itself are self-destruction, total ignorance of itself and non-recognition of its own attributes;

    3. true and not true of it are divisibility and indivisibility (for in a way it is divisible, in a way indivisible), and eternal existence and non-eternal existence (for in way it is eternal, in a way subject to change), and everything that pertains to it as a property of its median status is of this sort.

Again, if soul exists,

    4. there is true of it in relation to bodies that it is productive of life, that it initiates motion, that it holds together bodies as long as it is present to bodies, that it lords and rules over them by nature;

    5. not true of it are: being moved externally (for it is a property of ensouled bodies that they are moved from within), and being the cause for bodies of rest and changelessness;

    6. true and not true is its being present in them and apart from them (for it is present in them through its providence, but separate from them in its essence).

This is the first group of six. The second is as follows. *If soul exists*, the following is true for the rest of things—in this case bodies:

    7. in relation to themselves, sympathetic affection (for it is by reason of the life-giving causal principle that these have a mutual sympathy);

1005   8. not true is lack of sensation (for it is necessary that with the presence of soul everything should have sensation—some things as individuals, others as parts of a whole;

    9. true and not true is that bodies move themselves; for in a way bodies move themselves, through being ensouled, and[24] in another way not; (there are many modes, after all, of self-motion).

---

[24] Supplying e.g. ⟨πῶς μὲν γὰρ αὐτοκίνητα τὰ σώματα⟩ between σώματα and ψυχούμενα (West.). The text would seem to have suffered from homoeoteleuton.

Again, *if soul exists*, then

10. there is true for bodies in relation to it being moved from within by it, being vivified by it, and being preserved and held together through it, and in general being dependent upon it;

11. not true are being dispersed by it and being filled with lifelessness by it (for it is from that source that it partakes in life and cohesiveness);

12. true and not true are participation and non-participation in it (for both are true, both that in a way bodies partake of it, and that in a way they do not).

This, then, is the second group of six. The third is as follows: *If soul does not exist*,

13. there is true of itself, in relation to itself, lifelessness, non-being and mindlessness (for if it does not exist it will not possess either being or life or mind);[25]

14. not true will be the powers of self-preservation, self-creation, self-motion, and all such attributes;

15. true and not true will be not being an object of knowledge and reasoning to itself (for if it does not exist it will in a way be unknowable and irrational, inasmuch as it will not know or reason about itself at all, whereas in a way it will be neither irrational nor unknowable, if these attributes imply having some nature which is not rational nor participant in knowledge).

Again, *if soul does not exist*.

16. there are true of it, in relation to bodies, being incapable of generating them, being unmingled with them, having no care of them;

17. not true of it are the powers of moving them, of giving them life, and of giving them coherence;

18. true and not true are its being other than bodies and having no relation to them (for this is in a way true and in a way not true, if one takes otherness as implying existence, but total difference—in this way it would be other; not other, on the other hand, as not existing at all, but other in this respect, as being non–existent).

1006 This is the third group of six. The fourth is as follows: *If soul does not exist*,

19. there are true of bodies in relation to themselves immobility, non-differentiation in respect of life, lack of feeling for each other;

20. not true are being sense-perceptible by one another;

---

[25] Supplying ⟨οὔτε νοῦν⟩ after ζωήν.

21. true and not true is being able to affect one another (for in a way
    they will experience influences, and in a way not; they will ex-
    perience them only as material bodies, not as living things).

Again, *if soul does not exist,*

22. there is true for other things, in relation to it, not being watched
    over or being moved by it;
23. not true is being vivified or being held together by it;
24. true and not true is being like and unlike it (for in so far as, if it
    does not exist, they would not exist either, they would be like
    it—for they would be in the same state as it—but in so far as it is
    not possible for something which does not exist to be like any-
    thing, in this respect likeness of them to it will not be true).

So now we have gone through the method for our example in all the
proper modes, and we conclude from these arguments that soul is the
cause of life and motion and interaction for bodies, and in general of
their existence and preservation. For on the assumption that soul exists,
these things follow, and in the case of its non-existence the negation of
these follows. Only, then, from soul and through soul are these qualities present to bodies. This is the purpose of the whole method, to discover the properties of a thing, and of what things it is the cause both
to itself and to other things.

You may also observe that in these hypotheses our argument would
have gone more easily if we had not started from the soul itself, but
from bodies. For these are more familiar to us than the soul, and what
is true and not true of them more so than what is true and not true of
it, according as they participate or do not participate in soul. If they
participate in it they are living and moving and relate to one another,
whereas if they do not participate they are motionless and without activity or productivity.[26] Once, therefore, we have shown first those
qualities that are true and not true of bodies, in the case of the existence
1007 or non-existence of soul, in relation to themselves and to the soul, we
will more easily be able to show these qualities in the soul—for instance, that it is self-moved, that it is immortal, that it is incorporeal;
for on the basis of what bodies derive from it, we can demonstrate its
own properties.

So true it is, then, that those who wish to begin from the things most
familiar to us must take their beginning on different occasions from
different hypotheses, either from affirmative or from negative or from
what is given or from what is regarded as its opposite. I know, certainly, that Aristotle, in his imitation of this system (*An. Pr.* 1.27),[27]

[26] Reading ἄγονα for MS ἄπονα (West.).

[27] It is remarkable that Proclus should consider that Aristotle is "imitating" the system
of "Parmenidean" dialectic in the *Prior Analytics*, but the phraseology of 43b1–11, in particular, may have lent credence to this notion.

aims in the case of his categorical syllogisms to set out the predicates and the subjects and what is contrary to the subject and the predicate, stating what is true and what is not true of them. The system set out here, however, is far more complete, setting out as it does by the process of division all the modes through which one must proceed if one proposes to exercise one's intellect on each aspect of Being, arousing the investigative faculty of the soul through all the aforementioned hypotheses and perfecting the power which discovers the truth about each. When we are in pursuit of metaphysical truth, we are more likely to discover it through this system than through that of Aristotle, since through this multiplicity of hypotheses we can track down more accurately the subject of investigation. For the most part we will employ hypothetical forms of argument, always setting forth what is true and what is not true of our postulated entities. For these acquaint us particularly well with the common properties of things, showing us what relation they have to each other, and also their bases of division from each other; but we will also make use of categorical reasonings, when we have to establish the conjunction of each hypothesis, or its minor premise.

> "How do you mean?" he said. "Take," he said, "if you like, this hypothesis which Zeno made: 'If there are many things, what consequences must follow both for those many things with reference to themselves and to the One, and also for the One with reference to itself and to the many; and again, if there are not many, to consider in turn what will follow both for the One and for the many, with reference to themselves and to each other." (136a)

1008

Socrates was unable to grasp the very compendious presentation of the whole method in the foregoing passage, so he asks further about it, so that Parmenides may more clearly explain it and set out an account of it. That is what he does in the present passage, practising it in a model case, though here also in strict logical form and compendiously; for of all those modes which we described, he gives the whole twenty-four here, but compressed into eight. For the expression "what consequences follow" covers both "is true" and "is not-true"[28] and "is both true and not-true," so that one can by means of these indications multiply the eight once again by three.

Let us, then, briefly consider these eight modes that I have mentioned, taking as our example Zeno's hypothesis:
If there are many things, there clearly follows for the many,
1. in relation to themselves, being divided, not being first principles, being unlike one another;

---

[28] Reading τὸ γὰρ "συμβαίνει" περιλαμβάνει καὶ. . . . lines 14–15 (West.).

2. in relation to the One, being contained by the One, being generated by the One, participating in likeness and unity from the One.

There follows for the One,

3. that it dominates the many, that it is participated in by them, that it is prior to them—all this in relation to the many;
4. in relation to itself, there follows partlessness, non-multiplicity, being superior to being, life, and knowledge, and all such attributes.

Again, *if there are not many*, there follows for the many,

5. in relation to themselves, being indistinguishable and indivisible from one another;
6. in relation to the One, that they do not proceed from the One, that they are not different from the One.

There follows for the One itself,

7. in relation to itself, having nothing in its nature capable of acting upon things or bringing them to perfection (for it is in virtue of such characteristics that it generated the many;
8. in relation to the many, not presiding over them, not acting upon them in any way.

Having set out all this, we conclude that the One is everywhere the unifying and causal and governing principle of the many. And you see 1009 that here the transition takes place from the thing under investigation to its cause, for the One is of this nature. There must always, therefore, be, after the multiplicity of elaborations and hypotheses, some one summary conclusion. So here Parmenides will show by means of all his propositions that the One is at every level the cause of existence of beings and of the henads among them, which we declare to be the purpose of the whole dialogue. For they are not simply hypotheses without conclusion; but rather, by postulating both "if *x* is the case" and "if *x* is not the case," we can arrive at some definite and accurate conclusion in accordance with the true state of affairs, out of these various and multifarious hypotheses.

"Or, once more, if you suppose that Likeness exists or does not exist, what will follow on either supposition both for the terms supposed for other things, with reference to themselves and to each other; and the same story with Unlikeness." (136b)

Again in the case of these we will go through the same procedure. *If Likeness exists*, there will follow for it

1. in relation to itself, singleness, eternity, productiveness, primacy;
2. in relation to sense-objects, assimilation of them to intellectual objects, not allowing them to dissolve into the sea of Unlikeness, linking of parts to their respective wholes.

358

There will follow for sense-objects,

3. in relation to themselves, community with one another, participation in one another, taking pleasure in one another (for like takes pleasure in and sympathises with and mingles with Like);

4. in relation to it, participation in it, assimilation to it, unification by virtue of it.

If Likeness does not exist, there follows for it,

5. in relation to itself, non-existence, having neither generative power nor primally causative substance;

6. in relation to others, not controlling them, not making them alike by virtue of its own form, but rather the destruction, along with itself,[29] of even the likeness present in them (for if the first principle of like things does not exist, there is not much chance of their being alike).

There follows for sense-objects,

7. in relation to themselves, being non-communicative,[30] unmingled, devoid of interaction;

1010   8. in relation to it, not being given form in accordance with it, nor given coherence by it.

We can go through the same procedure with Unlikeness.

If Unlikeness exists, there follows for it,

1. in relation to itself, being a pure, immaterial, and unitary form, possessing multiplicity along with oneness;

2. in relation to other things—in this case things of sense—there follows for it being the distinguishing cause of defined demarcation and division in each thing;

for the others,

3. in relation to themselves, there follows the preservation of the particular characteristics of each, and the non-confusion of their forms;

4. in relation to it, being dependent upon it and deriving its order, both in wholes and parts, from it.

If Unlikeness does not exist.

5. it itself will neither be a pure and immaterial form, nor in general one and not-one;

6. it will not possess, in relation to the others, the cause of distinct being of each thing;

as for the others,

7. they will experience every sort of confusion among themselves, and

---

[29] Reading συναναιρεῖν for MS συναιρεῖν.
[30] Reading ἀκοινώνητον for MS ἀκίνητον (West.).

8. they will not participate in any single power which distinguishes all things.

From this we conclude that Likeness is a cause of community and sympathy and mixture in this realm, and Unlikeness of distinction and of acquisition of Form and of the unmixed purity of the potencies within them, in and of itself; for all these conclusions follow from the positive attributions presented, and the opposites of these[31] from their negations.

"And with Motion and Rest, and with Generation and Corruption, and with Being and Not-Being themselves." (136b)

We must exercise ourselves in the same way as previously with these entities also.

If Motion exists, there follows,

1. in relation to itself, eternity, infinity of power;
2. in relation to the things of this world, being a source of motion to them, being productive of life to them, being the cause of progressions and of activities in all their variety;

for these things here,

3. in relation to themselves, there follows being active, being alive, being able to change (for each thing changes its being by virtue of motion, proceeding out of potentiality into actuality);
4. in relation to it, there follows being brought to completion by it, coming into control of their own potentiality, being assimilated to the eternally static through it (for those things which cannot attain the Good permanently gain some share of it through motion).

1011

If Motion does not exist,

5. it itself will be ineffective and inactive and powerless, and
6. it will contain no causal principle of things of this realm, nor will it have any creative powers, nor an essential being enabling it to create;
7. ⟨the others, in relation to themselves . . .⟩[32] and
8. in relation to it they will be without coherence, delimitation, or completion, since there is no primary motion.

As regards Rest, something similar may be said:

If the Form of Rest exists, there will follow for it,

1. in relation to itself, stability, eternity, and singleness of form;
2. in relation to other things, the fact of each remaining within its proper bounds, and being firmly established in the same measures or places; ⟨while

---

[31] Reading ἀναιρέσεσι for Greek MS διαιρέσεσι (Latin *interemptionibus*) to serve as the opposite of θέσεσι.

[32] A lacuna here, covering (7), "the others, in relation to themselves."

3. the others, in relation to themselves . . .)[33], and
4. in relation to it being on every side delimited by it; and dominated, and achieving from it firmness in their existence.

If it does not exist, there will follow

5. for itself in relation to itself, lack of stability or firmness;
6. for itself in relation to the rest of things, not providing them with permanence and safety and stability;
7. for the others in relation to themselves, aimless wandering, instability, imperfection, and baselessness;
8. in relation to it, not being subject to its measures, nor acquiring being by virtue of it; but being borne aimlessly in all directions, there being nothing to hold them together or pin them down.

So then, the Form of Motion is the director of effective power and life and activity in all its many forms; and Rest is the author of stability and permanent states and of being fixed within one's own boundaries.

We may proceed in the same way with Generation and Corruption, and with Being and Not-Being. Perhaps, however, before doing this we should examine the question of the origin of Generation and Corruption, and whether the causes of these are to be postulated as being among the Forms. This is surely necessary, not only because these are sempiternal processes (for it is neither possible for there not to be generation, nor for corruption to perish utterly, but these two processes necessarily coexist with each other in the cosmos, inasmuch as the cosmos itself also must be inextinguishable, being in a state of coming into being and passing away, as Timaeus teaches us (*Tim.* 28a); but also because we say that generation partakes of essence and being, and corruption of not-being (for each thing, in so far as it comes to be, is led towards essence and acquires being), while inasmuch as it perishes, it is led towards not-being and transference to another form. It is for this reason, after all, that one thing perishes into another, because preexistent to it is Not-Being, which is divisive of Forms; and even as in that realm Not-Being is hardly less real than Being, if one may so say, quoting the Eleatic Stranger (*Soph.* 258a), so here Corruption contributes hardly less than Generation to the make-up of the universe. And even as There that which partakes of Being also has a share in Not-Being, and this latter participates in Being, so in this realm both that which comes to be is receptive of dissolution, and that which is dissolving, of generation.

So then, this is the cause of Generation and Corruption, to wit, Being and Not-Being. But we must now practise the same method in

---

[33] A lacuna, similar to that above (n. 32), covering (3) "the others, in relation to themselves." Neither here nor above, it may be noted, is any lacuna indicated in the MSS. Cousin is misleading on this point. The contents of both lacunae can be easily supplied by studying their respective opposite hypotheses.

1012

regard to these also, postulating that Generation exists, and seeing what follows for itself in relation to itself and to others, and to them in relation to themselves and to it; and what follows upon its non-existence in the same way, as for instance:

If Generation exists,
1. it will be incomplete of itself, and
2. a cause for everything else of likeness to Being;

as for the others,
3. in relation to themselves, there will follow change out of each other's states;
4. in relation to it, always partaking of it as it exists in them.

If it does not exist,
5. it itself will be inopinable, and
6. not cause for other things of any form or order or perfection;

as for the others,
7. they will be ungenerated and impassive, and
8. will have no communion with it, nor will they participate through it in Being.

And if you wish to go through the same procedure with Corruption:

If Corruption exists, there will follow for it,
1. in relation to itself, being inextinguishable and of infinite potency and being filled with Non-Being, and
2. in relation to other things, being a measure of existence and cause of constant generation;

1013 for the others,
3. in relation to themselves, flowing into each other, not being able to hold themselves together;
4. in relation to it, always being different from it, having Not-Being in them joined with Being and, through it, participating in it wholly and as wholes.

If Corruption does not exist,
5. in relation to itself there will follow not being destructive of itself (for if it existed, it would destroy itself along with everything else);
6. in relation to other things, not scattering them, not turning them into each other, not leading them away from being and essence.

As for the others,
7. in relation to themselves, there will follow not being changed into each other, not being affected by each other, each maintaining its own position;
8. in relation to it, being unaffected by it.

It is, then, the property of Generation to rouse things to existence, of Corruption to lead them away from existence. This is our conclusion from the foregoing hypotheses, since these two entities revealed themselves to us as being, if their existence was postulated, causes of being or not being something to other things, and if their existence were denied, of lack of motion and lack of change.

Such exercises we have indulged in by way of preface to what follows, considering it better that we should exercise our minds prior to the divinely inspired presentation of Parmenides as he himself has reminded us, by means of repeated examples, to do. The hypotheses of the existence and non-existence of Being we are going to get from him in the form of the hypotheses as to the existence and non-existence of Real Being, so there is no need for us to bother with them now, since we will be examining them in conjunction with him, if the Gods so will. Just this, however, may be noted, that the degree of puzzlement increases according as one is dealing with more basic principles, such as the One, Being, Motion, and Rest. On more particular topics the puzzlement is less.

1014

> *"And in a word, whenever you suppose that anything whatsoever exists or does not exist or has any other attribute, you ought to consider the consequences with reference to itself and to each one of the other things that you may select, and several of them, and all of them together; and again you must study these others with reference both to themselves and to any one thing you may select, whether you have assumed the thing to exist or not to exist, if you are really going to win through to a sight of the truth after a complete course of discipline."* (136bc)

There are two ways in which we undertake the examination of things. Sometimes we consider whether each thing exists or does not exist, sometimes whether such and such an attribute applies or does not apply to it, as for instance, whether the soul is immortal. On this occasion we are enquiring not only as to the existence or otherwise of all the attributes of the thing hypothesised—itself with respect to itself and to others, and for others with respect to themselves and to it—but also as to their applicability or otherwise. For instance (let the following argument stand as an example),

If the soul is immortal,

1. its virtue has a life connatural with it, it is self-sufficient for its own happiness, and these attributes follow for it in relation to itself;
2. in relation to other things, there follows its using them as instruments, its exercising care for them while separate from them, its bestowing on them of life;

for the others

3. in relation to themselves, there follows the coming into being of the living and the dead from one another, having the cycle of generation as an externally bestowed immortality;

363

4. in relation to it, being set in order by it, participating in some degree of self-motion, being dependent upon it in respect of life.

If the soul is not immortal,

5. it will not be eternally in motion, nor will it be intellectual of its very essence, nor will it be essentially alive, nor will its learning be recollection; it will perish from the evil proper to it, and it will not have knowledge of true existents; so much will follow in relation to itself;

6. in relation to others, it will be mingled with bodies and material, and it will not be capable of ruling them nor of leading them wherever it wishes, it will be responsive to the physical composition of bodies, and all its life will be bodily and concerned with generation;

as for other things,

7. in relation to themselves, they will have such a rank as do those things which are formed of actualisation (*entelecheia*) and body (for they will be only living things put together, from indeterminate life-force and bodies);

8. in relation to it, they will be such as to carry it along and subject it to change in accordance with their own motions, to contain it within them, not presiding over them from outside, and to live with it rather than from it as a source.

You see, then, that by following this method we have discovered how it is possible not only to hypothesise existence and non-existence, but also any other attribute that a being may have, such as being immortal or not being immortal, so that this is now clear to us as a result of this. But since the attribute of relation can be taken in a variety of senses— either as a relation to one thing only, as for instance to hypothesise the relationship of Likeness to Unlikeness; or to more than one thing, as for instance to hypothesise what relation Being has to Motion and Rest; or to all things, as if we hypothesise that the One exists, and ask what is its relation to the whole of existence—therefore Plato did not neglect this either, but added "that one must consider the consequences for each one of the other things one may select, and for several of them, and for all of them together." The one or more things in question must, of course, be cognate with the subject under consideration—as for instance, the Equal with the Unequal, for these are coordinate with one another; and Motion and Rest with Being, for these exist in it and in connection with it. But now if, although there are differences in the relation to one other thing and to a number and to all, we nevertheless laid down twenty-four modes, treating relation as uniform, do not be astonished; for the attribute of relativity is a variation proper to the *matter*, according as the subject is one or not one. We, however, set out to

1015

communicate the *form* of the method, and the formal distinctions within it, not the material ones.

But what has he set before us as the end of this exercise? "The vision of the truth," he says. Let us not understand "truth" here in a general sense, but as being precisely that intelligible truth about which he has taught us elsewhere, for the sake of which there is the great struggle to see "the plain of truth" (*Phaedr.* 248b). So all our life is an exercise in preparation for that vision, and the "excursion" through dialectic strives towards that goal. So the expression "win through to a sight of" is excellently chosen; for it is through many intermediary steps that souls attain to the vision of those truths.

1016

But in order that the method may become clear through yet another example, let us examine the twenty-four modes in the case of Providence. Let us take as our hypothesis *that Providence exists.* So then, *if it exists,*

1. there will be true of it, in relation to itself, being of the nature of the good, being infinite in power, having effective capability;
2. there will not be true of it, its being turned aside from its purpose, its being bereft of will;
3. true and not true will be its being one and not one.
4. in relation to other things, there will be true of it ruling over them, preserving each one of them, containing the beginnings and the ends of all things, bringing everything perfectly to its conclusion;
5. there will not be true its being injurious to the things it watches over, its producing the unexpected, its being the cause of disorder;
6. true and not true is its being present to all things and transcending them, knowing them and not knowing them (for it knows them in a different way, and not through powers coordinate with the things known).

As regards other things,

7. in relation to themselves, there is true not suffering anything at each other's hands randomly, suffering no injustice from any quarter;
8. not true is that there is some element of chance in their existence, their being unrelated to each other;
9. true and not true is that they are all good (for this pertains to them in one way and in another way not).

For other things,

10. in relation to it there is true being dependent upon it, and in every way being guarded and benefited by it,

365

11. not true is that they oppose it or that they escape it (for nothing is either so small as to escape it nor so lofty as not to be beaten down by it);

12. true and not true is that each thing partakes of providence (for in a way each takes a share of it, but in a way it is not it that it takes a share of it, but rather the good things that are apportioned from it to each thing).

Let us postulate, on the other hand, *that providence does not exist*; in that case,

13. for itself in relation to itself there will be true incompleteness, non-productivity, ineffectiveness, existing for itself alone;

14. not true will be overflowing abundance, superfluity, sufficiency, self-extension;

1017

15. true and not true will be not being busy and not being bothered (for in way this will be true of that which does not exercise providence, and in a way not, since things secondary to it will not be controlled by it);

16. in relation to other things, it is plainly true that it is unmixed, has no communication with anything, and knows nothing;

17. not true is that it assimilates everything to itself, that it dispenses to all things their appropriate good;

18. true and not true that it is an object of striving for them (for this is in a way possible and in a way not possible; for if it is through its transcendent superiority that it is said not to exercise providence, as being superior to all relationship and activity, then there is nothing preventing it from being an object of striving to all things secondary to it; but if it is said not to do so through being deprived of this power, then it would not even be an object of striving).

For other things,

19. there is true in relation to themselves, being unordered, random in their activity, indefinite in their receptivity, receiving many uncoordinated impulses into their own natures, being subject to random and unorganised movement;

20. not true is convergence upon one goal, apportionment according to value, arrangement according to rational disposition;

21. true and not true is their being good (for by virtue of existing at all they must be good, and yet if providence does not exist, one would be unable to say whence they derive their good);

22. in relation to providence, true of them will be being unaffected by it, not being coordinated with it;

23. not true will be being measured and defined by it;

24. true and not true, being ignorant of it (for all things which have come to birth must know this much about it, that it does not ex-

366

ist if it does not exist, and yet not know it, for they will have nothing in common with it).

We have come, thus, to the conclusion of our argument about providence, exercising ourselves according to the method; and we urge those who would become fitting auditors of Parmenides' teaching to exercise themselves with many other examples. As for us, we must pass on to the next section of Plato's text.

1018   *"It is an unmanageable task, Parmenides, of which you speak, and I don't altogether understand. Why not postulate some proposition and go through it yourself, that I may grasp this more clearly?"* (136c)

Even as the essence of the Forms is easily grasped and thoroughly clear for those who are willing to contemplate it with their intellects, whereas for those who attempt to discover it by means of sense-perception and imagination and opinion it remains unknown and uncontemplatable, so also the teaching of Parmenides is easily managed by those who have developed the habit of looking at things in their totality and perfection, whereas for those less perfectly developed it is unmanageable (*amēchanos*). That is exactly the position of Socrates here, and, on seeing the veritable ocean[34] which this method is and the vast number of possible propositions and their handling and ordering, he consequently described it as "an unmanageable task." By "unmanageable" he wishes to point to both its difficulty of comprehension, and its natural beauty (cf. *Symp.* 218c2; *Rep.* VI, 509a 6); for there is nothing that one can see elaborately contrived about it, so that it is "unmanageable"[35] by virtue of its natural quality, while it is easily manageable (*eumēchanos*) inasmuch as it is intellectual and imitates the conjunctions and divisions of real being; by the word *task* he wishes to indicate that it proceeds through the use of actual metaphysical truths, and is not based upon mere logical rules. It is certainly difficult to grasp and to handle for those whose intellectual development is not complete, and that is why he added, "I don't altogether understand"; for he had certainly got some grasp of this theory, but a rather incomplete one, as Parmenides' words have shown; and that is why he says, "I don't altogether understand." He now lays hold of the understanding of it that much the more profoundly, in that he has realised that the method is difficult to grasp. This attitude is characteristic of those who are naturally akin to truth, as he has said himself in the *Letters* (VII, 344ab), that is, the quality of reacting to the difficulty and unpleasantness that becomes apparent when one approaches these topics by attacking the

---

[34] Here, and elsewhere in the text (e.g. 1020.19) Proclus reads πέλαγος for πλῆθος at *Parm.* 137a6, but his lemma has been "corrected" to πλῆθος.

[35] Ἀμήχανος is here being etymologised as "being free from μηχαναί," which I find untranslatable. Also εὐμήχανος, which is used to mean "well-contrived."

study of them all the more vigorously, and not shirking the exertion
1019 resulting from the enquiry, but, as if competing under the umpireship
of the gods, enthusiastically to set about the understanding of the subject matter. It is even thus that the soul, in looking towards Intellect,
and beholding its unitary and simple and eternal intelligising, considers
that to be "unmanageable"; for it is within itself that reside all the types
of devices (*mēchanai*) and interweavings of the Forms; but nevertheless
it yearns for the perfection of Intellect, even if it cannot unravel its
thought nor the simplicity of the life of that level, but, circling round it
and clinging to it, through its own variety it seeks to imitate its uniformity, and in its divided state its undividedness in thinking.

It is the same thing that Socrates is doing here. For he does not run
away in a panic on seeing the difficulty of this method and the synoptic
quality of the exposition, and flinch from the labour[36] of practising
himself in it; rather, he admits his lack of ability and his falling short of
this knowledge, and cleaves still more enthusiastically than before to
the whole theory of it, and exhorts Parmenides to descend from the intuitive level to rational exposition and from the general level to some
particular example in order to practise the method with this. Even
thus, in the case of the realm of reality and of the gods themselves,
when we cannot attain to the knowledge of their inner activities we can
conclude their existence from those which proceed outwards, and we
recognise the more universal through the more particular; and even
thus also does Parmenides reveal himself through his discourse, proceeding forth from unified intellections to this variegated exposition,
which now Socrates requests of him, taking a position in this analogous to the tertiary ranks of being, who participate in the primary
through the powers that proceed from that quarter to them, and not
even in these immediately, but through the mediation of the classes in
between.

*"That is a heavy task, Socrates," he said, "to lay on a man of such an
age." (136d)*

On the one hand he is provoking Socrates to greater and more per-
1020 fect receptivity, both exaggerating the difficulty of the task and trying
to beg off this exposition—a thing, indeed, that Socrates himself is
found doing on other occasions, when young men are eager to hear
something from him, imitating his own spiritual fathers; and at the
same time the remark has a good deal of truth in it, whether you consider it in reference to his soul, or to him as a living being. If in reference to his soul, you would say that it is not fitting for one who is able

---

[36] Reading πόνον for πόρον with Latin translation (*laborem*).

to cognise things divine to operate through verbally expressed imagination (*lektikē phantasia*) and the body but rather to remain "in his own conning-tower" and "in his own habit of life." It is a "task," therefore, for one living on the level of intellect to act by means of discursive reason and imagination, and for one turned towards himself to direct himself towards other things, and for the simplicity of intuitive knowledge to turn to the variegation of discursive reasonings.

If it is said with reference to him as a living being, you could say that it is a considerable task for an old man to undertake such contests. For "to traverse so various and vast a sea of discourse" requires also an instrument which is unremittingly at the service of this activity, and plainly, therefore, that of a man in his prime. So we can take the words *task* and *of such an age* in two ways, and in each case we will see that the statement is true.

The statement also has much truth in relation to the subject matter. In many cases general rules of procedure are easily grasped; it is about their use that not a little difficulty arises for those who try them out, as in the case of geometry those who have learned the general[37] theorems still experience difficulty in using them to solve the problems that are presented. A sign of the difficulty involved in using this method is the fact that none of those who followed Plato set out any of their own works in this form (we leave aside Ammikartos,[38] whoever he was). For this reason we have tried above to employ it by using a number of examples.

Well then, let this serve to make clear the point that, though the knowledge of general principles is often easy to acquire, their employment is difficult. For which reason it is reasonable that Parmenides says that "a heavy task" has been laid on him by Socrates, not only for the reasons that we have mentioned, but also because of the nature of the subject of enquiry being what it is.

1021

"But you, Zeno," said Socrates, *"why don't you give us the illustration?"* (136d)

In all cases those beings which are held third in honour gain a share in the primary level through the median classes; but that which does not achieve this immediate participation and is separated from its next highest is excluded from the company of the gods.[39] In imitation of this situation, Plato in the discussions makes Socrates, in wishing to be

---

[37] Reading κοινοὺς for καλοὺς, with Chaignet, or καθόλου (West).

[38] This personage is mentioned nowhere else. The name sounds Carthaginian, or possibly Cyrenaic.

[39] Reading ἄτευκτον for ἄτακτον (line 9), χωριστὸν for χωρὶς (line 10), and ἑκὰς for ἑκάστοις (line 10) (West.).

369

filled directly with the thoughts of Parmenides, to be cheated of his hope, but doing this same thing through Zeno and succeeding to a preeminent degree in his request. Zeno, as has been said often before, represents divine mediation. The causal principles have been set out often before,[40] and to what entities the three are analogous, of whom Zeno is the middle one. It is by appealing to him, then, and desiring through him to be united to the father of the discourse (*logoi*), and stirring him up to help with his difficulty, that Socrates gains participation in Parmenides himself. As far as the discussion of the theory of Forms, Socrates has partaken immediately in communion with the old man because he himself on his own initiative was provoked to the consideration of the Forms; but when the pouring forth of deeper thoughts takes place, he necessarily relies on an intermediary, whom now Socrates rouses to action, and begs that he should become for him what Parmenides had been for him (Zeno). So then, Parmenides is an image of the paternal causal principle, for he is the common Father of all in the discourse—Zeno, of the Power of the Father, for which reason he is extended before the Father and beats down all multiplicity which has revolted from the One; Socrates, of the Intellect which reverts towards its Father through the medium of Life and Power. If you are willing to approach the passage with these analogies in mind, you will find a great deal of theory hidden within it.

1022   *He said that Zeno laughed and replied: "Let us beg Parmenides himself to do it, Socrates. What he means is no light matter, I'm afraid. Or do you not see what a task you are setting?"* (136d)

Even so among the gods the third joins himself to the second, and strives for fulfilment from him; whereas the second, inasmuch as he is situated in the first, draws forth the benefactions deriving from him upon all. It is remarkable also to note in this passage that earlier, when there was question of a smile, they both smiled, Zeno and the great Parmenides, whereas here, when there is talk no longer of smiling, only Zeno laughs, Parmenides remaining in his state of calm. This is because in the presence of the master he is exhorting the pupil to take in hand a discourse which seems difficult to the master himself; for this would not be the behaviour of a man who was observing the respect due to a master. This is also the reason why, when he was reading his treatise, he did it in the absence of Parmenides, as has been said in the Preface, for the reason that it would be tasteless to read it in the presence of his master.

The smile, then, represents the invisible and hidden activity of the

---

[40] E.g. Book I, 627.39-630.14.

divine, whereas laughter represents its progression onto a more visible plane; for laughter is more perceptible than smiling. So the one represents the permanent and quiescent and hidden god, the other a god who remains above, but is already in the process of proceeding forth and becoming manifest.

And there is something more remarkable still than this. Zeno, when he smiles, looks at Parmenides (this was stated explicitly earlier), but when he laughs, he addresses himself to Socrates. This is because in the divine realm the mediating class is hidden in so far as it is united with what is above it, but becomes manifest in so far as it consorts with what is below it. So therefore when Zeno laughs, he is manifesting himself to Socrates by ranking himself with him, through this union calling forth the thought of Parmenides. For he turns back Socrates also towards his own master, and in every way, leads him towards him as being the primal cause of theoretical knowledge and generative of all intellection deriving from him. And the reason for this he adds himself; for he says "you are setting a great task"; great and transcendent achievements require similar causes; middling entities are the causes of middling goods, not of the highest goods or those which transcend the many.

1023

> "If we were a greater multitude than we are, it would not be fair to ask him. Such a discourse would be unsuitable before a large audience, particularly in a man of his age; because most people are unaware that you cannot hit upon truth and gain understanding without this discursive wandering over the whole field. So, Parmenides, I join with Socrates in his request, in the hope of being an auditor of yours once again after all this time." (136de)

One of our predecessors[41] has already made the reasonable comment that Plato everywhere preserves propriety in his portrayal of his characters, as is plain from the present passage. In the *Gorgias*, for instance, where he is presenting a gathering of Sophists, he portrays the pupil as butting in on the replies of his master and leaping into the argument in a premature and disorderly manner; for such a character is Polus in that dialogue, unbridled and unmannerly even towards the father of his art. Here, however, when he is representing philosophers, he portrays Zeno as yielding place to Parmenides, and begging him to be the one to speak and to benefit the company. The gathering of Sophists reflects the whole material system, in which the offspring often even rise up

---

[41] This sounds like the sort of thing Longinus would say. Cf. Proclus *In Tim.* I, 14.7ff, 59.10ff, 68.3ff., etc., where he is recorded as commenting on the excellence of Plato's style and its suitability to its subject matter. If so, this is probably relayed through Porphyry.

against their own causal principles and try to lord it over their betters, whereas the community of philosophers reflects the order of the gods, in which the inferior orders summon forth the powers of the superior, and give way to their boundless generative abundance.

1024 　　But let this be enough about the ethical position of the characters. It is hardly necessary to state that the most divine type of doctrines are unsuitable to be conveyed to the hearing of the many, since Plato himself has said that all these things are objects of ridicule to the many, but thought worthy of admiration by the wise. Even so the Pythagoreans declared some of their discourses to be mystical, and others "open-air,"[42] while the Peripatetics made some esoteric, others exoteric. And Parmenides himself wrote one part of his work "according to Truth," and another "according to Opinion."[43] Zeno, in turn, called some of his arguments "valid," and some "tactical."[44] So it is reasonably stated here that such a discourse is "unsuitable" in the presence of the many, since they are incapable of comprehending what they would be hearing. And if someone already advanced in years were to enter into a discourse on these subjects in the presence of the many, it would seem still more unsuitable to them and shameful. In a young man such manifestations are less mocked at, as is remarked by Callicles (*Gorg.* 484c), who is one of the many affected by their sentiments; but they consider that for someone advanced in years to spend time in these activities is of all things the most worthy of ridicule. What the cause may be of such an attitude one does not need to turn elsewhere to seek; for Plato himself has given his verdict that they are afflicted by this through ignorance; ignorance indeed is the cause of great evils to souls. He shows also, again, that the failings of the many are involuntary; for every error committed in ignorance is involutary and deserving of pardon. The many, then, are ignorant of the extent of the power of dialectic, and that the end-result of this "wandering" is truth and intuitive knowledge; for there is no other way whereby we may ascend from the lowest levels of being to the first, apart from proceeding through the intermediary paths of Life. Even as our descent took place through many intermediary levels, as our soul proceeded always towards the more composite from the simpler levels of activity, so also our ascent will

1025 come about through many intermediary levels, as the soul dissolves the structure of life which it has compounded for itself.

　　We must, therefore, first recognise that the senses are able to cognise

---

[42] Ὑπαίθριοι. Cf. Iamblichus *V. Pyth.* 245-247, though he does not use this terminology.

[43] Cf. Diog. Laert. IX, 22, and Parm. fr. B1. 28-30 D-K.

[44] Zeno's distinction between ἀληθεῖς and χρειώδεις λόγοι does not seem to be recorded elsewhere. Could it have been in the *Forty Logoi*?

nothing accurate or sound, but contain a great deal that is confused and material and subject to passion, inasmuch as they make use of organs which are of this nature. Then we must dispense with thinking through images, those Stymphalian birds which fly about within us,[45] inasmuch as they present to us evils of form and shape, not being able at all to grasp the non-figurative and partless Form, but hampering the pure, immaterial cognition of the soul by breaking in on it and causing disturbance to it in its investigations. Thirdly, as well as these, we must eradicate multiform opinions and the "wandering" around them in which souls are involved; for they do not fasten upon the causal principle of things, nor do they implant in us knowledge or participation in the transcendent Intellect. Fourthly, we must ascend to the "great sea" of sciences (*Symp.* 210d), and there contemplate by means of dialectic their divisions and combinations and in general the variety of the Forms within us, and by means of this contemplation, having perfected the weaving together of its structure, our intellect will behold that it must separate itself from composite things and apply itself already on the level of intuition to true reality. For intuitive knowledge is superior to scientific, and life lived according to intuitive knowledge is more honourable than a life of science.

So then, many are the wanderings and whirlings of souls. There is one at the level of imagination, another above this at the level of opinion, another again at the level of discursive intellect. Only life according to intuitive intellect possesses freedom from wandering, and this is the mystical mooring-place of the soul, to which the poem brings Odysseus after the multifarious wanderings of his life (*Od.* 13.101), and to which we, if we wish to be saved, as we presumably do, will conduct ourselves.

But enough about these matters. It has already been stated that Zeno is contiguous to Parmenides, and that he is a kind of monad of all those who have been gathered together; and that he primarily reverts towards him through Socrates, who has superiority over the rest. He 1026 himself says that he has heard the discourse that is about to be presented on another occasion, whereas these will be hearing it for the first time—Plato indicating through this that in the divine realm the causes contiguous to the Fathers partake of some things from the Fathers transcendently and secretly, of which they solely and primarily partake through their ineffable unity with them, whereas there are other things that they partake of in common with the other entities which proceed from the same source. The first session of Zeno with Parmenides, then,

---

[45] An elaborated reference, perhaps, to the ὄρνιθες ἄγριαι of *Theaet.* 197c. The whole passage, however, is based upon *Phaedo* 66bff., with φαντασία substituted for σῶμα. Cf. Olympiodorus *In Phaed.* 6.2.

is analogous to the mystical intellection experienced by the secondary entities, while the session shared with the others is analogous to those progressive departures from reality which extend[46] to all things equally. Since the second session is inferior to its prior, inasmuch as Parmenides set out the system, as was reasonable, more comprehensively to Zeno on that occasion inasmuch as he was more familiar with his methods of argument, whereas he sets it out in more varied detail for the whole company by way of indicating, obviously, the lower level on which they are now operating, he says he has come to hear him "after all this time." For this is symbolic of the different levels of activity, the "junior" and the "senior," among the gods, not so termed by order of temporal succession but rather of worth. And if you note the precise terminology used by Zeno, "So, Parmenides, I join with Socrates in his request," and this is put by Plato not casually, nor simply for artistic effect, but he has put it in to indicate how Zeno derives all his own usefulness from the will of Parmenides. He says no more than he "requests"; what follows and what is owing to his request, he leaves out, even as the sentence seems lacking in something, imitating in this the state of mind of the speaker, who is observing the reverent attitude which he considers to be due to the father of such discourses.

1027 *When Zeno has said this, Antiphon said that Pythodorus said that he himself begged Parmenides and so did Aristoteles and the others, not to disappoint them but to indicate what he has been describing.* (136e)

Parmenides is the monad of all those who comprise this meeting, even as the One Being is the monad of the realm of Being. Zeno is the monad of all those who are going to participate in Parmenides. It is for this reason that he makes the request on their behalf, since be represents the power of recalling towards his Father those who have proceeded forth. Of those who have come in to visit them, Zeno said that he joined with Socrates in requesting Parmenides, thus bearing witness to his transcendent superiority over the others. Once these two have requested, all the secondary entities are set in motion towards laying hold of the primaries. For Pythodorus and Aristoteles and all the others, while Socrates alone was making his request, remained silent; for he was not the most primary among the participant entities. But once Zeno had made his request, they are all automatically stirred up. Even thus, among the gods, when the encosmic gods follow their "detached"[47] leaders, all entities follow along with them, angels and

---

[46] Reading προιούσαις for MS ποιούσαις, with Latin (*procedentibus*).

[47] The ἀπόλυτοι θεοί are the lowest rank of supracosmic, transcendent gods, identified by Proclus with the gods of the Phaedrus myth (e.g. *In Tim.* I, 18.8). They come between the ἐγκόσμιοι and ἡγεμονικοί, being the second element of the demiurgic triad (*ibid.* 269.24ff.).

daemons and individual souls; for all wish to act in concert with their own highest elements.

What the request is, then, he himself has added, "to indicate what he has been describing." The method of instruction, then, is going to employ symbols and indications and riddles, a method proper to the most mystical of doctrines, not employing logical proofs and conducting its procedure according to commonly accepted rules of argument.

> Parmenides replied, "I must obey; although I feel like the old race-horse in Ibycus, who trembles at the start of a chariot-race, knowing from long experience what is in store for him, to whom the poet compares his own reluctance on finding himself so late in life forced into the lists of love."
> (136e–137a)

1028   All those things, as has been said before, which are about to enjoy participation are moved to conjunction, and fasten avidly to the power which effects participation with them, and on this principle join themselves to their own coordinate monad—thus preparing themselves to enjoy participation in the transcendent monad. For this is always the way in the realm of true Being, in which those which are perfectly dependent on secondary entities can participate to an adequate extent also in the entities above them again.

So then, the others have gathered together with Socrates, are petitioning together with Zeno, and are going along with Parmenides, and thus even before the exposition begins there appears in the characters a kind of divine ordering, so to speak, in images. We see how all the secondaries depend upon the triad that pervades the whole divine realm, and are established and brought to completion by it; and how the primal among the causal principles are made manifest to those which ascend in an orderly way through their immediate superiors; and how for those who avidly cling to the divine there is prepared an ungrudging dispensation from that source. For even so will Parmenides subsequently assent to their requests, and he has already given the reason for his assent, putting the blame on "necessity"—*divine* necessity, obviously—against which, as the Athenian Stranger says (*Laws* VII, 818b), not even the gods can fight. It is, after all, a property of the godlike cause and of divine power to be available to all who are able to partake of it. But that he may demonstrate to them again how great is the task and how serious a struggle, he declares himself to be unequal to this long exposition, and to be in the same state as Ibycus, who because of advanced age is hesitant to give himself up to love-making, but yet is forced to do so, and who compares the compulsion with which he is confronted to that of an old horse who has competed in the race many times before, and now through excess of experience is trembling at what is before him. The poet writes somewhat as follows (fr. 2 Bergk):

Love once again, glancing at me meltingly from under dark lids,
has cast me by its various wiles into the inescapable nets
of the Cyprian. Indeed I tremble at its onset, like a horse which has
    often
borne the yoke to victory before, but now through old age
enters unwillingly the contest amid the swift chariots.

1029   That is the passage from the poem *Chariot* which is relevant to Parmenides' statement.

Again, one may gather from this passage how in all cases the superior entities project their own images onto the ranks of Being inferior
to them. Parmenides has presented Ibycus as an image of his own sensation; Ibycus is turn presents the horse; for the Forms proceed from
Intellect into the rational soul, and from this into nature, which exercises domination over irrational animals. Contests of horses and love
affairs are proper to souls in the process of ascent; for among these the
horse which partakes of evil weighs them down (*Phaedr.* 247b), the one
whose charioteer has not trained it well, while the one which is able to
struggle through to real Being is borne along lightly, and for those
souls ascent and salvation comes about through love. For this reason
also is their chariot winged, symbolising that which soars aloft by
means of erotic madness to intelligible beauty and the vision of true
reality.

So much may be said about the subject matter of the passage, with
which the present text is constructed analogously. As for Ibycus, it is
clear to those who have read his work that he was a songwriter, that he
was much concerned with matters of love, and that, when old and provoked to writing love songs, he says in one of his own songs that he
shrinks from the writing because of the strain involved in love.

"*And my memories too make me frightened of setting out, at my age, to
traverse so vast and various a multiplicity*[48] *of arguments. However, I
must gratify your request; for after all, as Zeno says, we are just among
ourselves here.*" (137a)

He knows how great is the wandering of the soul, not only on the
level of sense-perception and imagination and opinion, but even in the
discursive peregrinations of the reasoning faculty; and knowing this,
and remembering his own struggles, he fears to descend again into
1030 such a wandering, like some Odysseus, who when he has reached his
home and is already in possession of his proper good, is summoned
forth to some wars with barbarians such as he has already been

[48] The text of the lemma has πλῆθος, in accord with all Plato MSS, but, as we have seen
(n.34 above), Proclus reads πέλαγος in his text, so this must be a scribal correction.

through, and through experience does not choose to depart from his fatherland, inasmuch as he remembers what troubles he had in his wars and in his wanderings over a long space of time. Having ascended, therefore, into ratiocination (*logismos*) from imagination and sense-perception, and into intuitive cognition from ratiocination, he reasonably fears to descend again into ratiocination and the wandering of the discursive intellect, lest it should lead him unawares back down into imagination and sense-perception. For the descent from intuitive intellection is not a safe one, nor should one find oneself unawares remaining at a worse level. Even so in the *Phaedrus* Socrates, under Phaedrus' compulsion, describes both physical beauty and that which is manifest in the median level of Forms, and then, having departed ⟨from these, and through⟩[49] divine love extending our souls towards intelligible beauty, he calls "daring" and "impiety" and "sin" (242bff.) the descent from this to the secondary level, and the declination from the intellection of the primal beauty.[50]

It is because Parmenides is trying to avoid this, and remembers his own wandering and is now safely in port, that he shrinks from once again descending into "the multiplicity of arguments" from his intellectual and simple form of activity. Nevertheless, he makes the descent, for the sake of the good, for the benefit of the beings secondary to him; this grace of his is an image of the providence of the gods. Such, then, should be the descents from the intelligible of divine souls, still in dependence upon the divine and knowing well the evils consequent upon wandering, and descending only for the purpose of benefaction, not for any fulfilment of a love of generation, and not tumbling into the depths, nor attaching themselves to indeterminate[51] forms of life. For being "on one's own" is a symbol of a life free from all material multiplicity.

"Whence shall I begin, then? And what hypothesis shall I propound first?" (137a)

1031   Parmenides, having given himself up to the convolutions of the arguments, and descending from his intellectual "conning-tower" into scientific expositions and from the non-relative form of life to the relative, asks those who are about to partake of him once again, where he shall begin, and on the basis of what sort of hypothesis should he found

---

[49] Supplying e.g. ⟨τούτων, καὶ διὰ⟩, as seems required by the sense, between ἀποστὰς and τοῦ θείου ἔρωτος (West.).

[50] This reflects the interpretation of the *Phaedrus* first worked out by Iamblichus, and reported in Hermeias *In Phaedr.* 9.6ff. and 11.16ff. Couvreur (=Iambl. *In Phaedr.* fr. 1 Dillon).

[51] Reading ἀορίστοις, with Latin (interminatis) for ἀρίστοις of Greek MSS.

377

his argument; not that he is making his intellect dependent upon their judgment, nor wishing that his proper course be defined for him by them (for it would not be right for the better to have their activity regulated by the worse), but by way of causing them to turn towards him and rousing them up to the recognition of his nature, in order that he may not be implanting his reason-principles in them as unintelligent recipients, as Nature does to bodies, but that they may elevate themselves and join him in striving towards Being. For this is the way that Intellect elevates souls, as they are not only borne upwards by its agency, but prepared by it to help themselves. He urges them, then, to keep a watch on his procedure, and see where he takes his start from and whence he leaves off and through what middle terms he proceeds, but he does not seek to learn the correct procedure from them. Obviously so, because he does not wait for their answer, but goes on to announce his decision, and makes his discourse in relation to that.

It seems to me that the phrases, "Where shall I *begin?*" and "What hypothesis shall I propound *first?*" are both proper to the One, about which he is going to make his exposition (for "beginning" and "first" are the most suitable of all names to that entity), but they differ from one another inasmuch as, in enquiring whence he shall begin, he is plainly insisting that he should not look outside himself, but should weave together this great enterprise of discourse from himself and his internal store of knowledge. And in any case, seeing that there is a variety of possible methods, it is reasonable that he should enquire whence he should take his beginning; for one should not start from the same point in the case of every subject, as I have said previously in laying down the principles of the method.

He enquires also as to what hypothesis he should propound first. Since there are many hypotheses concerning both the intelligible and the sensible realms, he enquires what hypothesis he should propound 1032 in order to be able to speak of the whole range of being, and leave nothing at all univestigated either of intelligibles[52] or of things of sense, so as to give the name of "hypothesis" to the propounding of the subject as a whole, while terming "the beginning of the hypothesis" the first part of the whole setting forth of the proposed argument, many-faceted as it is.

"Would you like me, since we have decided to play out this laborious game, to begin from myself and my own hypothesis, hypothesising about the One itself, that is, what must follow if one assumes that the One is, or that it is not?" "By all means," said Zeno. (137b)

---

[52] Adding μήτε τῶν νοητῶν, from Latin translation (neque intelligentialium).

The actual method of Parmenides takes up one hypothesis and builds his whole argument on that, not an hypothesis which would appear to be one among a multitude of others, but one which comprehends all other hypotheses and is one prior to the many; for it reveals the total range of being and the whole order of things both intelligible and sensible, and furthermore their henads, and the single ineffable henad which is the source of all of them. For the One is the cause of all things, and from it he will generate all things as he proceeds.

But perhaps someone might raise this very question, how Parmenides, who did not deal with the One, can have called the One "his own hypothesis," and say that he will take his start from this beginning proper to himself. Before this some authorities have indeed declared that, whereas Parmenides did in fact concern himself entirely with Being[53], Plato, when he discovered that the One was superior to Being and to all existence, by way of correcting Parmenides, presents him as taking his start from the One. For even as Gorgias and Protagoras and each of the other philosophers sets out their theories in a better form in Plato's works than in their own, so also Parmenides is a more accomplished and visionary philosopher in Plato than we see him to be on his own. In this passage, as we see, he says "If there is a One," not "If there
1033 is a One Being," as if he is conducting his argument about the One alone, and not about the One Being. And in the case of the subsequent hypotheses, "If there is not a One," and in the conclusion of the whole discourse (166c), "If there is or is not some One, all things are the case and are not the case," assuming the One to be subject in all all these, not the One Being. Parmenides is being Platonic, then, in calling his hypothesis one which postulates the One. For what Plato has added to Parmenides' doctrine, they say, he has attributed to Parmenides himself. Those who maintain this would say that there is no need to be surprised if Parmenides does not seem to say anything in his poetry about the One itself (it is, after all, ineffable), inasmuch as he is defending his own poetry, which traces the generation of all existent things from Being; but in his unwritten discourses to Zeno he gave some indications on that subject, inasmuch as that is possible in words. He is justified, then, in calling his own hypothesis the exposition of the One.

But if one is to get nearest to the truth, one must follow the line of our Master, that Parmenides begins from the One ⟨Being⟩[54] (for the proposition "If there is a One," since it contains besides "One" also the concept of existence, belongs to this rank of things), and ascends from the One Being to the One, thus demonstrating clearly that the One in

[53] Reading ὄν for ἕν, of Greek MSS with Latin (ens).
[54] Supplying ⟨ὄντος⟩ after ἑνός.

379

the strict sense wishes only this, to be One, and "snatches itself away"[55] from Being; and that the One Being is second to this by reason of its descent towards Being, whereas the One itself is superior even to the designation "is," and the hypothesis "if it is"; for as soon as we add *is*, the One in the strictest sense will no longer remain. So that it is true that he hypothesises Real Being and One Being, and that by means of this hypothesis he ascends to the One itself, which he himself in the *Republic* (VI, 510b) describes as "non-hypothesised." For he says that it is necessary always to proceed through hypotheses, in order that we may culminate our ascent at the non-hypothesised One; for every hypothesis starts from a principle other than itself. But if one were to make the

1034 hypothesis a first principle, one would have to say about it something which he (Plato) has said about geometry; if something has a first principle which one does not know, and a conclusion and middle terms, therefore, built up from what one does not know, in no way can such a thing be an object of scientific knowledge (*Rep.* VII, 533c). The only thing, then, that is non-hypothesised is the One, so that whatever is hypothesised is something else and not the One; but he ascends from this to the One, as from an hypothesis to the non-hypothesised. One might thus properly admire the whole structure of Parmenides' discourse here; for if on the one hand he had assumed as an hypothesis that which was non-hypothesised, and taken what has no first principle as proceeding from one, then he would not have been following his method, which calls for in every case hypothesising something and seeing what follows from it; or, on the other hand, if he assumed what was not the non-hypothesised, but something more or less remote from the One, it would not have been easy for him to make the transition to it, nor would he have been able to reveal to us the cause of Being naturally and without strain. In order, then, that the One might remain non-hypothesised, and yet that he might ascend easily to the One from an hypothesis closely akin to it, he postulated the One Being, as being next in order to the One, and in which the term "one" finds, perhaps, its first proper use; for in the case of the One itself which is "beyond," not even this term is proper. And in this way, as he says, he both begins from his own hypothesis, which is the One Being, and this is the significance of the hypothesis "If there is a One;" and moving thence to the non-hypothesised, he makes manifest the derivation of all things from the transcendent henad of beings. That is why, when he has said that he will "hypothesise his own One," by way of showing what follows and what does not follow from it—at one moment, taking the concept of the One by itself—he chooses to demonstrate its ex-

---

[55] Chaldaean terminology; cf. *Or. Chald.* fr. 3 DP.

istence by means of affirmative propositions, while at another he assumes along with it also the idea of existence, but everywhere looking,
as it were, towards the One, whether unparticipated or participated, in
order to demonstrate that all things exist due to the One, and that without the One their existence would vanish; for the existence of Being
itself is due to the One.

How, then, you might say, does it come about that there is a plurality of hypotheses, if the whole discourse continues to be about the
One? Because, I will say, "the One" can be used in three senses. We
have the One that transcends all beings, and that which is present together with all beings, which also, with the One, produces all the orders of beings, and thirdly we have that which is inferior to Being and
which is, as it were, "swallowed down" by it.[56] Since, then, the One is
used in three different senses, in the first three hypotheses the subject
for discussion is the relation of each of these both to itself and to everything else. In the two remaining hypotheses of the first group, the subject is how the others are related both to themselves and to the One,
seen both as partaking in the One and as non-participant in it. Again,
since the remaining four take as their hypothesis that "the One" is not,
and not-being has two senses, either absolute not-being, or that which
is in one way and not in another, he considers the first two of the second group, in relation to either of these senses, both to themselves and
to everything else, while the latter two in relation to everything else,
both in so far as they partake of not-being, and in so far as they do not.
Thus he completes the tally of the nine hypotheses, producing as a final
conclusion that the One is the cause of all things; and that if the One is
not, nothing is; for it would not be right for the effects to remain in
existence once the cause is done away with.

We shall have an opportunity for examining these matters in more
detail later. I must say, though, that it seems to me that the present text
answers well to what has gone before, the phrase "from myself" answering to "Whence shall I begin?" and "my own hypothesis" to
"What hypothesis shall I propound first?" They do not both signify the
same thing. In the first case[57] he is defining the mode of his activity,
that it is from within outwards, and proceeds from his unitary intelligising into the variegation of discourse; while in the second case he is
proposing to specify the subject matter about which he is about to develop the aforesaid method.

And this is not the only message you may derive from the present

---

[56] Καταπίνειν, κατάποσις, Orphic terminology, based originally no doubt on Hesiod's
description of Kronos swallowing down his offspring. Cf. *In Tim.* I, 313.6; II, 93. 18-25;
III, 99.20.
[57] Reading οὐ μὲν for οὐ μὲν of Greek MSS, with Latin translation.

passage, but also that the mode of this activity of his is analogous to the divine. Each of the divinities, after all, begins his activity from himself—the conservative class first conserves itself, the anagogic raises itself up before anything else, the generative generates itself, and so it goes with all the others. So Parmenides utters these phrases in imitation of the divinity, and not these only, but also the phrase "to play out this laborious game." This also is divine, to call his clear and many-faceted procedures "games"; for each of men and other things is a "plaything" of the gods (*Laws* VII, 803c), all such as are brought to being by their outgoing energies. Every external argument is thus a "game," compared to the calm and unitary intellection of Being, but it is nevertheless "laborious" because it has to do with the contemplation of real beings, and unfolds the simplicity of the intellection within, and is nothing else but, as it were, an unravelling of intellections and a "rending apart"[58] of undivided cognition. This is what Parmenides offers; and Zeno accepted it readily, knowing the profundity of the doctrine. It had to be he who was the one to assent, as standing in the role of monad in relations to all alike who are going to partake in the arguments about to be uttered, and particularly as having often before heard his doctrines on these subjects and knowing their greatness.

"Then who will answer the questions I shall put? Shall it be the youngest? He will be likely to give the least trouble, and to be the most ready to say what he thinks; and I shall get a moment's rest while he is answering." (137b)

His general reason for wanting someone to respond to him is that his task is to practise the dialectical method. One must therefore have someone to express affirmation and denial. He chooses the youngest of the company, in order that he may serve just this basic purpose and not cause trouble by raising problems. For the old are like veterans of the law-courts, who have through their wider experience come to prefer their own doctrines. He chooses him also that he may speak from the heart, not giving responses against his conviction through contentiousness, but from unperverted thoughts, from which he himself will also be composing his arguments, producing replies that are unfabricated. And thirdly, he chooses him that he himself may get through his discourse with ease, working upon a complaisant, tender and unspoiled character.

These, then, are the reasons he himself has given for his choice of the youngest. One might, however, consider all this also on the level

---

[58] Σπαραγμός, again an Orphic term, deriving from the myth of the rending of Dionysus by the Titans; cf. *In Tim.* II, 198.7.

of the One Being and in general on that of the primal causes, how their power causes even the lowest strata of being to turn back towards the primary. For what is there that does not participate in the One? Even if you were to mention privation itself, you will find that it bears the image of the One. And what one of beings is there that does not derive benefit from Being? Even if you mention Matter, there is a way that Being exists potentially even in it. And in general the most comprehensive of the causes both bring into being and cause to revert to themselves even the lowest grade of being. It is in imitation of this that Parmenides chooses out the youngest as his interlocutor, in order that he may turn him back also to his own discourse (*or* creative reason-principle).

And if you care to see something even more arcane in this, in images, consider how the secondary and tertiary grades of the divine enjoy the influence of the primary monads—they do it mystically, calmly and unvaryingly; and how the summits of the angelic realm receive it, in a manner worthy of gods, in that they have situated themselves next to the divine; and how individual souls do, transitively, with a certain element of wandering. And having considered this, go on to consider how it applies here; all the others are filled with the doctrine in silence—Zeno, Socrates, Pythodorus. But Aristoteles undergoes motion, being cast in the role of the soul which is led upwards but will later be borne down again into material life. It is plain here too, as in the most holy rites, how some of those present are being initiated, others are possessed of the full vision, some are hearing it for the first time, while others have heard it also before. Note also how Parmenides is concerned for ease in his discourse, because this ease is operating is a 1038 divine characteristic. For they possess unwearyingness, to whom Hebe pours out the nectar, and their providential care arises after the drinking of the nectar, being free and unimpeded.

> *"I am ready at your service, Parmenides,"* said Aristoteles, *"for you mean me when you say 'the youngest.' So ask away, and I will answer."* (137c)

Parmenides made the general and indefinite statement that the youngest should be the one to reply to him. Aristoteles has brought himself into the category described, thus joining the particular to the general; for if he is the youngest, he should be the one to answer. Again, these statements bear some indications of divine things. The general and unified content of the intellection of divine beings is received on the particular level by souls, according to their own rank, and not souls only, but also the secondary ranks of the gods themselves receive on a particular level the general intellections of the higher. Thus also in the most divine Poet, when Hera says indefinitely and absolutely, "But if some one of the gods should summon Thetis to my presence" (*Iliad* 24.74), the goddess who is the chief of the angelic order makes the task hers in particular: "So she spoke; and storm-footed Iris sprang up . . ." (*ibid*. 24.77). And yet the remark was not addressed explicitly to her by Hera, but she, comprehending the order, both recognised it as pertaining to her and, recognising this, performed her proper task. For it is proper to her to gather together secondary entities to their own causal principles, according to the dictates of the demiurgic Intellect, and especially to the leader of the female divinities in the cosmos. It is this which Plato is representing in images when he causes Aristoteles to present himself and submit himself to the orders of Parmenides; and Parmenides, turning this youth to himself, addresses himself to the proposed discourse.

BOOK VI

◻

INTRODUCTION

◻ ◻ ◻

PROCLUS NOW turns to the exegesis of the First Hypothesis. He prefaces this with a long discussion (which I have distinguished as *Section A*) of the reasons for discerning no more nor less than nine hypotheses, against various predecessors who had postulated different totals. An excellent survey of the history of this controversy in Platonism may be found in the Introduction to volume I of Saffrey and Westerink's Budé edition of the *Platonic Theology* (pp. lxxix-lxxxix), but a certain amount must be said here.

Proclus' position (following Plutarch of Athens and Syrianus) is that, if one pays proper attention to the different senses of "One" and "Not-Being," one must arrive at five positive hypotheses and four negative ones. "One" has, as he maintains (1039.28ff., and cf. 1035.1ff.), three senses—one as superior to Being, a second as coordinate with it, and a third as inferior to Being—representing, respectively, the levels of One, Intellect, and Soul. "Not-Being" ("the Others," in this context) has two senses, that of Relative or Contingent, and that of Absolute Not-Being—representing respectively the physical world and pure Matter. The five positive hypotheses arise first from the postulation of the One in its three senses, and then from the postulation of the relation of it, first, to "the Others" which participate in the One, and secondly to "the Others" which do not. The four negative ones (6-9) are arranged rather differently on the basis of the absolute and relative non-existence of the One (in all its senses) and of the Others (1040.10-19).

It is clear to Proclus, at least, that if the various senses of the One are not properly differentiated, we get intolerable contradictions (1041.1-20), and yet in the past, he says, there have been those who would take the One in only one sense. These he characterises as τινὲς πραγματειωδεστέρων ἁπτόμενοι λόγων, who argue that the same sense of "One" must be assumed in all the hypotheses; otherwise Parmenides would not have achieved his declared aim, which was, after all, to practise his method on some single object of enquiry, to wit, his own One (137b).

385

The identity of these commentators (whose view corresponds much more closely than that of Proclus to that of modern critics) remains obscure. They cannot be Proclus' Neoplatonic predecessors, from Plotinus on, since they all, whatever their other differences, saw the first three hypotheses (or more) as concerning different entities. The general Middle Platonic view, as represented by Albinus in the *Didaskalikos*, was that the *Parmenides* was an exercise in logic, so either we must postulate some pre-Plotinian Pythagorising school of Platonists, of whose interpretation of the *Parmenides* we have otherwise only the dim evidence afforded by the speculations about the One of Moderatus of Gades—or there is the possibility that this was the position taken up by Plotinus' contemporary, the Platonist Origen, of whose views we hear more below, at 1064.21ff., and VII, 36.8-31 and 64.1-16 Klibansky (see notes *ad loc.*). Certainly Origen held that the subject matter of the first two hypotheses was the same, the first being purely negative in its conclusions.

At any rate, Proclus dismisses their position as leading to contradictions. The process of refutation of this school of critics, however, leads him to an exposition of his doctrine of henads (1043.4-1051.33). The doctrine of henads, as E. R. Dodds remarks in his useful discussion in *Elements of Theology* (p. 259), is "an attempt to bridge the yawning gulf which Plotinus had left between the One and reality. The doctrine of henads represents an attempt to account for the existence of individuality by importing plurality into the first hypostasis, yet in such a manner as to leave intact the perfect unity of the One. They are the transcendent sources of individuality; in them the whole Plotinian κόσμος νοητός already exists κατ' αἰτίαν, or in a seminal form."

There is a certain perverse logic in deciding that, even as there is Soul and individual souls, and Intellect and individual intellects, so, beside the One, there must be individual henads—even though the essence of the One is to be unitary. There is also the consideration that the first principle of any class of thing, by virtue of which that class is *one* class, should have the characteristic of absolute unity, and that is the thought that Proclus puts forward here (1043.16ff.):

> The first principle of everything, then, as being the provider to all things of the greatest of goods, we term unifier of all and for that reason One, and hence we say also that every principle, in so far as it has a share of this honour among beings, is a henad of some class, and the most unitary of things in each class.

He takes as examples light, nature, and knowledge, and traces these up to their respective henads.

However, it is not his concern here to present the whole doctrine of henads—for that we must turn to Book III of the *Platonic Theology* (chs. 1-7). He only wants to make the point that the subject of the *Parmenides* does not have to be one single One, but can perfectly well be a series of them, the monad of Intellect and the monad of Soul, as well as the One itself, being the subjects of the various positive hypotheses.

He next (1051.34–1064.17) enters upon an extremely important survey and discussion of the various views of his predecessors as to the subject matter of the hypotheses. The Middle Platonic interpretation of the dialogue he dismisses without discussion, presumably because it did not envisage separate subjects for each of the hypotheses, and begins his survey of his predecessors with Plotinus' senior follower Amelius, followed by Porphyry and Iamblichus (none of these, we may note, mentioned by name, but all identified satisfactorily by a knowledgeable scholiast). These three authorities saw a level of reality corresponding to each of the hypotheses—Amelius identifying them as eight in number, while his two successors saw nine. Amelius and Porphyry, despite differences further down the scale, basically follow Plotinus in identifying the subjects of the first three hypotheses as the One, Intellect, and Soul. Iamblichus, typically, is more subtle, making his subjects "God and the gods" (the latter taken as henads), "the intellectual and intelligible beings," and τὰ κρείττονα γένη, that is, angels, daemons and heroes, while rational soul is relegated to the Fourth Hypothesis, and "souls of inferior rank attached to rational souls" to the Fifth.

All these three authorities, however, err, in Proclus' view, by envisaging levels of reality corresponding also to the last four, negative, hypotheses. Proclus, following the lead of his more immediate predecessors, especially Syrianus, condemns this view as misguided. The last four hypotheses should not be seen as introducing new orders of reality, but rather as reflecting negatively on those set out in Hypotheses 2-5 (1056.16–1057.5).

The first of those who grasped this is a totally mysterious figure, whom Proclus refers to simply as "the philosopher from Rhodes" (1057.6). Here the knowledgeable scholiast is of no help. If we are following a chronological sequence, as we seem to be, this man is a predecessor of Plutarch of Athens and may even be seen as a sort of "missing link" between the Syrian School of Iamblichus and his successors, and the Athenian School. He presumably came to Athens from Rhodes, since he is described as being "*from* Rhodes." Theodorus of Asine might suggest himself, as being chronologically suitable (though not, so far as we know from Rhodes), but we know his hierarchy of Being (*In Tim.* II, 274.16ff. = Test. 6 Deuse), and it is not reconcilable with the scheme presented here.[1] Another possible candidate would be the philosopher Hierius, pupil of Iamblichus, teacher of Maximus of Ephesus, and uncle of Libanius' friend Aristophanes of Corinth (*Or.* 14.7), who was active in the mid-fourth century, but, again, we do not know that Hierius had any connection with Rhodes—or that he ever had an original thought! However, it is curious that Plutarch of Athens called a son of his Hierius (Damasc. *Vit. Isid.* 88.122 Zintzen), which might betoken some spiritual connection.

Such speculations, however, are hardly profitable. More important is the doctrine. The philosopher from Rhodes actually discerns *ten* hypotheses, the last five countering the first five. Thus, the first and sixth concern the One, the second and seventh Intellect and the Intelligible, the third and eighth the objects of discursive intellect (*ta dianoēta*—presumably the realm of Soul), the fourth and ninth the entities which follow on these (adopting the emendation μετά for μέν in 1057.26), and the fifth and tenth the Receptacle (*hypodochē*) of bodies, i.e. Matter.

Proclus feels that this scheme is on the right lines, but goes wrong in trying to produce an hypothesis to balance the First, since that has already shown that the One does not exist, as being superior to existence; it does not, therefore, need to be balanced by the Fifth (this man's sixth—presumably 160b5-163b5), which postulates its non-existence. This is more properly paired off with the Second, and one does not have to make artificial divisions in order to carve ten hypotheses out of the text (where this man made his divisions we are not told).

Plutarch, son of Nestorius, Proclus' "spiritual grandfather," improves on this theory by restoring the number of hypotheses to nine, and giving them each a separate subject matter, though the last four present their subjects *negatively*, drawing absurdities from the postulate that the One does not exist (1058.21-1061.20). Plutarch sees this division of reality reflected also in other passages of Plato, particularly the Simile of the Line in the *Republic*.

Syrianus accepts this scheme (1061.20-1064.12), but adds to it the remarkable elaboration that guides Proclus through his own exposition of the first Hypothesis (and of the Second in the lost part of the Commentary, reflected in Books III through VI of the *Platonic Theology*), that the First and Second Hypotheses actually run through the whole extent and variety of the divine world (1061.31ff.), from the intelligible monad down to τὰ κρείττονα ἡμῶν γένη, as Iamblichus called them—daemons, heroes, and angels dependent on the divine Soul. This preposterous notion gives occasion for much ingenuity of exegesis, as we shall see.

---

[1] But see now n. 27 below.

After this extensive introduction to the hypotheses in general, we turn, with the next lemma, 137c4-5, to the introduction to the First Hypothesis in particular, which I have designated Section B-I of the Book (1064.21-1097.20). This is divided by Proclus into nine topics, and I have marked these off in the text by subheadings for the convenience of the reader.

The first (1064.21-1071.8) is the *skopos*, the subject matter, of the Hypothesis. Here—after an initial dismissive glance at Origen the Platonist, who held that the One is *anhypostaton*—Proclus begins by addressing himself, at some length, to a refutation of Iamblichus' view that the subject is "God and the gods." The One exists (ὑφεστώς, 1066.5) but it does not possess being (*ousia*)—that is a property of the Intelligible, and of nothing higher. The One is above being—but so also, it is claimed, is all divinity. Iamblichus argues that "since every god *qua* god, is a henad (for it is this element, the One, that divinises all being), for this reason he thinks it right to join to the study of the First a discussion of all the gods; for they are all supra-essential henads, and transcend the multiplicity of beings, and are the summits (*akrotētes*) of beings" (1066.22-28).

I give this verbatim, as it is a matter of controversy whether or not Iamblichus had a doctrine of henads—that is to say, of divine, supraessential first principles of the various chains of being. Saffrey and Westerink have devoted much space to this question in the Introduction to volume III of their edition of the *Platonic Theology* (ch. 1, pp. ix-x1), and wish to deny, in refutation of an article of mine,[1a] that the doctrine of henads in its Procline form goes back further than Syrianus.

Their argument against an Iamblichean origin for the doctrine is that the "gods" that Iamblichus postulates as subjects of the First Hypothesis are described by him as "intelligible" (νοητοί)—at least as it would seem from Proclus' criticism of his position in *PT* III, 23. This would certainly indicate that Iamblichus saw no contradiction between describing his gods as henads and as "objects of intellection," which means that his distinction between the henadic and the noetic was not as rigid as that of Proclus, but it does not, I think, disprove that he had described some class of beings as both gods and henads. After all, Iamblichus' henads are "participated" (μεθεκταί, 1067.3ff.), in contrast to the One itself, by lower orders of being, so that to that extent they could be described as "objects of intellection." I am not satisfied that I have fully understood Iamblichus' position, but I am not yet quite prepared to deny him *any* doctrine of henads.

[1a] "Iamblichus and the Origin of the Doctrine of Henads," *Phronesis* 17 (1972): 102-106 (reprinted as Appendix B of *Iamblichi Fragmenta*).

At any rate, Proclus condemns Iamblichus for associating these participated divine entities with the One, arguing that because of their participated status, they could not properly be the subject of all the negations which are here laid upon the One (1068.1ff.). Only of the One itself could all these attributes be denied.

Proclus ends this section by rejecting the doctrine, which is attributable both to Origen the Platonist and to Porphyry, that the One is the summit of the intelligible world—"for this entity," he says (1070.19), "is a participated henad." It is interesting that here he describes the same entity, the "Father" of the noetic world, both as intelligible and as a henad, throwing some light, perhaps, on his use of the terms in his critique of Iamblichus.

The next topic is "the type of discourse suitable to the subject," discussed briefly, from 1071.9-1072.18. The correct type of discourse, we learn, is one that will arouse the "One" of the soul to a vision of the One itself. This is the path of logic and syllogistic proof.

Thirdly (1072.19-1074.21), Proclus discusses the nature of the negations used in the First Hypothesis. Unlike other negations, these are actually superior to their corresponding affirmations, since the Not-Being they are describing is superior to Being.[2]

Fourthly, and following logically upon this, he discusses the suitability of negations to the First Cause (1074.22-1077.18). Negation of a characteristic, he points out, need not simply imply lack of the characteristic concerned (as would negations applied to Matter, for instance); there is also a "higher" type of negation, implying non-possession of an attribute of which an entity is the cause to things lower than it on the scale of being (as, for instance, the power of utterance and of silence may be applied to soul, 1076.14ff.), and this is the sense in which negations are suitable to the One.

Proclus next tackles, as his fifth topic, an *aporia* which must have exercised exegetes of the *Parmenides* from the beginning, to wit, why does Parmenides not begin with his own first principle of One Being, instead of this supra-existent One, the negation of his own? Proclus' defence of this is slightly curious, since he generally seems to want to maintain the fiction that Plato is presenting in the *Parmenides* the views of the historical Parmenides (if one does *not* hold this, of course, the *aporia* ceases to have any force). He makes the point (1078.13ff.) that the Eleatic Stranger in the *Sophist*, who, after all, is a faithful disciple of Parmenides, in fact makes the same sort of criticism of the Master's first principle as does "Parmenides" here—that a first principle which

---

[2] On this passage, and on 1076.8-10 below, see the comments of Werner Beierwaltes, *Proklos, Grundzüge*, pp. 341–343.

was both One and Being, and a whole, could only possess one-ness as an attribute, and thus not be absolutely primary. Parmenides is therefore using his first principle of the Poem as a basis for ascending to the true first principle of all things.

It appears from 1079.18ff. that Proclus may be countering here the argument of a particular predecessor, and this could be Origen the Platonist, who is recorded at the beginning of the discussion of the subject matter of the hypotheses as saying that the One of the First Hypothesis is ἀνυπόστατον (1064.9, cf. *PT* II, 4)—that is to say, that the First Hypothesis does not have a real entity as its subject. In this case, the *aporia* would be of something more than historical interest, as Origen is reckoned by Proclus in the *Platonic Theology* still to be an authority worth refuting by name.

The sixth topic (1079.27-1082.19) concerns the status and purposes of the negations. Is it a sign of weakness peculiar to our human souls that we must talk of the One in such terms? No, says Proclus, even Soul and Intellect can only apprehend the One by supra-intellectual negation. So it is inherent in the nature of the One, non-existent as it is, to be apprehended through negativity.

The seventh problem (1083.1-1088.3) arises from the fact that, although absolutely every attribute should be denied of the One, Parmenides appears to be rather selective in the First Hypothesis. This was plainly a long-standing *aporia*. Proclus first mentions, dismissively, those commentators who opined that what is being denied of the One is the two types of quantity, the discrete and the continuous. For one thing, he says, Plato recognises more than two types of quantity (cf. *Phil.* 55e); for another, not all the attributes denied of it are quantities, e.g. shape, motion, rest. A second class of commentators (among whom we may perhaps rank the Middle Platonist Albinus, cf. n. 57 below) try to identify Aristotle's ten Categories here; a third see the five greatest genera of the *Sophist* (possibly Plotinus, though he nowhere explicitly denies them of the One). To both these latter one must reply that they have the truth, but not the whole truth.

Superior to these, but still not quite right, are those who point out that all the attributes Plato produces are true of the "monad", which I take here to mean the number one. In that case, they would be denied of it in the First Hypothesis, presumably, as only being in it κρυφίως (1084.12), or potentially, while in the Second Hypothesis they would be asserted of it for the same reason—that they *are* contained in it, if only potentially. Such an interpretation seems most suitable to a pre-Neoplatonic Pythagorean commentator, since Proclus indicates that this school of thought does not connect these two aspects of the monad with Intellect and the One, which no one after Plotinus, one would think, could fail to have done.

On the other hand, since the sequence of commentators is about to culminate in Syrianus, one would expect to see the views of Porphyry and Iamblichus criticised here somewhere. However, in this case we are not discussing the subject matter of the hypotheses, but simply why only these particular attributes are used for assertion and denial, and in answer to this problem Iamblichus, for instance, might well seek for a guiding thread in attributes that could be both denied and asserted of the unit. At any rate, of all the theories stated, this is the most likely to commend itself, I think, to the modern critic.

Not so the solution of Syrianus (1085.12-1086.9), the remarkable nature of which I have alluded to previously, in connection with the subject matter of the Second Hypothesis. He came to the conclusion, we recall, that the key to the selection of attributes by Plato was that each of them symbolised a type of intelligible being, and this is the guiding principle of his, and Proclus', exegesis of the first two hypotheses.

The eighth topic for discussion (1088.4-1089.16) is the rationale behind the order of the negations. This leads on from the previous question, especially if Syrianus' theory be accepted. Why, for a start, does Parmenides begin by denying plurality of the One, and only finally deny Being of it, though Being might seem the "noblest" or most essential attribute? Because, says Proclus (1089.2ff.), "in the case of negations, one should proceed from the most alien, and through these demonstrate that the less alien do not follow from the hypothesis"—and the most alien thing from One is Many.

The ninth, and final, topic (1089.17-1092.15) arises directly out of the eighth. What, asks Proclus, is it that is denied of the One first? Obviously, it is "many," but what precisely is this "many"? Some commentators assert that it is "the many at every level" (τὰ πανταχοῦ πολλά), that is, both intelligible and sensible multiplicity. The problem with that, though, is that "many" is attributed to the One in the Second Hypothesis, and that cannot include sensible multiplicity.

We have two sets of commentators after this, the latter of whom is then modified in a manner redolent of Syrianus or Proclus himself, lending likelihood to the conjecture that they are Porphyry and Iamblichus. The first set of commentators might then be indefinite Middle Platonists, criticised by Porphyry. The former commentator (Porphyry?) declares that what is denied of the One here is the *intellectual* multiplicity (τὸ νοερὸν πλῆθος). Proclus criticises this as too vague. If it is meant to include the intelligible as well as the intellectual level, well and good, but he should have said so; whereas if *noeron* is used in the strict sense, as pertaining to Intellect, as opposed to Life or Being, then it is simply wrong. It is not quite clear, I think, that Porphyry contrasted "noetic" and "noeric" in the technical sense observed by Iamblichus and those after him, so Proclus' criticism here may be simply anachronistic. At any rate, the second commentator (Iamblichus?) explicitly distinguishes the intelligible from the intellectual level of multiplicity (probably deliberately contradicting Porphyry), and declares that it is specifically the former which is denied of the One, as coming next after it. Proclus accepts this view, simply adding the reminder (following Syrianus) that there are many *taxeis* in the intelligible realm—three triads of them, indeed, each presided over by a henad—as well as many at the intelligible-and-intellectual level, and all these are implicit in "Many." (In the parallel passage of *PT* II, 12, p. 66 S-W we learn that this Many is actually the summit of the intelligible-and-intellectual realm.)

So ends this lengthy introductory passage, after which we turn to the consideration of the text (Section B-II). Proclus continues with some comments on the text of the first lemma (we may note here a particularly clear distinction being made between *theōria* and *lexis* at 1092.16-18), which stretches from 1092.16 to 1097.20. Proclus notes first that Parmenides adduces no proof for the proposition that the One is not many, since that is a *koinē ennoia* and does not require proof. Proclus then enunciates the basic (Aristotelian) dictum that "the beginning of every process of proof must be the indemonstrable (τὸ ἀναπόδεικτον, *An. Post.* I, 2), and common intuitions (κοιναὶ ἔννοιαι) must come before demonstrations, as the geometers also assert" (1092.27-30). All of which does not, however, prevent him from producing a sort of proof, to the effect that whatever is primally anything has no truck whatever with its opposite; but this is really just an analysis of what it means to be primally or absolutely anything as being the first cause of that quality, be it oneness or beauty or existence, in the rest of the world.

He goes on from this (1093.17ff.) to address again the problem already raised in the fifth *aporia* above—what sort of One Parmenides is assuming when he says "If One exists." Not the One of his Poem, necessarily, since that is One-Being, and One-Being is "many." Proclus' answer is, of course, the same as before: Parmenides is using his own first principle as a starting-point for ascent to the truly One.

After a brief commendation of the anagogic quality of the initial εἶεν of the Hypothesis, he goes on (1095.2ff.) to raise the *aporia*—why, only in the case of the first negation, that of "many," Parmenides does not emancipate the One from its opposite as well, namely "one," even as he frees it from both sameness and otherness, for example, or "whole" and "having parts." He answers this, as so often, first on the logical, and then on the metaphysical (πραγματειώδης) level. Logically, he is beginning from *koinai ennoiai*, and while the proposition that the One is not many is common sense, the proposition that the One is not one is not immediately obvious. So we must work up to that at the end, in 141e.

On the metaphysical level, Proclus appears rather to miss the point, or at least to leave it behind. He points out that the One here is not the One opposed to the Many, since that is involved with multiplicity, even as, say, Sameness is involved with Otherness. Quite so, but why, the *aporia* asks, does he not deny that "one" of it, at the same time as denying "many" of it? In fact, Proclus' first answer serves very well; it is not intuitively obvious that the One is not one, and it would abort the whole course of the hypothesis to demonstrate it at this point.

The next section concerns the denial to the One of part and whole (137c5-d3). It runs from 1097.28 to 1110.15, and is divided into two lemmata. (In *PT* II, 12, p. 66, 20ff. S-W, "whole and part" are associated with the middle triad of the intelligible-and-intellectual gods, but that is not made clear here.) Proclus begins, on the level of logic, with the observation, ultimately derived from Aristotle,[3] that when a syllogism derives the validity of the negation of the consequent from the negation of the premise, the premise is the more general concept (1098.5ff.). He follows this with the principle (more metaphysical than logical, one would think) that everything which is more comprehensive in its power than something else is nearer than that thing to the One (1098.29ff.). The purpose of adducing this pair of principles is to show the logical correctness of Parmenides' deriving the more particular denial of part and whole from the more general details of multiplicity.

All this is on the logical level, though. The consideration of *ta pragmata*, or metaphysical realities, only begins at 1100.12. He begins with the proposition that every "many" derives from the One as its cause. If we trace any multiplicity, even the multiplicity of henads, back to its primary cause, we arrive at the One. Whole and parts, on the other hand, are proper to the realm of Being, not of the One (1101.8ff.). The One Being, as we hear in the Second Hypothesis, is a whole and has parts. The One, therefore, is beyond "whole" and "part," as it is beyond all things essential (οὐσιώδη), and even unitary (ἐνιαῖα). Furthermore, "many" is also prior to "whole" and "part," because each of them is in a way many, but the primary Many participates only in the One (1101.36ff.).

Proclus here seems to be expatiating on the obvious at tedious length, but he plainly takes great delight in showing the logical sound-

---

[3] Cf. *Topics* VI, 4.141b28ff.; *Met.* K, 1.1059b30ff. Συναναιρεῖν is the technical term.

ness of Parmenides' procedure. The discussion of the proof continues to 1103.10. He then ends the lemma with two remarks, only the second of which need detain us. The question had, it seems, been raised as to whether Parmenides is denying these attributes of the One *in relation to itself*, or *in relation to others*. At least one previous commentator had argued for the latter alternative, as "many" and all subsequent attributes are *other* than the One, but this, Proclus argues, misunderstands Plato's procedure, which passes from what is not true of the One in relation to itself to what is not true both in relation to itself and to others ('same', 'different', 'like', 'unlike', 'in contact', 'apart'), and finally to what is not true in relation to others ('expressible', 'opinable', 'knowable', etc.): "So, when he says the One is not many, he is not saying that the Others besides the One are not the One, as though he were denying those of the one, but he is merely saying that it does not possess multiplicity in itself, and that the One is not, together with being One, also Many, but that it is solely One and essentially One, pure of all multiplicity" (1104.6-11).

He begins the second lemma, after a summary of the logical form of the proof, by calling attention to the distinction between being partless (ἀμερές) and not having parts, only the latter condition being proper to the One. The problem is that the highest level of Forms can be described as "partless"—what Plato in the *Timaeus* (35a1) calls *ameriston*. The fact that he describes the One as *ameres* in the *Sophist* (245a8) does not bother Proclus. This merely indicates that all that has no parts is also partless, but it is still true that not all that is partless has no parts (1105.9ff.). The point, after all, is partless, but it is made up of certain elements (the components of its definition) which may count as parts; and the monad similarly. Only the One has not even any components which would make up a definition, and so no "parts" whatever.

This, on the other hand, must not lead us to regard the subject of the First Hypothesis as absolutely non-existent, as do some commentators (1105.32ff.). Normally one would expect such criticism to be directed against Origen the Platonist, but the culprit or culprits in this case sound distinctly Neoplatonist, and would more naturally be identified with Porphyry and Iamblichus, as I hope to show.

At any rate, these authorities feel that one should attach some "nature and characteristic" (φύσις καὶ ἰδιότης) to the One. To do this, the first authority postulates, above Nous, something called *noötēs*, "intellectuality," envisaged as being something "simpler" (ἁπλούστερα) than, and presumably causative of, Nous; above this, *to nooun* (with the sense, Proclus is careful to explain, not of "intelligising," but rather of *causing* intellection, and thus more properly from νοόω rather than from νοέω!); and above this in turn, *to noēma*, which he claims to be primal.

More remarkable still, this person postulates prior to each of the Forms a causative entity of the same type (with ending in -ōma), and declares that all these are hen ("one," or "a One"), though what precisely he means by that is not clear to Proclus. Are they just different aspects of the One, or are they intended to introduce a real multiplicity into the realm of the One? Either way there are difficulties.

Pierre Hadot, in *Porphyre et Victorinus* (I, 355-375), provides a most useful discussion of this passage, and attributes the above doctrine, with great plausibility, to Porphyry. Where I am unwilling to follow him, however, is in his desire to attribute all the subsequent views reported here to Porphyry as well. Marius Victorinus does, admittedly, seem to make use of all three doctrines. The passage Hadot adduces for the third (*Adv. Ar.* IV, 23.27-34) propounds the remarkable view that the One possesses *praeexistentia, praeviventia, praecognoscentia* (which should be translations of a series of remarkable neologisms—προουσία, προζωότης, προνοότης), and these seem to answer pretty well to the "causes" of Being, Life, and Intellect which the third authority postulates within the One (see below). But if these are *all* Porphyry, then Proclus is presenting them in a most misleading manner. The alternative is that Victorinus had some access to other Neoplatonists than Porphyry, such as Theodorus of Asine or Iamblichus, though there is, unfortunately, no evidence of this.

At any rate, the next authority (1106.33ff.), wants to make a distinction between God and the state of "being God" (τὸ θεῷ εἶναι), the latter being the proper designation of the One (cf. Victorinus, *Adv. Ar.* I, 33.4-9). Proclus objects strongly to this, on the grounds that Plato denies Being (ἔστιν) of the One, but this is not quite giving credit to the intentions of the author of the doctrine, who presumably meant his (Aristotelian) formulation to signify "god-ness," without particular emphasis on *being*. More cogent is the argument that in the case of non-composite, immaterial entities, there can be no valid distinction between '*x*' and '*being x*'.

Since I would prefer to claim the next authority after this as Iamblichus, I have no convincing suggestion as to who this commentator may be, except that he is presented by Proclus as being different from the previous one. He could be Amelius, or Theodorus of Asine—or the first could actually be Amelius, and this one Porphyry. All that seems clear is that Victorinus knows both formulations, and that Proclus presents them here as distinct doctrines.

The third authority (1107.9ff.), whose terminology I find distinctly reminiscent of Iamblichus (see n. 90 to Book VI, below), wishes the One to contain within itself, in an incomprehensible way, the causal principles of Being, Life, and Intellect, and indeed of all the Forms, as "paradigms prior to paradigms," itself being "a whole prior to wholes," without need of parts. Proclus dismisses this sort of talk as being a needless duplication of reality, issuing in an infinite regress, since all multiplicity of whatever kind must be preceded by a One (although one might argue that what this authority is postulating are remarkably akin to henads!).

Better, he says in conclusion (1108.19ff.), to rest content with the negations, as being the only correct way of expressing the One's transcendent superiority. Not even the epithet *autotheos* (1108.36-37) is adequate to describe it. We might, cautiously, term it "the fount of all divinity" ($\pi\eta\gamma\grave{\eta}\ \vartheta\varepsilon\acute{o}\tau\eta\tau o\varsigma\ \pi\acute{a}\sigma\eta\varsigma$), but even then we are not saying what it is in itself, but only describing its relation to what follows it.

Having settled this question, he turns briefly to the *lexis* (1109.20ff.) simply pointing out that the negations here (and particularly the use of $\delta\varepsilon\tilde{\imath}$ in connection with them) are not privative, but rather indicate superiority to the corresponding assertions.

The latter part of Book VI is devoted to the section 137d4-38a1, which denies of the One (a) beginning, middle and end, and (b) shape, both straight and round. It is divided into five lemmata, and runs from 1110.16 to 1134.12.

We learn from the *Platonic Theology* (II, 12, p. 67, 14ff. S-W) that this is the third triad of the intelligible-intellectual realm, and indeed that Proclus sees each member of the triad represented, respectively, by "beginning, middle and end," "limits" and "shape," but once again, these distinctions are less than clear here.

Proclus begins by demonstrating that "having beginning, middle and end" is symbolic of a more partial rank of beings than simply having parts, since one can have a being which has just two parts, such as the Dyad.

He notices next (1111.23ff.) a tendentious *aporia*, which challenges Parmenides' assumption that everything which has a beginning, middle, and end has these as *parts* of itself. A line, after all, begins and ends in a point, but the points cannot be parts of the line, for nothing which has a limit has an unlimited number of parts; but points are unlimited, so the line cannot be made up of points *as parts*, although they constitute its beginning and end. Proclus' first response is that such an argument is irrelevant to the One (or to any immaterial being), which, if it had anything analogous to a beginning, middle, or end, would have them as parts—and further, if anything has limits at all, it will inevitably have parts which are bounded by such limits. His second response (1112.23ff.) is to declare the term "part" ($\mu\acute{\varepsilon}\rho o\varsigma$) to be ambiguous, having at least three senses: (1) that which mirrors the composition of the whole of which it is a part—a "homoeomer," one might say; (2) a non-

397

homogeneous part, as, for instance, *dianoia* and *doxa* are of the soul; and (3), in general, "anything that is in any way linked with other things for the completion of some one entity"—the sense in which we are "parts" of the universe. All of these senses of "part," he says, are here being denied of the One.

A second *aporia* is raised (1113.33ff.) by those who adduce the well-known passage of the *Laws* (IV, 715e), where the Athenian Stranger says that God "possesses the beginning and middle and end of all existent things," which would appear to be in contradiction to the present passage. Before giving his own (or Syrianus') solution, Proclus mentions two earlier essays at solution. Normally, one would assume Porphyry and Iamblichus, in that order, but the first (1114.1-5) seems from the terminology very like something that Iamblichus would say (see n. 92 below), that the One does in a sense possess beginning, middle, and end, but possesses them κρυφίως (a Chaldaean term), and in a way inconceivable to us. This suggestion Proclus has little use for, but the second he treats more politely (1114.20ff.), and for this reason I would conjecture that it is that of Plutarch of Athens. This suggests that Plato in the *Laws* passage is referring, not to the primal God, but to the Demiurge. Proclus does not reject this suggestion outright, but prefers the solution of Syrianus (1114.35ff.) that we must distinguish between descriptions of the One *in relation to itself* and *in relation to others*. It is in the latter sense that Plato is giving this description in the *Laws*, and also in the *Second Letter* (312e), while here the One is being described in relation to itself. A good example of Syrianus' creative exegesis!

The next lemma, 137d6-8 (1116.21-1124.37), concerns the denial to the One of Limit (πέρας), consequent on its having no beginning, middle, or end. Proclus begins by reminding us once again of the orderliness of Plato's argument, and then is stimulated by the question "in what sense the One is unlimited" into an extended discussion of Limit and Unlimitedness, showing how they pervade reality at all levels (1118.9-1124.37), which becomes almost a brief sketch of his philosophical system (although, as so often, the doctrine is actually that of Syrianus, cf. 1118.35-36).

He discerns ten levels in the universe at which first Unlimitedness, and then Limit, are manifested, and describes their characteristics in turn. From Limit and the Unlimited themselves, through Eternity, Intellect, Soul, Time, the revolution of the aether, forms-in-matter, quantity and quality in the material realm, unqualified body, and Matter, both informed and formless, all things partake in Limit and Unlimitedness. Where does this leave the One (1123.22ff.)? If it were unlimited in any sense proper to existent things, one would also have to term it "*not* unlimited," as not being exempted from both sides of the antithesis. It can only be "unlimited" as not having any final cause which would limit it, and so being outside the whole "chain" (σειρά) of Limit (1124.15).

The next lemma (137d8–e1) concerns the denial to the One of shape, both the straight and the curved or round (στρογγύλον). Proclus makes much of the fact (1126.6ff.) that Plato says, not "*is* neither straight nor curved," but "*partakes* neither *of* the straight nor the curved"—the latter expression, he claims, as against the former, also implying possession of no intermediate kind of shape (assuming that intermediate stages on a spectrum "partake of" the extremes in some proportion, as all colours are regarded as partaking of white and black). Again, he is able to maintain (1126.31ff.) that "having shape" is a more restricted category than having ends and middle, since things can have ends and middle without having shape—lines, for instance, time, number, or motion. This, then, preserves the progression from more general to more particular.

He then (1127.26ff.) notices an *aporia* arising from the *Phaedrus* (247c6–7): Is the One "without shape" in the same sense as the "supra-celestial place" of the myth? Plainly it must be in a different sense. Of the *hyperouranios topos*, after all, he has denied some attributes, but he asserts others (e.g. it is the "helmsman of the soul"), whereas of the One he denies all attributes. Also, we must note that the former entity is described as "shapeless," while the One is said to be "partaking in no shape," a more absolute denial of all shape, even "intelligible shape."

The fourth lemma (137e1–4), running from 1129.22 to 1132.29, raises the question in what sense one should take "straight" and "round" (στρογγύλον now seems to take on this sense, rather than "curved"). The answer is that "straight" refers to procession, and "round" to return. Since the One neither proceeds from itself nor returns to itself, it has no part in the straight or the round.

The fifth lemma (137e5–138a1), running from 1132.36 to 1134.12, briefly summarises the course of the argument and reminds us how far down the scale of Being we have reached, to wit, through the intelligible-intellectual realm, the role of which is to link the intelligible to the intellectual proper. The ramifications of the latter we will meet in the next Book.

COMMENTARY

◻ ◻ ◻

A. GENERAL INTRODUCTION TO THE
HYPOTHESES

1039 *"Well then," said Parmenides, "if there is a One, of course the One would not be many." "How could it?" "So there cannot be any parts of it, nor can it be a whole." "Obviously." (137c)*

The first question to be considered, making a new beginning to our enquiry, is how Parmenides came to establish the number of the hypotheses as he did. For whether there are four, or six, or eight, or nine, or ten, it is worth seeing how this number arose. For one might first raise the logical question as to whether the majority of the other hypotheses are not redundant, and contribute nothing to the advertised method. Deriving from this, we have, if anything, two hypotheses only: "If there is a One," and "If there is not, what follows?" More than this there are not, if we remember the canons we laid down. How, then, have so many arisen instead of two?

(i) On the Number of the Hypotheses

I wish to answer this question first, and only then to deal with the metaphysical realities. I would maintain that the number of the hypotheses is revealed clearly to be in accord with the defining terms on which the hypothesis is based. For if, on the one hand, the One exists, five hypotheses would arise in virtue of the different natures of the One—a fact that we have indicated previously.[1] If, on the other hand, it does not exist, four would arise, in virtue of the different concepts of Not-Being. For "One" has three senses—one as superior to Being, another as coordinate with Being, and another as inferior to Being. "Not-Being," likewise, has two senses—one as Absolute Not-Being, the other as that which exists in one way and not in another. Necessarily,

[1] Cf. above, 1035.6ff.

then, the argument, proceeding in accordance with all the senses of
1040 these two defining terms, causes the hypotheses to proliferate. In the
First Hypothesis it enquires into the relations of the One superior to
Being to itself, and to all other things, in the Second, those of the One
coordinate with Being; in the Third, the relations of the One inferior
to Being to itself and other things; in the Fourth, what are the relations
of the others which participate in the One to themselves and to the
One; in the Fifth, what relations the others which do not participate in
the One have to themselves and to the One. In the Sixth Hypothesis,
we investigate the relations of the One, if it does not exist, in the sense
of existing in one way and not in another, to itself and to other things;
in the Seventh, the relations of the One, if it does not exist, in the sense
of absolute non-existence, towards itself and others; in the Eighth, the
relations of the others to themselves and to the One, when taken as
non-existent in the sense of existing in one way and not in another; in
the Ninth, the relations of the others to themselves and to the One,
when taken as absolutely non-existent.

And so the procedure attains its fulfillment in this Hypothesis, having gone through all the senses of both One and Not-Being, and having by means of all of them brought to completion its investigations,
arranged in nine hypotheses. For it was impossible for all the affirmative and negative and both affirmative and negative propositions to be
true of the One taken in only one sense—for example, the proposition
that the One is neither the same nor different; and again, that it is both
the same and different, and once again, that it is both the same and not
the same, different and not different. So then, anyone who wants to
draw all these conclusions about the same subject is truly engaged in
1041 idle sport, and is "pursuing a game proper" not "to old men"[2] but to
children, when indulging in that. If in fact all the propositions are to
come out true, such as are concluded about the One on the assumption
of its existence, following necessarily on the existence of the One, so
that what follows from the non-existence of the One is false (for it is
impossible either for true conclusions to follow from both sides of a
contradiction, or for contradictory propositions to be true of the same
thing, unless the conclusions are necessarily true of different things in
each case), it is plain, surely, that the One must be taken in a variety of
senses, in order that the negative propositions may be true of one, and
the affirmative of another, necessarily following in each case from the
postulation of the One. And in this way the multiplicity of the hy-

---

[2] A reference to *Laws* III, 685a, παίζοντας παιδιὰν πρεσβυτικὴν σώφρονα. The word
ἀθυρεῖν used just before ("engage in idle sport"), originally Homeric (*Iliad* 15.364), and
otherwise poetical, may be for Proclus a vox Platonica (cf. *Laws* VII, 796b, and above,
Book V, 982.16).

potheses may be brought into unities, even though they are all about
the Parmenidean One, according as the argument considers it as One
or as Being or simultaneously as One and as Being, making different
inferences in each case. And again, when the One is postulated as not
existing, whether we take it as the non-existent in some sense or as the
absolutely non-existent, and draw impossible conclusions in both cases
by means of all these bringing up to nine the number of the hypotheses,
as we set out already.

It is clear, then, that the One has three senses, either the One pure and
simple, or that which is participated in by Being, but remains independent, or that which is participated in, but as an inhering characteristic. For of Intellect also we have the unparticipated, the participated
but essential, and the participated but as a state (of the recipient); separate from its participants, and the inseparably participated. All these
senses, both of Intellect and of Soul, are set out by him distinctly in the
Timaeus.[3] Further, that Not-Being also has two senses, either the non-
existent in some sense or the absolutely non-existent, he himself has
made clear in the *Republic*.[4] So that if the one has three senses and the
other two, it is reasonable that such should be the number of the hypotheses. For the Others, when one postulates that the One exists,
must have two possibilities, either to participate in the One or not; and
again, when one postulates that it does not exist, two possibilities,
either being other than the One which exists to some extent, or to the
One which in no way exists, and having either that which is in some
way existent and one, or that which is in no way one. So that the number of the hypotheses would necessarily be nine.

1042   That this is the number of the hypotheses has been sufficiently confirmed also by those who have paid attention only to the logical aspect
of the dialogue and have, as it were, chased after the traces of Plato's
arguments. For from these very traces, as one might term them, our
predecessors did not fail to grasp the true position of the philosopher
and the serious structure of the work. I need hardly labour the point.
The philosopher himself will make clear to us the division, when we
enter upon the study of his actual words; since of those who have either
contracted or extended the number of hypotheses incorrectly, the one
set have confused distinct ones, while the other set have split up ones
that are unitary and dependent on a single first principle. Let us, however, abide by these defining terms, and declare the hypotheses to be
just so many as we think that Plato himself will acquaint us with as the

---

[3] Cf. Proclus' discussion in *In Tim*. II, 250.22ff. (on *Tim*. 36c).
[4] Presumably a reference to *Book V*, 478bff.

argument proceeds. For one should not take one's principle of division from anywhere else but the text before us.

There are, then, nine hypotheses, the total being arrived at according to the principle, outlined above, of the different senses of One and Not-Being. So for the purpose of the present enquiry there is no need to say more, but what has been said already is sufficient for the logical study of the subject matter. However, there have been in the past some commentators, very much concerned with the reality behind the text, who do not accept that there are a plurality of hypotheses, nor in general that the manifold and various conclusions concern a plurality of different subjects, but they ask whether one and the same sense of One is to be assumed in all the hypotheses, or not one, but different senses in each. If the One were to be taken in only one sense, then there would not be a number of hypotheses, but only one (for there should be one hypothesis for each subject), and the dialogue is not about first *principles*, as you claim (they would say), but about the first principle; for the One which is the subject of discussion is a first principle and certainly not a number of first principles. If, on the other hand, the One has various senses, and he is weaving together his conclusions about different entities at different stages, and varying his hypotheses, he is failing of the object of the declared method. For the task was to examine the consequences of postulating and denying one and the same thing, not to jump from one sense of the word to another.

1043

(ii) On Principles and the First Principle: Doctrine of Henads

So then, as I said, this line of enquiry is more concerned with the underlying realities, while the previous one is of a more logical nature. But before I turn to its refutation, I must say a few words about the first principle, such as will suffice for the elucidation of our present problem. When we say that the One is the first principle of things existent and non-existent (since being unified is for all things a good and indeed the greatest of goods, while to be sundered completely from the One[5] is an evil and the ultimate of evils; for such a separation becomes the cause of Unlikeness and disconnectedness and of departure from the natural state), the first principle of everything, then, as being the provider to all things of the greatest of goods, we term unifier of all and for this reason One, and hence we say also that every principle, in so far as it has a share of this honour among beings, is a henad of some class and the most unitary of things in each class. First of all, we place

---

[5] The πανεπόπτου of the Greek MSS is a mirage. Moerbeke gives *omniquaque ab uno*, which confirms Taylor's excellent suggestion of παντελῶς τοῦ ἑνός.

this entity which has the status of principle, not on the level of parts, but of whole, nor in any single one of the Many, but in the monads which hold together the multiplicity, and further, among those monads, we see as being particularly in the summits that which is most unitary in them, in so far as these are themselves united to the One and are divinised and do not depart from that single first principle. As for instance[6]—to transfer our discussion to the realities themselves—we

1044 see many causes of light, some in the heavens, others below the moon; for different types of light are projected into this realm in various ways from material fire and from the moon and from the other stars. But if one were to enquire after the single monad of all the light in the cosmos, from which all the other objects derive which are lighted or productive of light, he will not fix upon any other candidate for this than this visible circuit of the sun. For this entity, proceeding forth from some higher level, from the "hidden", as they call it (*Or. Chald.* fr. 148), and supracosmic realm, has distributed to all the cosmic entities the light that is suitable to them. Or where else would both the heavenly bodies and the lightlessness of Matter derive their share of light? Well then, are we to call this visible body a first principle of light? But it is spatially extended and divisible, and projects different light from each separate part of it. We, however, are seeking the single principle of light. Perhaps, then, it is the soul, which "leads the body to existence" (*Laws* X, 899a), that we may take to be the generative principle of light? This generates light, certainly, but not primally; for it is itself a multiplicity, while light gives the impression of arising from a simple and unitary source. Perhaps, then, it is Intellect, the causal principle of Soul? But this too, though it is more unified than Soul, is not yet a first principle in the proper and primal sense. What is left, then, is for the One, the cause of existence and, as it were, the 'flower'[7] of this Intellect, to be the first principle of this light also; for this is the true sun "ruling in the visible realm" (*Rep.* VI, 509d), "offspring of the Good" (*ibid.* 507a). Every henad derives from this source, and every divinity

1045 from the henad of henads and the fount of gods. And even as that is the first principle of light there in the intelligible realm, so the henad of the solar order is the first principle of light here in the visible realm; so that if one is to choose one single cause and principle of all light in the cosmos, one must take this henad, analogous as it is to the One, established hidden within it and never departing from it. Since this henad is

---

[6] The passage from 1043.30 to 1049.37, which expounds Proclus' doctrine of henads, has been translated and discussed by Saffrey and Westerink in the preface to vol. III of their Budé edition of *PT*, pp. lx-lxxii.

[7] Ἄνθος, a Chaldaean term (*Or. Chald,* fr. 1.1, etc.), much used by Proclus, e.g. *In Tim.* I, 419.9, and III, 118.26; *In Crat.* 47.15ff.; *PT* l3, p. 15.3ff. S-W.

established above the solar intellect, there is also in Intellect, in so far as it is Intellect, the One participated in by it, like a seed sown in it, through which it is joined to the henadic realm; and not only in it, but in the solar Soul as well. For this too is drawn up to it in virtue of its own One, through the mediation of the One in Intellect. In the same way even in the solar body there is at least some echo of it; for this too must participate in what is above it, in Soul by virtue of the life that is sown into it, in Intellect by virtue of its form, and in the henad by virtue of the unity in it, since Soul too participates in both Intellect and the henad, and things participated in are different from what participates in them; you might actually say that the immediate cause of the solar light is this one, which it possesses through its participation in that henad.

Even thus, if we were to seek for the root, as it were, of all bodies, from which have sprouted all those both in the heaven and beneath the moon, both wholes and parts, we would not unreasonably say that this was Nature, which is the principle of motion and rest for all bodies, established in the things themselves that move and are at rest (I mean by Nature the single life that permeates the whole cosmos, participating after Intellect and Soul, and by means of Intellect and Soul, in unity).[8] This we would say is the principle, rather than any of the many particular things. And yet not even this is a principle in the true sense; for it has a multiplicity of powers, and by means of different ones it controls different parts of the universe. However, we are at present seeking the single common first principle of all things, not a multiplicity of separate principles. But if we are to discover that single first principle, we must ascend to the most unitary element of Nature and its 'flower,' in virtue of which Nature also is a god, which is dependent upon its own fount, and which holds together the universe and unifies it and renders it sympathetic with itself. That, then, is the One, the first principle of all generation both for the manifold powers of Nature, and for particular natures, and for all those things under the sway of Nature.

Thirdly, we may take the case of knowledge. We say that there is a first principle of knowledge, by which we certainly do not mean imagination and sense-perception. For there is no object of knowledge in these that is partless and immaterial and without shape. Nor yet will we call knowledge derived from opinion and discursive intellection a first principle. For the former kind does not have knowledge of causes, but is irrational, as Diotima says (*Symp.* 202a); for it only investigates the fact of things. The latter, again, even if it knows the cause also, yet grasps facts part by part, and does not comprehend the whole, nor the

---

[8] Reading ἐνώσεως, with S-W (*PT* III, p. lxii), for γενέσεως of MSS.

eternal and invariable aspect of reality, nor the simultaneous and non-composite and simple. So these likewise are not to be postulated as first principles of knowledge. Might intuitive intellect, then, be the first principle of knowledge? The knowledge inherent in it, after all, is simultaneously omnipresent and non-transitive and incessant and partless. If the knowledge of intuitive intellect were without multiplicity, so as to be totally non-multiple and one, perhaps we would have postulated it as the first principle of knowledge. Since, however, it is not only one, but also variegated, and there are a multiplicity of intellections within it, and that which is the intellection of something else is not necessarily also that of the rest of the objects of intellection (for as intelligible objects are distinguished from one another, so too are intellections), necessarily none of these are the first principle of knowledge; for they are all equally intellections.

1047   If, however, we are to state the single principle of knowledge, we must fix upon the One, which generates Intellect and all the knowledge both within it and what is seen on the secondary levels of being. For this, transcending the Many as it does, is the first principle of knowledge for them, and is not the same as them, as is Sameness in the intelligible realm. This is coordinate with its Otherness and inferior to Being. The One, on the other hand, is beyond intellectual Being and grants coherence to it, and for this reason the One is God and so is Intellect, but not by reason of Sameness nor Being. And in general Intellect is not god *qua* Intellect; for even the particular intellect is an intellect, but is not a god. Also, it is the proper role of Intellect to contemplate and intelligise and judge true being; but of God to unify, to generate, to exercise providence, and suchlike. By virtue of that aspect of itself which is not intellect, the Intellect is God;[9] and by virtue of that aspect of itself which is not God, the god in it is Intellect. The divine Intellect, as a whole, is an intellectual essence along with its own summit and its proper unity, knowing itself in so far as it is intellectual, but being "intoxicated on nectar," as has been said,[10] and generating the whole of cognition, in so far as it is the 'flower' of the Intellect and a supra-essential henad.

So, once again, in seeking the first principle of knowledge, we have ascended to the One. And not in the case of these only, but in every other case we would likewise discover the monads being the most proper principles of things; for everywhere the first principle is the One. It would be about this first principle that Socrates in the *Phaedrus* is speaking when he says (245d), "the first principle is ungenerated."

[9] Cf. *ET*, props. 120 and 134.
[10] Cf. *Enn.* VI, 7.35, where we find the reference to "intoxication with nectar"; *PT* I, 14, p. 67.2-5 S-W; and below, 1080.10-11.

For if it is impossible for any species to be wholly extinguished, far more so, surely, is it necessary that the single first principle of each of them should be preserved and remain eternally, in order that around it there should come into existence the whole multiplicity which proceeds properly from each one.

1048   It is the same to say "henad" as to say "first principle," if in fact the first principle is in all cases the most unificatory element. So anyone who is talking about the One in any respect would then be discoursing about first principles, and it would then make no difference whether one said that the thesis of the dialogue was about first principles or about the One. Those men of old,[11] too, decided to term incorporeal essence as a whole "One," and the corporeal and in general the divisible, "Others"; so that in whatever sense you took the One, you would not deviate from the contemplation of incorporeal substances and the ruling henads; for all the henads are in each other and are united with each other, and their unity is far greater than the community and sameness among beings. In these too there is compounding of Forms, and likeness and friendship and participation in one another; but the unity of those former entities, inasmuch as it is a unity of henads, is far more unitary and ineffable and unsurpassable; for they are all in all of them, which is not the case with the Forms. These are participated in by each other, but they are not all in all. And yet, in spite of this degree of unity in that realm, how marvellous and unmixed is their purity, and the individuality of each of them is a much more perfect thing than the otherness of the Forms, preserving as it does unmixed all the divine entities and their proper powers distinct, with the result that there is a distinction between the more general and more particular, between those associated with Continuance, with Progression and with Return, between those concerned with generation, with induction to the higher, and with demiurgic administration, and in general the particular characteristics are preserved of those gods who are respectively cohesive, completive, demiurgic, assimilative, or any of the other characteristics of theirs which our tradition celebrates.[12]

    Whereas, then, there exists there both indescribable unity and yet the
1049 distinctness of each characteristic (for all the henads are in all, and yet each is distinct), we gain knowledge of their unity and their distinctness from things secondary to them and dependent upon them. For in the case of the visible gods we discern a difference between the soul of the

[11] Sc. the Pythagoreans. Cf. *PT* V, 332.19-22 Portus, and Damascius *In Phaed.* I, 154.3.
[12] The various orders of gods, or henads, are dealt with at *ET*, props. 150-159 (see Dodds' notes *ad loc.*).

sun and that of the earth,[13] seeing that their visible bodies have a large degree of variety in their essence and their faculties and their rank in the universe. So then, even as we take our start from sense-perception in acquiring understanding of the differentiation of incorporeal essences, so it is on the basis of the variation in incorporeal essences that we cognise the unmixed distinctness of the primal, supra-essential henads and the particular characteristics of each. For each henad has a multiplicity dependent upon it,[14] in one case intelligible, in another intelligible-and-intellectual, another intellectual simply,[15] and within this one having an unparticipated multiplicity, another a participated one, and within this latter one having a supracosmic one and another an intracosmic. And thus far extends the procession of the henads.

So then, as we contemplate the extent of the whole incorporeal realm which is spread out beneath them and the measured series of variations down from the hidden level to that of distinctness, we declare our belief that there exists particularity and order even in the henads themselves, along with their unity. For it is on the basis of the differences in the participants that we discern the distinctions within the participated; for things that participated without variation in the same thing could not have exhibited such differences relative to each other.

So much, then, may be said concerning the situation of the primal henads and their communion with and distinction from one another, of which we are wont to call the one particularity, the other unity, distinguishing them thus also by name from the sameness and difference manifested at the level of Real Being. For these henads are supra-essential, and, to use technical terms, are 'flowers' and 'summits'.[16] Since, then, as we have said, there is within them both unity and distinctness, it is to this that Parmenides is addressing himself, that he may make 1050 clear their whole progression, right from the summit of the transcendent henad, and he thus takes for his hypothesis his own One, that is the One which is seen at the level of Being, and he considers this now as one, now as participated. The antecedent he preserves always the same by taking it in various senses, while the consequent he keeps changing, so that through the identity of the antecedent he may demonstrate the unity of the divine henads; for whichever of these you take, you can assume the same for the rest because all are in each other and are rooted

---

[13] I do not find the concept of a specific soul of the earth (χθόνια ψυχή) mentioned by Proclus elsewhere, but there is no reason why the earth should not have a soul.

[14] This doctrine is set out at *ET*, props. 135-140, and in *PT* III, 1-7.

[15] Reading ἡ μὲν νοητὸν ἔχουσα, ἡ δὲ νοητὸν ἅμα καὶ νοερόν, ἡ δὲ νοερὸν ἁπλῶς for ἡ μὲν νοητὸν, ἡ δὲ νοερὸν, ἐχούσης τῆς μὲν καὶ νοητὸν ἅμα καὶ νοερὸν ἁπλῶς of MSS., which is plainly confused. Moerbeke's translation is no help here, and Saffrey and Westerink (*op. cit.*, p. lxviii, n. 1) have not solved the problem.

[16] Chaldaean terms, ἄνθη and ἀκρότητες.

in the One; for even as trees by their 'topmost' parts are fixed in the earth and are earthy in virtue of that, so in the same way the divine entities also are by their summits rooted in the One, and each of them is a henad and one through its unmixed unity with the One. Through the changing of the consequent, on the other hand, taking it now as a 'whole', now as 'shape', now as something else again, and this both affirmatively and negatively, he seeks to demonstrate their distinctness and the particular characteristics of each of the divine orders. By means of the whole syllogism, in turn, he seeks to show both the communion of the divine entities, and the unmixed purity of each. For these reasons, then, the antecedent is one, the consequents are many, the syllogisms are many, and the hypotheses are more than two, since Parmenides through his hypothesis of the One Being at one stage ascends to the One that is prior to the participated henads, at another passes through the whole extent of those which are on the level of beings, and at another reveals the existence of those of them which are inferior to Being. And in general, since it has been stated previously about this method that its purpose is to postulate a given entity or proposition and then see what follows for itself in relation to itself and to others, and what does not follow, and again for the others both in relation to each other and to the postulate, we shall see how he himself in the first hypothesis examines what does not follow for the One both in relation to itself and to others, in the second what follows, and in the third what follows and does not follow; and how in the two following hypotheses he examines what follows for the others in relation to themselves and to the postulate and what does not follow; and how in the remaining four sections he varies his hypotheses similarly. So one should not be disturbed at contemplating the multiplicity of hypotheses, nor think that he is going beyond the proper limits of his proposed method, nor that he is deviating from the study of the henads in their capacity as first principles,[17] but that it is demonstrating simultaneously both their unity and their distinctness; for they are all united, in so far as they "remain in one" (*Tim.* 37d), while they are distinguished according to the different degrees of progression that they have accomplished from the One. And do not be astonished if we say this about the divine henads; even at the level of intellectual essences we are accustomed to call the whole intellectual realm a partless and single essence, and all the intellects one, and the one Intellect all, by reason of the sameness which draws and holds together the intellectual hypostasis as a whole. If we can talk of this level of being in this way, what should we think about

1051

[17] Excising ἑνάδος before θεωρίας, as virtually meaningless and grammatically difficult. It is presumably a gloss on ἀρχῶν.

the actual henads in the sphere of Being? Should it not be that they are unified to an especial degree? That they are in one another? That their mingling is insurpassable? That they do not proceed forth from the One? That they all have the imprint of the One upon them? Certainly at every level primal entities have on them the imprint of their own causes. Even in the case of bodies the primal is most full of life, like Soul, and the first among souls has the character of Intellect,[18] and the primal Intellect is a god. So also among numbers the first is of the nature of One and henadic and supra-essential, even as the One is. If, then, the henads also constitute a number, then there is both multiplicity and unity in that realm.

(iii) On the Subject Matter of the Hypotheses

So much, by way of introduction, on this subject. But since Parmenides denies and asserts different propositions in the different hypotheses, and often denies and asserts the same things at different stages on different subjects, and is in general clearly indulging in a "serious game" and working his way through the whole nature of things, and 1052 is not, as some have absurdly held, simply pursuing a soulless and empty logical exercise, nor showing off grandly his command of plausible arguments, it occurred to those of our predecessors who have approached the works of Plato with genuine insight[19] to fit the proper subject matters to these hypotheses, in order that there should be evident in each hypothesis a certain order of entities uncovered by Parmenides' method, and this on examination should turn out to be different for things that have different ranks of subsistence, and should have the same relation as they do to things other than them. This being their intention, they took various different paths in their apportioning of subject matters. We must first, however, specify what they call an hypothesis whose concern it is to fit the proofs to specific subjects. They are not simply looking to the structure of Parmenides' procedure (for according to it there are two hypotheses, one asserting the existence of the proposed entity, the other denying it), but they call an hypothesis that which takes up a part of the procedure and produces similar conclusions, either all affirmative or all negative or both. It makes no difference to them whether we draw these conclusions in relation to itself or to something else, but only that the quality of the proposition

---

[18] Cousin emends the MS ἐνοειδής to νοειδής (better νοοειδής). Latin translation reads *unialis*, but the sense seems to require νοοειδής.

[19] This would include all the commentators from Amelius on, as will become apparent. The whole passage that follows is excellently discussed by Saffrey and Westerink, *PT* I, Intro., pp. lxxv-lxxxix.

is the same. Thus they make different hypotheses concerning the One and concerning the Others than the One; and in the case of each simply, given the same premises, if the conclusions differ in quality, this they call an hypothesis.

Having made this definition clear, let us pass on. Some authorities,[20] then, divide the hypotheses into a total of eight, declaring that in the first he is discussing the One; in the second Intellect and the intellectual level of reality; in the third rational souls; in the fourth irrational souls; in the fifth Matter, in so far as it possesses some capability for participation in Forms; in the sixth Matter again, now in its ordered aspect, in so far as it has received the Forms in actuality; in the seventh Matter in its aspect as totally devoid of Forms and the capacity to participate in them, taken absolutely on its own; and in the eighth Form-in-Matter— for this is the only remaining one among the principles after the One, Intellect, the two classes of Soul, and the much-discussed Matter.

But this arrangement, while being correct in its ensuring that each of the subjects is a principle (for even the Form-in-Matter is a principle, even if it has also the characteristic of an element and of matter; and Soul is at all events a principle, even though the irrational soul is so differently from the rational; and on top of these the revered Intellect certainly is also, and far more than this God himself)—while ensuring this, then, it goes wrong about the number of the hypotheses and their order. For whereas there are clearly nine hypotheses, as will be demonstrated from the relevant texts of Plato as we come to them, it contracts their number inappropriately. It also disrupts the order of reality, by bringing in Form last, whereas it is superior to Matter, which is devoid not only of the Forms, but even of capacity for receiving them, and besides that by ranking prior to Matter which has undergone ordering that which is unordered and possesses mere impressions of Forms. This view, indeed, has received some support even from its critics. They say that the hypothesis concerning Matter in its receptive capacity is brought on first, because it is more perspicuous than that which has not even acquired this receptivity, though more obscure than that which has been already brought to order, and is better able to demonstrate the nature of Matter than that which is already occupied by Forms, and is less incomprehensible than that which is considered entirely as a negativity.

Quite a few other commentators, however, have opposed these authorities and written against them. Of those who have made the division of the hypotheses into nine, one set distribute the subjects as fol-

---

[20] The scholiast *ad loc.* identifies this as Amelius; cf. S-W, *ibid.*, p. lxxx.

lows:[21] the first concerns the primal God (all authorities agree on this,
1054 in fact); the second concerns the level of the Intelligible; the third is
about Soul (and about all soul, not just rational soul, as their predecessors asserted); the fourth is about Body ordered in one way or another;
the fifth about unordered Body; the sixth about ordered Matter; the
seventh about Matter *qua* unordered; the eighth about Forms-in-Matter, taken, however, as being in their substratum; while the ninth is
about Forms-in-Matter, considered by themselves apart from Matter.
The proponents of this scheme observe in many respects a correct order and principle of division, but they take the same things twice; for
we would be unable to say in what respect ordered Matter differs from
either unordered Body, nor yet from ordered Body. For if in becoming
qualityless body it is ordered, it is the same as unordered body, and if
it takes on qualification it will be the same as ordered body. Further,
they are not introducing the first principles of things; for how can some
ordered body be a principle? How is this not something constructed
from first principles? And how can the fifth hypothesis be about unordered Body? The explicit conclusion of this hypothesis is that the
Others neither are at rest nor in motion if they do not partake of the
One. But according to the *Timaeus* (30a) unordered Body is in motion,
even though "of an inharmonious and disorderly sort." And how
could Form, taken purely conceptually, without Matter, be a principle
of anything? Principles do not possess their existence conceptually, but
in reality. For in the case of things dependent on our conception, when
the conception is removed the existence of the thing conceived is abolished; but principles are principles through their own authority and not
in virtue of our conceptions. In general, then, there are many clear objections to this scheme, and in particular the fact that the ninth hypothesis overturns all possibilities, and allows nothing to exist even conceptually, and argues specifically against this so-called conceptual Form.

The next set of commentators,[22] following on these, follow a different method of presenting reality. The first hypothesis they declare to
be concerned with God and the gods—for the discussion is not only
about the One, but about all the divine henads; ⟨the second will concern
1055 the intellectual realm, rather than the⟩ intelligibles;[23] the third no longer

[21] Identified by the scholiast as Porphyry; cf. S-W, *op.cit.*, pp. lxxxi-lxxxii. As they
remark, this seems to confirm that Porphyry wrote a commentary on the *Parmenides*—
whether or not, as Pierre Hadot would claim (*Porphyre et Victorinus*, I, pp. 102-143; II,
pp. 59-113), the *Anonymus Taurinensis* is a part of it.

[22] Identified by the scholiast as Iamblichus. On the question as to whether Iamblichus
may be credited with a doctrine of henads, see J. M. Dillon, "Iamblichus and the Origin
of the Doctrine of Henads," *Phronesis* 17 (1972): 102-106, and *contra*, Saffrey and Westerink, *op.cit.*, pp. xxviff.

[23] Accepting Saffrey and Westerink's supplement for a lacuna here (cf. *PT* III, Intro.,

about Soul, as previous commentators had declared, but about the classes of being superior to us—angels, daemons, and heroes[24] (for these classes of being are immediately inferior to the gods and are superior even to the universal souls; this is their most remarkable view, and it is for this reason that they assert that these take a prior rank to souls in the hypotheses). The fourth hypothesis they take to concern rational souls; the fifth those secondary souls which are woven onto the rational souls[25] the sixth Forms-in-Matter and all the seminal reason-principles; the seventh, Matter itself; the eighth, Body in the heavens; and the ninth, generated Body beneath the Moon.[26]

This school of thought is correct in that it does not take the same thing twice, but it slips in the "superior classes of being" quite improperly. For if these are at the intellectual level, we have a treatment of the whole intellectual level in the second hypothesis; whereas if they are on the level of soul, it is plain that the treatment of them should be included in the hypothesis about Soul. A further objection to this school also is that they bring in products, rather than first principles, in the latter group of hypotheses.

1056   All these commentators share a common misconception, in that they do not see that the first five hypotheses produce true conclusions, whereas the last four lead to absurdities. This, after all, was Parmenides' stated purpose, to demonstrate how, if the One exists, all beings are generated, and how, if it does not exist, it eliminates everything and leaves nothing existent anywhere; and the whole procedure announces that this is what it is demonstrating, both through the postulation of true propositions and through the refutation of false ones. We may take as an example the postulate: "If Providence exists, all beings will be as they should be; if Providence does not exist, nothing will be as it should be, but both wholes and parts will be administered badly. Providence therefore exists; for its existence is the cause of goods, and its non-existence the cause of evils." These theorists should therefore have realised that Parmenides' aim was to show that through the existence of the One all beings acquire their share of substantiality, while through its non-existence the nature of things would be utterly eliminated (which indeed is what he states unequivocally at the conclusion of all the hypotheses), and seeing this, they should certainly not have

---

p. xix, n. 2). Porphyry has previously been listed as considering that the Second Hypothesis concerns "the whole intelligible level," and a contrast is appropriate here. We know from just below (line 21) that Iamblichus saw the Second Hypothesis as concerning the intellectual level.

[24] Cf. Damascius *De Princ.* II, p. 247.25-16 Ruelle, where this doctrine is explicitly attributed to Iamblichus (= Iambl. *In Parm.* fr. 12 Dillon.)

[25] Cf. Damascius *De Princ.* II, p. 286.19-21 (= Iambl. *In Parm.* fr. 14 Dillon).

[26] Cf. Damascius *De Princ.* II, p. 292.7-9 Ruelle.

introduced other subject matters also in the remaining four hypotheses,
1057 nor, as it were, kept right on on the same road, but rather should have
discerned the first principles of things in the first five hypotheses, and
in the last four should not have sought to find specific entities, but
should have realised that they prove that, if one removes the One, then
many impossible conclusions result from propositions that seem to us
possible.

The first man, as far as I am aware, to avoid this misconception was
the philosopher from Rhodes,[27] who himself arranges the hypotheses
according to a different principle. He makes them out to be ten in all,
and balances the first five with the last five. He takes the first as showing that, if the One exists, all the most ecstatic doctrines of philosophy
follow from this, such as Plato has taught us in other passages of his
works; while the sixth shows us that, if the One does not exist, nothing
of those things that can be stated about the One will agree with this hypothesis. In the second and the seventh hypotheses propositions about
Intellect and the intelligible realm are examined—on the one hand that,
if it exists, all the most excellent beliefs about these are true, on the
other that, if it does not exist, we overturn all true statements about
them. In the third and eighth, the subject is the objects of discursive
intellect; for these come next after the intelligibles, the one hypothesis
showing that, if they exist, they are in accordance with our conceptions, the other that they are shown to be discordant with them, if they
do not exist. In the fourth and ninth, the subject is embodied Forms;
these follow on[28] the objects of discursive intellect, according to the division of the Line in the *Republic*. The hypotheses demonstrate respectively that if the One exists, these do also, and if the One does not exist,
neither is it possible that these should. The remaining pair, the fifth and
1058 the tenth, concern the receptacle of bodies: in the one, the fifth hypothesis, the receptacle being harmonised through the existence of the One;
in the other, excluded from such harmony through the non-existence
of the One.[29]

This scheme is to be admired both for its structural neatness and its
intelligence, for concluding that conclusions are reached which are al-
ternately absurd, and true and concordant with the nature of things. In
other respects, however, because it innovates as regard the number of
hypotheses, and fabricates one hypothesis which contributes nothing,

---

[27] On the vexed question of the identity of this figure, see now the persuasive article of
H. D. Saffrey, "Le 'Philosophe de Rhodes': est-il Théodore d'Asine," in *Mém. A-J. Festugière*, Paris, 1984, pp. 65–76, showing that there is no serious reason to doubt the identification with Theodore of Asine.

[28] Reading, μετὰ for μὲν of MSS.

[29] This last clause is missing from Greek MSS, but found in the Latin translation.

it is to be rejected, and particularly because it strives to match another five against the first five, one to one. In general, it is not actually absurd to state the One does not exist, nor, if one posited such an hypothesis, would one draw impossible conclusions from it. For in fact that One which is first before all entities does not exist, for it is superior even to existence. But it is necessary that absurd conclusions follow from what comes after it, so that we could not pair the sixth hypothesis with the first; nor, therefore, the others with the others. This scheme has even persuaded him to cut up one hypothesis and thus increase the number.

Following on this, Plutarchus, our "grandfather,"[30] accepting from the teaching of ancient authorities the number of the hypotheses as nine, and from this newer theory that in the first five, true conclusions are drawn from the postulate that the One exists, while in the remainder absurdities are shown to follow from the postulate the One does not exist, and that the treatise is about first principles, derives the primary hypostases which rule all beings from the proposition that the One exists, both those that are transcendent and those that are manifest as inherent in things, and on the basis of the proposition that the One 1059 does not exist discovers that the order of reality is utterly demolished.

Making these assumptions, then, he ordains that the first hypothesis is about God, the second about Intellect, the third about Soul, the fourth about Form-in-Matter, the fifth about Matter—in the last two the Others than the One are the subject (for it was the custom also of the Pythagoreans, as we have said ([above, 1048.6ff.]), to call all incorporeal and transcendent being "One," and that which is corporeal and inherent in bodies "the Others"); so that it is reasonable that the first three, which ask what relation the One has to itself and to others, should concern the three transcendent ruling principles, while the last two, which ask what relation the Others have to each other and to the One, introduce immanent Form and Matter; for these are truly "other" and belong to others rather than to themselves, and are contributory causes rather than true causes, following the distinction made in the *Phaedo* (98bff.).

Having surveyed in these five hypotheses these principles, both those external to things and those immanent in them, which are introduced by Parmenides on the assumption that the One exists, he declares that it is shown in the latter four that if that One present in beings does not exist, if you take non-existence as implying existing in one sense and not in another, then only the sensible will exist (for if there is no intelligible, then the One will only be sensible), and among modes of knowledge only sense-perception (which is the intentionally absurd

[30] That is, the teacher of Proclus' teacher, Syrianus.

conclusion of the sixth hypothesis, that there exists only sense-perception among the modes of knowledge), and only sense-objects among the objects of knowledge. If, on the other hand, the One really does not exist, in the sense of absolute non-existence, then every mode of knowledge and object of knowledge is abolished, which is the absurd conclusion of the seventh hypothesis. The Others, if the One does not exist in the sense assumed by the sixth hypothesis, are in the state of dreams and shadows, which is the absurd conclusion of the eighth hypothesis. If the One is non-existent in the sense of absolute non-existence, the Others will not even attain to a dreamlike substantiality, as is clearly demonstrated by the ninth hypothesis. So if one were to say that the first hypothesis has the same relation to the rest as the single first principle of all things towards the rest of reality, that the four remaining ones of the first group deal with the principles following on the One, and that the four after these draw the conclusion that, if the One is removed, all the things indicated in the former four are utterly eliminated, one would probably be giving a correct explanation. For where the second ⟨shows that, if the One exists, then the realm of Intellect exists, the sixth shows that, if it does not exist, then only sense perception and perceptibles exist; where the third⟩[31] shows that, if One Being exists, the whole level of Soul will exist, the seventh shows that, if it does not exist, this means the destruction of every faculty of knowledge, whether sensible, imaginative, or rational; where the fourth shows that, if that One exists, the Forms-in-Matter have existence of a sort (for these in some way participate in the One Being), the eighth shows, if that entity only does not exist, the objects of sense will be multiple and mere dreams, in no way participating in real being and formal distinction; where the fifth shows that, if the One exists, Matter also will exist (although not participating in the One Being in so far as it is Being, yet it does so in so far as it is One), the ninth shows that nothing at all will exist nor participate in Being, if the One does not exist; for how, if that causal principle is removed, is it possible for any item in the whole universe to exist?

We have, then, according to this arrangement, the First Hypothesis as being about the One, which Plato in the *Republic* (VI, 509b) firmly placed beyond existence and Being; and the four following about beings, of which the first two concern things eternally existent while the latter two concern created beings, following the distinction made in the *Timaeus* (27d), between those things apprehensible by intellection through reason, and those things known by opinion through

1060

---

[31] This whole passage is omitted in the MSS, possibly by homoeoteleuton. I have suggested its probable content.

sense-perception—or, if you wish, the four follow the division of the
Line in the *Republic*, of which he apportioned one section to the intelligible realm, the other to the sensible realm, one to the henads, the
other to the things here termed the Others; and of the larger section,
one part to the objects of intuition, the other to the objects of discursive
intellection, even as of the two former hypotheses the one is about In-
1061 tellect, the other about Soul; while of the smaller section, he apportioned one part to things of sense, the other to things imaged, even as
here we have said that the fourth hypothesis is about Forms-in-Matter,
which are the proper objects of sense, while the fifth is about Matter,
which is analogous to things imaged by reason of the indefiniteness of
the knowledge of it attainable by us.

So then, there are four principles after the first, two transcendent and
two complementary;[32] and there are four hypotheses after the first,
based on the postulate that the One exists, and another four which
show the absurdities that follow on the elimination of the One. Such is
the theory of this man, who has scientifically distinguished from each
other the subjects of the hypotheses, has introduced, without leaving
any gaps, all the chief principles, has thoroughly understood the whole
object of Parmenides' exercise, and has articulated clearly all the rather
confused contributions of the older commentators.

What, then, are we to say, following on such a vast company of such
distinguished commentators, and what are we to add from our own
store? It may well be that it will suit our case to exclaim, in the words
of Homer (*Iliad* 23.536), "the best man is last!" in the person of him
who became my guide in philosophy at Athens,[33] and who kindled in
me intellectual light. In his treatment of this subject, he in some cases
brings a more theological level of criticism to bear, while in others he
makes minor adjustments, in conformity with Plato himself and the
text of Plato.

His view, then, also is that the first hypothesis is about the primal
God, and the second is about the intelligible world. But since there is a
wide range in the intelligible world and there are many orders of gods,
his view is that each of these divine orders has been named symbolically
1062 by Plato, and all have been expressed by philosophic names, not by
such names as are customarily celebrated by those who compose
theogonies, but which do not reveal their essences, such as are the epithets of the divine classes given out by the Gods,[34] but rather, as I said,
by names familiar to philosophers, such as Whole, Multiplicity, Limitlessness, Limit, which are suitable for application to them, all having

---

[32] συμπληρωτικαί, i.e. joined to a substratum to make up a physical object.
[33] Sc. Syrianus.
[34] Sc. the Chaldaean Oracles.

their proper rank, and portraying without omission all the divine stages of procession, whether intelligible, intellectual, or supra-cosmic, and that thus all things are presented in logical order, as being symbols of divine orders of being; and also that the fact that all those things which are presented positively in the second hypothesis are presented negatively in the first indicates that the primal cause transcends all the divine orders, while they undergo various degrees of procession according to their various distinct characteristics. For the One in the second hypothesis is neither the primal One (for it is complex, being all things) nor is it that which is inseparable from Being and thus, as being a state of it, is in it. He thus clearly distinguishes this One from the first and declares that this One, being such as it is, is distinct. It is plain, in fact, that this term signifies an autonomous divine henad; for every transcendent cause at the head of a multiplicity produces a double multiplicity, one which is transcendent like itself, and another which is immanent in its participants.[35] Even as the single Soul has generated some souls separate from bodies, and some which are inseparable, and as the one and whole Intellect has given substance to some intellects separate from souls, and others which are in them as functions of them, so also the One has produced some autonomous henads which transcend their participants, and others which act as unifications of other entities which are unified in virtue of them and in which they inhere. The whole second hypothesis, therefore, he says, reveals to us a multiplicity of autonomous henads, on which are dependent the entities about which the second hypothesis teaches us, revealing to us in its terms all

1063 their specific characteristics in turn. If this is true, we must examine each of the conclusions to see to which of the divine orders it is appropriate, and thus make division of the second hypothesis "limb by limb" (*Phaedr.* 265e).

As for the third, it is not about all Soul pure and simple, but such as has proceeded forth from the divine Soul; for the whole divine Soul is comprised in the second hypothesis.[36] For Plato himself has clearly stated there that the One partakes also of Time; and partaking of Time is the property first of souls, and not of intellectual beings, among whom there is neither "was" nor "will be," but only the eternal "is" (cf. *Tim.* 37eff.).

So then, having divided the whole of being into the divinised, and that which is taken on its own, he declares that the whole of divinised being is presented in the second of the hypotheses, be it intelligible, intellectual, or psychic. So if you would like to hear the subjects of the

[35] A basic principle of Procline metaphysics; cf. *ET*, prop. 28.
[36] Cf. *PT* I, 11, p. 49.17ff. S-W.

hypotheses in order according to this theory also, the first he declares
1064 to be about the One God, how he generates and gives order to all the
orders of gods. The second is about all the divine orders, how they
have proceeded from the One and the substance which is joined to
each. The third is about the souls which are assimilated to the gods, but
yet have not been apportioned divinised being. The fourth is about
Forms-in-Matter, how they are produced according to what rankings
from the gods. The fifth is about Matter, how it has no participation in
the formative henads, but receives its share of existence from above,
from the supra-essential and single Monad; for the One and the illumination of the One extends as far as Matter, bringing light even to its
boundlessness.[37]

So much, then, will suffice as a general introduction to the hypotheses. We must now give to each separately the discussion due to it.
Let us take our start, therefore, once again from the beginning of the
text of the first hypothesis, and consider the argument contained in it.

B. THE FIRST HYPOTHESIS

*"Well then," said Parmenides, "if there is a One, of course the One
would not be many." "How could it?" (137c)*

I. THEORETICAL EXPOSITION

(i) The Subject Matter

First we must state what is the subject matter of the first hypothesis.
1065 Is it about God only, or is it about God and the Gods, as some say? The
discourse is about a subject which has subsistence (*hyparxis*), and it is
not the case, as some have supposed,[38] that this One in its absolute form
is without substance (*anhupostatos*), and that the hypothesis produces
impossible conclusions. Even if they produce as evidence what is said
at the end of the hypothesis (142a6-8), "Or are these things not possible
in relation to the One?"—what the meaning of that phrase is in that
context will be discussed by us later; so, as I said, it is plain that that of
which the argument here denies all attributes is not without substance.
For everything which demonstrates some impossible conclusion by

[37] Cf. *ET*, prop. 57, which states the general principle of the extension of hypostases:
"Every cause both operates prior to its consequent and gives rise to a greater number of
posterior terms."
[38] This appears to refer to the view of the Platonist Origen. Cf. *PT* II, 4, where such a
doctrine is attributed to him (fr. 7 Weber), and Saffrey and Westerink's remarks, *PT* II,
Intro., pp. x-xii. Proclus returns to a criticism of this position in Book VII 64.1-16.

means of a conjunction of premises demonstrates that the impossibility follows either from the hypothesis itself or from the sequence of propositions; but since both of these are possible, the thing being proved is possible also.

Now the hypothesis that the One exists is true. The Eleatic Stranger also demonstrates this when he is countering[39] as absurd the thesis that the One does not exist, the only thing in existence being that which experiences the One as an attribute, whereas in fact in all cases that which truly is preexists that which experiences it and which does not truly exist; for he also, in that passage (*Soph.* 245a), defined that which is truly One as being absolutely partless; and this is what is demonstrated first in this hypothesis, that the One does not have parts, and all the other conclusions follow in order upon this, being demonstrated on the basis of necessary premises. If, then, it is necessary that that which is truly One exists (for everything else that truly exists is prior to what does not truly exist—it is absurd, after all, to say that that which truly is, is without essential existence); but the truly One is the partless (that is, that which has no parts),[40] and that is what is demonstrated in the first hypothesis as being beyond all things, seeing that all the propositions on the basis of which it is shown that the One is prior to all things follows from its having no parts. It is therefore absolutely necessary that this One of which everything is denied exists; for after all it itself exists necessarily, if indeed the partless is truly one. For such, as is said in the *Sophist*, is the truly One, even as here also the One is shown to be. The sequence of the syllogisms also shows this, being, as it is, necessary. Everything, then, is demonstrated through this about any of those things which have subsistence.

If, then, it is something which has subsistence (*hyphestōs*) about which the argument is, it is in turn plain that it is not something that has Being (*ousiōdes*); for the argument will deny Being itself of the One. One can only conclude, then, that either this thing is one of those things that are inferior to Being, such as the realm of generation or Matter, or it is one of those things which are superior to Being; but it cannot be one of those things which are inferior to Being, for every such entity partakes of time, as for instance does generation (but the argument denies this very characteristic of participating in time of the One); and exists in some way, as does Matter, for instance (but this entity the argument shows not even to exist). So then this thing, about which the proofs are presented in the First Hypothesis must be above Being.

[39] Reading ἀπαντῶν for the ἀπάντων of the MSS. In general, I follow in this passage (1064.21-1066.16) the emendations proposed by Saffrey in *PT* II, Intro., pp. xii-xv.

[40] Added from the Latin translation.

Necessarily then, if indeed only the Divine is above Being, and all that is Divine is above Being, the present argument could be either only about the primal God, who surely is the only entity above Being, or else it is about all the Gods also which are after him, as some of those whom we revere would hold.[41] So they argue that since every god, inasmuch as he is a god, is a henad (for it is this element, the One, which divinises all being), for this reason they think it right to join to the study of the First a discussion of all the gods; for they are all supra-essential henads, and transcend the multiplicity of beings, and are the summits of beings. But if we were to say that both the primal Cause and the other gods are one, we would have to allot one and the same hypothesis to all of them; for we would have to say that the discussion concerned the primal One in no way more than it concerned all the rest of the henads. But if this primal One, as indeed is very much the view of these authorities, is simply and solely One, and unconnected with everything else,[42] and unparticipated, as they say, "snatching itself away"[43] from everything, and unknowable to everything, as being transcendent, whereas each of the other henads is in some degree participated, and is not only a henad but also partakes in the multiplicity proper to it, and in some substance either intelligible or intellectual or psychic or even corporeal (for participation proceeds even down this far)—why should that One which is not reckoned with beings, nor ranked at all with the Many, be placed in the same hypothesis with henads which are participated in by beings, and serve to confer coherence on the Many?

After all, we do not get the same account given of the unparticipated and the participated soul; for the properties of the participated would never accord with those of the unparticipated, nor those of the superior with those of the inferior; otherwise the former would not have been distinct from the many alone by itself, while the latter is involved with the multiplicity of souls. Neither is one to count the unparticipated Intellect in with the many intellects, nor are the characteristics of all of them the same, for if they were, it would not be the case that the former holds the rank of monad, while the latter that of number which has come into being around this monad.

But if those who have fathered these arguments about the First Hypothesis want the three kings of the *Letters* (*Ep.* II, 312e) to be second-

1067

---

[41] Iamblichus; cf. above, 1054.37ff. This passage does seem to credit Iamblichus with a doctrine of henads, but see on this question the discussion of Saffrey and Westerink, *PT* III, Intro., pp. xxviff.

[42] Cf. Damascius *De Princ.* I, 43, p. 86.3ff. Ruelle, where Iamblichus is quoted a describing his *second* One as ἀσύντακτος πρὸς τὴν τριάδα (which follows it), the primal One being πάντῃ ἄρρητος.

[43] Chaldaean terminology; cf. *Or. Chald.* fr. 3.1 D.P.

ary to the One (even as, in their discussions of these entities, those who say that the First Hypothesis is not only about God but about all gods absolutely do wish to assert), for this very reason, that the One may not be numbered with things secondary to it, that it is superior to all reckoning of it with what follows it, and is not capable of being ranked with anything else (at least this is what they say when they are writing about the theology of Plato),[44] how are we any longer to rank both God and the gods in the one hypothesis and fit the same negations similarly 1068 to all of them?

For let us accept that every god is one; yet the "one" in each god is not separate in the same way, nor in the same way knowable, nor in the same way uncircumscribable, as is the primal One itself. And if Plato himself at the end of the First Hypothesis (141e7-10) says that the One does not participate in essence or in being, and that that which is participated in by any being is not one, how can this be attributed suitably to the other henads? For they are all participated in by beings. So even as, if someone said that the Soul did not make use of any body, he would not be speaking of every type of soul, but only of the unparticipated soul, and if he said that Intellect is not at all participated in by Soul, he would only be speaking of the unparticipated intellect, by the same token also he who postulated the supra-essential One as being entirely transcendent over all essence and all being is speaking only of the primal unparticipated One, not every one of whatever rank. And if he himself actually says that the One is beyond oneness and essence (for it is not even properly to be termed "one") how would the statement be true of those henads following on the first? For that one which is participated in by a multiplicity and which consorts with beings is not superior to even being termed "one" at all, seeing that it is not even transcendent over being. It is the same as if someone were to say that even the soul which consorts with the body is superior to being soul. And if in fact we have the whole level of gods and all the One which is participated in by Being presented to us in the Second Hypothesis, this very circumstance which they are seeking for, who try to squeeze the whole discourse about the gods into the first hypothesis, what need is there to cause confusion in this part of the discourse by joining on to speculations about the first principle an exposition about the multiplicity of the gods? For what else is that One which is ranked with Being and pro-1069 ceeds forth together with Being, than the multiplicity of gods, which gives divinity to the whole hypostasis of Being and coherence to the whole multiplicity of essential things? For every divine essence is sub-

---

[44] Sc. Iamblichus, presumably in his *Platonic Theology*. Plainly there he stressed the absolute transcendence of the One, distinguishing it sharply from the "three kings" of the Second Letter. Cf. Saffrey-Westerink, *PT* II, Intro., pp. lv-lvi.

ject to the henads of the gods, and each participated One is a principle of unification for all Being whether intelligible or intellectual or, beyond this, even psychical or corporeal, and each of the gods is nothing else than the One in its participated aspect. For even as man in the strict sense is so in virtue of his soul, so god in the strict sense is so in virtue of the One; for in each case it is the dominant element in all those which make up the totality of the entity which each properly is.

It follows necessarily, then, that the First Hypothesis is about God alone, in so far as he is the generator of the plurality of gods, he himself being transcendent over their multiplicity and unconnected with those gods who have proceeded forth from him. It is for this reason that everything is denied of this One, as being established as superior to all things and transcendent over all things, and producing all the characteristics of the gods, while itself being undefinable and uncircumscribable in relation to all of them. For it is not a particular one, but One in the absolute sense, and it is not intelligible or intellectual, but it produces both the intelligible and the intellectual henads. For in every ruling order the participated multiplicity should be presided over by the unparticipated and primal form,[45] or even a causal principle superior to form; in this way, after all, prior to the forms-in-matter there are the immaterial Forms, and prior to that life which comes to be in something else we have that which is separate and on its own and unmixed, and everywhere those things which come to be in something else are presided over by those which subsist on their own. For instance, the multiplicity of souls which have taken charge each of its own body are

1070 presided over essentially by the unparticipated Soul, which goes about in "the place above the heaven" (*Phaedr.* 247c); and the multiplicity of intellects are presided over by the single unparticipated Intellect, that one which is separate and eternally established in itself and gives coherence from above to all intellectual essence; and the multiplicity of intelligibles are dominated by the primal intelligible object, which is unmixed and established singly on its own, for that object of intellect in the individual intellect is distinct from that which is established prior to this on its own, and this latter is the intelligible object pure and simple, while the former is an intelligible object in relation to intellectual entities. Even so, then, beyond the multiplicity of participated henads there is the unparticipated One, transcendent, as has been said, over all the divine realms.

We shall, therefore, be very far from making the primal god the summit of the intelligible world, as I observe to be the practice of some

[45] A basic principle of Procline metaphysics; cf. *ET*, prop. 21. At *In Tim.* II, 240.6-7 it is attributed to Iamblichus (fr. 54 Dillon).

423

leading theologians,[46] and making the father of that realm the same as the cause of all things. For this entity is a participated henad. After all, he is called an intelligible father and the summit of the intelligible world, and even if he is the principle of coherence for the whole intelligible world, yet it is as its father that he is so. The primal god, however, who is celebrated in the First Hypothesis, is not even a father, but is superior also to all paternal divinity. The former entity is set over against its Power and its Intellect, of whom it is said to be the Father, and with those it makes up a single triad;[47] whereas this truly primal god transcends all contrast and relationship with anything, so *a fortiori* it is not an intelligible father. For it is not involved with any entity secondary to it, nor is it participated in any way, falling neither in the category of intellectual, nor yet of intelligible, essence, but it transcends in unity all the participated henads, and is "snatched away"[48] beyond all the processions of Being.

1071

Let this, then, be reckoned as the subject of the First Hypothesis: the ascent from One Being to the very One itself in the truest sense, and the consideration of how it is transcendent over all things, and how it is to be reckoned together with none of the divine orders.

(ii) The Type of Discourse Suitable to the Subject

Secondly after this let us consider what type of discourse will suit such a subject as this, and how we might properly take a grasp of the exegesis of the present topic, and how we may be able, I would say, to operate logically and intellectually and at the same time with divine inspiration, in order that we may be able to grasp the demonstrative power of Parmenides and to follow his conceptions, dependent as they are upon real Being, and that we may ascend by divine inspiration to the unspeakable and incomprehensible consciousness of the One. For we do possess, inasmuch as we rank as souls, images of the primal causes, and we participate in both the whole Soul and the plane of Intellect and the divine Henad; and we must stir up the powers of those entities within us for the comprehension of the present subject matter. Or how else are we to become nearer to the One, if we do not rouse up the One of the soul, which is in us as a kind of image of the One, by virtue of which the most accurate of authorities declare that divine pos-

---

[46] It would seem, from a comparison with *PT* II, 4, p. 31 S-W, that Proclus has Origen the Platonist in mind here, but the criticism applies also to Porphyry; cf. Hadot, *Porphyre et Victorinus*, I, pp. 258-259.

[47] Cf. *Or. Chald.* fr. 4 DP, and Damascius *De Princ.* I, 48, p. 95.20ff. Ruelle.

[48] *Or. Chald*, fr. 3 DP.

session most especially comes about?[49] And how are we to make this One and flower of the soul shine forth unless we first of all activate our intellect? For the activity of the intellect leads the soul towards a state and activity of calm. And how are we to achieve perfect intellectual activity if we do not travel there by means of logical conceptions, using 1072 composite intellections prior to more simple ones? So then, we need demonstrative power in our preliminary assumptions, whereas we need intellectual activity in our investigations of being (for the orders of being are denied of the One), and we need inspired impulse in our consciousness of that which transcends all beings, in order that we may not slip unawares from our negations into Not-Being and its invisibility by reason of our indefinite imagination, but rousing up the One within us and, through this, warming the soul (cf. Phaedr. 251b) we may connect ourselves to the One itself and, as it were, find mooring, taking our stand above everything intelligible within ourselves and dispensing with every other one of our activities, in order that we may consort with it alone and perform a dance around it, leaving behind all the intellections of the soul which are directed to secondary things.[50] Let this, then, be the manner of our discourse, logical, intellectual, and inspired, for in this way one might take the grasp that one should of the present hypothesis.

(iii) The Nature of the Negations

The third thing that we must consider is the nature of these negations, and whether they are superior to the corresponding assertions or inferior. It is generally felt that an assertion is a more worthy thing than a negation. A negation, after all, is a deprivation of something; whereas an assertion, they say, involves the presence, and, as it were, the possession, of Form. Now certainly for Forms and for things possessed by Form, assertion is preferable to negation; for this very thing is a necessary attribute of Forms, namely possession of themselves and repulsion of their corresponding negation. And in general for all beings, existence is preferable to non-existence, and assertion is more proper than

---

[49] This probably refers to Iamblichus, who seems to have been the first to develop the doctrine of a "One" of the soul; cf. Hermeias In Phaedr. 150.24ff. Couvreur (= Iambl. In Phaedr. fr. 6 Dillon). This he identified with the Chaldaean "flower of the intellect."

[50] Reading τὰ δεύτερα for τὰς δευτέρας of MSS. This ascent to the One is eloquently described also at PT II, 11, pp. 64–65 S-W. The image of "dancing around" the One, just above, is found in Plotinus, Enn. VI, 9.8.44 (cf. I, 8.2.24—Soul dancing around Intellect), and frequently in Proclus, e.g. below, 1080.18; PT IV, 5, p. 21.2 S-W. It probably derives ultimately from Epin. 982c (the dance of the planets). Cf. J. Trouillard, "La figure de chœur de danse (περιχορεύειν) dans l'oeuvre de Proclos," in Permanence de Philosophie (Mélanges Joseph Moreau), Lausanne, 1977, pp. 162–174.

negation. Being, after all, is the classic case of assertion, whereas Not-Being is of negation. It is quite clear what relation Plato himself in the *Sophist* (258ab) declared Not-Being to have towards Being, and that he declared Being to be superior; for there he says that Not-Being is hardly less existent than Being,[51] though by adding the phrase "if it is permissible to say so," he demonstrated the superiority of Being. So then, in every class of Being, assertion in general is superior to negation. But since Not-Being has a number of senses, one superior to Being, another which is of the same rank as Being, and yet another which is privation of Being, it is clear, surely, that we can postulate also three types of negation, one superior to assertion, another inferior to assertion, and another in some way equally balanced by assertion. It is not, then, simply true that assertion is always superior to negation, but there is a case where it takes second place to it, when negation expresses that type of Not-Being which is beyond Being. But since this type of Not-Being also is twofold—the one being possessed by Being, the other not being reckoned together with anything that is—it is plain that in the case of this latter neither assertion nor negation is properly relevant, whereas in the case of the former, negation is more appropriate, and also assertion, in so far as it has connection with Being. Yet even if no statement is properly true of that other (I mean that entity which is unconnected with Being), at least negation is more properly uttered of it than assertion. For even as assertions are about things that are, negations are about what is not; for in general an assertion wants to lay hold of some Form, and when the soul says that one thing is present to another and makes an assertion, it postulates something which is akin to itself. The primal entity is, however, above Form, and it is not suitable to apply to it any of those attributes which are proper to secondary things, nor to transfer to it attributes proper to us. For all unawares we will find ourselves talking about ourselves and not it. So then we must use in relation to it not assertions, but rather negations of those attributes which are proper to secondary things. For assertions strive to ascertain that some one thing is true of some other; whereas the First is both inaccessible to cognitions which are related to anything existing, and it is not possible to take anything as applying to it, but rather as not applying to it; for it transcends all compositeness and participation.

In addition to this, assertions present something defined, while ne-

---

[51] It is noteworthy that, in quoting *Sophist* 258b1-2, Proclus repeatedly uses the phrase οὐ παρ᾽ ἔλαττον (τὸ μὴ ὂν τοῦ ὄντος), which is not in Plato's text. See Saffrey's excellent note on this in *PT* II, p. 39, n. 1 S-W. The text is quoted also above, 999.34-36, 1012. 11-13, and below, 1076.8-10, 1184.37-39, always with παρ᾽ ἔλαττον. Either Proclus is following a variant reading, or he has developed a fixed false recollection of this text (Cousin's text, here, by the way, needs correction).

gations have an undefined field of reference; for the concept "not-man" is of a more indefinite nature than "man." So then, it is more proper to reveal the incomprehensible and indefinable cause which is the One through negations; for assertions slice up reality, whereas negations tend to simplify things from distinction and definition in the direction of being uncircumscribed, and from being set apart by their proper boundaries in the direction of being unbounded. How then would these latter not be more suitable to speculation on the One? One might, indeed, go so far as to say that it is only possible by these means to reveal the power of the One, which is incomprehensible and ungraspable and unknowable by partial intellects. So then, negations are superior to assertions, and are suitable to those who are being drawn up from what is partial towards the whole and from the aligned towards the unaligned and from the sliced-up type of knowledge towards that type of activity which is uncircumscribable and unitary and simple.

(iv) Suitability of Negations to the First Cause

The fourth thing we must consider is how and according to what mode these negations will fit themselves to the First Cause. I would not say that they would do so as to something which was receptive of assertions but did not happen to be in receipt of them, as if we were to say that Socrates is not fair-skinned; for the One is receptive of nothing, but it transcends all Being and all participation. Nor would it be in the way that it would attach itself to something which was absolutely non-receptive of assertion, and which possessed privation and inability to be mixed with the Form in question, as for instance, if one were to say that the line is not white because it has no capacity to participate in whiteness. For the first principle is not simply deprived of the things that are denied of it, nor are these things without any communion with the One, but they are actually derived from that source; and it is not true that, even as whiteness neither generates the line nor is generated by it, so the things following on the One are not generated from the One; for they derive their subsistence from it. Nor yet does it apply in an intermediate way between these, as if we were to say that the negation is predicated (of the One) in the way of something which is not itself receptive of a given characteristic, but is the cause of those things in which it resides, being receptive of the asserted characteristic; as for instance, Motion itself does not move, but rather the moved thing moves; yet the negation is applied to Motion, for it does not move, even though other things move by reason of it. And in general each physical attribute is itself free from the relevant characteristic; for it itself, being simple, either exists or does not exist, whereas what expe-

1075

427

riences the experience through it is the composite body. So then, not even in this sense are the negations uttered of the One; for the One does not come to be in any one thing, but although it is the cause of the assertions of which we apply to it the negations, it in no way comes to be in those things of which it is the cause.

Indeed, if I may state my view in summary, I would say that even as the One is the cause of all things, so these negations are the causes of the corresponding assertions. For this reason, all that the Second Hypothesis, as we have said previously, asserts, is denied by the First; for all those positive assertions proceed from these negations, and the cause of these is the One, as being prior to all other things. For even as the soul, being incorporeal, has produced the body, and as the intellect, even though unsouled (because after all it is not a soul) has given substance to the soul, even so the One, while not being itself pluralised, has given substance to all multiplicity, and although it does not possess number, to number, and not possessing shape, to shape, and similarly in the case of everything else; for it is none of the things to which it gives substance. For, after all, no other cause is the same as its own products. If, then, it is nothing of those things which it produces, and it produces everything, it is no one of all things. If, then, we know all things through assertions, we reveal the nature of that entity by negation from each other thing in the universe, and thus this form of nega-

1076 tion is productive of the multiplicity of assertions. For instance, the lack of shape in the case of the One is not the same as it is in the case of Matter, which is viewed as consisting in privation of shape, but rather it is that which generates and produces the order which involves shape. In the case of Matter, then, negations are inferior to assertions, since they are privations, while the assertions are participations in what Matter in itself is deprived of. In the case of real beings, on the other hand, negations are coordinate with assertions; for Not-Being does not participate in essence any less than Being, as is stated in the *Sophist* (258b). In the case of the One, the negations reveal its superiority as a causal principle, and in this respect they are superior to assertions. For this reason also the causal principles among those entities following upon the One have negations of what is secondary to them predicated truly of themselves. For instance, when we say that the Soul neither has the power of utterance nor is silent, we do not say these things about it in the sense that we would about stones or pieces of wood or any other thing without sensation, but in the sense that it produces voice and silence in the living being. And again, we talk of Nature as being neither white nor black, but colourless and, again, without extension. Do we say this, then, in the same way as we would about Matter? By no means (for Nature is superior to the things negated of it), but rather in the sense that it produces both colours and every sort of extension. In the same way, then, we talk of the Monad as being devoid of number, not in the sense of its being inferior to numbers and indefinite, but rather in the sense that it produces and defines numbers—I mean the primal Monad, and that which we say possesses all Forms of numbers.

Everything then, which is negated of the One proceeds from it. For it itself must be no one of all other things, in order that all things may derive from it, For this reason, it seems to me that often Parmenides denies opposite attributes of it, for instance when he says that it is neither whole nor part, neither same nor different, neither static nor in motion; for the One transcends all antithesis, rises above all relation, is 1077 pure from all duality, being itself the cause of all multiplicity and of co-ordinate pairs of opposites and of the primal dyad and of all relation and of all antithesis. For, after all, Nature is the cause of all corporeal antitheses, and Soul of all life-giving causes, and Intellect of all psychic classes of being, and the One of all divisions whatsoever (for it is not the cause of some and not others). The cause of all antithesis is not itself opposed to anything; for in that case there would have to be some other cause of this antithesis, and the One would no longer be the cause of all things. So then we say that the negations for this reason are productive of those which are going to be examined in the Second; for as many as the primal entity generates in the First, so many are produced in the Second and proceed forth in their proper order, and in this way there becomes manifest the structured realm of the gods, taking its origin from the transcendent henad.

(v) Why Does Parmenides Not Begin with His Own First Principle?

A fifth matter that one might reasonably investigate after this is how it comes about that, whereas Parmenides declared that he would take his start from his own One, he begins in fact from the negations of the One and not from the assertions of it, although he himself in his Poem speaks of it always in terms of assertions and not negations, for he declares it to be "whole-limbed" and "untremorous" (fr. 8.4 DK) and says also that it is "necessary" for it to be (fr. 8.30-31) and "unthinkable" (fr. 1.32)[52] for it not to be, and that he who says that it does not 1078 exist "fails of his purpose" (fr. 2.7-8); for the way which asserts that "it

---

[52] Ἀδόκητον sounds Parmenidean, but is not found in extant fragments. It may be a reference to fr. 1.31-32, ὡς τὰ δοκοῦντα χρῆν δοκίμως εἶναι. . . . In that case, how it is best translated is uncertain. The normal meaning "unexpected" will not serve. If Parmenides used the word, he used it in a special, Parmenidean sense—perhaps "not subject to opinion (doxa)," or "unthinkable."

is" is the way of persuasion, according to him; while that way which says that it is not, "and that it is necessary that it not be, this I declare to you to be a path totally without conviction" (fr. 2.5-6).

All in all, he directs many epithets at it, writing of it that it is describable and that it is intelligible (fr. 6.1). How then, when the Parmenidean One has such a nature as this, having said himself that he will begin his proposed exercise from that One, does he here set out through a series of negative propositions first, the positive versions of which he applied in his poetry to his own One? One must say in answer to this problem that even the Stranger in the *Sophist* (245a), when he set out to show, on the basis initially of his own master's teaching, that the One Being is beyond the multiplicity of beings and that for this reason Parmenides was right in placing the One Being before the many, went on to inquire whether the Parmenidean One is really One, and whether it is the same for it to be One and to be existent, or one thing to be one by its own nature, and another thing to be existent. And having raised this point, he shows that, if the One Being is a whole of some sort, as Parmenides said, and has a beginning and an end, being divided into these parts and being "whole-limbed," necessarily it experiences the One as an attribute and participates in the One by being a whole, but is not itself, however, the One in the true sense.[53] The true beginning of
1079 things, however, should not participate in anything else, because necessarily that which participates is secondary to what it participates in, inasmuch as it is in need of something else, namely, of that in which it strives to participate. So that if one is to follow this thesis, he will deny of the One all those propositions that he asserted, who postulated an attributive One.

Parmenides then, as we have said often before, has begun here too from his own One, which was attributively One (but looking away from it towards the One as itself alone and not as something which has oneness as its attribute), viewing the process of participation as one, he led the argument on to the pure intuition of the One, and through this gained knowledge of all things, necessarily, negatively, such as he had applied affirmatively to that which was one attributively, but not the very One itself. He actually began the negations from the idea of wholeness, by means of which the Eleatic Stranger also showed that the One had Being as an attribute (the Parmenidean One, that is, not the true One), and the first conclusion he comes to is that the One is not a whole. Platonists should observe how Parmenides demonstrates the same things in this passage through the notion of the One, which elsewhere the Parmenidean sage has demonstrated, by developing his

---

[53] Cf. Damascius' discussion of this point, *De Princ.* 13, 1, p. 24.10ff. Ruelle.

opinion in the direction of the truth, and should not condemn the First Hypothesis as being without content, but should rather inquire of what entity that hypothesis is true, and should take their guidance in this from Plato.

(vi) The Status and Purpose of Negations

This, then, was the reason for this discussion. But perhaps if some-one were to go on to ask us this question, whether we use negative expressions because of the weakness of human nature, which is unable to grasp the simplicity of the One through any positive mental act and vision and positively directed knowledge, or whether those things which are superior to our souls also know the One analogously through negations—to that we would say that Intellect also knows the Forms and grasps the objects of intellection by means of intellections which are coordinate with them, and this is a type of affirmative knowledge, for "being draws near to being";[54] and what it intelligises, it is, and what it says, that it intelligises; so then, what it is, is what in some way the Intellect states by means of its own intellection. Through the henad superior to Intellect, on the other hand, it is joined to the One, and through this unity it knows the One, knowing Not-Being by means of Not-Being; therefore, it knows the One through negations. For it possesses two types of knowledge, the one as Intellect, the other as non-intellect; and the one as knowing itself, the other as "being drunk," as someone says,[55] and inspiring itself with "nectar"; and the one type it knows as existent, the other as non-existent. So then even the much-celebrated Intellect itself has one type of knowledge which is negative, and another which is affirmative. If, then, the Intellect and the divine souls in virtue of their own summits and unities enjoy ec-static communion with the One and are divine souls primarily in virtue of this activity, while through their intellectual powers they are in de-pendence upon Intellect and dance about it, and in virtue of their noetic power they know themselves and their own essence, pure as it is from relation with what is below, and develop their own reason-principles, while in virtue of their doxastic powers they attain prior knowledge of all sensible things and order them suitably; and all these other types of knowledge of theirs are affirmative (for they know reality as it is, and this is characteristic of affirmation), but by their divinely inspired ac-tivity in relation to the One there is in these beings also a negative type of knowledge (for it is not what the One is that they know, but what it

1080

[54] Parmenides, fr. 8.25 D-K.
[55] Plot. *Enn.* VI, 7.35, with reference to the *Symposium* myth (203b5). Cf. above, n. 10.

is not, in virtue of its superiority to Being; and intellection of what something is not is a negation). If, then, both divine souls and the much-celebrated Intellect itself know the One through negation, why need we condemn our soul for impotence when it strives to express its incomprehensibility through negativity? For, as he says himself, there

1081 is nothing about the first principle such as we normally have cognisance of. For in truth, as he himself has stated in the *Letters* (312e), this is the cause of all evils for the soul, its seeking after the particular characteristics of the first principle and employing reasoning in the attempt to know it, whereas in fact one must rouse up the One in us, in order that we may, if one may so presume to say, become able to some extent, in accordance with our rank, to know like by like. For even as by opinion we know the objects of opinion, and as we know by discursive intellect (*dianoia*) the objects of that faculty, and as by the intuitive intellectual element (*noeron*) in us we know the object of intellect, even so it is by the One that we know the One. This is the same as saying that it is by Not-Being that we know the One, and this in turn is equivalent to saying that it is by negation that we know the One. For Not-Being is a negation, although not in the sense of absolute Not-Being; for that is Not-Being and, in addition to Not-Being, is nothing, for which reason it is devoid of all substantiality and is deprived even of unity. It is described, at any rate, as "not-even One" because on top of everything else, it is completely without participation in that which[56] non-participation in makes something entirely without substance; for it (sc. one-

1082 ness) is the last attribute to leave things; prior to it Being leaves, and prior to Being Life, and prior to this Intellection. So that something which has no intellection can still live and be, and that which does not live can still be, and that which has no being can at least subsist as One; but that which is not even one must necessarily fail of everything, and this is the absolutely non-existent. The One that is prior to Being, on the contrary, is Not-Being certainly, but it is not nevertheless nothing; for since it is one, it is impossible to say that it is nothing. Let us then declare it to be Not-Being, and let us cognise it by that in us which is similar to it (for there is in us a sort of seed of that Non-Being), and so let us call it "non-existent" as transcending all beings, lest we be seduced unawares into indefiniteness, and direct ourselves at Not-Being through imagination rather than through divine inspiration; for this will not only separate us from the One, but also from true knowledge.

It should be clear from this, then, how negations are proper to the

---

[56] Reading οὖ for ὄν of MS, and jettisoning Cousin's ἑνός. Moerbeke notes that he cannot decipher his text at this point.

One, and in what manner all things are denied of it, and that all knowledge of the One is through negation.

(vii) Is All That Exists Denied of the One?

1083   The seventh problem that we must investigate is whether all that exists is denied of the One, or not all, and if not all, why is there this randomness of selection and why does it go only as far as it does, and what purpose does the discourse have. First of all, perhaps, one should list everything that is denied of the One in the First Hypothesis. These are, in the order in which they are given, as follows:

> that it is not many, that it is neither a whole nor a part, that it has neither beginning nor middle nor end, that it has no limit, that it is without shape, that it is neither in anything else nor in itself, that it is neither at rest nor in motion, that it is neither the same as itself nor different, that it is neither like nor unlike, that it is neither equal nor greater nor less than itself, that it is neither older nor younger than itself, that, since it does not participate in time, it in no way participates in generation, that it does not even participate in being, that it is neither nameable nor expressible, that it is neither opinable nor knowable.

These, then, are what are denied of it, in summary. Our task now is to decide why only these were chosen; and if they do not represent all beings whatsoever, how they fall short of this and for what reason is something worth our while to work out. This problem caused great difficulty already to our predecessors. I do not bother to refute those,[57] first, who have said that what is being denied of the One are the two classes of quantity, the discrete and the continuous; for one thing, according to the Pythagoreans and Plato there are not just two classes of quantity, since he makes it quite clear in various places (*Philebus* 55e) that the classes of knowledge concerning quantity are three—arithmetic, mensuration, and statics; nor are all the things quoted of the nature of quantity, as for instance, shape, motion, or rest. Nor do I have much regard for those[58] who seek to ferret out the ten categories in this pas-
1084 sage; for not only the propositions here can be brought under the ten categories, but there are many other things also that one could mention of which Parmenides has made no use. Or again, if some people[59] want to allege that it is the five genera of being which are being made use of

---

[57] Unidentifiable, but presumably Middle Platonic.

[58] Albinus could be included here, on the basis of *Did.*, ch. 6, p. 159, 34f. Hermann: καὶ μὴν τὰς δέκα κατηγορίας ἔν τε τῷ Παρμενίδῃ καὶ ἐν ἄλλοις ὑπέδειξε.

[59] Plotinus takes the five μέγιστα γένη of the *Sophist* as the categories of the noetic world, but nowhere does he specify that they are denied of the One in the First Hypothesis. Amelius is a possible candidate.

here; certainly he had denied these of the One, namely Being, Sameness, Otherness, Motion and Rest, but he is not denying these alone, but also shape and wholeness and time and number and likeness and unlikeness, which are not genera of Being.

Those commentators, on the other hand, are most convincing who seek to demonstrate that all these things are present in the unit;[60] for the unit is many things covertly, both whole and parts, and comprehends various shapes, and is present both in itself and in another, as it is present to all the things that follow from it, and is at rest and in motion, simultaneously both remaining in its state and proceeding forth, and yet in the process of its self-multiplication, never departing from itself; and the likeness is also plain in regard to it, and similarly everything else. It is easy to show that these things are present in the unit, but it must be added to them that the unit is also a representation of Intellect, so that all these things are contained even beforehand in Intellect and for this reason are denied of the One, because it is above Intellect and all intellectual essence. Indeed it is because Parmenides saw all this that in his poem about Real Being he gives it the epithets of sphere and whole and same and other; for he describes it both as "like unto the bulk of a sphere, equally balanced in all directions from the middle" (fr. 8.43-44) and "whole-limbed" (fr. 8.4) and "unwavering" (*ibid.*); so that all these characteristics are primarily present in Intellect, and secondarily and on the level of image both in the unit and in the whole sense-world, but in this latter in a physical way, in the former mathematically; for the sphere on the intelligible level is Intellect, on the level of discursive thought it is the unit, and on the level of sense-perception it is this cosmos, which bears within it images of the eternal gods. Only thus, then, will those who introduce the unit into the discussion have

1085 attained the whole truth if they go on from it to Intellect; for there is nothing great and remarkable if the One is superior to the unit, seeing that Intellect is superior to it, but it would be remarkable if it were superior to Intellect and the totality of the intellectual realm.

Not even these, however, state the reason why only these characteristics are chosen, and not either more or less than those laid down. For these are not the only characteristics proper to the unit, but one might discover many others as well; for it is both odd and even, and contains each of the genera subordinate to these. They have no clear explanation, then, as to why only these out of all are chosen. As far as I know, only our own master (sc. Syrianus) out of all the commentators, closely according with Plato himself in the knowledge of things divine,

---

[60] I take μονάς here to mean the unit, the number "one." This class of critics might thus be seen as Neopythagoreans—such men as Moderatus or Nicomachus of Gerasa, but perhaps also Iamblichus.

has seen that all the things in order which he asserts in the Second Hypothesis he denies in the First, as has been stated often before, but that each of these there is a symbol of some divine order, namely Many, Whole, Shape, "Being in itself" and "in-another," and each of the others in order; for all things do not become manifest in the same way in every order of being, but at one level multiplicity appears, while at another some other characteristic of the divine. For as we have learned in the *Sophist* (245a), first of all is the One-Being, second is the Whole, and third is the All,[61] and as we see in the *Phaedrus* (247c), following on the intelligible gods, first of all there is the "colourless and shapeless and intangible essence," second comes colour, third shape, and simi-
1086 larly in the case of the other characteristics, and in different levels of Being we find the manifestation of different things. If, then, all these characteristics serve to reveal the level of One-Being, all in order and with nothing left out, and the One wishes to place itself beyond all beings, then it is reasonable that only these things should be denied of the One. How each of these characteristics is allotted to the divine orders, we will learn more accurately when we come to study the Second Hypothesis.

So then, what those things are that are denied of the One, and that they are necessarily just this many (for this is just the number of orders of real beings), has now been made plain. This much is also now clear, that all these characteristics have been taken from the distinctive property of Being, and not from that of Life or of Knowledge; for wishing and striving and all suchlike activities are characteristic of living things, while intelligising and thinking things out or exercising sense-perception are proper to knowing subjects; these, however, are common to everything that exists at all. So then, all the above-mentioned characteristics are true both of ensouled and soulless beings, as being consequents of mere existence, and reasonably so; for the hypothesis was, "If there is a One, what follows." All these things are denied of the One, in order that he may end by denying the very proposition that the One exists, with the words, "If then there is a One, then this One does not exist," on the grounds that it is superior even to existence; for it is not receptive of any of the consequent characteristics of existence, and it seems that these are the only characteristics that pertain to beings *qua*
1087 being, the ones which are asserted by the Second Hypothesis and are denied by the First, and we will not discover any things which are common to all beings except these, and of these the first mentioned are more general, while these later mentioned are more particular. For this reason, by eliminating the earlier ones, he eliminates those that follow

---

[61] Cf. the discussion of this triad in *PT* III, 20, pp. 67-73 S-W.

them in the hypothesis. He has, therefore, uncovered in an admirable way what follows as consequences as being *qua* being, and these things he has asserted in the Second Hypothesis and has denied in the First, wishing to show that the One is beyond beings, through showing that it is beyond all the common characteristics of all beings, and these are all the things that are denied of the One in the First Hypothesis, so that, if it is non-receptive of these, it is also non-receptive of Being in general.

If anyone considers that this hypothesis is drawing impossible conclusions, let him recall what is written in the *Sophist*, where the Eleatic Stranger, in putting to the test the doctrine of Parmenides about Being and showing that it cannot be One, especially according to Parmenides himself, who says that Being is a "whole," concludes explicitly: "For the truly One should surely be without parts" (245a). But perhaps the criticism of Parmenides here is undeserved: for he after all referred to "the truly One," which implies partlessness, which in turn implies not having parts; so that all the conclusions of the First Hypothesis demonstrated in consequence of this follow logically. So it is all true and harmonises only with the truly One that is the cause of all beings. And the negations do not lead us to the absolutely non-existent, but rather to the One itself in the true sense; for it is illogical that Real Being should exist (and we need not confine ourselves to Being; there is also the truly Equal, and the Beautiful, and each of the other Forms), while the truly One should be nowhere at all but be a mere name, that thing through which all beings are preserved and have their existence. And if it exists, it is plain that it is not many; for it would not be truly One if it were filled with not-one-ness; for the many are not one; and if it is not many, then it follows that the whole First Hypothesis is valid if one

1088   accepts this principle, and one should not criticise it as stating impossibilities. This, then, should settle this question.

(viii) The Order of the Negations

The eighth topic which requires examination is that about the order of the negations. If, on the one hand, they begin from the highest and primary propositions, how does it come about that he first disposes of plurality, and only finally of existence and the One itself (after all, the One seems to us to be more noble in status than multiplicity, and Being is the most honourable entity among beings)? If, on the other hand, he is proceeding from the lowest characteristics, how does it come about that he takes up likeness and unlikeness after the genera of Being, and also equality and inequality and greater and less; for these are inferior in status to the genera of Being? It is best to say that he starts from the top and proceeds through his negations to the lowest level. For even so also in the *Phaedrus* (247c), where he is denying of the summit of the intellectual orders all those which follow in order on it and proceed from it, he begins the procedure from the top, first declaring it to be without colour and then next without shape and thirdly untouchable;[62] for it was ruling over three intellectual triads—the cohesive, which he groups under colour, the perfective secondly, which he takes under shape, and the intellectual, which he has revealed symbolically to us under the heading of touch, as has been discussed in my commentary on the Palinode[63]—and these triads have been allotted this order, which is that of the negations. Even so, then, in this passage also, the negations begin from the top and proceed in accordance with the order of the divine realms, of all of which the One is the producer. And let us not be surprised that he has left to the end the negation of the One itself and of existence. If we follow through the whole order of the argument, this too will be perfectly clear to us; indeed I think it is already plain that, in the case of affirmative conclusions, one should begin from the classes which are most cognate and demonstrate through these the

1089 less cognate conclusions which follow from the hypothesis; while in the case of negations, one should proceed from the most alien, and through these demonstrate that the less alien do not follow from the hypothesis; for, as we said, those who employ this method should begin from the things most familiar. For this reason, then, he first denies the Many of the One, and when this has first been denied there follows all those things in order such as he denies between the Many and the One; last of all comes Oneness itself, which in position is most akin to it, but is participated in by Being, and for this reason is "a one" (*hen ti*), and therefore, not simply One. It was necessary, then, since the conclusions were negative, for the beginning of the whole hypothesis to be "not Many," and the end to be "not One."

(ix) What Is It That Is Denied First?

Having sorted this out, the ninth question that we must examine is what it is that is denied here first. He himself says that the One is "not many"; it is "many," then, that he first denies of the One. Where, then, are these "many," and what is the multiplicity which the One is not? There are some commentators who say that it is the Many on every level that he is denying of the One because the One transcends all multiplicity both intelligible and sensible; therefore, the One is not any

---

[62] Cf. the discussion in *PT* IV, 12.
[63] Not extant, but cf. *PT* IV, 12.

multiplicity, either intelligible or sensible. But we would ask them to recall that in the Second Hypothesis the Many are also asserted of the One; what sort of sensible multiplicity, then, are we to see in that hypothesis? For everything there is being said of real beings, because the One there is equated to Being.

Other commentators more august than these[64] wish the multiplicity denied of the One to be intellectual multiplicity; for the primal One is without multiplicity, they argue, whereas Intellect is One-Many, and Soul is One *and* Many, held together by the conjunction[65] by reason of its divisibility, while body is Many and One, as being divided, and thus characterised by multiplicity, and Matter is Many alone. This "Many," then, removes the intellectual multiplicity from the first cause, in order that it may be One alone and superior to Intellect. We would ask these commentators, though, what it is they mean here by "intellect." If they mean Intellect proper, which is secondary to the Intelligible, it is not only the One that is beyond the intellectual multiplicity, but the Intelligible also, inasmuch as it is superior to Intellect. If, however, it is the whole intelligible realm that they are calling Intellect, they are ignorant of the basis of distinction within the divine realms and the measured procession of the generation of beings.

However, other commentators more divinely inspired even than these,[66] dismissing sensible multiplicity and not even accepting intellectual multiplicity, declare that far prior to intellectual numbers there are the intelligible monads, from which there has appeared all the intellectual multiplicity arranged in its many orders; it is that multiplicity, then, which is removed from the One, that is to say, the intelligible, inasmuch as it is next after the One, which the intellectual is not. Nor is this to be wondered at, if the One transcends intellectual multiplicity, seeing that the intelligible monads also rise superior to it. This doctrine, then, is divine in its ascent to more simple causal principles; one must also, however, bear in mind[67] that among the intelligibles there are many orders, and, as the theologians tell us in song,[68] there

[64] Possibly Porphyry, if the first set can be taken to be Middle Platonist commentators. The distinctions made here accord with those of Plotinus in *Enn.* V, 1.8.

[65] Reading τῷ συνδέσμῳ δεθεῖσαν for MS τῶν συνδέσμων δεηθεῖσαν (West.).

[66] Probably Iamblichus, whom Proclus elsewhere (e.g. *In Tim.* I, 156.31) refers to as proceeding "in an inspired manner" (ἐνθεαστικῶς), and contrasts with Porphyry as speaking "rather more with insight" (ἐποπτικώτερον, *In Tim.* I, 204.26). The mention of "intelligible monads" here accords with Iamblichus' attested doctrine in Damascius, *In Phileb.* 105, p. 49-51 Westerink (= Iambl. *In Phileb.* fr. 4 Dillon) that the "monads of the Forms" reside at the level of the primary or "pure" Intellect (which is the Intelligible).

[67] This sounds like an amplification of Syrianus, but possibly comes from Proclus himself.

[68] Triads are certainly a characteristic feature of Chaldaean theology (e.g. frs. 2.3, 22, 23, 27, 28 Des Places), but no extant fragment mentions *three* triads as such. On noetic triads, cf. *PT* II, 24-26.

are three triads among them, which we shall reveal clearly as they are exemplified in the Second Hypothesis; there are also among the intelligible-and-intellectual an analogous number of triads to these. If, then, this is the case, it is obvious that this "Many" here is to be assumed to be in the primal and intelligible multiplicity;[69] for this "Many", *qua* Many, is generated only from the One, and from this Many the triadic format proceeds downwards to the lowest grade of being, manifesting itself in the intellectual realm, in the supra-cosmic, and in the sensible, and everything which on any level partakes in Being participates in this triad. For as one of the gods says (*Or. Chald.* fr. 22 DP):

1091

> For the intellect of the Father declared that all things be divided in
>   threes
> and He nodded his assent to this,
> and all things were so divided.

This, then, is the primal multiplicity, the intelligible, which stands forth manifest from the One, which he would seem first to deny of the One; and some commentators, ascending as far as this level, have identified the highest point of it with the One.[70] Either, then, the Many which are now being denied of the One are to be placed for this reason in the intelligible multiplicity, or in the foremost multiplicity on the level of the intellectual-and-intelligible; for the many henads, they say, are not situated among the intelligible gods, but rather in those directly beneath them. For there is one henad to each intelligible triad;[71] a multiplicity of henads is discernible first in the first rank of the intelligible-and-intellectual, as will also become plain in the Second Hypothesis from what we will demonstrate there.[72] For the present, then, let us take it that Plato removes the One from the whole multiplicity of henads as generating them and bringing them to existence, and he does this by taking as a first premise, following the common concepts established within us, that the One is not Many. So he begins his negations from this position, in which the primal multiplicity of henads has appeared from the first henad. Where the primal multiplicity of henads occurs, as we have said, will be made plain by the Second Hypothesis. The argument will show, at any rate, that it is in the first rank of the intelligible-and-intellectual gods, and not in those that are celebrated as solely intelligible; even if there is multiplicity among them also, it is

---

[69] Cousin's supplements are unnecessary here. Instead, delete ἡ (line 33) (West.).

[70] This could refer to Porphyry, who is reported by Damascius (*De Princ.* 43, I, p. 86 Ruelle) as equating the first principle of all things with the Father of the noetic triad, but might also refer to Origen the Platonist; cf. n. 46, above.

[71] For the general principle, cf. *ET*, props. 21 and 125.

[72] Cf. *PT* II, 12, p. 66 S-W: "Multiplicity is met with initially at the summit of the primal intellectual gods and in their intelligible 'watchtower,' as the Second Hypothesis will teach us."

1092 there in another mode, and not in such a way that the One should also be Many, but in such a way that the Many should be One; for it is plain that the contradictory of the statement that the One is not Many is that the One is Many, and the contradictory of the statement that One-Being is Many is that One-Being is not Many, so that if he said that One-Being was not Many, this Many we would have assumed to be of the class of intelligible Manys. But since he said that the One was not Many, we will situate this "Many" wherever it is first shown that the One is Many, and not One-Being. This will be shown to be after the intelligible orders, as we said, and among the so-called intelligible-and-intellectual orders of gods, at which point the argument shows the One and Being being pluralised separately, and will remove the intelligible multiplicity itself from the One last, linking the end to the beginning at the place where he demonstrates that the One is neither One-Being nor Being,[73] as we will learn at the relevant place (141d12).

II. Details of the Text

So much, then, about that. We must now turn to examine the details of the text, in order to connect it also with the consideration of the subject matter. The first thing to be said is that Parmenides does not think that the statement that the One is not Many requires either proof or argument to support it, but he has assumed it on the basis of our common and uncorrupted intuition (koinē . . . ennoia); for in our speculations about the first principle we should especially stimulate the common intuitions, since everything is naturally and unaffectedly related to it, both what operates according to intellect and what operates only according to nature. And, in general, the beginning of every process of proof must be the indemonstrable, and common intuitions must come before demonstrations, as the geometers also assert. Now nothing is more familiar or obvious to us than the statement that the One is not Many, for which reason he assumed this as not requiring introduction or further argument. It is assumed on the basis of common intuition that the One is not Many; if one is to demand some argument for this also, we may say that in all cases each thing which is anything primally

1093 transcends what is as it were its opposite, and is purely what it is; and so even as, for instance, the primally Beautiful is never not beautiful and real Being is never also not existent, so also the primal One is never also Many. This One, then, is only One and not also a multiplicity. For if there is some sort of multiplicity in it, it will be a thing unified and

---

[73] Reading οὔτε [τὸ] ἕν ὄν ⟨οὔτε ὄν⟩ to bring the text into line with 141d12 (τὸ ἕν οὔτε ἕν ἐστιν οὔτε ἔστιν), which seems to be what is being referred to here (West.).

not One in the simple sense; but prior to what is unified there must be the unifying agent, even as prior to that which is given form must be that which gives form. So there would be, then, something beyond the One which is itself first, which is impossible. If that in turn were to have multiplicity, we would have to seek something else prior to it, and either we will proceed to infinity, or we will discover that which is only One and declare that that is absolutely the sole causal principle. The unified multiplicity is akin to the first principle, but it is not the first principle; the One, then, is not Many, but the cause of the Many; for it is not-many in such a way as, not being many, to be the generating principle of the Many.

This, then, may be said about the negation which, as has been said, was accepted on the basis of common sense. We must now rather investigate this question, what sort of One Parmenides is assuming when he says, "if One exists." For if it is his own One, the statement "then the One would not be Many" is false; for the One-Being is Many. But if it is the primal, unparticipated One, then the conclusion is true, but this is not the Parmenidean One; for that was One-Being. But as has been said before, let us also recall now that when he announced that he would take as his hypothesis his own One, and having hypothesised this by saying "if it exists" (for the term "exists" is properly said of this), making use only of the concept of "One," he goes on to ascend from this to the One itself, which is neither Many nor any of the other things that exist; for taking the One-Being as a whole, at one stage he strains his intellect towards the One, using the term "exists" only in so far as its appearance is necessary to make a statement at all, and discovers the cause prior to the One-Being, while at another stage he puts equal emphasis on both parts and unfolds the whole multiplicity of divine Being down as far as the lowest level, while at yet another stage he puts primary emphasis on the term "exists," employing the term "the One" simply in order not to deprive Being of Oneness and thus reveal it as nothing, and makes manifest the entity which follows upon divine Being. It is possible for the One not to partake of Being, but it is not possible for Being not to partake of Oneness. For it is possible for Not-Being to subsist, for the One is of this nature, but that which is not even One is, so to speak, helpless to exist in any way, being completely deprived of unity. So then, from the One-Being one may proceed either upwards or towards itself or downwards; on the upward path the One itself in the truest sense appears, having transcended all Being, for which reason he deprives it in the last place also of the proposition "the One exists," on the grounds that not even this is suitable to the One.

So much, then, on this subject. The beginning of the First Hypoth-

1094

esis makes clear the enthusiasm of the speaker, with all his striving towards the subject and his directing of the listener towards it. For this
expression "come now" is of a nature to arouse the soul and lead it upwards, not allowing us, as it were, to go to sleep in face of the inquiry
about to be undergone, nor to approach it filled with sluggishness, almost saying that which is said by the gods, that "a releasing of the god
is the sluggish mortal / who tends to this realm" (*Or. Chald.* fr. 141
DP).[74] For, if we are to approach the One by means of these negative
conceptions and to emancipate ourselves from our accustomed ways of
thought, we must strip off the variety of life and remove our multifarious concerns, and render the soul alone by itself, and thus expose it to
the divine and to the reception of divinely inspired power. in order that
1095 having first lived[75] in such a way as to deny the multiplicity within ourselves, we may thus ascend to the undifferentiated intuition of the One.

This, however, is obvious. But one might raise the problem why he
does not, as in the case of all the other pairs of opposites—for instance,
Same and Different, "at rest" and "in motion"—remove also from the
truly One not just Many but One, but rather has only proposed this
much, that it is not Many, and has not gone on from this to demonstrate that it is not One, in order that it might be shown to be pure from
all opposites, since it is neither able to be both (for it would not be the
One if it were both), nor is it at odds with either one; for in that case
we would need a prior One which would make it and the other One.
We may say in answer, on the logical level, that he had to preserve the
hypothesis from which the argument takes its start. This hypothesis is,
"if there is a One," and it follows from this that one should conclude
the proposition that "it is not Many" (for the concept of "one" rejects
multiplicity), and it does not follow from this that "it is not One," even
though it is a different One which is opposite to multiplicity; and if it
is possible to remove this from the truly One, which is what he will do
at the end (for he will deny the proposition "that it is one" along with
denying that "it is" (141c10-11), but it was not possible to use it as an
assumption in the same way as he used the assumption that it is not
Many, because the argument had to in every case proceed from indis-
putable premises and not from those which themselves required argument. This, after all, was one exhortation made to those who proposed
to enter upon this exercise.

[74] Emending ἐς τάδ' ἔχων to ἐς τάδε νεύων as Cousin suggests (but Lewy's ἐς τάδ' ἔχων
⟨νοῦν⟩ would be acceptable as well). The verse seems to refer to the belief, in theurgy,
that a slackening of attention (or attention to mortal things) on the part of the practitioner
of a rite serves to release the god who has been summoned up from his or her compulsion
to perform. If so, that is not how Proclus is understanding the verse here.

[75] Reading ζήσαντες for ζητήσαντες (West.), which makes unnecessary Cousin's addition of τὸ ἕν in line 36.

On the logical level then, as I said, we may make this reply. If, however, we look to the realities, we may say that that One which has Many opposed to it is in any case involved with multiplicity, even as sameness is with otherness, and it is not a One that is exempt from multiplicity, even as there is no multiplicity without unity. For that One is inherent in multiplicity, thanks to which multiplicity experiences oneness as an attribute. So then, Parmenides has denied Many of the One and has passed over that One as being denied along with it; for if that One were one in the true sense, it would not only be Not-Many, but also Many, inasmuch as it coexists with Many, and though in itself it is not Many, incidentally it would be Many, and nowhere would we have that which is simply Not-Many, but only that which is in a way Not-Many, and that although in every case our thought demands that prior to what is in a way something there should be that which is simply that thing, and refuses to take its start from those things which are only what they are in a way; for this reason, it postulates the intelligible Forms also prior to sensible objects, seeking for things which are absolutely what they are prior to those things which exist in a way and have the same names as they. Assuming, then, that the One is not Many, and taking this Not-Many as being simply Not-Many, it is reasonable that he should not have been expected to remove also that One which was in a way Not-Many and not simply so.

Proceeding from this, then, to the realities,[76] we declare that this is the One which he said in the *Sophist* (245a) to be truly One, being partless and different from that which has One as an attribute, and in the *Letters* (II, 312e) the first of all things, to which one should not apply the question, "What sort is it?" For everything that is qualified is not what it is absolutely—for example, that which is qualifiedly beautiful or qualifiedly equal; quality, being a characteristic, makes something beautiful or equal in a particular way, so that quality is not to be applied to the One in the essential and absolute sense, in order that it may not become a particular kind of One instead of the One itself. If, then, the One Itself and the primal entity are the same, and the primal entity is God, it is plain that the One Itself and God are the same, and that is not some particular God, but God Himself (*autotheos*). Those, then, who say that the first God is Demiurge or Father are not correct;[77] for the Demiurge and the Father is a particular god. This is obvious, for not every god is demiurge or father, whereas the first principle is simply God and all gods are gods through it, but only some, such as are demiurges, through the Demiurge, and fathers, through the primary Demi-

[76] This refers us back to the course of the discussion before the *aporia* raised at 1095.2.

[77] This criticism is probably directed at Origen the Platonist. Cf. *PT* II, 4, and S-W, vol. II, Intro., pp. xff.

urge or Father. Let the One then be termed simply God, as being the
cause for all gods of their being gods, but not for some particular gods,
1097 as for instance demiurgic or paternal or any other particular type of
godhead, which is a type of qualified divinity, not divinity in the simple sense. For this reason he condemned in the *Letters* (II, 312e) the
practice of asking of the first principle, "What sort is it?" in order that
we might not make the first principle some particular thing instead of
being simply what it is. For it is valid to predicate the qualified animal
of a particular animal, but not of animal in the absolute sense; for
everything absolute is unqualified, as being prior to differentiation,
which is what makes it possess a particular something, and not absolutely that thing; for the particular animal is a qualified animal.

We gather, then, from this that the first principle and the One are the
same. Let us add that this is also the Good in the *Republic* (VI, 509c),
beyond existence and being, as it is described there, and which is supra-
essential; for the One and the Good are the same, if at least, as it is stated
in the *Phaedo* (99c),[78] the Good is that which holds everything together,
and that which holds everything together is the same as the One. If it is
not the same, then either it is beyond the One, or it is nothing, or it is
not One, and each of these alternatives is absurd, so the first principle
is that which is truly One and the king of all and the Good.

*"So then, neither is there any part of it, nor should it be a whole." "Ob-
viously." "A part is a part of a whole?" "Yes." "How about a whole?
Is it not the fact that a whole would be that from which no part is absent?"
"Yes indeed." "In either way, then, the One would be composed of parts,
both as being a whole and as having parts." "Necessarily."* (137c)

The first thing negated of the One, then, is "that the One is not
Many." For on the primal level the One is generative of the Many,
seeing as the primal Multiplicity itself proceeds forth from the One as
the summit of all things. The second negation after this is "that the One
neither is a whole, nor does it have parts"; for the One generates this as
a second order of being after the primal Multiplicity which he denied
1098 first of the One.

In order that we may apprehend this most clearly, let us deal with it
first on the logical level. What we mean will be made plain correctly to
someone who approaches the text from this angle. So then, this much
is plain to everyone, is it not, that when a syllogism derives the validity
of the negation of the consequent from the negation of the premises,
the premise is the more general concept? For instance, in the proposi-

[78] Here we find the principle stated indirectly, in that Socrates accuses his physicist
predecessors of not believing this; but this must be what Proclus is referring to.

tion, "If something is not an animal, it is not a man; but it is not an animal; therefore, it is not a man," we see that animal is more general than man. How else, indeed, would it in being denied also involve the denial of the other term, if it did not have a more general force? Even among terms which are said to be coextensive,[79] there is a certain superiority of terms that cause the negation of other terms over those other terms, in this very respect of initiating the negation of the other and through itself demolishing the other, even if not on a quantitative level, then at least in virtue of its potency. Let this, then, be taken as agreed, that in negative syllogisms, when through the denial of the premise we negate the consequent, and thus draw a negative conclusion for the syllogism, the premise is of greater potency; and when through the denial of the consequent we negate also the premise, it is the consequent that is the more powerful. And in general that which by its own negation also negates its partner, whether it be premise or consequent, is more dominant and powerful than the other.

Let this, then, be one point of agreement. The second principle, similar to this, is that everything which is more comprehensive in its power than something else may reasonably be concluded to be nearer the One; for since the One itself is, if we may use the expression, the most comprehensive of all things, and nothing is outside the One, not
1099 even if you cite privation and the most feeble of things—if they subsist at all, they are to some extent one—it is necessary that whatever is nearer to the One is more comprehensive than what is further from it, imitating in this the uncircumscribed causality and unlimited superiority of the One. Even so Being, in that it is more comprehensive than Life and Intellect, is nearer than the One, and Life is nearer than Intellect.

So then let these two axioms be regarded as established, and let us see how Parmenides concludes on this basis that the One is neither a whole nor has parts, and let us follow his line of reasoning. If it is a whole, he says, or has parts, then the One will be Many; but it is not Many, as has been said previously; so it will not then be a whole, nor will it have parts. And if the One is not Many, then neither is it a whole nor does it have parts. In both these lines of reasoning the negation of parts and whole follows from the negation of Many; for we established that that which along with itself negates also its partner in syllogisms is more powerful and comprehensive; and what is more comprehensive is nearer to the One; so this "Many" is nearer to the One than parts and

---

[79] Proclus presents ἐξισάζειν as a technical term of logic, but it does not seem to occur in the surviving fragments of the Stoics. Cf., however, Asclep. *In Metaph.* 381.31, where it seems first to occur, and Proclus *In Remp.* I, 29.28, where it is used, similarly, of equivalent expressions.

whole. For after all, parts are many, while many are not in all cases parts, so that "many" is a more comprehensive concept than parts; therefore, it ranks above parts. "Many," then, holds first rank among beings, and second comes whole and parts, and for this reason the One produces the former first, and the latter second, through Many; always primary entities in proceeding forth produce those following on them together with their own causal principles. If, then, the negations generate the affirmations, it is plain that the first negation generates the first, and the second the second; the Many, therefore,[80] is more general than that which is a whole and has parts; for what if the Many were infinite, while that which has parts would in all cases be composed of a finite number of parts? So that if something has parts, it will be in need of Manyness, but if it is a multiplicity it is not necessarily a whole. And observe the geometrical order in this, how the proposition that the One is not Many has been taken as an axiom and as a common intuition, whereas the proposition that it is neither a whole nor has parts is established by means of that common intuition; and again the proposition that it has neither beginning nor end is established by means of the proposition before it, and so on in order throughout, following the truly "golden chain" of beings,[81] among which everything derives from the One, but some immediately, others through one intermediary, others through two, and others through more than two, but all alike from the One.

1100

In this way, then, on the logical level, these Many are shown to be correctly ranked as prior to the whole and the parts. If you wish, though, let us consider the question from the perspective of metaphysical reality also. The Many *qua* Many have a single cause, the One. For every multiplicity springs from no other source than the One, seeing that even the multiplicity of beings, in so far as they are beings, derives from Being, while in so far as they are a multiplicity, they derive from the One. For if multiplicity sprang from any other cause than the One, necessarily that cause would be in turn either One, or nothing, or not One; but if it were nothing, it would not be possible for it to be a cause; and again, if it were Not-One, being Not-One it would differ in no way from the Many, whereas a cause must in every case differ from what derives from it. The remaining possibilities, then, are either that the Many be causeless and unrelated to one another and infinite infinitely-multiplied, having within them no One; or the One is the cause of Being for the Many; for either it is not the case that each of the Many

---

[80] A small lacuna in the Greek MS, filled from Latin.

[81] For the concept of the Golden Chain, derived from Zeus' speech in *Iliad* 8.19ff., cf. *In Tim.* I, 314.17ff., and below, Bk. VII, 48.24, with Klibansky's note *ad loc.* in his edition. *ET*, props. 21-30, sets out Proclus' doctrine of *seirai*.

is one nor the totality of them all, and thus the Many will be infinite infinitely-multiplied or each will be one, but the totality of them all will not be one, and they will have no relation to one another (for if they were related they would necessarily partake in One); or the other way about, and each individual will be infinite infinitely-multiplied since it will partake in no One, or both will partake of One, and there must be prior to them something to give unity to both parts and whole, which itself has neither whole nor part; or again this too will be lacking oneness, and so to infinity, or we will arrive at the One, before whole and parts. In addition to this, if there were any other cause of the Many besides the One, there would not have been a multiplicity of henads, which the One produces while maintaining its oneness.[82]

1101

If, then, there are many henads, the cause of their manyness, in so far as they are many, is the One; for the One is the primary cause of henads, which is why they are called henads, and the multiplicity of beings derives from the multiplicity of henads, so that every multiplicity is from the One. Whole and parts, on the other hand, are proper to the realm of beings; for if we take the One Being as a whole, it is surely plain that it is a whole in conjunction with Being, and if we take it as the One in a participated state, in this case also it is certainly in communion with Being, and if we regard it solely as Being, in this capacity too it is a substance. If, then, Whole and Part are in some way beings either essentially, or by participation, then these too are produced from the One, but also from Being, if indeed Whole and Part are beings.

This, then, is what Parmenides meant when he placed them in the One Being, saying, "The One Being is itself a whole and has parts," and making Being dependent on the One, and seeing the Whole in the One Being, and thus reasonably making the Whole a particular aspect of Being. Everything, then, which partakes of essential wholeness, also partakes of essence; but not everything which partakes of essence also partakes of wholeness. For the very parts of Being, in so far as they are parts, while partaking in essence, do not partake in wholeness in so far as they are what they are. If this is the case, then essence is beyond essential wholeness; the essential whole, then, partakes of essence and is not the same as essence. And so, then, if there is such a thing as unitary wholeness, it partakes of the One, and the unitary part necessarily partakes of the One, but it is no longer necessarily a whole—that is actually impossible in so far as it is a part; but whole and part are either essential or unitary (for whole and part occur both among essences and among henads). The One, therefore, is beyond Whole and Part and

---

[82] Accepting Saffrey's conjecture ⟨ἠνωμέν⟩ως for ὡς in 1101.3. As emended, this is a useful statement of the One's relation to the henads. Cf. *ET*, prop. 132.

things essential and things unitary. And not only this, but the Many also is prior to Whole and Part; for either of these is necessarily in a way 1102 many, as we have shown, but Many taken in the primal sense partakes only of the One. The Many is, therefore, prior to Whole and Part.

That is the way, then, in which we must go about our demonstration. But we must also examine the truth of these proofs. If they are really proofs, they will show that every whole necessarily holds together some multiplicity. All wholeness, then, contains some suggestions of its own parts. The wholeness that is in the part is necessarily also ranked with the part, and is not only a whole, but also a part; while that wholeness which arises from the parts is composed from its own parts; and that wholeness which is prior to its parts contains the causal principles of the parts, and so also of multiplicity. In no way, therefore, will the One be a whole. For if every whole is involved with multiplicity, and the One is without multiplicity, then the One will not be a whole. Again, the part is a part of something else, so that that which possesses parts possesses multiplicity; for every part desires to make one complete thing along with other parts; and these others are clearly Many. If, then, the One partakes of no multiplicity, and that which possesses parts possesses multiplicity, it is obvious that the One itself would not have parts. But it has been shown that it is not a whole either; the One is, therefore, neither a whole nor something which has parts; for whether it is a whole or has parts, it is Many; but it is not Many; so neither is it a whole nor does it have parts.

You see, then, that this is the first thing proved through the fact of not being Many, even as in the realm of Being wholeness is produced through the primal multiplicity. Now, proof through a cause is the most authoritative kind of proof. If, then, the whole exists through the Many, not being many is in turn the cause of not being a whole, and the solitariness of the One is exempt from both of these. This was just what the Eleatic Stranger was showing (*Soph.* 244e), that the truly One could not be—I mean, a whole. For he says that there is nothing to prevent wholeness having "one" as an attribute, but it was impossible for 1103 it to be the One itself. The same thing as he was demonstrating there, in demonstrating that the Parmenidean One is not One in the truest sense, he has proved here by showing that the truly One is not a whole, making the first principle advanced here the contrary of the proof there; for there he showed that, if something is a whole, it is not truly One, while here he shows that, if something is truly One, it is not a whole. So either one must disbelieve that that passage is true Platonic doctrine, or one must accept this passage also, and hold that according to Plato this is the first principle of all, and that the truly One is the primal entity.

So much for this, then. But, if the whole and that which has parts in some way appear to be the same thing, this should occasion no surprise. For we may view it both as unified and as articulated (*diakekrimenon*). In its unified aspect we term it a whole, while as articulated we describe it as having parts. The One is neither unified, and so is not a whole, nor is it articulated, so that it does not possess parts; for whether it was unified or articulated, in either case it would be Many; for the unified is a multiplicity dominated by the One, whereas the One itself is beyond all multiplicity, both that which is regarded as unified, and, far more so, that which is articulated.

So much for that, then. It remains for us to address the problem whether Parmenides denies these things of the One by taking what is not true for it in relation to itself, or in relation to others. For this latter has been the view of some commentators,[83] who argue that the Many are other in relation to the One, and that these are being denied of the One, and the same goes for Whole and Shape and all the rest. The philosopher makes it plain, however, at the beginning of the hypothesis, that he is taking these characteristics as not following for the One in relation to itself; for that it is without multiplicity and that it is not a whole we see in relation to itself, even if none of the others existed; in the case of the middle epithets he is examining, such as are not true of the One either in relation to itself or to others, as for instance that it is neither the same as itself nor different from itself, nor the same as others nor different from others, and neither like nor unlike in the same way, and neither in contact nor apart similarly. At the end, on the other hand, he considers such attributes as are not true of the One solely in relation to others, seeing that it is shown there that it is neither expressible nor opinable nor knowable, nor cognisable in any way by any of the others, but is transcendent from the others by itself, from both modes of cognition and objects of cognition, if one may so express it, remaining by itself ranked with none of the others, but unbounded in all respects. And so when he says that the One is not Many, he is not saying that the others besides the One are not the One, as though he were denying those of the One, but he is merely saying that it does not possess multiplicity in itself, and that the One is not, together with being One, also Many, but that it is solely One and essentially One, pure of all multiplicity. For when, in the Second Hypothesis, he proceeds to assert that the One is Many, denying that it is without multiplicity and solely One and thus neither a Whole nor having parts, he treats the One there in relation to itself.

[83] This *aporia* is based on the distinction made in 136a. As to who these commentators are, we have no clue, but they are presumably Neoplatonist.

1104

"In either case, then, the One would be Many, and not One." "True."
"But it has to be not Many, but One." "Yes it must." "So then, the One
will neither be a whole nor have parts, if it is to be One." "No indeed."
(137cd)

Here he sums up for us the whole proof which we have just been discussing, and it would be perhaps appropriate now to remind ourselves
of it. The One is not Many; a whole is Many; so, therefore, the One is
not a whole; and again: the One is not Many; that which has parts is
Many; so then, the One does not have parts. There is a syllogism, then,
here in the second figure, to the effect that the One does not have parts.
We can also construct an hypothetical syllogism as follows: if the One
is a whole, it has parts; if the One has parts, it is Many; but the One is
not Many; therefore, it is not a whole, nor does it have parts.

And behold here the carefulness of Plato, in that he did not say that
the One was partless, but that it did not have parts; for being partless is
not the same thing as not having parts. This latter may be said of the
One, but "partless" cannot be unequivocally said of it; for what is partless on occasion exhibits a sort of nature and a kind of form, or rather
it is none other than a unitary form, and it is nothing else than what
1105 Timaeus calls "undivided" (35a1). Timaeus, at any rate, in that passage
plainly means the same thing without distinction by undivided (*ameriston*) and partless (*ameres*) as we find written at the beginning of the account of the creation of the soul (35a5). In the *Sophist* also (245a8) he
calls the truly One partless when he says, "For presumably the truly
One must be partless," meaning by "partless" here the same as what in
this passage he has designated "not having parts," so that if there is
something that has no parts, according to him it is "partless"; but it
does not follow that if something is partless, it therefore has no parts,
if in the case of each of the genera of being there is one that is partless,
another divided into parts, and another median between the two. So,
for instance, the point is partless, as not having parts, in the way that
there would be parts of something specially extended, but it is not partless in the absolute sense, as having nothing that could be called a part;
for the definition of the point is made up of certain components, and all
the elements comprising it hold the rank of parts in relation to that
which is comprised of them. Similarly the monad, because it is not
made up of distinct parts as is every number derived from it, ⟨is part-
less⟩[84]; but because it is comprised of certain elements which make it a
monad and make it differ from a point, one would not be wrong in calling these components of the definition of the monad "parts"; for those
things that make up the definition of each form are assuredly parts of

---

[84] Accepting Taylor's addition ἀμερής ἐστι.

it, and it is made up of them as of parts, and it is a whole experiencing oneness only as an attribute, but not being the One itself, whereas only that which is simply One is composed neither of continuous parts nor of distinct ones nor of component ones[85] being solely One and simply One, not something unified.

All this could not be otherwise. But I see here a great fuss being stirred up by those who think that these negations lead us into the absolute non-existent or something such, since by reason of the lack of definition our imagination does not have anything definite to grasp onto, inasmuch as nothing is proposed to it, but everything absolutely is removed from the One, and for this reason they are persuaded that one must establish some nature and characteristic for the One. Various commentators make this assumption.[86] Some proceed upwards from Intellect and intellectual Being to the One, and want to place above Intellect "Intellectuality" (*nootēs*), as being something simpler than Intellect, and as it were the condition of intelligising taking place. For, they say, activities are prior to essences, as being more unitary than them, and so prior to Intellect they rank that which intelligises, not calling this the active agent, but rather the cause of activity as causing intellection, as if one were to speak of the ensouling or moving agent. And prior to this again they place the thought (*noēma*), and this they claim to be the first as being most partless, even as a movement (*kinēma*) is more so than the moving agent. And they do not do this in this area only, but in the case of each of the Forms, so that they always end up with similar entities,[87] I mean for example "goodity," "beauty-ness," "virtue-ness," "sameity,"[88] and similar constructions to these, and every such entity they claim to be One. One must ask them whether all these many things differ from one another in nature, or in name alone. For if they differ in name alone, they do not say what the One is, as they set out to do, but they babble emptily about the most divine class of things; whereas if these things differ from one another in essence, they would be leaving a multiplicity in the One, although Plato denies this before all other things unequivocally of the One. And where did they get these names from, in any case, and what theologians are they following who place essences second to activities? For Plato and

1106

---

[85] Translating συμπληρούντων αὐτό. The meaning is "parts" which, as in the case of the monad, go to make up its definition.

[86] On the whole passage 1106.1-1108.19, see Hadot's translation and discussion in *Porphyre et Victorinus*, I, pp. 355-375. The term νοότης turns up in Victorinus (along with ὀντότης and ζωότης, at *Adv. Ar.* IV, 5.33 and 539, and so is plainly Porphyrian, but the compounds in -μα below, ἀγάθωμα, κάλλωμα, ἀρέτωμα, ταύτωμα, occur nowhere else in Greek before Proclus.

[87] Or possibly, "always have the same endings" (i.e. -ωμα)?

[88] By such barbarisms I try to render the neologisms listed in n. 86 above.

all other theologians everywhere declare that activities depend upon potencies, and potencies upon essences.

But there is no need to discuss these further, as they have already been refuted by others. There are other commentators, who wish to distinguish between God and the state of being God,[89] and to allot to the primal reality the state of being God, and to give this as the distinguishing characteristic of the One. One must ask these how we are to understand this "being" of the One, seeing that Plato has removed existence from it, and how in the case of those entities are we to distinguish each from the being of each, and how we are to transfer these distinctions from composite entities to things that are simple and divine and most unitary of all things. For neither in the case of the Soul would we accept that Soul is different from "being Soul,"[90] nor in the case of any other of the immaterial Forms. Far more so, then, should we decline to introduce such distinctions into the realm of the Gods themselves. How, after all, can the One be different from the state of being One? If we postulate that, without realising it we would be making the One Not-One, if it is going to be made distinct from "being One," and will thus partake in it as something superior to itself.

There are other authorities,[91] however, who have said that since the first principle is cause of all things, situated above Life, above Intellect, above Being itself, it possesses within itself in some way the causes of all these things unutterably and unimaginably and in the most unified way, and in a way unknowable to us but knowable to itself; and the hidden causes of all things in it are models prior to models, and the primal entity itself is a whole prior to wholes, not having need of parts. A whole prior to parts has in some way need of the parts, and it is this that Plato has denied of it here, whereas a whole prior to wholes has no need of parts.

But those who say this are paying no attention to Plato, who considered that one should use only negation in connection with the One; nor do they bear in mind what is written in his letter to Dionysius (*Ep.* II, 312e), and the exhortation there to apply nothing to the One, but to remove everything from it, in order that we may not unawares attrib-

---

[89] Rendering το θεῷ εἶναι. Once again, who these commentators are, who made use of this distinctively Aristotelian formulation (e.g. *Met.* H, 6.1043b2) is obscure, but Porphyry seems a probable candidate, since Marius Victorinus makes the same distinction at *Adv. Ar.*, I, 33.4-9. Cf. Hadot, *op. cit.*, p. 359.

[90] Cf. Plot. *Enn.* I, 1, 2, where the same point is made, itself a development from Aristotle, *Met.* H, 3.1043b3ff.

[91] If the two previous views criticised are those of Amelius and Porphyry, then the probability is great that the present view is that of Iamblichus, but of course nothing is certain. Victorinus also seems to entertain this view (*Adv. Ar.*, IV, 23.27-34), but this need not disqualify Iamblichus. For ἡμῖν μὲν ἀγνώστως, cf. Iambl. *In Tim.* fr. 88 Dillon.

ute to it what is akin and proper to us; for it is this that in that passage he declared to be the cause of all evils, the enquiry as to what sort of a thing the One is. And apart from these considerations, how are we any longer to preserve the One? For the "whole of wholes" is more comprehensive than wholes and is, therefore, one-like, but the One itself transcends and exceeds all wholeness; and the whole of wholes belongs properly to the middle rank of intelligibles (if even to that), as we shall show (for this ranks above intellectual wholeness, and embraces it on all sides); but the One is beyond the intelligibles.

1108   But if we ascend not only from Intellect and Life and Being to place the unknowable causes of all things in the One, but also from each of the real Beings, such as Beauty, Virtue, Justice, and each of the others, the One will be equal in multiplicity to Intellect; and it would not any longer at all be one, and thus we would have inadvertently ended by doubling the totality of beings; for there would be the beings themselves and their causes subsisting in the One, and in the case of these we would be enquiring how, being many, they become unified, and we will necessarily postulate that there is a One prior to these, and either we will preserve it as One in the proper sense and remove all things from it, or once again we will place all things in it, and we will be tripling the totality of beings, and thus we will proceed to infinity without ever making a stand anywhere, maintaining that the One also contains multiplicity. This, indeed, is what some friends of Plato have before this ventured to assert, even though every multiplicity demands something else to give unity to the multiplicity, or, if there is no such thing, the multiplicity, having as it does a unity brought in from outside, will not be sufficient to count as first because of its deficiency in unity.

It is better, then, as Plato did, to rest content with the negations, and by means of these to exhibit the transcendent superiority of the One— that it is neither intelligible nor intellectual, nor anything else of these things which are cognisable by us by means of our individual mental activities; for inasmuch as it is the cause of all things, it is no one of all things; and it is not the case that it is unknowable to us while being knowable to itself; for if it is absolutely unknowable to us, we do not even know this, that it is knowable to itself, but of even this we are ignorant; for even to say that it is the "fount of divinity"—even as the Beautiful Itself and the primally beautiful is the henad of all beautiful things, and Equality Itself and primary equality is the henad of all equal things (for not even in the case of these do we enquire what Beauty Itself is, but we recognise that it is the fount of beautiful things, and we think this to be sufficient), even so, then, also the One is the fount of all divinity, inasmuch as it is God Itself (for every god, inasmuch as it

is god, derives its subsistence from the One)—not even this is abso-
1109 lutely correct. For if, as Plato says (*Parm.* 142a), "There is not even any
name to it," how should we call it God Itself or anything else? But in
fact this epithet and all others are inferior completely to the unknowable superiority of the One. But if we are to state anything at all positive about it, it seems to me that it is better, following the decision of
Plato, to call it the fount of all divinity, but only in the sense that we
term it the beginning and the cause of all things and the end of all things
and object of striving for them; for, for its sake all things are, and it is
the cause of all things, as he says himself in the *Letters* (*Ep.* II, 312e); by
using these terms we do not say what it is in itself, but what relation to
it those things have which are after it and of which it is the cause. In a
word, then, all divinity is a henad, but the One itself is nothing else
than Divinity Itself, through which all gods derive their quality of
being gods, even as all intellects derive their qualities as intellects from
the primary Intellect, and souls derive their quality of being souls from
the primal Soul; for that which primarily is something is the cause for
all other things of their being secondarily what it is primarily.

So much then for that. We must now turn our attention to the text,
and observe how Plato makes clear about these negations that they are
not privative, but express rather a transcendent superiority to corresponding assertions. For, he says, "The One must neither be a whole
nor must it have parts." This use of "must" demonstrates superiority
in the direction of goodness. And a proof of that is that we do not attach
"must" to privative expressions. For who would say, "The soul *must*
be ignorant of itself?" For ignorance is a privation for those things
which have the faculty of knowing. And so he himself declared about
all evils that it was necessary for them to exist, in the *Theaetetus* (176a).
So the expression "must not be" should not be applied to privative
1110 expressions, but to those states which are superior to positive states; as
for instance, "The first principle *must* not intelligise itself," inasmuch
as it is superior to intellection, and "It must not be many," as being superior to being many, and "It must not be a whole nor have parts," as
being superior to these also; for the expresion "must" is not characteristic of privation, but rather of superiority. This then, as I said, is what
Plato is demonstrating when he adds "must," which is sufficient to remind us of the special property of these negations, and at the same time
he wants to show through this that he is discussing something that has
real existence and not a thing without substance. For who could say
about something insubstantial that it *must* be insubstantial? For the
expression "must" refers only to those things which possess substance
at all.

454

"So then, if it has no parts, it has neither a beginning nor an end, nor a middle; for such things would already be parts of it." "Quite right." (137d)

Earlier he distinguished the One from the primal multiplicity. Secondly, he removed from the One wholeness, which holds together the combination of the intellectual gods; and that it was this that he removed from it, and not only the intelligible wholeness, will become quite clear to us from the Second Hypothesis.[92] And we will discover more clearly, as we go on, this also, for what reason he began his negations from this multiplicity, which we have talked of before, and not from the summit of the intelligible world, which is the One Being itself, but it is this that he will remove from it last, in showing that the One is beyond the whole intelligible world. And thirdly, he now removes from it beginning and middle and end, this being a symbol of a rank inferior to that which is a whole and has parts; and we shall understand how he demonstrates this in turn on the basis of what precedes it, pursuing his canons of proof. For if the One does not have parts it will have neither beginning nor middle nor end; for everything that has beginning and middle and end has parts. But the former; therefore, the latter. So when the former is abolished, so is what follows it. Having beginning and middle and end is, then, the symbol of a more partial rank; for the more general is more akin to the cause, while the more particular is further from the first principle, agreeing in this with the facts of life; for as regards that which has parts, it is not yet clear if it has a beginning and a middle and an end. For what if it is a whole made up of two parts? The dyad, after all, is a whole in a way, and in such a way as to be the first principle of all particular things; the feature of having a beginning and middle and end arises first in the triad. If one says that every whole is triadic, yet even so there is nothing to prevent that which has parts from being in itself and not yet complete, since the complete and the whole preexist it. For this reason he did not commence his proof from the whole, but from the notion of having parts.

This, however, is obvious from what has already been said. Some commentators raise the problem as to how Parmenides can unequivocally draw the conclusion, "for such elements would then be parts of it." For this demonstrates to us clearly that everything which has a beginning and a middle and an end has its own beginning and middle and end as parts. But this is not true; the line, after all, has as its beginning and end a point, but such, our opponent claims, are not parts of the line; for nothing which has a limit has an unlimited number of parts,

92 Cf. *PT* IV, 35.

and the points are unlimited, so a line is not made up of points, nor in general is it possible for a magnitude to be composed of points.

In reply to this difficulty one may say first that since Plato is talking about the One, it is reasonable for him to say, "If it has beginning and middle and end, such elements would be part of it"; for the One is not lumped together out of unlike elements, as is the line, nor will it have such limits as that does, but if one is at all to postulate in it an end and a middle and a beginning, these elements will be such as to make up the content of the One, so that they would have the relation of parts to it; for it will have these as parts, in the way that the triad has a beginning and middle and end as parts of it. One might reply secondly that, even if something has limits, these in turn would have other parts in any case which are bounded by these limits; for if things are limits, they must be limits of something, and that which has them will surely be composed of those elements within which those limits fall, and will have those as parts; so that we may understand the expression "such elements would be parts of it" as referring not to limits, but to things limited. For if something has limits it also has parts; it is not, however, the case that if it has parts, it in all cases has limits also; it may just have other parts, as is the case with each of the numbers. He was right, then, to say that "everything which has a beginning and a middle and an end would have parts," for it is either these, or it is what is within these.

This, then, is the first reply one might make. The second, which would also be far truer, is that the word *part* is subject to ambiguity. So that which has the same elements as the whole, and has everything partially that the whole does holistically, we term a part, as for instance each of the many particular intellects is a part of the whole Intellect, even though all of them are in each of the Forms, and the sphere of the fixed stars is a part of the universe, even though it also encircles everything, but in a different manner from the cosmos. The second meaning of the part is that which goes to make up the totality of something, as we call all the spheres parts of the universe, and the discursive intellect and opinion parts of the soul; for the one set makes up the totality of the universe, the other set that of the soul. In addition to these meanings, we use a general meaning of part to describe everything that is in any way linked with other things for the completion of some one entity. For in the way one might call each one of us a part of the cosmos; not that the universe as universe is made complete by means of us (for the universe does not become incomplete when one of us perishes), but because we are linked together with the universal parts of the universe, and we are administered along with everything else, and we are present in the universe as in a single living thing, and we ourselves are parts of the universe and help to make it up, not in so far as it exists, but in so far as it is an agent of generation.

Since, then, the word *part* has three senses, Plato in proclaiming that the One has no part is plainly removing from it *part* in all its senses; for everything that is any kind of part has multiplicity, but the One does not have multiplicity, so that it would in no way have parts; if this is the case, it would not have a beginning or a middle or an end. For these one would call parts of that which possesses them according to the third meaning of *part*, according to which a part of something is anything which is in any way linked to it, the whole being made up through the conjunction of those elements; for the line *qua* line inevitably has other things which are parts of it; but in so far as it is a limit, it is inevitably composed of these elements as making up its whole; for by reason of these it is termed limited, and these would be called limited things, even if they were not parts of a line.

To this difficulty, then, we respond by making the distinction between the various senses of *part* and specifying in what way beginning and end are described as parts of that which contains them. On another subject, however, some people raise the problem how it is that the Athenian Stranger in the *Laws* (IV, 715e) says that God possesses the beginning and middle and end of all existent things, whereas Parmenides in the present passage shows that he has neither beginning nor middle nor end. These two statements, they say, are somehow contra-
1114   dictory to each other.

There are some, again, who say in reply to this difficulty that the first principle both possesses beginning and middle and end and does not possess them; for it possesses them in a hidden mode, whereas it does not possess them distinctly; for it contains everything within itself in a manner inexpressible and inconceivable to us, but knowable to itself.[93] Once again, we will not accept these theorists, since they in their turn are multiplying the One to some extent or other; for this hidden and undivided multiplicity belongs to some other order of secondary entities and not to the primal entity itself, which is pure of all multiplicity. For in general, of divisions, some are monadic and extend only to the intelligible realm, while those extending into numbers are to be viewed in connection with the orders of being subsequent to this; but the One is prior to all division and all multiplicity, both the unified and the distinct, being exclusively One.

[93] This commentator is to be connected, through this phrase, with the third of the commentators on the previous lemma (1107.9ff.), whom I have identified tentatively with Iamblichus, but whom Hadot would see as Porphyry. A difficulty for my view is that there is a further commentator below (οἱ δὲ, 1114.20), between this one and Syrianus.

But let the argument of this group be set aside as unsound;[94] for it is not our intention to indulge in controversy with others, nor to examine the views of others, except incidentally. There are others,[95] however, who make a more attractive reply to this difficulty, saying that both the Athenian Stranger and Parmenides are talking about God, but the latter is talking about the God that is primal and transcendent over all things, while the former is talking about a particular god ranked in another order; for why should we not put it in plain words, calling him, with perfect accuracy, the Demiurge and Father? For the phrase "going about his circuit" is not proper to the One, and the statement that Right follows upon him demonstrates to us that quite another order and a different god is being talked of; and it makes sense to refer those statements to the Demiurge, seeing that he divides the universe three ways according to the demiurgic triad, and encompasses everything with his intellectual cognition, while he orders everything else with the help of Right.

These views, as I have said, are quite correct. But our own Master has solved the objection still more perfectly, saying that it is not the same thing for us to examine how the One is related to itself and how 1115 it is related to others, as we have indicated many times before this. Once these problems have been sorted out, it seems reasonable that Plato here, where he is considering what does not follow for the One in relation to itself, has denied it beginning and middle and end; for these would as far as we are concerned have introduced with them multiplicity into the One. The Athenian Stranger, on the other hand, is not saying what relation God has to himself but what relation he has to others, and that he possesses beginning and middle and end, these things being present in the universe and not in God, while God himself, because he is prior to everything, is pure from having beginning and middle and end, but holds together all existing things, in which these three elements exist. So that even if the discussion does concern the first God in that passage also, it does not contradict what is said here. For the Athenian Stranger is not saying that god possesses this triad in himself and in relation to himself, but that he transcends all the beings in which these three elements are. And if in the *Letters* (II, 312e) he declares that all things are about the king of all, and for his sake all things are and he is the cause of all nobility, it is plain that he says this because that entity is the beginning of all things and their end and their middle, but he is not because of this himself possessed of beginning and middle

---

[94] σαϑρὰ φϑεγγόμενος, cf. *Theaet.* 179d.

[95] If we maintain that the previous view is that of Iamblichus, we might see this commentator as Plutarch of Athens, especially as his view is entertained so hospitably by Proclus.

and end; for that passage teaches what relation God has to others, and not what his relation is to himself. Of other things, then, the first principle is beginning and middle and end, but he is not himself divided into beginning and middle and end; for he is the beginning of all things because all things proceed from him; and their end because all things are directed towards him; for all pangs of desire and all natural striving is directed towards the One, as the sole Good; and he is the middle because all the centres of existent things, whether intelligible, intellectual, psychic, or sensible, are established in the One; so that the One is the beginning, the middle, and the end of all things, but in relation to himself he possesses none of these, seeing that he possesses no other type of multiplicity; but not in relation to anything else either, for he neither has beginning, because nothing is superior to him, nor does he derive from a cause; nor does he have end, for he does not exist for the sake of anything, but everything that has an end in all cases exists for the sake of something, and the One is only that for the sake of which things exist, even as Matter, and in general the lowest element in all things, is only for the sake of something; nor is there a middle of the One, around which as middle the One exists, that the One may not be a Many of which there is a middle element. The One is, then, transcendent over all these things, and one should not apply any of them to it, but, as Plato instructs us, we should rest content with the negations. For when we say that it is an object of striving or an end, we are indicating the efforts of other things towards it; for by the compulsion of nature all things after the First strive towards the First. How indeed, if they are centred and rooted in the First, could they not strive towards their own cause? These, then, are things which have acquired a relation towards it, but it is transcendent over all things equally.

"And further, the end and the beginning are the limits of each thing."
"Obviously." "So then the One is unlimited, if it has neither beginning nor end." "It is unlimited." (137d)

In the Second Hypothesis, in the interests of establishing this triad—I mean beginning, middle, and end—he establishes, after the One and Many and the Whole and that which has parts, the Limited and the Unlimited, ranking these three pairs of opposites together; for these are indicative of a single divine order, in its aspects of resting where it is and proceeding forth and returning towards itself and holding itself together in its peak of superiority. And then he generates in this way first that which has ultimate points, and then what has beginning and middle and end, and thirdly the straight and the curved and the mixture of the two as being marks, after the first, of a second divine order. In the present passage, after the whole and that which has parts, he denies of

1116

1117

459

the One the triad dependent on this, that of beginning, middle, and end, and from this he has concluded that it is also infinite, "infinite" signifying that which does not have an ultimate point. For in the infinite there is no ultimate point, neither as beginning nor as end. He could, indeed, have shown that the One is without beginning and end also from its not having ultimate points, and its not having ultimate points from the fact of its neither having parts nor being Many; but it is in order to lead the argument forward by means of more familiar concepts that he has begun by demonstrating from its not having parts that the One is without beginning and without end, in order that we may not have three instead of one. From the demonstration of this he has derived as an additional conclusion (*porisma*) that the One is also infinite, if it is without beginning and without end, substituting for beginning and end "limit," which is the same as the ultimate point. It seems to me, then, that this infinity here does not simply indicate the negation of limit, but the removal of all ultimate points. Since, then, in the Second Hypothesis he asserts that it has an ultimate point, it is reasonable that here, by denying it, he should demonstrate that the One is infinite as not having ultimate points, which we are accustomed to term limits; for that very characteristic of limitedness and its opposite of unlimitedness, which he will assert of the One after whole and parts in the Second Hypothesis (145a3), he leaves aside, as having it removed *a fortiori* along with the whole and the parts, or even before this by means of the Many. For every limited and every unlimited multiplicity is either Many alone, or at the same time is a whole and has parts; if it possesses its unlimitedness potentially, but is in actuality limited and is some whole, and something which has parts, then through this it is Many; if it is separately limited and separately unlimited in actuality (this being impossible simultaneously), it is in one way a whole and possessor of parts, while in another way there is no reason why it should not be many; for the unlimited, although it is not a whole, is yet many; therefore, when he denied whole and possession of parts of the

1118 One, it was also possible to deny of it limitedness and unlimitedness.

But what the sense of this is, and how the whole and the parts are coordinated with each other by means of the limited and the unlimited will become clear to us later on, when we are talking about the multiplicity of the gods. Now our task is to discuss in what way the One is the cause of all things, and how it gives rise to all the divine numbers. In this connection, people are accustomed once more to raise the question in what sense the One is unlimited. Some declare[96] the One to be

---

[96] Plotinus criticises this view in *Enn.* VI, 9.6, while adopting the second view listed below, but the criticism of this view here, and the second view itself, are probably those of Porphyry (see General Introduction, p. xx). The first view will then be that of some pre-Plotinian commentator; cf. the parallel passage in *Anon. Taur.* I, 20ff.

termed unlimited in this sense, that it is untraversable and is the limit of everything else (for the term "unlimited" has two senses, the one as being incomprehensible and unencompassable, the other as being the limit of all things, and not having any other limit); and the One is unlimited in both senses, both as being incomprehensible and unencompassable by all that is secondary to it, and as being itself a limit of everything and not itself being in need of any other limit. Others[97] take its unlimitedness to refer to its being of unlimited power and that it is generative of all things, and that it is cause of all unlimitedness in existent things and extends the gift of itself through the totality of beings; for all things are contained in the One and exist through the One, and none could come to be unless they become One by their own nature. Others, again, take its unlimitedness in this sense: since Intellect is limit, and the One is above Intellect, for this reason they have termed it unlimited; for, they say, it is only these two things that Plato predicates of the One, unlimitedness and motionlessness, since Intellect is limit and Soul is motion, and he wants to show that it is superior to both Intellect and Soul; for there are three ruling hypostases, of which the first dominates the other two.

We, however, accept all these suggestions as having a certain attraction, even though we incline to some more than to others; but we are very strongly indeed influenced by our own Master, who in this passage as well has very accurately tracked down the intention of Plato, and we would recommend all lovers of truth to see first how many orders of unlimitedness there are among beings, then what processions of limit there are, as it were, set over against these, and after that to turn to the consideration of what unlimitedness is being referred to here; for if one treats the inquiry into the present question in this way the whole intention of Plato will readily become clear.

Unlimitedness, then, if we start from below, may be viewed in Matter because it is unlimited and shapeless and formless of itself, whereas the forms and shapes are limits of Matter. It may be seen also in unqualified body in respect of division; for this is the entity which is primally divisible to infinity, in so far as it is the first which is extended. It may be also viewed in the qualities which come into being primally about the unlimited, which are the first things to contain the more and less; for these are the elements by which Socrates in the *Philebus* (24b) characterised the unlimited. It may also be seen throughout the whole of the realm of generation; for this possesses unlimitedness, both in re-

[97] It may be noted that this commentator is credited with the term ἀπειροδύναμος, whose first recorded user is Porphyry, though he uses it of the soul (*Sent.* 37, p. 43.9 Lamberz). On the other hand, Porphyry also describes τὸ ὄντως ὄν as ἄπειρον καὶ ἀδιεξίτητον, *ibid.* 34, p. 39.10-11, but this is not a very serious objection, since he is not referring to the One. The following commentator is probably, therefore, Iamblichus.

1119

spect of its constant coming into being and in the ceaseless cycle of this, and in respect of the unlimited exchanges with each other of generated things as they constantly come into being and perish, among which also unlimitedness in respect of multiplicity has its origin, since it only has existence in the process of coming to being, never attaining true existence.[98] And prior to these the unlimited may be observed in the circuit of the heavens; for it also possesses unlimitedness by reason of the unlimited power of that which moves it; for body, in so far as it is body, does not have unlimited power, but through the presence in it of intellect even body exists eternally, and its motion is unlimited; it is unceasing and continuous, having the same thing as its beginning and end. Prior to these again, the unlimited may be perceived in the Soul; for as it thinks transitively, it possesses the power of unceasing motion and is eternally mobile, joining its circuits one to the other, and producing an activity which is unwearied and always one and unfailing. Further, prior to Soul, the unlimited may be perceived in the case of Time itself, which measures the whole circuit of the Soul; for this is limitless as a whole because its activity, through which it unfolds the motions of souls and through which it measures their circuits as it proceeds according to number, is unlimited in its power; for it never stops resting and going forward, both clinging fast to the One, and unfolding Number, which measures the motions of all things. But indeed, even prior to Time, behold the infinite in Intellect itself and intellectual life; for this is non-transient and always a totality and present as a whole, and eternal and infinite in power; its eternal motion and unfailing continuity is a mark of an essence and power which does not give out, but always preserves unsleeping life, through which also everything that is in motion is able always to move, participating through its motion in stable infinity. And the unlimited does not extend only as far as these, but also, prior to Intellect, the much-celebrated Eternity itself is necessarily infinite, seeing that it comprehends the whole intellectual infinity. For whence would Intellect derive its eternal life if not from Eternity? So then this is unlimited, prior to Intellect, in respect of power; or rather all other things are infinite in power, but Eternity is power itself; for indeed the primal Eternity is nothing else than Power.

1120

Ascend then to the primal fount of infinity, cognising the hidden cause of all other infinite things of whatever kind, and when you have thus ascended you will see that all things are infinite in respect of power from that source. For such, if you will, is Essential Infinity; such is what is termed by Orpheus "chaos," about which he himself has said,

---

[98] Reading περὶ τὸ ὄν (West.), for meaningless περιδεομένου of Greek MSS (there is a gap of six letters in the Latin translation here).

"Nor was there any bound beneath it" (fr. 52 Kern).[99] For Eternity, even if it is unlimited in respect of everlastingness, nevertheless as being the measure of things eternal is also a limit; chaos on the other hand is primally unlimited and solely unlimited, and is the fount of all infinity—intelligible, intellectual, psychic, corporeal, or material.

You see, then, how many orders of infinity there are, and how in each case the secondary depend upon those prior to them; for material unlimitedness is held together through eternal generation, while eternal generation is unfailing by reason of the eternal motion of the aether, and the eternal motion of the aether is brought about by the unceasing circuit of the divine Soul; for it is an imitation of that entity, and the circuit of the Soul is unfolded through the continuous and unfailing power of Time, which makes the same things to be beginning and end by means of the temporal present, and Time exercises its activity without limit by virtue of the unlimitedness of Intellect, which is always static; for that which proceeds according to Intellect, when it is infinite, is infinite by virtue of an eternally static cause, around which this unfolds itself and about which it performs its eternally uniform dance. And Intellect possesses eternal life by virtue of Eternity; for eternality comes to all things from eternity, and it is this on which all depend, some more manifestly, others more obscurely, for their being and life; and Eternity is infinite by virtue of the fount of infinity, which from above provides unfailingness to all essences and powers and activities and circuits and generations. Up to this, then, there ascends, and from this there descends, the order of things infinite; for even as the order of things beautiful descends from Essential Beauty, and the order of things equal from Primal Equality, even so the order of things infinite descends from Essential Infinity.[100]

Enough has now been said about the orders of Infinity. We must now turn to examine the chain of Limit which proceeds parallel with this. For these two causal principles were produced simultaneously by God—Limit and the Unlimited, or, if you wish us to express them in Orphic terms, Aether and Chaos. For the infinite is Chaos, in so far as it is receptive of every power and every type of unlimitedness, and in so far as it encircles everything else, and is as it were the most infinite of all things infinite. Aether is limit because this (visible) aether too limits and measures all things. The primary limit is Essential Limit, the fount and foundation of all limits, intelligible, intellectual, supracosmic, encosmic, preexisting itself as the measure and bound of all things. The second limit is that associated with Eternity; for Eternity is

1121 (marginal line number at left, aligned with "circuit of the Soul")

---

[99] Cf. the discussion of this fragment at *In Tim.* I, 385.17ff.

[100] Cf. *ET*, prop. 92, and Dodds' comm. *ad loc.* There, αὐτοαπειρία is declared to be neither First Principle nor Being, but between the two.

1122 simultaneously both unlimited, as has been said, and limit; in so far as it is the cause of unfailing life and the power which bestows everlastingness, it is unlimited; inasmuch as it is measure of all intellectual activity and the bound of the life of intellect, bounding it from above, it is limit. And in general it is one of those mixed entities which are formed of limit and unlimitedness, for which reason we do not see fit to call it the primarily Unlimited; for that which is primarily anything is transcendent over either of every pair of all mixed entities, as Socrates says in the *Philebus* (23c).

The third class of limit is to be seen in Intellect; for in so far as it remains in itself in virtue of its intellection and possesses a life which is single and eternal and the same, it is bounded and limited; for that which is non-transitive and static belongs to the limited nature, and in general in that it is a number it plainly in this respect partakes of limit. Fourthly, Time is limit, both in so far as it proceeds according to number, and in so far as it is the measure of the circuits of the soul; for everywhere the measuring element, in so far as it measures, and that which sets bounds to other things, partakes of the causal principle of limit and is a measuring and limiting element of other things. Fifth after these comes the circuit of the Soul, and its cycle as it is uniformly completed, which is an invisible measure of all visible motions; for it is on the basis of the circuit of life that all the unfolding of those things which are moved by an external agency is given definition.

The sixth form of limit is the motion of the aether on the same terms and in the same place and about the same centre, which bestows limit from all aspects upon the disorderly element in material things, and rolls them together in one cycle and is itself limited by itself; for its unlimited element consists in its happening again and again, but not in its not turning back on itself, nor on the grounds that it is unlimited in one direction, nor does unlimitedness here too consist in the fact that it is devoid of limit; but the single circuit is unlimited in that it occurs many times. Seventh is the unfailing creation of the forms in matter, and the

1123 fact that nothing of all things perishes, and the fact that all things are bounded, individual things by common terms, parts by their wholes. All this shows in this realm the opposition of limit and unlimitedness; for although generated things alter in unlimited ways, nevertheless their forms are limited and persist the same, becoming neither more nor less.

As an eighth type of limit let us mention all quantity as it particularly appears in material things, even as quality was previously stated to be unlimited; for it does not allow of the more and less, as Socrates says in the *Philebus* (24b). Ninthly, unqualified body as a whole is limit; for it is not unlimited in size, but it is of the same extent as the universe; for it must as a whole be said to be the substratum of the universe. A tenth type of limit is the form-in-matter itself, which holds together matter and bounds its boundlessness and shapelessness, and it is this, indeed, solely that some people think of when they refer limit and unlimitedness to matter and form alone. So many, then, are the orders of limit; to sum up, we shall see many different characteristics of these.

It remains to examine how the One shall be termed unlimited, whether in the sense that we apply unlimitedness to existent things, positively, or in some other way. But if unlimitedness is predicated of it in this way, we would even more have to describe it as "*not* unlimited"; for in the case of each antithesis it is necessary that the One either be exempted from both of the opposites and not be either of them, or that it should be called rather by the name of the superior of the two; for one must apply the best term to that which is best of all, but not any predicate which expresses any kind of inferiority. So, since there is an antithesis between the One and multiplicity, we call it "one," and there being a contrast between cause and effect, we term it "cause"; for the cause is superior to the effect and one to multiplicity; it was necessary, then, that one call it either "above cause" and "above one,"or "one" and "cause," but in any case not "multiplicity" and "effect"; for to what entity would we allot the more honourable terms if we refer the worse terms to the One? If then also Limit is superior to the Unlimited, we will not apply to it a name derived from the Unlimited; for it would not be right to apply epithets to it from the worse side, but rather, as we have indicated before now, by negation of the better; for "unlimited" in this sense is the same as "not having limit," even as "partless" is the same as "not having parts," when we predicate partlessness of the One. And if it is neither derived from any other cause, nor does there exist any other final cause of it, it is reasonable to describe it as unlimited; for each thing is given by its causal principle and comes to rest, having attained its proper end. So then, whether one imagines an intelligible limit or an intellectual limit, the One is beyond the whole chain of Limit.

And if in the *Laws* (IV, 716c) God is described as the measure of all things, one should not be surprised; for there he is called the measure of all things, as being the object of striving for all things and as providing a defining limit for all things of their existence and their power and their perfection; here, on the other hand, the One is shown to be unlimited as itself, requiring no limit or other measure; for all relations of it to itself are denied of it in this passage. It is unlimited, then, as being superior to all limit; for there is not within it any limit in relation to itself; for there is no beginning in it, as we said, nor middle, nor end. For which reason we identified this unlimitedness with having no ex-

1124

treme points, even as partlessness was identified with having no parts, and that quality of having no extreme points is what we say is denied of it by the term "unlimited," which does not involve applying to the One any potentiality, or any unbounded multiplicity, or anything else of those things which are usually meant by unlimited, but only the quality of being bounded by nothing, nor having in it any beginning or end, which we call the extreme points of those that have them—only this is what we apply to the One, in conformity with those epithets which will be affirmatively demonstrated of it in the Second Hypothesis.

"And it will be without shape, then, for it would not participate either in the curved or in the straight." "How would it?" (137d)

1125   He first removed from the One the epithet "many"—this on the basis on our universal conception of oneness. Secondly, he removed from it the quality of having whole and parts—this by reason of the fact that the One is not many. Thirdly, he declared that it did not have beginning and middle and end—this by reason of the fact that it did not have parts; and in addition to this, he derived an extra conclusion that it is beyond both that limit which is connected with parts and which makes something to have an ultimate point; the term "limit" has two senses, after all, both the sense of "beginning" and the sense of "end." Now, fourthly, he removes from it straightness and curvedness, which in the Second Hypothesis too he will rank after that which has a last point and a beginning and a middle and an end. But before he demonstrates the fourth point syllogistically, he begins by stating the conclusion, with the words, "And it will be without shape, then"; for intellectual intuitions should precede scientific syllogisms, since intellect also embraces the first principles of science.[101] So the stating in advance of the conclusion imitates the immediate comprehension of the intellect; whereas the procession through the parts of the syllogism represents the unfolding of scientific knowledge, which proceeds forth from the intellect. And observe how the conclusion is more general than the syllogisms, for they take separately the straight and the curved and thus construct their proof, whereas it simply postulates that the One is without shape.

This is clear enough, then. We should go on now to discuss the concepts themselves. These, then, are forms common to all extended things; for we distinguish lines into straight and circular and mixed, and surfaces in the same way and solids, except that the straight and the curved in lines are without shape, whereas those in surfaces or solids are receptive of shape; the one lot are called straight-lined, the other

---

[101] For this principle, cf. Aristotle *An. Post.* II, 19.101b5ff., and *EN* VI, 6.1141a 7-8.

curved-lined, and the others a mixture of these two. Plato seems, then, to be thinking of such as exhibit shape, not of anything which might be straight or curved only, without shape; for the One has already been
1126 declared and shown not to have limits, so that the type of straight that is being denied of it here must be that which has limits; and such is that which has shape; for by limits here he understands those which are comprehensive of what they limit, which is only the case with things that have shape.

And one may admire in other respects also the accuracy of his terminology here. For, he did not say that it was "neither straight nor curved" (this would not prove the conclusion that it is without shape; for what would prevent it from being one of the intermediate shapes, for instance, a cylinder or a cone or some other of the mixed shapes?), but he says that it partakes neither of the straight nor of the curved. For if we were to grant to it a shape from one of the mixed forms, it would partake of both of these. What I mean is, if we were to enquire whether the nature of something is white or black, if I then show that it is neither white nor black, it has not yet necessarily been demonstrated that it is without colour. But if I show that it partakes neither of the white nor the black, it is necessarily shown that it is without colour; for if it posesses one of the median colours, it will partake of both of these, since the median colours make use of their participation in both these colours, as the median are derived from the extremes. So he declares that the One does not partake of the curved and the straight in order that it may possess both neither of these and none of the intermediate shapes, the possession of which would entail necessarily partaking of these. For the cone and the cylinder have inevitably some ultimate points and a beginning and an end, because these partake in some way of the curved and of the straight, so that the argument which does away with these and participation in these does away at the same time with participation in the shapes intermediate between them. And this is also clear, that this conclusion is more particular than the one before it; for if something partakes of shape, it has both ends and a middle; it is not, however, the case that whatever has ends and a middle already partakes of shape; for a line can have ends and a middle, and so can time, and number and motion in the same way, all of which are without shape.
1127 So this conclusion is more general than that of partaking of shape; for which reason this conclusion eliminates along with itself the quality of partaking in shape. But this is not the cause of the denial of that.

The progression from shape to circular and straight is entirely reasonable; for it would have been possible to deny shape in general of the One, demonstrating that shape has limit and bound, and the One in no way admits of limit or bound; but he wants to carry on the argument from the top down the two columns of opposites, and so he takes at the outset after the Many, whole and parts, and again extremities and middle, and then in turn straight and curved, and then again being in itself and in another, and in turn after that being at rest and in motion, and through the treatment of all of these he demonstrates that the One is none of them. For it is not possible for it either to be both of the pairs of opposites (for in that case it would not remain one, according to the hypothesis), nor can it be either one of them; for it would then have an element within it which was in some way at war with and opposed to itself; but the One must be prior to all antithesis, or it could not be the cause of all things; for it could not be the cause of those things to which it is in opposition. So then it is reasonable that he should proceed down along the two chains of beings, and thus should now proceed from dealing with shape to dealing with the curved and straight, and in so proceeding should so construct his argument as to deny along with these also every other shape of the One, employing the notion of participation, which is characteristic of all mixed shapes.

Enough has now been said about the text. But the question arises, since he has also in the *Phaedrus* (247c) described the intelligible summit of the intellectual realm, which he there called the "supercelestial place," as "colourless, shapeless, and untouchable," are we to say that he has described that order as shapeless in the same way as the One or in a different way, and if so in what way? In fact, it is not possible that the same type of negation should be employed in the case of this as in the case of the One. For of the former class he has denied some attributes, but has asserted others; for he described it as essence, and as really existent and as visible only to the "helmsman of the soul,"[102] and has declared that "about it is the nature of true knowledge," because prior to it there is a further realm; some attributes it transcends, while others it partakes of. But of the One he denies all characteristics, and asserts none; for there was nothing prior to the One, but it transcends equally all beings whatever. So the mode in which this attribute is denied is different in each case, and if you care to pay proper attention to the terminology, you will see that it is not accidental that that realm has been described as "shapeless," which the One is described as "partaking in no shape." These descriptions are not identical one with the other, even as the epithet "partless" is not identical with "having no

1128

---

[102] It is interesting that, like Hermeias (*In Phaedr.* 150.23 Couvreur), Proclus does not appear to read νῷ after θεατή, which allows of wider speculation as to the identity of the "helmsman of the soul." Iamblichus (*In Phaedr.* fr. 6 Dillon) identified it as the One of the Soul, which he could hardly have done had νῷ been in his text. Proclus does, however, assume that νοῦς is referred to here, cf. *PT* IV, 13, p. 43.1ff. S-W, and *In Alc.* 77, where he quotes the passage with νῷ, which complicates the situation.

parts"; in the same way, then, that essence he described as shapeless, while he describes the One as partaking in no shape. If, then, one is to state one's view unequivocally, that essence, inasmuch as it produces intellectual shape, may be described as shapeless, as being in all respects superior to it and as being generative of such shape. But it is inferior to another kind of shape, intelligible shape, for the intelligible Intellect comprises the intelligible causes of shape and of the whole and of multiplicity and of all things; and of shapes, some are entirely unknowable and inexpressible, the manifestation of which takes its start from the intelligible world, but they are knowable only to the intelligible Intellect, and if in other gods there is something similar (as is actually the case) its presence in all of them comes from that Intellect.

Other shapes are knowable and expressible as pertaining to the powers of the gods, not to their substances, in virtue of which they possess the characteristic of being gods, and to their intellectual essences, and it is through these (shapes) that they become manifest to the intellectual eyes of souls. Of all these, then, the intelligible Intellect comprises the unitary and single cause, and the "supercelestial place," being the highest element in the intellectual realm, is the first principle of all intellectual shapes, as we show in our commentary on the *Phaedrus*.[103] Therefore it is shapeless, but not absolutely exempt from all shape; it has proceeded according to the summit of the Father, and his inexpressible symbol;[104] but it is inferior to the shapes within him. The One, on the other hand, rises superior to the whole realm of shapes, both the "hidden" and the intellectual, and transcends all shapes, both known and unknown. What distinction there is between these, is known to those who have hearkened to the Gods, and that Plato knew those shapes also we have shown elsewhere. Wherefore it is reasonable that he should say that the One partakes of no shape. For the intelligible cause of shapes and the "shape" of intellect is inferior to the One. It is not, therefore, the same to be shapeless as to have no shape, even as it is not the same to be partless as to have no part, as has been said above.

> "Round is that whose extremity is everywhere equidistant from its centre?" "Yes." "And straight is that of which the middle is in front of both extremities." "So it is." (137e)

As to this use of the terms "straight" and "round," and as to how the above passage is true of things divine, it is plain that we should not un-

---

[103] The substance of his exegesis in this lost commentary is no doubt represented in his discussion of the same matter in *PT* IV, 4-26, esp. 10-16, on the ὑπερουράνιος τόπος.

[104] σύνθημα, a Chaldaean term, cf. *Or. Chald.* frs. 2.3 and 109.3 DP, but used frequently by Proclus, like σύμβολον, to describe the "traces" planted at lower levels by higher hypostases, by which ascent to them may be stimulated.

derstand them in any vulgar mathematical sense, but in a way suitable to the subject matter before us. Some commentators before this have declared "straight" here to refer to the unbendingness and unchangeableness of the Intellect, and "round" to refer to its turning back upon itself and its acting upon itself. This Parmenides makes mention of in the words (Fr. 8, 43-4 D-K):

> Like unto the bulk of the sphere,
> equally balanced in all directions from the middle,

where he is referring to Being. On the basis of which some commentators declare that Plato through this demonstration is reminding Parmenides of the poems that the One transcends all shapes both circular and straight.

1130   We, however, do not accept this interpretation. It drives a wedge between the philosophies of the ancients and makes Parmenides refute himself, and this on the Platonic stage, upon which there have been many declarations about Parmenides, proclaiming the reverence in which Plato held him. In fact the former is referring to one sort of One, while the latter is looking to another, when they deny or assert, respectively, the spherical shape of the One. We interpret this "straight" and "round" with reference to procession and return; procession may be seen as represented by "straight" and by the illumination which proceeds from causal principles; return is represented by "round," as reflecting back upon its own principle and as making this its end. Each of the intellectual entities, then, both proceeds to all things upon a straight path, and is turned back towards its own good, which is the midpoint in each because each equally folds in upon it from all directions, and presses together upon that, as upon a centre, all its own multiplicity and all its own powers. One might, then, want to say that each of the intellectual entities was "round" as being in all cases equidistant from its midpoint; for all of its parts are equally united to their proper good, and it is not the case that they are in one aspect more distant from it, and in another less, as is the case with our souls, where one of the horses leads towards the good, while the other bears down towards the earth (*Phaedr.* 247b), but each of them from every aspect has an equal grasp upon it, holding as it does the position of central point. And one might describe it as straight, that being that of which the middle is in front of the extremities, on the grounds that it is in virtue of procession that things are distinguished from one another—that which proceeds from that which remains static, the pluralised from the unified—and one would thus be striking the mark if one applied this epithet to that realm as well; for if you want to consider the matter, you would discover that it is procession which distinguishes entities from one another, and which makes some first, some median, and others last, and those things which are median have the faculty of distinguishing the last from the first, and are, as it were, "in front of" them; while the process of return joins everything together again, and rolls them into one, and leads them together to one single common object of striving for all beings.

1131 So then, each of these qualities exists also in that realm, in which the intellectual classes of gods participate primally, as they simultaneously proceed forth and turn back towards themselves; for these classes are chiefly characterised by their tendency to turn back upon themselves. And in a secondary degree after these, souls participate in the straight and the circular, as they proceed forward in a line, but again turn back on themselves in a circle and return to their own first principles; and ultimately also objects of sense participate in them; for there exists in these both straight line figures in a spatially distinct and individual way, and the spherical shape which comprehends all the cosmic shapes; for which reason Timaeus (*Tim.* 54a–55c) has given the whole cosmos a spherical shape, while he has arranged its five parts by the use of the five figures, which are only of equal sides and equal angles, by inscribing all these within the sphere and within each other; by which he makes clear that these figures have come down from some exalted divine order, since they have the capacity to organise all undivided things such as Intellect, and divisible things such as the visible cosmos, and median things such as Soul.

One may also see on the level of generation these two qualities. One may view in the cycle of existence here (for generation returns to itself cyclically, as is written in the *Phaedo* [70cff.])[105] the circular; while the straight one may see in the procession of each thing from its birth to its decline, and the middle here, which is in front of the extremes, as its peak of development. For how else could one come ⟨from one⟩ end of life to the other ⟨than through the middle⟩,[106] even as in the case of the straight line the road from one of the extremities to the other is through the middle? So then, these qualities penetrate down from the intellectual realm to the realm of generated things, the straight becoming the cause of procession, the circular of return.

If, then, the One neither proceeds from itself nor turns back to itself because both that which proceeds is secondary to that which produces it and that which turns back is in need of what it is striving for, it is plain

1132

---

[105] Presumably this is a reference to Socrates' argument from the cyclical reciprocity of life and death in this passage of the *Phaedo*. Cousin in his edition reads ἐν Φαιδρῷ and wishes to refer to 247d, but that passage, on Proclus' theory, does not refer to this world.

[106] Accepting the supplement here of Thomas Taylor, though not confirmed by Latin translation.

that it partakes neither of the straight shape nor of the round. How, after all, could it proceed, since it has no creative first principle for itself, either within itself or prior to it, lest it be deprived of oneness, becoming secondary or dyadic? And how could it return to itself, since it has no end or object of striving? So, as has been demonstrated previously here, neither does shape pertain to the One, since it has neither end nor beginning. There is no need, then, to enquire for what reason he demonstrated on the basis of species of shape, that is to say, the round and the straight, that the One is beyond all shape, without first defining the genus itself, as for instance laying down that shape is a limit which encloses something, or that which is contained by some bound or bounds; for he had decided to proceed by means of opposites, and to show that the One transcended each of these, and by the use of that argument which is common to all, that it is neither possible for the One to be the worse of the two opposites, in order that it may not have anything better than it, nor can it be the better of the two, in order that it may not have any element that is in discord with it. In this way, then, he shows that it is pure from both straight and round, and you see again how here too he has derived his conclusions from what has gone before, that is to say that the One has neither beginning nor middle nor end, always demonstrating the subsequent by means of arguments of geometrical validity from what precedes it, and over and above this, imitating the orderly procession of beings as they make their descent always from the primal to the secondary and the more particular.

"So then, the One would have parts and would be Many if it partook of either straight shape or round?" "Indeed it would." "Therefore, it is neither straight nor round, inasmuch as it has no parts." "Quite right." (137e)

So now here we see the completion of the whole mediating order of
1133 the so-called intelligible-intellectual realm, since all the processions within it have been shown to be ranked below the One, and, as we have often said, to be dependent upon the One, since negations, as has been demonstrated, are the mothers of assertions. It is reasonable, then, that in this conclusion he should turn back the whole order into one summation and ascend again as far as his first negations; for if the One had shape it would also be Many; so he links shape to "being many" through the mediation of "having parts," and shows that all these classes are secondary to the One. For such is the distinction in his mind of the divine orders, that he did not tolerate joining on the negations
1134 that follow unless he had first turned back this order upon itself, both joining shape to "being many," and demonstrating the connection of all the aforementioned classes. In what rank of beings the straight and

472

the round actually are, we shall learn more clearly in what follows, and we shall also learn that the intelligible-and-intellectual classes of things extend as far as this. Now, however, this much alone is clear, that we must not postulate this rank of Being either of the One, but must see it also as being derived from the One, even as was the case with the others which have been dealt with before it.

BOOK VII

◻

INTRODUCTION

◻ ◻ ◻

BOOK VII (1133-1244, Cousin, 34-76 Klibansky) proceeds from *Parmenides* 138a2 (καὶ μὴν τοιοῦτόν γε ὂν οὐδαμοῦ ἂν ἔτι εἴη) to 142a10 (οὔκουν ἔμοιγε δοκεῖ), thus taking us to the end of the First Hypothesis. Of this, only the commentary up to 141e10 (οὐ φαίνεται) is extant in the Greek, the remainder being available in William of Moerbeke's Latin translation (on this, see further General Introduction pp. xliii-xliv). Book VII thus covers the great majority of the First Hypothesis, Book VI having concerned itself largely with general introductory issues.

The first section extends from 138a2 to 138b6, and concerns the denial to the One of the attributes "being in another" and "being in oneself." It is divided into five lemmata. Proclus sees these attributes as characterising the summit of the intellectual gods, which *taxis* of entities is hereby excluded from the One. He first of all disposes of a troublesome objection, to the effect that the real Parmenides, at fr. 8.29-32, describes his One as being "in the same place," which would seem to contradict the present text, by reminding us again that Parmenides in his Poem is really talking of Being. Then he turns to a detailed discussion of the significance of οὐδαμοῦ. Both Soul and Intellect, after all, are described in Platonic theory as being "nowhere." Prop. 98 of *ET* lays down that "every cause which is separate from its effects exists at once everywhere and nowhere." Plotinus begins *Enn.* III, 9.3 by declaring, "Universal Soul did not come to be anywhere or come to any place, for there was no place," and at V, 2.2.21 Intellect is described as being οὐδαμοῦ as well as πανταχοῦ. But, says Proclus, neither Soul nor Intellect are *absolutely* nowhere, only the One is that:

> for it is neither in what is subsequent to it, in so far as it is transcendent over all things, which is not the case with either Intellect or Soul, which are the principles after the One; nor is it in itself, in so far as it is simple and non-receptive of any multiplicity. (1135.40-1136.3)

Discussion of "nowhere" leads him next (1137-1139) to address the

474

problem of whether the expression "everywhere" is superior to, and more perfect than "nowhere," or inferior to it. The *aporia* is: if being "everywhere" is inferior to being "nowhere," then (since exercise of providence involves being, in some sense, "everywhere") would it not be better for the One not to exercise providence? Proclus distinguishes two senses of "everywhere," "one which relates to what follows a given entity, as when we say that providence is everywhere present because of the fact that it is absent from no one of things secondary to it . . . ; the other sense is that which refers to everything which is both prior to a thing and subsequent to it." He remarks also that one can have a sense of "nowhere" which is coordinate with "everywhere," as in the case of Being, which is "nowhere" because it is present to all things equally. The One, however, transcends any of the senses of being "in" something (Proclus here borrows Aristotle's list of senses of "in" from *Physics* IV, 3), and so is absolutely nowhere.

The next lemma (138a3-7) is chiefly concerned with the sense to be assigned to κύκλῳ ("in a circle"), and runs from 1140 to 1144. Here, as often elsewhere, Proclus presents a sequence of three commentators, in ascending order of acceptability, culminating with his revered "father," Syrianus. It is, as usual, tempting to see the other two as Porphyry and Iamblichus, especially as the first one views the topic *merikōteron* ("in a rather restricted sense," 140.27), while the second "looks towards *ta pragmata*," and "speaks correctly," a contrast very reminiscent of that which Proclus makes in his *Timaeus Commentary* (I, 204.24ff. Diehl), where he speaks of Porphyry as discussing the introductory portion of the dialogue *merikōteron*, as opposed to Iamblichus, who treats it *epoptikōteron*; while elsewhere (*ibid.* I, 87.6), Iamblichus is praised, in distinction from his predecessors, for referring μᾶλλον εἰς τὰ πράγματα (cf. also *ibid.* III, 168.4-5).

At any rate, the first commentator takes this passage as simply denying that the One is "in a place." But, as Proclus says, "there is nothing special about a characteristic which is shared even by individual souls." The second commentator takes the view that Plato is denying of the One every sense of "being in something." This interpretation seems to be open to the objection that the One might be "in" all things in the way in which the point is in the line, since the point is not contained κύκλῳ by the line, nor is it touched πολλαχοῦ. However, this is to take things too literally, as Proclus says. The line comprehends the point, since it contains all its characteristics. He then goes on, rather laboriously, to prove that the point cannot be the same as the One.

However, even this interpretation does not exhaust the meaning of the text. Only that of Syrianus, in Proclus' view, does that. He, as mentioned above, takes the οὔτ᾽ ἐν ἄλλῳ οὔτ᾽ ἐν ἑαυτῷ to refer specifically to the One's transcendence of the highest class of intellectual gods, such as are asserted of the One-Being at 145b6ff., in the Second Hypothesis, and Proclus gives his argument in full from 1142.10 to 1143.34.

The third lemma (138a7-b2, 1145.1-1147.4) deals with the second half of the disjunction, οὔτ' ἐν ἑαυτῷ. This leads Proclus to a discussion of *authupostata*, "self-constituted entities," the definitive statement of which is to be found in *ET*, props. 40-51. Here, à propos the meaning of περιέχειν, "encompass," he says the following:

> For a start, everything is said to be "in itself" which is cause of itself and which is self-constituted, for we do not agree with those authorities who state that everything which is produced is produced by a cause other than itself, but even as we are accustomed to rank the self-motive prior to the externally moved, even so one must rank the self-constituted as prior to what is produced by another agent. (1145.34-1146.2)

The One does not count as "self-constituted"; only the hypostases subsequent to it are that. So it is not "in itself."

The lemma ends (1146.27-1147.1) with some interesting, if confusing, textual criticism. It seems to Proclus that one might make clearer the meaning of οὐκ ἄλλο ἢ αὐτό, εἴπερ καὶ ἐν ἑαυτῷ εἴη, if one transposed the καί after εἴπερ to before οὐκ (and made it mean "and," instead of "actually"). Presumably he would then understand the whole as: "On the other hand, if it were in itself it would also be encompassing of itself, *and* none other than itself (would be the encompasser), since it would be within itself." (It is clear from this, by the way, that he does not read the ὄν before οὐκ which appears in the lemma.) This indeed might make things simpler, if one could move the καί about in this way. The second suggestion, not of Proclus himself but of "some authorities," is less awkward, but still quite radical. They suggest that the phrase οὐκ ἄλλο ἢ αὐτό, εἴπερ καὶ ἐν ἑαυτῷ should be assigned to Aristoteles, assenting to Parmenides' argument. Parmenides then continues with ἕν τῳ γάρ τι εἶναι. . . . All this is provoked, it seems, by the pleonastic nature of οὐκ ἄλλο ἢ αὐτό.

The next lemma (138b1-5, 1147.5-1151.34) first raises the problem, arising from the principle that "the same thing cannot as a whole both be acted upon and act in the same way at the same time," of the status of the soul as self-moved, since this seems to imply the same thing both moving and being moved.

Proclus feels that he can avoid contradiction here by pointing out that the soul has different faculties, by virtue of which it is both generative (γεννητική) and self-reversionary (ἐπιστρεπτική). An entity like the soul is not free of multiplicity (1148.35ff.) "for it will be produced as a whole, but not in the same respect as the producer will it also be produced. For the productive element in the primary sense will be the generative element of the soul, since after all it is possible for one part to generate and another to be generated . . . ." None of this, however, is true of the One.

Proclus next (1149.26ff.) turns to an attack on those Platonists who wish to make the One "self-constitutive" (αὐθυπόστατον). In Plotinus' case, this is bound up with his doctrine, in *Enn.* VI, 8, of the One's will (βούλησις), which brings about its self-generation (cf. VI, 8.13.50ff.). For Proclus, self-constitution seems inevitably to involve a duality of creating and created aspects. Plotinus, however, is second to no man in his insistence on the complete simplicity of the One, so the dispute here is really a matter of semantics, with, if anything, Proclus not appreciating the subtlety of Plotinus' reasoning.

The argument goes back behind Proclus, however. At 1150.22, he mentions another thinker or thinkers, who follow Plato more accurately and declare that the first principle is superior both to self-constitution and to all causality and potency. From the manner of his reference (simple οἱ δέ), I feel that Syrianus is not in question here. The most likely candidate otherwise is Iamblichus. It would be he, then, who first challenged the more traditional doctrine, the history of which both within and outside Platonism is well traced by John Whittaker in an important article.[1] This would accord well with Iamblichus' postulation of a One which is completely ineffable (ἄρρητος), as reported by Damascius in the *Dubitationes* (I, 86.3ff. Ruelle).

The *authupostata*, then, are neither the highest nor the lowest rank of beings (1151.10ff.). Below them are entities which create other things, but are themselves created by others, and above them what creates other things, but is somehow superior to self-creation.

The whole passage 138a2-b7 on the Syrianic theory, as I have said, asserts the transcendence of the One specifically to the summit (ἀκρότης) of the intellectual order of gods. The next, long passage (138b8-139b3) proves that the One can neither be at rest nor in motion. This, Proclus, following Syrianus, sees as denying of the One the second intellectual order, the "lifegiving" (ζωογόνος τάξις, 1153.26), the characteristics of which are motion and rest. His commentary on this is divided into eight lemmata.

He first (1154.3-1155.11) deals with the question as to why Motion and Rest are dealt with before Sameness and Otherness (which follow, at 139b-e). The reason is that the former are more substantial qualities

---

[1] The Historical Background of Proclus' Doctrine of the Αὐθυπόστατα," in *De Iamblique à Proclus, Entretiens Fondation Hardt* XXI (1975), pp. 193-237.

of beings than the latter. The *Sophist*, he notes, also preserves the same order.

He next (1155.15ff.) turns to the division of types of motion, both physical and spiritual. In the *Laws* (X, 893bff.), he notes, we find a ten-fold division of motions, since the *Laws* is more concerned with the philosophy of nature; but the *Parmenides* is content with a two-fold division, as set out in the *Theaetetus* (181d), into alteration (ἀλλοίωσις) and locomotion (φορά); locomotion may in turn be divided into circular motion and linear motion. All of these motions may be applied not only to bodies, but to souls and to the Intellect as well.[2] Souls transfer their attention from one Form to another, which is a type of locomotion, and they are affected by their contact with the Forms, which constitutes alteration. Even Intellect is altered by its contemplation of the intelligible, and it performs a sort of cyclic intellectual motion about it as about a centre. So from all these spiritual motions, and not just physical ones, the One is free.

Someone, it seems, had made the suggestion that Plato leaves out self-motion on the grounds that the One is not exempt from this (1158.17ff.). Proclus dismisses this as absurd. This school of thought has been mentioned before, at 1150.2ff. As I commented there, it is hard to see what Neoplatonist thinker could have made such a suggestion; it is more suitable to a Stoic-influenced Middle Platonist.

He continues (1159.1ff.) with a rather laborious proof that the One cannot undergo alteration without admitting multiplicity, and thus absolutely ceasing to be itself, whereas Soul and Intellect are not destroyed by alteration. As for locomotion, it is even less probable that the One would be subject to it, but once again we have a laborious proof of this (1160.10ff.). Likewise, proofs are provided that the One is subject to neither of the subdivisions of locomotion, circular and linear motion (1162.16ff. and 1164.24ff.).

He continues to be bothered by those who would assign some form of motion to the One (1167.10ff.). "Let us," he says, "make some brief reply to their arguments. They say that it is absolutely necessary for the First to act on the things that are secondary to it, for it gives them all unity, and it is the cause among beings of all the unitary forms (ἐνιαῖα εἴδη) which are participated in by them. Why, then, should one not describe this activity of the One as motion?"

Proclus' reply is that one should not put activity (ἐνέργεια) before essence (οὐσία), nor should one attribute *energeia* at all to the First Principle. This seems to be a criticism of Aristotle's doctrine in *Met.* Λ

[2] For a good discussion of the concept of "spiritual motion" in Proclus, see S. E. Gersh, Κίνησις Ἀκίνητος: *A Study of Spiritual Motion in the Philosophy of Proclus* (Phil. Ant. XXVI), Leiden, 1973.

(7.1072b26–8), but presumably also of some more recent authority. Activity in the One would involve also attributing potentiality (δύναμις) to it, and the resulting triad of *ousia, dynamis*, and *energeia* would introduce multiplicity into the One. So no activity; therefore no motion. Presumably Proclus would not accord such attention to this position were it not still a live issue, but no one seems prepared to own up to it, among his more immediate predecessors.

At any rate, this question leads Proclus to a discussion of how the One gives rise to the existence of everything else, without its *acting* (1167.36ff.). "By its essence as One" (τῷ εἶναι ἕν) is the answer, even as do Soul and Intellect give life and existence respectively to what follows them by their essences alone. At 1169.4ff., Proclus actually brings in Aristotle to support his position, suggesting that Aristotle made his first principle a final cause only, in order not to have to grant it activity!

The final lemma of this section (1169.12–1172.26) discusses the proof that the One is not at rest, by virtue of not being ἕν τινι (which Plato can leave vague, but which we must fill out with "state" or "condition," though it can also be interpreted to mean "in a container"). In this connection he quotes (1169.33–35) the interesting remark of an unidentified predecessor, that "it is because the One is not at rest that Being is in motion, and because the One is not in motion that Being is at rest"—the idea being that the One must have the potencies of both conditions within it, while being superior to both. So all talk of the "calm" or "quiet" or "rest" of the One must be taken as poetic licence.

Following on this section of the *Parmenides*, Proclus turns to the section 139b3–e6 (1172.31–1191.9), which Syrianus identified as expressing the One's transcendence over the third, or demiurgic, order of the intellectual realm. This is characterised by Sameness and Otherness, and finds its positive equivalent at 146a8–147b8, in the Second Hypothesis. Proclus divides his commentary, as in the previous section, into eight lemmata.

We begin with an *aporia* on the place of the five *megista genē* of the *Sophist* in the hierarchy of beings. Since there is, once again, a sequence of three commentators culminating in Syrianus, it seems probable that the previous two are Porphyry and Iamblichus. It would be Porphyry, then, who seems to have raised the question as to the proper place of the *megista genē* and to have declared that they are present at every level. This is easier for Porphyry to argue, since he made the summit of the intelligible world his supreme principle (Damascius *Dub.* I, 86.8ff. Ruelle). For him, then, there is no specifically henadic realm. Iamblichus, on the other hand, who does postulate such a realm, and who postulates it with a variety of entities, wishes to limit the *megista genē* to the level of Intellect, and even, perhaps, within that, to rank them lower than the summit of the intelligible order (cf. n. 31 below). Syrianus is then brought in to resolve the controversy with one of his characteristically comprehensive solutions (1174.21ff.).

Proclus goes on (1175.30ff.) to develop the point that the order of negations corresponds to the relations of the One with itself, with itself and others, and with others, respectively.

In the next lemma (1177.27-1179.21), he sets out four propositions in turn, in order, as he says, of increasing difficulty: the One is not different from itself; the One is not different from others; the One is not the same as itself; the One is not the same as others. The next six lemmata deal with these in turn.

A series of *aporiai* are raised in the course of the discussion, but from the manner of their introduction ("Someone *might* raise the point . . ."), they do not sound like difficulties actually raised by previous commentators. Of these, the most significant is one which manifests itself at two places, 1184.9ff. and 1190.4ff., in slightly different forms: (1) "How can the One be said to be transcendent over all things if it is not *different* from them?" and (2) "Are the others than the One not different from it?" At least ἑτερότης from everything else, it would seem, should be predicable of the One.

Not so, Proclus maintains. The transcendence of the One is not to be regarded as "difference" or "otherness," since otherness implies *some* relationship to the other in question. In the case of the One, what we have is "unspeakable superiority" (ἄφραστος ὑπεροχή; 1184.19, 1190.37), which involves no relationship with what follows it. As for what follows on the One, this had indeed "declined" (ὑφιέναι) from it, but this ὕφεσις does not necessarily involve ἑτερότης (1190.19ff.).

If Proclus seems here to be indulging in some semantic maneuvering, we must concede to him that he is struggling with a difficult exegetical problem, how to express the state of non-reciprocal otherness which obtains between the One and all of its "products." The author of the *Anonymous Parmenides Commentary* (probably, though not certainly, Porphyry) expresses it well (fr. III) by comparing our concept of the One's "difference" from everything else to our talk of the sun's setting, when in fact the sun is experiencing no darkening, but the earth is falling into shadow, or the passengers on a ship having the sensation that the land is moving, when in fact it is they who are being carried along. It is interesting that *Anon. Parm.* uses the similar phrase ἀσύμβλητος ὑπεροχή (III, 7) to express the One's total transcendence (see also on this, General Introduction, p. xxix).

The next section, which is a commentary on *Parm.* 139e7-140b5, runs from 1191.13 to 1201.21. It concerns the denial that the One is like or unlike either itself or others. This passage Syrianus took to refer to the "assimilative" (ἀφομοιωτική) order of gods in the supra-cosmic realm, whose role it is to connect the lower orders of gods with the intellectual realm, and in particular with the demiurgic monad, on which they directly depend. The section is divided into four lemmata, and the course of the exposition follows fairly closely that of the section on sameness.

Once again, Proclus takes in turn the four propositions: (1) the One is not like itself; (2) the One is not unlike itself; (3) the One is not like the others; (4) the One is not unlike others. Again, he denies that Plato is following the Aristotelian categories (1192.1ff.). Likeness follows on Sameness naturally because it is presupposed by it; something is "like" which has sameness as a characteristic (πάθος) of it (1195.31). The One has no pathē of any kind; therefore it cannot be like anything else, even if some other things can be said, loosely, to be "like" it. Plotinus is chided mildly, at 1199.3ff., for calling Nous an eikōn of the One, as he does at Enn. V, 1.7.1 (cf. n. 66 below), though later (1200.22ff.) it is allowed that one may speak thus, with suitable reservations. "Even if, then," says Proclus (1199.16ff.), "you were to say that all things are like to the One, yet you will not say that they are like it in virtue of this likeness, but rather only in virtue of the unity which proceeds from the One to all beings, and the natural striving of all things towards the One."

The next section of the text, 140b6-d8, which argues that the One is neither equal nor unequal, poses Syrianus, and Proclus after him, a slight problem. At the corresponding stage of the Second Hypothesis (148d5-149d7), we have an argument asserting that the One is both in contact and not in contact with itself and with others. This characteristic Syrianus deemed proper to a median class of gods, partly supra-cosmic and partly encosmic, called the apolytoi, which may be translated "absolute." This stage Plato skips over in the First Hypothesis (or rather, I suppose, adds in the Second), for some reason not obvious. Proclus promises rather airily to explain the reason "later" (1202.9-10), presumably in commenting on the later passage. What we now come to, on the Syrianic scheme, is the class of encosmic gods, both above and below the moon, who are characterised by varying degrees of equality and inequality.

The commentary on this section extends from 1201.25 to 1212.4 and is divided into five lemmata. Apart from showing that "equal" and "unequal" follow on logically from sameness and otherness, he is chiefly here concerned with the concept of "measure" and commensurability which Plato introduces here. First, as he notes (1206.1ff.), Plato produces definitions of "equal," "unequal," and "incommensurable," in a proper geometrical manner, before going on to his proofs.

First we have the proof that the One is not equal either to itself or to others (1206.36–1208.2), this following from the fact that the One is not the same as anything else; then that the One is not unequal either to itself or to others (1208.11–1210.23), the argument being that being unequal involves a multiplicity of measures or parts, and the One has no measures or parts. Here an *aporia* is envisaged to the effect that, although the One does not have measures, it might be thought to be its own measure, and thus to have *one* measure. But that would make it equal to itself, and *qua* equal, it would not be simply One. So it cannot be or have measure.

This, however, leads to another *aporia*, arising from Plato's statement in the *Laws* (IV, 716c) that the divine is the measure of all things. But how can it be a measure, since it is beyond all limit and boundary and unity (1210.1ff.)? It can only be a measure, we must say, in the sense of being an object of striving for all things, but not as being co-ordinated with any of them, even to the extent of being "unequal" to them.

The next section covers the passage 140e1–141d6, which argues that the One is neither older nor younger nor the same age either as itself or as anything else, on which the commentary stretches from 1212.9 to 1233.19, comprising nine lemmata. This brings us clearly into the realm of Time, and so to the encosmic gods and the World Soul, which has its existence in Time.

The proof that the One transcends Time involves Proclus in some interesting doxographical discussion. After dismissing those early philosophers who thought that all things, including God, were comprehended by Time (1213.17ff.), he turns to the question of precisely what kind of Time is intended here by Plato. We find here a five-part doxography (1214.24–1219.9) ending with Syrianus, and with its third and fourth members therefore identifiable with some probability as Porphyry and Iamblichus. There is, as can be seen from notes 81 and 82 below, some confirmatory evidence for this from other quarters. The first two are less clear, but the first, at least, may be Plotinus.

The problem is that the transcendence of ordinary time would not be any great distinction for the One, since Intellect also transcends ordinary time (1215.29ff.). The One must also transcend the state in which Intellect exists, Eternity (Αἰών). This is the view of the second and third sets of commentators (the first had seen no problem). In this connection, Proclus criticises the third commentator (Porphyry?) for identifying the One's state as *Kairos*, "Occasion," or "the right moment," an ingenious, Pythagorean-influenced deduction from such passages as *Philebus* 66a, *Politicus* 284e and *Laws* IV, 709b. Proclus brushes this aside, his main objection being that this commentator does not explain how *chronos* can be understood to include *aiōn* as well.

The fourth commentator (Iamblichus?) declares "time" here to refer to "the causal principle of the intellectual order" (1216.37ff.). Proclus professes not to understand what is meant by this, but if we consider it against the background of Iamblichus' known doctrine of Time,[3] we can see that it corresponds to the πρῶτος καὶ ἀμέθεκτος χρόνος, or χωριστὸς χρόνος, which is, as it were, the monad of the time in the physical world, or at the level of Soul. This is a curious concept, certainly, but Proclus in fact understood it perfectly well, since he discusses it himself in the *Timaeus Commentary* (III, 30.30ff.). Here, however, he dismisses it in favour of the comprehensive solution of his master Syrianus, which actually sounds very little different. He also seems largely to adopt this commentator's interpretations of the "younger," "older," and "of like age" of the lemma, as indicating superiority, inferiority and equality of essence.

The next three lemmata (1219.16-1225.22) comprise demonstrations of the three negative statements about the One: (a) that it is not of the same age as itself or others; (b) that it is neither older nor younger than itself or others; and (c) that it does not participate in time. In connection with this last proof, problems are again raised. The first is why Plato has not also specified that the One transcends eternity (1224.2ff.). Proclus suggests, first, that the denial that the One is at rest is also a denial that it participates in eternity. The second returns to the question as to why the One might not be Time itself, as it is in fact termed by Orpheus, while the Pythagoreans, as we have seen, call it *Kairos* (1224.29ff.). The Orphic term is a problem for Proclus, but he explains it as simply a symbolic term for the One's generative power.

The next lemma (141a7-b3), running from 1225.30 to 1228.18, presents the problem as to whether Plato is being merely sophistical, as some commentators have considered, in his argument that what is becoming older than itself must also be becoming younger than itself. Following on the initial set of commentators, we have a sequence of two, answered by Syrianus, so Porphyry and Iamblichus are once more in prospect, but they say nothing which would serve to identify them. Syrianus' solution is that we are dealing here with souls, which are entities possessing cyclical rather than linear life, so that even as they become older, they also become younger, since their end is also their beginning—a good example of Syrianus' creative interpretation of the text to suit his elaborate metaphysical scheme.

[3] The texts relating to this are collected by S. Sambursky and S. Pines, in *The Concept of Time in Late Neoplatonism*, Jerusalem, 1971.

The next three lemmata are summative in nature and contain nothing worthy of special note.

The next section covers *Parm.* 141d7-e7, and runs from 1233.28 to 1239.21, divided into two lemmata. This passage, which dissociates the One from the three divisions of time—past, present and future—Syrianus takes as relating to the classes of being dependent upon the divine Soul, that is, according to a triadic distinction first attested in Iamblichus, *De Myst.* I, 3: daemons, heroes and pure souls. He sees this triadic division also observed in *Rep.* X, 617c, with Plato's description of the three Moirai, since they are allotted past, present, and future respectively. It would be incorrect, however, he says (1235.4ff.), to suggest that these entities act in any partial way, and not over the whole of time. Rather we must say that transcendent Time has within itself three *dynameis*, the perfective (τελεσιουργός), represented by the past, the cohesive (συνεκτική), represented by the present, and the revelatory (ἐκφαντορική), represented by the future, and these beings are allotted one or other of these. The whole scheme, he claims, represents the three triads of the intelligible realm (1237.3ff.), the first being *on, aiōn*, and *to protōs aiōnion*, constituting *ousia, dynamis*, and *energeia* respectively, and the other two depending upon each of these. Syrianus is explicitly credited with this theory of the powers of Time at *In Tim.* III, 38.12ff., which makes clear how much Proclus is indebted to him here.

The second lemma (1238.24ff.) shows that the One participates in none of these aspects of Time, and so transcends every order of souls.

Having descended this far down the scale of being, even to the divinised level (ἡ ἐκθεουμένη οὐσία, 1239.27), Plato, in Proclus' (and Syrianus') view, now turns back to the monad of the intelligible world, to deny Being of the One. This is set out in *Parm.* 141e7-142a1, the commentary on which is covered in 1239.27-1242.33 Cousin, and 34.1-42.29 Klibansky, since the Greek text gives out half way through. It is divided into two lemmata.

In the first (1241.15ff.), Proclus raises the question why Plato does not begin by denying Being of the One, and only gets round to doing so now. His answer is that the denial of Being at the outset would have appeared to checkmate the dialectic process straight away, which would be ridiculous. For this reason he starts with the proposition that the One is not many, and is prepared to use "is" loosely until he reaches the final stage of the argument. Its non-existence thus becomes obvious gradually, by the elimination of all other attributes.

Proclus also sees a metaphysical suitability in this order of negations:

Thus Plato copies the circle described by the whole of existence, which not only proceeds from One but also returns to One. He comes to procession by means of the concept of multiplicity, . . . and he gets back to One by way of "being one." . . . Where, then, should he have started his construction of the scale of beings in this account of the procession from the One, if not with many? And from what other point could he have made his reversion than through "being one"? (34.6ff. Klibansky)

This scheme, he notes, is concordant with that of the theologians—in this case, presumably, Hesiod and Orpheus—who begin their accounts with theogonies, and culminate in the matings of Zeus and the other gods!

Proclus begins the second lemma (34.30 ff.) with a distinction between two senses of "one," the first one transcending, and the second coordinate with, Being. It is the first, of course, with which we have to do here, and so the verb "is" cannot properly be used of it. This leads him to renew his attack, on the one hand, on Iamblichus' association of "the gods" with the One in the First Hypothesis, since all the henads of the other gods coexist with Being; and on the other, on the view of Origen the Platonist that the subject of the First Hypothesis is *anhypostaton*, harking back in this to the beginning of Book VI (1054.37ff. and 1065.1ff., respectively).

He then embarks on a laborious proof that One and Being cannot be coordinate, but that the One must be prior to, and the cause of, Being (36.32-38.27). This being proved, however, we are left with a problem as to what "one" it is in which Being participates. This requires the postulation of the One Being, or "the One that exists," which is the subject of the Second Hypothesis.

In this connection, Proclus produces an apparent quotation from Speusippus (40.1-5), which gives rise to considerable difficulties. Suspicions might be raised, for a start, by the fact that he mentions Speusippus by name at all, considering how completely he suppresses explicit reference to authorities in the rest of the commentary. However, he does mention Xenocrates once, at 888.36, in giving his definition of a Form, and he is quite prepared to quote Zeno and Parmenides by name, as well as other "ancient" authorities such as Orpheus and the Chaldaean Oracles, so that this is not quite without parallel. It is certainly probable that Proclus has no direct acquaintance with Speusippus, but is borrowing the reference from an intermediary—Iamblichus, Porphyry, or even Nicomachus of Gerasa—but there is no reason, I think, to doubt the substantial accuracy of the quotation.

A more serious difficulty arises over the subject matter. If this is a verbatim quotation, then to what is Speusippus referring? Plainly Proclus takes the Indefinite Dyad here to be in some way identified with the One of the Second Hypothesis. They seem to have the same role in producing the universe, and One Being can be seen, presumably, as a dyad composed of "one" and "being." But we need not assume that Speusippus is commenting on or referring to Plato's *Parmenides* (though such a reference, I suppose, cannot be excluded). Klibansky, in his notes (p. 86), suggests that the fragment comes from Speusippus' treatise *On Pythagorean Numbers* (of which we have a long extract on the Decad preserved in Iamblichus'(?) *Theologumena Arithmeticae* (82.10–85.23 De Falco = fr. 28 Tarán), and this is a reasonable conjecture. It is Proclus, therefore—or perhaps a predecessor—who is making the connection with the subject of the Second Hypothesis. Speusippus is brought in here because he isolates a first principle, the One or Monad, which is above Being, and not itself, by itself, counting as a principle. It is this last statement (in Moerbeke's Latin *et ab ea que secundum principium habitudine ipsum liberaverunt* (sc. Pythagorei), rendered by Klibansky καὶ ἀπὸ τῆς κατ᾿ἀρχὴν ἕξεως αὐτὸ ἠλευθέρωσαν, that has caused the most trouble. I do not agree with Tarán[4] that this is in contradiction with Aristotle's testimony in *Met.* 1092a14–15 (fr.43 Tarán). All Speusippus need be saying is that the One by itself would never have created anything, and that even after the generation of the Indefinite Dyad, it is the Dyad, rather than the One, which performs the role of creative principle. But further discussion of this interesting question would be out of place here. Suffice it to note that Proclus thinks he can adduce Speusippus as testimony to the distinction between the One itself and the One Being.

The One is, then, shown to be above knowledge of any sort, even the sort of knowledge possessed by Soul or Intellect. In this connection, an *aporia* is raised (42.12ff.) as to what Plato means here by "belief," in the phrase "if one is to believe this argument" (εἰ δεῖ τῷ τοιῷδε λόγῳ πιστεύειν). Proclus suggests that *pistis* here may be taken in the Chaldaean sense of "faith," rather than in the "normal" Platonic sense of a level of knowledge lower than *epistēmē*, dependent upon sense-perception. He does not absolutely commit himself to this solution, however. It may be that Plato is just saying that reason cannot entirely grasp the nature of the One. No matter how near a lower principle gets to apprehending it, there is always something more.

The next lemma (142a1–2) establishes the point that nothing can be in any relation to the One, since the One has no existence, and relations can only obtain between things existent. Proclus' attention is attracted (44.13ff.) by the inclusion of the rather pleonastic phrase "this non-existent" (τούτῳ τῷ μὴ ὄντι). This provokes him once again to a distinc-

---

[4] *Speusippus of Athens (Phil. Ant. XXXIX)*, Leiden, 1981, pp. 352–356.

tion between the various degrees of non-existence, but also to an ec-static, Plotinus-like, description of the soul's striving towards the One, which may yet contain, interestingly, a criticism of Plotinus, as Klibansky suggests:

> For the mind is tormented by the unlimitedness and indefiniteness of the totally non-existent; it experiences difficulty in grasping it and is happy to be ignorant of it, fearing to step out into the limitless and measureless. But it mounts towards the incomprehensible supereminence of the One itself, borne in its direction by a longing for its nature, revolving round it, wanting to embrace it, seeking with supreme passion to be present to it, unifying itself as far as possible and purging all its own multiplicity, so that somehow it may become perfectly one. (44.32ff.)

Plotinus, in *Enn.* VI, 9.3.4ff., describes the approach of the soul to the One as follows:

> The soul reaching towards the formless finds itself incompetent to grasp where nothing bounds it or to take the impression where the impinging reality is diffuse; in sheer dread of holding to nothingness, it slips away. The state is painful; often it seeks relief by retreating from all this vagueness to the region of sense, there to rest on solid ground, just as the sight distressed by the minute rests with pleasure on the bold. (MacKenna's translation)

If Proclus is in fact "correcting" Plotinus in making this distinction between the soul's horror of the non-existence of Matter and its longing for the One, then he would seem to have the worst of the argument, and even to call into question how far he himself is a true mystic. Plotinus, who was, knew whereof he spoke, and his experience is confirmed copiously from the testimony of other mystics, Eastern and Western.[5] The approach to unqualified Being, or Non-Being, or whatever the goal of meditation is taken to be, is initially attended by feelings of terror, until the mystic becomes familiar with the sensation. Proclus plainly revolts against this notion, feeling that the approach to the One should be a purely joyful experience. But the dance of the moth round the flame is not a purely joyful experience.

The next lemma (142a2-3) specifies the forms of description and knowledge that are inapplicable to the One. Proclus notes that two modes of description are denied of it, *onoma* and *logos*, and three modes of knowledge—*epistēmē*, *aisthēsis*, and *doxa*. This leads to a long dis-

[5] See e.g. Evelyn Underhill, *Mysticism*, Part II, ch. 9: "The Dark Night of the Soul," London, 1910.

quisition on, first, the various levels of knowledge, and then, the doctrine of names, drawing largely on the *Cratylus*.

He begins (48.11) with a reference to the famous passage of the *Seventh Letter* (341cd), which refers to the "light suddenly kindled in the soul." This plainly refers to the sudden illumination about a problem in philosophy which may result from the process of dialectic, but Proclus takes it as referring to our apprehension of the One, regarding Plato's expression φῶς ἐν τῇ ψυχῇ as a description of the "One of the soul."

In connection with the discussion of *aisthēsis* (48.20ff.), he makes reference to the interesting concept of divine "sense-perception," that is, the analogue of sense-perception present in the Demiurge and in the gods of the noetic realm, by which they apprehend things in the cosmos. This notion of a sort of archetype of sense-perception in the noetic world may arise from speculation on how the gods cognise the world (a problem put by Parmenides in *Parm.* 134d), was certainly stimulated by speculation as to what the second horse of the divine ξυνωρίδες of the *Phaedrus* myth might correspond to, and was given a proof text in *Or. Chald.* fr. 8 (quoted here):

$$νῷ \ μὲν \ κατέχειν \ τὰ \ νοητά,$$
$$αἴσθησιν \ δ᾽ \ ἐπάγειν \ κόσμοις.^6$$

The phrase δημιουργικὴ αἴσθησις (the presumed original of Moerbeke's *conditivus sensus*) seems to occur nowhere else in Proclus.

He then (50.1-22) takes in turn *doxa* and *epistēmē*, and runs through the whole *seira* of each, from our own level of opinion and knowledge right up to that of the Demiurge, in the case of opinion, and of Being itself, in the case of knowledge, and declares the One to be inapprehensible to all forms of either of these.

There next follows, at 50.23-25, a confused passage which seems to contain a lacuna of some length, because when we come out of it we are already embarked on a discussion of names. Names, also, and therefore language, must be seen as present at the divine level as well as the human; we have evidence that this was Plato's doctrine at *Cratylus* 400d, *Phaedrus* 255c, and *Timaeus* 36c. But not even divine language can describe the One, since, as he says (52.9-10), "every name which can be properly said to be such by nature corresponds to what is named, and is the logical image of the object." This leads him to refer to a bizarre doctrine of Theodorus of Asine (also quoted at *In Tim.* II, 274.10ff.) that the letters of the name ἕν, including the rough breathing, refer not to the essence of the First Principle itself, but to all that proceeds from it (52.10-21).

---

[6] On this see my article, "The Concept of Two Intellects: A Footnote to the History of Platonism," *Phronesis* XVIII (1973): 176-185.

Why, then, do we call it "One" at all, or what are we naming when we use this term? Proclus suggests (54.4ff.) that what we are naming is actually "the understanding of unity which is in ourselves":

What else is the One except the operation and energy of this striving (after the One)? It is therefore this interior understanding of unity, which is a projection and, as it were, an expression of the One in ourselves, that we call "the One." So the One itself is not nameable, but the One in ourselves (54.11-14).

We call this element in ourselves "the One" because it is unity that protects and preserves us, and it is thus our most valuable element, as it is for all created things (56.1ff.). Even a multiplicity must have a share in some sort of unity, if it is not to dissolve into infinity. So we name our conception of the First Principle "the One," because unity is that for which all things strive.

The One is the same as the Good (56.34ff.), since we cannot conceive of one being prior to, or distinct from, the other, and neither of them are properly knowable. If Socrates in the *Republic* (VII, 540a) speaks of the Good as knowable, he qualifies this by talking about "inclining the light (αὐγή) of the soul towards it"—and Proclus takes ἡ τῆς ψυχῆς αὐγή as referring, once again, to the "One of the soul."

He ends the lemma (58.25ff.) with a most interesting appeal to the evidence of the Chaldaean Oracles as to the One of the soul. There is some problem about the exact form of the quotation—Klibansky's punctuation is plainly wrong in one place (see n. 120 below)—but they constitute a useful addition to our store of fragments, even if they do not mean exactly what Proclus wants them to mean. The information about Adad, since it is found also in Macrobius, *Sat.* I, 23.17, probably derives from Porphyry.

The penultimate lemma (142a4-6) simply reinforces the previous one, with a list of verbs corresponding to the nouns. Proclus takes the opportunity to present here the passage on logic and language from the *Seventh Letter* (342a-344a), to make the point that if names and definitions are incapable of conveying the essence of objects of intellection, how much less will any name or definition convey the essence of the One (62.9-14)? The only justification he can find for the apparent repetitiveness of this sentence is that it emphasises that the One is unknowable *by its own nature*, and not just by reason of the feebleness of all other things.

He does however, wish to specify that οὐδὲ γιγνώσκεται here only refers to *epistēmē*, rational knowledge, which does not exclude suprarational *cognitio indivinata* (ἐνθεαστικὴ γνῶσις?), such as the One of our soul would employ for cognising the One (62.21-28).

The final lemma (142a6-8) seems at first sight to permit only a negative conclusion to the whole First Hypothesis: "Is it possible that all this should hold good of the One?" "I should say not!" This, it seems, was used by Origen the Platonist as a firm indication that there is no subject of the hypothesis, and that, in turn, provokes Proclus to attack him once again. To Proclus it is obvious that the One above Being must be discussed somewhere, and it is certainly not discussed in the hypothesis following, so it must be discussed in the First. Of course, Origen does not believe in such an entity, so Proclus' argument is irrelevant to him.

Proclus proceeds (64.25ff.) to a doxography of those who accept that the subject of the First Hypothesis is the One, but are bothered by the final conclusion. As so often, we have a sequence of three authorities, culminating in Syrianus, encouraging again the conjecture that the previous two are Porphyry and Iamblichus. Certainly the contrast at 68.15-16 between those who follow λογογραφικὴ ἀκολουθία and those who follow ἡ τῶν πραγμάτων θεωρία is characteristic of the contrasts which Proclus makes in the *Timaeus Commentary* between these two (see n. 127 below). Be that as it may, the first authority wants to take this passage, not as the conclusion of the First Hypothesis, but as the beginning of the Second! This is not in fact an entirely unreasonable suggestion, as the passage reads just as smoothly if taken in that way, but Proclus, though polite to it, does not feel that it is on the right lines.

Better, he feels, is the view (66.25ff.) which sees this as the generalising conclusion of the whole argument: "So the general negation represents at the same time the whole progression of all from the One and the manifestation of individual beings taken together and separately in the order that appears fitting" (68.11-13).

This is on the right lines, but needs further development, and this it receives at the hands of Syrianus (68.16ff.). Syrianus prefaces his solution with a reminder to us of the different senses which negation takes on at lower levels of reality, in order to make clear how none of these applies to the One:

But negative propositions about the One do not really express anything about the One. For nothing at all applies to it, either specifically or privatively, but, as we have said, the name "One" names our conception of it, not the One itself, and so we say that the negation also is about our conception, and none of the negative conclusions that have been stated is about the One, but because of its simplicity it is exalted above all contrast and all negation. (70.5-10)

Proclus has said this before, in the course of the general introduction to the First Hypothesis in Book VI (1076.35ff.) à propos the suitability of negations to the First Cause. This passage shows, if demonstration were needed, that the doctrine is that of Syrianus. Proclus goes on (70.19ff.) to endorse it further, from a slightly different point of view, by pointing out the One cannot even properly stand as subject to any proposition, even a negative one, as it has been doing throughout the First Hypothesis, so it is only proper to undercut all these propositions at the end of the argument.

A third way of approaching the problem, to which he turns at 72.23ff. (after a sideswipe at Aristotle for not rising above Intellect in his search for the First Cause), is to take the statement that these things are not possible (δυνατόν) for the One as expressing the truth that the One should not even be credited with the power (δύναμις) of generating all things, which is one significance of negation, and thus that it transcends even this.

His final approach to the problem (74.3ff.) is to draw attention to the suitability of Parmenides' procedure here to the mystical ascent of the soul to the One. The soul must leave behind all reason and deliberation, and set aside even the dialectical method which has brought it to the threshold of the One, in order to make the final leap to union with it. That leap should be characterised by *silence*, and so "it is with silence," as Proclus says in the final sentence of the surviving part of the Commentary, "that he brings to completion the study of the One."

COMMENTARY

□ □ □

"Further, being such as we have described, it cannot any longer[1] be any-where; for it cannot be either in another or in itself." "How so?" (138a)

The discussion passes to another order of beings, the summit of those gods termed intellectual in the strict sense, and it denies this of the One, showing that the One is nowhere, neither as being contained in any other cause, nor as being comprehended by itself and belonging to itself. But before he enters upon the necessary chain of syllogistic proof, he has once again announced in advance the conclusion, employing, before efforts at scientific demonstration, intellectual intuitions, and this is how he will proceed also in all the subsequent steps. That he is beginning on another order, he has made sufficiently clear to us both by the phrase "any longer" and "being such as we have described"; for how would that which has been demonstrated to be beyond all the median orders of gods and of the intelligible-intellectual order be any longer the participant in any of the intellectual entities or

1134 even in the summit of the intellectual beings? After all, that which is transcendent over the more divine causes will far more outstrip those which follow on subsequent to these.

So much may be said, then, about the organisation of the argument in general, according as it follows the order of reality. But once again, when some critics say at this point that Plato is contradicting the Parmenidean One of the poems, we do not accept their argument. For Parmenides says about his own One that:

> It remains the same in the same place, and rests by itself;
> And so it stays ever stable; for strong Necessity
> Holds it in the bonds of limit, which constrains it round about.
> Because it is not right that Being should be without end.[2]
>
> (fr. 8.29-32)

---

[1] Proclus reads ἔτι before εἴη, against MSS of Plato, and indeed uses it just below (line 27) as "evidence" that Plato is moving here to the description of a new *taxis* of beings.

[2] Proclus' MSS read τούνεκεν οὐκ ἀτέλευτον τοῖον, εἰ θέμις εἰπεῖν, which is incoherent. I follow D-K (and Simplicius): οὕνεκεν οὐκ ἀτελεύτητον τὸ ἐὸν θέμις εἶναι.

492

But, as this text demonstrates, he is giving here a philosophical description of Being and not of the One; and these characteristics will be asserted of that entity in the Second Hypothesis, where Being is linked together with the One. So if in the present passage he demonstrates that it is the One, and not Being, that does not have limit and is not situated anywhere, neither in itself nor in anything else, this is not a refutation of the philosophy of Parmenides, but leaves that as it stands and adds to it a higher doctrine.

1135

This is the distinction we would make about that. But that we use the term "nowhere" in its strictest and simplest sense in reference to the primary cause, we must now explain. The Soul, for one thing, is often said to be nowhere, and especially the non-related soul; for it is not possessed by any of those things secondary to it, nor is its activity constrained by any relation, as if it were bound through some relation to what is subsequent to it. Intellect is also said to be nowhere; for it is everywhere alike, and is present equally to all things far more (than Soul), and by reason of this sort of presence it is not contained by any of the things which participate in it. God also is said to be nowhere, because he transcends all things, because he is unparticipated, because he is superior to all conjunction and all relation and all linking to anything else. Now, as I said, each of these things is correctly said about the three ruling hypostases, but the term "nowhere" is not used in the same way in all cases. The soul is nowhere among those things subsequent to it, but it is not nowhere in the absolute sense; for it is at any event in itself, as being self-moved, and it is in its own cause, since everywhere the cause contains in a prior way the potentiality of its product and comprehends it unitarily. Intellect too is nowhere among those things subsequent to it; but it too is not simply nowhere, as it is also in itself as being self-hypostatising, and further it is contained by its own cause—if you want to speak in theological terms, by the paternal cause (for every intellect is an intellect of the Father,[3] one of the universal Father, another of the father of its own triad: at any rate Intellect is contained by the Father); and even if you prefer not to describe it in this fashion, at least it is so because every intellect strives towards the One and is held within the One; for this reason too, it is incorrect to state that the Intellect is nowhere. Only the One is nowhere in the absolute sense; for it is neither in what is subsequent to it, in so far as it is transcendent over all things, since this is not the case with either Intellect or Soul, which are the principles after the One; nor is it in itself, in so far as it is simple and non-receptive of any multiplicity; nor is it in what is prior to it because nothing is superior to the One; this, then, is what is absolutely nowhere, whereas all other things are nowhere in a

1136

---

[3] For the expression νοῦς πατρός, cf. Or. Chald. fr. 22.1 DP.

secondary sense, and in one way they are nowhere and in another they are not nowhere. If you will consider the whole order of beings, you will see, first, that the forms in matter are solely in other things and of other things, and established in certain substrata; and then that natures, while also being in other things (for they descend into bodies and are in a way in a subject), yet already bear some echo and image of being in themselves, in so far as they are lives already and essences; and when one part of any of them has some experience they share the experience themselves; and then souls in relation, in so far as they have a relation, are themselves also in another (for this relation towards what is secondary involves inevitably being in another); yet in so far as they are able to turn towards themselves, they are more purely in themselves (for natures exercise all their activity about bodies, and whatever they do, they do to something else; but souls exercise some of their activities in relation to the body, while others they exercise in relation to themselves and direct themselves towards themselves); non-related souls are already in themselves, and are no longer in others in the sense of what is secondary to them, though in another in the sense of what is prior to them; for "being in another" has two senses, that of having relation to what is secondary to one, which is inferior to being in oneself, the other which is superior to being in oneself, and of these the former extends as far as souls in relation, whereas the latter begins only with divine and generally with non-related souls; and the former sense applies to the former category; for all things are in their own causal principles, or otherwise they would not exist, if they had gone forth completely from their causes; and the second sense belongs to the latter category, for the former meaning would have implied a deficiency of power. Or is it not otherwise necessary that if it is in the lowest of any order it should also be in the first? So then, we may say that divine souls are only in what 1137 is prior to them, that is to say in the intellects upon which they depend. Intellect, further, is both in itself and in that which is prior to it, by which I mean the Father and, if you wish, the power of the Father; for all things up to this point have the characteristic of being in another, but as for the Father himself, how would he have it? Whether Intellect is only in itself or also in another is a question that will have to be looked into later, when we come to speak of self-hypostatisation.[4]

The expression "nowhere," then (for this is what we are meant to be considering), can in no way apply to those things which have the characteristic of being in another (that is, in the sense which is inferior to being in oneself); for how will the characteristic of being nowhere fit

[4] Presumably in the (lost) discussion of the Second Hypothesis. Cf. *ET*, props. 40-51, and Damascius, *Dub.* 78, I, 173.20ff. Ruelle.

the situation of these things which are in something else when it conflicts with the idea of being in anything at all? As for those entities
which are in another in the sense which is superior to being in oneself,
being nowhere is present to them, but not absolutely; for each of them
are in their own causal principles. Only to the One is the epithet "nowhere" applicable primally and absolutely; for it is neither in what follows it, for that would not be right; nor is it in what is prior to it, for
there is no such thing; nor is it in itself, for that is not its nature—the
first, because it is without relation, the second, because it is primal, and
the third, because it is simply One; so that it is nowhere.

This, then, is absolutely correct. After this, however, we must inquire into the expression "everywhere," as to whether it is superior and
more perfect than "nowhere," or inferior to it. If it is superior, on the
one hand, why do we not assign what is superior to the first principle,
whereas we have given it the characteristic of being nowhere, but in
fact, we say simply that it is nowhere; if on the other hand it is inferior,
how would it not be better for the first principle not to exercise providence than to exercise it? For that which exercises providence is present
to all those things which merit providence; whereas that which does
not exercise providence is not compelled to be anywhere among what
is secondary to it.

We may say in reply that the expression "everywhere" has two
senses, one which relates to what follows a given entity, as when we
say that providence is everywhere present because of the fact that it is
absent from no one of secondary things, but preserves and holds together and orders all things, penetrating through them by virtue of its
sharing of its power; the other sense is that which refers to everything,
both that which is prior to a thing, and that which is subsequent to it.
1138 For that thing is "everywhere" in the proper sense which is both in
what is secondary to itself and in what is prior to it because it is also in
the proper sense all these things; and it is of this sense of "everywhere"
that the "nowhere" in his passage is a negation, having the sense of
what is neither in itself nor in what is prior to it, and this sense of "nowhere" is superior to "everywhere" and is a particular epithet of the
One alone.

There is another sense of "nowhere" which is coordinate with
"everywhere," which we are accustomed to apply only to secondary
entities, and either of them is true by virtue of the other. Being, for instance, is "nowhere" because it is "everywhere"; for that which is possessed by some particular place is in something, whereas that which is
present equally to all things is nowhere exclusively; and again because
it is nowhere, for this reason it is everywhere; for because of the fact
that it is equally transcendent over all things, it is equally present to all

things, as being equally distant from all things. These meanings are co-ordinate with each other, but that other meaning of "nowhere" is superior to all meanings of "everywhere" and can only be applied to the One, as being the negation of every sense of being *in* something.[5] For whether you understand "in something" as being "in a place," or as being "in a whole," or as being a whole in parts, as being "in an end or purpose," or in the sense that the affairs of those administered are "in the hands of" the administration, or in the sense of a genus in species, or of species in genera, or in the sense of "in time," all these senses equally are transcended by the One. For neither is there any place which contains the One, in order that the One may not appear as a multiplicity, nor is there a whole which comprises the One; for it is not a part of anything, lest, being a part, it should also be in a whole, which would involve the One in being a quality of something; for every whole has oneness as a quality, and it is deficient in comparison to the truly One, since it itself is not truly one; nor is it itself in parts; for it does not have any part, being partless; nor is anything else an end which has power over it, for it has been shown to have no end or purpose beyond it whatever; nor is it in anything as a species is in a genus; for of what would it be a species, since there is nothing greater than it?

1139 Nor is it in time, for that which is in time is a multiplicity; it will be shown, then, not to partake of time either. So then the One is superior to all the meanings of "to be in something." If, then, every sense of being in something is false of it, the corresponding negation, "being nowhere," is true; for being in something is the contrary of being nowhere, even as someone is contrary to no one, so that the One would therefore be nowhere.

So much for that, then. Once again, to sum up, he divides the idea of being in something into two, into being in oneself and being in another, summing up all those well-known varieties of meaning in these two, in order that, if he can show that the One can neither be in itself nor in another, he would have shown that it was nowhere. For if it is in something, he says, either it is in itself or in another; but it is neither in itself nor in another; therefore it is not in anything. And if it is not in anything absolutely, it would be nowhere.

Once he has demonstrated this, it will become clear that the One is transcendent over that order to which this designation belongs, I mean, "being in itself and in another." When this has become clear, we are then able to conclude that Intellect cannot be the primal entity; for there is proper to it its being in itself, its knowing itself, and its turning to-

---

[5] The following distinction of meanings of ἐν is borrowed from Aristotle, *Physics* IV, 3.210a14ff.

wards itself, even if this appears particularly at the summit of the intellectual realm, along with the turning towards the first principles, and the entry into itself and, as it were, the "crookedness" of being in itself, which always wishes to possess and embrace itself.[6]

> *"If it were in another, it would be encircled all round by that in which it was contained, and would have many contacts with it at many points; but it is impossible for there to be contact at many points all round in a circle with a thing which is One and has not parts and is not round." "It is indeed impossible."* (138a)

1140

The summary of the proof of the conclusion here presented is more or less as follows: the One is neither in itself nor in another; but everything that is in something is either in itself or in another; therefore the One is in no way in anything, and that which is in no way in anything is nowhere. Further, he demonstrates the first of the premises as follows: the One cannot touch anything at many points; that which is in something else touches that which it is in at many points; therefore the One is not in anything else. Again, the One has neither beginning nor end, nor is it in general something that contains and is contained; but if the One were in itself, it would have an element which contains and an element which is contained. Therefore, the One is not in itself; but it has been shown that it is not in anything else either; therefore the One is neither in itself nor in anything else. Such, then, are the syllogisms which demonstrate the present text, proving to us what is required with geometrical force on the basis of what has previously been agreed.

Let us turn next to the consideration of the doctrine behind this, and let us consider in what sense Parmenides says that everything which is in something else is contained "in a circle" by that in which it is, and touches it in many ways at many points. Of the commentators previous to us, some have taken the phrase "in something else" in a rather restricted sense, understanding it as meaning only "in a place" and "in a container," and reconciling the text to this interpretation plausibly enough; for what is in a place touches that place and what is in a container touches the container and it is contained on all sides by it; for the expression "in a circle" is equivalent to "on all sides," indicating the force of the containing entity which holds the contained element within it. This, then, is what they say is being demonstrated to us, that the One is not in a place, if being in a place must involve being many and touching its container at many points, whereas it is impossible for the One to be Many.

1141

---

[6] There is a reference here to Κρόνος ἀγκυλομήτης, or rather ἀγκυλόμητις, Kronos symbolising the summit of the intellectual realm, cf. *In Crat.* 66.25-27 Pasq., and *PT* V, p. 290 Portus.

I would say to this, "What is there remarkable in the One not being in a place?" For there is nothing special about a characteristic which is shared even by individual souls. But what is being proved should be a special quality of the One and of the causal principle which is set above all beings.

Other commentators,[7] looking to the facts, have stated that he is denying here of the One every sense of being in something, and they are right; for in no sense is the One in something, as we have said earlier. But how are we to reconcile the text with the various senses of being in something, many as they are? For the point is said to be in the line, obviously as being in something else; for the point is one thing, and the line is another, and yet just because it is in something else it is not for this reason contained on all sides by the line, nor does it touch the line at many of its parts. One may reply to this difficulty by saying that even if the line does not contain the point spatially, yet it contains it in some other way; for it contains its characteristics; for the point is merely a limit, whereas the line is both a limit and something else besides that, being a length without breadth. Again, the point has no extension, whereas the line is both without extension and in another direction is extended. And in general, since the point is not the same thing as the One, it is necessary that the point should be multiple, not as having spatially distinct parts, for in this respect it is partless, but as having a number of characteristics which go to make it up, and in this way having the equivalent of parts, and since the line comprehends these, it may be said to touch the point in many places. That the point and the One are not the same is plain; for the latter is the first principle of all things, whereas the former is first principle only of magnitudes; but the point is not on the one hand prior to the One; for the monad is one, and so is also the partless unit of time. The remaining possibility, then, is that the point is subsequent to the One, and partakes of the One, so that it is also not One, but if this is the case, then there is nothing preventing it from having a number of incorporeal characteristics which are present in the line, and for it to be contained by this. One can, then, answer the difficulty in this way, but that does not get us nearer to a view of how Plato took the sense of being *in* something, and what class of beings he is looking to when he denies this characteristic of the One.

Better then, following the lead of my own father (sc. Syrianus), to

1142

---

[7] Since these commentators come second in a series of three, culminating in Syrianus (1142.10ff. below), and since they meet with Proclus' qualified approval for their attention to τὰ πράγματα, one is tempted to identify them with Iamblichus. We may note a similar concern with the various senses of ἐν in Iamblichus' *Commentary on the Categories* (*ap.* Simpl. *In Cat.* 46.14-21).

proceed along that most sensible and safest course, and say that he is denying of the One here just what is asserted of the One Being in the Second Hypothesis and he is denying it in the same way as it is asserted there, and indeed one should view the meaning of being "in another" as being the same as that which the philosopher clearly understands it to be in that place. Since it is clear, then, that there he is manifesting a certain class of gods, and says that this class is "in itself and in another," in virtue of the fact that it is both turned towards itself intellectually and remains eternally in monadic form in its causes; for that class is the monad of the intellectual gods, resting in virtue of its own superiority in the intelligible gods prior to it, but revealing also its intellectual characteristic by activating itself in itself and about itself—the sense of "in another," then, is that of remaining at rest in its cause and being comprehended by its own cause. This, therefore, is also the reasonable sense in which to take "in many ways," and touching its own cause "at many points"; for because it is surrounded by it, it is more particular than it; and everything that is more particular is more pluralised than its own cause which comprehends it, and being more pluralised it is joined to it by its own various powers and in different ways by different of them, and this is what is meant by "in many ways"; for in virtue of its various powers it is variously united to the intelligible which is prior to it.

But this order of beings, to which "being in itself" along with "being in another" properly applies, is also a multiplicity (for it par-
1143 takes of the intelligible multiplicity), and it has parts (for it partakes of the median classes among the causes prior to it), and it is in a way circular (for it partakes of the ultimate class of the middle gods—I mean the shape that is proper to that order). Wherefore it is not one absolutely, but many, nor is it partless, but has parts, nor is it beyond all shape, but circular. And, as being many, it is able to touch what is prior to it at many points; inasmuch as it has parts, it is able to communicate with its priors in many different ways; and as endowed with shape, it is surrounded in a circle by them; for everything which is shaped is surrounded by that which gives it shape, whereas the one neither has parts nor participates in circularity. So that it is not possible for there to be a cause prior to it which touches the One in many places and in a circle, but it is beyond all things, as having no causal principle superior to itself; for it is impossible for there to be anything which touches it in a circle and in many places, since it is One and partless and not partaking in circularity; all these things he has added in order that there should appear the characteristics of multiplicity, having parts and partaking in circularity, all of which are proper to this class of beings, in which we also locate the characteristics of being in oneself and in another; for this

class is many in comparison with the intelligible unity, and has parts and partakes in circularity, since all secondary things must partake in what is prior to them. Since even when it is called a monad, it is a monad in a mode proper to the intellectual realm; otherwise, it is a multiplicity in comparison with the noetic monads; and when it is said to be a whole and partless, that is in relation to the intellectual realm, and this is said from our perspective; and even if it does not have parts, yet it has parts in comparison with intelligible wholeness; and when we say it is without shape, once again this is in the intellectual realm, since in any case it is necessary for it to partake in the shape that is prior to it.

So then, one must remove also this class from the One, and one must say that the One is the cause of it also; all classes whatever owe their existence to the One, and that which is above all beings as their cause is the One, and of it there is no cause whatever. For if the One had a cause, this cause prior to it would necessarily have to be the cause of greater and nobler things to what follows it; for those which are higher among the causes are providers of more lofty goods to those things secondary to them. What, then, that is more divine than the One and unity would things receive from that cause, which we see fit to rank above and beyond the One? If, on the one hand, it is going to give nothing to what follows upon it, it will be unproductive and have no basis of community with all things, and we will not even know that it exists, seeing that we have no basis of community with it; for in fact all of us by nature seek after the One and strain upwards towards it, but we would not have any element which would connect us with that other cause if we derive nothing from it. If on the other hand, it also is going to give something to beings, is it going to give something inferior to the One? But it is not right for something which is superior to be only the cause of inferior things. Well then, will it be the cause of superior effects? And what will be superior to the One it is not even possible to conceive; for everything else is called "better and worse" in virtue of its greater and less participation in this cause; and indeed the very concept of being better is so through participation in the One. And in general this One would not be an object of striving at all for all things, if we had something superior to it; nor would we despise all other things as we do and pursue the One, both overlooking Justice and not attaching ourselves to Beauty because of our desire to preserve what seems to us to be One. If, then, we despise all other things in favour of the One, and never overlook the One for the sake of anything else, the One might reasonably be regarded as the most honourable of things; inasmuch as it holds together and preserves everything in our conception of it. That, then, which provides unity to things would reasonably be the first of all things; this entity, then, is the first of all things; there is

500

not, therefore, any cause at all which is superior to the One; therefore the One is not in anything else. It is nothing trivial, then, that is being proved here, nor such as could at all apply to souls or to anything secondary.

What is made clear here, then, is that the One does not derive from any other cause. That it is also superior to self-constituted entities, he makes clear in the arguments that follow next.

1145 *"On the other hand, if it were in itself, it would have to encompass it, none other than itself, since it would actually be within itself; and nothing can be within something without being encompassed by that thing." "Indeed it cannot."* (138ab)

The second part of the latter of the premises is examined in these words; for the proposition that everything which is in something is either in itself or in another being entirely true, he does not deem worthy of mention; for if something is in something, it is plain that this something in which it is is either itself or not itself and identical with something else; so that either it is itself or something else that that which is in something is in. But, to the point where the One is neither in another nor in itself, he devotes some further comment and some special attention; he has already proved, before this, that the One is not in anything else, and now he is going to argue that it is not in itself, and he will be constructing his argument by taking the start of his proof from what is more honourable. For this sort of being in another is more honourable than being in oneself, since being in one's cause is superior to being in oneself.

And this is the nature of the organisation of the argument in general. That the One is not in itself, he demonstrates in this way: the One does not have one part of itself which encompasses and another which is encompassed; but that which is in itself has one element which encompasses and another which is encompassed, for which reason it is in itself in a way that what is encompassed is in what encompasses it; so then the One is not in itself. This, then, is the argument; and of these two premises, we will examine the second at a later point, when Plato makes mention of it again. But as to how that which is in itself has one element of itself which encompasses and another which is encompassed, this we must now discuss.

We must consider, after all, what is meant in this context by these terms 'encompass' and 'the encompassing'. For a start, everything is said to be in itself which is cause of itself and which is self-constituted; for we do not agree with those authorities who state that everything which is produced is produced by a cause other than itself, but even as we are accustomed to rank the self-motive prior to the externally

moved, even so one must rank the self-constituted as prior to what is
1146 produced by another agent. For if there is something which brings itself to completion, there is also something which constitutes itself, and
if there is such a thing as a self-constituted entity, it is plain that it
would be of such a sort as to produce itself and to be produced by itself;
for this is what it means to be self-constituting and self-generating. For
I class as self-generative not that which nothing produces (in view of
which some authorities have declared that the First Principle is self-
generative as having no cause of itself; and then, as having no cause,
they dare to say that it derives its subsistence from chance), but what
produces itself.[8] Since, then, an encompassing power always causally
encompasses that which is produced by it, it is necessary that that
which produces itself should be both encompassing of itself in so far as
it is a cause, and encompassed by itself in so far as it is an effect, and
because it is simultaneously cause and effect, it is necessary for it to be
encompassing and encompassed. If then, that which is "in another" is
that which is produced by another, superior cause, that which is "in itself" must be declared to be that which is self-begotten and produced
by itself;[9] and even as the former was encompassed by its cause, so the
latter will be encompassed by itself, and it will be encompassing and
cohesive of itself, through the same thing being both agent and object
of cohesion and encompassment; for in preserving itself it will encompass itself.

So much, then, for the subject matter of the present passage. As regards the text, we may note that the phrase "none other than itself,
since it would actually be within itself" could be given a clear sense if
one were to transpose the conjunction *kai*, so as to make the whole
phrasse mean "and none other than itself, since it would be within itself"; for if it is in itself, it itself is the container, and nothing else, for
such is the nature of the self-substantiated. Some commentators have
actually assumed that another speaker is saying this, i.e. that Aristotle
is here assenting to Parmenides' argument, and have based their exegesis on assigning what follows to Parmenides: "For nothing can be in
1147 something without being encompassed by that thing." But even if this

---

[8] For a useful discussion of this topic, see John Whittaker, "The Historical Background
of Proclus' Doctrine of the Αὐθυπόστατα," in *De Iamblique à Proclus, Entretiens Fondation
Hardt* XXI; pp. 193-237. The reasons against regarding the One as αὐθυπόστατον are
well stated by Proclus at *In Tim.* I, 232.11ff. It is not clear who Proclus is criticising here.
Plotinus speaks of the One as ὑποστήσας ἑαυτόν at *Enn.* VI, 8.13.57, but he denies in the
same breath that it came into being from chance.
[9] Cf. *ET*, prop. 41: "All that has its existence in another is produced entirely from another, but all that exists in itself is self-constituted." It is noteworthy, however, that ἐν
ἄλλῳ in the *ET* always seems to mean "in something *lower*," whereas here it means "in
something higher." Cf. 1136.29 above, where the two senses of the term are contrasted.

is so, as we have said above, that is of no significance for the subject matter in hand. So we may pass on to the next section of Plato's text.

"Thus the encompassing thing would be one thing, the encompassed another; for the same thing cannot as a whole both be acted upon and act in the way at the same time; and so, in that case, the One would no longer be one, but two." "No indeed." (138b)

The whole syllogism, as has been said before, is pretty much as follows: the One does not have one part of itself which contains, and another part which is contained, lest it become two instead of one; that which is in itself has one part of itself which contains itself, and another part which is contained; So then, the One is not in itself. Such being the nature of the syllogism, he had already taught us in what has gone before about one of the premises; but in adding here both what would make this one clearer and would make the other one also, he produces the conclusion set forth in the text; for if that which contains is one thing, and that which is contained is another, the One could not be both containing and contained by itself; for it would surely then have to be two, and not one; and even if it is "in itself," it is the sort of thing of which there is one part that contains and another that is contained. So then, that which is in itself must at the very least be a duality; for the container is different from the contained; for it is impossible for any one and the same thing to be containing and contained in the same respect.

The sequence of the arguments, then, is of this sort. We must now examine each part of the text in detail. First of all, then, let us consider how it is impossible for something to be simultaneously acting and acted upon as a whole; for this he has taken as something of common knowledge and agreed on all hands. Might this not eliminate for us the self-moving element in the soul? For in what is self-moved it is not the case that what moves is different from what is moved, but the whole simultaneously is moving and moved, as we have demonstrated elsewhere at great length.[10] We must, therefore, try to argue as convincingly as possible how this fact and the former can both be true.

1148 Of the faculties of the soul some we declare to be generative, and others which cause the soul to revert back upon itself[11] (even among the gods, after all, we have learned that there are similar differences of characteristics); and the generative faculties, beginning from the soul

---

[10] This is demonstrated at *ET*, prop. 17. If, as seems likely, this is a reference to that, it is an indication that the *In Parm.* is later than the *ET*.

[11] At *In Tim.* II, 204.21ff., à propos the divisions of the soul in *Tim.* 35b we find the number Two associated with its γεννητικαὶ δυνάμεις, the number Three with its ἐπιστρεπτικαί.

itself, produce its proper life, and following upon this, that life which proceeds into the body and has its being in the substratum; the reversionary faculties, on the other hand, concentrate the soul upon itself in virtue of a sort of vital cycle, and turn it towards the intellect which is established prior to the soul. For even as the generative faculties produce a double life of the soul, one which remains within it, and another which proceeds in our direction from it, even so the reversionary faculties produce a double reversion, both towards itself, and towards the intellect which is above it.

These, then, are the faculties which in particular generate the whole of the life of the soul; and the whole soul partakes in them because the faculties extend through each other and act in concert with each other, for which reason it is said that the whole soul generates itself; for as a whole it participates with the whole of itself in its generative faculties, even as it reverts towards itself, and neither is the generative element devoid of reversion, nor is the reversionary element non-generative, by reason of their participation in each other, so that one might say that each of the statements is true, both that which states that the soul generates itself and, what is said here, that it is not possible for something to be simultaneously acting and acted upon as a whole; for the generative power is one thing, ⟨and the generated life is another⟩,[11a] and even if the producing and the produced elements are one, yet along with unity there is also difference, by virtue of which such an entity does not remain free of multiplicity; for it will be produced as a whole, but not in the same respect as it is the producer will it also be produced. For the productive element in the primary sense will be the generative element of the soul, since after all it is possible for one part to generate and another to be generated, even as in the cosmos we say that the heavens generate and create, whereas the realm below the moon is generated; and again that no part, but rather the whole, is generated and generates at different times, and again that the whole acts and is acted upon in the same time, but one part acts, and another part and not the same part in turn is acted upon. And what if while heating it becomes cold and while becoming pale it becomes dark? For this reason, in order to dispose of all such objections, he, with attention to accuracy, added the words *whole, simultaneously,* and *the same,* in order that it should not act in one way and be acted upon in another, nor at various different times, nor with various aspects of itself.

So then, that he has shown that that which is self-moved and all that is in itself partake in duality, and that that which is in itself is not one, is plain from this; for there is no duality in the One, first of all because

1149

[11a] Accepting a supplement of Westerink.

all multiplicity has been eliminated from the One, and the dyad is the fount and cause of multiplicity and contains in a way within itself the whole of multiplicity; and secondly because it would have to have both a containing and a contained element in itself. It has been shown that there is no such thing in the One; for it is not possible for it to be a container as a whole is of parts nor in the way that a particular shape partakes in shape, so that it will contain itself with one part and be contained with another. We have previously seen it denied, after all, that the One has parts; even if it had not already been proved separately that the One could not partake in duality, yet this also follows upon what has been said, which is the reason why Parmenides makes use of it here.

Everything else in the passage has, I think, been adequately proved by what has already been said; there is this point also here that, it is worth pointing out, Plato is demonstrating, which indeed some of his followers have sufficiently established, but others have not acceded to, although they wish to be initiates in Plato's mysteries and desire to join in the dance around him. For some want to say that the first principle is self-constituted, arguing that even as the first principle of moving things is the self-moved, even so the first principle of all those things which have any sort of existence is self-constituted;[12] for all things subsequent to the first principle also derive from the first principle. This first principle, then, is self-constituted in the proper sense, as deriving

1150 its substance from nothing else, whereas as they say, everything must either be created by itself or, inevitably, by something else. Indeed, some other thinkers, developing a certain recklessness,[13] have before now even declared it to be self-moved, proceeding to this from the concept of self-constitution by reason of the kinship between the two concepts; although this self-moved entity would necessarily be in motion and could not be properly one, but a multiplicity; and what is self-constituted must necessarily be divisible into a superior and an inferior element; for it is superior in so far as it creates, and it is inferior in so far as it is created; the One, on the other hand, is entirely indivisible and non-multiple; for it is neither a unified nor a distinct multiplicity; for if it were distinct, it would be in many places and not one, whereas if it were unified there would have to be something else prior to it which unified it; for what is unified is something which has unity as an attribute, but is not itself unity, as the Eleatic Stranger says (*Soph.* 244e). If,

---

[12] Presumably Plotinus, on the basis of his doctrine in *Enn.* VI, 8; cf. n. 8 above. There, however, the authority concerned was accused of postulating the One's existence (or supra-existence) as a matter of chance, whereas Plotinus attributes it to will (βούλησις).

[13] It is hard to imagine what Neoplatonist thinker might be rash enough to aver this, but it could refer to the Stoics, whom Plotinus actually criticises for this at *Enn.* III, 1.2.17ff.

then, the self-constituted is in any way divisible, while the One is not divisible, the One would not be self-constituted, but rather the cause of all self-constituted entities, by virtue of the fact that all things are preserved by the agency of the One, both such things as are generated by themselves and such things as are generated by others.

Other authorities,[14] following Plato, have uncompromisingly declared that the first principle is superior to this function also, and superior, again, to every paternal and generative cause, inasmuch as it is superior to all potency—this in spite of the fact that Plato is loud in asserting that it is the cause all good things,[15] though not cause in the way that it makes use of any potency by means of which it is productive of everything. For a power generates what it generates as inferior to its own powers; of those things following upon the One, those which are nearest the One shine forth from it ineffably and in a hidden level,[16] possess paternal and generative rank in respect of all beings, and produce other things by virtue of their own powers from themselves, and in this way are more multiple than the One by generating those beings which are self-constituted, while those that are already distinct and 1151 multiplied take in to themselves the power of the self-constituted, receiving their substance from the primal causes, but being produced also by themselves; and these are dependent upon the paternal causes which generate the forms, while they in turn are dependent upon the One which is superior to all such causality, but makes shine forth from itself in a manner unknowable to all in all directions according to the first principles of beings.

If this is the case, then, it is plain that everything which creates itself is also productive of other things; for the self-constituted entities are neither first nor last among beings; that which is productive of other things without being productive of itself is twofold, one sort being superior to the self-constituted, the other inferior. Productive things, then, are of this sort; but of things produced from a productive cause the primary sort are the self-constituted, which are produced indeed, but generated self-productively from their own causes; the second order, dependent upon a substantiating cause other than itself, but not able to produce itself and to be produced by itself—this order of beings enjoys a procession from above as far as the ultimate orders. For if that which generated other things but does not generate itself is last on the

---

[14] Since this is a rather offhand way to refer to Syrianus, Iamblichus seems the most likely candidate.

[15] *Ep.* II, 312e2-3; cf. *PT* II, 9, p. 58.11-59.4 S-W.

[16] Κρύφιος, κρυφίως, a Chaldaean term (fr. 198 DP); cf. 1026.5ff. above. The κρύφιος διάκοσμος is the model of the universe in the mind of the Demiurge (cf. *In Tim.* I, 430.6; II, 70.7). It is equated with the πρωτογενὲς ᾠόν of the Orphics.

scale, and if there is something which generates itself and generates other things, then there must exist also prior to those things which generate themselves things that generate other things; for entities which are more comprehensive are more first principles, and if we were to seek where that which generates itself is situated finally, we would say that it is where actuality first comes into play; and actuality first occurs at the level of being, even as potentiality occurs in the henad prior to being and existence in the henad prior to this, so that the primal being is productive of itself, and this it does essentially, while the third from this does it intellectually, and that which is midway between the two does it vitally.

"So then, the One is not anywhere, being neither in itself nor in another?" "No, it is not." (138b)

Quite in accord with geometrical practice, he in each of the theorems first states the proposition, then the proof, then finally the conclusion—through the proposition, imitating the unified and stationary activity of the intellect; through the proof, the procession of thoughts into multiplicity as it unrolls itself; through the conclusion, the circular turning of the intellect back towards its first principle and the single perfection of the whole activity of intellect. Although he has done this in all theorems before this he does it particularly clearly in this one; for it is proper to this order (of beings) to be both of itself and to remain in what is prior to it; therefore he represents by means of the course of the argument the concept of being in oneself, while by the conclusion and the turning back to the beginning he represents the idea of being in another.

"Consider then, whether, such being the case, it is possible for it to be at rest or in motion." "Why not?" (138b)

With this he turns to another question, demonstrating that the One is neither in motion nor stationary, the latter of which characteristics Parmenides asserted of it in his poems, reasonably enough, inasmuch as there he is theorising about the One Being, even as Plato himself will assert these things in the Second Hypothesis. Parmenides, at any rate, says on one occasion:

Whole-limbed and unmoved and ungenerated[17] (fr. 8.4 D-K)

and again

But it is motionless in the toils of great bonds (fr. 8.26)

[17] Reading ἀγένητον for Simplicius' ἀτέλεστον, probably borrowed from line 3 above.

and again

> And it remains the same in the same, and stands on its own (fr. 8.29)

and again

> Thus there it stands fast (fr. 8.30)

and on another occasion

> It is the same there to think and to be (fr. 3).

and again

> For not without being, on which it is predicated, will you find thought . . . . (fr. 8.35-36)
> Behold how what is absent is nevertheless firmly present to the mind (fr. 4.1)

1153 Since in these passages he has situated intellection in Being, he obviously accepts that there is a certain type of motion therein, namely intellectual motion, which Plato also recognises; for it is he who says it is not even possible to conceive of intellect without motion (*Soph.* 249a1-2); so that if there is intellection in the One Being according to Parmenides, then there is also motion, since inevitably there must be life along with intellection; everything after all that lives moves by virtue of living. In the above verses, admittedly, he says that the One Being is motionless, calling it "unshakeable" and "steadfast" and explicitly "unmoving." So also Plato declares that where there is intellect there is not only motion but also stability (*Soph.* 249bc). And in respect of One Being each of them postulates these characteristics, as will become plain in the course of the Second Hypothesis, and Parmenides could not be convicted of error by means of these negations, but would rather accept the addition of another level of philosophical theorising concerning itself with the truly One.

This, however, has been gone into in my previous discussions; now, following my own system, it must be said that, the intellectual orders being also divided in three, Plato, by negating in what has gone before the "in itself" and "in another," has shown the One to be superior to the summit of the intellectual realm; now, in here denying motion and rest of it, he has moved on to another order, from the intellectual monad to the life-giving one, and shows that the One transcends this too. We must, therefore, examining the characteristics of this order also, show that the One is superior to such characteristics.[18] The proper

[18] Cf. *PT* II, 12, p. 68.23ff. S-W.

characteristics, then, of this life-giving divinity[19] are motion and rest, the one showing forth the founts of life, the other establishing it firmly as transcendent over its own streams. If, then, we demonstrate that the 1154 One is situated above all rest and all motion, we would then understand how it transcends this whole chain.

But we may go into this on another occasion. Here we may note that he shows that one must not only negate physical motions of the One, when he says, "The One is motionless in respect of every type of motion" (139a). If according to him every actualisation is a motion, the One will also be prior to actualisation, so that it will also be prior to potentiality, lest it should possess a potentiality which is incomplete and not actualised; these consequences follow necessarily. For everything that proceeds from the One must have what the One itself has, even as what proceeds from Being must have what Being has. But Matter is without activity; for that which acts acts either upon itself or upon something else; and Matter, inasmuch as it is one, derives from the One; no activity therefore is to be postulated in the One, and so no potentiality, but just Oneness itself alone.

As to why he has dealt with Motion and Rest before Same and Other another reason will be given later, deriving from the logical sequence. But we may say here on the basis of the subject matter that Motion and Rest are seen in the substances of beings and in their activities (for procession is the motion of a substance, and rest is its establishment in its causes; for every being proceeds forth while remaining in place) and, as substantial causes, are prior to Sameness and Otherness; for beings are made Same and Other as they proceed from their causes along with remaining in them, being made Other by the whole process of proceeding, but being made the Same by the process of turning back towards what has remained static, and for this reason Motion and Rest are placed before Sameness and Otherness, as arising at an earlier stage to them. For this reason also in the *Sophist* he places Motion and Rest 1155 directly after Being, and then Same and Other; for Being is unitary, not having an opposite; whereas Motion is dual, since all procession is from somewhere to somewhere; and Rest is triadic, since it turns back and comes to rest after proceeding forth; and Sameness is tetradic, for the number four is the first of numbers which is of the same length and breadth; and Otherness is pentadic, for this number divides the even and the odd absolutely. This, then, may be derived from a consideration of the metaphysical realities; the necessary nature of the sequence

---

[19] Theologically, this is denominated Rhea; cf. *In Crat.* 81.2ff. Pasquali, where a passage from the Chaldaean Oracles is quoted (fr. 56 DP).

of the propositions will become clear a little later in what we are about to expound.

"Because if it were in motion, it would have to be either moving in place or undergoing alteration; for these are the only types of motion." "Yes." (138c)

Since we are inquiring whether the One is in motion or not, for this is the first thing that we have to examine, let us make a comprehensive division of motions. We found such a division also in the *Laws* (X, 893bff.), according to the perfect division of the decad, identifying eight passive motions, and one that was active indeed, but which required the mover and the moved to be different, and constructed one motion out of both of them; and the final one which is active and also arising from itself and having a moved element and a moving element which are identical, which is what we term the self-moving motion. Here, however, it is suitable to make a different and more abbreviated kind of division, in order that we may not involve ourselves in using physical concepts when talking about the divine realm. How, then, are we to comprehend all these motions in summary form other than by dividing them all into two?

For that the motions here mentioned are not to be considered only as material ones, but also as taking in all immaterial motions, he himself has made plain with the words, "For these are the only motions there are." So then, whether we postulate motions of the soul or of the intellect we must understand how these are to be brought under these two headings, namely spatial motion and alteration. It is obvious, for one thing, that the whole life-giving class of gods is the cause of all such motions, if indeed all life is motion, as Plato judges it to be (*Laws* X, 895c), and every motion is brought under these motions, as the present 1156 argument asserts.

Let us consider, therefore, the whole range of what moves. Let our discussion take its beginning from bodies, either those which move some part of themselves or which move something external. For those things that change one place for another experience change of something external to themselves; whereas what comes to be or perishes or grows or lessens or is combined or distinguished, is said to come to be and perish and suffer all these other alterations through some change in itself. That which changes in its external relations is said to move spatially; for such motion traverses place, for place is external to bodies; all that which moves in relation to something internal to it is said to suffer alteration, whether it experiences generation or destruction or growth or lessening or combination or dissolution. Nothing suffers qualitative alteration simply by being moved in space; in particular such motion is appropriate to the divine bodies, and they are essentially unalterable; for since they also had to be in motion because the state of being always the same in identical relation is proper only to the most divine of all things, and the nature of body is not of this order, as we have learned in the *Statesman* (259d), but being the first among all visible things they possess a being which is eternal (for those things which are primary in each order have the shape of what is prior to them),[20] they are moved, but only according to the motion which preserved the essence of the things moved unaltered.

What is moved spatially is of this nature, but that which is changed in respect of one of its internal parts becomes "altered." Such a state is most proper to forms-in-matter, as Timaeus has taught us (*Tim.* 50c), so that "alteration" is proper to the changes which these undergo, as the forms "enter and exit."

So much, then, for bodily motions. All such motions are comprehended in the notion of locomotion (*phora*) and alteration (*alloiōsis*) which Socrates in the *Theaetetus* (181d) is looking to as the sole type, 1157 inasmuch as he is contending against Heraclitus when he there makes this division of motions. But if we ascend to the level of souls, we see that in these also one can distinguish between locomotive and alterative change. In so far as they at different times confront different Forms— through their contact with various Forms assimilating themselves to their own intelligibles—they themselves also in a way appear multiform, inasmuch as they partake in the activities of the objects of their intellection, constantly differing as they do, and alter their state in accordance with them, to this extent, in my view, there is alteration in these also.

On the other hand, in so far as they are active around "the intelligible place," and traverse the whole range of the Forms, which is both external to them and encompasses them on all sides, to this extent in turn they perform locomotion, as witness Plato, who shows knowledge in the *Phaedrus* of the "intelligible place" (247c)[21] and terms the activity of the souls and their going about it a "circuit" (247d), so that they experience both alteration and locomotion, experiencing alteration in respect of their living aspect (for it is this that is affected by its objects of vision and is assimilated to them), while undergoing locomotion in changing from one object of intellection to another and going about in its intellections and turning back to the same ones again; or rather they contain within themselves the causal principles of alteration and locomotion.

---

[20] Cf. *ET*, prop. 112: "The first members of each order have the form of their priors."
[21] Plato in fact terms it, of course, ὑπερουράνιος τόπος, not νοητὸς τόπος, but he uses the latter term at *Rep.* VI, 508c, 509d, and VII, 517b.

And if you turn to consider the much-hymned Intellect,[22] you will find in this also the models on an intellectual level of both alteration and locomotion; for by participating in the nature of the intelligised, in the process of intelligising and becoming an object of intellection itself by intelligising, it becomes altered in respect of its character as intellect; for participations are said generally to bestow something on the participator rather different from its nature, and Intellect participates in the intelligible, but not vice versa.

1158   Then by intelligising in relation to the same thing on the same terms and in the same way, and activating itself about the intelligible object as about its own centre, it has assumed antecedently the model of locomotion in this realm. Thus in the *Laws* (898a) Plato likens the motion of Intellect to the motion of a "well-turned globe," by reason of the fact that Intellect moves "on the same terms and in the same way and around the same things," even as does the globe. For there is in Intellect also, as they say,[23] a "dancing" and a "procession," not, however, as there is in souls, but rather a dance[24] and procession which consists of their *having* danced and *having* proceeded according to the simple and concentrated activity of Intellect.

At all levels, then, we find motions to be alterations and locomotions, intellectual at the level of Intellect, psychic at the level of Soul, and bodily and disparted at the level of sense-objects, so that one should not be surprised that these are the only motions; for they are all comprehended in these two types. Nor should one claim that he has left out self-motion, on the grounds that the One is self-moved; for he himself clearly in what follows (139a), will say that the One "is unmoving in respect of every kind of motion." Indeed it would be ridiculous to declare the One to be self-moved, if in fact it is impossible for the One to be many and to have parts and to be in itself, while the self-moved is both mover and moved, and in all cases moving is a separate thing from being moved; for which reason such an entity cannot be absolutely one, but it too will experience oneness as an attribute, multiplied along with its unity. But in fact both Socrates, when he thus divides motions in the *Theaetetus*, and Parmenides, in the present

---

[22] This is a slightly curious phrase, ὁ πολυύμνητος νοῦς. Cf. above, 1080.13, and *In Tim*. I, 191.17. It is a variant of πολυτίμητος νοῦς, an expression of Syrianus, *In Met*. 25.4, 90.32, which Proclus also uses, e.g. *In Alc*. 247.7, and 1053.14 above. Its precise significance is not clear to me, but it should refer to its celebration in poems, Orphic or Chaldaean.

[23] Who speaks of a χορεία; of Intellect I do not know (not Plato, certainly), but Plotinus, at least, speaks of a διέξοδος of Intellect at *Enn*. III, 8.9.33. Porphyry, at *Sent*. 44, p. 58.4ff. Lamberz, explicitly denies διέξοδος of Intellect. Normally, χόρος νοῦ is an "etymology" of χρόνος.

[24] Reading ἀλλ᾽ ἡ (sc. χορεία / διέξοδος) for the meaningless ἄλλη of the MSS. With the use of the perfect tenses here, cf. Damascius' use of ὠδευκέναι at *In Phil*. 136.9.

instance, do not omit any other type of motion, when dealing in the former case with bodily ones, and in the latter with all, but with this pair he here takes in the set of ten motions listed in the *Laws* (X, 894aff.).

"Now if the One alters from itself, it is presumably impossible for it still to be one?" "Impossible." "Therefore it does not move in the sense of alteration." "It seems not." (138c)

1159　He began by enquiring if the One moved. In making this enquiry he divides motions into alteration and locomotion, and having shown that the One neither alters itself nor moves spatially, he draws the conclusion that the One does not move as follows: "The One is neither altered nor moves spatially; but everything that moves is either altered or moves spatially; therefore, the One does not move." How then, first, are we to demonstrate that the One does not undergo alteration? If it is altered, it would possess multiplicity; for if it changes from itself, it will inevitably change into multiplicity, even as Being changes into Not-Being; whereas if it itself remains fixed, and some element of it changes, then inevitably again it will not be one, but a multiplicity; for the One itself will have to be both a substratum and an element that changes. But it has been shown that the One in no way partakes of multiplicity.

The Soul, then, as it alters through its motions about real being, has been shown necessarily to be a multiplicity, likening itself at different times to different aspects of reality, and receives an impression of the vital characteristic relating it to each; and Intellect likewise, in striving towards the intelligible and partaking of it, is multiplied along with remaining Intellect, becoming and being as many things as is the intelligible multiplicity. So the One, if it were to alter itself while remaining One, as, of the others, the one remains Soul and the other Intellect, in participating in something different from One would no longer be One only; but as the one (Soul) becomes intellectual through partaking in the nature of the Intellect, and the other (Intellect) intelligible through being no longer simply Intellect intelligising itself, but also intelligible as intelligised by itself; so then, if the One also suffered alteration, it would no longer be simply one; for what it took on, since it would be something else other than One, would no longer permit the oneness of the One to remain. Far more so, then, if the One itself had changed from itself, would it have become not One; for everything that is altered must change into what it is not.

The One, therefore, does not alter; for either the One itself will change, or even if it stays fixed (as a whole) it will not be one but many, since one part of it will change, and another stay fixed. But all this Plato

1160 does not even bother to go into, since it had already been dealt with by the argument that the One has neither parts nor multiplicity; he contents himself with mentioning that the One cannot even be altered, lest it lose its quality of being One.

"Does it, then, move in place?" "Perhaps." "And yet if it does, it must either be carried round in a circle in the same place or shift from one place to another." "Necessarily." (138c)

He has turned to the other type of motion, that of locomotion, and demonstrates that the One does not move according to this mode either, first of all dividing locomotion into motion around the same place and transference from one place to another; for everything that moves in place either keeps to the same place, remaining unchanged as a whole and moving only as regards its parts, or moves both as a whole and in its parts, coming to be in one place after another. There are four possibilities here:

1. moving as a whole and in one's parts from one place to another;
2. moving neither as a whole nor in one's parts;
3. moving as a whole, but not in one's parts;
4. moving in one's parts, but not as a whole.

Of these four, the third, moving as a whole while one's parts remain stationary, is impossible, for if the whole moves the parts of which the whole is formed must also move; while (2) moving neither as a whole nor in one's parts is the property of things which are static. The remaining possibilities, then, are (4) not moving as a whole, while moving in one's parts, and (1) moving both as a whole and in one's parts. But the former of these produces the motion of a sphere or a cylinder, when these things move about their own axes; while the latter produces transferral from one place to another when some whole object alters its situation and occupies one place after another.

That the division of types of motion follows these lines should be clear from this discussion. And we see these two motions not only at the level of sense-objects, the circular in the case of the heavens, change of place as a whole in the case of things beneath the moon, but also in 1161 the realms superior to these, since the individual soul, by reason of its movement upwards and downwards and its changing activity on the same level, provides a model for motions of whole bodies, while the Intellect, through its unchanging reversion towards the intelligible, anticipates causally circular motion; and not only the Intellect, but every divine soul, by reason of its "dance" round Intellect, takes on incorporeal circular motion. For which reason we have already said that the Athenian Stranger in the *Laws* (898b) likened the activity of the Intel-

lect to the imitation of a "well-turned globe." And indeed Parmenides himself, in calling Being a "sphere," and saying that it "thinks," will plainly be prepared to characterise its thoughts as circular motion. Timaeus, as well (*Tim.* 36c), having bent into a circle the linear progress of the soul, and making one of the circuits inner and the other outer, in both cases according to the demiurgic causal principle, granted to them an eternal and intellectual procession prior to bodies. The theologians also know of incorporeal circular motion, seeing that the theologian of the Greeks (sc. Orpheus) declares about the primary and hidden god, who is prior to Phanes, "And he was borne unceasingly about / In an endless circle" (fr. 71 Kern). And the Oracles lay down that "all the founts and the beginnings whirl, and yet always remain fixed in an unwearying eddy" (fr. 49.3-4 DP). For since everything that turns in a
1162 circle has rest mixed in with its motion, it is reasonable to say that it also remains ever fixed in the process of turning about, the term "unwearying" signifying its immaterial nature. So then, we have the motions of incorporeal entities also comprised in this division, and so the One is shown to be motionless as being situated superior to all motion, and not as in one way motionless, while being in another way moved.

"If it turns round in a circle, it must rest on a centre, and have those parts which revolve around the centre as different parts of itself. But in the case of a thing which cannot have a centre or parts, in what way could this ever be carried round on its centre?" "In no way." (138c)

After the division of spatial motion, he shows that the One does not move according to either of these motions, neither according to the circulation of its parts, nor according to the transferral of the whole. And he first shows that the One does not move according to the circulation of its parts; for one characteristic of this is to have some central point, while the extremes move around the centre, and another is to remain static as a whole, while moving by reason of the reciprocal replacement of one's parts; but the One is neither a whole having parts, nor can there be in it any central or extreme point. How, then, could it undergo circular motion, since it is not in receipt of either of the characteristics of circular motion?

These conclusions, therefore, have been drawn in what has preceded, according, as they say, to geometrical necessity. As regards the
1163 details of the text, we may go on to note that the phrase "to rest upon a centre" is reasonably applied to the sphere because its centre is what provides a fixed point for its whole circuit, and because when this is moved the whole moves, and the whole is founded upon this, as upon a hearth and cohesive principle, even as in the *Statesman* (270a) the Sage there states that the universe is founded upon a very small footing—"a

very small footing" meaning its centre. In the phrase "having those parts which revolve round the centre as different parts of itself," we must alter the word-order slightly for the sake of clarity, in order that the whole may read, "And everything which is carried round in a circle must have different parts of itself," such as are these parts which are carried around about the centre; for only the parts of it are moved, while the whole remains static. The phrase "that which has neither a centre nor parts" clearly makes a distinction between the centre and the parts, the centre not being a part; for the centre is something different from all the parts of a mobile object, since it remains static while all of them move. The phrase "carried round upon its centre" must be said to mean something such as the following: "being external to the centre and being borne round upon it, but not towards it (for this is a characteristic of things that move in a straight line), but embracing the centre by circling it from all sides." For things that move in a straight line move either towards the centre or away from the centre. That which moves in a circle might be said also to move around the centre even, as he said before, "having its parts moving around the centre," and again in another way, "upon the centre," as floating upon it and spread out upon it by reason of its striving for a place at the centre. Unless, indeed, one might say in another sense that it moves in a circle upon the centre as being positioned upon it, and moving in a circle, just like the phrase in the *Statesman* about being based on a very small footing, such that one part remains static and the other is borne about the middle, even 1164 as it was said above that the thing which moves in a circle rests on a centre. So much, then, for the text. We may now pass to the next passage of Plato.

> "It must move, then, by changing its place, and coming to be in different places at different times." "Yes, if it moves at all." "But we say that it could not be anywhere in anything." "Yes." "Is it not then even more impossible for it to come to be there?" "I don't quite understand how you mean." "If a thing is coming to be in something, is it not necessary that it cannot be in that thing so long as it is still coming to be in it, nor yet can it be altogether outside it, since it is already coming to be in it." "It is necessary." "If, then, something else should experience this, only that thing would experience it of which there would be parts; for part of it will be already in the other thing and part of it outside it at the same time, and a thing which has no parts surely cannot possibly be at the same time neither wholly inside nor wholly outside something." "True." "Is it not still more impossible that a thing which has no parts and is not a whole should come to be in anything, since it cannot do so either part by part nor as a whole?" "It would appear so." (138de)

This is the remaining type of motion, when the thing moved as a whole changes from one place to another. And it is this that we are concerned now to demonstrate as in no way applying to the One, and once again this has been proved by means of what has been proved previously; for we have denied to the One the attribute of being in anything, and it has been shown that the One is in nothing. But everything which moves as a whole from place to place comes to be in something; so the One does not move as a whole from place to place. That it is impossible for the One to come to be in one place through changing from another is also clear. For either it must be as a whole inside each place, or as a whole outside each, or one part of it must be in one place and the other in another. But if as a whole it is outside each, being in neither it would not be conveyed from one to the other; on the other hand if as a whole it is inside each, it would not once again be moved from the former place to the subsequent place. And if one part of it is in one situation, and the other in the other, it will be divisible; but the One is in no way divisible; for if it is going to be divisible ⟨it will not be One; since, however, it is indivisible⟩,[25] it is necessary that the One should come to be either outside both places as a whole or inside both; but these alternatives are impossible. The One does not therefore come to be in anything.

That this is even more impossible than being in something is quite plain. For you might imagine some kind of being which is a whole and is neither external to nor internal to anything, but both external and internal; for it is in this way that the Soul and Intellect are said to be both in the cosmos and outside the cosmos; but for some whole to come to be in something, while being neither outside it nor inside it, is impossible. It is even more impossible, then, for the One, both as a whole and as having parts, to come to be in something than to be in something. If by soul we are to understand not just our soul, but also the divine Soul, and say that it contains the cause of such motion by reason of its transitive activity, we are looking here to its divisible aspects, and in virtue of the fact that it contains different reason-principles we will say that it takes up its stand at different times according to different ones, neither being as a whole at any one focus of activity nor being entirely external to it; for it does not present itself as a whole to the thought processes of Intellect all at once (for it is not its nature to behold them in one comprehensive act), nor is it wholly separated from Intellect, but it comes to be in some way in virtue of its different intellections in the different forms of the Intellect, and as it were establishes its own intellection in the Intellect as in its proper place.

[25] Westerink's suggested supplement, since text as it stands makes no sense.

For this reason Timaeus (*Tim.* 35a)[26] did not shrink from describing the soul even as generated, when he termed it divisible; for it does not possess simultaneity in its thought, but all its activity is in a state of coming to be, and its thoughts are given substance in the process of transition; for which reason also Time takes its origin from it, and serves as the measure of its primary activities. The Intellect, then,
1166 seems in the purest sense to contain the model of circular motion, having as a centre the static part of itself, whereas the many processions of the Forms from this Being and, as it were, Hearth of itself may be likened to the straight lines leading out from the centre, and all its intellectual activities, the intellections of ⟨true beings⟩[27] and of Being itself, may be seen as the single surface which runs round the radii from the centre and the centre itself. The divine Soul also has been allotted the paradigm of both motion in a straight line and circular motion in its progress through the intelligible realm, the latter remaining static as a whole, but unravelling the intelligible realm by its transitions, while to the extent that it is always striving as a whole towards the object of its intellection it is paradigmatic of the former; for in this aspect it both remains static and moves as a whole. Finally the individual soul clearly by its lateral motions expresses the incorporeal cause of motion in a straight line, and by its reversionary motions expresses that of circular motion.

> "Hence it does not change its place either by travelling anywhere and coming to be in something, or by revolving in the same place, or by changing."
> "It seems not." "Therefore the One is unmoving in respect of every kind of motion." "It is unmoving." (139a).

In the present passage he brings together all the previously stated conclusions about motion, and, having formerly enumerated them separately, he now makes one conclusion of all of them in general, instructing us also by means of this ascent how one should concentrate one's view of the One by always gathering together multiplicity into what is common to it, and taking the parts together in wholes. For what he previously divided into fragments, distinguishing motion into three motions—alteration, circular motion, and straight motion—and concluding in the case of each that the One does not move in respect of it, now having enumerated each of these separately by saying, "neither by travelling anywhere nor by revolving nor changing," and having made the enumeration orderly, by returning from what has just been

---

[26] Cf. Proclus' discussion of *Tim.* 35a at *In Tim.* I, 147.23-154.26 Diehl. He takes ἡ αὖ περὶ τα σώματα γιγνομένη μεριστὴ (οὐσία) to refer, not to the material world, but to one aspect, and component, of the Soul.
[27] Accepting Westerink's supplement ⟨ὄντων⟩, superior to Cousin's ⟨εἰδῶν⟩.

1167 demonstrated to what comes before that, in order that he may join the end to the beginning and imitate the circular nature of Intellect, he has produced a common conclusion which embraces all of them, that "the One is unmoved in respect of every kind of motion." You see once again[28] how the premise and the conclusion are general, and the proofs proceed by means of divisions; for the static intellections and reversions bring together the multiplicity, while those that are involved with procession divide the whole into its parts and the One into the number proper to it.

But enough has been said now about his general procedure. Since, however, some authorities are accustomed to raise difficulties about the arguments which deny motion to the One, let us make some brief reply to these. They say that it is absolutely necessary for the First to act upon the things that are secondary to it, for it gives to all of them unity, and it is the cause among beings of all the unitary forms which are participated in by them. Why, then, should one not describe this activity of the One as motion? Because, I would say, one should not rank activity as prior to essence, nor in general grant activity to the first principle; for everything which acts has the potentiality corresponding to its act. It will therefore be necessary for those who allow activity to the first principle to grant it potentiality as well. But if potentiality and activity are situated there, we will once again have multiplicity appearing in the One, and the One will no longer be one. But we (for let us state our own opinion here) would see even subsequent to the One something which is superior to potentiality and productive of the substance of potentiality and even more so of activity; for the subsistence (*hyparxis*) of the primary triad of the intelligibles is beyond all potentiality and actuality. How much more so, then, is the One, which, as rising above all subsistence, we postulate as being superior to actualisation.

And we shall not wonder how all things arise from the One without its acting. For it is possible to argue that that which produces something by acting experiences this through deficiency of power; of a superior nature is that which produces in virtue of its existence alone; this 1168 thing, then, will be free of the burdens of creation. Even so, the Soul also vivifies everything to which it is present by being life only and not having any other activity besides living, but in the process of living only communicating life to everything that is capable of living. And Intellect produces what is subsequent to it by being what it is, not having any other activity besides existence which gives existence to those things to which it gives it. But since being Intellect it does not act only

---

[28] Cf. 1151.39ff. above.

by existing, but also intelligises what it creates, and Soul also knows that what it creates lives and knows it by living, it seems that both Intellect and Soul create by means of cognitive activity; but they create in reality with the accompaniment of cognitive activity; and if you remove this, while leaving to the one the fact that it is life, and to the other its existence, both Soul and Intellect will still produce what they produced to the accompaniment of cognitive activity.

If, then, these entities produce by their existence alone, far more so does that One which is above them produce all things by the very fact of being one, not requiring any other activity to accompany its being one. For if it created through activity, it would be necessary to enquire, since it acts, whether it creates its own activity or does not create it; for if it does not create it, the first principles will be two, the One and the activity of the One, differing from each other; but if it creates it, it is necessary that the One should create this prior to activity, or else we ascend to infinity, postulating an activity before activity, so that it is necessary that the One produces activity itself prior to activity. And if this is the case, there is no cause for wonder that that which is the cause of all things should thus be prior to all activity, unless perhaps one wants to call that primal production from itself prior to all activity an activity of some sort, since in many cases in the affairs of this realm we call the finished products activities of those who have brought them to completion. Even if someone were to say this, it is obvious that the activity is not in the One, but after it, so that the One created what it first created having no need of activity; and even as it created what it created first, even so did it create everything; so then it created all things without employing activity. But if in using these very words *created* and *pro-*
1169 *duced*, we use terms proper to activity, even this should be no cause for surprise; for we apply these terms to the One from the realm of beings, signifying through terms denoting activity the activity-less manifestation of all things from it. And indeed the inspired Aristotle seems to me for this reason, in preserving his first principle free of multiplicity, to make it only the final cause of all things, lest in granting it to create all things, he should be forced to grant it activity towards what follows upon it; for if it is only the final cause, then everything exercises activity towards it, but it towards nothing.

> *"On the other hand, we also assert that it cannot actually be in anything."*
> *"We do." "Consequently, it is not ever in the same (condition)."*[29]
> *"How so?" "Because then it would be in that very (condition), in the process of being in the same (condition)." "Certainly." "But we saw that*

[29] It is necessary in English to add some such filler, but the force of the argument in the Greek is strengthened by the circumstance that no such noun is necessary.

it could not be either in itself or in anything else." "No, indeed." "The One, then, is never in the same." "It would seem not." "But what is never in the same is not at rest or stationary." "No, it could not be." "The One, then, as it would seem, is neither at rest nor in motion." "No, it would seem not." (139ab)

What was requiring to be demonstrated at the beginning of this was that the One has no need of rest or motion, and is superior to both and the cause of them. For the characteristic of being neither at rest nor in motion is not true of it in the sense that it is true of Matter, for Matter participates in them all only to the point of mere seeming, but the One is deprived of them as being superior to both, and in virtue of the fact that it is through it that these genera make their appearance among beings. For, as one of our predecessors has remarked,[30] it is because the One is not at rest that Being is in motion, and because the One is not in motion, that Being is at rest; for by its static aspect it imitates the motionlessness of the One, and through its active aspect it imitates the fact that the One is superior to any resting and situation in itself, and through both aspects it imitates the One, which is neither of these.

The subject before us, then, is as I have stated; but the argument, in 1170 dividing up the propositions, demonstrates, first, "that the One is not in motion" by means of the syllogisms set out previously; then in turn it demonstrates "that it is not at rest" by means of the syllogisms set out now in the following manner: "Everything that it at rest wishes to be in the same place, even as that which is in motion is in different forms or places. But everything that is in 'the same' is in something—that, obviously, by being in which it is in the same. So then, everything that is at rest is at rest in something; for that which is at rest in the mode of life is in itself, whereas that which is at rest corporeally is in something else. And being in oneself and being in another in each case do not escape being in something. But if everything that is at rest is in something, that which is not in something is not at rest, by virtue of the antithetical contradiction of the premise. If, then, the One is not in something, as has been shown previously, and that which is not in something is not at rest, it is surely plain that the One is not at rest." This, then, is the final conclusion that he draws; with the statement, "And we also assert that it cannot actually be in anything," he takes up the minor premise, that the One is not in something, whereas with the statement, "Then it is never in the same (condition)," he takes up the major premise. Or rather, the conclusion is the combination of the two; for the major premise was that that which is not in something is not in the same thing either, which he proved next after the interlocu-

[30] I am unable to identify this predecessor, but he is presumably a Neoplatonist.

tor had said, "How so?" and asked him to demonstrate also the major premise; which Parmenides having done, he then goes on to conclude, "The One is, then, never in the same (condition)," which is no different from saying, "The One, then, is not ever in the same (condition)," because in both cases it is expressed after a reminder of what the premises were, in order that the argument may be of this sort: "The One is not in anything; that which is not in anything is never in the same place." Then the second argument is of this sort: "The One is never in the same (condition); that which is never in the same (condition) is not stationary; so then the One is not stationary."

He adds in, "nor is it at rest"; for that which is established in another 1171 seems also to be stationary, and that which can remain in itself seems to be at rest. But he has denied both of the One, inasmuch as it is neither in anything else, as has been shown previously, nor in itself. So whether we hear of some "intellectual calm" being celebrated by the wise,[31] or a "mystical haven," or "paternal silence," it is plain that the One transcends all these states, being beyond both activity and silence and rest, and all those symbols of stability which are celebrated in the realm of beings. Through this, then, he demonstrated that the One is not stationary; and he added the conclusion which is common to all these and to what has gone before, that the One is neither stationary nor in motion, producing a conclusion for the whole argument that corresponds to the original proposition.[32]

Someone might perhaps raise the difficulty against us, that the fact that the One is neither in motion nor stationary has been sufficiently stated already; for who could raise any objection to the preceding arguments? But there is no objection to calling it "Rest" or "Motion." In reply to this problem, we must state the general rule on these matters which has often been stated before, and which is as follows, that if there are two opposed principles of any sort, then the One is neither both of them together, lest it become non-one and there would be something prior to it, causing the mixture of these opposites; nor is it simply the superior of these two opposites, lest it have something in conflict with it, and that should not be one, and not being one, should be composed of infinite parts infinitely multiplied, through its privation of oneness; nor can it be the inferior of the two, lest it should have something superior to it, and that this superior thing in itself should once again be composed of infinite parts infinitely multiplied. We must state, then,

---

[31] Proclus considers all these terms as relating to entities below the One. All the expressions—νοερὰ γαλήνη, πατρικὸς ὅρμος, and πατρικὴ σιγή—have a Chaldaean ring to them and recur frequently in Proclus. Cf. Saffrey and Westerink's notes at *PT* IV, 9, p. 30, n. 1, and *ibid.* 13, p. 43, n. 3.

[32] 139b2-3 corresponding to 138b6-7; cf. 1151.39ff. above.

that primary Rest and primary Motion take their start from themselves, and the one is stationary, and the other is in motion, as is the case with each of the Real Beings. So then, one and the same argument proves both that the One is not stationary and that it is not Rest Itself, for Rest is stationary, not as participating in some other rest, but as being of itself and taking its static power from itself. For rest in another is itself not at rest, even as motion in another is not in motion, but that which is so in itself is at rest, even as the corresponding motion is in motion; for after all, how would each of these, being superior to that which is in others, not be of itself and act towards itself?

1172

And so the One is prior to motion and before everything moved, and prior to rest and before everything stationary, so that not even if one were to talk of it as the most static of stationary things or the most active of things in motion, will we accept such terminology; for extreme cases of participations do not destroy the participation, but rather strengthen it. If, then, it does not remain stationary at all, it is not the most static of things; or else the phrase "the most static" is only empty words, and does not say anything about the One, or if it denotes the most stationary thing, it grants a higher degree of stationariness to something which is not in fact stationary at all. And again, if it is not in any way in motion, it is not the most active of all things; for if the phrase "most active" signifies nothing, it says nothing about the One; if on the other hand, it signifies that which participates most of all in motion, then it would not be the most active; for activity is a type of motion according to Plato, even if according to other authorities activity differs from motion. But it has been shown by us previously that the One is prior to all activity, since neither because of itself nor because of what it produces does it require activity.

"Further, the One cannot be either the same as another or the same as itself, nor yet other than itself or other than another." "Why is that?" (139b)

He is going through all of what are called the "genera of being" in the *Sophist* (256aff.) but figure here as symbols of divine and intellectual orders, and he shows how the One, while itself the cause of so-called transcendent negations,[33] yet does not participate in any of them, nor is any of them, in order that by means of this removal of all of these

---

[33] Ὑπεραπόφασις, a technical term of Stoic logic (Diog. Laert. VII, 69 = *SVF* II, 204), properly used of such a double negative as "It is not the case that it is not day," or ∼∼P. Presumably, in the case of the One, such a "hyper-negation" would be e.g. "It is not not at rest" or "not not the same." For the Stoics, the double negative simply equalled an affirmative, while in this case it signifies the One's transcendence of both sides of the opposition.

attributes he may show the One to be fixed above all the intellectual realms. For this attribute of "being same and other than itself and others" will appear clearly to characterise the whole demiurgic order,[34]

1173 even as what went before it characterised the life-producing and what went before that the highest level in the intellectual world; and these characteristics appear to be most fitting for the level of demiurgy according both to the teachings of Plato about it and also to those of the other theologians.

And yet some commentators[35] raise a difficulty here, taking these terms in an exclusively philosophical sense—Motion, Rest, Sameness, and Otherness—and not seeing that these things are to be seen in the context of the One, first of all, and not of Being, and that even as two kinds of number exist simultaneously, both the supra-essential and the essential, even so each of these pertains in a primary way to the henads, and only then to the realm of beings, and that these are symbols of actual divine orders and complete realms, and not just genera of being or Forms.

For how would it be possible, seeing that the Forms are of comprehensible extent, that these alone should be denied of the One, and not all Forms? Why, then, did he not go through all the Forms? But, as I said, some people, in calling these "genera of being," ⟨have declared⟩ that the genera of being are ⟨at every level⟩;[36] for they are classes of all things, they say, and they penetrate all levels of being, and the Primally Existent, whatever that is, comprehends all of these classes, in so far as it has proceeded forth from the supra-essential, having become Being, and in so far as it has assimilated itself towards what has produced it, acquiring Sameness instead of unity, while in so far as it has distinguished itself from the One, not being the One, it becomes Otherness. For where Sameness exists, there also is Otherness, distinction also having arisen by reason of the declination from unity in the Same. In so far as it proceeds forth, it is established in motion, while in so far as it is established in the One, even while it proceeds it has a share in stability. For in general processions, as they say, are the causes of motion

1174 and otherness in Being, while reversions are causes of sameness and rest.

Others[37] ⟨situate⟩ these genera in the intellectual realm, while main-

---

[34] That is, the third level of the intellectual realm. Cf. the parallel discussion in *PT* II, 12, p. 69.15ff. S-W.

[35] Again, the first of a threesome culminating in Syrianus, so probably Porphyry; φιλοσόφως μόνον ταῦτα λαμβάνοντες sounds like an anti-Porphyrian gibe.

[36] Accepting an emendation of Westerink, to give sense to the sentence.

[37] Probably Iamblichus. Cf. Proclus, *In Tim*. I, 230.5ff. (= Iambl. *In Tim*. fr. 29 Dillon), where Iamblichus is reported as declaring τὸ ἀεὶ ὄν to be on a higher level than τὰ γένη τοῦ ὄντος.

524

taining ⟨that these are genera of Being⟩;[38] for such a number could not derive its existence immediately from the One; it is necessary, then, as has often been drawn attention to elsewhere, that the multiplicity which manifests itself immediately from the One should be most akin to the One, constricted in quantity and incomprehensible in power, in order that through the constrictedness of its quantity it should imitate the quantitylessness of the One, and through the incomprehensibility of its power, the infinity of the One which is prior to power; but the pentad is remote from the One and goes beyond even the first order of numbers, by which I mean the triadic; but Plato has termed the summit of the realm of beings the One Being, as being the monad of Being; whereas the theologians celebrate intelligible monads and triads, but not pentads or other numbers; so then, the genera of being do not come immediately after the One.

Such, then, is the argument of those who raise these difficulties. But if we are to arbitrate the arguments of such famous and divine men, and that in spite of the fact that such an enquiry is beyond what is relevant to our present concerns, and that this matter has been examined by us at greater length elsewhere,[39] on the basis of the teaching of our master, we may at any rate make clear his judgement that considers both schools of opinion to speak rightly, both those which place the genera at every level and those who do not allow this number to be ranked directly after the One; for the genera are in the intelligible and in the intellectual realms according to the rank proper to them in each case, but in one way among the primal entities, and in another among the secondary—here intelligibly, there intellectually. And this is the same 1175 as to say here unitarily and indivisibly, and there divisibly each according to their own number, so that one should not wonder if the intelligible monad comprehends the whole intellectual pentad indivisibly and unitarily, where we find that subsumed under unity both Rest in some way and Motion are one, and also Sameness and Otherness, all being undivided "in the darkling mist," as the theologian says.[40] For where also the monad which is the cause of monadic numbers is shown to comprehend all the reason-principles which the decad comprehends decadically, and the tetrad tetradically, why should one wonder if on the plane of beings, the intelligible monad comprehends all the classes of being monadically and indivisibly, while some other order comprehends them dyadically, and yet another tetradically, since the Ideas are

[38] Accepting an emendation of Westerink.

[39] Perhaps a reference to the various discussions of the status of the γένη τοῦ ὄντος in the *Timaeus Commentary*, e.g. II, 135.21ff. where their operation at the level of Soul is discussed, or II, 160.6ff. where they are attached to the demiurgic level of Being.

[40] Orpheus *Hymn* 6.6.

also in the intelligible realm; but nevertheless we do not say that they exist in the same way as in the intellectual realm, but there as wholes, unitarily and paternally, whereas in this latter realm they exist separately, individually and demiurgically, but it is necessary that everywhere the number of the Ideas be dependent upon the genera of being? If, then, the intellectual Ideas partake of the intellectual species, it is plain that also the intelligible Ideas will partake of the intelligible species. If, then, at the limit of the intelligibles the primary ones among the Ideas are four,[41] there must be prior to the tetrad of Forms a monadic creation of the genera (genē);[42] for thus also in the intellectual realm prior to the decadic generation of the Ideas there exists a pentadic cause of the classes of being (genē).

About the classes of being, however, we will say more later on.[43] For the present, let us, if you will, examine the order in obedience to which he first denied Motion and Rest of the One, and then Sameness and Otherness. I have earlier myself stated the cause of this when I said that Motion and Rest are double, and that one form of them is prior to Sameness and Otherness, namely that according to which each thing proceeds from and returns to its causes, while another variety is subsequent to Sameness and Otherness, being observed in the activities of beings. Let us now state this in another way, taking our point of departure from the theses of the method earlier stated. In the First Hypothesis he denies things of the One; but the first things denied, as we made clear earlier, were "of itself in relation to itself," while the next test were "of itself in relation to itself and others," and yet another set simply "of itself in relation to others"; for multiplicity and wholeness and shape and being-in-something and motion and rest he denies of the One itself in relation to itself, whereas sameness and otherness, and like and unlike, and equal and unequal, and older and younger, he denies of it in relation to itself and to others (for the One is the same neither as itself nor as others, and it is other in the same way, and so for each of the other characteristics); while being an object of opinion or knowledge, or being nameable or utterable is denied of it in relation only to others; for it is unknowable to all things secondary to it in respect of all these cognitive activities.

Since, then, the negations are divided into three groups, the first of itself towards itself, the second of itself both towards itself and towards

---

[41] A reference to *Tim.* 39e7–40a2, the Essential Living Being being τὸ πέρας τῶν νοητῶν for Proclus; cf. *PT* III, 19, and *In Tim.* III, 105.14–107.26 Diehl.

[42] The word-play between εἰδητικῆς τετράδος and γενῶν I find it impossible to convey in translation, but Proclus is making a kind of contrast here between genera and species.

[43] Presumably in the exegesis of the Second Hypothesis.

others, the third towards others alone, the first being primary, the second being median, the third last, Motion and Rest are denied of the One of itself towards itself, whereas Sameness and Otherness are denied of it doubly, both in relation to itself and in relation to others, for which reason the former pair are ranked among the first set of negations, while these are ranked among the median set, and quite reasonably does he give an account first about the former and later about the latter. In the same way he will go on to deny like and unlike and equal and unequal and older and younger of it both in relation to itself and in relation to others, thus denying all these attributes of the One and, as they say,[44] depriving the One of substance, quality, quantity, and temporality; for these attributes pertain to these categories—sameness and otherness to substances, likeness and unlikeness to qualities, equal and

1177 unequal to quantities, and older and younger to temporal beings. And observe how here he denies these things, I mean sameness and otherness, of the One, knowing as he does that Parmenides in his Poem attributed these to the One Being. For he says, "It remains same in the same, and lies on its own" (fr. 8.29 D-K).

The One itself, then, established above One Being, must be shown to be in no way the same and, far less, other; for Sameness is more akin to the One. But he denies both this and Otherness of the One, in order that it may be shown to transcend One Being, in which Sameness is placed by Parmenides in his Poem, and Otherness as well[45]—not that those facts are disproved; rather these are added because of the acceptance of the former. For if that which partakes of Sameness and Otherness is not yet One in the true sense, it is necessary that the truly One should exist prior to these as being pure of these, or else in its participation in these it will not be solely One, being filled with what is alien to the One, for whatever you add to the One by its addition causes oneness to vanish, since it rejects the addition of everything that is alien to it.

"Were it other than itself it would be other than One, and so would not be One." "True." (139b)

There being four negative theses in respect of the One concerning Sameness and Otherness, he begins from those which are further from the One and more easily grasped by us, and thus proceeds through the rest. There are four of these theses: (1) that the One is not other than

---

[44] It is not clear to me to whom φασίν refers—perhaps to the sum-total of previous commentators. At any rate, they are connecting the genera of Being with the main four Aristotelian categories.

[45] In Parmenides' One there is, of course, no Otherness. Proclus can say this only because he equates it with his own ἓν ὄν.

itself; (2) that the One is not other than the others; (3) that the One is not the same as itself; and (4) that the One is not the same as the others. The clearest of these are the two extreme theses, for it is plain that it is not the same as the others, and that it is not other than itself; the remaining two are difficult to grasp, for how could one accept that it is not the same as itself, seeing that it is One, or how could one be persuaded that it is not other than the others, seeing that it is transcendent over them?

1178   Parmenides, then, starts from the clearest propositions and shows first that the One is neither other than itself nor the same as the others. And since of these two the more obvious is that the One is not other than itself, he first establishes this point by demonstration. For, as I said, Sameness is nearer to the One, while Otherness is more remote; and what is nearer is more difficult to remove, while what is more remote is easier, as being more separate from it. It is for this reason, indeed, that the dialecticians are accustomed to say that he who wishes to train himself must seek the dissimilarities in kindred things and the similarities in divergent things.

So much may be said, then, concerning the order of the theses. We must now say how he goes about demonstrating this first of the four, that the One is not other than itself; then in turn, if we can, we will speak about each of the others. He demonstrates it, then, in this way: if the One is other than itself, it would be necessarily other than one; for it itself is one, and that which is other than one is not one; for after all, that which is other than man is not man, and that which is other than horse is not horse, and in general that which is other than each thing is not that thing; if the One, then, is other than itself, the One is not one. But this is an absurdity, since it leads us round to a contradiction, viz. that the One is not one; therefore, the One is not other than itself.

One might raise against this proof the objection that Otherness also will be proved by this not to be other than itself; and yet this it must necessarily be. For each of real beings takes its start of activity from itself, as has been said many times, and the Eleatic Stranger (*Soph.* 258d) stated that the nature of the Other, in being other than the other classes of being, was in this respect itself not-being, even as were Motion and Rest. But if Otherness is other than itself; it will be other than Otherness, and it will not be Otherness, even as the One would not be one; therefore, Otherness is not other than itself. One might reply, perhaps, that Otherness takes its start of activity from itself and makes itself
1179 other, but not other than itself, but rather than others; for it is able to distinguish those too from each other, and itself far more so from them, and thus it acts upon itself by preserving itself unmixed with the others. And if you wish to speak still more truly, you could say that

Otherness, in so far as it is other than itself, is not otherness; for it is other than itself by participating in the other classes of being also; in this respect therefore it is not otherness, in so far as it participates in other things than itself; and this is not an absurd conclusion in the case of Otherness, because it is a multiplicity; but in the case of the One it would be absurd, for it is only one and nothing else. But the negation must be made in respect of something itself, and not something else; I mean, for instance, if something is other than man, one may say that it is not man, and if it is other than white, one may say that this is not white; but one should not say, since Dion is other than Man, seeing that the one is an individual and the other a Form, that Dion is not a man; for he is not the Form itself, of which he was said to be other; for he is not Man; but he participates in the Form, and thus he is man, as being by participation an individual man.

"And if it were the same as another, it would be that other, and not be itself; so that in this case, again, it would not be just what it is, one, but other than one." "In no way." (139bc)

This is the second of the four propositions, easier to grasp than those which follow it, but more difficult than that which preceded it. It also rests firmly on the fact that the One accepts no characteristic from other things; for this axiom is supremely true, both of the One and of all the other divine causes. For neither does the heaven accept anything of mortal unpleasantness into itself, nor does the Demiurge accept anything from the creation in the cosmos, nor do the intelligibles from the intellectual multiplicity and from the division that is proper to them, so that it is not possible either for the One to be filled with any characteristic of beings. In no way, then, is it the same as the others; for then either it would participate in them, or it would be participated in by them, or else both it and they would participate in some other One. But it is not possible on the one hand for them both to participate in some One; for there is nothing superior to the One nor more one than it; for in that case there would be something prior to the One; for ascent is to the One, not to a multiplicity. Superior principles are always more unitary, as Soul is than body, ⟨Intellect than soul, and the One than Intellect. Nor does it in turn participate in others;⟩[46] for it does not accept anything from them, since they are worse. Nor is it participated in by them, for it transcends all beings equally, and the participated One is something else than it, while the primally One and the object of striving for all beings stands unparticipated, prior to the totality of things, in order that it may remain one, devoid of multiplicity; for that which

1180

---

[46] Lacuna in Greek, filled from Latin.

is participated in is not completely one. So then in no way is the One the same as the others.

This conclusion, indeed, one might reach from common sense, to conclude that the argument is true; but let us also examine the proof of Parmenides, which is as follows: if the One is the same as any other of all things, it would be the same as something which is not one; for it itself is the One, and at the same time it is clear through this that it is inconceivable for the truly one to be two; for it is plain that these two would be different from each other. Each then, being one and differing from the other, by reason of this difference would no longer be one. The One, then, is only one; that which is other than it is therefore not-one. If, then, the One is the same as another, it is the same as a thing which is not one; for that which is the same as the One is one, even as that which is the same as not-man is not a man. If, then, the One is the same as something other than itself, the One will not be one; if it is not one, it will be other than one, which was shown before to be absurd.

It would have sufficed for the proof of the hypothesis to reduce the statement to a contradiction by means of the "three-term argument."[47] Nevertheless he adds this point also, that of its being other than one, in order that by means of demonstrating the immediately ensuing absurdity he may reveal this hypothesis also as being unsound. In the same way, one might demonstrate that Sameness Itself is in a way not sameness, if it were shown to be in some way the same as Otherness, or some other of beings apart from itself. For let it be postulated that Sameness is the same as Otherness in so far as it partakes of Otherness. 1181 If, then, that which is the same as Otherness is other and not the same, Sameness will be other and not the same. And there is nothing strange in this; for it is Sameness by its own essence, but other by participation in Otherness; and that becomes the same by participating in it; and this is perhaps the most paradoxical consequence, namely that that which has come to be the same as the nature of the Other should become other.

Thus the argument when conducted in the case of the One is true, because the One has neither any genus prior to it nor any species, whereas those things which have prior to them a genus or a species— as for instance Man and Horse, or Socrates and Zeno—being the same

---

[47] The argument-form διὰ τριῶν is part of Stoic logic, but authorities differ as to its nature. Michael Frede, *Stoische Logik*, p. 182, first seems to favour the form: "If *p*, then *q*; if *r*, then q; either *p* or *r*; so *q*," but that does not fit here. The immediately preceding argument, if that is what Proclus is referring to, runs: "If *p*, then ~*q*; if ~*q*, then r; so, if *p*, then *r*," and an argument of this form is given this name, as Frede also points out (p. 183) by Alexander of Aphrodisias, (e.g. *In An. Pr.* 326.9 Wallies) and by Themistius, Philoponus, and Ammonius, so this seems more likely to be correct. Chrysippus wrote a treatise on the subject, Diog. Laert. VII, 191.

in respect of genus or species, are no longer completely the same as each other; but it is necessary that there should not be prior to the One either genus or species, lest the One should come to be, by participating in genus or species, not one. For that which participates in a genus has something over and above the genus, and that which participates similarly in a species has something over and above the species; and in general everything which participates in something has something over and above that in which it participates; for if it had nothing, it itself would be completely that thing, and would not merely participate in it. If, then, the One is neither in a genus nor in a species and is the same as some other thing, it would be that thing with which it is the same, since it would not be the same as something that is other than it.

"Therefore the One will not be the same as another, or other than itself."
"No indeed." (139c)

This comes as the common conclusion of the two first propositions, which have a connection with each other in so far as they may be taken as complementing each other, the one expressing otherness to itself, the second sameness towards the others; for Otherness would seem to call rather for being connected with the others, while Sameness, with relation to itself. Therefore these former propositions are easier of proof; for they are more inappropriate to the One. The following propositions are more difficult, for otherness towards the others is nearer to the One by reason of the transcendent superiority of the One, and sameness towards itself is nearer to it because of its unutterable and indescribable super-unity[48]—"sameness" and "otherness," of course, having two senses, for we call "same" both Sameness and that which participates in Sameness, and "other" similarly both Otherness and that which participates in Otherness. The argument will show as it proceeds that in neither sense is the One other or the same; for neither as Otherness nor as other is it other than the others; nor either as Sameness or as participating in Sameness is it the same as itself; in what sense we are to take this we will learn as we proceed.

"Nor can it be other than another, so long as it is one. To be other than something properly belongs, not to 'One,' but only to an 'Other than another,' and to nothing else." "Correct." "So in so far as it is One it will not be Other; or do you think so?" "No indeed." "But if not in this way, then not in virtue of being itself; and if not in virtue of being itself then not as itself; and if as itself it is not in any sense other, it cannot be other than anything." "Correct." (139c)

[48] Proclus here uses, it seems uniquely, the term ὑπερένωσις.

531

Of the two remaining propositions, he once again takes for proof the easier before the other; and it is easier to deny of the One itself that which lies further from the One. And such is Otherness, as has been often stated; for Sameness is more akin to the One, for which reason it has a nature which is difficult to distinguish from it and which requires more argument. For this too should be noted in this connection, that it is the length of the argument that is the measure of the clarity or obscurity of the subject matter, in order that he may not be indulging in anything uselessly or without substantive need. So then, for this reason, he will say more about the fourth proposition, and he has said least about the first, and less about the second than about the third.

So much, then, about the order of the argument. So, as we have said, since "other" is taken in two senses, in regard to each he denies that the One is other; and first he denies it as not participating in Otherness, for the One as One does not participate in Otherness—otherwise, it would not be one through such participation—but everything that is termed 1183 "other than another" is so termed because of its otherness; for the One as One is not other because it does not partake in Otherness; for only to what is other is proper the quality of being other than another, but not to the One; and such is that which partakes in Otherness. But if the One is going to be other by virtue of Otherness, it will participate in Otherness; for "one" is one thing and "other" is another, the one being an absolute expression, the other a relative one, so that the other is not other to the One, but to that which it makes other.

He goes on from this to show that the One is not Otherness either; for what if it is not other as participating in Otherness, but is Otherness itself? But neither is this, he says, true; for if it is not other as being One, it will not be other to the One; and if it is not other to the One, neither will it be itself Otherness. A most inspired conclusion; for Otherness is other to itself and through itself, but the One is not other to itself, but in fact the concepts of One and Other are entirely different; so therefore, the One is not Otherness.

If, then, the One is not other than itself, it is not Otherness either; and this is what he himself has said so succinctly: "If it is not in virtue of being itself, then it is not as itself," that is to say, if it is not other in relation to itself as being One, because "one" is different from "other," then neither is it Otherness itself; for in that case it would be one and the same thing to say that it is other to the One, and other than Otherness, if indeed the One is to be Otherness, which the argument has disproved.

Having said this, he produces a general conclusion as follows: that if as itself it is not in any sense "other," neither as Otherness nor as participating in Otherness, then "it cannot be other than anything." For

everything which is other than something is either Otherness itself or participates in Otherness; but the One neither is Otherness nor participates in Otherness; therefore it is not other than anything. And in general, if Sameness is the contrary of Otherness, and Sameness is superior to Otherness, it is in no way proper to associate the worse of the pair with the One; but it is either identical with neither or with the better of the two, as we have said above. Otherness, then, is in some way in the
1184 position of contrary to the One, if such an expression is not improper, in so far as the One is the cause of unity, while Otherness is the cause of division. Sameness, on the other hand, through its holding together of beings and bringing them into community, imitates the unity which proceeds from the One. In no way, then, is the One other, but it is rather more same than other. However, it is not same either, as will become plain as we proceed.

Someone might perhaps raise against us a difficulty by asking how the One can be said to be transcendent over all things if it is not other than them; for what is transcendent is distinct from those things which it transcends, and it will be separate from everything which is divided from it; and everything which is divided is divided in virtue of Otherness; for as we said, Otherness is divisive, while Sameness is cohesive.

In reply to this I would say that the One does transcend beings and is separate from them, but it does not hold this separate and transcendent position of seniority in virtue of Otherness, but rather through another unspeakable superiority, and not such as Otherness provides to beings. It is like the use of the word *always* in connection with the cosmos, and in the case of Intellect; this *always* is not used in the same way for both of them, but in the one case it is temporal, and in the other eternal and beyond all time; even so, Intellect is transcendent over Soul, and so is the One over beings in general, but in the case of Intellect this transcendence is achieved through Otherness, which causes distinctions among beings and, in the case of the One, in a mode prior to Otherness; for Otherness imitates the transcendence and the unmixed nature of the One, even as Sameness imitates its unspeakable unity; so it is separated from all things in a different way to the way in which Otherness separates beings from each other. And this is clear also in the case of what we may term opposites; for one cannot say that the absolutely non-existent is other than being, because what is other, although non-existent in one sense, is yet existent;[49] and that which is non-existent in this sense is no less existent for that, as Plato says (*Soph.* 258a); and how
1185 if it were in no way existent could it participate in any genus of being?

---

[49] The μὴ ὄν of Plato, *Sophist* 257b is simply "not-x," and distinct from the μηδαμῶς ὄν of 240e. For the misquotation παρ᾽ἔλαττον in *Sophist* 258b1-2, cf. above n. 51 to Book VI (at 1072.34).

⟨Therefore, even as the absolutely non-existent is not⟩ other ⟨than beings⟩,[50] lest in becoming other it should be banished from all sorts of being, so the One is transcendent over all beings, but is not transcendent because it is other, lest in being other it should no longer be transcendent over all beings; for one must not transpose the negation according to which it is no one of all things into an assertion arising from the negations; for being other is an assertion; in fact, even the notion of transcendence we do not use in a proper sense in speaking of the One nor any other of those terms which properly refer to beings.

> *"Nor yet can it be the same as itself." "Why not?" "That which the nature of the One is, such will surely not be the nature of the same?" "Why not?" "Because when a thing becomes the same as something, it does not become one." "But why?" "For instance, if it becomes the same as the many, it must become many, not one." "True." "Whereas if there were no difference whatever between unity and sameness, whenever a thing became the same it would always become one, and whenever one, the same." "Certainly." "So if the One is to be the same as itself, it will not be one with itself; and thus it will be one and not one." "But this is impossible."*
> (139de)

This is the fourth of the propositions, that the One is not the same as itself, neither as Sameness nor as participating in Sameness. And first of all, he shows that it is not as Sameness; for if the One is Sameness, then everything that participates in Sameness by that very token becomes one, in so far as it partakes of the same—for it must inevitably become one in other respects, and to the extent that Sameness is secondary in rank to the One,[51] for there is nothing without unity; for even Otherness creates everything that it creates with the help of unity; since for anything at all to exist without participation in unity is utterly impossible. So, in so far as anything will be the same, to this extent it will be necessarily one, if Sameness is the One. But in fact there is something which in so far as it partakes in Sameness becomes many, as for instance "that which becomes the same as the many and not one"; so, therefore, the One is not identical with Sameness. For even as that which has become the same as horse is horse, and that which has become the same as white is white, and the same as black, black, and in the case of everything whatever, that which has been assimilated to some species receives in every case the form of that to which it is said to be identified, so that which has become the same as the many by becoming many has become the same as the many. So then that which

---

[50] Adopting Westerink's supplement for what is plainly a lacuna in the MSS.
[51] A tentative rendering of a corrupt passage.

has become the same as the many, in so far as it is many, is the same as them; but in so far as it is many it is impossible for it to be one. Therefore, the One is not Sameness; for in that case all things that partook of Sameness by the same token would also become One. But it has been shown in the case of the many that Sameness is not the One, by reason of the, as it were, oppositeness of the many to the One.

Having demonstrated this, he goes on to show that the One is not the same, either, in the sense of participating in Sameness; for if it is the same as itself in the sense of participating in Sameness which is something other than it, the One will not be one; for it will be, through participating in Sameness, both one and something else which it is not, and it will no longer preserve the characteristic of the One, since it will have become a multiplicity instead of one. And all this he has summed up succinctly by saying that "if the one is to be the same as itself, it will not be one with itself"; for Sameness has been shown to be other than the One. Therefore, the whole argument is contained in this potentially; everything that is the same as something either partakes in Sameness or is itself the same; but the One neither partakes in Sameness as something other than it, lest in partaking in something else besides the One it should not be One, nor is it itself Sameness, for it is not the case that what are true of Sameness are also true of the One. For it is possible for the Many to be the same as the Many, but not possible for them to be one as long as they are many. So then, the One is not Sameness, neither as participating in Sameness, nor as being able to be the same (as anything).

The argument as a whole is more or less of this sort. But someone 1187 might raise against us the objection—to begin from the last section—as to where and in what passage he has shown that there is something that becomes one and not the same. That that which becomes the same does not in all cases in virtue of this become also one let us assume to have been demonstrated, because that which becomes the same as many does not become one, but many; but once this alone has been demonstrated, why does he bring on two more inferences, saying, "Whenever something would become the same, it would always become one, and when it became one, the same," if Sameness and One were the same.

It may be said in reply that following the same line of argument we shall add this also: "For if anything becomes one, it becomes other than the many; and yet if Sameness and One were the same, it would be necessary that that which became one would straightway become the same also, and not other; for even as that which is the same as the many is not one, so the One is not the same as the Many."

But one might say that that which becomes one, not being one previously, becomes different from those things which are not one, and becomes the same as itself, and the reason why it is other than what is not one is that it is the same as itself. One might answer to this that that which becomes one of necessity becomes other than those things which are not one, but does not bring with it the notion of sameness in so far as it is one; for it becomes other than what is not one in virtue of contrariety, but it is *qua* one that the One is one; since it is not a relative concept; for it is absolute, while "the same" is a relative term. So for something to become one does not imply sameness; for in all cases absolute concepts preexist relative ones, for which reason that which becomes one is not in every case the same, because absolute terms are prior to what is relative; and "same" is one of the relative terms, for something may at the same time be both not the same and one. So then, Sameness and the One are not absolutely one.

For this reason Plato, relying on this argument, has added that if the One were Sameness, then what is the same would be one *qua* the same, and the One same *qua* One; but that which is the same as the many was plainly many and, in virtue of this, not one, and that which becomes one is not yet the same as anything.

Again, some will raise the problem as to how we say that something "becomes the same as the many"; for it would seem more proper to say "equal," not "same." One may reply to them that there is an essential Multiplicity among beings, and there is another multiplicity which comes in from the outside and is accidental, and the one is to be found among Forms, while the other exists in material things; when essential Multiplicity and Number come to have the same number, not that number which exists in numbered things, but that which is number in the pure sense, then multiple *A* is said to become "the same" as multiple *B*, but not "equal"; for community in essence is sameness, whereas equality in respect of some quantity is not essential quantity. For even as in the sphere of quality, there is one thing which is quality alone, and there is another which defines quality in respect of essence, even so, in the sphere of quantity, there is one thing which is quantity proper, and another which is quantity in essence; and when two such quantities join with one another, they join through sameness, even as also essential qualities join to one another through sameness, not through likeness. So much, then, for that problem.

The philosopher indicates in this passage also that it is possible for Sameness to coexist with Otherness and Multiplicity. But Unity, and the One, is said to be above any linkage with Multiplicity; for if it is possible for the Many to partake in Sameness, but not for them to be one in so far as they are many, although they are by reason of this the same as others because they are many, it is plain that Sameness exists

536

also in multiplicities, but Oneness desires to transcend multiplicity. Whence it is with reason demonstrated that the One is not Sameness; for Sameness does not stand apart from Multiplicity, whereas the One is outside all things multiple. For each order of beings brings in something also with itself in every case which did not exist prior to it; for instance, the realm of generation has change of essence which the heavenly realm does not have, and the heavens possess circular spatial motion which the Soul of itself does not have, and Soul has transitive thought which Intellect does not have, and Intellect has a striving towards the intelligible which Being does not have, and Being has Sameness and Otherness, which the One itself transcends, having no need of either of these, either Sameness (for it has a simplicity which is superior to Sameness) nor Otherness (for it has a superiority which is greater than Otherness).

1189

> *"Consequently it is equally impossible for the One to be either other than another or the same as itself." "It is impossible."* (139e)

He has produced here a common conclusion for the two propositions just demonstrated; for he says that "it is impossible for the One either to be other than any things or the same as itself"; One must not take this either as indicating weakness and deficiency of power, nor on the other hand as superfluity of power; for there is also an impossibility of this kind (even as we are accustomed to say that it is impossible for the good man to sin), but rather the transcendence which is superior to all power. For in this sense impotence may be truly predicated of the One, as being superior to all potency which proceeds from it, both that which is productive of otherness and that which is productive of sameness among beings; for thence proceeds both that Limit which is the author of all sameness in beings, and the Unlimitedness which is generative of all distinction and division. Even as, then, it is above all Limit and above all Unlimitedness, even so it is above all Sameness and far more so above all Otherness, both the divine and that which exists in beings.

If, then, there were some divine order which should be characterised by them,[52] most of all the divine orders, the One would be transcendent over this also; and being same or other would make manifest the order of the gods which proceeds from it, particularly according to these two modes.

> *"Thus the One cannot be other than, or the same as, either itself or another." "No indeed."* (139e)

[52] Sc. Sameness and Otherness. The order referred to is the third intellectual order, which the One is shown here to transcend.

This is the common conclusion of all the four propositions, reverting back to the first premise,[53] but expressed somewhat differently. For there he said that the One was "neither the same as another nor as itself," separating off first of all the same from the other, and then the other (from the same); but here he has added the other and the same together to produce a division comprising both, adding, "either to itself or to another," and he has begun from the other and ended with the 1190 other, both through his conciseness and through his beginning and ending with the same element imitating the cycle of intellectual activity.

So much, then, for that. Perhaps, however, someone would ask us again, after these proofs have been presented, if perhaps the others than the One might not be other than it; for the others seem to bring along with them also the suggestion that they are other than the One; for they are certainly not the same; for they are not also One. But perhaps, as we said, the fact is that the Many[54] *qua* other are necessarily also in all ways "other" (*alla*), but are not other (*hetera*) than the One. For as he himself has declared, what is "other than" (*heteron*) is other than another; and so, even if they should be called "others" (*alla*) and other than the One, one would not say it in the sense that they have made a procession from it by means of Otherness; for in that case Otherness would be second after the One and median between the One and the Many, in order that these should proceed in accordance with it. But let us grant that there is a declination[55] from the One to these; but not every declination is the product of Otherness, but only that declination which is in the realm of the Forms. Wherefore everything that is other than its proper cause is also in declination from it, but not everything that has declined is in a relation of Otherness to that cause of itself.

Perhaps also one might express it thus, that the others than the One are other than the One by virtue of having made their departure from the One, which has been rendered other than them by means of the Otherness which has entered into them; for by being differentiated from that which is exempt from differentiation by reason of its simplicity, they have been allotted an inferior rank, so that they will also be called other than the One, since by becoming other than each other, they are separated from the One, which absolutely rejects the title of reciprocal otherness. So then, since there are two, or rather three, types

[53] Cf. 1151.39, and 1171.14 above.

[54] Excising τὸ πολλὰ τοῦ ἑνός, line 10, with Westerink. It is meaningless as it stands, and probably a gloss (Moerbeke reads τοῦ πολλὰ τοῦ ἑνός, which is no help).

[55] The concept of ὕφεσις as a technical term seems to go back to Porphyry (e.g. *Sent.* 11, p. 5.2 Lamberz; ὑφέσει δυνάμεως) but not to Plotinus. For the theory of declination, cf. *ET*, props. 28-29, 36, 63-64.

of otherness in beings—the one that of superiors, the other that of inferiors, the third that of coordinates—in the supra-essential realm, instead of the otherness of superior forms to inferior, we must postulate transcendence, instead of that of inferior to superior, declination, and
1191 in place of the distinction of coordinates from each other, individual peculiarity. Everything, then, is in declination from the One, and the One is transcendent over all things, and neither is the One other than the others nor are the others other than the One. If, then, by chance we use terms loosely in talking of the others than the One, we must be pardoned, in view of popular usage. For that in fact we say nothing in the proper sense about the One, we will hear the philosopher demonstrating a little later. Nevertheless, we do talk about it because of the natural striving of the soul towards the One.

"Nor can the One be like or unlike anything, whether itself or another."
"Why ever not?" (139e)

He has moved at this point from one order of being to the next one after it, as we shall show in the Second Hypothesis, and specifically from the demiurgic order to that order which is celebrated by other authors as the assimilative,[56] the characteristic of which is that it is the sole supracosmic entity through which both everything in the cosmos and all the transcendent classes are assimilated to the intellectual gods, and are joined to the demiurgic monad, which transcendently rules over all and shows how the One by transcending this also yet is generative of it, if it is permissible to say so, showing forth this whole order along with those prior to it and not denying any single intellectual form. For there is nothing remarkable or awesome in this, if the One transcends some one single form, Likeness or Unlikeness for instance, nor must the present argument be thought to concern itself with these; for the Forms are very numerous, and it would not be possible to say for what reason he has left some out, while using others apart from the rest in connection with the separation of them from the One. But it is plain to those who have made divisions among the divine classes that he is showing the One to be superior to all classes, raising up to the One a single theological hymn by means of all these negations. We are, then,
1192 not going to accept the argument that he is simply following the ten categories,[57] taking same and other from substance, like and unlike

---

[56] The ἀφομοιωτικὴ τάξις of gods (otherwise known as ἡγεμονικοί) is discussed by Proclus in *PT* VI, 1-14, while their separation from the One is stated *ibid*. II, 12, p. 70.15-28 S-W. Since the title for them used here seems to derive from the identification with the present conclusion (or rather, with its equivalent in the Second Hypothesis, to which Proclus refers), the "other authors" referred to here can only be Syrianus, since he is the inventor of this exegesis.

[57] He has alluded to this view above, 1176.30ff. Cf. n. 34.

from quality, equal and unequal from quantity, and older and younger from time. And yet this is true and we have already said so ourselves but all these categories are among the things of sense and concern the sense world; but since Plato is dealing with supracosmic orders of being and showing that the One transcends them also, there would be nothing worthy of note even if one were to show that the One was free of every one of the categories, and especially if one follows those who make the categories inferior to the intelligible realm.[58] For how would there be any accidental quality there, and how are we to postulate substance there, which is such as to have especially the characteristic of "being the same and numerically one while being receptive of opposites?"[59] For neither is it the case that such a unity has any place in the intelligible and eternal nature, nor do the genera and species which are less honourable than such substances, seeing that neither do these substances themselves, though they are more honourable than them, nor far more so do the accidents which are dimmer in nature than such genera and species. So even if we say that the whole intelligible essence is free from such celebrated categories, what superiority would this removal of these show for the One which is above the intelligible world? So then let us leave aside for these reasons the categories, whether or not those who make much of them distinguished them properly; for it matters nothing for the present purpose. But if someone thinks that what is being negated here is certain intelligible or intellectual Forms, we have already said to such a one that there would be nothing astonishing even in this, if the One were to transcend any one Form, seeing 1193 as it is the cause of all the intelligibles. For even the henad of Intellect[60] transcends these, in virtue of which Intellect is one-like and is, as it were, especially rooted in the One itself, and all beings are connected with it through the One in themselves, but especially Intellect, seeing that this comes (directly) after the One.

But if we are to make any statement to reveal the nature of the present negations also, one must say that the whole assimilative order proceeds from the demiurgic monad and imitates the sameness there by means of its likeness, showing forth its collective and universally cohesive aspect in a more partial manner, while it imitates the demiurgic otherness by means of its unlikeness, mirroring its divisive and distinguishing aspect by means of its purity which is unmixed with the extreme points of its realm. To call, as some of our predecessors have

---

[58] As does Plotinus, for example, in *Enn.* VI, 1-3.
[59] Aristotle *Cat.* 5.4a10-11 (quoted by Plotinus, *Enn.* VI, 1.2.16-18).
[60] For this entity, see *ET*, props. 160-161, and *PT* III, 9.

been pleased to do,[61] likeness a "slack" form of sameness, or unlikeness a "slack" otherness, must, however, be avoided; for there is no such thing among the gods as slackening or tightening up, nor is there any unboundedness in the direction of more and less, but all things are fixed in their own bounds and their own measures, and are not capable of entertaining any tightening or slackening. What would be more suitable would be to use expressions which clarify the analogical relationships which hold among the divine realms; for Plato himself has applied analogy to the gods, when he makes the sun analogous on the visible level to its counterpart on the intelligible level. So then, likeness is in the secondary realms what Sameness is in those prior to them, and unlikeness similarly answers to Otherness, ⟨and what Sameness is on the level of whole and source, that⟩[62] likeness is on the level of part and, as it were, "principle," and the first offspring of Sameness and Otherness are the like and the unlike. For the equal and the unequal spring from there, but prior to these are likeness and unlikeness; but the like is more general among the Forms than the equal and the unlike than the unequal, ⟨and even as these depend immediately upon the Same and the Other, so does the assimilative or hegemonic order⟩[63] immediately depend upon the demiurgic monad; for in it in general the whole assimilative causal principle has its prior existence. Therefore it is that Timaeus presents the Demiurge there not only as creating the cosmos, but also as assimilating it to the Essential Living Being to a greater degree than before (*Tim.* 37d), and for this reason he presents the whole of time as being a measure of the circuits of the universe, even as eternity preexisted as a measure of the nature of the Essential Living Being.

It is with reason, then, that after dealing with the demiurgic monad he proceeded to the assimilative order, removing this also from the One; and the order of the propositions is the same as in the previous section; for there are four propositions here too, namely, (1) if the One is like itself, (2) if the One is unlike itself, (3) if the One is like the Others, (4) if the One is unlike the Others. The proofs of these, that none of them is suitable to the One, all take their start from Sameness and Otherness, since according to the canons of demonstration the

1194

---

[61] Possibly a reference to Iamblichus, who makes use of the concepts of ἄνεσις and ἐπίτασις in his Commentary on the *Categories* (*ap.* Simpl. *In Cat.* 231.6ff.), in connection with distinguishing between ἕξεις and διαθέσεις in the category of Quality. It would not be like Iamblichus, one would think, to postulate degrees of relaxation and tension in connection with gods, but then he would not be doing so here, as such an identification is an innovation of Syrianus!

[62] Adopting Westerink's necessary filling of a lacuna. The contrast between πηγαίως and ἀρχικῶς can be explained by the fact that in *PT* VI, 1, the ἡγεμονικοί or ἀφομοιωτικοί θεοί are designated ἀρχαί, as opposed to their superiors, who are πηγαί.

[63] Lacuna here in Greek MS filled from Latin translation.

middle terms are in the proper sense the causes of the fact. For which reason in many cases he does not base his proof upon what has previously been proved; for it is not always the case that those which are higher and prior in order are generative of what are secondary to them, but they may be completive or protective or in other respects exercise providence over them, but they do not in all cases generate them. For consider back from the beginning, if you will, the order of propositions. He demonstrated the thesis that it had neither whole nor parts on the basis of the concept of many, for thence proceeds the totality of the intellectual realm; that it has neither beginning nor middle nor end he derived from the fact that it is neither a whole nor has parts, for it is from these that they are produced immediately; that it is neither straight nor curved he derived from the fact of its neither being a whole nor having parts, for being in itself and in another proceeds from that order and not from that of shape, although it is ranked immediately before it in the order of propositions. That it is neither at rest nor in motion he derives from many sources, both from its not being in anything and from its not having a middle and from its not having parts; for the order of being at rest and in motion proceeds from all these orders.

1195

All these things we shall make clear when we coordinate each of these propositions to the teachings of the theologians about the divine processions. Even as, then, he has made his proof in the case of these from those entities which lie before the order under examination in each case as causes, even so also in his discussions of likeness and unlikeness he has produced his conclusions negating these of the One from Sameness and Otherness, since the order of their procession is from those. Having said this by way of introduction, we must now next examine the proofs themselves, dealing with each in order.

> "Because a like thing is a thing which has an identical character." "Yes."
> "But we have seen that the character 'same' is distinct from the character 'one'." "We have." "Now if the One has any character distinct from being One, it must have the character of being more things than One; and this is impossible." "Yes." "So it is quite impossible that the One should be a thing 'having the same character' as either another or itself." "It seems not." "Therefore the One cannot be like another or like itself." "It seems not." (139e–140a)

The syllogism asserting of the One that it is not like either itself or another is somewhat of this sort: according to the geometricians, once we have first defined what "like" is—namely, that that which has the same character as something we say is "like" that which it has the same character as; for we say that two white things and two black things are like, as having the same characters, black and white, and again if you

say that black and white are like one another, you will be saying that
they are like by reason of the fact that they partake in the same genus,
colour. So the syllogism is as follows: the One has no character the
same either as itself or as another; that which is like either itself or another has some character the same; the One, therefore, is not like either
itself or another. Such being the syllogism, then, he has deemed only
one of the premises to be in need of defence, that which states that the
One has not any character the same either as itself or as another. How
and in what way? The One, he says, is plainly separated from Sameness; for it has been shown that it is no way the same; but that which is
separate from Sameness, if it were to have the same character as something, will be many and not one; for everything that has any character
whatever is many, both what it is and the character it possesses. And
what is there astonishing in that, seeing that the One itself, if it acquires
a character, is many? For even the One itself does not have the character
of oneness, but that is reserved for the many which partake in the One;
the One itself is one, and does not partake of the character of one; if it
has any character beside itself, it would be more and not one. And
again it must be said: if the One is separate from Sameness, it does not
have the character of same, lest it then come about that it has some
other characteristic which is not itself and thus becomes not one; but in
fact the One is separate from Sameness; in no way, then, does the One
have the character of Sameness either towards itself or towards another; from this it follows that the One is like neither itself nor another;
for what is like has some character which is the same.

Enough, then, about the order of the premises; but observe how
carefully he has not said that the One has the character of one, but that
it has no other character except "being one"; for it *is* this, and does not
have it as a character; for everything that has any character is many; for
by characteristic he means participation in some other thing. We may
assume also that in saying that the One has no other characteristic than
being the One, he is hinting in a truly remarkable way that even the
One is an inadequate description of the first principle of all things,
which is what he is going to say at the end of the present hypothesis
(141e), and that human discourse attributes even this to it as an unsuitable title, even though it is more suitable than others, because it is not
even possible to conceive anything more august than the One, so that
even the One will be characterised by that highest principle. But discourse must come to a halt at this point and not add anything more, lest
unawares we involve that which is superior even to oneness in multiplicity.

But if someone were to enquire this in turn, whence comes it that
that which has the same character is "like," we must reply that Likeness

543

is the offspring of Sameness, even as Sameness is of the One. Sameness, then, participates in the One, and Likeness participates in Sameness; for "having a characteristic" consists in participating in another and proceeding forth in accord with another causal principle senior to itself. And observe how—since he is talking of participating and not participating now in the case of the One, not as in something superior to it, but as in something inferior and dependent upon the One, as will be the case in the Second Hypothesis, or not dependent on it, as in this one— in order that he may not cause confusion by using the same word, he has described participation in something superior as a "character" (*pathos*), saying that the like has the "character" of sameness, and the unlike that of otherness; for the latter are more universal than the former; for as we said, the equal and the unequal are same and other in the sphere of quantity. And in the same way in the *Sophist* also (244e) he called participation a character and said that the whole had oneness as a character, not being the One itself but participating in the One.

> *"But neither is it true that the One has the characteristic of being other; for in that case again, the One would have more characteristics than being one." "More, indeed." "But that which has the characteristic of otherness either than itself or than another would be unlike either itself or another, if it is the case that that which has the characteristic of sameness is like." "Correct." "So the One, as it seems, through in no way having the character of otherness, is in no way unlike either itself or another." "No indeed."* (140ab)

Here in turn the syllogism is more or less of this sort: the One does not have the character of other, either in relation to itself or to another; that which is unlike has some character of otherness either in relation to itself or to another; the One therefore is not unlike. Whence, then, does he derive that the One does not have the characteristic of Otherness? That it in no way partakes in Otherness has been said already. But that which has been made other plainly of necessity participates in Otherness. If, then, it is not possible for the One to be anything else but one, in order that the One may not become more than one, it would not suffer the characteristic of being other. But whence comes it that the unlike suffers the characteristic of being other, either than itself or than another? Because the unlike is on the same side of the list[64] as Otherness. So then, even as Otherness participates in Unlimitedness, so Unlikeness partakes in Otherness; for everything that is unlike is also other, while not everything that is other is automatically also unlike; for essential Otherness is not unlikeness but the community of po-

1198

---

[64] That is, of the Pythagorean Table of Opposites.

tencies brings about likeness and their differentiation brings about the unlikeness that is its opposite.

So it appears from these arguments that it is not the case that Likeness is the same as Sameness, or Unlikeness as Otherness; nor are they other than the latter but established as superior to them in rank; but each of them is secondary after their counterpart, even as Plato has ranked them. For Sameness is more comprehensive than Likeness, and Otherness than Unlikeness, and they have the same relation to these as "founts," in the terminology of the theologians, have to the principles that proceed from them, or which the most universal monads have to more particular monads, which are generated in a primary way from them but exhibit an inferior essence and power; and even if some authorities,[65] slightly deviating from the notion of descent, term this "slackening," they are perhaps not being unreasonable.

> *"Therefore the One cannot be either like or unlike either another or itself." "It seems not."* (140b)

This is the common conclusion of the four propositions, and he has preserved the same form in presentation as the premise (139e7-8); for there, having presented like and unlike, he added in common to both of them the phrase "neither to itself nor to another." He has done this in a manner suitable to this assimilative order of being, here also assimilating the end of the discussions about it to the beginning. He proceeded differently in the case of the first conclusions, inasmuch as each of these orders turned in upon itself and did not depart from itself.

If someone were to raise the problem whether the others than the One are like the One or not (for indeed some[66] are accustomed to call Intellect an image of the One as being unitary and partless, seeing as the One is partless)—if, then, one were to raise this point, what such likeness would be and how it would not also be the case that the One would not be like the others, we will say that Likeness, whether we regard it as genus or species of being, or whether on the other hand it is said to be the whole assimilative order of gods, does not make all things like to the One; for it is not the summit of beings or the Form of Forms or the order of all divine orders, but they have a median degree of progression, both among Forms and among the divine genera. Even if, then, you were to say that all things are like to the One, yet you will not say that they are like it in virtue of this Likeness, but rather only in virtue of the unity which proceeds from the One to all beings, and the natural striving of all things towards the One; for all things are what

[65] Again, perhaps, Iamblichus; cf. n. 61 above.
[66] E.g. Plotinus, in *Enn.* V, 1.7.

they are through desire for the One through the agency of the One, and in virtue of this striving each, being filled with its proper degree of unity, is likened to the single cause of all things, and is not likened to something like it, lest that cause should appear to be like the others, but, if it is proper to say so, it is likened to a paradigm of those things which are like to it.

Beings are indeed likened to the One, but are likened by means of an inexpressible striving for the One, and not by means of this assimilative order or the single Form of Likeness; for it is not possible for this to join all things to the One and draw them upwards to him, but it is the job of this order to drag up everything subsequent to it towards the intellectual demiurgic monad, as it is the job of another agency to draw them towards the intelligible monad, which possesses the "transportive" force, as the theologians call it,[67] of all things from it down as far as Matter and, in turn, of all things back to it.

So the characteristic of this is to turn all things by means of likeness towards the intellectual monad and draw together all the orders of 1200 beings which have been separated from it; for even Like itself and Unlike itself are in need of the One, and each of them participates in it and is what it is in virtue of it, and is cause to others which participate in them of their being, and this communion with all beings does not come about for them through likeness, but through oneness, as does also their communion with the One itself which is beyond all things. So even if we say that all procession is accomplished through likeness,[68] and even the procession of beings from the One similarly, we must excuse ourselves for looseness in terminology, since we are using terms that we are accustomed to use in the case of Being, such as model and image, also in the case of the One and of the apparition of all things which exist from it. For even as we term it itself the One, attaching to it the most divine of names, since we see nothing among beings more venerable nor more holy than this, so we characterise the procession of all things from it by the term of "likeness," since we have no more appropriate term than this to attach to the notion of procession.

And since, as we said, even if one were to say that the others are like the One in so far as each participates in some one, it does not follow by this token that it is also like the others; for not even in the case of the Forms do we agree that what are like the Forms are like what are like

---

[67] Διαπόρϑμιος; cf. Or. Chald. 78 DP. Proclus uses the term also at In Alc. 68.12-13 (West.), and In Crat. 33.14-15. It seems from this latter passage to have been an epithet of the class of ἴυγγες in Chaldaean theology. No doubt the term is derived from διαπορϑμεῦον of Plato Symp. 202e.

[68] Cf. ET, prop. 29: "All procession is accomplished through a likeness of the secondary to the primary."

themselves (indeed this is one of the problems which Parmenides raises), but rather are like to models; so also when we postulate that those things which partake in the One are like the One, we will not declare in return that it is also like what participates in it, but if one may properly so say, it is like a model to them; for elements of unity (?)[69] in these are gifts and as it were images of the One.

If certain authorities called the One an "Idea" on the head of this, they were not far wrong, only provided they spoke of it with caution and were not by means of the use of the terms "idea" and "model" either to make it a multiplicity or to count it in with the Forms, but call it an idea only by analogy, even as Socrates called the Good the Idea of the Good, since it bore that relation to all beings which each of the intelligible Forms bears to its own chain which derives its existence from it and relates to it.

1201 And indeed one may gather from the definition of "like" the solution to the problem; for he defined "like" to be that which has the character of same, and the One has no character either of same or not same, but is One itself alone. Those things which participate in it have the same characteristic as each other of participation in the One, so that they are like each other in virtue of each other, but are not like to the One, because it does not have oneness as a characteristic, but is Oneness itself. So it is very far from true that the One is like the others, seeing that it is not even the case that the others according to this definition are like the One, since they do not experience in any way the characteristic of likeness, in so far as that is restricted to things which experience some characteristic the same, to the extent to which they experience it. For something is not said to be like another thing if it experiences that to which it is like, but rather if it experiences the *same* as that other, so that both should have the same experience.

Enough, then, has been said by us in reply to this problem. Let us now pass on to the next passage of Plato.

"Further, the One, being such as we have described, will not be either equal or unequal either to itself or to another." "How is that?" (140b)

After the assimilative order of gods which is solely supra-cosmic, the theologians see fit to rank that order which is particularly called the "detached,"[70] the characteristic of which is, as they maintain, to be both transcendent over things in the cosmos and to be in communion

---

[69] A lacuna in both Latin and Greek MSS. Something like this must be the meaning. Possibly read τὰ γὰρ ἁ⟨πλᾶ⟩ ἐν τούτοις ῥ⟨ιζώματα⟩?

[70] The ἀπόλυτοι θεοί, identified particularly with the gods of the Phaedrus myth (e.g. *In Tim.* I, 18.8). It is a slight embarrassment for Syrianus' scheme that they are omitted here.

with them and to be placed immediately superior to the cosmic gods; for which reason they declare that they have been allotted the median position between those gods which are solely supra-cosmic and those in the cosmos. This absolute order, then, he will present in the Second Hypothesis (148dff.), and he will there say what the characteristic of it is and that this order can "touch and not touch" (*Parm.* 149d6) because

1202 it is in a way both encosmic and supra-cosmic, being a cause of coalescence for the encosmic gods properly so-called and also leading forth into multiplicity the unity of the whole assimilative and solely supra-cosmic chain.

There, then, as I said, he will present this order also. Here, however, he has passed it over and has gone on to those gods which are only in the cosmos[71] the reason for this we shall learn more accurately in that place; for there, if it is the gods' will, we shall make the acquaintance of their whole order; but in order that we may not be astonished at that place, we have given some advance indication here also, and at the same time in order that we may turn the lovers of truth to the search for the cause of this. He has, then, gone on to deal with the encosmic gods, the characteristic of which is the equal and unequal, the one epithet indicating their fullness and the fact that they do not admit of any addition or subtraction (for such is the equal, always preserving the same limit of itself), the other epithet alluding to the multiplicity of their powers and the superiority and inferiority inherent in them; for in the case of these we find most of all divisions and variations of powers and differences in degrees of processions and analogies and the bonds that arise by reason of these, from which, indeed, Timaeus has derived the existence of the souls dependent upon them (*Tim.* 41c), all of which derive their origin from equality.

But all these things will become more obvious to us in what follows if indeed it is clear, as we have just said on the basis of the passage of the *Timaeus*,[72] that souls, prior to bodies, are also established through analogy, and that their causes must preexist in the gods established immediately above them. So then it is reasonable that their characteristics should be the equal and the unequal.

He now produces the proofs relative to the negations of equal and
1203 unequal on the grounds of both Sameness and the Many, but not of the like and unlike, although these have been dealt with, correctly, immediately before; for the totality of the encosmic gods proceeds from the demiurgic monad and the primal multiplicity, which are the first

---

[71] Similarly, at *PT* II, 12, p. 70.27ff. S-W, Proclus passes straight from the ὑπερκόσμιοι to the ἐγκόσμιοι θεοί, since there too he is following the *Parmenides* closely.

[72] Cf. also *In Tim.* III, 225.13ff. Diehl, a comment on *Tim.* 41bc, and on ἰσάζοιτ' ἄν in particular.

things he denied of the One; in what way this is true will become clear
to us as we proceed. In any case, we must absolutely accept this much,
that the causes from which the proofs derive are the dominant causes
of those entities which the discussion is about, so that also the equal and
the unequal, in so far as they derive from the One and through Sameness and the Many, are in the same measure denied through these
things of the One; for which reason, indeed, he begins his exposition
here, "being such as we have described"—not such as we have just now
described, but such as was previously shown to be completely non-receptive of the same and the other and to be free from multiplicity.
Being of this nature, then, it is "neither equal nor unequal either to itself or to others"; for once again these conclusions also are double, even
as were those about the like and the unlike and the same and the other.
And if this is so, and if it is demonstrated that it is from the same and
the other that it is neither equal nor unequal, it is reasonable that the
same and the other should be beyond the like and the unlike, because
they are not true of these alone but also of the equal and unequal, and
in the same way are more universal than like and the unlike; for they
apply also to equal and unequal; for that which is participated in by
more entities is more universal.

So much, then, for the order of the propositions. It is plain also that
these two characteristics are dependent on the double column of divine
epithets; for the equal stretches back to the like and the same and the in-
another and the round and the whole, while the unequal goes back to
the unlike and the other and the in-itself and the straight and that which
has parts, and again of these the one set goes back to Limit, and the
other to the Unlimited. And indeed it seems to me that it is for this reason also that he carries the discourse on through a series of antitheses,
in order that he may show that the One is beyond all antithesis, being
ranked with nothing, but being entirely transcendent over each pair of
1204 opposites in the whole series. For again, as we have often said, if it is to
be the worse of any pair, that is unreasonable; for nothing that is better
is cause of the worse, but although it may have some communication
with it, it will not be its cause in the proper sense; for neither does
Sameness produce Otherness nor Rest, Motion, nor in general is it a
case of producer and produced, but rather a kind of encompassing and
unity stretches out from the better to the worse.

*"If it is equal, it will have the same number of measures as anything to
which it is equal." "Yes." "If greater or less, it will have more or fewer
measures than things, less or greater than itself, which are commensurate
with it." "Yes." "Or, if they are incommensurate with it, it will have*

549

had smaller measures in the one case, and greater in the other." "Inevitably." (140bc)

That the equal and the unequal which I have dealt with here are not to be taken as simply the physical, nor yet the mathematical, nor that which is established in the reason-principles of the soul, nor even the intellectual form itself, has been stated by us previously; for all these levels of being have only a partial hold on divine reality and are unworthy of an hypothesis which concerns the One. For what would be so impressive, as has already been said, about the One being superior to one intellectual form—never mind the others? No, as we have said, equality and inequality are to be taken as penetrating throughout the whole of divinity in the cosmos, even if the proofs also suit physical equals and mathematic equals and those in reason-principles of soul and those in the intellectual forms. For one must begin one's proofs from the top down through all levels, and extend them through all secondary beings, in order that the One may be shown to be transcendent over all divinities, over the intellectual realm, the psychic realm, and the mathematical and physical forms.

So all such axioms as are now stated about equals and unequals are to be accommodated to this order of gods; for since there are in this order 1205 also a multiplicity of potencies, some coordinate with each other and tending towards the same end and good, others differing in respect of superiority and inferiority, we must say that the former class are characterised by equality (for the good is the measure of each of them; and those things which are united to the same good are measured according to the same measure and are equal to each other), while those which are non-coordinate with each other we must postulate as performing their procession according to inequality, since we say that some of them are superior and others inferior. But since even of those that are unequal some are commensurate and others incommensurate, it is plain that we must fit these concepts into the divine realm, commensurability being taken as referring to those cases in which the secondary entities are mixed with those prior to them and participate in the whole of what is superior to them (for in this way also, in entities that are commensurate, the lesser desires to have a common measure with the greater, the same unit of measurement being applied to either of them as a whole); whereas incommensurability applies in those cases where the lesser entities, by reason of the transcendent superiority of the greater, participate in them up to a point, but are unable to be joined to them as a whole because of their own inadequacy. For in the case of partial causes which are at many removes from the primal, communion with them is incommensurate and so is the striving upwards for them towards the same intelligible good, and it would seem, if these things are symbols of the encosmic gods, I mean the equal and the unequal, that it is reasonable that this "commensurate" and "incommensurate" should appear at this point. For among incorporeal and immaterial entities such an antithesis can have no place, since everything there is rationally related and has its basis in pure forms; but where there is also a material substratum and a mixture of form and a formless element, then it is reasonable that there should also be an antithesis of commensurability and incommensurability between those things which the encosmic gods maintain directly—souls and bodies, Form and Matter. It is reasonable, then, that commensurability and incommensurability should arise at this point, in connection with the distinction of inequality; and this is the reason why the argument which raises the difficulty made mention of these.

1206   We will consider these matters, however, at more length later on; for the moment let us assert that he follows the methods of geometry in assuming prior to the proofs definitions of the equal, the commensurate, and the incommensurate; equal he states to be "that which is measured by the same measures," commensurate "that which is measured by the same measure—if it is greater, more times than less, if it is less, less times than the greater"; and the incommensurate is "that which is divided into parts which are equal numerically, but are unequal in size"—in the case that it is smaller, obviously into smaller parts, if it is bigger, obviously into bigger, and the smaller will be made up of smaller measures numerically equal, and the greater of greater. For if you take the side and the diagonal and you divide each in half, it is obvious that the one will have each of its halves larger and the other smaller. So, since in the case of both things commensurate and things incommensurate there is a comparison equally of larger and smaller, in the one case the measures being equal, but multiplied either more or less times, in the other case the division being made into equal parts but either into larger or smaller parts in point of size, in the one case the distinction is in terms of number, in the other case in terms of parts incommensurate in size. So, then, having established in advance these definitions, he next brings on the proofs, by means of which he shows first of all that the One is not equal either to itself or to another, and then that it is in turn not unequal either to itself or to another. His words are as follows:

> "Now a thing which does not partake in sameness cannot have the same number of measures or of anything else." "It cannot." "Therefore the One, not having the same number of measures, cannot be equal to itself or to another." "It would seem not, at any rate." (140c)

The syllogism which he has constructed about the equal which removes it from the One is of the following sort: the One partakes of nothing same; the equal partakes to some extent of the same in virtue of the power of measure; the One, therefore, is in no way equal because
1207 neither is it the same. "Same," after all, is used in many senses; for it is possible to have sameness in respect of form and subject matter and some measure or other and time and place; for it is possible for things to be the same as each other both in measure and in time and in form and in number and in many other respects, through all of which the power of sameness extends. The equal, then, as being secondary to sameness, takes its generation from the One in virtue of it; the One, on the other hand, being beyond sameness, is obviously far more transcendent over equality, seeing that, if something were a magnitude, but not of the same type as that with which it is compared, that other thing could never be described as either equal or unequal; for these relationships are only possible in the case of things of like form. Who, after all, would consider a line and a surface to be equal and unequal to one another, or a plane and a solid? For these things have no ratio common between them, and Aristotle, in his discussion of motion (*Phys.* VII, 4), is right to lay down that motions of like kind are commensurable, while those of unlike kind are not, as for example growth and change or generation and spatial motion. The One, therefore, being incommensurable with any of those things which come into being after it and derive their existence from it, cannot be either equal or unequal to them, nor yet to itself, since it has an existence which is unitary and superior, and has no need of equality; in which respect it is plain that the One is not so called as being a quantity such that it would be receptive of equality, but only because its simplicity and partlessness can only be signified in this way; for it is through wishing to indicate its transcendence over all other things that we term it "one," not as being of the same rank as things multiple nor as placing it as one of the monads in numbers, but signifying that it is an essence having nothing in common with everything else, only by participation in which will one attain any inkling of how it is one.

It has been shown, then, thus far that it is in no way receptive of
1208 equality because it does not tolerate sameness, either in respect of time or of number or in any other mode, as being totally non-receptive of sameness.

"On the other hand, if it had more or fewer measures, it would have as many parts as measures; and thus, once more, it would no longer be one, but as many as its measures." "Correct." "And if it were of one measure

552

it would be equal to that measure; but this we saw to be impossible, that it
should be equal to anything." "We did indeed." (140c)

A second syllogism, removing inequality absolutely from the One,
is produced here on top of the preceding in the following form: the
One is not receptive of a multiplicity of measures or parts; but everything that is unequal is receptive of a multiplicity of parts; the One
therefore is not unequal. For whether the unequal is made up of a
greater or lesser number of measures, it has at all events a multiplicity
of measures; but we have removed all multiplicity from the One, both
the lesser and the greater; therefore the unequal is inferior to the primal
multiplicity and comes into existence in virtue of it, but it partakes also
of the causal principle of unity; for, as has often been said, negation is
the origin of assertion.

By these means, then, he has shown that the One also transcends inequality. But since someone might raise the problem, "But perhaps it
will not be either of lesser or of more measures, but of one measure, in
order that we may not leave a multiplicity in the One and so let it be
itself its own measure"—to counter this objection he has added the further qualification, that if someone were to postulate that the One was
of this sort, it will be equal to something inevitably, to wit, its own
measure; and if the equal and the One are not the same because the latter is absolute while the former is relative, it is obvious that in being
equal the One will also be not one because the equal is not one; for
whatever is added to it removes oneness from it, since the truly One
1209 rejects the addition of anything else, by the addition of which it will no
longer be one alone, but one with something else, nor the One itself,
but rather some particular one, since it will appear with the addition.
Therefore, since it is equal it will not be one, and this will be so whether
it is measured by some other one or by itself. But it has been shown that
the One is equal to nothing; so then, the One will neither have one
measure nor many; for if it were the measure of itself, ⟨this would produce a distinction within it, and it will not, therefore, be⟩ inexpressible,[73] being both a measure of itself and measured by itself, and it will
not be one in the true sense, but of dual nature.

It is this that has persuaded us to deny also that it is in itself, for which
reason it is plain that the epithet of "absolute" is to be granted to the
One, but not the designation "relative to itself," in order that we may
not take it as being doubled and bring it about that the One has some
characteristic but is not Essentially One. If, on the other hand, it is the
measure of what is below it, it will be ranked together with the things

---

[73] A lacuna here, with which the Latin is no help. I give the approximate meaning required.

measured and will be among them, measuring them also by itself as the monad in numbers measures number; but it must exist as transcendent over all things; and it must be a part of nothing, lest it be less perfect than the other things of which it is a part; for every part is incomplete. If, then, it were to be the measure of things measured as a part, it will be less complete than other things—the One is not, after all, "beyond" those things of which it is a measure; while if it is some part of other things, it will be a one and not the One itself; for its distinctness in respect of the other parts will make it a one; for each of those, being a part, is inevitably a particular one.

If, then, the One Itself is not even a whole, in order that it may not possess oneness as a characteristic, as he has shown in the *Sophist* (244e), far more so will it not be a part, lest it be also incomplete, on top of having the One as a characteristic. From this it is clear that the One Itself is not any one of the Forms, for every Form is a part of the totality of Intellect, but the One is transcendent over both the whole intelligible realm and over all the Forms in it, which are parts of it.

How, then, can it be called the measure of all things? Surely in that it provides measures for all things; for it is given the title of "one" for this reason also, as being the cause for everything of unity and coherence, since in itself it is none of these things. And how would it be a measure, since it is beyond all limit and boundary and unity? Every measure, after all, is the limit and boundary of what it measures. So when Plato in the *Laws* (IV, 716c) says that the divine is the measure of all things, and far more so than man, as one of his predecessors dares to declare (sc. Protagoras), one must understand in what sense he says that it is a measure, if he is making his statement about that which is beyond all things, and we must realise that he is using it in the sense of apportioning to all beings both their being and their well-being, being the prior cause of the measures in each of them. Certainly Socrates shows this in the *Philebus* (66a4–c10) in the enumeration of goods of this kind,[74] when he places measure among the goods which are primally participated in and not yet of the nature of Limit, even as he has placed the appropriate and the measured (66a), and in saying that in connection with these we find the primary Good, but not that which is beyond all things which are said to be in any way mixed or of the nature of limit or the unlimited; so that if one were to venture to say that it was a measure, it must be taken as being a measure in the sense of an object of striving for all things, but not as being coordinate with what is meas-

---

[74] Cf. Damascius' account of Syrianus' exegesis of this passage of the *Philebus* at *In Phil.* 253-254, p. 119 Westerink.

ured by it; and being such as this, it will not be even unequal to those things with which it is unconnected.

"Therefore, since it partakes neither in one measure nor in many nor in few, nor does it partake in sameness at all, it appears that it can never be equal to itself or to another, nor yet greater or less than itself or another." *"Absolutely so."* (140d)

We may note here how in the conclusion he goes back in order from what has been demonstrated immediately before, through the middle demonstrations to the beginning of the propositions; for he says, "since the One partakes neither in one measure," this being the last of the propositions previously proved; "nor in many, nor in few," and these were what we demonstrated in the middle; "nor does it partici-

1211 pate in sameness at all," this being what was stated first of all. He shows nevertheless that the One is in no way equal, and then after that the actual proposition that it is neither equal nor unequal. And he has divided the unequal in the conclusion, describing it as "greater and less," which he called by one common name in the proposition under the term "unequal," demonstrating to us in this order of being also that the class of the encosmic gods, to which this terminology of equal and unequal is proper, in its upper extremity and at its summits is unified, while at its lower extent and in its processive aspect is divided, and in proceeding to the most individualised levels it goes from the same measures to the many and the few; at which point the unmeasured, being overcome by equality, turns back[75] and reverts to its beginning; for all inequality among them is dominated in every aspect by equality.

The One has been shown, then, to be beyond all the encosmic gods, seeing that the equal and the unequal are properties of these. In what way we say that this antithesis is proper to this order of beings we will find out in what follows, by following the statements of Plato; let us now gather from what has been said this much, that one must not talk of the One either in terms of unity, nor in terms of partlessness, nor in terms of having the relation of cause to those things following upon it, nor as being greater nor smaller nor equal; for these qualities only have place in things which are subject to comparison. Such comparison is doubtful enough in those things in which there is some same element which is receptive of tension and relaxation; but where there is no same element, how is it possible to talk of it in terms of comparison or analogy? Nor is it proper to apply to it the superlative forms of all other epithets, as some are accustomed to do, wishing to communicate something more about it than is done by means of negations, celebrat-

---

[75] Reading ἀνακάμπτει for ἀνακάλυπτει, (West.).

ing it as most stable of all things and most endowed with energy; for it is superior even to such superlatives, being non-receptive of all those 1212 qualities on the basis of which such superlatives are inevitably formed; for there is no way in which one can describe that which is in no way white as being superlatively white, and that which is no way black as superlatively black; for superlatives are secondary to simple participations in a quality.

"Well then, can it be held that the One can be older or younger than anything, or as the same age as anything?" "Why not?" (140e)

The discourse has now proceeded as far as the gods in the cosmos, always removing in turn the next layer of characteristics from the One through the intermediacy of the classes in between; rather, to express myself more clearly, producing at each stage secondary entities through those which are nearer to the One from the transcendent cause of all things. He is now going to go on to separate off divine being itself, that which primally partakes in the gods and receives their procession into the cosmos, from the One, or rather produce this also from the so-to-say "unspeakable fount of all beings," through which all things divine partake in this characteristic, both those which are primally divine and those which are divinised from these. For even as everything which has any sort of being is produced from the monad of beings, both real Being and that which is assimilated to it, while not enjoying being in itself but through its communion with real Being receiving some dim impression of being in the same way also from the single henad of all divinity, the characteristic of which, if I may make so bold as to say, is to divinise all things according to a certain transcendent and unutterable superiority, there is produced both the totality of divine number, in virtue of which is the being, or rather prebeing,[76] of the gods and of the whole divinised order of being.

The aim of this argument, as we have said, is to declare the One to be transcendent over this level of Being as well; and I would like those to pay attention who have declared the first principle to be Soul or anything else of this sort, how Parmenides nullifies their hypothesis, showing that the One is non-receptive of Time, while that which is non-receptive of Time cannot be Soul; for all soul partakes in time and 1213 uses periods measured by time. The One, indeed, is superior to and beyond Intellect because all Intellect both moves and is at rest, whereas the One has been shown to be neither in motion nor at rest; and it is

---

[76] For the term προεῖναι, cf. *ET*, props. 116 and 122 (102.16 and 108.9 Dodds)—not a Plotinian usage in this sense. It first appears (in Neoplatonism) in Iamblichus, *Myst.* VIII, 2 (προούσιος, τὸ προόντως ὄν), perhaps borrowed by him from the Hermetic tradition (Stobaeus *Exc.* XXI, 1).

superior to Soul because all Soul partakes in time, and the One will be shown now not to partake in time; but Intellect also is different from Soul for the same reasons, being pure from all temporal activity, so that by means of these distinctions we are able to discern and recognise the three ruling hypostases.[77]

That the One is entirely non-participatory in Time he shows by demonstrating first that it is neither younger nor older nor of the same age as either itself or anything else; for everything which partakes in Time must partake in these things, so that, if the One is shown to be free from these which are characteristic marks of all things which partake in Time, it will have been shown that it does not partake in Time. This view has seemed incredible to many, and especially to those physical philosophers before him who considered that all things were comprehended by Time and if anything is eternal, then it was time that was without limit, and that nothing of all things was not measured by time; for even as they thought that all things were in space, thinking all things to be body and nothing to be immaterial, so they thought all things were in time also, inasmuch as they were moved, and nothing was unmoved; for the idea of bodies brought with it that of space, and motion that of time; therefore even as the One has been shown not to be in time either by means of the present postulates, and for this reason it is neither soul nor anything else of those things that have need of time and partake in time either in their essence or in their activity, so through all these propositions it is demonstrated that the One is neither body nor soul nor intellect, the first because it is not in another thing, the second because it does not partake in time, the third because it does not experience motion or rest.

All these doctrines are normally propounded by the majority of commentators about the One, and considering it the First Principle, they say that it is not body, as the Stoics maintained, nor incorporeal soul, as Anaxagoras claimed, nor motionless intellect, as Aristotle said later; by this, they claim, the philosophy of Plato is superior to the others, in that it rises up to the causal principle above Intellect.

At any rate, this being his thesis, by way of indicating to us the procession of the argument towards multiplicity, he is not content to rest in the same way as he had in his previous statements with a duality, but has enumerated the characteristics of this level of being as a triad, that is, "the older," "the younger," and "that which has the same age," although here too he could have presented it as a duality, in the form of "of equal age" and "of unequal age," even as above he had distinguished between equal and unequal; but there he placed a dyad first,

1214

[77] A reference, perhaps, to Plotinus' tractate of that title (*Enn.* V, 1).

and then went on from the division of the unequal into a triad, while here he has actually taken his start from a triad; for there unity was dominant over multiplicity and the whole over the part, while at this level of being both multiplicity and division into parts is the most
1215 prominent aspect, as Timaeus says (*Tim.* 35a), and it is this that Parmenides is imitating here when he begins from a triad and proceeds to a hexad; for the notions of older and younger and equality of age are doubled by being distinguished into "in relation to itself" and "to others." And it is obvious enough how the triad and the hexad are proper to this order of being; for its triple nature arises from Being and Sameness and Otherness; and its triple power made up of the charioteer and horses shows its affinity to the triad, while its having an essence which is even-and-odd, woven together from both, demonstrates its natural connection to the hexad.[78]

So much, then, is easy enough to grasp. But perhaps it is suitable to raise at this point first of all the question as to what, after all, this "time" can be, which he declares that this order of beings partakes in, and from which he exempts the first principle itself. For this is no small problem, but, as it is generally agreed, it is difficult to indicate its characteristic nature; and this is shown by the explanations of commentators before us and their disputes with one another; for the majority of those who have exercised themselves with this problem have concluded that Plato is here referring to the obvious and generally known sort of time, since he clearly states that coming to be is proper to those things that participate in time (*Parm.* 141a).[79] But one must ask these where would be the honour or wondrousness of the One being shown to be superior to this sort of time, seeing that souls are superior to it— that is, the time which measures the motions of sensible things, since they are prior to bodies—and how then, further, is it that this time is in the Second Hypothesis asserted of real being, as they themselves admit, and that although intellectual being does not admit of such time;
1216 for he says at the same time that that is to be attributed to Being and also the agreed-upon sense of time; for "was" and "will be" are parts of time, and, as Timaeus himself asserts (*Tim.* 37e), these categories have nothing to do with real beings.

Another group of commentators,[80] having regard to this difficulty, and taking the statement in the Second Hypothesis that the One participates in time (*Parm.* 152a) as referring to nothing other than the much-

---

[78] Six is the first "even-odd" number, being divisible both by two and by three.

[79] At *Enn.* VI, 9.3.42, Plotinus declares the One to be exempt from Time without specification, so he may be among those referred to here.

[80] Identity unclear, if the following two commentators are to be taken as Porphyry and Iamblichus. Perhaps Amelius?

celebrated Eternity, have concluded that the expression "time" should be referred to this, in order that, we may assume, Plato, along with his general tendency to refer to things in hidden ways, should be here secretly indicating eternity through the mention of time. It will not be difficult to counter this school of thought by contrasting with it the terminology of Plato, which declares that everything which partakes in time comes to be and has come to be, both of which expressions Timaeus bids us not to transfer to real being and the eternal class of things.

Other commentators, again,[81] have seen fit to make a distinction, and call the primal God "Occasion" (*kairos*), the second "Eternity," and leave to the third here the appellation of "Time," in order, forsooth, that the One may be preserved beyond both time and eternity. Now their situation is attended by certain particular problems over and above what they necessarily inherit from their predecessors. For the addition of the doctrine that the One is infinite would not remove from them the ignorance that surrounds this sort of time, along with the fact that Plato, as we learn in the *Philebus* (66a), does not leave Occasion and Measure as characteristics of the first principle, but rather as characteristics of that which primally participates in it, even if the Pythagoreans saw fit to denominate the first principle of all as "Occasion" for some reason or other. For even if one were to assent to this, it would be impossible to link together Time and Occasion, especially if one is going to place Eternity between the two of them, and still to maintain that the One does not partake in Time because it is Occasion; this, after all, would be more appropriate to maintain about what is eternal and can be truly said about Eternity, whereas in the case of the One, one must say that it is neither Eternity nor eternal.

Others again,[82] hold that it is not Eternity either that is being referred to, nor are they inclined to identify it with time in its generally agreed sense, but rather seek to establish some intermediate nature and are of

1217

[81] Presumably Porphyry. Proclus reports (*PT* I, 11, p. 51.4ff. S-W) that in his περὶ ἀρχῶν, Porphyry declares the highest aspect of Nous (which is, for him, the Supreme Principle) to be προαιώνιος, while Nous itself is αἰώνιος. The denomination of the Supreme Principle as Καιρός is interesting, as being attested only by Proclus, here and at *In Alc.* 121 (though the Pythagoreans are reported as attaching the epithet to the number seven). However, a Platonist could derive stimulus from such passages as *Laws* IV, 709b and *Pol.* 284e—Plotinus, at least, took inspiration from the latter (*Enn.* VI, 9.18.44). As for the *Philebus* passages, we learn from Damascius (see n. 74 above) that Syrianus took the three elements, not as constituents of the Good, but as primary participants in it.

[82] Presumably Iamblichus. There is a useful collection of texts on Iamblichus' theory of Time in Sambur+sky and Pines, *The Concept of Time in Late Neoplatonism*, pp. 26-46, mainly from his *Commentary on the Categories* (*ap.* Simplicius). Iamblichus had a concept of "primary and unparticipated Time" (Simpl. *In Phys.* 792.20ff.), which seems to be that referred to here. See also Iambl. *In Tim.* fr. 63 Dillon, and note *ad loc.*

559

the opinion that the "time" alluded to here is the causal principle of the
intellectual order, whatever that is; the expression "older" indicates superiority in essence, the expression "younger," inferiority, and that
which is established at the same level of being is indicated by the
expression "having the same age," but not even these authorities make
clear what is the causal principle of this order, nor how Plato uses the
expressions "come to be" and "have come to be" (141c) about things
which are free of all generation, but differ merely in order.

It is after all better, then, in this case also to call attention to the teaching of our master (sc. Syrianus), to the effect that the text here concerns
divine souls; for these are divinised by participating eternally in the
gods, and it is to these that the most primal time properly refers, not
that which has proceeded into the visible realm, but that which is absolute and non-relative, according to which are measured all the circuits of souls, and their dances and encirclings around the intelligible.
For it takes its beginning from above, imitating that eternity which
comprehends all things and holds together all motion, whether it be
psychic or vital or however it be said to arise, and it unfolds it and
brings it to completion, and it is itself in essence an intellect, while acting as cause for divine souls of their "dance," and of their infinite motion around the intelligible, and by means of which there also arises that
in them which is "older" and "younger" and "of the same age." And
all these terms can be taken in two senses, for "older" in them can be
understood in relation to themselves, in so far as by virtue of their superior powers they get more benefit from the infinity of time and take
a larger share of it; for they are not filled with the same degree of completeness from the orders more divine than themselves in respect of all
their powers, but more in virtue of some and less in virtue of others,
and that which partakes of more time we call "older"; and in relation
1218 to other things, inasmuch as some of them accept the whole measurement of time and the whole extension of it which proceeds into souls,
while others are measured by its more particular circuits. Those, then,
are "older," the circuit of which is more general and extended over
more time.

And indeed the expression "younger" has a similar range of meanings; in relation to itself, it is such as to participate less in time than
powers inferior to it; for being younger than itself, in its relation to
what is above it, it is as it were grown ancient by extending itself in
parallel to the whole power of time; while in relation to what is below
it, it is still youthful by reason of its more partial enjoyment of time. In
relation to other things, the term has reference to the declination of its
activity, for that which has its circuit measured by a lesser circumference is "younger" than that which has it through a larger one.

As for the concept of being "like in age," both in relation to itself and to other things, it is plain how one should relate it to things at the same level, which enjoy the same method of participation and the same measure of perfection. Every divine soul, after all, even if its circuit is measured according to a different time from that of its dependent body, yet has the same period of return, and this is always measured by its own time, while that of the body is measured according to the time proper to it; for which reason in turn it is of equal age both to itself and analogously to the body also.

We will not then be forced to resort to the normal sense of time merely because of the mention of coming to be and having come to be; for these also are to be found in the circuits of divine souls; nor on the other hand will we have to resort to identifying it with eternity, because the Second Hypothesis asserts time of the One; for we declare that there we find set out in order the procession of Being right from the intelligible monads through the intellectual and supracosmic and encosmic orders down to an encounter with divinised incorporeal being.

We are following here the doctrine of Plato, who both declared in the *Timaeus* (36e) that time is the measure for all things of transitive life, and that Soul is the first principle of divine life and intelligent living for the whole of time; and who has declared in the *Phaedrus* (247d) that the souls behold Being because they view things in time, not in eternity. And there will be no need for us to understand the expressions "younger" and "older" and "of the same age" as referring to order of being and the difference between the cause and the caused, nor will we need to enquire what is the cause of that order,[83] but we can take such expressions in their natural sense as referring to measures of time, greater and less and equal to others, as the case may be.

> "If it is of the same age with itself or another it will partake in equality of time and likeness; and we have said that the One does not partake of either likeness or equality." "We did indeed." (140e)

Even as in the case of the other sets of antitheses before this he first demonstrated that the One was not like anything, next that it was not unlike, and in turn that it was not equal, and then that it was not unequal, so in the case of these propositions also he first shows that the One is not of like age with anything, and then in turn that it is neither older nor younger either than itself or anything else. For the One must be shown to be beyond also the whole divine Soul which is prior to all other souls, even as it has been shown to be prior to all real beings and

---

[83] A reference back to the doctrine of Iamblichus(?), 1217. 2 above.

the cause of all of them; and for this reason we should not demand that it encompass the causes of all things and that it should be for this reason a multiplicity; for every causal principle is cause of some particular property, as for instance Essential Living Being is cause only of the existence of living beings, and each of the intelligible principles likewise.

The One, then, is causal principle of henads and of unity to all things, and all things derive from that source, as being either henads themselves or deriving from some henads; for Being itself, and in general every entity, is either one or deriving from units of some sort; for if it is unified, then it plainly consists of some units; and if these are henads, then the conclusion is obvious. If they themselves are unified, then in turn one must go back to those things from which they derive, and one must either be involved in an infinite regress, or come to rest with some henads, from which as elements the unified entity derives. From all of which one may gather that all things are either henads (units) or 1220 numbers; for that which is not a unit, but is unified, if it derives from some limited amount of henads, is a number, and this would be a primary number as deriving its existence from indivisibles; for each henad is indivisible; the other is a number of beings and is made up of beings and not from indivisibles, so that if something is the cause of beings, it is very reasonable that it is not the cause of all things, while if something is the cause of the henads from which all things derive, it is reasonable that it should be the cause of all things; for nothing exists which is not either a henad or composed of henads. One should not, then, say that the causes of all things are in the One, or otherwise, only in the sense that one may consider the One the cause of all things as being the cause of henads, seeing that all things derive their existence from these.

Since, then, it is the cause of the divine Soul also, inasmuch as the essence of this as of all beings is derived from henads, it is reasonable that it should be demonstrated to be beyond this also; for divine souls, inasmuch as they are intellectual, have intellect as their causal principle, inasmuch as they are Being, and inasmuch as they are unitary, the One, deriving their substance from it, inasmuch as each of them is a multiplicity of certain henads; these henads it has as elements, but each individually also has a one as unifying its multiplicity, for which reason, indeed, each is what it is as a whole and not as a disorganised multiplicity.

That the One is beyond these also, therefore, is being demonstrated in the propositions above. All the proofs, we may note, from equality and inequality and from likeness and unlikeness (from which derive the categories "equal in age" and "like in age," and their opposites) proceed from the causes of the divine Soul, both those which are generative and those which divinise it on the immediate level, through which as means they depend also on the primal gods and participate in the One itself. The expressions "equal" and "unequal" would be proper to the encosmic gods, from whom the divine souls in all cases derive their divinity; for it is through taking on divine Intellect that they are divine, as we learn in the *Laws* (X, 899b). The qualities of being like and unlike they derive from the assimilative gods, in which the souls participate primarily; for these are the primal images of beings, of which the souls being images, they take their substance in all cases, so that it is reason-

1221 able that equality and inequality in age, and likeness and unlikeness in age, should derive their characteristics from equality and likeness. As to how it is demonstrated that the One is neither older nor younger than itself or anything else we will consider a little later; we must now consider in what way it is not of equal age to itself or anything else.

The One, then, he says, partakes of the equal and the like neither in relation to itself nor in relation to anything else; for both propositions have been proved. But everything that is of like age, whether it is such in relation to itself or to something else, partakes in equality and like-ness in relation to that with which it is of like age; the One, therefore, must be said to be of like age neither with itself nor with anything else of all existent things; for both things are required for sameness in age, both equality and likeness; for things which have an equal time span, if they are not of like nature, would not be said to be of the same age. So a man of thirty years is not of equal age to a palm tree[84] of thirty years; for there is nothing to prevent the latter being already old, while the former is young, because the whole life span is not the same for both of them. And those things which are like one another, if they have not lived for an equal time, would not be of the same age; for it is plain that an old man is like an old horse, but he is not of the same age; for, pre-sumably, equality of time does not produce sameness of age. One must therefore take both together, both the like and the equal, for something to be of the same age; wherefore one thing is said to be of equal age, and another of like age, the one as a result of equality in the amount of time, the other from likeness in the sort of age level.

Thus much on the physical level of exegesis. On a nobler level, one might say that divine Soul as a whole depends upon these two orders of being immediately, and through these is likened to the divine level, and is drawn up and divinised and partakes of the One in so far as it is divinised, needing the encosmic gods which divinise it, while in so far as it is likened, it has need of the supra-cosmic gods, whom we have stated to be the first to assimilate all things to beings. From there, then,

1222 both equality and likeness go forth to those things which have the same

---

[84] Or, possibly, a phoenix, since φοῖνιξ can mean either.

age; for both orders generate Time, the one as being the first to illuminate those things in this cosmos which partake in Time, the others
inasmuch as things measured by Time are the first images, or rather, in
as much as Time is the first image, as is also stated in the *Timaeus* (37d);
for prior to those things which are measured by Time, Time itself is an
image of Eternity, as Timaeus says.

"And that it does not participate in unlikeness and inequality, this also we
said." "Indeed we did." "How then will it, being such as it is, be able to
be either older or younger than, or of the same age with, anything?" "In
no way." "Therefore the One cannot be younger or older than, or of the
same age with, either itself or another." "It would seem not." (140e-
141a)

The remaining propositions are indicated in the above passage, to
the effect that the first principle is neither older nor younger than itself
or than anything else. The proof is derived from the opposite of what
has gone before, I mean unlikeness and inequality, being produced in
some such manner as the following.

The One is neither unequal nor unlike itself or another, as has been
demonstrated previously; but everything that is older than either itself
or another is unequal in time unlike that than which it is younger or
older; therefore the One is neither younger nor older than either itself
or another. For that which does not partake of inequality in time and
unlikeness is not prevented from being unequal and unlike in some
other way. So inequality in time and unlikeness are not present in eternal
things, but there is nevertheless another way, not according to time, in
which they are present in their multiplicities and in their powers; but it
is plain that that which is in no way receptive of the unequal and the
unlike would not partake in inequality or unlikeness in time either. Far
more so, then, is the One transcendent over divine essence which op-
1223 erates according to time, by as much as it surpasses even those causes
which are perfective of it; for it is to make this clear that he has added
the phrase "being such as it is"; for how could that which is beyond
likeness and unlikeness partake in those things which partake in likeness and unlikeness? And how would that which transcends equality
and inequality be ranked with what partakes in a more partial manner
of these? For that which is unequal and equal in time does not participate in the whole power of the unequal and equal.

So then, after bringing to a conclusion these last two propositions as
well, that the One is neither older nor younger, he produces a common
conclusion for this triad: that the One is neither older nor younger than
itself nor anything else, nor is it the same age, bringing together the
whole multiplicity into one common principle; and by adding the

phrase "neither than itself nor anything else" he has conveyed to us the division into six[85] and has shown the way of ascent through the triad to the divine dyad. Having previously revealed to us through the dyad all the divine orders, he has here produced through a triad the manifestation of the divine soul, and we have said why. So then, that we may once again behold this also being produced dyadically, he has added in the conclusion the phrase "neither to itself nor to another."

> *"Would it not be the case, then, that the One could not even be in time at all, if it were such as I have described? Or is it not necessary that, if something is in time, it must be always becoming older than itself?" "Necessarily."* (141a)

After the triad which he has initially examined in connection with the divine soul, he wishes also to deny of the One all temporal participation. The proof, then, is as follows: the One is neither older nor younger than, nor of equal age with, itself, as has been demonstrated previously; but everything which participates in time is simultaneously older and younger than, and of the same age as, itself; therefore the One does not participate in time. And indeed how could it, since it is transcendent over the whole of time and over eternity itself, participate in any particular periodic measurements of time? Indeed this is also 1224 worthy of investigation, why he has not shown that the first principle is beyond eternity, but only beyond time; for nothing prevents that which has its existence prior to all time being eternal. Perhaps the answer is that the argument will demonstrate this also as it proceeds, when it demonstrates that it is not even dependent on existence, and far more, when it shows that it is not even possessed of the unity which goes with existence; for everything eternal subsists in existence as well, if indeed the attribute of eternal existence is proper to things eternal. Here however, since he has made the beginning of his negations from the many, which are subsequent to the intelligible realm, and since eternity is actually *in* the intelligible realm,[86] it is reasonable that he should demonstrate that the One transcends what partakes in time and all time, but should remain silent on the subject of eternity and things eternal, although both are measures, the one among real beings, the other in the realm of generation. And whereas there are many types of eternity and time, the first principle is superior to all these measures, by reason of its very oneness being itself the measure of all eternities and times, by which both real beings and generated things come to be measured. One might also add, if you like, to the present enquiry, that

---

[85] Discussed above, 1214.16–1215.15.
[86] Inserting ⟨νοητῷ⟩ (West.) to complete the sense.

since he has shown in what precedes that the One is not at rest, he has already proved that it is not eternal or eternity; for eternity "remains at rest in one place," and everything eternal is at rest in the same state; so since this has already been proved by those arguments, it is reasonable that he does not consider it to require separate argument here.

But, someone might say, might it not be that although the One is in no way participant in time, it could itself be Time; for the Pythagoreans used to term it "Occasion,"[87] and Orpheus calls his first principle of all, "Time." But it cannot be Time, lest the perfection emanating from it extend only to souls and in general to all things in motion; for things eternal are superior to those things whose activity is in time, and it could not be generative of worse, while not being the cause of the better. It was called "Occasion" by the Pythagoreans because it is the cause of the good[88] and the requisite; for such is "Occasion," appor-

1225 tioning to each thing its proper benefit according to what is suitable; it has been said earlier on, how according to Plato "occasion" is one of those things which follows on the first principle, relying on the proclamation in the *Philebus* (66a), and it is called Time by Orpheus (fr. 50 Kern) in virtue of a certain admirable analogy.[88a] For having handed down to us an account of mystical generations of what is ungenerated, the theologian also symbolically names the cause of the manifestation of divine things "time." For where there is generation there also is time; both the generation of things of sense is according to encosmic time, and that of things eternal in virtue of the One, since we have called this also generation to conceal the ineffable procession of these from the One. Even as, then, we put up with them calling the unsleeping activity of divine things which is transcendent over what they have providential care of, "sleep,"[89] their unity, "binding," and their procession, "loosing," even so when they apply the terms "time" and "generation" to things outside time and generation, we must also put up with Plato's denying time, in the present passage, in its normally accepted sense of the One.

"Does not, then, 'older' always mean older than something younger?"
"Obviously." "Well then, whatever is becoming older than itself, must also be at the same time becoming younger than itself, if it is to have some-

---

[87] Καιρός; cf. n. 81 above.
[88] Cf. Olympiodorus *In Alc.* 39.8-9: "As Aristotle declares (*An. Pr.* I, 36.486 35-36), occasion is time *plus* what is required (τὸ δέον) and time *plus* the good (τὸ εὖ)." Also Olympiodorus *In Phaed.* 9.9.11.
[88a] Cf. Proclus *In Crat.* 59.81ff. and 67.2ff. Pasquali.
[89] This and the following expressions are references to allegorical interpretations of famous passages of Homer, the sleep of Zeus after union with Hera (*Iliad* 14.346ff.), and the story of the binding of Zeus by the other gods, and his freeing by Thetis (*Iliad* 1.396ff.).

thing than which it is becoming older." "What do you mean?" "This."
(141ab)

His purpose in this and the following passage is to establish that
everything that partakes in time is older than, and of equal age with,
itself: and since he wishes this, he necessarily begins by demonstrating
that something is older than itself; and in so far as it is older than itself,
it is plain that it is also younger than itself; for it is in relation to itself
that it is called both younger and older. Now this argument might
seem to be problematic in the extreme, one might even say sophistic;
for how could something be simultaneously older and younger than itself? Surely the Socrates who has become older than himself is not also
younger than himself; at any rate being older is present to him, while
being young is gone from him.

1226   So some commentators have given up in face of this argument, and
have not scrupled even to say that Plato is appearing here to indulge in
sophistry, all too readily transferring their own ignorance to the argument. Others,[90] again, in trying to stand up to these critics, have
championed the truth rather too weakly for they say the same
thing is at the same time younger and older; in respect of future time it
is younger, for it has not yet attained to that; in respect of past time, on
the other hand, it is older, since it has already lived through that. But
this is not what it is to become both simultaneously younger and older
than oneself, but rather younger than one thing and older than another;
so that the argument of this commentator is quickly revealed to us as
being weak. Another set, again, declared that everything is both older
and younger than itself, what is now existent being older, and what
was before younger, and that what is now older can be said to be older
than what was formerly younger; but these too fail to understand the
sense of Plato's statement (141b), which puts what is against what is,
what will be against what will be, and what has been against what has
been, these in all cases being relative expressions; so then, it is not possible to say that that which now is older has become older than that
which had become younger; for this is to mix up times and not to preserve
the rule which he himself laid down regarding all relative expressions.

We must therefore turn once again to our Master, and bring to bear
upon the problem his discussion, which throws light upon the whole
preceding argument. That which partakes in time is of two sorts; the
one which, as it were, proceeds in a straight line, beginning from one
point and ending in another; the other which travels round in a circle,

---

[90] Presumably Porphyry and Iamblichus are among these latter commentators since,
once again, they lead up to Syrianus, but there is nothing distinctive that would serve to
identify either of them.

and pursues its motion from the same point to the same point, so as to have a beginning and an end which are the same and a motion which is unceasing, since each point of its progress is both beginning and end, and is no less a beginning than an end. That, then, which enjoys cyclical activity partakes in time by circuits, and since the same point is for it both an end and a beginning of motion; in so far as it departs from a beginning, it becomes older, whereas in so far as it arrives at an end, it becomes younger; for as it comes to be nearer to its end, it comes to be nearer to its own beginning; and that which comes to be nearer to its own beginning becomes younger; so then, that which arrives cyclically at its end becomes younger, while at the same time and by the same process also becoming older; for that which draws near to its own end proceeds towards being older; so for that which has a beginning different from its end, becoming younger is different from becoming older; but for that of which its beginning is the same as its end, its youngness is no younger than it is older, but as Plato says, "It becomes simultaneously younger than itself and older." For that which is moved in a straight line does not have this characteristic, because end and beginning are different in its case, whereas that which moves in a circle has the quality of being younger than itself by reason of the fact that its motion comes about in relation to the same point as both beginning and as end. So then, everything that partakes in time, if it becomes older than itself, also becomes younger than itself; and what is of this sort is that which moves in a circle.

For this reason the ancients were understandably disturbed lest this argument be in some way sophistical, since they were looking to things that moved in a straight line, whereas they should have made the distinction and considered what things have the characteristic of having their beginning and end the same, and what have them as different, and they should have considered that the subject of discussion now is divine souls, which partake in time in the respect that they have a periodic time of their proper motion, as indeed do the vehicles which are dependent upon them.

This, then, is the argument of our Master. How it comes about that everything that becomes older than itself also at the same time becomes younger than itself will be explained by means of two mean terms[91] by the Second Hypothesis (153bff.), which discovers the necessity of the inseparable coexistence of these in the case of all things that partake in time, and not only in the case of those which move in a circle. For the present, however, let what we have said stand as sufficient, since it re-

---

[91] It is not clear to me what this means if the passage referred to is, as it seems to be, 153bff. Possibly the δύο, which is strangely placed *after* τῶν μεσοτήτων, is a gloss.

lates properly to the present subject matter and to the circuits of divine souls.

But if we are even here briefly to relate the argument, which is of universal application, to all those things which come to be other than themselves, let us pause for a moment to say that everything in truth which becomes older than itself, while it becomes older, becomes younger also in so far as it becomes older; for example, that which comes to be ten years old comes to be older than what is nine years old; but while it is becoming this, the nine-year-old entity is becoming younger than itself, as even before this the nine-year-old became older, while the eight-year-old became younger than that which was then coming into existence; for either of the two in the process of generation becomes constantly different from the other and never remains the same. And if we take coming to be in this sense, we shall find that everything truly comes to be older than itself, by reason of always being taken as being in some other state, and, even as it becomes older, so, changing our perspective, it becomes younger also, even as it transfers itself from one aspect to another, becoming older than what it formerly was.

"If one thing is already different from another, there is no question of its becoming different: either they both already are now, or they both have been, or they both will be, different. But if one is in the process of becoming different, you cannot say that the other has been, or will be, or as yet is, different; it can only be in process of becoming different." "Necessarily." (141bc)

Since the interlocutor has enquired how the same thing can simultaneously be older and younger than itself, Parmenides brings to bear on the pursuit of this enquiry a certain general rule about all pairs of opposites whatever, that they are relatives, not, however, in the sense of synonyms like *like* or *equal*, but of heteronymous terms such as *son* and *father*; for such entities are different in reality, not just in name, but in formal aspect; for synonyms are such as are the same in form. These things, then, they term different, and what he means is this, that whatever be the case with one of a pair of real opposites, such must be the case with the other, so that if the One is one of those things which are existent or future, then the other must be future, while if the one of them is past or present, then the other too must be present. For if one of them were such and such and the other were not, it would be obvious that that would be what it is in virtue of its own nature, and not as one of a pair of opposites; for anything which is in any way an opposite, in that very respect in which it is said to be an opposite partakes

569

of the nature of relativity; for it is opposed to an opposite. Such, then, is the rule.

But perhaps someone might inquire how it is that although we say that image and model are relative to one another, we declare that the one enjoys true existence, whereas the other comes to be and is generated. One must say in reply that the image as an image does not come to be, but comes to be something else by being imaged and coming to be an image of its own model; for in so far as it is an image of some real being, it is that which it is actually called imagistically, and it is always an image even as that other is always a model; and even if an image has its being in the sphere of generation, yet the coming to be of the image is in constant community of existence with the being of the model, and while the *always* of the model is eternal, that of the image persists for an infinite time.[92] If we are right in saying this, we will not accept those who postulate models of corruptible things;[93] for there would be then a model of an image which does not exist. But if it is not, then, going to be a model, it is plain that it was not a cause essentially or in virtue of its being; for that which is a cause in virtue of its being, so long as it is the same, by nature performs the same activity. Therefore, there is one of two possibilities: if we are to agree that there are paradigms of some sort for things that exist contingently and come into being and pass away, we shall be compelled to say either that they have in them some element of generation, coming to be as paradigms at that time when their images come to be, and are not either before or after that time paradigms, and for this reason this quality does not pertain to them essentially but accidentally, as we have said; or on the other hand that their images are always in existence, those same things which have contingent existence and are borne about in generation; that is to say, if the aforementioned principles about relative entities and in general about opposites are true.

But this we may take as a sort of corollary to the main argument. There should be no cause for astonishment if, in taking the three divisions of time, after mentioning being and having come to be and being about to be, he has added also coming to be; for this signifies continuance in procession and subsistence, not just simple existence, as do the verb *to be* and being, and it is for this reason that he has added in this verb also as being proper to those things which participate in time. And perhaps also the expression "what already is" means to him that which is seen prior to all motion in the present moment as imaging what is in

1230

---

[92] The distinction, presumably, between "eternal" and "sempiternal" existence.

[93] This must refer to the postulate of paradigms of *individual* physical objects; otherwise, it seems incomprehensible. All Forms of natural objects, after all, are paradigms of ἐπίκηρα πράγματα, taken generally.

the eternal; whereas "coming to be" signifies that which is extended along the infinity of time. For the eternal is all together at all points in both the partlessness and the infinity of eternity because eternity remains in the same state in its infinity, whereas that which partakes in time is always in the present instance, but it comes to be according to the infinity of time; wherefore time also is in one respect partless and in another respect infinite.

"Now the difference signified by 'older' is always a difference from something younger and from nothing else." "It is." "Consequently, what is becoming older than itself must also at the same time be becoming younger than itself." "It would seem so." (141c)

From the general rule he proceeds now to the present statement. For if the older is one side of an antithesis, which he has just called in the present passage a "difference," and it has been said that if one of a pair of opposites is the case, then the remaining one must be the case, then the conclusion from this is obvious—that if something is to become older, it also becomes younger; for that which becomes older than itself at the same time becomes younger than itself; for it itself is that thing than which it becomes older, so that it itself is also younger, and both relate to the same thing, as we said before. And if someone were to say that Socrates becomes older than himself but not younger, we will reply that Socrates does indeed become older, in the strict sense, but at the same time the same Socrates becomes also younger than himself, because the younger element in him becomes different at each moment, even as does the older element; for since they are in process of generation they suffer permanent joint permutations, as we have said. If there is also some other way in which something while becoming older than itself simultaneously becomes younger than itself, it will be revealed to us in the Second Hypothesis; for the same addition according to the arithmetic mean makes older than itself what takes on this additional amount of time, whereas according to the geometric mean the same thing becomes younger through having its proportion lessened, as will become clear when we come to that point.

"Now, in the process of becoming it cannot take a longer or shorter time than itself, but must take the same time with itself, whether it is becoming, or it is, or has been, or will be." "Certainly, this too is necessary." (141c)

It has been shown that that which partakes in time, which is a characteristic that he wishes to deny to the One, simultaneously becomes younger and older than itself, and we have said how this may be, relating the argument sufficiently for the present purpose to those things which enjoy periodic life, because that which pursues its activity in cir-

1231

571

cles has the same point as a beginning and an end of its circuit; and in so far as it comes to be nearer to its end it becomes older, while in so far as it comes nearer and nearer to its beginning it becomes younger, and even as its beginning and its end are one, so its becoming older and younger than itself is one. It has also been shown in what way the argument is true also of everything which partakes in time, both of the older and the younger as they move and are in process of generation, and how the younger necessarily appears differently to a different older aspect because of the necessary alteration of the relationship between the older and the younger. He wants now, therefore, to add to what has already been said the principle that such an entity is also of equal age with itself; for everything has come to be and is about to be and comes to be and is during an equal time with itself; for if Socrates is seventy years old, he is of the same age as himself, and if he has been thirty, he has come to be for the same extent of time as himself, and if he comes to be this age, similarly he comes to be for the same time as himself; for since he comes to be in relation to himself he possesses the same time span as himself. There is nothing complicated in all this, but it is plain how it is the case also in those entities which progress according to linear development; for it is possible for one thing to be and to become and to have become of greater or lesser time span than another and inevitably also of equal time span to it, and thus neither greater nor lesser.

> *"So, it seems, any one of the things that occupy time and have temporal character must be of the same age as itself and also be becoming at once both older and younger than itself." "It may be so." "But we saw that none of these characters can attach to the One." "No, they do not." "Therefore the One has nothing to do with time, nor does it occupy any stretch of time." "No indeed, at least as far as the argument goes."* (141d)

By means of these steps, then, he produces the present conclusion, and this is that the One does not partake in time nor is it in time; for we must remove from it also all types of divine being and not just the summit of them; for these are those entities which have their activity in some time, and not in eternity, and partake in time of some sort, such as we mentioned above. The One, on the other hand, partakes in no sort of time, for it is totally transcendent over these entities which partake in any sort of time. How he demonstrates that the One partakes in no time has been stated previously, but nevertheless, let us state now the actual syllogism: "The One is in no way older or younger or of equal age with itself; but everything which partakes in time is simultaneously older and younger and of the same age as itself; therefore the One in no way partakes in time." This conclusion he has just drawn himself in saying, "Therefore the One has nothing to do with time";

and then more comprehensively by saying, "and does not occupy any stretch of time"; for it is completely transcendent over time, and is established above every temporal order.

1233   This characteristic of not partaking in time is true not only of the One alone, but also of all those entities which do not move according to motion in space; for those also do not move in time, and even if they move while time exists, time does not concern them, but rather what is subsequent to them; for existing at a time when time is proceeding is not the same as being in time; for being in place is not the same as existing when place exists, or in that case everything immaterial would have to be said to be in a place because it exists when place exists; so then, even as the immaterial is not in a place, even though it exists when place exists, so it is not in time. And perhaps it should not even be said to be when time is, because it is prior in essence to that which is itself prior to what is in time, and the expression "when" would have absolutely no place in the case of this which exists prior to eternity, which is itself the model of time. For how could one use the expression "when" of that which is neither in eternity nor in time, but rejects any connection with both of these? For even as the One is not in time because it is not in motion, so neither is it in eternity because it is not at rest; for eternity is at rest, as Timaeus declares (*Tim.* 37d).

> *"Well now, the words 'was,' 'has become,' 'was becoming,' are understood to mean connection with past time, are they not?" "Yes indeed." "Again, 'will be,' 'will be becoming,' and 'will become' are connected with future time." "Yes." "And 'is' and 'is becoming,' with time now present." "Certainly."* (141de)

He has denied all attributes of the One in order: the attribute of partaking in time from being neither older nor younger than itself; that of being older and younger than itself, from partaking neither in likeness nor equality nor in unlikeness nor inequality; that of being equal and unequal and like and unlike, from being neither the same nor other; and this in turn, from the quality of in no way being either in motion or at rest; and this, from being neither in itself nor in another; and this from 1234 neither encompassing itself nor being encompassed; and this, from that of not having parts; and this in turn from that of not being a whole; and this from not being a multiplicity; and this in turn, from not being anything else than One.

So having denied all these attributes and coming down as far as participation in time, which is a condition proper to the multiplicity of divine souls and the divine classes of being which are involved with them (for it is particularly to these that we declare this distinction to be proper), he proceeds from above as far as these, first making a triadic

573

division into past, present, and future, and then a nine-fold division, subdividing each of these three again into three. He has himself provided us with a clue to the order of these divisions elsewhere; or is it not so that Socrates in the *Republic* (X, 617b) says that the Fates divide up time, and that one sings of what is past, another of the present, and another of the future? This triple division of time we may take to refer to certain triple hypostases among the classes superior to us, which Parmenides wishes the One to transcend; for the monad of souls is united to Time as a whole, while the many souls participate in it only in a secondary way. And some of these participate as wholes, such as do so in the past or present or future, and others in a partial way, as are those which are given essence according to the differentiae of these; for to each of the wholes there is ranked a multiplicity divided into first and middle and final elements; for in connection with that soul which is established in the past there is a multiplicity proper to it, of which the summit is represented by *was*, the middle represented by *became*, and the final element by *was becoming*; and associated with that which operates in the present is another second multiplicity, of which the dominant element is characterised by *is*, the median element by *has become* and the final element by *is becoming*; and with that which operates in the future there is associated yet a third multiplicity, of which the highest element is represented by *will be*, that in the middle is associated with 1235 *will become*, while the final element is defined by *will have become*; and thus these three triads will be immediately dependent upon these three wholes, and all these upon their own monad.

What, then, are we to make of this? That those orders which are divided according to the parts of time act in a partial mode, and not all throughout time as a whole, but some only in the past, others only in the present, and yet others only in the future, and to which of these we should assign each part of time we will not be able to say; up to what point extends the present or the past, and from what point begins the future? But perhaps it is better to say that all these entities act throughout the whole of time, but since time as a whole has within itself three potencies,[94] the one which is perfective of all motion, the other which is such as to gather together and preserve all things which are beneath its rule, the third revelatory of the divine (for in bringing round all things in a circle it gives perfection to the non-eternal among things and gives connection to their essence and reveals the unified infinity of eternity to them, unfolding the multiplicity which is packed together on the level of eternity; for which reason this manifest time, as Timaeus

[94] Cf. the similar exposition in the *Timaeus Commentary*, III, 38.12ff. Diehl (*ad Tim.* 37de), where Proclus makes it clear that this is Syrianus' doctrine.

says [*Tim.* 37d], reveals to us the measure of the divine circuits and brings to completion the things of this realm and guards them as they come to be, according to their own numerical formulae); so then, since that time which is prior to souls has three powers—the perfective, the cohesive, and the revelatory—in virtue of its likeness to eternity (for eternity, as we have shown elsewhere,[95] holding the middle rank in the intelligible world, brings to completion the order of beings after it by conferring unity upon it, and on the other hand makes manifest that which is prior to it, producing its ineffable unity into multiplicity, and also holds together the median bond of the intelligible world, and preserves all things without change through its own proper power); so time receives these triple powers from eternity above it, and gives them also to souls; but eternity holds this triad in itself unitarily, while time 1236 possesses it both unitarily and dividedly, and souls possess it dividedly. And for this reason some of them are characterised by one power and others by another, some representing the revelatory aspect of time, others the perfective, and others the cohesive; even so also of the Fates some are connected properly with bringing to completion and perfecting and are thus said to sing what is past, always acting and always singing their own songs which are cosmic intellections and creations, for the past is completive; others are directed towards holding together the present, for they guard the substance and generation of things present; and others again are concerned with showing forth the future, for they bring into existence and to perfection that which does not yet exist. So it is not unsuitable, then, that we should customarily divide this time of ours three ways, into past and future and present, by reason of the triple powers of time, the revelatory, the perfective, and the cohesive, understanding these faculties in one way in the case of eternity, in another way in that of time, and in yet another way in the case of souls.

And if you wish to look at things in another way, since the ordering of those souls superior to us is divided into those which are primal and intermediate and ultimate, the most universal of them are connected properly with the past, as comprehending both the present and the future; so even as the first of these comprehends the two latter, even so do those souls comprehend the two remaining categories; the intermediate souls are related to the present, for this was once future, but is not yet past; so even as the present comprehends the future, so also the median souls are comprehensive of those following on them, but are comprehended by those prior to them; the third group is connected

---

[95] A reference, probably, to the *Timaeus Commentary*, III, 14.16ff. Diehl (*ad Tim.* 37d), where the doctrine is credited to Syrianus.

with the future, for this has not traversed the present, nor yet has it become past, but it is still future only, even as also this third category of souls exist only for themselves and, because of their descent into the extreme of partialness, are not yet comprehensive of any others; for these comprise the lowest limit by reason of the division into three parts of the classes of being following upon the gods, since for each in
1237 turn of these three universal categories, there is a triadic multiplicity dependent upon it. But the rest of these categories we will consider at a later point; for the moment let us just examine the first triad.

This has, as being common to all of it, the characteristic of being "once upon a time";[96] for this is the characteristic of the past and of completion; and this is divided into *was, became, was becoming*; so again of these three the one signifies the summit of the triad, *was*, which is characterised by substantiation; the other signifies the point of completion, to wit, *became*; and the remaining one signifies extension in the process of completion, *was becoming*, these things being also images of intelligible things—*was* being an image of being, *became* of eternity, and *was becoming* of the primally eternal entity; for being comes to all things from the first aspect, the quality of being simultaneously total and whole from the middle one, and that of being pluralised and extended in any way from the third one. And to these three the subsequent triads of aspects are analogous both in relation to the future and to the present and to the past; for to *was* are analogous *will be* and *is*, the one belonging to the future, the other to the present; and to *became* are analogous *will become* and *has become*; for this tense of *become* is different from the preceding, the one having past sense, the other present; for *has become* has a cohesive sense, and we see it both as having been perfected and as perfect *now*, in a timeless *now*; as for instance, "an eclipse has happened" (*gegonen*), for this means the same as "it is now completed." Since, then, *gegonen* has two meanings, he initially only mentioned two categories in the present, *is* and *is becoming*, in order that he should not confuse the argument; but later (141e5) he is going to add *has become* also as a present category. To *was becoming*, thirdly, he takes as analogous *is becoming*, and secondly, *will have become*; for this is not the same as *will become*—let us not think that it is; for *will become* signifies the timeless indivisible existence in the future, as for instance "there will be a flash of lightning" (*genēsetai*): whereas *will have become* expresses progression along with extension, as in the case of "he will have become a man"; in the case of lightning, it would be false to say "it will have become."

1238   These two triads, then, are analogous to the one before them, and the

---

[96] An attempt to render the ποτέ of *Parm*. 141d8.

position between *was* and *will be* is occupied by *is*, whereas that between *became* in the past sense and *will become* is occupied by *has become* in the present sense, and that between *was becoming* and *will have become* is occupied by *is becoming*. And in every case the first monads are proper to substantiality, the middle ones to total and simultaneous potency, while the third are proper to activity in extension; and characteristic of all of the first triad is *once upon a time*, of all of the second, *now*, and of all of the third, *later on*; and indeed he uses the corresponding number of expressions for them. And if he has ranked the future triad second, one should not wonder at that, for he is imitating the cycle of time in connecting the end to the beginning, since when he proceeds he will rank in the middle the triad connected with the present, and last that connected with the future.

> "*Consequently, if the One has nothing to do with any time, it never has become nor was becoming nor was ever, nor can you say it has become now or is becoming or is; or that it will become, or will have become or will be hereafter.*" "*Very true.*" (141e)

How the syllogism proceeds here is plain enough; the One participates in no time; everything which once was or became or was becoming, which in the present is or has become or is becoming, and which in the future will be or will become or will have become, participates in some time (all these categories, after all, have portioned out between them the totality of time); the One, therefore, transcends and rises above both the temporal triad and its henad. But the proof of this is clear enough by reason of what has been said before; however, in the enumeration of the three triads one should note how he has preserved their order in relation to each other, first listing that which relates to the past, second, that which relates to the present, and third, that which relates to the future, even as in the *Republic* (X, 617b) he has allotted the past to the first of the Fates, to the middle one the present, and to the third the future, on the grounds, plainly, that time as a whole is contained intellectually by their Mother, Necessity. But in each classification he does not begin with *was* and *is* and *will be*, but rather from the middle term, that is to say, *became* once upon a time, and now *has become* and *will become*; for this is proper to them, inasmuch as they imitate eternity, and it is possible for us to begin from here and thus to call to mind the other categories.

So much then for that. One should now draw together this single summary from all that has been said here, that the One is established above all Soul and divine Being and all that has constant and identical activity, such as is the class of the beings superior to us, whether it is to be divided into triads or into enneads or into any other number, and

1239

nothing of this sort is to be applied to the One; and that thus the argument has proceeded to this point in its denial of all the orders, both the intellectual and the others, of the One. Where it will lead us in its further progress, we shall learn if we journey along with his instructions, and examine closely everything of what is said.[97]

> *"Now, can anything participate in existence except according to one of these modes?" "No." "So the One does not participate in existence in any way." "Evidently not." "So the One does not exist at all." "Evidently not."* (141e)

By way of everything that has been said so far, we have arrived at the existence that is deified and whose activity is unvarying; and by negation we have removed from the One all orders of existence, the divine and the intellectual and the psychical. And now again, by way of the nature that is common to all these orders, we get back to the intelligible monad of beings, and we will exalt the One beyond this too. For as we said before, the starting-point for his negations was not the summit of the intelligible world, but the summit of the intellectual. For it is in the sphere of the intellectual that "many" originates, as will be clear when we go on to the Second Hypothesis. But "existence" at the level of the
1240 One Being is prior to this "many" and belongs to all these orders, to what is many, to what is a whole, to what has shape, and to all the rest. And so we get back from all these, which have existence in common, to existence itself.

This is why in introducing this negation he says, "Everything that participates in existence participates according to one of these modes," referring not merely to the last mentioned predicates but to altogether everything that has been enumerated in the First Hypothesis; e.g. "it is a whole" or "it has parts" or "it has a beginning, a middle, and an end" or "it is in itself or in something else" and so on, i.e. to all the predicates that he has denied of the One. Thus it becomes clear (as we have said from the first) that he is considering those predicates which belong to beings *qua* beings, and not *qua* living or intelligent. For he says, "Everything that in any way participates in existence participates according to one of these modes; ⟨but the One participates in none of these modes⟩;[97a] so it does not participate in existence."

Similarly, Socrates said in the *Republic* (509b) that the first principle is beyond existence and is not existence but cause of existence, and that

---

[97] From this point on, the translation is based, with their kind permission, on that of Prof. G.E.M. Anscombe and L. Labowsky, with some minor adjustments to bring it into terminological accord with what goes before it, and others based on a reconsideration of problematic passages in the text, with the help of Westerink and Steel.

[97a] Adding ⟨τὸ δὲ ἕν οὐδενὸς μετέχει⟩ after μετέχει, as is necessary for the text (West.).

it is beyond both everything that intelligises and everything that is intelligised; just as we say that the sun is the cause, both of those who see and of what is seen. And by "existence" he means nothing but "being." For he states clearly here also that it is not possible for anything to be without participating in existence, both in this dialogue and in a similar way in the *Timaeus*. If, then, the first principle is above existence and above all Being, then the use of the very word *is* is wrong, for it transcends even "Being." And this is where the Platonic Parmenides differs from the one who speaks in the Poem, for the latter had the One Being in mind and said that it is the cause of everything, but the former is thinking of the One, and mounts from the One Being to the One alone which is prior to existence. At any rate, having denied that the One

1241 participates in existence, since it is clear to him that it could still be existence itself—for participation means secondary possession of a characteristic—he adds, "So the One does not exist at all," a position which he no longer reaches demonstratively. Indeed, it would not be possible to prove this in itself because of the kinship of existence and unity. For the more akin characters are, the more difficult it is to prove anything about them by the negative method, as we have already said (1088-1089).

But that the One is not the same as Being, Plato will show demonstratively at the beginning of the Second Hypothesis; and if this is true, it is evident that the One does not even "be"; for everything apart from "one" that is added to the One depreciates the transcendent supereminence of the One. And so, with the "is," which he takes from what is common to all kinds of existents, he gets back to their cause, and he says that it is not compatible with the One even to be this cause.

Perhaps someone will ask why he began by denying "many" and not "is" itself. Why did he not prefer an order progressing from the term next after the One to the remotest terms, or from these back to the "is" which is the acme of beings, but chose instead to begin with "many"?

The answer to this question is that the denial of existence would have been in contradiction to the hypothesis. For this speaks of the One as "being . . . , but the negation in question would say that it is not. It would have been extremely ridiculous to say right at the beginning, "If the One is . . . , the One is not," for the argument would have seemed to cancel itself. For this reason he uses the word *is* loosely and says, "If the One is . . ." as if this *is* made no difference, and finds that "many" is clearly what is most opposed to "one." He is also bearing in mind that the real Parmenides said that being is one and not many.

Beginning, then, with "many" as the most familiar starting-point, he sees, when he has separated the other predicates from the concept of the One, that it has to be conceived as independent even of existence

579

and that *is* itself cannot be said of it. There are two terms involved, namely, *one* and *is*, and he recognises that it is more useful to begin with the contrary of the subject than of the predicate. But the contrary of 1242 "one" is "many"; so he argues, "If the One is one, it is not many," and not, "If one, the One is not." And as we have said, he shows at the beginning of the Second Hypothesis that even the One treated there is not the same as Being, however closely connected they may be; so is it not abundantly proved that the first One is in itself uninfected by existence?

This will also be clear from what will be said there. The imparticipable must always precede the participated. (This is Plato's doctrine in the theory of Ideas, and it is for this reason that he says that a character as it is in itself is prior to its existence in something else.) So if even that One in which being participates is distinct from being, the unparticipated One must of necessity transcend Being still more. So the One does not participate in existence, not even the supreme existence which is nothing but existence, or Being itself which is nothing but being and is prior to the various genera of being.

In all the preceding discussion he understood "participation" in the sense of the organisation into unity of the things that come after Being itself. Here, then, he understands it in the same way, and says, "Everything that participates in existence participates in it according to one of these modes." He means either as "being a whole" or as "having a shape" or as "being the same and other," or as any of the other things that he has denied of the One.

To this statement he adds that "the One does not participate in existence in any way," meaning participation according to one of these modes. But it remained possible to say, "The One does not indeed participate in existence according to any of these modes, but may it not have some share in the existence which is prior to these modes, and be joined to it?" And this is why he adds,[98] "And so the One does not ex-34K ist," here for the first time showing that it is not existence itself; for "is," i.e. the first existence, is not predicated of the first One. To this he will presently add that the One is not even one, i.e. it is not the One that has existence, which participates in Existence itself, as does the One of the historical Parmenides.

Thus Plato copies the circle described by the whole of existence, which not only proceeds from One but also returns to One. He comes to procession by means of the concept of multiplicity (for in the sphere of being, multiplicity is the principle of procession, and every procession is accomplished according to the manifoldness of what proceeds),

[98] Here the Greek text breaks off. What follows is preserved in the Latin translation only.

and he gets back to "One" by way of "being one." For this is the source of the unification of all things, and it is according to the unity of their own kinds that they are severally joined together into one. Where, then, should he have started his construction of the scale of beings in his account of the procession from the One, if not with "many"? And from what other point could he have made the reversion than through the "being one"? For processions multiply beings, while reversions bring them together and unite them. For all things are connected with the One Being inasmuch as they all participate in existence: the One Being is the monad of beings. Through it they move mystically to the One which it contains, and then through this to the One that transcends the existent. What can one say but that here, too, Plato imitates the theologians who speak first of the original procession and procreation of the gods, then of their progression, and afterwards tell how they are united first severally with their unifying causes and finally with the first One?

"It cannot then be even to the extent of being one, for then it would be a thing that is and participates in being; but it seems that the One neither is one nor exists at all if one is to believe such an argument as this." "There seems to be no way out of it." (141e)

It has been said that the One does not participate in being in the way that "many" and "whole" and "part" and "shape" and so forth, do; then, that it does not exist even in that way that the first Being does. But the One that is lower than the One itself is said to participate in being inasmuch as it is bound up with it. And so he adds these words, "the One is not even one." For he knows that *one* has two meanings— in one sense it transcends, in the other it is coordinate with, *is*. In the latter sense, it is in a way comparable with existence as participating and being participated in by it. But in the former, it is incomparable and is imparticipable by everything.

36k So he shows that the first One is not like the One that coexists with Being. For if it can truthfully be said of it that it "is one," this "being one" involves "being"; of the transcendent One he says that it is not even possible to say that it is one. For the One of which we say "is one" is really the One that goes with Being. So we must not say that it is the One, for the "being one" that belongs to the one that goes with "being" and has a part in existence and has not remained "one" but has turned into "One Being."

But if this is true, then how can anyone say that the First Hypothesis treats not of the first God alone, but also of all the other gods?[99] For all

---

[99] The doctrine of Iamblichus; cf. above 1054.37ff.

the henads of the other Gods coexist with being; and so each of them is a god. But only the One should be called "one itself" and is above existence and unparticipated, so as not to be *a* one as opposed to the simply one. For what is "one" together with some other predicate is a one, just as "being" together with "life" is a being, and not "being itself," and "life" together with "intellect" is "intellectual life" and not "life" pure and simple, and everything taken with some differentiating addition is other than that thing considered as it is in itself and before differentiation. So "one" in itself must be before the "one" that goes with "being." For this reason one cannot say that this hypothesis is about the gods also, as some people have thought.

On the other hand, in discussing the One he is not treating of something that is not a real substance. We amply proved this at the beginning (1065.16ff.) when we referred to the Eleatic Stranger's statement that what is really one is indivisible. We showed (*a*) that Parmenides' deductions are necessary consequences from the premise "the one has no parts"; (*b*) that what follows from a possible premise must be possible; and further (*c*) that the hypothesis is not about something unreal. But if we show at the beginning that the hypothesis is concerned with the One, which is real, and at the end that it does not deal in an indeterminate way with all the gods, then we have proved that it deals with the first One only, throughout. Nor is the One such as to be participated by Being, or to be the One Being; for that "one" is participable, and it is the "one" which takes on to itself "being"; but both of these Plato has denied of the One, meaning, evidently, the transcendent One. It is neither one in the way in which that *one* is which goes with the *is* in "is one," nor does it exist like existence itself and the being that exists. As it is neither of these, the One altogether transcends the One Being.

Let us make a series of deductions.

If the One and Being were immutably the same, they would not be distinct. But not even the Second Hypothesis permits us to say that there is no distinction between them; therefore they differ from one another.

38K But if things are different, either (1) they are coordinate, and one is not prior to the other; or (2) they are not coordinate.

(1) If they are coordinate, either (*a*) neither communicates in the other, and so there are two principles of all things; or (*b*) there is some connection between them.

(1*a*) If there is no connection, then Being will be deserted by unity, and every not-one will be in no way one and will consist of infinities;

(1*b*) Or they communicate and are mixed together, and the One will be existent and Being will be one. Then there must be something prior to both which mixed them and makes "being plus one" into "one being." For we learn in the *Philebus* (23d) that before the mixture and the mixed there must necessarily be the mixer. And that will therefore be either (1*ba'*) existent without unity; or (1*bb'*) one without existence. If both together, the same argument holds good.

(1*ba'*) But if it is existent without unity, it is either (1*ba'*1) not one; or (1*ba'*2) nothing. But it is impossible to call it nothing, while calling it existent.

(1*ba'*1) Therefore it is not one. But if it is not one, then everything of which it consists must also be not one; and so the existent, which is not one, consists of infinities because there is no "one" that is prior to "being one."

(1*bb'*) But if it is one without existence, it will prove to be a one that is participable by the existent while it does not itself participate in existence.

(2) But if Being and the One are not coordinate, then either (2*a*) Being is higher and is before the One; or (2*b*) the One is higher and is before Being.

(2*a*) And if Being is before the One, itself producing the One as prior to it, then again Being will not be One, and the same deduction will hold good, the same infinite regress.

(2*b*) But if the One is prior and is the cause of Being, then it belongs to its mode of reality not to be existent (for it produces the existent), and not to participate in the existent. And this is the solution required.

For if the first One participated in Being in some way, although it is higher than Being and produces it, it would be a one which took over the mode of reality which belongs to Being. But it is not *a* one, and is the cause not just of Being but of everything, though of Being before the rest. And if everything must participate in its cause, there must be a "one," other than the simply One, in which Being participates; and this "one" is the principle of beings. This is also how Speusippus understands the situation (presenting his views as the doctrines of the ancients).[100] What does he say?

40K   For they held that the One is higher than being and is the source of
        being; and they delivered it even from the status of a principle. For
        they held that, given the One, in itself, conceived as separated and

---

[100] This testimony is most interesting, but has suspicious aspects. Proclus does not generally quote authorities by name in this commentary, but Xenocrates appears at 888.36, so there is no reason why Speusippus should not do so now. See further on this, Introduction to Book VII, pp. 485–86.

alone without the other things, with no additional element, nothing else would come into existence. And so they introduced the Indefinite Dyad as the principle of beings." (fr. 48 Tarán)

So he too, testifies that this was the opinion of the ancients about the One; it is snatched up[101] beyond existence, and next after it comes the Indefinite Dyad. Here too, then, Plato proves this One to be beyond the existent and beyond the unity that is in the existent and beyond the whole One Being.

In the Second Hypothesis he is going to say that the One Being, too, is a principle. It is constituted by distinct predicates, "one" and "being," and beyond it, he says, is the One Itself. For the unity that has existence through the unity of the One Being is not the One, but a particular one; yet in no case is the particular identical with the undifferentiated character . . . or Being.[102] But this too presents difficulty, because the "one" and the "being" must clearly be two, and so they cannot be purely one. For two are not one. So here we have something that is both one and not one; but this is not purely one, as what is both equal and not equal is not simply equal. So it is right to preserve the simplicity of the purely One, placing it beyond the "one" which is in "being" and beyond that "one" which is constituted by "one" and "being."

Having got so far, he rightly observes that, since the One is such as we have described, it is unknown to all particular kinds of knowledge and is inexpressible and unutterable. For what is first nameable and knowable is the one that is one by existing, and, in general, any character unifying, though not participated by, its series. To give an analogy: sense-perception helps us to reach some knowledge of the cosmic gods, for it sees their visible dwelling places and thereby reminds us of their characters; but it does not in the least help us to know the gods that are beyond the heavens. In the same way, intellect and knowledge of being help us to attain to the One Being; but our powers of knowing kinds of being do not in the least help us towards union with the One itself, except in so far as they are a kind of predisposition to the upward movement towards it. For it is not participated in any way or by any kind of being.

"If," Plato says, "one is to believe an argument like this." Proceeding by means of negations, we have declared the One to be exalted above everything; above intelligible and intellectual objects, above the 42K hyper-cosmic and cosmic gods, above the nature that is made divine.

---

[101] *Sursum raptum est.* Probably translates ἄνω ἡρπάσθη, Chaldaean terminology; cf. *Or. Chald.* fr. 3.1.
[102] Cf. 1096.21ff. above. There is a lacuna in the Latin MSS here.

"If," then, "one can believe an argument like this," the One is imparticipable. Obviously the reasoning is human and therefore particular. But neither does divine reason say anything but that the One is imparticipable. For as we have said before, everything strives to imitate the One by way of its own highest element. For souls, what is imparticipable is the first Soul: this is the universal which unites souls into a kind. Again, for intellectual substance the imparticipable is the divine Intellect, which is the universal uniting intellects into a kind. And in the same way, for all the divine henads the imparticipable is the One itself.

Whence, indeed, do the second in rank derive their imparticipability except from the One? For transcendence belongs to what comes first more than to what follows. So the One transcends the kinds of existence more than the universal Intellect transcends souls, or the universal Soul, bodies. So if the first, divine Intellect is imparticipable, it is obvious that the One itself is not on a level with any being.

But what is belief? It looks as if Plato were opposing the argument because, as he himself says, belief founded on persuasion is weaker than knowledge got by learning. But perhaps "belief" here is not the same as the belief we have spoken of elsewhere in connection with sense-perception, but is what the theologians[103] mean when they speak of the preservation of love, truth, and firm and immutable faith in the first principles, and say that faith binds and unites us to the One. These words, then, are to be believed, and to be relied on steadfastly and constantly, not assented to doubtfully and as a matter of opinion.

But suppose he did speak doubtfully when he said, "If one is to believe such reasoning"; this would not be strange, when he is trying by means of negations to hint at the supreme reality of the One. For one cannot allow that reason may entirely grasp it. Even the purest forms of knowledge are unable to comprehend it. The nearer they get to it and the more they attain to what is connatural to them, the more they find that it remains beyond the scope of their own operations, though they achieve participation †in whatever can be comprehended.†[104]

But whatever they apprehended, they desire something greater than that because of the travail inborn in them, the yearning for the supereminence of the One; and that is why there exists in us so great a devotion to it. But this yearning is always repulsed as falling short of its

[103] The Chaldaeans; cf. *frs.* 46-48 DP. The Chaldaean triad of virtues is mentioned above, 927.26ff., and frequently elsewhere, by Proclus. $\pi i \sigma \tau \iota \varsigma$, here, must be translated both as "belief" and as "faith."

[104] *Aliquid ut subtile*, corrupt. Perhaps William is reading $\lambda \varepsilon \pi \tau \acute{o} \nu$ for $\lambda \eta \pi \tau \acute{o} \nu$, as Klinbansky suggests. Or perhaps read *et si participant . . . , sed quia—contrasententiant . . .* (West.).

object, for knowledge is struggling to gainsay the peculiar unapproachability of the One.

44K   *"And if a thing does not exist, can this non-existent have anything that either belongs to it or is of it?" "How could it?"* (142k)

It is obvious that everything which stands in a relation to something must first itself be something and must exist on its own account (cf. *Soph.* 247aff.) for how could the non-existent endow anything else with existence? This is the nature of real relations. So if it has been shown that the One is beyond existence, nothing at all, such as a name or description, belongs to it, nor will there be a single thing, such as knowledge or sensation, that is of it. For if so, it would be knowable and sensible and nameable and expressible and would stand in relation to something else. But what stands in a relation has some kind of existence. For even the intelligible stands in a certain relation to the intellect, and the knowable to knowledge, inasmuch as they are mutually coordinate. But that which transcends all cannot, as has been shown, be susceptible of even a hint of relationship to anything else.

But what is meant by the careful addition of "this non-existent"? What is the meaning of "not being"? It has various meanings. For what does not exist in any way at all, and what has come to be, and "rest" and "movement" (this follows from the properties of "other"—and the One itself: all of these "are not" (cf. *Soph.* 255aff.), but not everything that "is not" is unknown and inexpressible. "Rest" and "movement" are known, and so in general are all the things that "are not" which belong to the sphere of the intelligible. For just that is meant by calling them intelligible. Neither is "what has come to be" unapprehended, for, as the *Timaeus* says (27dff.), that is the object of sense and opinion. The things that "are not" which are unknown are (a) the One itself and (b) what does not exist in any way at all; the former as superior to all knowledge of kinds of existence, the latter as falling short of any possibility whatever of being apprehended. Thus in the *Republic* (V, 477aff.) Socrates called non-existent what does not exist in any at at all, and said that it was unknown. ⟨He distinguished it from the "not being" of what has come to be⟩,[105] which is the object of opinion and comes after perfect being which is the object of real knowledge. And on the other hand, he called the Good non-existent because it is above being. He says that it is superior to being and existence and better than intelligible objects, and that it is the light of truth which brings the intelligible before the intellect (509b).

So "non-existent" and "beyond belief" can be taken in two ways.

---

[105] Not in Latin, but supplied by Klibansky to complete the sense.

And this is correct. For the soul is tormented by the unlimitedness and indefiniteness of the totally non-existent; it experiences difficulty in grasping it and is happy to be ignorant of it, fearing to step out into the limitless and measureless. But it mounts towards the incomprehensible super-eminence of the One itself, borne in its direction by a longing for its nature, revolving round it, wanting to embrace it, seeking with supreme passion to be present to it, unifying itself as far as possible and purging all its own multiplicity so that somehow it may become perfectly one. Impotent to comprehend its incomprehensibility or to know the unknown, yet according to the manner of its own procession, it loves its inexpressible apprehension of participation in the One. For in order to receive something, the soul must first coexist with that thing; but what would it mean to touch the intangible?

Thus the One transcends all analysable knowledge and intellection and all contact. And only unification brings us near the One, since just because it is higher than any existence, it is unknown. And this is why in the *Letters* (*Ep.* VII, 341c) Plato speaks of "a learning different from all other kinds of learning." Such is the One. But the totally non-existent is unknown as falling away from all things in its indefiniteness and as incapable of having real subsistence.

So it is ridiculous to say that because it is not an object of knowledge or opinion, the One is the same as the totally non-existent. For the totally non-existent is nothing, since one cannot apply the expression "something" to it, the opposite of which is "nothing" (cf. *Soph.* 237c). But it is impossible to say that this is the One, for "nothing"—i.e. "not a thing"—is the negation of "one" as well as of everything else. Indeed Plato did not deny "one" absolutely of the One, but the "one" of "being one," as well as "being."

"Therefore no name or description or knowledge or sensation or opinion applies to it." "Apparently not." (142a)

You could distinguish these negations into two kinds, and say that the One is declared to be (a) inexpressible, and (b) unknowable. Make a further division of the expressible and the knowable, and you will say that it is inexpressible in two ways, unknowable in three.

For the expressible is expressible either by a description or by a name; but the name is prior, and the description is by nature posterior to the name. For the name imitates the simplicity and unity of objects, but the description their complexity and variety of aspects. So the name is related to the single thing as signifying the whole subject at once; but the description circles round the essence of the thing and unfolds its complexity. The thing is the starting-point for both name and

46K

description, but the secret essences of intelligible objects, which are united with One, are preserved "in god-nourished silence":[106] they imitate the inexpressibleness and unutterableness of the One. But the One has its place above the silence and the intellect and the knowledge of the intellect, which form a triad.

48K   Again what can be known is the object either of ⟨sense-perception or of⟩[107] opinion or of scientific knowledge. For all cognition is either without concepts or with concepts; and, if the latter, it either brings in causes or makes no mention of causes. So we have three kinds of cognition: sense perception, opinion, and scientific knowledge. And so what is completely unapprehended by us is neither scientifically knowable nor judgeable nor perceptible.

Now, starting from the kinds of cognition in ourselves, we must also take their totalities and realise that all being known is denied of the One. For how could what is beyond all that exists be sensibly perceived? And how could it be the object of opinion, when it is not such as in one way to be, and in another way not? And how can what has no cause be an object of science?

So it is rightly said in the *Letters* (VII, 341c), as we have said, that it is to be learned in a different way; that when we have given much care and attention to it, a divine light is kindled in us through which there comes about—in such a way as is possible to us—a glimpse of it, which makes us participate in it in respect of that part of ourselves that is most divine. But the most divine thing in us is the One in us, which Socrates called the illumination of the soul, just as he called the truth itself light. This illumination is our individual light, and so, if it is not impious to say this, here also like is apprehensible by like: as the sensible is by sensation, the opinable by opinion, the knowable by science, so by the One in ourselves do we apprehend the One, which by the brightness of its light is the cause of all beings, by which all participate in the One.

Take, then, all sense-perception, not merely ours but that of the demons, and that of the cosmic gods, and that of the sun itself, and that of the "absolute" gods, and that of the assimilative gods,[108] and the very fount of sense-perception that is its demiurgic cause.[109] "For with the intellect he lays hold of the intelligible, but sensation he applies to the worlds" (*Or. Chald.* fr. 8 DP). If you consider step by step this whole series which springs from the fount of sensation, you will find not one member of it to have knowledge of the One. Just as, in Homer, Zeus is said to be invisible even to the perception of the Sun, "which

---

[106] Chaldaean terminology, *Or. Chald.* fr. 16. Cf. 1171.6 above, where we find a reference to the "paternal silence."

[107] Omitted in Latin, but added by Klibansky as necessary for the sense.

[108] That is, the ἀπόλυτοι and the ἀφομοιωτικοί.

[109] For the demiurgic, as opposed to the paternal, cause, cf. *ET*, prop. 157.

has the most penetrating light." (*Iliad* 14.343-344). And Plato says that the One is known by no sensation, for, he says, no being senses it— evidently not even the divine sensation, nor the primary cause of sensation; nor, in general, is there any mode of cognition in the divine Intellect that is coordinate with the One. Neither, therefore, does the demiurgic sense-perception perceive the One, for even that is a perception of things existent.

50K   Secondly, consider opinion; first, ours, then that of the demons, then that of the angels, then that of the cosmic gods, then that of the absolute gods (for these, inasmuch as even they have something to do with the world, contain the rational principles of sensible objects), then that of the assimilative gods (for in these are the causes of the cosmic gods); and, finally, the demiurgic opinion, Opinion itself, for this is the fount of all opinion and is the primary cause of the things that exist in the world, and from it the circle of difference has its origin. Consider this whole series and say: the One is unknowable to all forms of opinion.

There remains knowledge. Do not regard only what we have; for it is particular and there is nothing venerable about it—it does not know the One—but regard also the knowledge of demons, which sees the kinds of existence; and the angelic knowledge, which sees what is prior to these; and that of the cosmic gods (by which they follow their "absolute" leaders); and that of the absolute gods themselves, which operates transcendently in the sphere of the intelligible; and, higher still, that of the assimilative gods, through which they are the first to assimilate themselves to the intellectual gods; and in addition to these, consider the original knowledge which is united to the intelligible themselves, which in the *Phaedrus* (247d) is also called "knowledge itself"; and, above all these, consider the intelligible union which lies hidden and unutterable in the interior recess of Being itself. Consider all these kinds of knowledge and understanding of existence, and you will see that they all fall short of the One. For they are all knowledge of Being and not of the One. But the argument has shown that the One is above Being. Therefore all cognition, whether it is knowledge, or opinion, or sense-perception, is of something secondary and not of the One.

But we have said that the ⟨One is also inexpressible⟩ . . . so much the more ⟨do we say⟩ that it is unknowable to any reason-principle that comprehends a multiplicity (?) . . .[110]

---

[110] There must here be a lacuna of some considerable extent, since when we resume we are well into the second part of the division which Proclus has made, that the One is *inexpressible*, and are discussing the question of names. For the latter bit, I adopt an excellent suggestion of Westerink, that *multa circumcurrens aliquid dico* is Moerbeke's misreading of τῷ πολλὰ περιτρέχοντι λόγῳ as τ.π. περιτρέχων τι λέγω. But that does not solve the main problem.

Names may be human or demonic or angelic or divine—for there are divine names, as the *Cratylus* says (400d), which the gods use in addressing each other, and in the *Phaedrus* (255c) Socrates, himself divinely inspired, says, "whom Zeus named *Himeros* when he was in love with Ganymede." And the *Timaeus* (36c) says, referring to the Demiurge, "He named the circles of identity and difference."[111] For I believe that these passages agree with the theologians inasmuch as they signify by the words quoted that there is also an order of divine names.

52K   All these things belong to what comes after the One, and not to the One itself. No attribute of other things is applicable to the One. For they are all inferior and fall short of its transcendent super-eminence. What could be made commensurable with it, since it is not among the kinds of existence but is beyond them all alike? For if a thing is commensurable with anything else, this means that there are some things that agree with it more and some less; but the One transcends all things equally. So none of the things that come after it is commensurable with it, or corresponds to its nature, or can be compared with it.

Further, every name which can be properly said to be such by nature corresponds to what is named and is the logical image of the object. So there is no name of the One but—as somebody has said[112]—it is even beyond breath. But the first of the things that emanate from it is represented by the rough breathing with which we utter *"hen."* Itself, it is unnameable, just as the breathing by itself is silent. The second is represented by the utterable vowel which now becomes utterable with the breathing, and it itself becomes both utterable and unutterable, unspeakable and speakable; for the procession of the second order of existence has to be mediated. Third comes *hen* which contains the unsoundable breathing and the soundable force of *e* and the letter that goes with this, the consonant *n*, which represents in a converse way the same thing as the breathing.[113] And the whole is a triad formed in this way: from this one derives a dyad, but behind the dyad there is a monad. But the first principle is beyond everything and not merely beyond this triad which is the first thing that comes after it.

This, then, is the context of his argument which deduces the trinity by way of the names from the first principle. While he is theologising in this way, he is thinking only of the very first development of names, declaring that "one" is the very first of names, which is subordinate to

---

[111] Cf. *In Crat*. 19.24ff. Pasquali.

[112] A reference to Theodorus of Asine (*Test*. 9 Deuse). Cf. *In Tim*. II, 274.10ff. (= *Test*. 6 Deuse), where the doctrine on the letters of the One is explicitly attributed to him, and Deuse's commentary *ad loc*.

[113] Presumably in the sense that consonants are non-sonant, even as the rough breathing is, but conversely.

the simplicity of the One. He is working purely with an understanding of what is designated and he discovers these two assuming to themselves utterable sounds, and prior to these, and given these, he discovers thirdly that prior breathing which is the silent symbol of Being (*hyparxis*).

Clearly we must first enquire how it is that no name of the One is really spoken. We shall learn that if names are natural, the first principle has no name, not even the name "one," understanding that everything that is by nature a name of something has meaning as being congruous to its object, either by analysis into simple names or by reduction to its letters. If this is so, then "one" has to be reduced to its letters, since it cannot be analysed into any simpler name. So the letters of which it is composed will have to represent something of its nature. But each of them will represent something different, and so the first principle will not be one. So if it had a name, the One would not be one. This is proved from the rules about names which are plainly stated in the *Cratylus* (390d).

54K

The question arises, however, how it is that we call it "one" when the thing itself is altogether unnameable? We should rather say that it is not the One that we call "one" when we use this name, but the understanding of unity which is in ourselves. For everything that exists—beings with intellect, with soul, with life, and inanimate objects and the very matter that goes with these—all long for the first cause and have a natural striving towards it. And this fact shows us that the predilection for the One does not come from knowledge, since if it did, what has no share in knowledge could not seek it; but everything has a natural striving after the One, as also has the soul.

What else is the One in ourselves except the operation and energy of this striving? It is therefore this interior understanding of unity, which is a projection and as it were an expression of the One in ourselves, that we call "the One." So the One itself is not nameable, but the One in ourselves. By means of this, as what is most appropriate to it, we first speak of it and make it known to our own peers.

Since there are two activities in us, the one appetitive and the other reflective (the former existing also in those beings that are inferior to ourselves, but the latter only in those that are conscious of their appetites), that abiding activity that is common to all may not be absent from our own souls, but these must be responsive to the energies that concern the first principle, and so the love of the One must be inextinguishable. This is indeed why this love is real, even though the One is incomprehensible and unknowable. But consciousness labours and falls short when it encounters the unknown. So silent understanding is before that which is put into language, and desire is before any under-

591

standing, before that which is inexpressible as well as before that which is analysable.

Why, then, do we call the understanding of unity within ourselves "one" and not something else? Because, I should say, unity is the most venerable of all the things we know. For everything is preserved and perfected by being unified,[114] but perishes and becomes less perfect when it lacks the virtue of cleaving together and when it gets further away from being one. So disintegrated bodies perish, and souls which multiply their powers die their own death. But they revive when they re-collect themselves and flee back to unity from the division and dispersal of their powers.

56K   Unity, then, is the most venerable thing, which perfects and preserves everything, and that is why we give this name to the concept that we have of the first principle. Besides, we noticed that not everything participates in other predicates, not even in existence, for there are things which in themselves are not existents and do not have being. And much less does everything participate in life or intellect or rest or movement. But in unity, everything.

Even if you mention "many," this cannot exist without having a share in some sort of unity. For no multitude can be infinite, so if a multitude occurs, it will be finite. But a finite multitude is a number, and a number is some one thing. For "three" or "four" (and so for any of the numbers) is a sort of unity. It is indeed not a monad, but at any rate it is a unity, for it is a kind, and a kind always participates in unity, for it unites its members. Or how could we say that "three" is one number and "four" another, if they were not distinguished from one another as distinct unities? So everything participates in some unity, and that is why "one" seems to be the most important of predicates.

It was therefore correct to give the name "one" to the conception which we have of the first principle. And as we know that unity is common to everything and preserves everything, this will guide us in naming that which is the cause and the desire of all things. For it had to be named either after all things or after those that come next after it; so it can be named "one" after all things.[115]

Why do we not say that the other names also are names of the concepts that we have, and not of the things themselves—e.g. "intellect," "the intelligible," and so on? I would say because the concepts of other things give knowledge of the things of which they are concepts, and they arise in us cognitively; and for this reason they are sometimes (though not always) projected into language. But our concept and ap-

---

[114] Cf. Plotinus *Enn.* VI, 9.1.
[115] Cf. *PT* III, 21, p. 74.5-11, S-W.

prehension of the One, i.e. our travail, is in our nature per se, and not in the manner of a perception[116] or cognition. The other concepts, being cognitions, coexist with their objects and are capable of naming them, for their objects can somehow be grasped by them. This concept, however, is not cognitive and does not grasp the One, but is essentially an operation of nature and a natural desire of unity. This is proved by the fact that the desire of everything is desire of the One, but if our concept were of something known, then its object would only be the object of desire to the cognitive powers and not to things without knowledge.

58K From this it is clear that the One and the Good are the same.[117] For each is the object of desire to all things, just as nothingness and evil are what all things shun. And if the One and the Good are different, then either there are two principles or, if the One is before the Good, how can the desire of the One but be higher than the desire of the Good? But how can it be better, if it is not good? Or if the Good is before the One, since it will not be one it will be both good and not good. If, then, the One is the same as the Good, then it is right that it should be an object of desire before any cognition and that the apprehension of it should not be of the same kind as of knowable things. This is why our concepts of these really name their objects, for they know them; but this other apprehension desires something unknown and, impotent to comprehend it, it applies the name "one," not to the unknown—for how could it?—but to itself, as somehow divining the reality of what transcends itself and everything else. But it is unable to reflect on the One itself; for, as we have said, the desire of the One, the incessant movement of striving, is in all things by nature and not by representation. Even the divine Intellect, as I have said before, does not know the One by direct vision[118] (i.e. intuitively) or intellectually, but is united with it, "drunk with its nectar" (*Symp*. 203b), for its nature, and what is in it, is better than all knowledge . . . (*Lacuna*) Thus the One is the desire of all, and all are preserved by it and are what they are through it, and in comparison with it, as with the Good, nothing else has value for anything.

So Socrates says at the beginning that it is knowable, but immediately adds a qualification, saying how it is knowable, namely, "to him who inclines his own light towards it" (*Rep*. VII, 540a). What does he

---

[116] κατ' ἐπιβολήν (*secundum adiectionem*). Originally an Epicurean term, ἐπιβολή is taken up by later Platonists, beginning with Iamblichus (e.g. *Protr*. 22.4, 118.29 Pist.), with the general meaning of an act of "attention" or "apprehension."

[117] Cf. Book VI, 1097.10ff. above.

[118] ἐπιβλητικῶς, transliterated by Moerbeke ("intuitively"—*iniective*—is his translation) a rare word, used by Proclus elsewhere only at *De phil. Chald. Ecl.* 4. 3 Jahn. Adj. first used in this sense by Iamblichus, *Protr*. 18.2 Pist.

mean by "light," except the One that is in the soul?[119] For he said that
the Good can be compared with the sun, and that this light is like a seed
from the Good planted in souls. Besides, before speaking of the light,
he too made it quite clear that the way to it is by negations: "As if in
battle one has to rob it of everything and separate it from everything"
(*Rep.* VII, 534b).

So it is right that it should not be possible to apply a name to it, as if
one could be made to fit what is beyond all things. But to it "one" only
can be applied if one desires to express what not only Plato but the
gods, too, have called inexpressible. For they themselves have given
oracles to this effect.[120] "For all things, as they come from one and revert to one, are divided, intellectually, into many bodies." They coun-
sel us to get rid of multiplicity of soul, to conduct our mind upwards
and bring it to unity, saying, "Do not retain in your intellect anything
which is multiple," but "direct the thought of the soul towards
the One." The gods, knowing what concerns them, tend upwards towards the One by means of the One in themselves. And this precisely
is their theological teaching; through the voice of the true theologians
they have handed down to us this hint regarding the first principle.
They call it in their own language, *Ad*, which is their word for "one";
so it is translated by people who know their language.[121] And they du-
plicate it in order to name the demiurgic intellect of the world, which
they call "Adad, worthy of all praise." They do not say that it comes
immediately next to the One, but only that it is comparable to the One
by way of proportion; for as the former is to the intelligible, so the latter is to the whole visible[122] world, and for that reason the former is
called simply *Ad*, but the other which duplicates it is called *Adad*. Orpheus has also pronounced which god was first named, saying: "The

60K

---

[119] On the "One" of the Soul, cf. above 1071.25-33 and n. 49 *ad loc.*

[120] What follow are quotations from the Chaldaean Oracles, but they do not survive in
Greek. However, W. Theiler has tentatively restored the first from Moerbeke's literal
translation:

πάντα γὰρ ἐξ ἑνὸς ὄντα καὶ ἔμπαλιν εἰς ἓν ἰόντα
τέτμηται, ὡσεὶ νοερῶς, εἰς σώματα πολλά.

The latter quotations (lines 30-33) are obscured by Klibansky's punctuation. The true
quotation seems to be "Neque in tuo intellectu detinere multivarium aliud," which
might be retranslated as μηδὲ . . . ἐν σῷ νῷ κατέχειν πολυποίκιλον ἄλλο. For πολυποίκιλος as
a Chaldaean term, cf. fr. 34.1. As for the third quotation, it might be a free rendering of
fr. 112: Οἰγνύσθω ψυχῆς βάθος ἄμβροτον· ὄμματα πάντα | ἄρδην ἐκπέτασον ἄνω—or a dis-
tinct fragment on the same lines. On this passage, see H. D. Saffrey, "Les Néoplatoni-
ciens et les Oracles Chaldaïques," *Rév. des Ét. August.* XXVII (1981), pp. 220-225.

[121] This must still refer to the Chaldaeans, but in this case we have a piece of real Chaldaean lore, not attested as such in the surviving fragments of the Oracles (though the
terms ἅπαξ ἐπέκεινα and δὶς ἐπέκεινα, for the supreme god and demiurge respectively,
may well allude to Ad and Adad). On Adad cf. Macrobius, *Sat.* I, 23.17, where he gives
"unus unus" as a translation of Adad.

[122] Reading *visibilia* for MS *invisibilia*, which gives no proper contrast.

594

gods called Phanes by name first on great Olympus" (fr. 85 Kern). He himself speaks of things that existed before Phanes and symbolically applies names taken from the lowest levels of reality[123]—"Time" and "Ether" and "Chaos" (fr. 60 Kern), and, if you will, "the Egg," but he never says that the gods used these names. For these were not their names but he transferred to them names that belong to other things.

If, then, one must give a name to the first principle, "one" and "good" seem to belong to it; for these characters can be seen to pervade the whole of existence. Yet it is beyond every name. This feature of the One is reproduced, but in a different way, by the last of all things, which also cannot be represented by a name of its own; how could it, since it has no determinate nature? But it is named *dexamenē*, i.e. "receptacle," and *tithēnē*, i.e. "nurse," and "matter" and "the underlying," after the things that come before it, just as the first is named after the things that come after it.

> *"Therefore it is not named or spoken or judged or known, and nothing perceives it." "Apparently not."* (142a)

It is stated clearly in the *Letters* (VII, 342a-344a) that no name can with certainty comprehend an intelligible object, nor can a visible picture, nor a definition, nor any rational knowledge of it. The intellect alone is capable of grasping an intelligible essence certainly and perfectly. Plato works out the argument for one example, the circle.

For when does this mere name "circle" grasp the whole essence of the intelligible circle? When we hear the name, what do we know but the name?

Nor does an impression drawn in the dust by a geometrician comprehend it. For this is merely one of the copies multiplying it, not first known by reasoning but by sense and imagination.

Nor yet the definition, which does indeed circle round its essential nature; but it is complex and composite and so cannot seize upon the simplicity of that essence.

62K Nor does the theory of it grasp it, even if it meditates a thousand times things that themselves belong accidentally to the circle, and one might as well call it knowledge of these other things.

All these are about it but are not itself. But the intellect and intellectual knowledge knows the essence itself and comprehends the Form itself even by simple intuition. So it alone is capable of knowing the circle. And similarly for "the equal" and "the unequal" and the other characters severally.

---

[123] William would seem to have misread χρόνον in his text as χρόνων, translating this as *temporibus*.

If, then, we have shown that names and definitions and rational knowledge are worthless for grasping intelligible objects, what should we say about them with regard to the One? Surely that all names and all discourse and all rational knowledge fall short of it? So the One is not nameable or expressible or knowable or perceptible by anything that exists. This is why it is beyond the grasp of all sensation, all judgement, all science, all reasoning, all names.

But, you will say, what is the difference between this and what he has already said? For he said before that there is no apprehension of the One. But there he said that the One ⟨is not knowable⟩ by others . . .[124] He is showing by this very insistence that it is not unknowable because of the weakness of other things, but by its own nature. By what he said before, he indicated the inferiority of other things in relation to the One, but here its super-excellence with regard to itself.

But we must attend to the fact that when he says that the One is not known, by "knowledge" he means "rational knowledge." Before, he mentioned three things—rational knowledge, opinion, and sensation—and as in this sentence he takes up two that are the same as in the previous one, namely sensation and opinion, it is obvious that by the third, "knowledge," he means only rational knowledge, so that if there is a divinely inspired knowledge that is better than rational knowledge and which leads the One in ourselves towards that One, obviously the argument did not eliminate this, and learning it is the "final discipline," as Socrates rightly says (*Rep.* VI, 505a), because it is discipline in the final knowledge. But this final knowledge is not science, but is higher than science.

"Is it possible that all this holds true of the One?" "I should say not."
(142a)

To all his negative propositions he now appends this very unexpected conclusion, which raises a grave doubt. In what sense is it impossible that these things should hold true of the One? Are not all the foregoing arguments dismissed by this single remark?

64K   Some people[125] have therefore been persuaded by this passage to say that the First Hypothesis reaches impossible conclusions, and so that the One is not a real subject. For they associate all the negations into one hypothetical syllogism: "If the One exists, it is not a whole, it has not a beginning, middle, or end, it has no shape," and so on, and after all the rest, "It has no existence, is not existence, is not expressible, is

---

[124] Klibansky's supplement here seems unjustified, but there is plainly some corruption or lacuna. Presumably we must supply a clause which mentions the difference between what is being asserted now and what was asserted before.

[125] Origen the Platonist. Cf. above 1065.1ff. and n. 38 *ad loc.*

not nameable, is not knowable." Since these are impossibilities, they concluded that Plato himself is saying that the One is an impossibility. But this was really because they themselves held that there is no One that is imparticipable by existence and, therefore, that the One is not different from Being nor from the One-Being, and that "one" has as many modes as being, and that the One that is beyond Being is a mere name.

In reply to this interpretation, it must be stated that impossibility must lie either in the premise or in the reasoning. But the deduction was a necessary one, as every consequent statement was always proved by what went before, and the premise was true. For there must be a One that is simply one, as we have shown both from what is said in the *Sophist* and also from objective necessity.

So the hypothesis does not lead to a conclusion that is impossible or that conflicts with Platonic doctrine. What more need we say to these people, who are already refuted by what is said about dialectic in the *Republic* (VII, 534bff.), namely, that it treats of the cause of all the intelligibles, which approach differs in no way from the negative method?[126]

If this view is true, where does Plato discuss the One negatively? Not in the Second Hypothesis, where he discusses "all" affirmatively, nor in the third, where he discusses "all" negatively. The alternative remains, that the discussion of the One is either in this hypothesis, or nowhere. But the latter is unlikely, as Socrates said in that passage that it was the main subject of dialectic.

But others admit[127] the validity of the hypothesis, because the *Republic* also says about the first principle that it is what is beyond intellect, and the intelligible and beyond existence (VI, 509b), and these are what Plato here denies of the One, while in the Second Hypothesis he begins by affirming existence. So if the first does not deal with the One that is beyond Being, what other hypothesis is there besides it that does so? And so their reply to this doubt is that Parmenides believes all the foregoing conclusions to be true, but that this statement is not the close of the discussion of the First Hypothesis, but is put down as the starting-point of the Second; in order to show the way to the Second Hypothesis, he says that someone may find these conclusions impossible 66K as concerning the One. He had to bring in what was needed to pass

---

[126] Adopting an emendation of Westerink.

[127] Once more we are in a sequence of three authorities, culminating in Syrianus, so one may conjecture that this is Porphyry. Note the significant contrast below, 68K.25-26 between following *consequentia logographica* (λογογραφικὴ ἀκολουϑία), and *rerum theoria* (ἡ τῶν πραγμάτων ϑεωρία), a contrast made also at *In Tim.* I, 73.28, and 339.18. Though no contrast is made in those pages between Porphyry and Iamblichus, it is the sort of contrast which Proclus does make between them; cf. e.g. I, 87.6ff, 195.22ff.

over to the Second Hypothesis so that we should not find anything superfluous. For these things only seem impossible because of the inexpressibleness of the One, since it is obvious to any one that, as far as truth goes, they are not impossible. For possible premises do not lead to impossible conclusions, but the premise is possible, unless the really-One is incapable of being real. The Stranger in the *Sophist* reminds us of this (245a-b) where he refutes those who say that the first is the whole, by showing that the really-One is not a whole. If the premise is granted that there is the absolutely-One, then everything follows necessarily from this by necessary hypothetical syllogisms. So this statement, "These things are impossible," is made as a constructive introduction, in order to show the way to the Second Hypothesis, because they are impossible on account of the super-excellence of the One. For what is to follow is more commensurate with our understanding and easier to communicate to us that what has gone before, as it has more affinity with our minds. Plato himself in the *Letters* (II, 312e) replies to someone who asks what the first principle is, that such a question is unsuitable. For nothing that has any affinity with us should be attributed to the first principle, and one should absolutely not ask "what is it like?" That is dealt with in the Second Hypothesis, which asks what the One Being is like and shows that it is a whole, that it is a finite and infinite manifold, that it is in motion and at rest, and that it is everything, in due order, that agrees with these characters. But the First Hypothesis which takes the absolutely-One for its subject does not tell us what it is like, but removes everything from it and assigns nothing to it because nothing that has any affinity with us ought to be said of it. From this it is obvious that what has been said will seem impossible (though, as has been shown, it is all possible), because it is so far from our own nature and so totally foreign to Plato's own rule for speaking about the first principle.

This, then, is the argument of these people. But others,[128] later than these, think that this conclusion is a generalisation which contains all the previous negations. For just as there are conclusions rounding off every theorem, so this conclusion is appended to the rest, "that all these things are impossible of the One," namely, "many," "whole," "shape," "being in itself or another," the various genera of Being, "like" and "unlike," "equal" and "unequal," the property of being older than, younger than, and the same age as itself, the three- and nine-foldness of the parts of time, and after all these, also participation in substance, being existence itself, being participable by existence, expressibleness, knowableness. All of these, as has been shown, are im-

---

[128] Perhaps Iamblichus. See previous note.

possible of the One. This is why he asks if it is possible to say these
68K things which he has asked about of the One, and Aristoteles denies it.
For whatever you add to "one," any kind of existent whatever, is
something other than one. If "one" has something else added to it besides what it itself is, it becomes "something that is one" instead of
being simply "one," just as, if "animal" has something else added to it
besides what it itself is, it becomes "a particular animal." And so with
everything considered in itself: "good," or "equal" or "like," or
"whole," if they have anything else added to them they are no longer
just those characters themselves but have become "something good,"
"something equal," "something that is like"—in general one should
say the same about all these characters considered in themselves as
about "one." This is, then, a single negation summing all the rest and
added to them. The One, not being one among all things, is the cause
of all.[129] So the general negation represents at the same time the whole
progression of all from the One and the manifestation of individual
beings taken together and separately in the order that appears fitting.
And this interpretation, too, is correct.

Of these solutions, the former aims at literary consistency, while the
latter does not depart from the consideration of reality, However, following our Master, we must also say that negative propositions in the
sphere of the existent have different meanings according to their subject matter. Sometimes they have only a privative, sometimes also
specific[130] significance. E.g. we say "is not" in speaking of rest because
it is not movement or identity or difference, and similarly we say "is
not" in speaking of movement because it is not any of the other things;
and in general each thing is in a single way, inasmuch as it is itself, but
in many ways it is not, inasmuch as it is distinguished from other
things. But though we deny other things of it, these negative propositions are in a particular way tied up with positive propositions. For it
does also participate in each of the other things, yet it keeps its own integrity and is what it is. In this case, then, the negative propositions are
specific, for not being *that*, it will be the other; now this is intellectual
form. For it has been shown that it is the character of difference as
distributed[131] in this sphere that makes "not being" true in it; this is
what constitutes negation here.

On the other hand, in speaking of sensible objects we say that Soc-

[129] Cf. 1075.17-34 and 1076.30-32 above, and Plotinus *Enn.* VI, 9.6: "That which is
cause of all is none of those things (of which it is cause)."
[130] *Specionaliter*, presumably translating εἰδητικῶς. Cf. 68K.26 and 70K.4 below.
[131] Cf. Plato, *Soph.* 255e: "And we shall say that (the character of difference) pervades
all (the forms) . . ."; and 257e: "The character of difference seems to me to have been
parcelled out."

rates is not a horse and not a lion, and is not any of the other things, for he lacks all the other characters. For, being one particular thing, he is not an infinite number of others, and in him there are lacks, which are nothing but lacks, of all of those characters. For he does not in a partic-
70K ular way participate in the other things, as we said was true of intelligibles. And this non–participation is not due to the purity of the idea "Socrates," but to the weakness of a material and corporeal subject, which is incapable of a simultaneous participation in everything. For this reason negative propositions in the intelligible sphere really express something about the predicates. The same holds true also of negative propositions about objects of sense; but in the former case they are specific, while in the latter they are merely privative.

But negative propositions about the One do not really express anything about the One. For nothing at all applies to it, either specifically or privatively, but, as we have said, the name "one" names our conception of it, not the One itself, and so we say that the negation also is about our conception, and none of the negative conclusions that have been stated is about the One, but because of its simplicity, it is exalted above all contrast and all negation.[132] So he rightly added at the end that these negative propositions do not express anything about the One.

It is not the same thing to refer to the One and to express something about the One.[133] The argument does not express anything about the One, for it is indefinable. So the negative propositions that have been stated do not express anything about the One, but do refer to the One. This is why they resemble neither those which occur in the intelligible sphere nor those which are about the objects of sense. For the former are about the same things of which the negations also are predicated, while the latter do not in any way express anything about the One.

This, then, is the solution of our first doubt. But from another point of view one must say that he first denies everything of the One, thinking that negations are more suited to it than assertions, and keeping the hypothesis which says "is" of the One. But since, as he advances, he has taken away from it not only everything else but also participation in substance and Being, which itself is of high value, and has shown that it is neither expressible nor knowable, now at the end he rightly removes from it even the negations themselves.[134] For if the One is not expressible and if it has no definition, then how will the negations be

---

[132] Cf. 1076.35ff. above.
[133] Cf. 1191.5ff. above.
[134] Accepting Westerink's emendations. William must have misread his text here. (ἕν for ὄν in line 24; and *utique dicet* in line 25 must conceal or mistranslate a word for "remove." Cf. 70.1-2).

true for it? For every proposition says that "this" belongs to "that." ⟨But as nothing can belong to the One⟩,[135] it is totally unnameable. But there has to be some name as the subject of a negative proposition, and so even the negations are not true of the One, but negations are truer than assertions; yet even they fall short of the simplicity of the One. Indeed all truth is in it, but it is itself better than all truth. So how would it be possible to say anything true about it?

72K   He is therefore right in ending with the removal even of the negatives, saying that it is impossible that they should express anything about the One, which is inexpressible and unknowable. And one should not wonder that Plato, who always respects the principles of contradiction, says here that both the assertions and the denials are false of the One at the same time. For with regard to what can be said, assertion and denial make the distinction between true and false: but where no proposition is possible, what kind of assertion would be possible? It is clear to me that he too, who after Plato refused to admit a One above Intelligence for the reason that he was convinced of the validity of the principle of contradiction, and saw that the One was inexpressible and unspeakable, stopped short at the intellectual cause and the Intellect, ⟨making that⟩ the cause superior to all things;[136] however, by asserting that the Intellect is the cause, he eliminates providence; for it is providence that is characteristic of the One that is beyond Intellect, not mere thought such as is proper to Intellect. And by abolishing providence he does away with creation, for what can provide for nothing is sterile. And by rejecting creation he is rejecting the hypothesis of the Ideas according to which the Demiurge fashions his work, and consequently—not to enumerate everything—he does away with the whole of dialectics . . .[137] introducing new doctrines into his inherited philosophy. In order to escape this, we say that, for the inexpressible, contradictory propositions are both false, that they make the distinction between true and false only in the sphere of the expressible, and that in no sphere are they ever both true.

   To give, as they say, the third cup to Zeus the Preserver,[138] we take the negative propositions about the One as generating positive propositions, as has often been said; but do not think that the One has the power of generating all things, both productivity and existence having

---

[135] Added by Klibansky to fill a lacuna in the Latin.

[136] There is a gap of eight letters after *supra*, line 9, which may have contained something like *sedentem*. Klibansky's supplement of four lines of text is altogether too elaborate. It is Aristotle, of course, who is being referred to.

[137] Once again, a gap of eight letters. Klibansky punctuates wrongly. New paragraph should begin with *Ut igitur*. . . .

[138] A proverbial expression, but used by Plato at *Philebus* 66d, *Rep.* IX, 583b, *Ep.* VII, 340a.

been removed from it. For power is a middle term between these . . . the last negation referring to the One removes also such negations from it.[139] And "these things are not possible of the One" means that even the power of generating all things, which we said was a characteristic of negation, does not belong to the One, and therefore, even if it is said to generate and to produce, these expressions are transferred to it from the sphere of the existent, since they are the most distinguished names of powers. But it is better than all these names, just as it is better than

74K the things that are named by us. Indeed, if I am to state my opinion, positive propositions apply rather to the monads of kinds of being, for the power of generating things is in these. The first principle is before every power and before assertions.

Next, then, let us take up the fourth way of solving the problem. The soul ascending to the level of Intellect . . . [140] ascends with her multitude of faculties, but sheds everything that dissipates her activities. Now going further and having arrived there she comes to rest in the One Being, and she approaches the One itself and becomes single, not becoming inquisitive or asking what it is not and what it is, but everywhere closing her eyes, and contracting all her activity and being content with unity alone. Parmenides, then, is imitating this and ends by doing away both with the negations and with the whole argument, because he wants to conclude the discourse about the One with the inexpressible. For the term of the progress towards it has to be a halt; of the upward movement, rest; of the arguments that it is inexpressible and of all knowledge, a unification. For all these reasons it seems to me that he ends by removing the negations also from the One. For this whole dialectical method, which works by negations, conducts us to what lies before the threshold of the One, removing all inferior things and by this removal dissolving the impediments to the contemplation of the One, if it is possible to speak of such a thing. But after going through all the negations, one ought to set aside this dialectical method also, as being troublesome and introducing the notion of the things denied with which the One can have no neighborhood. For the intellect cannot have a pure vision when it is obstructed intelligising the things that come after it, nor the soul distracted by deliberation, of the things that are lower than the soul, nor in general is it possible to have perfect vision with deliberation. Deliberation is the mark of thought's encounter with difficulties: this is why Nature produces and knowledge says

---

[139] Sc. essence and activity. But there is plainly some corruption in the text here.

[140] A gap here of eight letters in the MS, but no apparent break in sense. Perhaps just an epithet of Intellect which William could not read.

what it says without deliberation.[141] It deliberates only when it is doubtful and falls short of being knowledge.

Just as there deliberation ought to be eliminated from our activity, although it is brought to perfection by deliberation, so here all dialectical activity ought to be eliminated. These dialectical operations are the preparation for the strain towards the One, but are not themselves the strain. Or rather, not only must it be eliminated, but the strain as well. Finally, when it has completed its course, the soul may rightly abide with the One. Having become single and alone in itself, it will choose only the simply One.

76K   This seems to be the point of the last question that Parmenides asks when he concludes this long development of the argument about the One. And so it is right that Aristoteles also, following him, ⟨passes from⟩[142] the nature of Being to the inexpressible itself; for by means of a negation he too removes all the negations. It is with silence, then, that he brings to completion the study of the One.

[141] Ἀνεπιστάτως transliterated by Moerbeke. The term ἐπίστασις, for "attention," "deliberation," seems first to occur in Philodemus and so is presumably Epicurean in origin, but brought into later Platonism. It is used already by Plotinus (*Enn.* III, 7.1.7), and fairly frequently by Proclus.

[142] Accepting Westerink's tentative filling of a small lacuna here.

BIBLIOGRAPHY

THIS IS NOT a comprehensive bibliography. I have included only works to which reference has been made in the Introduction or Notes. Abbreviations are given for works frequently cited.

A. TEXTS AND COMMENTARIES

(i) Proclus

In Alc.	*Commentary on the First Alcibiades of Plato*, ed. L. G. Westerink. Amsterdam. 1954.
In Crat.	*In Platonis Cratylum Commentaria*, ed. G. Pasquali. Leipzig: Teubner, 1908.
	In Primum Euclidis elementorum librum Commentarii, ed. G. Friedlein. Leipzig: Teubner, 1873.
In Parm.	*Procli Commentarium in Platonis Parmenidem*, in *Procli Opera Inedita*, ed. Victor Cousin, pp. 617-1258. Paris, 1864.
In Parm. VII	*Procli Commentarium in Parmenidem, pars ultima adhuc inedita, interprete Guillelmo de Moerbeke*, ed. R. Klibansky, L. Labowsky. London, 1953. Reprinted 1973. (Plato Latinus III)
	Proclus, Commentaire sur la Parménide de Platon, trad. de Guillaume de Moerbeke, ed. C. Steel. 2 vols. Leuven/Leiden, 1982-85.
In Remp.	*In Platonis Rempublicam Commentarii*, ed. G. Kroll. 2 vols. Leipzig: Teubner, 1899-1901.
In Tim.	*In Platonis Timaeum Commentarii*, ed. E. Diehl. 3 vols. Leipzig: Teubner, 1903-1906.
ET	*Proclus, Elements of Theology*. ed. with translation and commentary by E. R. Dodds. Oxford, 1933. Second edition 1963 with Addenda and Corrigenda.
	In Platonis Theologiam libri sex, ed. A. Portus. Hamburg, 1618.
PT	*Proclus, Théologie Platonicienne*, ed. H. D. Saffrey and L. G. Westerink. 6 vols., 4 published so far. Paris: Budé, 1968-1981.
	Procli Tria Opuscula, ed. H. Boese. Berlin, 1960.
	Proclus, Dix Problèmes concernant la Providence, ed. Daniel Isaac. Paris: Budé, 1977.

Proclus, Providence, Fatalité, Liberté, ed. Daniel Isaac. Paris: Budé, 1979.

(ii) Others

Dub.   Damascius, *Dubitationes et Solutiones in Platonis Parmenidem,* ed. C. A. Ruelle, Paris, 1899. Reprinted Hakkert, 1966.

Hermeias, *In Platonis Phaedrum Scholia,* ed. P. Couvreur. Paris, 1901. Reprinted Olms, Hildesheim, 1971, with index verborum by C. Zintzen.

Iamblichi Chalcidensis in Platonis Dialogos Commentariorum Fragmenta, ed. J. Dillon. Leiden: Brill, 1973. (Philosophia Antiqua XXIII)

VP   Marinus, *Vita Procli,* ed. V. Cousin. In *Opera Inedita,* pp. 1-66.

Numenius, *Fragments,* ed. E. Des Places. Paris: Budé, 1973.

Enn.   Plotinus, *Opera,* ed. P. Henry and H. R. Schwyzer, 3 vols. Brussels: Museum Lessianum, 1951-1973.

Sent.   Porphyry, *Sententiae ad intelligibilia ducentes,* ed. E. Lamberz. Leipzig: Teubner, 1974.

Or. Chald. (DP) *Oracles Chaldaiques,* ed. E. Des Places. Paris: Budé, 1971.

Orphicorum Fragmenta, ed. O. Kern. Berlin, 1922.

SVF   *Stoicorum Veterum Fragmenta,* ed. J. von Arnim. 4 vols. Leipzig: Teubner, 1903-1924.

Syrianus, *In Metaphysica Commentaria (Commentaria in Aristotelem Graeca,* VI:1), ed. W. Kroll. Berlin, 1902.

Theodoros von Asine, Sammlung der Testimonien u. Komm. W. Deuse. Wiesbaden, 1973.

B. TRANSLATIONS

Proclus le Philosophe, Commentaire sur le Parménide, par A. Ed. Chaignet. 3 vols. Paris, 1900-1903.

Proclus, A Commentary on the First Book of Euclid's Elements, translated with introduction and notes by Glenn R. Morrow. Princeton, 1970.

Plato and Parmenides: Parmenides' Way of Truth and *Plato's* Parmenides, translated with an introduction and running commentary by F. M. Cornford. London, 1939.

C. Modern Works

Beierwaltes, W. *Proklos, Grundzüge seiner Metaphysik.* Frankfurt am Main, 1965.

Beutler, R. "Proklos." In Pauly-Wissowa, *Realenkyklopaedie der klassischen Altertumswissenschaft,* Band XXXIII, 1 (1957), cols. 186-247.

Bielmeier, A. *Die neuplatonische Phaidros-interpretation.* Paderborn, 1930.

Dillon, J. M. *The Middle Platonists.* London and Ithaca, 1977

Dodds, E. R. "The Parmenides of Plato and the Origin of the Neoplatonic One." *Classical Quarterly* 22 (1928): 129-142.

Entretiens Fondation Hardt, XXI: De Iamblique à Proclus (contributions by Beierwaltes, Whittaker and Trouillard). Vandoeuvres, 1975.

Festugière, A. J. "Modes de composition des commentaires de Proclus." *Museum Helveticum* XX (1963): 77-100.

Frede, M. *Die Stoische Logik.* Göttingen, 1974.

Gersh, S. *Kinesis Akinetos: A Study of Spiritual Motion in the Philosophy of Proclus. Philosophia Antiqua* XXVI. Leiden, Brill: 1973.

———. *From Iamblichus to Eriugena,* Leiden, Brill, 1978.

Hadot, P. *Porphyre et Victorinus.* 2 vols. (including text and translation of *Anonymus Taurinensis in Parmenidem* in vol. 2). Paris. 1968.

Klibansky, R. "Eine Proklos-Fund und seine Bedeutung." *Sitzungsberichte der Akademie der Wissenschaften Heidelberg* 1928/9, Abh. 5. Heidelberg, 1929.

Klibansky, R. *Plato's Parmenides in the Middle Ages and the Renaissance.* Mediaeval and Renaissance Studies, vol. 1, no. 2, Warburg Institute. London, 1943. Reprinted with *The Continuity of the Platonic Tradition during the Middle Ages,* Kraus International Reprints, New York, 1982.

Lloyd, A. C. "Procession and Division in Proclus." In *Soul and the Structure of Being in Late Neoplatonism,* ed. H. J. Blumenthal and A. C. Lloyd. Liverpool, 1982.

Rutten, C. "La doctrine des deux actes dans la philosophie de Plotin." *Revue Philosophique* 146 (1956): 100-106.

Rosán, L. J. *The Philosophy of Proclus.* New York, 1949.

Sheppard. A.D.R. *Studies on the 5th and 6th Essays of Proclus' Commentary on the Republic. Hypomnemata* 61. Göttingen, 1980.

Trouillard, J. *L'Un et l'âme selon Proclus.* Paris, 1972.

Wallis, R. T. *Neoplatonism.* London, 1972.

INDICES

In the case of certain frequently repeated names or topics (e.g., Plato, Parmenides, Zeno, Socrates, the One, Intellect, Soul), the entry is selective.

INDEX OF PROPER NAMES

Academy, New, 7, 121n, 304n
Adad (Chaldaean god), 594
Albinus, xxv, xxxv, 25n, 30n, 281n, 386, 391, 433n; on Forms, 151, 212n
Alexander of Aphrodisias, 74n, 202, 304n, 530n
Amelius, xiii, xxvii, 96, 116n, 150, 155-156, 189, 191-192, 197, 217n, 231n, 387, 396, 410n, 433n, 452n, 558n; views on subjects of hypotheses, 411
Ammikartos, 10, 329, 369
Ammonius Saccas, xxvii
Anonymous Parmenides Commentary (Anon. Taurinensis), xxvii-xxx, 460n
Anonymous Prolegomena to Platonic Philosophy, xii n, 3
Anonymous Theaetetus Commentary, xxv n, 4
Anscombe, G.E.M., x, 74n, 578n
Aristophanes, 45
Aristotle, xxv, 10, 44n, 68, 74, 87, 107, 146-147, 157, 160, 165-167, 202, 207, 208-209, 240n, 245, 253, 254, 255n, 281n, 285, 294, 305, 306, 309, 314, 320n, 334, 356-357, 393, 452n, 466n, 479, 486, 491, 520, 540, 601; *De Anima* read by Proclus with Plutarchus, xii; *Topics*, 9, 32, 43, 325, 338n, 343, 394n; on homonyms, 292; his attack on Ideas, 284; Third Man Argument, 249; No-Man (*outis*) Argument, 249; distinction of senses of "in," 475, 496; on motion, 552
Armstrong, A. H., xvi n
Asclepiodotus (dedicatee of *In Parm.*), xxxvi, 5, 20n
Athena, 11, 49, 71, 134, 174, 189, 221, 293

Beierwaltes, W., xviii, 390n
Beutler, R., xi, xxiv
Blumenthal, H. J., 185n

Chaignet, A. E., xliv, 19n, 297n, 369n
Chaldaean Oracles, xii, 27, 39, 50n, 99, 107, 109, 135, 140, 148, 152, 168-169, 180, 183, 255, 280, 289, 293-294, 312, 343, 380, 404, 408, 417, 421, 424, 438n, 442, 469, 488, 493, 506n, 509n, 515, 522, 546, 584n, 588 (*bis*), 594; doctrine of prayer, 13, 55n; concept of "faith," 486, 585; *synocheis*, 294; triads, 424, 439
Chrysippus, 74n, 249n, 530n
Cousin, V., xliii, 65n, 78n, 117n, 125n, 132n, 135n, 158n, 173n, 215n, 216n, 217n, 311n, 361n, 410n, 432n, 442n, 471n

Damascius, xxi, xxx, xxxviii, 20n, 59n, 271n, 421n, 439n, 477, 494n, 554n
Dillon, J., xxxvi n, xli n, 12n, 129n, 229n, 389n, 412n, 488n
Diodorus Cronus, 219n
Dionysus, 140, 174, 382n
Dodds, E. R., xvii, xxv-xxvi, xxxii, xxxvi, 85n, 386, 463n
Domninus (colleague of Proclus), xiii

Empedocles, 101-102, 139n, 219
Epicurus, Epicureans, 107n, 245, 304n, 593n, 603n
Eucleides of Megara, 96, 121n
Eupolis, 45
Euripides, *Troades* 887-888 quoted, 231

Festugiere, A-J., 25n
Frede, M., 74n, 530n

Gersh, S., 102n, 158n, 478n

Hadot, P., xxvii-xxx, 396, 424n, 451n, 457n
Harpocration of Argos, 152
Hegel, G.W.F., ix, xliii n, 326
Hephaestus, 153, 183n, 189
Heraclides of Pontus, 47
Heraclitus, 23
Hermeias, 58n, 152, 236n, 296n, 300n, 377n, 468n
Hesiod, 46, 59n, 381n, 485

SUBJECT INDEX

(Passages of particular importance are given in italics.)

* Proclus uses εἶδος and ἰδέα more or less indiscriminately. I have tended to follow him in this, but inconsistencies remain. Glenn Morrow favoured "Idea"; I favour "Form," which may have caused inconsistencies to go unnoticed, but no substantial confusion should result.

Sense-perception (αἴσθησις) (*cont.*)
376-377, 588; "intellectual," 312, 488
(demiurgic); subject of sixth hypothesis, 416

Soul (ψυχή), xvii, xxiii-xxiv, 27, 151-152,
180-183, 245, 363-364, 482, 493, 503-
504; definition of, according to "Parmenidean" method, 354-356; "soul" of
a dialogue, 4, 6; divine souls, 560-561,
563; soul of the Earth, 408; divides
Forms, 173-174; as place of Forms, 253;
individual soul, 53-54, 71, 256, 376,
494, 592; as "image" of Intellect, 117,
152; relation to Intellect, 517, 602;
Forms of irrational souls? 182; levels of,
181; "One" of the soul, 390, 424, 432,
488, 588; partakes in Time, 556-557;
unitary principle of, 307; unlimitedness
in, 462; unparticipated Soul, xxiii

Textual criticism, variants, 226n, 230,

236, 468, 476, 492, 502, 516

Theology, theologians, 83, 148, 168, 174,
204-205, 218, 270-271, 280-281, 285-
286, 294, 312, 313, 417, 451-452, 493,
515, 524-525, 542, 545, 546, 547, 581,
590, 594. *See also* Orpheus, Chaldaean
Oracles

Theurgy, xv, 100, 154, 187, 194, 218,
342, 442n

Time, 90, 117, 418, 482-483, 556, *557-
578*; unlimitedness of, 462; what
"time" is denied of the One, 558-561;
Orphic conception of, 566; *dynameis* of,
574-577

Unlimited. *See* Limit

Whole and Part, 444-448; senses of
"part," 456-457

INDEX OF PLATONIC PASSAGES

(This index is confined to those parallel passages quoted by Proclus himself. References
are to Cousin columns, as providing a more accurate indication than pages of the present
edition; numbers with *K* affixed refer to Klibansky's edition of the last part of Book VII.)

LIBRARY OF CONGRESS CATALOGING-IN-PUBLICATION DATA

Proclus, ca. 410–485.
Proclus' Commentary of Plato's Parmenides.
Translation of: In Parmenidem.
Bibliography: p.
Includes indexes.
1. Plato. Parmenides. 2. Socrates.
3. Zeno, of Elea. 4. Reasoning—Early works to 1800.
I. Morrow, Glenn R. (Glenn Raymond), 1895–1973.
II. Dillon, John M. III. Title.
B378.P6913 1986   184   85-43302
ISBN 0-691-07305-8 (alk. paper)